Toward a Grand Strategy Against Terrorism

About the Editors

Dr. Christopher C. Harmon Dr. Harmon has long-held interests in the two subjects of this text: strategy and terrorism. His first book, coedited with low-intensity conflict expert David Tucker, was *Statecraft and Power* (University Press of America, 1994), a work in honor of a teacher of strategy, Harold W. Rood. Harmon taught for four years on the Strategy and Policy faculty of the Naval War College, Newport, Rhode Island, and then wrote and directed a strategy syllabus for two hundred Marine majors, foreign allies, and US civilians at Command and Staff College, Quantico, Virginia, where he later held Marine Corps University's Kim T. Adamson Chair of Insurgency and Terrorism (2005–2007). He is the author of two editions of the graduate-level textbook *Terrorism Today*—published by Frank Cass (2000) and Routledge (2007), as well as chapters on terrorism and counterterrorism for *Fanaticism and Conflict in the Modern Age* (2005) and *The American Military Tradition* (2007). Two of Dr. Harmon's articles have appeared in the journal *Vital Speeches*. The US State Department gave him a Distinguished Public Service Award. From March 2008 through September 2009, Dr. Harmon was executive director as well as curricula chief of the Marshall Center's Program on Terrorism and Security Studies; he is now Director of Studies.

Andrew Nichols Pratt Since August 1996, Professor Pratt has been the Professor of Strategy and International Politics in the College of International and Security Studies in Garmisch, Germany. Following the 9/11 terrorist attacks, he developed the Program on Terrorism and Security Studies (PTSS) and was named its first Director. In February 2008, he served the US Special Envoy for Middle East Regional Security (SEMERS) in Jerusalem and on the West Bank. Returning to the college and Marshall Center that June, he resumed duties of Director, PTSS in October 2009. Prior to his retirement from the Marine Corps after twenty-six years, Colonel Pratt served as Director of the Marine Corps Command and Staff College and the Marine War College. Throughout his career, he was privileged to command extensively and at every level, from a CIA Special Operations Group team that conducted covert operations in denied areas in support of US national security objectives overseas, to a Battalion Landing Team deployed in the Persian Gulf. "Nick" Pratt graduated from the US Naval Academy and holds two Master of Arts degrees. His involvement with counterterrorism matters began in 1967 and continues apace.

 **Dr. Sebastian L. v. Gorka** Dr. Gorka is an internationally recognized authority on issues of national security, terrorism, and democratization, having worked in government and the private and NGO sectors in Europe and the United States. A graduate of the University of London and Corvinus University, Budapest, he was Kokkalis Fellow at Harvard's John F. Kennedy School of Government and holds a Ph.D. in political science. He was the first Director of the Institute for Transitional Democracy and International Security, and also spent four years as Adjunct Professor for the PTSS program of the Marshall Center. Dr. Gorka has published in excess of 120 monographs, book chapters, and articles, many for the JANES Group of the United Kingdom, and his work has appeared in the *Financial Times*, the BBC, CBS, REUTERS, the *Washington Post*, *EuroNews*, and *Newsweek*. Dr. Gorka advises and briefs the US Special Operations Command and NATO; recently he advised the Pentagon on Secretary Gates' draft guidance on strategic communications in the war on terrorism. Dr. Gorka is a frequent lecturer at institutions such as the FBI's International Law Enforcement Academy, USMA West Point, and the School of Advanced Military Studies, Fort Leavenworth. He teaches in the Irregular Warfare Department, College of International Security Affairs, National Defense University, Washington.

Acknowledgments

The authors wish to recognize, with gratitude, the expert advice and assistance of the following reviewers:

Kristian P. Alexander, Zayed University, Abu Dhabi, UAE

Katherine Cleary

BG (RET) Russell D. Howard, Joint Special Operations University

Charles A. Loftus, Arizona State University–Polytechnic Campus

George Michael, The University of Virginia's College at Wise

Stacy R. Neal, The Fletcher School, Tufts University

The three Editors gratefully acknowledge the assistance of Larry Loeppke, Debra Henricks, Robin Reed, and the full McGraw-Hill team, which did exacting and expert work. At the Marshall Center, Mary Ann Peters and Michael N. Schmitt, successive Deans of the College of International and Security Studies, were directly and positively engaged in this project, doing much to shape the good will in which it unfolded. The Editors are equally grateful to: Rick Steinke; Jeannie Callaghan, Lisa Murphy, Sonya Acuff, and Laura Harmon for their sound judgment and skills in publishing within federal guidelines; Ms. Callaghan (again) for thoughtful advice at all stages; Kevin Kelly for a chapter translation from French; and Leigh Ann Truly for proofreading. Some drafts were studied and improved by Ken Duncan, John Sawicki, Behram Sahukar, and Bob Johnson—all gifted adjunct professors in our counterterrorism program.

Toward a Grand Strategy Against Terrorism

Christopher C. Harmon, Ph.D.
George C. Marshall European Center for Security Studies

Andrew N. Pratt, M.A.
George C. Marshall European Center for Security Studies

Sebastian Gorka, Ph.D.
College of International Security Affairs, National Defense University

The McGraw·Hill Companies

TOWARD A GRAND STRATEGY AGAINST TERRORISM

Published by McGraw-Hill, a business unit of The McGraw-Hill Companies, Inc., 1221 Avenue of the Americas, New York, NY 10020. No part of the design, format, layout, art work, or typeface used in this publication may be reproduced or distributed in any form or by any means, or stored in a database or retrieval system, without the prior written consent of The McGraw-Hill Companies, Inc., including, but not limited to, in any network or other electronic storage or transmission, or broadcast for distance learning. Copyright © 2011 by The McGraw-Hill Companies, Inc. All rights reserved.

Some ancillaries, including electronic and print components, may not be available to customers outside the United States.

This text is published by the **Contemporary Learning Series** group within the McGraw-Hill Higher Education division.

❊   This book is printed on recycled, acid-free paper containing 15% postconsumer waste.

1 2 3 4 5 6 7 8 9 0 DOC/DOC 1 0 9 8 7 6 5 4 3 2 1 0

MHID 0-07-352779-3
ISBN 978-0-07-352779-6

Managing Editor: *Larry Loeppke*
Developmental Editor: *Debra A. Henricks*
Editorial Coordinator: *Mary Foust*
Editorial Assistant: *Cindy Hedley*
Production Service Assistant: *Rita Hingtgen*
Permissions Coordinator: *Lenny Behnke*
Senior Marketing Manager: *Julie Keck*
Senior Marketing Communications Specialist: *Mary Klein*
Marketing Coordinator: *Alice Link*
Director, Specialized Production: *Faye Schilling*
Project Manager: *Robin A. Reed*
Design Coordinator: *Margarite Reynolds*
Buyer: *Sherry Kane*
Cover Concept: *Carl Shelton*
Compositor: *S4Carlisle Publishing Services*
Cover Images: *Map: © Soldeandalucia / Dreamstime; Chess: © Scifisnake (Ryan Jones) / Dreamstime.*

All credits appearing on page or at the end of the book are considered to be an extension of the copyright page.

The contributions of all article authors are personal works of scholarship and professional expertise; these texts do not necessarily reflect the views of the US or German governments or their relevant ministries, offices, and departments.

Library of Congress ISSN: 2151-7487

www.mhhe.com

Contents in Brief

Unit 4

Case Studies   313

Contents

Unit 1   The Problem and Its History   1

Misunderstanding the essence of terrorism virtually guarantees policy failures. To place counterterrorism in a proper context, this text commences with an essay that serves as a précis of the problem. Terrorism is a complex phenomenon; challenging to all. A tactic used to socially, politically, and psychologically fragment a targeted population, terrorism demonstrates a line of development beginning in ancient times that can be traced and from which we will gain insights and knowledge. Understanding terrorists' behavior and their goals in order to craft counterterrorism policies stipulates a sense of terrorism's history. Terrorism, like a persistent cancer, has invaded our societies in the past; it afflicts us today, and it may destroy our descendants correspondingly if we fail to grasp its fundamentals.

To understand how many terrorist groups have met their end and to know why, it has been necessary to make an extended study of such organizations of the twentieth century. This essay takes shape in nine categories. There is a grid of groups based upon their impact: defeated, successful in limited ways, or wholly successful. This is laid over another grid measuring duration or life span: groups that last a few years, groups extant for eight to fifteen years, and terrorists that wage campaigns lasting decades. An unpalatable teaching of this research is that terrorism often works—or works well enough to keep militants trying terrorist methods. Fortunately, many groups do fail and are largely forgotten; their demise is equally instructive to governments and to counterterrorism professionals.

The Cold War reinforced the systems and architecture of national security developed under the international Westphalian order of nation-states. Since the collapse of the bipolar balance, new or revived threats have emerged that are ill-matched by the existing "legacy structures" of national defense and security. Consider "hyper-terrorism"—political violence that is more interested in extent of damage caused than in simply the inculcation of fear. While its existence is limited to a small subset of non-state actors—transcendentally motivated irrational terrorists—the threat exists. Radical reform of the security structures of many countries is required if we are to effectively meet the challenge of threats such as al Qaeda. Such a reform entails new divisions of labor and will require a significant revision of constitutional strictures, as well as new levels of international cooperation. This will not be easy and will require a high level of political will to implement. Should such reform be delayed, the developed democracies will remain too vulnerable.

Unit 2   Law, Force, and the Military Option   85

International law and the use of force are two vital subjects for counterterrorism professionals. Prior to 2001, international law tended to point toward a criminal law paradigm in response to counterterrorism. However, the al Qaeda attacks of 9/11 evoked a global response that confirms the emergence of a new normative paradigm in which a military response is often viewed as an appropriate complement to law enforcement in cases of large-scale transnational terrorist attacks by non-state actors. The law enforcement option is still preferred, if it can be effective, and there has been vast improvement in international cooperation in the form of expansive international agreements and the establishment of formal and informal cooperative law enforcement systems.

There is a beguiling paradox in the resolution of terrorist crises. Patience, negotiations, or both, have served government in certain tactical cases, while in other instances, the opposite has been true, and force against terrorism has been decisively successful. In our liberal societies, the force attempted is most often discrete—that is, careful, selective, and coming swiftly but after deliberation and planning. Democracies also place a premium upon return to "normalcy"; once used, the sword is sheathed. The lengthy record of successes using force includes actions against such substate groups as Congolese kidnappers of Belgians, South Moluccans in Holland, MRTA in Peru, FARC in Colombia, and a series of skyjackers—the PFLP (Entebbe), the Red Army Faction (Mogadishu), and the Algerian GIA (Marseilles).

Competence in counterterrorist operations demands at least three skill sets—a kind of "iron triangle." One arm is a specialized counterterrorist force. Intelligence and investigative capabilities are at least as vital—a second side of the triangle. Finally, there must be sound and decisive national political leadership. The chapter surveys a number of related qualities desired in the right counterterrorist team, including components of diplomacy, interagency rehearsals, law enforcement, and emergency services.

Insurgency and terrorism are not identical. Insurgency is a struggle between ruling authorities and a substate group using politics and violence—which may or may not include terrorism, the deliberate and systematic abuse of civilians. Counterinsurgency methods may help in a global counterterrorist campaign, if, for example, they deprive the terrorists of root causes of propaganda, hinder a populace from supporting terrorists, counter ideological support to terrorism, create or maintain splits within the militant movement, and so on. The "Al Anbar Awakening" in Iraq, and the author's own recent experiences in Afghanistan, are examples of how effective counterinsurgency did notably reduce terrorism.

Unit 3   Instruments of National Power   153

Diplomacy is a major instrument of national power and should be seen as the first and preferred policy tool for countering international terrorism. Diplomacy is preferable to the use of force, which is limited under international law and in any case is costly, dangerous, and uncertain. The Irish peace process and the coaxing of Libya away from terrorism are examples of diplomacy's track record in helping to counter terrorism. The principal tools of diplomats include bilateral and multilateral diplomacy to strengthen weak states and help gird political will to take a stand against terrorists and their supporters. Other instruments include mediation, public diplomacy, and track-two diplomacy.

There is often an option: talking to terrorists. Here we analyze the potential advantages and disadvantages of such engagement and address the questions of whom to talk to, when to talk, how to talk, and what to talk about. Also worthy, and examined here, are potential "lessons learned" from the experiences of recent engagement with terrorist groups throughout the world. The final section assesses the extent to which productive dialogue can or cannot be established with contemporary terrorist groups that frequently lack the clear chain of command and internal discipline associated with so-called traditional, nationalist-separatist movements.

Intelligence collection and analysis have proven historically to be critical weapons in identifying and neutralizing terrorist individuals and organizations. Intelligence activity conducted in secret has often proven significantly effective in uncovering and countering the plans and actions of terrorist organizations and in degrading terrorist capabilities. Indeed, the record indicates that intelligence is an indispensable tool both in the context of an overarching national counterterrorism strategy and at a tactical level. Intelligence agencies are well structured and equipped by training, method of operation, and internal culture to attack and defeat terrorist groups—whether national or international in nature. The sharing of intelligence on an international basis has also proven effective in countering a networked, transnational terrorist threat.

As grand strategy deploys the full range of a government's tools, pursuing terrorist funding is a new requirement of governments. The United Nations recognized this in a treaty entering into force in 2002. With fuller implementa-tion, this convention promises the impounding of terrorist money and closure of certain funding paths and vehicles to a degree hardly contemplated in 1970, 1980, or 1990. Moreover, the forensics of terrorist money are immensely help-ful to intelligence and law enforcement. A single ATM receipt broke open the well-hidden cell of Bali bombers who had murdered more than two hundred people. The work to be done by counterterrorism professionals is arcane and specialized. The world community must improve—and is improving—in such areas as legal frameworks, financial regulation, financial intelligence, law enforcement, and prosecutorial and judicial processes.

Radicalization processes have led—or pushed—a small minority of Muslims on a downward path into unforgivable violence against the innocent for "Isla-mist" ends. Analysis of what these terrorists themselves write and say, as well as learning from defectors and critics from the inside, makes it apparent that the ideological struggle with these contemporary terrorists and their mentors must be very firm. The world community must reverse the violent extremists' impact on the thought and politics of legitimate Muslim communities. In addition to a struggle of ideas, we must gain allies within the Muslim world as well, includ-ing progressives, liberals, and the secular minded. Terrorist ideology is a toxin; it must be combated directly and explicitly with antitoxin.

In older days, security experts and military historians spoke of four realms of battle: land, sea, subsurface naval, and air. Space has since been added. Now comes cyberspace. Political groups and several governments have already opened cyber fronts of conflict. Palestinian groups and the Israeli government have warred in this realm for years. Worldwide, political actors now pursue influence making, hate speech, fund-raising, and other strategies with great effectiveness in cyberspace. Attacks on infrastructure, including the cyber sorts, have been proven possible, to the surprise of several governments. Such attacks are probable as parts of present and future war. While democracies are often neither able nor willing to systematically close ugly websites, much less the servers they use, a range of cyber defenses is available. These include the technical, the legal, and the structural. With funding, planning, rehearsal, and occasional offensives, governments can better contain the growing threats in this new terrorist frontier.

Experts have argued that terrorists and the media are in a relationship of mutual dependence: Terrorists seek press coverage that will further their propaganda goals, and the media relish stories of drama and violence that will maximize their audience. Yet this symbiosis is not inevitable. To be sure, reckless coverage can play into the hands of the terrorists. But responsible reporting is a valuable tool that can help society understand the threats and formulate an effective counterterrorism response. Counterterrorism professionals need to take this into account. They must have a media strategy, and they can look for ways to use the media to their advantage.

Terrorist attacks are, by definition, unexpected events that may give rise to a crisis. The ability of governments to manage these crises may determine their future success or failure as governments. Successful management of an attack-induced crisis is expected; any errors by the government will be magnified, particularly if the attack is one employing a weapon of mass destruction. This chapter is designed to assist in understanding the fundamentals of successful management of terrorism crises, with particular focus on the procedures necessary to anticipate, manage, and resolve any crisis arising from terrorism.

There is no mistaking the threat to Germany: Citizens have been abroad for terrorist training; authorities dismantled a 2007 plot in the Sauerland; and in September 2009, al Qaeda published a direct threat—based on German foreign policy. The Federal Republic must be a "democracy capable of defending itself," but it knows the shadow of the years 1933 to 1945, so parliament and other authorities work hard to attain the balance of security with protection of civil liberties and liberal institutions. These ideals are visible in German institutions: There is no national gendarmerie; military and police forces are strictly separated; the federal structure keeps the sixteen *Länder* separate; and the federal interior ministry is minimized. Within these restraints, intelligence and police work to catch and convict terrorists, while abroad the policy is "effective multilateralism." While the latter is politically popular, it also bumps the republic up against the limitations of all international security institutions.

Critical infrastructure protection in the face of terrorism and natural or health hazards can be seen as a joint task of public and private stakeholders working in threat and hazard prevention, vulnerability mitigation, crisis planning, and handling crisis situations. The chapter outlines a new approach in Germany to vulnerability mitigation and crisis planning for critical infrastructures. The

approach to modernizing critical infrastructure protection is based on a strategy
for critical infrastructure protection that helps bring together various public
and private stakeholders in order to implement new protection measures and,
hence, make critical infrastructures more robust and more flexible than
in the past.

Beginning with phenomena in the Algerian War, the French have extensive
national experience with terrorism. Attacks on French interests and citizens
have occurred frequently within the country and overseas. But in recent years
the government has successfully evaded or preempted any major terrorist
catastrophe on French soil, and it is highly useful to understand why. Excellent
intelligence, special investigative magistrates, new legal procedures, seriousness about detaining suspects, robust special counterterrorism forces, and support from the citizenry and the central government are the leading reasons for
the "silent victories" in France.

The counterinsurgency in Afghanistan is different than past misadventures
there, and the prospects for a military defeat of the Taliban are good if six principles and two microstrategies are uniformly applied. First, prevent collateral
damage to avoid swelling the insurgent ranks. Second, focus on the expenditure
of development funds. Third, ensure there is persistent presence in the remote
and rural areas. Fourth, commit to the longer-term effort of developing a literate
population. Fifth, actively demonstrate respect for Islam. Sixth, apply a zero
tolerance approach to corruption. These measures must be complemented with
the implementation of microstrategies to expand the incidence of cross-border
shuras among Pakistani and Afghan subtribes and the construction of combat
outposts along dominant terrain just inside Afghanistan.

In any place where non-indigenous, national, and other local armed forces
operate in the same battle space, there is usually discord, and there may be
terrorism. One of the reasons is a fundamental lack of understanding of several
factors: identification of potential counterinsurgents, the main cultural conditions and perspectives that apply to the local security environment, and the
operational capabilities and limitations of the security actors. These factors can
be called the security architecture. The case study of Pakistan's Pashtun tribal
belt demonstrates that, although security architecture is complex and not a
panacea for military planning, it provides indispensible insight. There is clear
value to the study of terrorism's "root causes," and the vital region covered in
this case study is a necessary place to begin.

Foreword

Terrorism had already emerged as a major security challenge when the Marshall Center was established in 1993. Since that time, al Qaeda's declarations of war (1996, 1998) and many world tragedies have only underscored the need for vigorously resisting the terrorist threat—now a primary factor in strategic planning for most countries on the globe.

The body of literature on terrorism has grown immensely and quickly. What is still too slender is the published reading available to professionals in counterterrorism (CT). There are simply too few good books aimed at defeating terrorism, as against merely describing it further. The present volume responds to this pressing need.

The enclosed essays are a coherent product of intellectual labor within our Program on Terrorism and Security Studies, a CT course initiated in 2004 by Col. A. N. "Nick" Pratt (USMC, ret.). Marshall Center professors, regularly visiting scholars, and several other talented friends of our center have prepared these chapters. All these pages are new; none has appeared elsewhere.

Unit 1, "The Problem and Its History," offers this volume's assessment of the terrorist phenomenon, which has mandated the invention of "counterterrorism." Col. Pratt, who did more than anyone to shape our CT curricula, explores how terrorism has evolved over the ages, drawing out ancient cases before coming forward into contemporary times. Another of our editors, Dr. Harmon, makes a new contribution to a public discussion he literally helped start, or restart, with work of 2004–2006 in Washington and here in Garmisch: how terrorist groups end, and what their many and diverse histories suggest about tackling al Qaeda. Dr. Gorka, who has taught in three countries and regularly lectures for the US Joint Special Operations University, looks back over the development of institutions in the West and demands to know whether we possess the right ones to adequately address messy challenges by malevolent substate actors.

Given that the world community of 2010 has a serious and continuing terrorism problem, how should we face it?

That discussion commences in earnest with Unit 2, "Law, Force, and the Military Option," opening with coauthored work by our celebrated international lawyer, Michael Schmitt, and Navy Captain and lawyer, Dean Dwigans. Their chapter is followed by an essay by Dr. Harmon about past uses of force. If there have been failures, there are also glittering examples of successful CT—and these deserve closer study by CT practitioners as surely as they deserve better recognition by voting citizens.

Next comes J. Q. Roberts, who served the Marshall Center as Deputy Director between past and current tours in the Pentagon, dealing with special forces and low-intensity conflict. Years of experience allow him to lay out three keys to success in the use of CT forces, and they compel study. Another current practitioner, a US Army field force commander, closes the section with his well-organized thoughts on "stability operations" in conflict zones where insurgency and terrorism both occur. Colonel Christopher Cavoli, a brilliant success here as an academic fellow, may well be back in Afghanistan when this book appears.

Unit 3 turns to "Instruments of National Power." Many of these are nonmilitary and well suit our world of the moment—in which al Qaeda has been driven out of Afghanistan, Abu Sayyaf has been decimated in the Philippines, many Irish terrorists have "decommissioned" their guns and bomb factories, and the Iraqi insurgency has been winding down. Thus we begin with diplomacy—including public diplomacy and traditional sorts—addressed expertly by two former ambassadors: Mary Ann Peters and David Litt. The dangers of talking to terrorists are balanced out with the possible benefits in an exciting contribution by British Army veteran James Wither of the Marshall Center's faculty.

CT creates an insatiable demand for all kinds of intelligence. Acquiring and managing intelligence that is actionable and sound, and then knowing when and with whom to share it, is a preoccupation in counterterrorism. This is especially so for our author on the subject, Dr. John J. Le Beau, a former career intelligence operative as well as one of our Marshall Center's best lecturers. Some intelligence is financial, and countering terrorist finances is a field to which the Program on Terrorism and Security Studies (PTSS) has long devoted a special module, offering lectures on Hawala money exchanges, legal cases involving Hamas, Hezbollah's money-raising in Latin America, FARC's drugs, and the larger organized crime-terrorism nexus. Celina Realuyo was a financial specialist who ran the team at the US Department of State that won a rare high rating from the 9/11 Commission. Her essay draws on much work in the private finance sector, travels in scores of countries, and immense experience in "Following the Terrorist Money Trail" for the US government from 2002 to 2006.

Ideas matter. Clarification of our principles and serious debate are central to the struggle against the terrorists. We thus welcome the chapter by a leading British scholar on world religions and their relationships to political violence, Patrick Sookhdeo, a regular lecturer here; he writes on "Islamists" whose doctrines and deeds confound the religion they insist on calling theirs. The problems of propaganda and hate speech on the World Wide Web are explored by John Kane, who was PTSS Deputy until 2009 and remains our resource on cyber terrorism, internet radicalization, and the proper rebuttals to these. Closely related to these phenomena are the worldwide public media—which convey strong messages, of both good and bad men. Our lecturer from Reuters, Mark Trevelyan, has presented his ideas on whether there is a "right" way for media to report on terrorism. Understanding his subject, and thinking through his counsel, will help our readers, especially those engaged in crafting good public affairs postures as their ministries and security forces grapple with terrorist incidents.

Media policy is but one of the many fields touched on by John Clarke, our center's expert on crisis management, and editor of a book on homeland security. Dr. Clarke addresses "the day things go badly," because, invariably, on some days they will. His map for strategic thinking in emergencies also sets up subsequent case studies in the final section of this volume.

"Case Studies" of particular countries' counterterrorism issues make up Unit 4. Of intriguing diversity, these chapters are written by practiced hands, including two true experts (Mike Fenzel and Tom Wilhelm) on the fighting in Southwest Asia, where insurgency and terrorism are thoroughly intermixed.

Two German authors offer studies of their Federal Republic's policies and strategies. Our senior German professor, Dr. Ralf Roloff, writes on broad themes of democratic balancing and "the democracy which can defend itself." Longtime civil servant and PTSS lecturer Peter Lauwe brings his career's work on critical infrastructure protection into focus as he details German plans and policies and experience to date with various disasters and near-misses.

France, no less than Germany, has enjoyed many CT preemptions and successes. Why? A unique blend of special institutions, sound law, good intelligence, and serious policing, according to our authors. These are the outgoing French Chair, Marine Lt. General Jean-Paul Raffenne, and coauthor Jean-Francois Clair, whose career placed him in very high posts within DST, the domestic intelligence service of the French Republic.

There have already been 650 counterterrorism practitioners who have graduated from our Program on Terrorism and Security Studies, which has grown in size yet continuously must turn away candidates. Our students—if that word suits mid-career professionals—have come from ninety countries. As they graduate, they literally foster a living network of CT expertise—just the sort of successful program the world needs to match terrorist networks. They share something else too: The will to defeat this modern scourge of calculated political violence against the innocent. In this program we adhere to an instructive proposition, borrowed from a legend in modern terrorism studies: While relativists say "one man's terrorist is another man's freedom fighter," the truth is that one country's terrorist is another country's terrorist. That wisdom comes from Paul Wilkinson, a past lecturer here. We share what has been the preoccupation of Wilkinson's life work: That democracies find the proper balance between the mandates of security and the rights of liberty as they meet the terrorist's challenge.

This volume, good and scholarly on its own terms, will be a textbook for our internal use for the next five years. Its publication by as respected a press as McGraw-Hill makes the prudence and research and experience of the Program on Terrorism and Security Studies available to all who want to help in countering terrorism: graduate students, those at military schools, involved citizens, private experts on security in the business world, members of police forces and defense departments, conflict resolution experts, and many other sorts of practitioners seeking a sober and highly international approach. PTSS has helped make Garmisch one of the world's most well-known centers of thought and work on counterterrorism. I am glad to see this public offering by all our PTSS authors and their fine editorial team: Dr. Sebastian Gorka, Colonel Nick Pratt, and Dr. Christopher C. Harmon.

January 2010
Garmisch, Germany

Dr. John Rose, BGen. US Army (ret.)
Director, George C. Marshall Center

Introduction

We look at a global landscape dotted with local warlords who create and command sub-cultures of violence, conflicts that continue for decades, terrorists with global ambitions who are determined to kill in ever-greater quantities, and transnational criminal gangs that employ terrorist tactics to challenge state authority head-on.

In my first monograph on terrorism, written in 1974, I observed that, as a consequence of political developments and technological changes, power—defined crudely as the capacity to kill, destroy, disrupt, alarm, and compel society to divert vast resources to security—was coming into the hands of smaller and smaller groups. The power once possessed almost exclusively by national armies was being wielded by gangs whose grievances, real or imaginary, would not always be possible to remedy. Putting it another way, the tiny bands of political fanatics that have existed throughout history were becoming an increasingly potent force to be reckoned with as we approached the end of the twentieth century. How we, as democracies, would meet this threat—and remain democracies—posed one of the major challenges of our age.

This felicitous, although frightening, mental flash still haunts me. It is the focus of the essays of this book. They address both the use of military force and the employment of nonmilitary tools, the role of international cooperation, and the importance of the ideological contest. Collectively, they push toward a grand strategy against terrorism.

The Evolution of Strategy

Many years ago, a high-ranking official in the Defense Department asked me whether terrorists think strategically. I answered, No. What we called terrorism was a set of tactics employed by some groups. The members of these groups did not think of the tactics as a set. In fact, the analysts gave more coherence to terrorism than did those we labeled terrorists. Action-oriented extremists, the terrorists had some primitive notions about spectacular actions to attract attention to themselves, create alarm, free imprisoned comrades, and possibly provoke government repression that they hoped would, in turn, drive the masses to their barricades; but these notions were not really a strategy.

Asked by the same official if we had a strategy to counter terrorism, I again answered, No. We had an accumulation of security measures and policy statements. Each one had its origins in response to a specific event, but their original context was often forgotten, and they had become a kind of mantra, frequently repeated but not well understood.

Some countries developed strategies to defeat terrorist campaigns on their own territory, but the idea of a global strategy against terrorism meant something different before 9/11. The principal international concern, that of most western countries, especially the United States, was terrorism spilling over into the international domain in the form of airline hijackings, kidnappings of diplomats and other assaults on internationally protected targets, or terrorist attacks in other countries. In other words, a specific set of tactics and targets provoked the international response to terrorism. A diplomatic strategy was required.

To mobilize and maintain the necessary international support required keeping the focus on individual terrorist tactics and targets, out of the political realm where discussions of causes might complicate matters. The goal was the suppression of international terrorism, not the defeat of specific terrorist groups.

Like-minded governments did go further, cooperating in the exchange of intelligence, expertise, and technology to prevent terrorist attacks and improve response. Western European governments took the lead in forging a more unified response to what was seen as a mutual terrorist threat. But there was still no thought of a grand global strategy.

The attacks on 9/11 altered notions of strategy. The objective was no longer merely the suppression of terrorism as a phenomenon, but the eradication of a specific terrorist enterprise that operated globally. A Global War on Terrorism required a global strategy. Unfortunately, this is where things became muddled.

The Global War on Terrorism was at first a campaign to destroy the particular terrorist enterprise responsible for the 9/11 attacks—al Qaeda. Then Washington expanded it to include the elimination of all terrorist groups that had killed Americans or who might threaten US security, but to ensure international cooperation, it had to include other countries' terrorist foes. Just about all terrorist groups were to be destroyed. But the old quest of eliminating terrorism as a phenomenon was never abandoned, causing those trapped in the old conceptual cage to wonder how we could wage war on a set of tactics. The blending of the old and new campaigns also introduced the old policy mantras about not making concessions to terrorists holding hostages. To this already huge potpie were added concerns about nuclear proliferation, the spread of weapons of mass destruction, and rogue states, which brought Iraq, Iran, and North Korea into the mix. Instead of strategy, the result was a daunting list of serious concerns and ambitious goals, each of which seemed logical, but together constituted a hugely ambitious undertaking that went far beyond what we started with. That other countries, while sharing America's concerns, remained skeptical at this global project is understandable.

Déjà vu and Despair

I read the excellent essays in this book with a sense of *déjà vu* and, inevitably, a small measure of despair. As a young Special Forces officer in the 1960s, I pored over the writings of T. E. Lawrence, Mao Tse-tung, Ho Chi Minh, and Che Guevara. The US Department of Defense had sponsored a series of detailed case studies of counterinsurgency campaigns, and the RAND Corporation had translated the French General Staff's report on lessons learned from the Indochina War.

True, these works were about insurgency and counterinsurgency, not counterterrorism. The word "terrorism" appeared in the texts, but it had not yet acquired the currency it has today or its status as a unique and distinguishable mode of conflict. In the late 1960s, the term "urban guerrillas" was often used to describe those who used terrorist tactics and who today certainly would be described as terrorists. At that time, theoreticians of urban guerrilla warfare, including Carlos Marighela and Abraham Guillen, discussed the utility of terrorist tactics. Gradually, terrorism moved beyond guerrilla warfare to become its own domain.

My sense of *déjà vu* does not diminish the originality of the scholarship reflected in this book. It merely underscores the relevance of history. References in these chapters reach back to the Algerian War in the 1950s, the Philippine insurgency in 1902, the Northwest Frontier in the nineteenth century. It seems that we return to history, exploring it in new ways to relearn lessons that are still valid.

Intimate Local Knowledge

One lesson that comes through in the essays is the importance of detailed local knowledge. Strategies may set objectives, guide actions, and determine how resources should be allocated, but the implementation of strategy depends on the local situation and the terrain. This seems truer in terrorism than in conventional conflict. When conventional military forces can concentrate their full kinetic power on destroying other conventional forces, less local adaptation may be required. But where success depends on the orchestration of many tools of state—diplomacy, traditional law enforcement, military force, political warfare, psychological operations, economic development—tailoring to unique local situations becomes critical.

In this context, local means intimate, down to the tribe, the clan, family connections, the town, the neighborhood, local history, small-group portraits. If grand strategy is broad top-down thinking, counterterrorism is implemented bottom-up.

We are currently engaged in an effort to defeat and dismantle a global terrorist enterprise, but the nature of that enterprise in Algeria is very different from what it is in Iraq or Afghanistan or Indonesia. It arises from different soil in each place. Defeating it requires different combinations of tactics and policy tools. America's Global War on Terrorism—a now discarded term—in fact, consists of hundreds of little wars. That was true of counterinsurgency in the 1960s. It is true of counterterrorism in the twenty-first century.

My sense of despair comes from personal recollections of how difficult it is to engage high-level decision makers in this kind of detail. Leaders of vast government organizations, commanders of mighty armies, while realizing the importance of the particular, nonetheless find the descent into micropolitics difficult. They want to know how we prevent another 9/11, or 3/11, or 7/7, how we dismantle al Qaeda, how we defeat terrorism, not necessarily how inter- and intra-tribal politics shape the Taliban insurgency in Afghanistan and thereby the future fate of al Qaeda. Yet strategy must be informed by detail. And the global conflict will be fought in detail.

This places an enormous burden on intelligence, which is another theme that recurs in these essays. We need both current intelligence and contextual intelligence. It is not merely a matter of collecting bits of information or "connecting the dots," to use the now-famous phrase. These tasks are difficult enough by themselves, but we also need to know the local social geography, the very local politics, the belief systems, and the operational codes of our terrorist adversaries. This requires not only intelligence analysts but area experts, anthropologists, psychologists, criminologists, and others with an array of expertise. Since governments are unlikely to hold this diversity of talent, we must find ways to mobilize knowledge to get smart fast, just as we have developed ways to mobilize troops. Despite understandable sensitivities within academic communities, the social sciences have played and will continue to play a significant role in helping to understand terrorism and deal with it in a legitimate way.

Effective counterterrorism also requires understanding our terrorist foes. That proposition is not to be confused with being understanding of our terrorist foes—which implies sympathy. Until recently, we have not done well here. The Cold War prompted a rich scholarship aimed at understanding Soviet adversaries, their worldview, strategic thinking, views of war-fighting, operational codes. (Soviet scholars similarly carefully analyzed western behavior.) Mutual understanding helped prevent war between the two superpowers.

In contrast, at that time, terrorists were dismissed as mad dogs or evildoers, unworthy of serious inquiry. Attempts to understand what they were about risked being seen as subversive. That left us with a two-dimensional caricature of our terrorist foes, leading to two-dimensional KA-POW! strategies, politically appealing but ineffective.

There is now a growing and excellent body of work that focuses on terrorist belief systems, methods of recruiting, decision making, operations, and communications projects. And this knowledge is informing a more sophisticated approach to counterterrorism, as evidenced in the following chapters.

Law Enforcement or Military Force

The essays raise another fundamental point: The legitimate excuses for war have been greatly narrowed in the past half-century. Many disapprove of war under any circumstances, although war itself has not been outlawed. There are specific circumstances when the resort to arms is permitted by international law. In all circumstances, the conduct of warfare has rules. These are not always obeyed, but they are no less valid despite the breaches. We accept that wars will be fought. We demand that they be regulated. The fact that terrorists do not abide by these rules is not, as some argue, an excuse for us to abandon them. Counterterrorism is not just about defeating terrorists. It is about upholding the law.

Terrorism is regarded by most people, and defined by international law, as illegal, outside the norms of conflict, a crime in itself, unjustified by any circumstances. Counterterrorism does not recognize terrorism as a legitimate mode of conflict. A terrorist, by definition, is an outlaw. While we may sympathize with the terrorists' grievances in some cases, while we must operate within the constraints imposed by the rules of war, and while we should treat terrorist prisoners humanely, we still condemn terrorism and do not recognize terrorists as legitimate combatants.

This complicates counterterrorism immensely. We debate whether terrorism should be treated as a law enforcement problem or as a form of war. The operational differences between the two are significant. Treating terrorism as a law enforcement problem means precisely defining the crime in criminal codes, correctly identifying the perpetrators, gathering evidence that will stand up in a court of law, prosecuting the accused on the basis of individual culpability, not groups of persons on the basis of membership.

In contrast, dealing with terrorism as a mode of warfare, even while condemning terrorists as criminals, means collecting intelligence aimed at thwarting terrorist attacks and destroying terrorist groups. The target is the terrorist conspiracy and the enterprise that inspires, instructs, and supports the terrorist acts. Support is defined broadly. Treating terrorism as war also means a continuing campaign. The response is not linked to the individual terrorist act. The state may continue to strike again and again in a variety of ways until the group is isolated politically, impoverished financially, reduced numerically, disorganized and no longer capable of launching terrorist attacks, but kept on the run. Law enforcement seeks a conviction. War on terrorists is relentless.

History provides examples of both approaches and, more often, combinations of the two. Some countries have waged internal wars, often brutal, against domestic terrorists. Israel regards itself as being at war with terrorists. The United Kingdom deployed its army to Northern Ireland, but for the most part dealt with IRA terrorists through a modified criminal justice system. Until 2001, the United States treated terrorism primarily as a law enforcement problem, although on occasion it employed military force in response to terrorist attacks on US targets abroad. After 9/11, the United States redefined terrorism as war.

There were sound reasons for this conceptual redefinition. Military force was going to be used in Afghanistan, where al Qaeda found refuge. Putting America's response into a framework of war was a means of mobilizing national resources and expressing national will. Most important, a framework of war allowed the United States to take the initiative in going after al Qaeda wherever it could, without awaiting further provocation. This was not retaliation for an al Qaeda attack. This was a campaign to destroy al Qaeda. Many nations that had already been or would soon find themselves targets of al Qaeda attacks accepted this definition. For the United States, going to war against al Qaeda did not mean abandoning diplomacy or law enforcement. Where the rule of law existed and the long arm of law could reach, a law enforcement approach was preferred. Where it did not, military force was employed.

As we have seen, the initial idea of a narrowly defined campaign against al Qaeda, however, soon morphed into a more ambitious war on terrorism, which encompassed a diverse array of missions. With the invasion of Iraq, a dangerous and ultimately costly distraction from the effort against al Qaeda, America's counterterrorist campaign appeared almost exclusively military. Domestic politics encouraged this view.

The deliberate abandonment of the term "Global War on Terrorism" suggests that the United States will now revert to a law enforcement approach, but the United States and its allies are still engaged in Iraq, and they confront an expanding insurgency in Afghanistan, where military involvement in a counterinsurgency effort is justified primarily by a counterterrorist objective—the requirement to defeat al Qaeda.

Toward Super-Precision Warfare

The tasks of law enforcement and waging war are becoming blurred. The reluctance to go to war, especially in the West, is gradually creating a criminal predicate as the only legitimate *casus belli*. It is no longer accepted that nations go to war merely for the advantage of the state. Instead, many argue that limited military force may be used only to prevent crimes of great magnitude, such as genocide, or to bring perpetrators of great crimes to justice. From this perspective, the force applied must be limited and precisely targeted. A nation is not a target; not even its armed forces but only selected members of its leadership may be targeted. Similarly, military force to combat terrorism, if used at all, is to be aimed at tiny groups to prevent them from carrying out attacks or at designated individual terrorist leaders. This is super-precision warfare, required by today's sensitivities, enabled by today's precision weaponry.

At the same time, law enforcement organizations, facing well-armed adversaries, have been obliged to create tactical units and increase their armament. In a few countries where governments confront well-armed criminal syndicates willing to directly challenge state authority, armies have assumed law enforcement functions, which increasingly resemble low-level war.

The fusion of war fighting and law enforcement, especially in the area of counterterrorism, challenges institutions and rules that were designed for a clear separation of the two. At what point does precision targeting become assassination? While formally rejecting assassination, the United States has argued that targeted killings in a war context—using remotely piloted drones to kill terrorist leaders in Pakistan as part of its campaign against al Qaeda—is legitimate. Obviously, this raises some difficult questions.

At what point does the military interception of a terrorist team become an ambush?—an issue raised when British commandos killed IRA operatives in Gibraltar. What rules of engagement should govern the use of force in Afghanistan or against Somali pirates in the Indian Ocean?

How long can individuals be detained on suspicion of involvement in terrorism before they are formally charged?—a topic of debate in the United Kingdom. What rules govern the status of captured terrorists? Are they enemy combatants to be held for the duration of hostilities or must they be brought to trial in regular courts? Absence of clarity here has fed an ongoing mess in the United States.

Finite Goals or Perpetual War

This brings us to another salient aspect of counterterrorism. Combating terrorism—the term used in the United States years before the Global War on Terrorism—implied an enduring task. Law enforcement accepts this. Authorities try to prevent crime, reduce crime, contain crime; they never think that they will defeat crime.

War, on the other hand, at least in western thinking, implies a finite undertaking including desire to reestablish the peace. A war is to be fought and won or ended in a political settlement. Warfare is not intended to go on forever—except as considered by some terrorist foes. Does counterterrorism have an achievable finite goal or is it perpetual warfare?

One essay asks, How does terrorism end? Terrorists theoretically may achieve their own stated goals, gaining independence or taking power. Some would argue that the victories of the Khmer Rouge in Cambodia, the Sandinistas in Nicaragua, and the ANC in South Africa are examples of terrorists' successes. True, terrorism was clearly an important component of these struggles, but it was only one component. The Khmer Rouge and Sandinistas fielded guerrilla armies, and all three movements had large political bases, which they were able to mobilize. The case of the PLO is more complicated. Terrorism played a key role in creating a sense of Palestinian nationalism and mobilizing a measure of international support, but four decades of armed resistance has yet to create an independent, viable Palestinian state.

Lacking a large political base, the tiny terrorist armies active in Europe were unable to translate terrorist violence into concrete political achievement, although some contests continue. In many cases, terrorists are defeated—successfully suppressed by the authorities or obliged to abandon their violent tactics and enter the political process. But it is difficult to negotiate with terrorists, and with religiously inspired fanatics, it is impossible. Do counterterrorist campaigns end only when the last terrorist is killed?

Individual terrorist groups may eventually be defeated, although terrorists show remarkable resiliency, and contests may drag on for decades. But terrorism as a phenomenon, as a violent mode of political expression, as a component of armed conflict, is likely to persist, as do other forms of crime. In some cases, our goals are finite and achievable. In others, we must accept a continuing effort. In all cases, the contests are likely to be long, which poses a particular challenge for impatient democracies that are reluctant to support imperial tasks. Our strategies, therefore, must be sustainable and also thoughtful.

Brian Michael Jenkins

Unit 1

The Problem
and Its History

Andrew Nichols Pratt

Terrorism's Evolution:

Yesterday, Today, and Forever

In confronting the challenge of international terrorism, the first step is to call things by their proper names, to see clearly and say plainly who the terrorists are, what goals they seek, and which governments support them. What the terrorist does is kill, maim, kidnap, and torture. His or her victims may be children in the schoolroom, innocent travelers on airplanes, businessmen returning home from work, political leaders. . . . The terrorist's victims may have no particular political identity, or they may be political symbols, like Aldo Moro or, perhaps, Pope John Paul II. They may be kidnapped and held for ransom, maimed, or simply blown to bits. One defining characteristic of the terrorist is his choice of method; the terrorist chooses violence as the instrument of first resort.

William Joseph Casey, US Director of Central Intelligence[1]

Minoru Yamasaki, who designed the soaring World Trade Center that dominated Manhattan's skyline for three decades, intended this complex as a "living symbol of man's dedication to world peace."[2] On the beautiful clear morning of 11 September 2001, Osama bin Laden's al Qaeda—nineteen Salafi-Jihadist terrorists—simultaneously devastated this compelling symbol of peace while attacking a vibrant center of international cooperation, the cerebral cortex of American security and America's ordinary citizenry. Al Qaeda's actions that morning revealed at once the extent of their hatred for our democracy and our freedoms that this system protects. We must never forget the 2,975 souls from more than ninety nations who perished that day.[3] Like a virtual memorial, this attack should remind all democracies, not just the United States, that the price for freedom may reach as high as those sadly absent Twin Towers. However, of greater significance, 9/11 raised fundamental questions regarding how our societies must address this threat. The answers to these questions necessitate a thorough understanding of the history and causes of the terrorism phenomenon and of the extraordinary chapters that ensue in this text.

   Without compromising our ideals, how do democratic societies recognize quite ordinary and unremarkable men, who harbor a virulent hatred for democracy; counter an organization opposed to democratic freedoms, yet which itself mimics *Fortune* 500 companies; and protect themselves from an ideology rooted in fanatical, seventh-century social practices, which today are goaded into lethal action by base and pernicious prejudice?[4] How does a democratic society coexist with a struggling, traditional culture overwhelmed by immoral western influences? And perhaps most significant, how do democracies address the considerable security problem confronting countries with growing immigrant populations, an undetermined percentage of whom are radicalized to the point of threatening violence? How do we defuse these potential terrorists whose nationality inscribed on a passport is of little consequence to the bearer, who identifies himself primarily by religion and a sense of primary allegiance to a transnational community; a question a Program on Terrorism and Security Studies (PTSS) colleague once posed? Europe contends with a potentially violent fifth column movement, but to date has experienced considerable difficulty in acknowledging this threat, let alone in dealing with this politically charged menace.[5]

While the purpose of this book is to address counterterrorism—its policies, strategies, campaigns, and current patterns and trends—for context, this effort must commence with a précis of the problem. Terrorism is a complex phenomenon; challenging to understand whether one is a social scientist, a military commander, a diplomat, an intelligence officer, a political leader . . . or a student. Terrorism is a tactic used to socially, politically, and psychologically fragment a targeted population. These tactics created a line of development beginning in ancient times that can be traced and from which we will gain insights and knowledge. To begin to understand terrorists' behavior and their goals in order to craft counterterrorism policies, we must have a sense of terrorism's history. Terrorism, like a persistent cancer, has invaded our societies in the past; it afflicts us today; and terrorism may destroy our descendants correspondingly if we fail to grasp its fundamentals. Misunderstanding terrorism almost guarantees policy failures.

Of primary importance is our appreciation of how terrorism has mutated from a purely domestic, nation-specific problem into an "existential" threat to national security and international stability, as described by the former British Prime Minister, Tony Blair.[6] Terrorists' traditional motivation has been premeditated, political violence designed to influence an audience. The doyen of terrorism studies, Brian Jenkins, noted over thirty years ago, ". . . terrorists want a lot of people watching, not a lot of people dead." While his comment became an aphorism, Jenkins in 1999 acknowledged terrorism's dramatic transformation. The most recent attacks in New York, London, and Mumbai illustrate that terrorism's current goal is the achievement of the highest body count possible.[7] Four- or five-digit terrorism, or casualties greater than those of 9/11, appears to be the aim or measure of effectiveness sought by modern terrorists. But, while terrorism's blood craving has grown, terrorism's nature endures. The essence of terrorism remains the acquisition and retention of power. Terrorism is always political, a direct challenge to the polity, and to the state's legitimacy and authority, even when other motives such as religion, criminality, or psychology are involved.

To counter terrorism, one must understand what it really is—a deliberate choice—neither the product of inflamed passion, the environment of war, nor of the strength of feeling sustaining a cause. Terrorism is a method, not a description.[8] Since the dawn of history, all acts of terrorism or terrorist campaigns are designed to promote publicity while creating fear, panic, and the prospect to seize power.

But what makes terrorism so imperative for us to understand today as an existential threat, as the former British Prime Minister Blair warned, are the terrorists' modern weapons. In one sense, terrorism's history can be represented in a simple chronological progression that presents the terrorists' weapons of choice: daggers, garrotes, guns, explosives, and at present, weapons of mass destruction. We will commence our sojourn through terrorism's history by talking about the terrorists who discriminately murdered their victims with daggers, and we will conclude with comments about modern terrorists who combine a desire to attack indiscriminately on a global stage with both the capability and the motivation of using weapons of mass destruction.

First Quest: Defining Our Threat

We must begin our quest by developing a working definition of terrorism for this text; for use while at the Marshall Center; and—we suggest—for professionals. With seven simple cases we ask, "Was this an act of terrorism or some other form of violent activity?"

1. From 1933 to 1945, Nazi Germany slaughtered six million Jews throughout Europe and Eurasia;

2. In late December 1937, the Japanese Imperial Army raped and murdered over 260,000 Chinese in a senseless orgy of violence;

3. On 6 August 1945, a lone US Army Air Corps B-29 attacked Hiroshima with an atomic bomb; approximately forty-five thousand Japanese died in a flash and many tens of thousands died later;

4. On 12 October 2000, a small rubber boat with two waving occupants motored along-side the *USS Cole* (DDG 67), an American warship harbored in the Yemeni port of Aden, and exploded, blowing a hole in its side, killing seventeen sailors and injuring thirty-nine;

5. On 19 September 2006, Robert Redeker, a public high school philosophy teacher and writer near Toulouse, wrote in the newspaper *Le Figaro* that Mohammad was "a merciless warlord, a looter, a mass-murderer of Jews and a polygamist." He also called the Koran "a book of incredible violence," comparing Islam unfavorably with Christianity and Judaism and criticizing the hostile reaction to a speech by Pope Benedict XVI. Redeker, his wife, and children immediately received death threats by telephone, e-mail, and on the internet forum that published photos of him, a home address, directions to his home, and his cell phone number. That day's issue of *Le Figaro* was banned in Egypt and Tunisia and a contributor to *Al Hesbah* wrote "May God send some lion to cut his head."[9]

6. On 5 April 2007, Second Lieutenant Joanna Dyer and three other British soldiers perished from a roadside bomb while on patrol in Basra, Iraq. Former Prime Minister Blair labeled the ambush an "act of terrorism," suggesting its perpetrators were linked to Iran;[10] and

7. On 27 October 2008, Islamist rebels stoned to death thirteen-year-old Aisha Ibrahim Duhulow . . . for being raped. Begging for mercy moments before being buried up to her shoulders and her horrific execution, the Somali youngster is said to have pleaded "Don't kill me, don't kill me" in front of a thousand-strong crowd.[11]

We shall return to these seven cases later in this chapter.

Defining terrorism has proven to be difficult even for one country, let alone regional organizations or global bodies. A definition overtly describes our approaches to the problem

---

". . . the unlawful use of force or violence against persons or property to intimidate or coerce a government, the civilian population, or any segment thereof, in furtherance of political or social objectives." *Federal Bureau of Investigation (FBI)*

> "... premeditated, politically motivated violence perpetrated against noncombatant targets by subnational groups or clandestine agents, usually intended to influence an audience." *US Department of State*
>
> "... calculated use of violence or threat of violence to inculcate fear, intended to coerce or to try to intimidate governments or societies in pursuit of goals that are generally political, religious, or ideological." *US Department of Defense*

of terrorism and profoundly influences how we respond to it. If terrorism is always considered a crime (as distinct from war), then in America, the Justice Department and the police are responsible for combating it, and it is difficult legally to call on the military in incidents on US territory, even in situations (such as those involving chemical or biological agents) for which only the military is trained to respond.[12] If terms such as "unlawful," or "against persons or property," are found in the text as in the foregoing definition used by the Federal Bureau of Investigation, we can surmise a "legal" or "judicial" approach will be taken to the terrorism problem. This type of approach entails the application of the rule of law in which evidentiary practices apply; law enforcement means are practiced; and imprisonment will serve to bring the terrorist criminals to justice.

Terms such as "politically motivated violence" or "to intimidate governments" as depicted above imply a political-military approach. Evidentiary practices need not necessarily be followed. While intelligence could fail to meet the higher threshold of evidence, a democratically elected political leader can act on reasonable intelligence that might not meet the highest standards of a court. In fact, a leader may be morally or constitutionally obliged to act. While "politically incorrect" in some circles, the use of overwhelming military force can be a political-military solution to some terrorism, as the campaign against the Liberation Tigers of Tamil Eelam (LTTE) in Sri Lanka has so vividly demonstrated. And while not immediately a matter of definition, we should remember that no campaign intended to eliminate terrorism has ever been successful without first eliminating terrorists.

Concomitantly, a nation's definition normally reflects its history of fighting terrorism. The United Kingdom's decades-long campaign against the Belfast-based "Provisionals," who vowed to use violence as a catalyst for unification, played out in Northern Ireland, in Great Britain, in the Republic of Ireland, as well as in Europe. Consequently, both the United Kingdom's old and post-9/11 definitions of terrorism described "putting the public in fear" locally, as well as "outside" the United Kingdom.[13] One's experience with terrorism shapes one's definition of terrorism.

Additionally, geostrategic shifts can impact upon a definitional construction. Russia introduced a Security Council resolution in 2004 that expanded the definition of terrorism to include Chechen and Palestinian groups, enlarging the list of terrorist individuals and groups beyond those linked to al Qaeda and the Taliban by United Nations Security Resolution 1267.[14] Russia proposed terrorism be described as "any act intended to cause death or serious injury to civilians or taking of hostages" to compel action. Such acts "are under no circumstance justifiable by consideration of a political, philosophical, ideological, racial, ethnic, religious or similar nature." In so acting, Russia abruptly reversed decades of support for terrorists fighting for territory and self-determination. Foreign Minister Sergei

Lavrov declared, "The time has come to renounce the double standard once and for all when it comes to terror, no matter what slogans it uses."[15]

Our definitional challenge impels us to arrive at as complete and objective definition of terrorism as possible—one acceptable for academic research as well as for facilitating counterterrorist operations on an international scale.[16] To accomplish this, we can apply a Clausewitzian-like approach to defining terrorism based on three important elements:[17]

1. The aim of the action, which is always political—that is, to gain or to maintain political objectives, changing a regime, changing the people in power, or changing social or economic policies;

2. The essence of the action—that is, the use of or threat to use violence to influence a broader audience as opposed to nonviolent protest such as strikes, peaceful demonstrations, or tax revolts; and

3. The target of the action—that is, civilians. Terrorism is distinguished from other types of political violence such as guerrilla warfare and civil insurrection by the intentional targeting of civilians.

As Boaz Ganor has noted during his visits to the Marshall Center, terrorism exploits the relative vulnerability of the civilian "underbelly" and is not the result of an accidental injury inflicted on a civilian or a group of civilians who stumbled into an area of violent activity.[18] While a literal copy of this Clausewitzian-like approach to defining terrorism is not necessary, any sound definition of terrorism should address these three elements in some analogous manner. Furthermore, as a security official peruses an intelligence report or examines the scene of an attack, applying this definitional approach will be equally beneficial. However, our global community still cannot arrive at a simple definition that satisfies all.

The impasse in arriving at a universal definition of terrorism nurtured over time the myth that "one man's terrorist is another man's freedom fighter," which is twaddle[19] and a false dichotomy. The term "freedom fighter" has to do with ends such as Euskadi Ta Askatasuna's (ETA) secessionist goal of freeing the Basque people from control by Spain. Terrorism connotes the means of achieving this goal. To reiterate, terrorism is a tactic; it is a method. Hence, an individual can claim the mantle of freedom fighter using terrorism to achieve his purposes; however, in reality he is simply a terrorist.

The genesis of this enduring myth is in the United Nations' "crisis of identity" suffered during the Cold War. This saga plays out in the first pages of Rolf Ekeus's discussion of the United Nations' contemporary challenges. A portion of the UN's membership still adhered to ideologies or doctrines that rejected human rights and supported the absolute authority of the state. The United Nations' body fractured between the democratic West and the authoritarian East. The upshot found the Security Council evolving into a debating society and the General Assembly transforming into a stage for "a beauty contest in which both sides wooed for political favors from the nonaligned."[20] Aroused in the early 1970s by a wave of letter bombs, the Lod airport attack in Israel, and, finally, the Munich massacre, UN Secretary General Kurt Waldheim enjoined the United Nations to define terrorism in order to punish these perpetrators. Simultaneously, "wars of national liberation" were being discussed in New York and were perceived by the Soviet Union and many developing nations as classic cases of "just war." This argument was accepted, along with a perverted corollary that those "in the right" were released from the normative rules of warfare. Thus, it proved too difficult to outlaw the activities of international terrorists. The United Nations' Sixth Committee legal commentators at this time such as Mr. Joewono, an Indonesian, and Dr. Abu Lughod, a Palestinian, contended that national liberation movements, because of their legitimate *jus ad bellum*, should be treated as privileged belligerents and absolved from the restraints of the humanitarian rules of war. In a grotesque perversion of logic, they argued, "It would be unjust to expect such peoples to adhere to the same code of ethics as those who possessed more sophisticated means of advancing their interests."[21]

If one truly appreciates international law, one man's terrorist can never be another man's freedom fighter. Although fashionable at conferences and cocktail parties, this expression serves at best as a weak lecture transition sentence or merely an empty witticism between neophytes. Murderers of young children are never "freedom fighters." If they were ever entitled to such a distinction, we would then have to concede that international law itself was nothing more than an authorization to commit evil in world affairs.[22] So let us return to our seven cases that we questioned earlier.

Words have meaning and the term "terrorism" regrettably for decades has been used promiscuously. Nazi Germany's slaughter of 6 million Jews throughout Europe and Eurasia represented an unparalleled genocide. The rape of Nanking by the Japanese Imperial Army described a depraved war crime directed from the highest echelons of the Imperial Japanese Army. The first use of the atomic bomb by the United States on Hiroshima, which killed tens of thousands of Japanese, approached the model of war that Clausewitz once defined as "absolute" war and was the Allies' "best worst option" to end World War II. From extensive research, the United States' best course of action targeted the mind of Emperor Hirohito and his decision-making structure and not innocents.[23] The year 2000 attack on *USS Cole* (DDG 67) resists a facile description. The *Cole* sailed under "Threat Condition *Bravo*," the second-lowest condition on a scale of four, so only a handful of sailors were posted on deck as it refueled. Crucially, the weapons systems on the bow and stern were unmanned because of the relatively low level of alert. Reminiscent of TV's amusing but ineffectual deputy sheriff Barney Fife of Mayberry, two sailors patrolled the ship with pistols with two rounds each and instructions not to load their weapons or fire unless fired on, and then only after being given the captain's permission. Given the nature of the ship's duties, a terrorist attack best describes this case. However, some critics have pointed out that under US law an attack against a military target does not meet the legal definition of terrorism (see: 22 USC § 2656f(d)(2)). Nonetheless, at the end of the day, the intent of this attack furthered al Qaida's political goals.[24] The case of Robert Redeker, while not archetypal terrorism, threatened bloodshed for political purposes against civilians, which amounts to an act of terrorism. Second Lt. Joanna Dyer and her fellow British soldiers died fighting a sophisticated, Iranian-supported insurgency, though their deaths were not the result of an "act of terrorism" as suggested by an understandably emotional British Prime Minister Blair. Finally, the gruesome stoning murder of thirteen-year-old Aisha Ibrahim Duhulow before a crowd depicted a horrific act of terrorism by a group of Salafi-Jihadists that was designed to dramatically intimidate local Somali citizens.

"Terrorism" loses consequence and gravitas if misused, and words such as "genocide" are, in fact, more egregious. We should examine terrorist cases focusing upon the act itself and neither its perpetrators nor the alleged probity of its cause. Now with our definition of terrorism, we will examine the nature of this pernicious phenomenon.

Terrorism's Historic Roots: Today's Antecedents

The events of New York City, Bali, Beslan, Madrid, London, and Mumbai have placed terrorism's brutal realities on center stage before a global audience. An effective way to examine terrorism's nature is to see it as part of an unfolding historical process. Terrorism is a form of political warfare and, like war itself, retains its constant nature, but its causes, objectives, and motivations evolve. The following brief treatment of terrorism's history will illuminate its enduring nature.

With certain irony, the first known terrorist group was a Jewish group called the Sicarii, an extremist offshoot of the religious sect of Zealots who attempted to expel the Romans and their Jewish collaborators from the Judean region and introduced terrorism as a strategy from approximately AD 66 to 73. The name "Sicarii" comes from the short sword or *sica*, their preferred weapon. Josephus, a first-century Jewish historian, provides our sparse history of the Sicarii and their unorthodox tactics: killing during daylight in crowded places to demonstrate the Roman Empire and Jewish kingdom's impotence; attacking in order to strike fear beyond their immediate targets; and acting in an apparent random nature. The Sicarii's high-risk assaults were conducted to demonstrate the vulnerability of the region's ruling elites. When their tolerance expired, the Romans crucified two thousand people and thus ended our first case.[25]

Next, the Assassins, an offshoot of the Ismaili sect, terrorized the Middle East during the eleventh–thirteenth centuries. Founded by Hassan-es Sabbah in the Elburz Mountains in Persia, this cult later expanded to Syria following the Mongol invasion of Persia. Operating remarkably like today's Salafi-Jihadist enterprise, the Assassins killed apostates: Muslim prefects, governors, caliphs, and even Conrad, the Crusader King of Jerusalem. Twice their leader, known in legend as "The Old Man of the Mountain," attempted to assassinate Saladin. The Assassins preferred the dagger. They courted death purportedly motivated by hashish-induced visions of paradise and were encouraged to believe nothing and dare all.[26] The Assassins were initially suppressed by the Mongols and later destroyed in 1272 by the Muslim leader al-Malik Baybars al-Bunduqdari, an important Mamluk Sultan of Egypt and Syria.[27]

The third terrorist group worthy of mention is the Thuggee. Some question the extent of the religious dimension of Thuggee; however, most contemporary sources have described them as being a Hindi religious cult, devotees of Kali, a Hindu goddess of destruction whose aims were imperceptible. Some revisionist sources consider the Thuggee a specialized form of organized crime or paramilitary activity like a modern mafia lacking any particular religious dimension. The Thuggee's centuries-long campaign ended under British rule in the 1830s, but not before this criminal terrorist group had killed as many as two million people; the group would rivet our attention if only 10 percent of that figure had died. The Thuggee strangled their victims with silk garrotes; murdered travelers who were rarely English; and attacked large areas in an indiscriminate manner. Early attempts at prosecuting and eliminating the Thuggee failed due to the lack of evidence for their crimes. Their *modus operandi* yielded very little evidence: no witnesses to interrogate, no weapons to examine, and no corpses. Furthermore, the Thuggee usually made no confessions when captured. Another obstacle to prosecution was that Thuggee groups did not act locally, but attacked all over the Indian subcontinent, including territories not under British rule. In a survey of political terrorism, the Thuggee rate no more than a footnote except for the sheer number of casualties.[28]

The last historic terrorist group we treat is the Narodnaya Volya. They functioned from January 1878 until March 1881 and arguably represent terrorism's most successful organization.[29] Walter Laqueur writes that the moral and intellectual distance between Narodnaya Volya and contemporary terrorists can be measured in light years.[30] Their motto proclaimed, "Not one drop of unnecessary blood!"[31] Sofya Perovskaya, Narodnaya Volya's most famous terrorist—who directed Czar Alexander's murder—was not unlike leaders of the Baader Meinhof, Red Brigades, or even al Qaeda. A disaffected child of the ruling class with a grudge, she hated her own. Perovskaya wanted the Russian society to compress like an overtightened spring so when it finally popped, it would break.

This was the classic era of anarchist terrorism that lasted from about 1880 to the end of World War I. Some scholars suggest a comparison is warranted between present-day terrorism and its nineteenth-century predecessor.[32] In 1906 alone, approximately thirty-six hundred government officials were killed or wounded by terrorists. Acts of terrorism became so common during this period that many Russian newspapers introduced special sections devoted solely to printing daily lists of political assassinations and bombings throughout the empire.[33] As we now know only too well, the spring finally did break in 1917 with the Bolshevik revolution, but by then Perovskaya had been hanged for murder.

Terrorism: The Tool of the Radical Left and Right

Political terrorism—not to be confused with criminal terrorism and pathological terrorism—is systematic violence used in the furtherance of political aims, often by small groups dedicated to a specific agenda, usually involving attacks upon the governing authorities.[34] Political terrorism emanates from the left and right political spectrums and from political motivations in between. Thus, distinctions between political and ethnic terrorism occasionally blur as some separatist groups are influenced by, or receive support from, the left, despite being nationalists. Terrorism in an outlying region or colony is often assumed to be separatist in its logic, though loyalist terrorists have been opposed to the exclusion of Northern Ireland from the United Kingdom. The left and the right occasionally clash with right-wing terrorists seeking to defend the status quo. This has occurred, for example, in Colombia, where the activities of the leftist Fuerzas Armadas Revolucionarias de Colombia (FARC) and the Ejército de Liberación Nacional (ELN) precipitated terrorist atrocities by the preservationist rightist United Self-Defense Forces of Colombia, or the AUC, the country's largest paramilitary group.[35] Positioning themselves as a necessary counter to Colombia's leftist insurgents, ordinary Colombians were often victimized—instead of protected—by the AUC. The armed groups displaced indigenous communities from their land, massacred civilians, and kidnapped political figures. As human rights groups have documented, some paramilitaries even charged "taxes" in local areas and regulated how citizens could dress.[36]

In the United States, prior to the modern era of religiously motivated terrorism begun by terrorist attacks on the World Trade Center complex, the right wing represented

American law enforcement's greatest challenge. During the American Revolutionary War, Loyalists suffered being tarred, feathered, and lynched by revolutionary mobs. A form of political cleansing divided entire families with family members who remained loyal to the king escaping to Canada and members loyal to the fledgling revolutionary American government occupying their kin's estates to this day.[37]

America's most infamous right-wing terrorist organization, the Ku Klux Klan (KKK), emerged from the American Civil War and was initially led by the South's greatest tactician, General Nathan Bedford Forrest. Initially, the KKK opposed northern occupation, the Reconstruction, and the Black vote with lynching being the order of the day. The Klan became a nationwide phenomenon enjoying its largest political successes not in the South but in Colorado and Indiana and as far north as Maine, attacking not just Freedmen, but Jews and other minorities as well as intimidating and opposing Roman Catholics and labor unions. America contended with other manifestations of terrorism during the late nineteenth and early twentieth centuries: the Molly Maguires in the 1860s and 1870s; the Ludlow Massacre of Greek, Italian, and other immigrants; and, the infamous West Virginia Miners' Rebellion, which introduced the term "redneck" as well as the use of close air support by the fledgling US Army Air Corps.[38]

Right-wing extremists and terrorists appear to be experiencing a reincarnation of sorts. Our global economic downturn, the flood of illegal Third World migrants into the First World, and the election of America's first black president are contributing to a resurgence of right-wing extremist groups. In the United States, right-wing extremism had been on the wane since the Oklahoma City bombing in 1995. However, according to a US intelligence assessment distributed by the Department of Homeland Security, this trend has reversed.[39] Europe is also experiencing a similar resurgence in right-wing violence. The German Federal Police Office (BKA) affirmed Germany's far-right threat is increasing, with the number of violent offenses committed by neo-Nazis climbing steeply. Germany is witnessing a revival of indisputable xenophobic violence and racism—not incidents blown out of proportion by a media all too aware that headlines about Nazis sell newspapers. Between January and August of 2006 alone there were some eight thousand offenses by right-wing radicals reported to the BKA—20 percent more than the previous year and 50 percent more than in 2004. While many pundits dismiss the regular reports of xenophobic violence as scare-mongering, statistics published by the German Interior Ministry prove that the far-right's gloves are indeed off.[40]

Addressing the left, the late 1950s and early 1960s heralded the birth of global radical left-wing terrorism due in part to the availability of arms, the spread of mass communications, and the decline of substantive political debate. The world had suffered two world wars and numerous rebellions causing the globe to be awash with cheap weapons. What we call globalization today arguably developed during this period with cheap air travel permitting mobility and instant communications available to millions. Serious political debate succumbed to simplistic sloganeering: "Make love, not war," "Imagine No Religion," and "More power to the people." However, left-wing terrorists shunned this naïveté and were heavily influenced by anticolonial struggles in Indochina, Algeria, and Africa. A shared, loosely fashioned, vaguely defined socialist ideology developed during this period, allowing such odd temporary coalitions as the one that formed between Provisional Irish Republican Army (PIRA) active service units, Ilich Ramírez Sánchez (aka Carlos the Jackal), an affluent Venezuelan-born, leftist revolutionary, and his German partners. Carlos formulated the attack on the headquarters of the Organization of Petroleum Exporting Countries (OPEC) in Vienna in December 1975, leading an all-star cast of terrorists, which included Gabriele Kröcher-Tiedemann of the second-generation Red Army Faction in the assault seizing over sixty hostages. This militant socialist ideology did forge ties that still bind to this day. However, anti-Semitism and a pragmatic need for operational and tactical expertise also bound these anomalous bedfellows. Perhaps the most enduring regional relationship was forged by Northern Ireland's Republican terrorist movement and the PLO. This too dated from the early 1970s, when Fatah organized weapons and terrorist training for PIRA and INLA operatives in Libya and Lebanon.[41]

These left-wing terrorist groups mushroomed during this period, organizing themselves hierarchically while normally adhering to severe discipline and command lines. Their extreme security paranoia is best exemplified by the Abu Nidal Organization (ANO), also known as the Fatah Revolutionary Council. By 1987, Abu Nidal (the pseudonym of Sabri Khalil al-Banna) had turned the full force of his terror tactics inwards on the ANO itself. Members were tortured until they confessed to betrayal and disloyalty. According to recruits who were able to escape, victims were buried alive, fed through a tube forced into their mouths, then finally killed by a bullet fired down the tube. Some had their genitals placed in skillets of boiling-hot oil. There were several mass purges. During one night in November 1987, 170 ANO members were tied up, blindfolded, machine-gunned, and buried in a mass grave. Another 160 met the same fate in Libya shortly afterwards.[42]

Fortunately for us, left-wing terrorists lost sight of their intended audience and goals. For the left-wing terrorist of this era, terrorism was a tactic that became a strategy and a strategy that over time eventually became a *raison d'être*. Terrorism moved from being a tool, to an end, to finally a way of life without gaining any lucidity, coherence, or depth. These groups eventually collapsed under the weight of their own inadequacy, unable to accomplish the broad social tasks that their terrorist tactics were never meant to achieve. Left-wing terrorist groups such as the Japanese Red Army, an army of approximately forty terrorists, could never realistically achieve its goal to overthrow the Japanese government and emperor and start a global revolution. The more presumptuous a terrorist group's claim and the more extensive its desired constituency, the greater is the terrorist's chance of failure.

Nevertheless, while suffering from internal pathogens, these terrorist organizations and their successors waged and some continue to wage today a thriving psychological warfare campaign using the media and ". . . the oxygen of publicity."[43] Political terrorism became a form of psychological warfare waged through the media. On 10 September 1976, in New York City, five Fighters for Free Croatia (CFF) hijacked TWA Flight 355 and journeyed from New York to Canada, on to Iceland, and over London, dropping pamphlets. The flight eventually terminated in Paris, where the terrorists were arrested.[44] At the end of this thirty-hour odyssey, one of the terrorists, as he was being led away, off-handedly intoned, "Well, that's show biz." It certainly was theater. A $400 investment in five plane tickets from New York to Chicago leveraged millions of dollars of free publicity for the political cause of the Fighters for Free Croatia.[45]

Mass media do not merely cover terrorism; terrorists plan on such coverage. Yasser Arafat, a master terrorist and manipulator of the media, selected the 1972 Munich Olympics as a target to reinvigorate world attention on the plight of the Palestinians as these games were the first "live" internationally televised sporting event in history. The Red Brigades attempted to conduct their attacks to make the deadline for the much-favored Italian Sunday papers. American terrorist Timothy McVeigh selected the Murrah Federal Building specifically because it had "plenty of open space around it to allow for the best possible news photos and television footage."[46] That bin Laden demonstrated his ability to reach a global audience, foist his picture onto every cable news channel, displace presidential election chatter on nightly news, and garner the attention of the Sunday pundits, astounds. His videos are pure propaganda, designed to weaken American resolve, while fostering recruiting and fund-raising.

As a key component of psychological warfare, the media can also shape the outcome of a terrorist incident because sustained coverage of a hostage situation can protect lives by building international sympathy for the hostages' plight. However, a government can be pressured to resolve the situation, perhaps prematurely as was the case with the Ma'alot massacre in northern Israel on 15 May 1974.[47] The media can disrupt or even prevent a dynamic counterterrorism operation. During the Hanafi siege in mid-March, 1977, three buildings in Washington, D.C., were seized by twelve terrorists who were tipped off to the hostage rescue force's actions by live TV media coverage. Conversely, inadvertent assistance to law enforcement agencies by the media is also possible. The Unabomber's seventeen-year campaign ended when major US newspapers published his Luddite political manifesto, which Theodore Kaczynski's brother David fortuitously recognized.

Before we leave our discussion of terrorism from the left and right and begin our discussion of "Holy Terror" or killing in the name of God, be aware that religious terrorism also practices psychological warfare.[48] Violent Islamist doctrine requires its believers to accept *jihad* as continuous process warfare: psychological, political, and military.[49] This theme will recur later in this text.

"Holy Terror": Killing in the Name of God

While other forms of terrorism appear interested in influencing contemporary society through violence or the threat of violence against civilians, religious terrorists exhibit a fundamental difference when compared to their political cousins. Religiously motivated terrorists usually seek little or no dialogue with contemporary society and wish only to eliminate its modernizing influences. For the most part, religious terrorists are hierarchical and authoritarian. The true believer experiences no ethical conflict from his acts of violence because they are sanctified—legitimized—by some form of religious authority.[50] A divine being appears directly involved in determining ends and means or a terrorist's strategy. This religious stimulus is the inspirational source of most of the terrorist incidents we are experiencing today.[51]

Religious terrorism neither began on 9/11 nor is unique to Islam, having an ancestry arguably stretching back nearly 2,000 years; however, this text will focus on religious ter-

---

"I acted alone and on orders from God."
　　　　　　　　　　Yigal Amir, the young Jewish terrorist who assassinated Israeli
　　　　　　　　　　　　　　Prime Minister Yitzhak Rabin in November 1995

rorism's more modern and lethal manifestations. We begin our treatment of religious terrorism with an examination of "Islamism," a set of ideologies holding that Islam is not only a religion but also a political system that emerged as a branch of the Islamic reform movement of the nineteenth century. This movement concluded that its society's flaws were a result of Islam not presiding over the entire Arab world. Since the 1970s, modern Islamism has become prevalent at once in the Muslim power centers and on the "Muslim street."[52]

After the 1979 Iranian Revolution, the Middle East erupted in an orgy of political violence and terrorism that continues to this day. The early terrorists' targets were not American or European citizens; rather, they were Middle Eastern citizens. These terrorist incidents were dramatic, riveting events designed to provide maximum publicity to yet unfamiliar violent Islamist groups:

- The seizure by armed Islamic fundamentalist dissidents of the Al-Masjid al-Haram in Mecca in 1979;
- The assassination of Egyptian President Anwar Sadat by Egyptian Islamic Jihad's (EIJ) Khalid Islambouli on 6 October 1981;
- The 1981 plot to overthrow the government of Bahrain to install an Islamic Republic;
- The attempted assassination of Saddam Hussein of Iraq, 8 July 1982, in Dujail
- The plot to overthrow the Kuwaiti government in 1982;
- A bloody confrontation between the terrorist group al-Gama'a al-Islamiyah and the post-Sadat Egyptian government that concluded with a suicide attack on the Egyptian Embassy in Pakistan by EIJ on 19 November 1995; and
- Islamic uprisings in Saudi Arabia, Lebanon, Egypt, and Syria, which all generated considerable news coverage during this tumultuous decade and yet today are forgotten.

Skyjackings of Arab airliners, kidnappings of Arab government officials, assassinations of Arab civil servants, and attacks on Arab businesses and cultural centers became commonplace in the Middle East. Shiite groups like Islamic Amal (Hope) and Hezbollah concealing Imad Mugniyah's covert terrorist cell, Islamic Jihad, only began to attract media attention in the early 1980s. Shiites emerged as a new common denominator in terrorism, somewhat replacing the Palestinian groups of the "second wave."[53] While this period's growth of religious terrorism is highly complex and is afforded rather indifferent treatment here, certainly the Lebanese civil war contributed significantly as well as other social factors to be addressed below. As this cycle of international terrorism shifted from one group to another, terrorist attacks became more devastating. As Shiites of both Iran and Lebanon became convinced they had been treated unfairly by the Arab world as well as "colonized" and manipulated by the West, some sought martyrdom through suicide by killing Islamic apostates and western unbelievers.[54] Their anger has spread from the Shiite world of Iran, southern Lebanon, and the marshes of Iraq to the entire Arab world and larger Muslim community. Today, Islam is not the only source of religious terror; however, the vast majority of religious terrorists today are Muslim. This is simple fact; anything else is denial.

Religious terrorism descends from other religious communities as well. One needs only to walk through the mural-covered Catholic neighborhood of Bogside in London Derry where violence between Catholics and Protestants has proven difficult to eradicate to appreciate a Christian contribution to religious terrorism. Arguments are made that "The Troubles," approximately three decades of violence between elements of Northern Ireland's nationalist community (principally Roman Catholic) and unionist community (principally Protestant), represent strictly political terrorism. This is more than slightly disingenuous.

Catholic PIRA terrorists were able to take control of their communities by offering the residents protection from the Protestants and establishing their authority through coercion and torture on their own kith and kin. This particularly unpleasant form of confessional terrorism developed into the hallmark of the PIRA and its splinter groups over the past thirty years. Kneecapping—torture with a pistol or an electric drill—became a common punishment for nonconformists in the Catholic Republican areas. This punishment was meted out by appointment, which victims kept out of fear for their lives. Depending on the degree of punishment, one or both knees were destroyed. Sometimes elbows and thighs were included and the victim only survived if his family had made a prior arrangement for an ambulance to arrive on the scene at the time of the shooting. The PIRA preferred its Catholic victims to survive, as they then served as an example to others in the community. Protestant extremists also practiced punishment shooting as a means of maintaining discipline and loyalty. Still, the majority of these victims resided in the Catholic communities. Victims rarely cooperated with the British Security Forces and their distinctive plaster casts served as an effective visual deterrent to those who might otherwise have contemplated rejecting the PIRA's strangehold. Due to the highly developed skills of Belfast's surgeons, most of those crippled made remarkable recoveries from their traumatic wounds.[55] By way of additional examples of the depths to which this base prejudice descends, a highly skilled and legendary British counterterrorism unit commander once told this writer that he "could smell a Catholic" while Protestant farmers once swore "a Catholic can put the evil eye on your cattle."

The third Abrahamic religion, Judaism, also contributes to the annals of religious terrorism and provides some of terrorism's most despicable and destabilizing attacks. On 25 February 1994, that year's Purim Jewish holiday, Dr. Baruch Goldstein, an American-born Jew, entered the mosque in the Cave of the Patriarchs in Hebron in uniform with IDF rank insignia, creating the image of a reserve officer on active duty. Goldstein opened fire on eight hundred Palestinian worshipers, killing twenty-nine souls and wounding 150. After being subdued by worshipers and disarmed, Goldstein was beaten to death. His blatant act of terrorism in one of the most sensitive religious flash point on the West Bank provoked outrage across all communities. Yet, almost immediately, this horrific tragedy took on a distorted life of its own. A bloody atrocity became the source of conspiracy theories arising from all sides. Goldstein allegedly shot "179 Arabs with allegedly 140 bullets," convincing some there must have been other shooters and birthing yet another Middle East conspiracy theory. More nauseating, this cold-blooded Kahanist terrorist was described by his community as a tender person and caring doctor.[56] An inscription on his tomb proclaimed Goldstein "a martyr murdered in sanctifying God's name," and continues, "The holy Dr. Baruch Goldstein . . . gave his soul for the people of Israel." Like his coreligionist Yigal Amir, the assassin of Israeli Prime Minister Yitzhak Rabin, Goldstein was an archetypal true believer who experienced no ethical conflict killing in the name of God.

Religious terrorism blossoms from nearly all denominations if fortified with the necessary conditions such as the following:

- Today's ethnic-religious conflicts in places like Iraq, Kashmir, Palestine, and Sri Lanka;
- The impact triggered by the modern globalization of western values, economics, and popular culture, and by the extent to which the West, particularly America, captures the imagination particularly of Middle Eastern intellectuals and youths;[57]
- A lack of democratic legitimacy, especially in the Middle East. Sadly, while Latin America, eastern Europe, and Southeast Asia are gradually developing democratic institutions, the one region that has seen little increase in representative institutions over the past forty years, is the Middle East. With the exception of Israel, Freedom House does not list one Middle Eastern nation as "free";[58] and
- Political repression; economic inequality, and social upheaval, which foster a self-loathing, especially a result of exposure to the malaise of the Arab world.

Yet an inner logic exists that stimulates religious terrorism that we ignore at our peril. Today's religious terrorists, especially the Salafi-Jihadi variant, perceive a sense of crisis threatening their Muslim identity and consequently, their very survival. As a result, these terrorists use religion as a refuge from which centuries-old concepts such as the reestablishment of the Islamic caliphate become modern goals. Their religion is also employed as a physical or spiritual sanctuary against repression as was strikingly demonstrated during the Egyptian trials of the al-Gama'a al-Islamiyah in the 1980s.[59] Religion is exploited as an instrument for activism or political action, which can be frequently seen in various Friday sermons originating in the Middle East.[60] As a result of this religious sanctioning, terrorists maintain that their actions are purely defensive and reactive to the threat from secularization commencing with foreign influences; from modernizing contacts within their own culture; and in some cases within resistance movements themselves. The current bloody struggle between the Palestinian Authority and Hamas on the West Bank and in Gaza for the leadership of the Palestinian people is an unequivocal example.[61] This inner logic also motivates the evolving threat from al Qaeda.

While al Qaeda and its Salafi-Jihadist enterprise continued to lose ground, both structurally and before the court of world public opinion, they remain the most dangerous form of religious terrorism today.[62] Al Qaeda, once a model business organization with a multi-million dollar operating budget, has transformed into a hybrid model—a mix of centralized command and control emanating from the Pakistan-Afghanistan border, and global decentralization in which affiliated organizations have a great deal of autonomy. While al Qaeda's goal—uniting Muslims to overthrow apostate regimes and expelling westerners from Muslim countries—remains unaffected, it has transformed from an organization that planned and executed attacks to a more nebulous movement aimed at inciting global acts of terrorism. Arguably, the best description of al Qaeda today posits two variants: one nested along the Pakistan-Afghanistan border and being remnants of al Qaeda of the 1980s, and the other, the promoter of al Qaeda-ism. This terrorist ideology facilitates interaction and support of like-minded Islamic mercenaries in an international matrix of logistical, financial, and sometimes operational terrorist activity.[63] Practitioners of al Qaeda-ism, an ideology that has bonded together today more than a hundred Sunni affiliates or affinity groups such as al-Ittihad in Kenya and Somalia, the Islamic Movement of Uzbekistan, the Abu Sayyaf Group in Philippines, or al Qaeda in the Land of Islamic Maghreb (AQIM) practice a radical Salafi-Jihadi Islam, which actually predates the original movement.[64]

A classic affinity group, AQIM, named for their location in North Africa, evolved from the Algerian militant group, the Salafist Group for Preaching and Combat (GSPC). GSPC formed in 1996 as an outgrowth of the once-powerful and extremely violent Groupe Islamique Armée (GIA). GIA's popularity plummeted following a series of massacres in which it killed thousands of Algerian civilians, opening the door into the region for the al Qaeda-supported GSPC, which effectively eclipsed the GIA by 1998. Imitation of al Qaeda-ism is also the part of the process of self-radicalization during which individuals reconstruct their worldviews and create new identities linking them to other amoeba-like Salafi-Jihadist groups.

Al Qaeda and its affinity groups can be viewed as a network, a collection of nodes connected through links. Some nodes are more popular and are attached to more links, connecting them to other more isolated nodes. These more connected nodes, called "hubs," are important components of bin Laden's international Salafi-Jihadist network. Prior to 9/11, a few highly connected hubs dominated bin Laden's spiderweb. Marc Sageman captured this organization perfectly in *Understanding Terror Networks*: a central staff, core Arabs, Maghreb Arabs, and Muslims from Southeast Asia, which were large clusters built around hubs: Osama bin Laden, Khalid Sheikh Mohammed, Zein al-Abidin Mohammed Hussein, and Abu Bakar Baasyir. The central staff were connected to their major clusters by lieutenants in the field: Ramzi bin al-Shibh, Waleed Mohammed Tawfiq bin Attash, and Abd al-Rahim al-Bashiri for the Core Arabs; Fateh Kamel and Amar Makhulif for the Maghreb Arabs; and Riduan Isamuddin and Ali Ghufrom for the Southeast Asians.[65] Bin Laden's genius lay in tolerating this network's spontaneous and natural evolution, without interference and guided through his "leader's intent."[66] His networks to this day are not static; they evolve over time. Al Qaeda network growth is not a random process; rather, it is one of preferential attachment. Sageman humorously describes in lecture this networking occurring over dietary preferences and meal preparation in the Afghan camps of the 1990s: Arabs preparing kebab; Maghrebis preferring couscous; and, Southeast Asian terrorists gathered around curries. While amusing, Sageman's hypothesis is more than plausible. In Afghan camps run by Pakistan's Inter-Services Intelligence in the 1980s, this author observed Tajiks eating with Tajiks, Pashtuns eating with their fellow tribesmen, and Shiite Hazara, considered *kafir* [infidels] by their Sunni coreligionist Afghans, eating alone.

These networks resist fragmentation because of their dense interconnectivity making random attacks rarely effective. Hubs are vulnerable, but must be attacked simultaneously: five to fifteen hubs at once. The price of al Qaeda's robustness is susceptibility that can be observed in the numerous successful drone attacks along the Afghan-Pakistan border today. Al Qaeda sustains casualties; however, there is no knockout punch possible. A more traditional and vulnerable hierarchical network like Jemaah Islamiyah, organized top-down versus bottom-up, broke up when the Indonesian government decided to act after the Bali bombings.

How should we portray the evolving threat from al Qaeda and its Salafi-Jihadist enterprise? Clearly, there is no facile answer. Governments must develop their counterterrorism strategies to deal with competing, contradictory evidence; address multiple timeline horizons that deal with the present as well as the next generation; and eventually grapple with the very notion of what constitutes "victory" over this threat. Complicated subjects like how to suppress al Qaeda are rarely black and white, and this is no exception.[67] Al Qaeda and its enterprise capture the lion's share of media headlines and national security focus; however, we need to examine another terrorist manifestation that arguably is just as lethal.

Fringe Element Terrorism

Unlike the political and religious radicals who purportedly seek to transform society, fringe elements or "wacko-perps" have narrowly defined issues around which they are mobilized.[68] It is only their choice of terrorism, not the inherent threat posed by their views, that leads them to be accurately perceived as a threat to society. American terrorist Timothy McVeigh imagined the US government was trampling rather than protecting his individual rights when he detonated a truck bomb in front of the Alfred P. Murrah Federal Building in Oklahoma City, killing 168 fellow citizens and injuring more than eight hundred on 19 April 1995.[69] This date was the second anniversary of a standoff between FBI agents and Branch Davidians, which ended in a fire that destroyed their compound located near Waco, Texas, killing at least 74 people.[70] The Oklahoma attack also occurred on the 220th anniversary of the American revolutionary battles Lexington and Concord against British domination. McVeigh's date selection manifested his visceral hate of government.

A similar "wacko-perp" previously mentioned was Theodore Kaczynski, known as the "Unabomber," an American MIT graduate with a Ph.D. in mathematics whose neo-Luddite views led him to carry out a campaign of terrorist mail bombings across the United States from 1978 to 1995. Kaczynski sent sixteen bombs to targets including universities and airlines, killing three people and injuring twenty-three because he considered technology a dehumanizing force that was incompatible with his personal freedom.[71] Kaczynski was finally captured, found guilty, and diagnosed as paranoid schizophrenic. While his grievances were in essence nonviolent, his manner of protest was lethal.

Some of these bizarre causes attract a following. Members of an Oregon-based group of eco-terrorists who called themselves "the family" were indicted in January 2006 for various acts of destruction across the western United States. The federal indictment detailed a story of four and a half years of vandalism and fire bombings on seventeen sites in California, Colorado, Oregon, Washington, and Wyoming. US Attorney General Alberto Gonzales noted, "In all, their trail of destruction across the Pacific Northwest and beyond resulted in millions of dollars of property damage."[72]

However, the most lethal "wacko-perps" to date were Japanese. The Aum Shinrikyo cult, which has been renamed Aleph, represented the most lethal manifestation of a New Age apocalyptic religious sect.[73] Aum combined tenets from Buddhism, Hinduism, and Christianity and was obsessed with the apocalypse.[74] Shoko Asahara, Aum's founder and self-proclaimed "enlightened one," motivated his devotees to engage in bizarre rituals such as drinking his blood and wearing electrical caps that they believed kept their brain waves in tune with his brain. The group made headlines around the world when, on 20 March 1995, its members carried out a chemical attack in the Tokyo subway system. A nerve agent, sarin, was released in train cars, killing twelve and causing an estimated six thousand people to seek medical attention.[75]

While at first blush, we would immediately characterize Aum's followers as "wacko-perps," their organization and extent dictate our attention. At the time of the 1995 subway attack, the group claimed forty thousand members worldwide, with offices in the United States, Russia, and Japan, according to the State Department.[76] They conducted experiments with sarin, VX, anthrax, botulism, and crude radioactive dispersal devices (RDD). At the time of the Japanese police's much-overdue crackdown, Aum had accumulated as much as $1.2 billion in assets; purchased molecular engineering computer software; and attempted to recruit Volgograd weapons experts. Official reports from the US and Japanese governments and interviews with law enforcement agencies and intelligence officers conclude that the group staged at least twenty attacks between 1990 and 1995: ten with chemical agents and ten with biological ones.[77] For its terrorist attacks, the Japanese courts uncharacteristically have sentenced fourteen members to hang. Russian officials also arrested several Aum followers in 2001 for planning to bomb the Imperial Palace in Japan as part of an elaborate attempt to free Asahara.[78] Aum Shinrikyo has the distinction of being considered the first nonstate terrorist group to attempt to employ a modern weapon of mass destruction, and their activities benchmark the beginning of postmodern terrorism.

When we attempt to estimate who is most likely to use a weapon of mass destruction, the two groups that may experience fewer moral constraints are religious fundamentalist organizations and religious cults or closed cults sometimes erroneously called new religions.[79] Today, three requirements exist for a terrorist's use of weapons of mass destruction: the ability to acquire a weapon; the capability to disseminate a weapon; and the desire to use one. We are witnessing the confluence of these conditions, and, regrettably, all three conditions exist today.[80] The means and predisposition for a covert or a clandestine operation aimed at creating immense destruction are spreading. A clandestine nuclear attack is one such possible conjunction. Nuclear weapons technology is oozing out of control. Nuclear materials are spreading into hands hostile or potentially hostile to democratic states and into regions where the prospects for effective control to prevent loss and stem the continued spread are highly uncertain. A successful clandestine nuclear attack would have significance extending far beyond the immense immediate casualties.[81] We are in the midst of a potentially dramatic change in our current concept of national security. Once our nations were essentially secure from homeland destruction, unless our military was defeated. That may have changed:

> For would-be aggressors before 1945, a capacity to destroy always required a prior capacity to win. Without a victory, their intended aggressions were never more than military intentions. This is no longer the case. From the standpoint of ensuring any one state's national survival, the goal of preventing a classical military defeat has become secondary. The implications of this transforming development are considerable.[82]

Terrorist groups, non-state actors, can circumvent armies and deliver a catastrophic strike. Groups such as Avenging Israel's Blood, which sought revenge for the victims of the Holocaust in 1946, to Aum Shinrikyo in 1995, and now al Qaeda, with its stated intent to use weapons of mass destruction, reinforce the notion that we should not be musing whether we are going to be struck, but rather when such an attack will occur again. If we have failed to absorb the lesson to expect the unexpected, then we are losing ground, not gaining ground in this war on terrorism.

In Search of "Root Causes" of Terrorism

The question that should be foremost at this point is what causes a human to strike out at fellow humans using terrorist methods. Thus far, we have scrutinized the nature of terrorism, but what about its root causes? Visualize a beautiful oriental carpet, to introduce the tapestry of terrorism. A carpet is traditionally woven on a loom, a familiar weaving apparatus. The carpet's warp, the threads running the length of the piece, and its woof, the threads running crosswise or at right angles to the warp of the piece, provide the lattice for the carpet's knots, which create the design. These threads are the plinth of a carpet and, building upon our analogy, symbolize the essential root causes of today's more deadly forms of modern terrorism. The warp is the atavistic adrenalin rush, the associated physiological euphoric state that accompanies a terrorist's action. This is not unlike the euphoric state one experiences in combat, in a situation of extreme anxiety, or simply skydiving. Killing another human being—the ability to take life—produces intense excitement, elevating a human to nearly godlike powers.[83] The chief of Jaish-e-Mohammed, Maulana Masood Azahar, described caressing a Kalashnikov in his hands as being ". . . ready to talk to the enemy. The bullet was in the chamber and it was ready to fire and I felt ecstatic."[84] Committing murder becomes a thrilling decision: a peak experience; an elevation from meaninglessness to real consequence; and the chance to be a hero.[85] To further our analogy, the woof simply reinforces the warp because killing in the name of a divine being allows cold-blooded murder to be morally justifiable; sometimes required; and celestially rewarded. The gravitas of religious authenticity legitimizes an act of primordial murder.

Now we apply the knots to our piece, which represent the variety of preconditions, factors that set the stage for terrorism over the long run and precipitants, specific events that immediately precede the occurrence of terrorism, to borrow the terminology of Dr. Martha Crenshaw.[86] "Root causes" are not the proximate cause of terrorism. Rather, they are factors that establish an environment in which terrorism may arise. A basic distinction exists between root-cause factors that are preconditions and those that are precipitant. The former set the stage and the latter ignite the action. These preconditions and precipitants—our knots—describe: dreadful histories accompanied by humiliation; foreign repression; the love for a lost land or era; the lack of democracy, civil liberties, and rule of law; the lack of power sharing, ethnic or religious discrimination; illegitimate governance; a government's intolerance of minorities; extremist ideologies or zealotry; becoming a failed state; rapid modernization; or charismatic leaders, individuals who can whip a mob into frenzy by the power of their oratory or deeds and then set the mob loose to destroy. Two examples of the power of oratory are the Muslim Brotherhood's incitement causing the near destruction of Cairo in 26 January 1952 and the destruction of the US Embassy in Islamabad in 1979 by a mob goaded to believe a fatally erroneous Friday sermon stating America had bombed the al-Masjid al-Haram in Mecca. The Hebron Massacre mentioned earlier was a knot as was the start of the 28 September 2000 riots and injuries soon after Ariel Sharon's untimely visit to the Temple Mount, an area known to Muslims as al-Haram as-Sharif. An additional knot unique to the Middle East is what Christopher Dobson described in *Black September* as "a fatal flaw" or the Palestinian "disease," which has been woven through Palestinian history like a scarlet thread. Supporting this cultural propensity to violence, Ghazi Hamad, a member of Hamas who acted as the spokesman for the Hamas-led government in Gaza rhetorically queried in a sharply worded article, published in the widely read Palestinian newspaper *al-Ayyam*, "Has violence become a culture implanted in our bodies and our flesh?"[87]

Certain factors sustain a climate of terrorism, such as: cycles of revenge observed constantly in Chechnya fueled by *adat*; the need for a group to provide for its members or simply survive, as the remnants of the PIRA are discovering today; the discovery of profitable criminal activities as with the FARC's major role in the cocaine trade in Colombia; the perception that there are no exits given the bloodshed of the conflict; or, as Somalia's piracy reminds us once again, ungoverned spaces, failed or failing states. These factors provide a conducive medium for terrorism's root causes to ferment. Shortcomings exist in our current knowledge base on root causes. As context matters, data analysis argues for an interdisciplinary systems approach and access to classified or otherwise restricted material in order for us to recognize factors contributing to a terrorism-spawning environment. The issues of the Taliban in Pakistan are simply not very comparable to those of the PIRA or to those of Hezbollah and Hamas in Lebanon and the occupied Palestinian territories, or even the current terrorism in Baghdad.[88]

Myths imply that terrorism is the inevitable by-product of poverty. However, as Richard Miniter reminds us in *Losing Bin Laden*, terrorism is the derivative of individual spiritual poverty, but not mass material poverty.[89] Another myth suggests that terrorism is the result of hostility over the American involvement in Iraq, Afghanistan, or the global war on terrorism. Many argue that terrorism would disappear if only the Israeli-Palestinian conflict were resolved. This too is sadly a myth. Some self-absorbed observers suggest that terrorism is encouraged in response to the world's efforts to prevent terrorism. This is merely a political fig leaf that hides wanting capability, or worse, cowardice. These spurious conceptions are regrettably left frequently unchallenged at terrorism conferences and United Nations gatherings. One concluding caution about those who sometimes endorse research to discover the elusive root cause of terrorism: frequently, this is a subterfuge to excuse the inexcusable.

Conclusion: Or, Just the Beginning?

Why have we not been able to bring education to our children on our own? Fathers and parents, I implore you to dedicate your full effort and commitment to see that all your children are educated. Otherwise, they will merely graze like sheep in the field, at the mercy of nature and the world changing so terrifyingly around us.

Syed Abbas, Supreme Leader of Northern Pakistan's Shia, from *Three Cups of Tea*

Terrorism, like disease, is a perennial, ceaseless struggle we will never completely eradicate but must constantly treat. Like skin cancer, we must discover it; surgically incise it; conduct biopsy to determine its causes and malignancy; and scrutinize it constantly. The following chapters in this text will detail some of the necessary policies and strategies to "treat" terrorism. In addition to these prescient recommendations, consider policies that tackle just three issues. A group of thirty Arab intellectuals published the *Arab Human Development Report 2002* contained in the annual United Nations Development Programme (UNDP) report. Rima Khalaf Hunaidi, a former deputy prime minister of Jordan, and her team indentified three deficits within the region: knowledge, freedom, and womanpower.[90] Substantially reducing these three deficits will remove many "knots" from our terrorism tapestry.

Knowledge permits individuals to make informed decisions regarding the intellectual poverty of terrorism and not be led as like sheep as the prescient Syed Abbas warned. Al Qaeda and its Salafi-Jihadist enterprise are crystal clear about what they oppose, yet they have made no argument to prove they could offer a better tomorrow. Next, countries with established political freedom have been empirically proven to be less prone to terrorism.[91] The Middle East models many outward trappings of democracy. Elections are held and human-rights conventions are signed. Yet the great wave of democratization that has opened up so much of the world over the past twenty years seems to have left the Muslim world virtually untouched. Finally, no nation can improve its economic circumstances while disenfranchising over 50 percent of its population. One of every two Arab women still can neither read nor write. Female participation in their country's political and economic life is the lowest in the world. The diehard, self-righteous obscurantists of the Islamic world ensure its deepening malaise as female oppression in Islamic countries is manifestly getting worse.[92] Terrorism is not likely to disappear, but its appeal could lessen if these three deficits are narrowed, enhancing economic growth in the Middle East and reducing its attendant youth unemployment.[93]

Our adversaries in the long war on terrorism are dispersed around the globe. Al Qaeda and its Salafi-Jihadist enterprise are resilient, patient, ruthless, and dedicated to the mass murder of innocents. Ironically, the very democratic nature of our societies renders our citizens vulnerable. To ensure the continuation of our democratic blessings, we must create a zero-tolerance attitude toward terrorism and collectively defend ourselves. Beyond al Qaeda, we confront a protracted ideological conflict, of which the terrorist campaign waged by disconnected Salafi-Jihadists, is merely a symptom.[94] Violent terrorists will always be with us, so we must be capable and motivated to suppress and, when necessary, kill these individuals whose galvanizing dream is to destroy the West and those who emulate free ways of life, through the wonton murder of innocent civilians. When hatred is bred in the enemy's bone, the notion of exercising strategic patience will likely earn us a rest for all eternity. This book may illuminate a more prudent way ahead.

Professor Andrew Nichols Pratt Since August 1996, Professor Pratt has been the Professor of Strategy and International Politics in the College of International Security Studies in Garmisch, Germany. Following the 9/11 terrorist attacks, he developed the Program on Terrorism and Security Studies (PTSS) and was named its first Director. In February 2008, he served the US Special Envoy for Middle East Regional Security (SEMERS) in Jerusalem and on the West Bank. He reassumed the duties of Director, PTSS in October 2009. Prior to his retirement from the Marine Corps after twenty-six years, Colonel Pratt served as director of the Marine Corps Command and Staff College and the Marine War College. Throughout his career, he was privileged to command extensively and at every level, from a CIA Special Operations Group team that conducted covert operations in denied areas in support of US national security objectives overseas, to a Battalion Landing Team deployed in the Persian Gulf. A. N. Pratt graduated from the US Naval Academy and holds two Master of Arts degrees. His involvement with counterterrorism matters began in 1967 and continues apace.

Recommended Readings

Al Zawahiri, Ayman. *In His Own Words: A Translation of the Writings of Dr. Ayman al-Zawahiri.* Ed. and trans. Laura Mansfield. US: TLG Publications, 2006.

Cetron, Marvin J., and Probst, Peter S. *Terror 2000: The Future Face of Terrorism.* No publ. Initially printed as "For Government Use Only, Not for Public Release," 24 June 1994. Available at: http://www.dtic.mil/srch/doc?collection=t3&id=ADB201036

O'Neill, Bard E. *Insurgency and Terrorism; From Revolution to Apocalypse,* 2nd ed. Dulles, VA: Potomac Books, Inc., 2005.

Open Source Center. OpenSource.gov provides timely and tailored translations, reporting, and analysis on foreign policy and national security issues from the Open Source Center and its partners, https://www.opensource.gov

Poland, James M. *Understanding Terrorism,* 2nd ed. Upper Saddle River, NJ: Prentice-Hall, Inc., 2005.

Sageman, Marc. *Understanding Terrorist Networks.* Philadelphia, PA: University of Pennsylvania Press, 2004.

Stout, Mark E., Jessica M. Huckabey, John R. Schindler, and Jim Lacey. *The Terrorist Perspectives Project; Strategic and Operational Views of Al Qaida and Associated Movements.* Annapolis, MD: Naval Institute Press, 2008.

Notes

1. William J. Casey, "The International Linkages; What Do We Know?" *Hydra of Carnage: International Linkages of Terrorism: The Witnesses Speak,* Edited by Uri Ra'anan and others (Lexington, MA: Lexington Books, 1986), 5–15.
2. Jackie Craven, "The New York World Trade Center," *About.com.* Retrieved 24 August 2009, from http://architecture.about.com/od/worldtradecenter/ss/worldtrade.htm
3. "Official 9/11 Death Toll Climbs By One," *CBS News,* 10 July 2008. Retrieved 13 October 2009, from http://www.cbsnews.com/stories/2008/07/10/national/main4250100.shtml
4. Mitchell D. Silber and Arvin Bhatt, "Radicalization in the West: The Homegrown Threat," New York Police Department, 2007. Retrieved on 5 September 2009 from http://sethgodin.typepad.com/seths_blog/files/NYPD_Report-Radicalization_in_the_West.pdf. Their report uses the term "unremarkable" thirteen times in describing individual perpetrators within today's Jihadi-Salafi terrorist movement.
5. For more on this Islamist commitment to political activism and the legitimization of violence, see Dr. Patrick Sookhdeo's treatment of the subject in "How to Undermine the Extremist Ideology Behind Al Qaeda," chapter 3.5.
6. "Blair Warns of WMD Terror Threat," *CNN.com,* 5 March 2004. Retrieved on 5 September 2009 from http://www.cnn.com/2004/WORLD/europe/03/05/uk.blair/index.htm. According to Blair, the nature of the "global threat we face in Britain and round the world is real and existential and it is the task of leadership to expose it and fight it, whatever the political cost."
7. Brian Michael Jenkins, *Unconquerable Nation: Knowing Our Enemy, Strengthening Ourselves* (Santa Monica, CA: RAND, 2006), 8.
8. Christopher C. Harmon, "What History Suggests About Terrorism and Its Future," in *The Past As Prologue,* ed. Williamson Murray and Richard Hart Sinnreich (New York: Cambridge University Press, 2006), 218.
9. Elaine Sciolino, "Teacher in Hiding After Attack on Islam Stirs Threats," *New York Times,* 30 September 2006. Retrieved 15 October 2009 from http://www.nytimes.com/2006/09/30/world/europe/30france.html
10. Thomas Harding and George Jones, "Blair Links Iran to Brutal Act of Terror," Telegraph.co.uk, 6 Apr 2007. Retrieved 15 October 2009 from http://www.telegraph.co.uk/news/worldnews/1547852/Blair-links-Iran-to-brutal-act-of-terror.html

11. "Stoning Victim 'Begged for Mercy'," *BBC News,* 4 November 2008. Retrieved 24 August 2009, from http://news.bbc.co.uk/2/hi/africa/7708169.stm

12. Jessica Stern, *The Ultimate Terrorists* (Cambridge, MA: Harvard University Press, 1999), 11–30 and 164–168.

13. Terrorism Act 2000, Office of Public Sector Information (OPSI). Retrieved 13 October 2009 http://www.opsi.gov.uk/acts/acts2000/ukpga_20000011_en_2#pt1

14. "Security Council Committee established pursuant to UNSR 1267 (1999) concerning Al-Qaida and the Taliban and Associated Individuals and Entities," UN.org. Retrieved 5 September 2009 from http://www.un.org/sc/committees/1267/index.shtml

15. Simon Saradzhyan, "Kremlin Goes on a Western Offensive" *Moscow Times,* 27 September 2004. Retrieved 24 August 2009, from http://www.cdi.org/russia/johnson/8382-3.cfm

16. Boaz Ganor, "Proposing a Definition of Terrorism," *Defining Terrorism: Is One Man's Terrorist Another Man's Freedom Fighter?* International Institute for Counter-Terrorism. Retrieved 24 August 2009, from http://www.ict.org.il/ResearchPublications/tabid/64/Articlsid/432/currentpage/1/Default.aspx

17. Dr. Christopher Bassford, in a teaching note written on 3 January 2003, suggested Clausewitz's trinity comprises three specific elements. The identity of those elements is readily evident to anyone who reads the first paragraph of his description: It is "composed of primordial violence, hatred, and enmity, which are to be regarded as a blind natural force; of the play of chance and probability within which the creative spirit is free to roam; and of its element of subordination, as an instrument of policy, which makes it subject to reason. . . ." This set of elements is usually labeled "emotion/chance/reason"; sometimes "violence/chance and probability/rational calculation"; or, even more abstractly, "irrationality/non-rationality/rationality."

18. Ganor, "Proposing a Definition of Terrorism."

19. *Merriam-Webster Online Dictionary* 1 a: silly idle talk: drivel b: something insignificant or worthless: nonsense from http://www.merriam-webster.com/dictionary/twaddle

20. Rolf Ekeus, "New Challenges for the United Nations," in *Turbulent Peace: The Challenges of Managing International Conflict,* ed. Chester Crocker, Fen Osler Hampson, and Pamela Aall (Washington, DC: United States Institute of Peace, 2001), 517–528.

21. John Dugard, "International Terrorism and the Just War," from David C. Rapoport and Yonah Alexander, eds., *The Morality of Terrorism: Religious and Secular Justifications,* 2nd ed. (New York: Columbia University Press, 1989), 83–85.

22. Louis Rene Beres, "On the Difference Between Murderers and Freedom Fighters," Freeman Center for Strategic Studies, 29 January 2004. Retrieved 24 August 2009, from http://www.freeman.org/m_online/feb04/beres.htm.

23. Richard B. Frank, "The Best Worst Option," from "Would You Have Dropped the Bomb?" *Bulletin of the Atomic Scientists* (July/August 2005), 60. Frank, winner of the 2000 Harry S. Truman Book award for *Downfall: The End of the Japanese Imperial Empire,* argues that a sober assessment of US strategy demonstrates the atomic bombs were the worst way to end the Pacific War except all the others. The grim reality is that no other combination of events would have produced an enduring peace at less cost.

24. Stephen Robinson, "Bombed US Warship Was Defended by Sailors with Unloaded Guns," *Telegraph.co.uk,* 15 November 2000. Retrieved 24 August 24, 2009, from http://www.telegraph.co.uk/news/worldnews/middleeast/yemen/1374316/Bombed-US-warship-was-defended-by-sailors-with-unloaded-guns.html

25. John Gearson, "The Nature of Modern Terrorism," in *Superterrorism: Policy Responses,* ed. Lawrence Freedman (Oxford, UK: The Political Quarterly Publishing Co. Ltd./Blackwell Publishing, 2002), 14.

26. Philip K. Hitti, "The Assassins," Retrieved 15 October 2009 from http://www.alamut.com/subj/ideologies/alamut/hitti_Ass.html

27. Bernard Lewis, "The Ismalites and the Assassins," in *A History of the Crusades: The First Hundred Years,* ed. Kenneth M. Setton and Marshall W. Baldwin, 2nd ed. (Madison, WI: University of Wisconsin Press, 2006), 130.

28. Walter Laqueur, *A History of Terrorism* (New Jersey: Transaction Publishers 2001), 12.

29. Walter Laqueur, "A History of Terrorism" in *Confronting Fear: A History of Terrorism,* ed. Isaac Cronin (New York: Thunder's Mouth Press, 2002), 6.

30. Laqueur, 6.

31. Bruce Hoffman, *Inside Terrorism* (New York: Columbia University Press, 1998), 18

32. Richard Bach Jensen, "The International Campaign Against Anarchist Terrorism, 1880–1930s," *Terrorism and Political Violence,* Vol. 21, No. 1 (January 2009): 89–109.

33. Reiss, Tom. *The Orientalist: Solving the Mystery of a Strange and a Dangerous Life* (New York: Random House, 2005). Retrieved 15 October 2009, from http://catdir.loc.gov/catdir/samples/random051/2004050928.html

34. Sean Kendall Anderson and Stephen Sloan, *Assassins to Zealots,* 2nd ed. (Lanhan, MD: Scarecrow Press, Inc., 2002), 3–5. This is an excellent text to keep on hand as it contains a wealth of information regarding major terrorist groups, significant terrorist events, and terrorists' weapons systems of choice.

35. Bard E. O'Neill, *Insurgency and Terrorism: From Revolution to Apocalypse,* 2nd ed., Revised (Paperback) (Dulles, VA: Potomac Books Inc, June, 2005), 29.

36. Stephanie Hanson, "Colombia's Right-Wing Paramilitaries and Splinter Groups," *Backgrounder,* Council on Foreign Relations, 11 January 2008. Retrieved 24 August 2009, from http://www.cfr.org/publication/15239/colombias_rightwing_paramilitaries_and_splinter_groups.html

37. For granularity on terror and the American Revolution, see: John J. Tierney, "Terror at Home: The American Revolution and Irregular Warfare," *Stanford Journal of International Studies,* No. 12 (Spring 1977): 1–19. Note, however, there is no evidence that statesmen or senior army commanders of the American Revolutionaries endorsed terrorism or allowed it as calculated policy or strategy.

38. Lon Savage, *Thunder in the Mountains: The West Virginia Mine War, 1920–21* (Pittsburgh, PA: University of Pittsburgh Press, September 1990). The West Virginia mine war of 1920–21, a major civil insurrection of unusual brutality on both sides, even by the standards of the coal fields, involved thousands of union and nonunion miners, state and private police, militia, and federal troops. Before it was over, three West Virginia counties were in open rebellion, much of the state was under military rule, and bombers of the US Army Air Corps had been dispatched against striking miners.

39. Greg Miller, "Right-Wing Extremists Seen as a Threat," *Los Angeles Times,* 16 April 2009. Retrieved on 24 August 2009, from http://articles.latimes.com/2009/apr/16/nation/na-rightwing-extremists16

40. "Germany's Far-Right Rolls Up Its Sleeves," *Deutsche Welle,* 17 October 2006. Retrieved on 24 August 2009 from http://www.dw-world.de/dw/article/0,,2206348,00.html

41. Sean Gannon, "IRA-PLO Cooperation: A Long, Cozy Relationship," *The Jerusalem Post,* 7 April 2009. Retrieved on 24 August 2009, from http://www.jpost.com/servlet/Satellite?cid=1238562940033&pagename=JPost%2FJPArticle%2FPrinter

42. Duane "Dewy" R. Clarridge, *A Spy for all Seasons: My Life in the CIA* (New York: Scribner, 1997); cited in Michael Ledeen, "Dead Terrorist in Baghdad," *National ReviewOnline,* 20 August 2002. Retrieved on 24 August 2009, from http://www.nationalreview.com/ledeen/ledeen082002.asp

43. Margaret Thatcher, Speech to American Bar Association, 15 July 1985. Retrieved on 24 August 2009, from http://www.margaretthatcher.org/speeches/displaydocument.asp?docid=106096

44. "Bombs for Croatia" *TIME,* 20 September 1976. Retrieved on 24 August 2009, from http://www.time.com/time/magazine/article/0,9171,946611-1,00.html

45. James M. Poland, *Understanding Terrorism: Groups, Strategies and Responses,* 1st ed. (Upper Saddle River, NJ: Prentice-Hall, Inc., 1988), 45.

46. Brigitte Lebens Nacos, *Mass-Mediated Terrorism: The Central Role of the Media in Terrorism and Counterterrorism* (Lanham, MD: Rowman & Littlefield, Inc. 2002), 12.

47. Michael Stohl, "Demystifying Terrorism: The Myths and Realities of Contemporary Political Terrorism," in M. Stohl (ed.), *The Politics of Terrorism,* 3rd ed. (New York: Marcel Dekker, Inc., 1988), 11.

48. Dr. Jerrold Post, "Rogue Leader Profiles," Political Psychology Associates, Ltd. Retrieved on 24 August 2009 from http://www.au.af.mil/au/awc/awcgate/cpc-conf2000/post/sld001.htm, slide #13.

49. Majid Khadduri, *War and Peace in the Law of Islam* (Baltimore, MD: John Hopkins Press, 1955; Reprinted 2006), 64.

50. Dr. Jerrold Post, "The Mind of the Terrorist: When Hatred Is Bred in the Bone," Lecture, George Washington University, April 2008, Slide #32.

51. Dr. Tom Mockaitis, a PTSS lecturer, argues there could be a mistake in attributing the increased lethality of terrorist attacks today to lack of restraint brought on by religious extremism. Instead, the explanation may be that today's terrorists emphasize high body count due to a "threshold phenomenon." Numbed by decades of violence, people do not shock as easily as they once did. Mockaitis suggests today four- or five-digit casualties like September 11 are needed to produce the same effect once caused by a relative handful of murders. See Thomas R. Mockaitis, *The "New" Terrorism: Myths and Reality* (Westport, CT: Praeger Security International, 2007) at http://books.google.com/books?id=wGanuKh80WsC&dq=The+%E2%80%9CNew%E2%80%9D+Terrorism+by+Thomas+R.+Mockaitis.&printsec=frontcover&source=bl&ots=I3e8Y3Z9Lx&sig=9fGaLXyJNEcJY6EVbkbicJFIVok&hl=en&ei=xOQ4SrH9GsLJ_gaqu4TXDQ&sa=X&oi=book_result&ct=result&resnum=1#PPR1,M1

52. Patrick Sookhdeo, "How to Undermine the Extremist Ideology Behind Al Qaeda," herein.

53. David C. Rapoport, "The Four Waves of Modern Terrorism," in *Attacking Terrorism: Elements of Grand Strategy,* ed. Audrey Kurth Cronin and James M. Ludes (Washington, DC: Georgetown University Press, 2004), 46–73.

54. Apostasy in Islam is commonly defined as the rejection in word or deed of Islam by a person who was previously a Muslim. "Apostate regimes" are leading avowed targets of Islamist terrorists.

55. Major Alexander C. Roy, Royal Marines, United Kingdom, *The Roots of Terrorism in Northern Ireland* (United States Marine Corps Command and Staff College, Quantico, VA, 1991). Retrieved on 24 August 2009, from http://www.globalsecurity.org/military/library/report/1991/RAC.htm

56. The central claim of Kahanism argues the vast majority of the Arabs of Israel are, and will continue to be, enemies of Jews, and that a Jewish theocratic state, governed by *Halakha,* cleansed by the forced expulsion of Palestinians, from Israel, the West Bank, Gaza Strip, areas of modern-day Egypt, Jordan, Lebanon, Syria, and even Iraq-Eretz Yisrael, should be created. Kahanism is also associated with support for violence against Jewish opponents and against the Arab population generally. For a useful overview, see Raphael Cohen-Almagor, "Vigilant Jewish Fundamentalism: From the JDL to Kach," *Terrorism and Political Violence,* Vol. 4, No. 1 (Spring 1992): 44–66.

57. Meyrav Wurmser, "The Roots of Islamic Radicalism," Hudson Institute, 1 September 2001. Retrieved on 25 August 2009, from https://www.hudson.org/index.cfm?fuseaction=publication_details&id=1084

58. "Map of Freedom 2008," including Algeria, Bahrain, Egypt, Iran, Iraq, Israel, Israeli-Occupied Territories [Israel], Jordan, Kuwait, Lebanon, Libya, Morocco, Oman, Palestinian Authority-Administered Territories [Israel], Qatar, Saudi Arabia, Syria, Tunisia, United Arab Emirates, Western Sahara [Morocco], and Yemen, Freedom House, 2008. Retrieved on 24 August 2009, from http://www.freedomhouse.org/template.cfm?page=22&country=7534&year=2008

59. Magnus Ranstorp, "Terrorism in the Name of Religion," *Journal of International Affairs,* Vol. 50 (Summer 1996): 47.

60. The Middle East Media Research Institute (MEMRI) archives hundreds of these sermons: see "Palestinian Friday Sermon by Sheik Ibrahim Mudeiris: Muslims Will Rule America and Britain, Jews Are a Virus Resembling AIDS," Palestinian Authority TV-13 May 2005, MEMRI clip no. 669. Retrieved 5 September 2009 from http://www.memritv.org/clip/en/669.htm

61. For a thorough treatment of this struggle see Jonathan Schanzer, *Hamas vs. Fatah: The Struggle for Palestine* (Palgrave Macmillan, 2008).

62. US Department of State Office of the Coordinator for Counterterrorism, *Country Reports on Terrorism 2008,* "Chapter 1: Strategic Assessment," 30 April 2009. Retrieved on 24 August 2009, from http://www.state.gov/s/ct/rls/crt/2008/122411.htm; and "Al Qaeda Network Still CIA's Top Priority," *Middle East Online,* 19 May 2009, retrieved 5 September 2009 from http://www.middle-east-online.com/english/?id=32123. DCI Leon Panetta noted

"defeating Al Qaeda remained the CIA top priority as it "remains the most serious security threat we face."

63. For example, terrorists in North Africa threatened to execute a British hostage unless the UK released radical preacher Abu Qatada from jail. The unidentified hostage was captured earlier in 2009 in a remote region on the Mali-Niger border where he was attending a cultural festival as a tourist. The Foreign Office confirmed the threat issued by a group known as al Qaeda in the Islamic Maghreb. The group threatened to kill the British hostage within twenty days—a deadline that expired on 16 May 2009—and the hostage was murdered.

64. Eben Kaplan, "The Rise of Al Qaedaism," Council on Foreign Relations, 18 July 2007, Retrieved on 25 August 2009, from http://www.cfr.org/publication/11033/rise_of_alqaedaism.html

65. Marc Sageman, *Understanding Terror Networks* (Philadelphia, PA: University of Pennsylvania Press, 2004), 137–138.

66. Leader's intent can be defined as the purpose of a chosen action or direction so subordinates have a clear understanding of the desired end state of an assignment. Clear and concise, the leader's intent includes a mission's overall purpose and expected results. With clearly communicated purpose and direction, all can understand what they must do and why. Leader's intent consists of three parts: Task: What it is to be done, or the "objectives"; Purpose: Why it is to be done, or "sense-making"; and, End State: What it should look like when done, or "the goal."

67. Russell E. Travers, "Evaluating Progress in the War on Terror," *The Intelligencer, Journal of US Intelligence Studies,* Vol. 17, No. 1 (Winter/Spring, 2009): 11–14.

68. "Wacko-perp" is an FBI term that combines the slang term "wacko" meaning crazy and "perp," a law enforcement agency (LEA) abbreviation for perpetrator. "Wacko-perps" describes an organization of like-minded criminals.

69. "A Look at the Numbers," Oklahoma City National Memorial & Museum. Retrieved on 5 September 2009 from http://www.oklahomacitynationalmemorial.org/secondary.php?section=5&catid=145

70. Justin Sturken and Mary Dore, "Remembering the Waco Siege," ABC News.com, 29 February 2007. Retrieved on 5 September 2009 from http://abcnews.go.com/US/story?id=2908955&page=1

71. "The Unabomber's Brother Tells His Story," NPR, 30 May 2009. Retrieved on 5 September 2009 from http://www.npr.org/templates/story/story.php?storyId=104743973

72. Alicia Caldwell, "11 Indicted in Eco-Terror Investigation," *Denver Post,* 20 January 2006. Retrieved on 25 August 2009, from http://www.denverpost.com/news/ci_3421918

73. Jonathan B. Tucker, "Lessons from the Case Studies" in *Toxic Terror, Assessing Terrorist use of Chemical and Biological Weapons,* ed. Jonathan B. Tucker (Cambridge, MA: Belfer Center for Science and International Affairs, John F. Kennedy School of Government, Harvard University, 2000), 251.

74. "In the Spotlight: Aum Shinrikyo," Center for Defense Information, 23 July 2002. Retrieved on 5 September 2009 from http://www.cdi.org/terrorism/aumshinrikyo.cfm

75. US Department of State, "Country Reports on Terrorism 2007," 30 April 2008. Retrieved on 5 September 2009 from http://www.state.gov/s/ct/rls/crt/2007/103714.htm

76. Ibid.

77. David E. Kaplan, "Aum Shinrikyo, 1995," in Tucker, ed., *Toxic Terror,* 207.

78. US Department of State, "Country Reports on Terrorism 2007."

79. Dr. Jerrold Post, "Psychological and Motivational Factors in Terrorist Decision-Making: Implications for CBW Terrorism," in Jonathan B. Tucker, ed. *Toxic Terror: Assessing Terrorist Use of Chemical and Biological Weapons* (Cambridge, MA: MIT Press, 2000), 271–289.

80. Dr. Peter Katona's first lecture to Program on Terrorism and Security Studies on 20 June 2006 (PTSS 06-5).

81. Noah Feldman, "Islam, Terror and the Second Nuclear Age," *New York Times Magazine,* 29 October 2006. Retrieved on 25 August 2009, from http://www.nytimes.com/2006/10/29/magazine/29islam.html

82. Louis Rene Beres, "A New Military Reality: Existential Vulnerability Without First Losing A War," *PTSS DAILY* (21 April 2009): 61.

83. Celeste Katz and Corey Siemaszko, "NYPD, FBI Heroes Honored After Foiling Terror Plot to Bomb Synagogues," *New York Daily News,* 22 May 09. Retrieved 5 September 2009 from http://www.nydailynews.com/news/ny_crime/2009/05/22/2009-05-22_nypd_fbi_heros_honored_after_foiling_terror_plot_to_bomb_.html. This article describes how the NYPD arrested a gang of homegrown terrorists. We get a sense of this notion that killing another human being—the ability to take life—produces intense excitement and a sense of grandeur. Committing murder becomes a thrilling decision. The suspects were ordered held without bail and branded anti-Semitic would-be killers who dreamed of basking in the glory of their spectacular attacks. "I hate those motherf-----s, those f-----g Jewish bastards," suspect James Cromitie told the informant, court papers revealed. "I would like to get [bomb] a synagogue." Cromitie eagerly anticipated watching the devastation he wrought played out over and over again on TV. "I'm the one who did that," Cromitie congratulated himself after the planned attacks, an informant told cops. "That's my work." The group's diabolical dream was to create "a fireball that would make the country gasp," a law enforcement source said. Even though cops called Cromitie the ringleader, David Williams was singled out as the meanest, bragging he would shoot anyone who tried to stop him.

84. Rahimullah Ysufzai, Harinder Baweja, Amir Mir, et al., eds., *Most Wanted: Profiles of Terror* (New Delhi, India: Roli Books, 2002), 44.

85. Nira Kfir, "Understanding Suicidal Terror Through Humanistic and Existential Psychology," in *The Psychology of Terrorism: Volume I, A Public Understanding,* ed. Chris E. Stout (Westport, CT: Praeger, 2002), 143–157.

86. Martha Crenshaw, "The Causes of Terrorism." *Comparative Politics,* Vol. 13, No. 4 (July 1981): 379.

87. Nidal al-Mughrabi, "Hamas Official: Is Violence Palestinian 'Disease'?" *Reuters,* 17 October 2006. Retrieved on 25 August 2009, from http://www.memeorandum.com/061017/p58#a061017p58

88. *Social Science for Counterterrorism: Putting the Pieces Together,* ed. Paul K. Davis and Kim Cragin (Santa Monica, CA: RAND National Defense Research Institute, RAND Corporation 2009), xxi–xlix.

89. Richard Miniter, *Losing bin Laden: How Bill Clinton's Failures Unleashed Global Terror* (Washington: Regnery Publishing, 2003).

90. United Nations Development Programme Regional Bureau for Arab States, *The Arab Human Development Report 2002: Creating Opportunities for Future Generation* (New York: United Nations Development Programme, 2002), 27–29.

91. Alberto Abadie, "Poverty, Political Freedom, and the Roots of Terrorism," Kennedy School of Government, Harvard University and NBER (October 2004): 1. Retrieved on 25 August 2009, from http://ksghome.harvard.edu/~aabadie/povterr.pdf

92. Yasmin Alibhai-Brown, "Who'd Be Female Under Islamic Law?" *The Independent,* 4 May 2009. Retrieved on 15 October 2009, from http://www.independent.co.uk/opinion/commentators/yasmin-alibhai-brown/yasmin-alibhaibrown-whod-be-female-under-islamic-law-1678549.html. Safa Faisal, "Muslim Girls Struggle for Education," *BBC Arabic Service,* 24 September 2003. Retrieved on 25 August 2009, from http://news.bbc.co.uk/2/hi/middle_east/3130234.stm. For a regional discussion of this "malaise" view, see "Algerian Author Anwar Malek: The Arabs Have Lost Their Worth, Their Humanity, and Their Culture," 3 March 2009, MEMRI TV Clip No. 2063. Retrieved 5 September 2009 from http://www.memritv.org/clip/en/0/0/0/0/0/0/2063.htm

93. Atlantic Council, "Global Trends 2025: A Transformed World," Executive Summary of the National Intelligence Council report of the same name, November 2008. Retrieved on 25 August 2009, from http://www.acus.org/publication/global-trends-2025-transformed-world

94. Jenkins, 51.

Christopher C. Harmon

How Terrorist Groups End:

Studies of the Twentieth Century

Terrorism studies are too young to have their Arnold Toynbee. Scholar Walter Laqueur has perhaps come the closest. At this writing in mid-2009, there remains a need for broad and searching inquiries into why and how terror groups have declined or ended. The project requires detailed knowledge of scores of important groups, extant and extinct, worldwide. The project also demands originality, so for this chapter we have set aside the useful frame I developed in 2003 and worked publicly for five years.[1] It is hoped that a fresh sowing in this vital field will help with the understanding of what we have seen in the twentieth century.

The Early Twentieth Century

From the nineteenth century, the twentieth inherited several forms of violence that would dramatically influence politics and terrorism. Three that were important, and very different, were labor militance, anarchism, and communism. These three schools of thought and action profited from liberalism and rationalism; they were internationalist, and by degrees each supported workers and the poor. The most honest and credible of the three was the first, labor—the drive for the rights and wages of blue-collar working men, women, and children, but a drive that sometimes assumed violent means and took innocent lives.

Labor Militance and Violence

International labor organizations arose from, and sometimes parallel to, older and more local and national models. Their members were overwhelmingly partisans of a fair wage, decent hours, and protection of children from brutal factory work or endless hours. Novelist John Steinbeck wrote sympathetically of the California farmworker unionizers who organized strikes or demands for better wages or improvement in camp conditions. But other activists stepped well over the lines of public pressure and civil opposition. The organization called Workers of the World, or "Wobblies," conducted strikes but also sabotage[2] of property. Individual militants or groups of organized labor undertook the beating or killing of bosses, night watchmen, or "big capitalists." Cities as different as Seattle and New York witnessed laborites' assaults on the innocent. A few representatives for a union of iron workers and bridge builders coordinated an ugly bombing campaign in the United States in the fall of 1910 that took two dozen lives, injured others, and massively damaged property.[3] The labor movements also produced theorists and public advocates (e.g., in France,

Georges Sorel). They advocated violence—usually accompanied by other political aims and strategies that might appeal to the sympathetic mind and to the average citizen.

American labor violence succeeded, in its way, according to the best US historian of terrorist movements, Walter Laqueur. "The daily wage of American iron workers (AFL) went up from $2.00 to $4.30 (for shorter hours) between 1905 and 1910 as the result of the bombing of some one hundred buildings and bridges."[4] He adds that Spanish workers, using similar methods, improved their wages during the First World War.[5] To violence, and that powerful display the strike, labor militants added mediation, sweet reason, unions, and other factors. These combinations improved labor conditions and pay. There was steady growth and legitimization of unions. As this occurred over decades, sporadic labor violence did not end, but it came to be seen in the American public mind as separate from political notions such as anarcho-syndicalism or communism. All these are among the reasons labor violence overturned so few economies and political orders of the early twentieth century.

Anarchism

Although it often lauded the poor man or hated the rich man, anarchism was never essentially and directly about conditions in the workplace, or the economy. It was obsessed with the state, more than the state of the working man. Anarchism despises political authority as inherently repressive and antihuman; it thus drives to bring down government, all government. The Russian Peter Kropotkin, born a prince before becoming an anarchist, drew a line between his confreres and Communists on the issue of the state: "To this question the anarchists alone give the proper answer: 'No Government!' All the others say 'A Revolutionary Government.'"[6] In the last third of the nineteenth century, and during the early twentieth, anarchism was distinctively international for reasons that were philosophical, first, and operational, second. The important activists often traveled (or fled) abroad, knew one another or corresponded, employed each other at publishing houses and journals, read each other's broadsides with their internationalist rhetoric, and saluted the others' violent actions as laudable "propaganda of the deed." They helped foreign fugitives find haven from the law, find work, or find comradeship.[7]

Violence joined up with philosophical anarchism in Russia at the end of the 1870s. Soon, given the devolution implicit in arguments for both violence and anarchism, theorists such as Kropotkin and Mikhail Bakunin[8] praised all actions that destroyed, from petty crime to grave assault.[9] The spiral downward led to adulation for "infernal machines" (usually dynamite bombs). The Russia of the late nineteenth century saw anarchism embedded with both low crime and flaming political idealism. The movement targeted senior defense, intelligence, and police officials, not just political governors. The revolutionary concepts were exported, and the colluders turned up to write, preach, and kill in the United States, Italy, Spain, Germany, and France. Anarchists hid out for periods in Switzerland, supporting themselves in journalism, printing, or other trades; they thus lived ironically—in a prosperous country amidst donors' money, chemicals for bomb-making, printing presses and newspapers, transportation, and the like, while working daily and nightly to destroy it all for a vision. International anarchists believed they could win. They could at least kill and they could reduce a city to general fear. Historian Barbara Tuchman depicts Paris at one time in the grip of "mad bombers"—streets deserted, shops shuttered, panic evident in the public.[10]

Why did this anarchist movement die? Indeed it did end: incidence of violence fell off dramatically, as in Italy and France after 1900. In the United States, the movement appeared to peak about 1908, and touched another summit in 1919. But one hears little of new lethal attacks after 1920—the year of payroll robbery and murder in Massachusetts by Ferdinando Nicola Sacco and Bartolomeo Vanzetti. It is also important to recognize that it was a movement—not a freakish wave of public interest, or a political party, or a disciplined formation of cells. Anarchism was international; it was networked (to use a modern term); ideas drove the actors; there were clandestine levels as well as public faces; some adherents were lethal and some were utterly fearless. For these reasons, the movement suggests parallels with the contemporary Salafist Islamist movement, best known for the much-narrower al Qaeda organization. And how it perished is thus doubly important.

Until recently, little was asked about the mystery of, and few good answers delineated reasons for, the death of violent anarchism.[11] New studies of the terrorists by Richard Bach Jensen, as well as Ersel Aydinli, demonstrate how state intelligence units, policing agencies, and other governmental offices and legislatures had profoundly important roles. Italy and Russia took leads in multistate action to coordinate border control and extradition. American cooperation with foreign states came slowly, too slowly, but did come. Creating the Federal Bureau of Investigation at home helped: It meant that investigators of anarchists no longer had to borrow manpower from the minuscule Secret Service, and also that a national register could be kept to allow information exchange and coordination across hundreds of local, county, and state jurisdictional lines. Europeans adjusted internal laws, as in banning open anarchist meetings, and enhancing court powers over conspiracy (i.e., revolutionary activities short of attacks). Russian services performed ruthlessly, locking up suspects and executing anarchists. Russian police, much provoked, were very aggressive; after October 1917 their successors set new standards in the use of force. In short, governments worldwide stiffly countered the anarchists.[12] Thus, *The Economist* may well be wrong in its conclusion to a fascinating four-page review of the century-old phenomenon (published in 2005): "So why did their wave of terror pass? Not, it seems, because of the measures taken to deter them."[13] For *The Economist,* the arrival of The Great War in 1914, and the Russian Revolution soon thereafter, made the difference. And surely these were important, new, and perhaps overwhelming, robbing anarchists of public interest. But two titanic events do not displace all quieter workings of history: being much provoked, states focused, and then responded, and with good effect.[14]

Communism

The October Revolution brings our account to the third and final school of thought bridging the nineteenth and twentieth centuries and relevant to terrorism. After labor militance and anarchism, there came communism. It had been visible, by degrees, in Narodnaya Volya (People's Will), a Russian terrorist group of the late 1870s. Its Central Committee believed that if a dozen pillars of government and security would collapse, the whole of government would tumble as the masses rose up. But the group's ideology was hazy—as much anarchist or pro-farmer as communist. Purer political revolutionary forms, such as those filled by Mensheviks, Bolsheviks, and Social Revolutionaries, attended to how government would be reformed and would work, not only to how it initially would be destroyed. They dreamed of new gleaming towers but also had the maturity to plan for them.

Communists often debated the issue of terrorism, and later students of such debates have an inappropriate tendency to fix on deprecatory remarks of famous Bolsheviks about the foolishness of individual terrorism—as Vladimir Lenin suggested in titling a booklet *Left-Wing Communism: An Infantile Disorder.*[15]

Such vanguardsmen of the era as Trotsky and Lenin did make the argument, in the course of a career in politics, that terrorism could be stupid or self-defeating. But these same communists used terror, and argued for terror, when it served their revolutionary purposes. What they ridiculed was not "the deliberate and systematic murder, maiming, and menacing of the innocent to inspire fear for a political end."[16] What they opposed was individual terrorism uncontrolled by their tight party. The Lenin who could mock bomb-throwers as "infantile" penned a letter to the "Combatant Committee" of St. Petersburg in 1905 urging revolutionaries to robbery, arson, and other terroristic acts, insisting that they stop blathering about bombs and begin using them.[17] Leon Trotsky, commander of the Red Army, thrilled to the power of both communist dictatorship and terrorism against counterrevolutionaries, penning a book exalting both, three years after the revolution. When the Soviet secret service murdered Trotsky in exile, it served as one more demonstration of how, once in power, Bolshevik communists viewed terror as they had while rising to power: through the eyes of cold utilitarianism.

After 1945 a new chapter opened for communism—one of both remarkable state power and renewed interest in expanding the revolution abroad. Terrorism kept some of its roles. International terror had some links to communists, their international organizations, and certain of their capitals.[18] Rulers of communist East Germany criticized terrorism during the high Cold War, but for years they funded *Konkret,* the radical newspaper in Berlin to which Ulrike Meinhof contributed, and both parties helped this relationship grow into provision of counsel and safe-haven to her Red Army Faction (RAF).[19] Serious communists, like serious anarchists, long for the state to disappear; many in both schools are certain that much violence is required to bring this about. Study of only tactics may confuse; thus, some observers imagine that the German RAF was more anarchist than communist—a myth easily dispelled by reading their communiqués. While the two movements differ on what happens after the revolution, the communist knows that anarchism, revolutionary spirit, and terrorism all have their virtues; their utility will depend upon timing and circumstance, and upon who becomes damaged and who benefits. And so the German Democratic Republic was just one of many communist bloc states supporting terrorist cells abroad.

The twentieth century lived with and endured communism. Witnesses, participants, and victims saw its stages of nascence, its rise to power, its dangerous status as deliberator over half the world during the high Cold War, and its sudden decline in authority by 1990. During eight decades in which its adherents governed important states, terrorism, whether guided by, or aided by, communists, took unnumbered lives. A minority of these perished in classic, archetypal international terrorist attacks by communist groups with communist state sponsors. Many died in other kinds of violence when communists were seeking power. Many more died in communist states after power was successfully taken. The human damage has been chronicled (e.g., by a man such as Alexander Solzhenitsyn, or in long lines of zeros, as added by the team of French academics who compiled the *The Black Book of Communism,* 1997).[20] In the end, among the many and diverse classes of victims were individual industrialists and arms-makers and top politicians in Europe; tens of thousands of village leaders hunted down over time in Indochina from 1940 to 1975; peasants in Asia caught up within insurgencies; and certain whole villages in Colombia and Peru, which dared to resist the revolutionaries via poorly armed militias. Communist terror came to dozens of other places and in myriad conditions. In four or five years, gunmen with a revolutionary dream could turn a pristine, admired city of one million such as Montevideo, Uruguay, into a war zone of urban strikes and daily gun battles, as the Tupamaros did by 1970.

No scholar has thoroughly studied and described the many ways that late-twentieth-century communist terror groups came to their ends, but it is errant to assume that they fell when the Soviet bloc did, in 1989 and 1990. First, many communist militants did not fall; they fought on, as Revolutionary Organization 17 November did in Greece. It was never touched by the Greek state and was indeed only broken by a bomber's accident in 2002, allowing a wave of arrests.[21] Second, other communist state-supported groups fought on and live even now; for example, the National Liberation Army (ELN) in Colombia long ago became self-supporting. Today has outlasted the Soviet bloc by two decades and keeps several thousand men and women in the field. Third, certain communist groups did not fall with the Kremlin but perished well before. This was true of the Belgian Communist Combatant Cells. Most Italian leftist terror groups disappeared before 1990. Law enforcement was the usual primary reason.

The German Red Army Faction (RAF), or Baader-Meinhof group, did not quickly disappear, but it too failed. RAF did not announce its dissolution and failure in a communiqué until April 1992, proximate to the world-shaking fall of the wall. But the group's real end was signaled as early as 18 October 1977. On that day, four of the imprisoned RAF leaders—including lovers Andreas Baader and Gudrun Enslin—attempted suicide (three of four succeeded). The Lufthansa jet their comrades had hijacked to bargain for the freedom of the prisoners in Stammheim jail was recaptured by elite West German border guards (GSG-9), who shot all the hijackers in the action. With only a handful of quarrelsome confreres still operating inside the Federal Republic, the RAF experienced despair. The wiser of them understood that after eight years of terrorism they had made astonishingly few allies among sixty million normal Germans, people whose lives were democratic, whose self-governance centered in Bonn and more local places, and whose economy was a shining success. The RAF thus tottered along after 1990 and 1992, but few new members joined, and nearly all who did were uncovered by diligent police work.[22] The Federal Republic was no oppressor, and there were no profound "roots" to terrorism requiring excision, but only a shallow and shoddy malaise in some elites. In a tribute to how democracy may calmly mobilize, active security forces, operating carefully under the law with enhanced intelligence, they eventually reduced all remnants of the minuscule Red Army Faction.

Similar diligence by security forces and governments in France, Belgium and Italy undercut and effaced those countries' "Fighting Communist Organizations."[23] Regional cooperation by authorities developed as well.[24] Proper extraditions of fugitives thus gradually trumped older presumptions of the "asylum rights" of political terrorists, making foreign refuges challenging to find. When EUROPOL was born, it confirmed the best tendencies in European politics as well as developments since the Maastricht accords reduced national borders in 1992. If this maturing organization comes to move firmly against transnational terrorists—in the way that INTERPOL has done recently under Secretary General Ronald Noble[25]—the healthy effects of international action will be enjoyed more by European society.

Today communism is exhausted in most locales. But it has not died. "Naxalites" dominate great parts of central-eastern India. Counterparts of a Maoist calling have reached a peak of power in Nepal, entered parliament, and taken the Prime Ministry, shelving terrorist methods—at least in most places, at least for now. Their terrorism has been placed on "pause" while they share power. Colombia has badly damaged ELN and Revolutionary Armed Forces of Colombia (FARC)[26] regions, but neither insurgency is at an end. Peru's Sendero Luminoso, or Shining Path, decapitated by 1992 arrests, is reportedly attempting a "comeback" after a decade and a half of impotence. But in Europe, the United States, and some other regions, factors including the collapse of the Soviet Union have persuaded most that communism has little future, and thus that its violent methods cannot be justified. Mainland China seems only to underscore the decline of communism's foreign meddling of militant sorts. In the 1960s and 1970s, Chinese advisors serviced at least a dozen militant groups in Asia and Africa, including the genocidal Khmer Rouge.[27] Today, Beijing presides over new economic strength and military power, but this parallels a decline in ideological commitment. Beijing seeks allies and oil; few if any official Chinese actions include direct support to violent substate groups. This apparent absence of Beijing's state support for violent revolution has been one reason for notable declines, in some regions, of terrorism. In other areas—where indigenous Maoist revolutionaries might perform better if they could only have Beijing's aid—the lack of foreign state assistance is important.

Racism and Nationalism After World War II

Fierce nationalisms lay behind two global wars of the twentieth century and myriad attacks of smaller scale. The wars of nationalism include many long-simmering low-intensity conflicts featuring terrorism and insurgency in the post–World War II era. The Allies' crushing of fascism—a doctrine built upon racial and national exclusivity and superiority—could not prevent the rise of later racist or hypernationalist figures and movements. So while organized neo-fascist parties and movements of post-1945 years have often been small, they have had support of malcontents, reactionaries, and others.

A riveting example of "terrorist as political reactionary" was the Secret Army Organization (OAS), a last-ditch attempt by French and other Europeans to defend status quo European power in Algeria in the face of success by the indigenous National Liberation Front (FLN). Men of the OAS imagined themselves to be counterterrorists, protectors of many decades of French improvements in the Maghreb. In fact they swiftly descended into nihilism. Their quick end in failure has obscured some of their very real strengths, however. OAS was formed by savvy leaders, enjoyed considerable financing, conducted hundreds of *plastique* bombings and assassinations, and had international sanctuaries (especially in Spain). OAS was also defending the status quo—which is normally easier than overthrowing it. But it was defeated in less than two years by a combination of Charles de Gaulle's government efforts and a near-absence of public support for the OAS except in limited and white circles in Algeria. Political forces labeled them as "neo-Nazis" and "assassins." At the operational level, in France as well as North Africa, police and government outsmarted the rightists: "It has been estimated that ten determined men fought and won the battle against the OAS in France. What they brought to the struggle was intelligence, political acumen, level-headedness, and personal toughness," according to Paul Henissart's history *Wolves in the City*. IBM computers were exploited, as well as networks of human sources. "In addition to using police tipsters, double-agents, and anti-OAS groups, [police] received information from thousands of private citizens loyal to the government."[28] The Secret Army Organization was born in December 1960; it died in July 1962 when all but .02 percent of voting Algerians said "Oui" to independence.

It is not surprising that the OAS had found supporters among rightist European farmers and businessmen worried over loss of economic status in a prospective FLN-run Algeria. Similarly, many extremist and reactionary groups of the twentieth century have seen their ranks swell with economic crisis. The history of this pattern in Italy and Germany in the 1920s and 1930s is clear, and the rise of fascist street gangs of those days was clearly "terrorism." Waves of immigration into Europe and the fall of the Berlin Wall have had their own roles in spawning violent new racist or nationalist organizations. Today, smart analysts think about how the early twenty-first-century economic recession is affecting prospects of rightist and other terrorists. Economics is merely one driver of politics. Many times, social trends or legislative changes have added to economic worries, and thus added volume to the calls to action. One further and recent example in US history is when the 1983 "Brady Bill" making guns harder to acquire had this effect on some right-wing Americans already angered by general recession and an acute farm crisis.

Ghosts in the American Experience

Both immigration and economic trouble have been connected in the United States to the long run and continuing life of the Ku Klux Klan (KKK). This organization was founded in the mid-nineteenth century, prospered, and moved readily into the twentieth. The KKK was in Canada, as well as many US states, where membership peaked from 1915 to 1925. The first of those years marks the opening of the D.W. Griffith film *Birth of a Nation*—initially released as *The Clansman*, a powerful film seeming to idealize white supremacy and anti-black violence. The second date, a decade later, was that of a powerful political display: in Washington, DC, an estimated 40,000 Klansmen marched. Nor would the KKK disappear after the Second World War. Some American racists doubtless joined such groups as the KKK precisely in personal reaction against post-1945 liberalism, tolerance, and internationalism. US civil rights improvements and new laws could infuriate the serious kind of racist who joined the Klan; that paradox is instructive as to the nature of terrorism.

Mike German, a young FBI agent, penetrated several KKK and neo-fascist terror groups in the United States. He offers valuable research into how the Klan was forced into decline—though not defeated—beginning in the late 1920s. The complex of reasons includes (1) political infighting, which fractured the organization and has continued to do so even today; (2) scandals—as when violent episodes shocked the public, or an individual Klansman's actions tarnished the image of "protector of southern values"; (3) a change in American values, whereby the public's tolerance for racism declined, and many were moved by the exposure of fascism's atrocities and death camps overseas in the early 1940s; (4) federal government actions, especially a 1946 tax decision that damaged Klan business enterprises and the 1954 *Brown vs. Board of Education* Supreme Court decision on education that ended school segregation forever; and (5) the Klan murders of three civil rights workers in Mississippi in 1964, which horrified the US public. The cumulative effect was to thoroughly discredit an organization that since the 1880s had often lynched and terrorized with impunity.[29] During the last half-century, the KKK has not possessed half the powers it once had in America. Together these are a veritable roster of terrorist group vulnerabilities—and they should suggest all kinds of possibilities to clever counterterrorism specialists.

Unfortunately, racism and terrorism from the extreme right in America have never been limited to the KKK network. There is a lengthy and distressing chronicle of maiming, menacing, and occasionally even murder of the innocent by other US groups preaching narrow or eccentric forms of white power religion and politics. Tiny political minorities, and even "lone wolf" actors, militants—usually male—tend to imagine themselves to be heroic defenders of the racial majority in the fifty states. Consider only the last generation, and only lethal actions, often against black or Jewish victims. Among the earliest of these murderers was Gordon Kahl of Posse Comitatus in February 1983, in North Dakota. Richard Wayne Snell, of the Covenant, Sword, and Arm of the Lord (CSA), killed in Arkansas in 1983 and in June of 1984.[30] Members of The Order, a white supremacist group, killed a man in June 1984 in Colorado. Neo-Nazi David Tate of The Order killed in April 1985.[31] In Oregon, White Aryan Resistance–inspired skinheads of East Side White Pride beat a man to death in November 1988. A gap in lethal incidents followed, yet the far right returned: Timothy McVeigh, racist and anti-federalist, bombed and killed scores in April 1995 in Oklahoma. Militants hoping to found an Aryan Peoples Republic killed in Arkansas in 1997. A free member of the prison gang Confederate Knights of America, John William King, murdered in Texas in June 1998. Ben N. Smith of the World Church of the Creator killed twice in July 1999, in Illinois and Indiana. Buford O'Neil Furrow committed an August 1999 murder in California. In a testament to the significance of ideas—not just personalities—in terrorism, at least five of these latter acts are linked to the ugly racist novel, *The Turner Diaries*.[32]

What social and political forces contain and resist this modern-day terrorism from the racist right? One is federal leadership from Washington, be it in federal statutes or action against entrenched resistance in some states and localities.[33] We return to the KKK: after the Civil War of the mid-nineteenth century, federal intervention had controlled or suppressed many indigenous patterns of racist behavior. This activism by Washington (including locking up thousands of Klansmen) was abandoned after 1882, with deleterious effects; when resumed after World War II, it proved again to be a vital element in the desegregation of the 1950s, and in the successful prosecution of terrorists in courts. Successive US presidents, the Justice Department, and other organs of federal power used law, administration, rhetoric, and occasionally the deployment of soldiers to check violence and dampen the resistance of white citizens and institutions opposed to racial equality. Federal power has not ended the Klan or most related organizations, but it damages their prestige, discourages activists, and demonstrates these organizations' weaknesses.

Majority public opinion has been yet more important. It was not revolution but evolution that made Americans move toward fuller racial equality. Education, religion, and common sense played their parts. The decline of racism was indirectly recognized by William L. Pierce, propagandist, author of *The Turner Diaries*, and founder of the white racist National Alliance, when he told admirer and terrorist Robert Matthews that "White people are just not in a revolutionary mood now."[34] Indeed, what is most remarkable about American racists' public demonstrations of the most recent decades is not that they occur, for that is simply an unsavory aspect of a large country with political liberty; it is instead that whenever a racist organization's march permit becomes known, ten times as many citizens turn out on the named day to counterdemonstrate against racism or neo-fascism. This phenomenon has been common all across America.[35] Racism is publicly despised.

A third factor in the "containment" of such terrorism in the United States is the private legal suit. In singular victories that have come in a slow and compelling parade, civil suits are now used by public interest groups—usually in federal courts—to break individual terrorist organizations and hate groups. One leader of this legal offensive is Morris Dees, who in 1981 launched "Klanwatch"—now known as the Intelligence Project—at his Southern Poverty Law Center in Montgomery, Alabama. Three decades of work have provoked several murder plots against the attorney. It was a Dees suit, for example, that ended the reign of terror, hate-speech, and bogus religious rites conducted from a compound of Aryan Nations in Hayden Lake, Idaho. A woman and her daughter passing via automobile stopped near the compound, showed more than necessary interest, and were fired upon from within. In this case of assault, Dees beat the group in court, and Idaho took away Aryan Nations' legal status, money, and land.[36] Today the Hayden Lake complex has been leveled and the twenty acres are "Peace Park." With the death of Richard Butler, the group's leader, and the arrest of a purported chief financier, it can be said that the Aryan Nations gang has been broken, peaceably, by domestic legal means. The Southern Poverty Law Center takes credit for similar claims of decisive action against Imperial Klans of America with chapters in eight US states, and the White Aryan Resistance started by Tom Metzger.

Outside the United States, racism, neofascism, and extreme nationalism have many other homelands, and occasionally spawn terrorism. The Czechs, Poles, and Russians have each had unprecedented opportunities for liberal democracy since 1990, but that has not prevented race persecution, beatings, stabbings, and occasionally deaths, especially in Russia. The group Blood & Honour keeps alive the Nazi flame with members or affiliates in a number of European Union countries and the United States.[37] Germany had a hundred cases of bodily injury from right-wing attack in the twenty-four-month period 2006–2007, though perhaps no homicide. In Italy, where a center-right government is strongly against illegal immigration, an unforgivable pattern of individual attacks is also visible, causing one local newspaper headline to declare "a racism emergency."[38] These facts and fears evidence continued dreaming by right-wing supremacists, a dream which for most passed forever in May 1945. Rightist extremism has by no means ended in Europe, although it is much less dangerous than some newer forms of terrorism.

More from the Left: Revolutionaries of the 1960s and Beyond

Some Italians now fear a revival of their own militant left. This is unlikely, but it does speak to how vividly Italian adults recall the communist and anarchist terror groups of four decades ago. Much of Europe remembers. Those were times of violent upheavals, squatter communes, cocky splinter parties, and anarchism. Such things mixed and flourished in the German north in Frankfurt and West Berlin. French cities including Paris and Toulon saw riots and *"Aux Barricades"* cries beginning in May 1968. The late 1960s were years of racial and antiwar turmoil in the United States. Many around the world were mesmerized by the communist-led turmoil and purges inside China. In the narrower field of pure terrorism, 1968 was above all the year of the Popular Front for the Liberation of Palestine, including founder George Habash and foreign allies such as Hans Joachim Klein and Vladimir Ilich

Sanchez ("Carlos the Jackal"). They opened new fronts with international air piracy and lethal attacks in Paris. Many of the European groups networked, holding terrorist summits, meeting under foreign state auspices and in Middle Eastern training camps, buying arms from the same dealers, and occasionally carrying out joint missions, as against North Atlantic Treaty Organization targets.

Most of these later twentieth-century communist organizations failed—for two fundamental reasons. They could not successfully challenge the post–World War II success of capitalism and democracy. The second reason is that, as Lenin and Mao predicted, sporadic violence by small cells was unlikely to enjoy strategic success unless fully integrated with broader political and economic plans. For Lenin, this meant clandestine organization, a vanguard party apparatus, and understanding the perfect time to strike; for Mao, it meant protracted war and competition with the regime on multiple levels until, gradually, the strategic balance of power shifted and the long drive toward state power could conclude. Both men won. But their insight and prescience were not shared by Che Guevara. His school of simple "focoism" that stressed the mobilizational capabilities of small roving armed bands was a failure, after the singular victory in Cuba. Scores of Guevarist-type groups came and went, unsuccessfully and swiftly, especially on the Latin American scene.

Two of the continent's most celebrated terrorist groups, in Uruguay and Argentina, respectively, initially enjoyed years of success, until the military intervened and conducted systematic repression with all available assets. That is, powerful terrorists were defeated by greater power. Uruguay's bout with the communist Tupamaros led by Raul Sendic Antonaccio began in 1962, with their first manifesto appearing in 1965. Bank robberies paid for intelligence nets, a huge network of safe houses, weapons, and even underground medical clinics. Armed attacks bedeviled this liberal and admired country, sometimes called the "Switzerland of Latin America." After a few years of revolutionary work, the peace of the capital was in tatters, US personnel came under the gun, and British Ambassador Geoffrey Jackson suffered an infamous and long period in a "people's prison." The group was a founder of modern terrorism in more respects: Its partnership with the criminal underworld;[39] playing Robin Hood distributing cash and food to the poor; large numbers of female members; and the presence in Tupamaro ranks of substantial numbers of professionals and well-educated graduates.[40] The Uruguayan armed forces intervened in April 1972, later formally taking state power. They soon captured key revolutionary leaders as well as hundreds of cadre, and killed many Tupamaro gunmen. This was decisive; after 1973 the movement was never able to reorganize; after 1976, it had no serious presence at all. The Tupamaros had a successful run for about a decade and disappeared. Uruguay's armed forces defeated them and, years later, withdrew and handed power back over to civilian authorities. A once-flourishing democracy was thus returned to the democratic fold.[41]

Full-blooded state reaction also crushed the Montoneros in Argentina. These terrorists' ideology blended nationalism with Marxist-Leninism and populism, finding a balance of motives that accorded well with political trends in that country. Abroad they opened offices and conducted propaganda; at home they infiltrated Juan Peron's political organizations and conducted bold armed operations, drawing upon as many as five thousand armed guerrillas. These tactical successes stung and bled the authorities, while generating fantastic sums of money, especially via kidnappings of industrialists, including one ransom of $60 million;[42] some money would end up in Cuba, a patron state. But the Montoneros also evidenced vulnerabilities, especially an internal split between leftists and rightists that led even to gun battles. A series of spectacular actions occurred in 1974, but this marked the apex of success for the revolutionaries, as it led directly to a military decision for intervention. The generals took control of all civilian policing efforts in February 1975, and effected a full political coup in March of 1976. The successive months saw multiple and often ugly methods deployed to exterminate this powerful underground. Civilian authorities did not regain power; that would come only with the military despots' blunders and defeat in the Falklands War of 1982.

The Latin world of the late 1960s and the 1970s saw the rise and fall of many other groups, including the National Liberating Action (ALN) organization of Carlos Marighella. He turned from mainstream Brazilian communism into terrorist underground work, and published the 1969 pamphlet *Minimanual of the Urban Guerrilla*. Then he perished almost immediately in a gun battle with police. His successor lasted only months and the ALN disappeared. The fall of many such short-lived groups makes clear the pattern. Force was met with force, be it legal, covert, or martial. Latin America saw some cases of state appeasement of terrorists, but few instances of successful negotiation leading into satisfactory settlements. Most of the challengers to government were advocates of "absolute war"; they were serious revolutionaries in a hunt for state power, not compromise, and not limited reforms in favor of the poor or the workers. Terrorist parties of this time were creative, exciting to some citizens, and often well led, by charismatic figures or well-educated propagandists, or both, making them strong enemies. As such, Latin states tended to reply slowly but ultimately with great harshness. In Guatemala and Argentina, especially, the government offensive came with free use of torture[43] and extrajudicial killing. Attrition of the terrorists and victory for the state were normal outcomes. The pattern would remain during much of the 1980s and 1990s, as we shall see, but with two notable differences: efforts at negotiation would become more common; and in certain cases, large numbers of Latin undergrounders would fold pacifically into overt political parties, shaping their ambitions in more legitimate fashions. The Colombian M-19 and Salvadoran Farabundo Marti National Liberation Front (FMLN) cadre would do so, following defeats in the fields.

Events in Latin America had strong parallels in Western Europe by 1968 and 1970. Anarchism appeared, after decades of absence in major cities, and to a degree not known in Latin America. Michael "Bommi" Baumann's June 2 Movement in Germany helped reopen wars of youth, radicalism, and criminality against order. His mindless book of those days, *Terror or Love?*, suggests the lack of strategy in his political circle in Berlin, and thus anticipates the decline and failure of that dimension of the urban and student movement. Joschka Fischer and Daniel Cohn-Bendit did not do notably better in Frankfurt. These self-declared Sponti, or spontaneous ones, unrestricted by Leninist ideas of planning and revolutionary organization, attracted attention and sympathy, and police brutality on occasion, but never persuaded the German people they were all "latent fascists." A concentrated multiyear effort to infiltrate a large factory for Opel cars and bring about workers' rebellion flopped due to immaturity of technique.[44] Anarchism failed in northern Europe in the 1960s and 1970s, unless a loosening of lifestyles and culture is taken as the only standard of success. Yet Fischer's career is a notable example of one way terror groups end: folding into pacific life. He moved away from the violent underworld and sympathies for armed terrorism, toward the Green Party and elections, and even became the federal republic's foreign minister (1998–2005). Both Fischer and Cohn-Bendit remain regularly in the newspapers, but as personalities and politicos, rather than street fighters.

Europe's communist terrorist groups were more successful, longer-lived, and found more mainstream supporters, than competing anarchist groups. Italy's communists make for remarkable study. Prima Linea, or Front Line, was a large terrorist organization and force of the underground. Trotskyite and Maoist parties abounded, inside and outside the law. Lotta Continua, or Permanent Struggle, boasted some two hundred thousand adherents. The Red Brigades had "columns" in Rome, Florence, Turin, and Milan, even if the last of those turned restless and broke away, taking money and guns with them. Incident levels in Italy rose in the 1970s to shocking heights. There was chaos, perceived and actual, in the country through the early 1980s. Such power in terrorist hands is always to be judged in relation to other political power; in Italy, central government was weak, after decades of tumultuous parliamentary politics, enhanced Communist Party strength, and voter disillusionment with such matters as organized crime. Instead of teaching the value of democracy and the mechanisms of rule of law, some social science faculty were poisoning students with contempt of country. A powerful press like the Milan-based Feltrinelli's was no bulwark of the establishment; its heir, Giangiacomo Feltrinelli, was literally a paymaster of various international militant groups, including Italian terrorists.[45] Hard-working Italian politicians who labored to build working coalitions of disparate parties failed more often than succeeded, and when Christian Democrat Aldo Moro built a bridge to the legal communist left, in 1978, the Red Brigades immediately murdered him for it.

In hindsight, Italian incident levels make it almost incredible that republican democracy survived. That it did, and without even one month of tyranny, is a lesson for all times. No dazzling new computer software or police science was the key. No one leader from the political parties took the helm and showed the way. Security forces were key—but not the only answer. The country's response was a hesitating and uncollective one, but it did succeed. And the most important victory was on the legal front. Instead of sacrificing the law, as in Argentina and Uruguay, legislators studied and improved the laws on terrorism in several key ways.[46] By measures passed through parliament, police were given greater powers to investigate and to detain suspects. A new group of judges was created to specialize in prosecuting terrorists—as also occurred in France. Terrorism ceased to be considered an anomaly or a quirky expression of libertines and became a named offense in state codes. A new provision, however, pointed the terrorist toward a "golden bridge" even as it threatened longer years in jail and encircled his rear with policemen: this allowed any who confessed, and aided police, to dramatically reduce their own sentences. This last point capitalized on the very size of the underground by giving openings to weaker cadre. The terrorist movement contained not just hardened men and women but softer adherents, or comrades grown weary; some of these were willing to talk when captured; *pentiti* testimony locked up comrades for decades; and the more they gave away, the more the rigor of the terrorist left generally dissolved. The phenomenon illustrated the vulnerabilities of terror groups that seek to become broad insurgencies; counterintelligence and discipline problems escalate with growth. It was combinations of legal punches and law enforcement—not an end to Communist bloc aid or the dismantlement of the Berlin Wall, that knocked down so many Italian leftist terrorists during the four years 1979 to 1982. Italy also deployed a specialized police unit, which on 28 January 1982 freed NATO's General James Dozier from a Padua apartment staffed by Brigadists. Incident chronicles then fell nearly silent for the Red Brigades columns; most notations were of arrests of undergrounders, not attacks.[47]

In North America the early 1970s were notable for their violence. This followed the rise in civil rights activism and included several hideous murders of these activists by right-wingers. Problems were illuminated by arson and rioting in major US cities. The Vietnam War was a second source of domestic violence. It especially affected Americans below the 49th latitude, but the war also inflamed some eyes and ears in Canada.

The Quebec Liberation Front (FLQ) is one of those charted by Dr. Crenshaw's groundbreaking 1991 survey "How Terrorism Declines."[48] She lists the group as active from 1963; one may or may not argue whether her end-date of 1972 is too generous to a group another scholar announces as "dormant" after 1970. The early date marks out this nationalist, separatist, and also leftist revolutionary group as among the first to be active in the Northern Hemisphere. They broke away from a larger leftist group and took aim at military establishments and US economic and political influence in their country. Evading police, one young leader returned to his native Belgium, while Raymond Villeneuve made a pilgrimage to Cuba, helping initiate a long relationship between that island state and North American leftists going underground or seeking to land airplanes they hijacked. The organization survived initial police reaction, found support in anti-Ottawa sentiment in the French-speaking region, published the journal *La Cognee* (The Axe), and engaged new members such as part-time journalist Pierre Vallieres, who was to write two solid books of propaganda.[49]

Robberies and kidnappings built toward a peak that came between the summers of 1968 and 1969; there were a hundred bombings, including that of the Montreal Stock Exchange. These produced vigorous police action by a government long known as quiescent and liberal. In 1970 the FLQ tried to escalate its efforts but overreached with an elaborate plot to seize a British trade commissioner and swap him for prisoners. As this fell into shambles, the FLQ also seized Vice Premier and Labor Minister Pierre Laporte—soon strangled, and dismissed in a terrorist bulletin as "Minister of Unemployment and Assimilation."[50] Quebec separatism prompted the Canadian government to its own unique form of radicalism: a World War I–era "War Measures Act" was invoked for the first time during peace. This allowed a range of state actions that must have astonished the terrorists and their intellectually loose allies accustomed to chatter about the rightist "extremism" of Ottawa. Sufficiently provoked, Canadian authorities now introduced, against fellow Canadian citizens, such methods as *agents provocateurs*, systematic intelligence work, countless arrests, and detention without trial. Hundreds of FLQ cadre or sympathizers were entrapped. Within months the cause had been stalled; the country had become silent. Separatism still watered the soil of Quebecoise nationalism, but in legal and fruitful channels, yielding election of the Socialist and former separatist Pierre Trudeau as prime minister in 1968. This victory, by a leader the FLQ's Vallieres had mocked as a slavish compromiser, could just as well be said to show how the democratic path can be an effective path, that forgiving and indisciplined political culture (such as that of Weimar Germany) need not invite the empowerment of thugs (such as Nazis). Quebec separatists won "half a loaf" and it seems difficult to deny that terrorism was one cause of the change.[51] Now the separatist cause seems satiated; polling gives few indications of support for violence to further set the region apart from Canada. Terrorism ended in a combination of intelligence work, harsh law enforcement, and political accommodation.

Puerto Rico offers a related case, in which serious cultural, linguistic, and political differences may threaten division from a larger multinational country in North America.

United States control of the island of the Caribbean dates from the US war with Spain; Puerto Rico was a sort of spoil of war. Advocates of total independence have never been able to capture more than a bare minimum of the island's votes, but their track record of violent provocations is lengthy, reaching back to 1950, when they nearly assassinated President Harry Truman, and 1954, when the group shot up the House of Representatives. Arrests ended these cells. The thoughts and resentments that sparked the cases smoldered as embers, however, and produced new flame in 1974 when the Armed Forces of National Liberation (FALN) appeared. They stunned New York City with a tavern bombing of a type Americans associated with Ulster tragedies. Incendiaries were laid in department stores—in a suggestion of later German RAF arson of 1968, or partisans of Iraq who left dynamite in Paris stores in late 2008. Dozens of other attacks followed. Then the action jumped from the eastern United States to Puerto Rico itself, opening a fresh front. But arrests and convictions, as of ten perpetrators in December 1980, squelched the drive. It has been argued that the group ended in 1982; certainly after 1983 there was little to keep the FALN name in lights. Policing succeeded.

But the FALN case reveals the difference between a campaign and a war. One militant Puerto Rican campaign was finished—but not the war. A very similar group had been founded in 1978 and proved well prepared to succeed the faltering FALN. They called themselves the machete-wielders, or Los Macheteros. Displaying that mix of leftism and nationalism so visible in the twentieth-century terrorist world, the new group was an ally of the Marxist-Leninist Puerto Rican Socialist Party (PSP), which itself had connections to Cuba. Their greatest triumphs represented guerrilla war and terrorist robbery capabilities. The first was a 1978 simultaneous incendiary attack on nine US combat planes lined up at a military base near Isla Verde International Airport. The second, five years later, was equally impressive. Having placed a member inside the workings of the Brinks armored car service in Hartford, Connecticut, the group awaited the best day, brought other employees under control, and escaped with $7.2 million. Some of it emerged in Robin Hood–style giveaways in Puerto Rican communities; some of it doubtless bought weapons and supplies; much of it appears to have gone to Cuba in a vehicle driven over the US border with Mexico.

The Federal Bureau of Investigation (FBI) took apart Los Macheteros with the same patience and thoroughness it would show later against rightists and "militiamen" in the US "patriot movement" of the 1990s. With surveillance, wire taps, and other efforts (not to mention the special energy of an organization whose office in San Juan had been rocketed by Macheteros), the FBI disassembled this organization, brought its people to trial, and awarded lengthy sentences. Women and men, activists and journalists, social workers, and a Harvard University man were convicted in the late 1980s. The effect on the group was nearly terminal. William Clinton, in a legal but imprudent use of the powers of the presidency, pardoned many of these terrorists as he departed the White House in 2001. Of further concern to counterterrorists was the continued liberty of Filiberto Ojeda Rios, a long-time Machetero leader. Finally, in 2005, the FBI found him, armed, in a house on the island; he died in the subsequent gunfight.[52]

Los Macheteros may be counted among the "deceased" of late twentieth-century terrorist organs. The proximate cause of their expiry was devoted work by law enforcement and successful trials—the latter can never be taken for granted.[53] It is not irrelevant that the US Navy, after a century of use of Vieques as a bombing and gunnery range, ceased such practices, removing one cause of discontent in Puerto Rico. Perhaps a larger cause of the near-total containment of terrorism by government has been inadequate support for it by other Puerto Ricans. In the same way that a majority of Irish have long rejected IRA methods, the island of four million people,[54] as a whole, neither votes for nor supports bombings and killings for independence. There is no mass support, above or below the political ground level. On the other hand, Los Macheteros were a success for some years, and before them came other waves in this pool of ethnic and nationalist resentments, which may well be stirred by further storms. Such disturbances can sometimes have a cumulative effect. In tsarist Russia, for example, there were three waves of political terrorism; each of the first two subsided, yet all helped produce the Bolshevik Revolution of October 1917.

As the twentieth century closed, merging with the twenty-first, another nationalist-separatist fighting force with long tenure and a solid level of performance and skill seemed in profound trouble. Basque Homeland and Freedom (ETA) in Spain and France is unlike Los Macheteros because it still has fighters in the field and other operational capacities. But the ETA is at an all-time point of weakness. It survives, but barely; it strikes against Spain, but rarely; it makes headlines, but usually with the capture of ETA shooters or financiers by the more clever security forces of Madrid or Paris. ETA is still standing but may be on its last legs. If so, and ETA ends, it would be significant to world terrorism: The group is now a half-century old, has killed nearly nine hundred Spanish in its operations, and has represented a model, and been an occasional partner, to other terror groups. Among its greatest successes must be counted the attraction of foreign support—guns from Libya, perhaps advice from Soviet agents, certainly training grounds in Soviet-bloc client state South Yemen in the 1970s—without ever being soiled in its image as an indigenous and independent revolutionary force. This is a difficult balance to strike, but ETA has done it well.

Formed at the end of the 1950s, ETA focused on propaganda and political front activities, initiating systematic violence only years later. Principal Spanish political and security force personnel, and Civil Guards (the gendarmerie) were the most usual victims. Shooting was a preferred method; later would come the car bombs, with their far wider swathes of "collateral damage" to other Spaniards. Assigning a "revolutionary tax" to Basques who were, and were not, engaged in revolution was an innovative and successful financing means the group has never abandoned. But weaknesses were also present. Internecine quarreling over ideology was a plague of the early decades, with some leaders favoring pure nationalism while another strong wing wanted to rally behind declarations of Communism and global revolution. Two other problems were larger, also political. Spain emerged as a strong democracy, as the death of Francisco Franco in 1975 led into the benign monarchy of King Juan Carlos, who transferred some powers over to the National Assembly. Second, in a move largely ignored by terrorism analysts and much of the outside world, the central government bestowed on the Basque lands a high degree of autonomy as to matters of culture, local law, and language. This was quite simply a concession to Basque activism of many types. Initially, ETA reacted violently, probably sensing the subtle dangers (to a terrorist movement) in this prudent concession by Madrid. Over time the government work had its effect, helping to divide the ordinary Basque from his confrere in the terrorist underground.

Today the political fronts that were once so helpful to supporting ETA violence are gravely weakened. Several have been banned by Madrid, including Herri Batasuna (Popular Unity), which in the early 1980s was second in strength in Spanish political parties. Herri Batasuna changed its name to Batasuna, only to again be proscribed. In 2007, 2008, and 2009 the most noted spokesman for the front, Arnaldo Otegi, was under intense police pressure. The larger political challenge is that typical Basques no longer respond to ETA battle cries; indeed, the largest parade on the nationalist issue the country has seen in recent years occurred in January 2007 and it was against ETA terrorism.[55] A final problem is almost overwhelming for the dwindling ranks of ETA terrorists: Franco-Spanish cooperation. This began in small ways in the late 1980s, as France at last began making moves on its side of the border to arrest ETA activists and financiers. For example, a French raid of 1986 on a safe house unveiled much about the group's finances within France, and also captured varieties of international currency. More important was the impetus felt in Madrid to closely collaborate, in 1991 and 1992, to protect impending world tourist events in Spain such as the World Trade Fair, and the Barcelona Olympics of 1992. The late 1990s and early twenty-first century saw continued close cooperation, with arrests on both sides of the Franco-Spanish border. It seemed that new leaders served only months in their roles before capture. The president of France and the prime minister of Spain met in Elysee Palace in January 2008 to advance collaboration on counterterrorism, going so far as to announce creation of a small, combined policing unit.[56] This now continuous and high-level bilateral cooperation is wrecking ETA.[57] There is scarcely another case in recent times of two countries combining so well to snuff out terrorist cells—to the immense advantage of both states.[58]

Two other famous and long-standing terrorist entities of our world might have been comparatively studied, until May 2009. Both were Marxist-Leninist; both had enjoyed protracted periods of leadership continuity; both were wealthy; they have been successful as insurgents and leaders of "shadow governments," protecting large swaths of territory, and were thus much more than "bite and flee" attackers of civilian and military targets. Mao Tse Tung's "phase two" warfare, combining guerrilla efforts with semiconventional and positional warfare,[59] is the best descriptor of the character of these two very important organizations. The FARC of Colombia and the LTTE in Sri Lanka have been feared for their skills in varieties of fighting and terrorism. Now the latter appears finished. About the former, the Colombian government must be especially careful. One of the great yet common sins of counterinsurgency is overestimating successes, of which there were many during 2007 and 2008. But Bogota has more to do, and after FARC there is the smaller entity ELN.

The government and armed forces of Sri Lanka after 2001 were seized with a profound determination that has resonated with their polity and allowed concerted national effort against a powerful in-country enemy. The 1980s and 1990s had seen many ground battles, which together with LTTE terrorism had left over sixty-five thousand dead. A negotiated peace made for a few quiet years, but this was overturned in 2006 and replaced by the most intense fighting. As 2008 finished, regional newspapers were printing accounts of major advances by government ground forces, and the recapture of key towns, as well as the idea that founding leader Velupillai Prabhakaran was living on the run—from jet fighters and ground incursions into his traditional safe havens. In pursuit of him, according to the *International Herald Tribune*, was Defense Secretary Gotabaya Rajapaksa, a former army officer, a relentless opponent of negotiated concessions or halts in the military offensive, and a skilled coordinator of the air, ground, and naval forces now hunting LTTE night and day.[60] He is the brother of Sri Lanka's president. Now, it may be argued that this leadership duo and fine armed forces have wrecked the guerrillas and terrorists of LTTE. After thirty-five indomitable years, Prabhakaran and many top officers are dead.[61]

Some Groups of Religious Bent

Terrorism is always political. In the late twentieth century it also became more religious. The 1970s and 1980s offered several extreme versions of Christianity and of Hinduism, which caught up "true believers" in militancy. There were Sikh sects active—and killing—internationally in the mid-1980s.[62] There was long-running violence from the Jewish Defense League (in the eastern United States, sometimes by individuals with links to Israelis), which may now be spent. But by 1988 and 1990 one could begin to discern newer groups of religious bent—or bent religion. One study has determined that a definite numerical majority of the new groups founded since 1990 avow religious objectives—in front of, or parallel to, political ones.[63] Most such groups deserve to be taken at their word. Iran's officials supported (then and now) groups of both Sunni and Shia faiths. Beneficiaries include Hamas, which in its well-crafted charter took an integrated approach to conceptual support for struggle and violence that combined ideas of Sunni Islamism in realms of politics, culture, society, even the arts, and the place of women. There are, newly in evidence, many more religion-inspired political movements in the traditional "arc of crisis" from North Africa through the greater Middle East into Afghanistan and Pakistan.

The 1990s also saw the crest of Aum Shinrikyo ("Supreme Truth"), strong in Japan but also Russia. It offered an eccentric mix of worship of Shiva (Hindu goddess of destruction), certain precepts of Buddhism, fashionable mysticism and self-help, and the claims-to-deity of its founder, Shoko Asahara, who, among other innovations, expanded the Buddhist precept of *poa* into an excuse for mass killing for the "altruistic" purpose of releasing souls for reincarnation in higher forms and better status.[64]

Such perverse ideas and a cult of personality would lead directly to some of the first uses of weapons of mass destruction (WMD) by a substate actor. Asahara had not always obsessed over WMD, but his views darkened dramatically after efforts to openly compete in political elections to Japan's lower Diet in February 1990. The failed exercise brought in fewer than two thousand votes. Humiliation set arrogance and self-interest off together on the road to terrorism, and ultimately mass murder. This devolution is a fair rejoinder to the illogic in the oft-voiced apology for terrorism, that "minorities are driven to violence to be heard." In such cases as Aum, the terror groups are indeed minorities—because their ideas and platforms are simply unpopular; this hardly gives them rights to murder, maim, and menace the innocent until they receive more attention. Asahara hastened his scientific programs, which came to include beam weapons, and Ebola virus, and efforts to acquire uranium. Aum conducted its first WMD attack in April 1990—with botulism. Another dozen WMD attacks of varying type and considerable originality followed, including use of botulinum toxin (against the Imperial Palace) in 1993, a killing with sarin in Matsumoto in June 1994, and a subway attack the next year with briefcases dispensing toxin (botulism, again) through built-in fans. More failed than succeeded, but all prepared the cult well for 20 March 1995 and its mass-casualty success with sarin on Tokyo subways. The world was amazed; Japan was stunned. Maiming many more than it killed, the gas traumatized the Japanese national psyche.[65]

Aum's strengths included fanaticism, peculiarly combined with the high education levels and scientific training of many top cadres. There was as well a fruitful collaboration with Russia. Thousands of members joined in that country, but more importantly, high-level military and government and scientific circles in Russia sold or gave Aum many valued prizes, from commando training by former KGB experts to a military helicopter to a formula for sarin.[66] Finally, there was the remarkable budget of the cult, and its enormous infrastructure, especially in Japan; these were massive, and doubtless helped with political influence and deterred punitive suits. But the most important of Aum's strengths, the one that most prolonged the cult's life before 1995, was Japanese tolerance. A society long known to permit or indulge religious societies and cults, Japan is also a liberal democracy, as hesitant as post war Germany to display a heavy hand in domestic or foreign affairs. This religious, social, and political tolerance was stretched beyond all limits as Aum increasingly preyed upon wider circles of Japanese civilians in the early 1990s. There were kidnappings, druggings, shamelessly inept "medical treatments" in their clinics, disciplinary murders, illegal disposal of corpses, and outright attacks on public figures such as judges who had made anti-Aum rulings in property cases.

The cult's weaknesses, by contrast, were few. For example, Aum required a relative minimum of members, being flamingly elitist in its practices and planning. If public support could not be mustered in elections, it was enough to have the public ignore most of the cult's actions. Even the visions of the apocalypse that darkened Asahara's mind were a source of certain strengths: forcing cohesion; permitting discipline; eliciting tremendously long work hours from members. Only the excess of terrorist killing in the final, successful sarin attack brought the group's end. Once government and police were confronted with the act of 20 March 1995, they snapped to attention and dismantled the decade-old organization. Japan arrested some four hundred members; thousands quit on their own. The guru founder and many top leaders went to prison. Administrative proceedings immediately placed Aum in formal bankruptcy, although their legal charter to exist was not revoked, it seems. One can argue that Aum was decapitated by arrests.

Might Aum be a case of a terrorist group enduring exposure and setbacks by changing its name? This phenomenon, noticed by political scientist Harold W. Rood, accounts for many past actions by sophisticated terror groups—e.g., (1) the way the Palestine Liberation Organization (PLO) created and dis-used the entity Black September; (2) Irish militants moving from the "Official" Irish Republican Army, to the "Provisionals" (PIRA) in 1969, to "Real IRA" in 1997; or (3) the Kurdistan Worker's Party (PKK), which changed its name after its founder's capture in 1999 and then changed it again, to Kongra Gel, and perhaps most recently the Kurdistan Democratic Confederation.[67] Aum suffered through its public humiliation, mass arrests, and the loss of most of its facilities. It then reemerged as Aleph—the first word of the Hebrew language. On the surface it is different in character: peaceable, though still devoted to yoga, rites of self-purification, and other aspects of religion, psychology, and public attention-getting. In a classic exercise of democratic freedom of speech, and an unwitting reminder of how Japan allowed a killer cult such as Aum to develop, an earnest foreign newspaper columnist in Tokyo wrote in apparent anguish over how Aleph's "monks" and "laymen" are piteously "hounded" by police even though "no one can explain what the danger is." Police surveillance is attributed by this newspaperman to the logic that Japan "needs" another threat—that only "a potentially resurgent Aum justifies police budgets and staff levels."[68]

Aum changed its name; now observers ask whether it has changed its nature. Some Japanese security officials think Aum's successor does bear close watching: Two years after the sarin attacks, Aum publicity still advertised its interest in *poa*, and "official guru" duties once held by Asahara were said by adherents to be maintained by his two young children while he is in jail. If thousands of original members did leave the group in 1995, several hundred did not, or later returned, including several top officials who must be considered complicit in the former violence. These include Fumihiro Joyu, who was jailed for three years only to return, gain control of Aleph, and direct it for a half-decade—until a March 2007 schism. None of the capital sentences for murder have been carried out, and many lesser Aum criminals have long since left jail. The new group is also rebuilding physical infrastructure. The shell company that made computers never disbanded in official bankruptcy proceedings by the state, was soon prospering again, with tens of millions of dollars in sales by the late 1990s. In 2002, *Kyodo News* reported that such sales, and the way Aleph "places the highest level of importance on developing cyber skills" and "identifies itself as a cyber cult," were reasons for US intelligence concern about a cyber-attack by the group.[69] As of 2005, Aleph owned twenty-six facilities, as well as another 120 residences, according to Japan's national police, and 650 members were living collectively in compounds. Canada, the United States, and the European Union all classify Aleph as a terrorist organization.

Other religious terrorist groups of the late twentieth century have not merely evaded arrest for their crimes; they flourish. This success defies an undercurrent of certain academic writers counseling that "calm observers understand that terrorism always fails." Such a view is nonsense, and both Hezbollah and Hamas offer reproof to the idea. The former was born among Lebanese Shia in 1982; the latter is a Palestinian Sunni counterpart begun some five years later. The trajectory of each helps explain (1) how religion works with politics to produce a successful terrorist organization, and (2) how it is that some terror groups end: in success, for both have now achieved political power by degrees, even if their ultimate objects have not been won. Hezbollah and Hamas have proven they are as sophisticated as they are dangerous.

The so-called Party of God (Hezbollah) began by emphasizing a role as the "Organization of the Oppressed on Earth"—another of Hezbollah's many names. It prudently never abandoned this arm of activity. Human needs are one of the only abundancies of Beirut's Shia slums, and Hezbollah's effective shadow government is at work nourishing, nursing, educating, and propagandizing among those people. Such labors have always helped to make people ignore the rank hubris in calling themselves "The Party of God," on the one hand, and have helped to justify and excuse their terrorism, on the other. Indeed, the infamy of the 1980s days of kidnapping, torturing, and killing hostages including Germans, Frenchmen, and Americans has all but passed out of today's parlance; it has been some time since Hezbollah acted in such ways against westerners. Even after the death of intelligence chief Imad Mughniyah (in Syria in 2008), this remains an organization of capable terrorist operatives—but their emphasis is of other kinds: guerrilla war and politics.

Against any opponent, especially the Israeli Defense Force soldiers, the organization offers a sophisticated and developing array of methods and techniques, from well-disguised road bombs to anti-ship missiles to unmanned aerial vehicles (which may one day be armed). Several thousand men and women are armed by Hezbollah; many more thousands are trained or active supporters; its discipline and ability have been recognizable to military analysts for a decade and a half, and to the world after July 2006, when Hezbollah forces fired rockets into Israeli territory. Hezbollah has another arm, the political. Its skills well suit the freedoms of action offered in a relative vacuum of Lebanese life, where central government is weak and past official pronouncements about Hezbollah's existence and *de facto* rivalry to the state are permissive or even apologetic.[70] Finally there is the media arm of Hezbollah, outlets led by *Al Manar* television. When Israeli bombs destroy the antennas or studios, *Al Manar* swiftly resurrects—another proof of the way political infrastructure, religious motivation, and state sponsorship may enliven terror organizations under even the most intense pressure. Like FARC in Colombia, or the New People's Army in the Philippines, the Party of God can seemingly absorb any number of hard hits, year upon year, and carry on, planning for an indefinite future. Conceivably, Hezbollah might one day lead a Lebanese coalition government.

Hamas, the Islamic Resistance Movement, formed amid the clatter of stones and bullets in the first Intifada in late 1987. Like Hezbollah, it enjoys huge subsidies from Iranian coffers[71]—even while declining to walk the Shiite line in religious affairs. Individuals and groups of Palestinian expatriates worldwide supply other money and aid, as from the United States, Europe, and the Latin "Tri-Border Area." Secular Syria gives fulsome support, and always has, despite profound differences of political ideology. These Palestinian terrorists, politicos, and undergrounders began with the slingshot and the knife—and after all the knife was all that was needed in attacks by "The Assassins" of the twelfth-century Middle East. Swiftly, Hamas graduated to a wide array of weapons, especially the vehicle bomb—yet another "lesson learned" by watching Hezbollah.

While Hamas lacks its Lebanese counterpart's skills in complex guerrilla war, it is possessed of a smooth and practiced political touch. It campaigns and competes well at the polls, and did so well before stunning Fatah (and outside observers) with a January 2006 electoral victory in Gaza. That led in turn to a June 2007 formal political regime in Gaza, which rivaled Fatah's control of the West Bank and also allowed the periodic launching of rockets into Israeli towns.[72] Hamas, "owning" Gaza, had the power to gather rockets, the ability to launch them, and the responsibility for the war they produced with Israel. The organization also continues its many other forms of attacks on foreigners, especially Israelis, and its bloody rivalry with Fatah Palestinians. More than a few observers of history—or cynics—have said that some terrorists become sanctified once they attain state power. Hamas has some of each—power and legitimacy—and is grappling for more. In its charter, which lays down its views on society, religion, politics, the arts, etc., there is an absolute and oft-repeated proscription against compromise or any mediated solutions to "the Palestinian problem" that surrender any authority over any part of the land.[73] Negotiations, not to mention pathways out of violence, are never easy; it is most challenging to make inroads with a religiously motivated terrorist clan. But that is Hamas; its desirability as a partner—to Fatah or foreign parties—in any peace process is only slightly above nil. The end of Hamas is not near. The group is in fact a success.

Graphing Results, in Nine Parts

The sweep of the twentieth century proffers innumerable examples for the study of how terror groups end. There are hundreds of terrorist groups—too many to master, or even mention, in one essay. And there are different good ways to approach this considerable analytical challenge. We have excluded several notable false starts, such as the odd notion that terror groups have a natural life span. Arguing for the latter ignores the varied and important factors that limit or enable terrorism, ranging all the way from the governmental responses the present author often emphasizes, to the internal and strategic choices the leaders make, and that Martha Crenshaw's scholarship has illuminated.

My distinctive direction, in publications and public lectures of 2004, 2005, 2006, and 2007, was to classify the leading ways that most groups come to their demise: that is, defeat by security forces; defeat by decapitating the leadership; defeat by government's good grand strategy; folding into pacific political life; and terrorist success. The present, more chronologically oriented approach throws different kinds of light. It comes to conclusions about a given group under a pair of analytical rubrics: duration of the group's life, with emphasis on significant actions or years of "main violence"; and extent of successful results. Studied under the first rubric (I) are terror groups whose campaigns are of short duration (five years or less). Groups that ran for a medium length (eight to fifteen years) are rubric II. Rubric III shows protracted terrorist campaigners whose efforts last for two, three, four, and even five decades. With cross-cutting analysis, we identify, first, organizations that expire defeated; second, others that achieved or are achieving limited success and third, groups that have largely succeeded, or appear to enjoy strategic successes now. A chart at the chapter's end graphs these nine sections of results, and a footnote follows here on methodology.[74]

Short-Lived Organizations

I A: Scores of twentieth-century terrorist groups have had very brief life spans, as little as three to five years. This fact, and the swiftness with which the public forgets them, ought not mean neglect of <u>how</u> they were defeated or brought into decline. Analysts and strategists have often declared that it is best if government can interrupt terrorism or insurgency in its incipient stages. This is usually a regretful post facto complaint about a government's lapse. It can instead be an optimist's observation about how quickly a dangerous terror group has disappeared or been defeated.

Among the first of these, in post–World War II history, was the Secret Army Organization, founded to save European settlers' status and French power in Algeria, but that totally failed within a year and a half—by mid-1962. Certain other European rightist groups were to have life spans of similar brevity, or do only marginally better. In 1980, for example, there was the aforementioned neo-Nazi scare, a natural result of massive bombings in quick succession in Bologna, Munich, and Paris. But the Paris assault was by Palestinians using an invented French cover name, the Federation of National Action. In Germany the "Military Sports Group" of Karl Heinz Hoffman did exist. But it had barely begun to operate when one of its bombs killed thirteen visitors at the *Oktoberfest* in the Therese Meadow in central Munich; by a year later, the little clan was on the ropes. Peter Janke's admirable dictionary of guerrilla and terrorist organizations devotes a mere eight lines to the Wehrsportgruppe Hoffman. Members went to the Near East for Palestinian training and "were arrested on their return to the Federal Republic . . . Hoffman was jailed in 1981, after which the group ceased to exist."[75]

American examples of total failure and precipitous decline are too numerous to chart. Illustrative are four groups of the 1970s and 1980s, at different ends of the ideological spectrum: the Symbionese Liberation Army, the United Freedom Front, The Order, and the Army of Aryan Resistance. The first two of these gun gangs were black-dominated leftists who held up banks and shot patrolmen while dreaming of status as a revolutionary vanguard. The other two were white-power groups on the political far right. None of these enjoyed even three good years of real power in their respective undergrounds. A common theme of such cases, in Europe and America, is good and aggressive police work, and resultant attrition through both arrests and gun battles, sapping the vigor of these secular, racist and militant organizations.

Myriad fragments of militant life have burned briefly and expired shortly. Consider Latin America. In Bolivia, the endlessly romanticized Cuba-veteran Che Guevara started a "National Liberation Army" that never exceeded fifty-one troops. It formed in 1966 only to see Che and another leader killed the next year. That drama inspired a successor in Brazil, named the October 8 Revolutionary Movement, which a wave of arrests swiftly reduced to virtual invisibility in 1969. Later, as remnants folded back into Brazil's official communist party,[76] a further Brazilian spore failed to flower, let alone take root: "National Liberating Action" existed from 1968 until 1971.[77] To consider Europe is to rediscover many such flickers and flights. In Holland alone, now-long-gone entities include the Free South Moluccan Youth Organization (1975–1979), and Red Youth and Red Help groups of the early 1970s. Italy's rightist Revolutionary Action Movement ran for half a decade only, in the mid-1970s. There was the New Force, which lasted six years in Spain, passing from the scene in 1981, and there was Portugal's yet-shorter-lived New Order. Belgium's Communist Combatant Cells surely hold some form of European record for brevity. They operated only from October 1984 to December 1985, whereupon arrest of all four members terminated their tactically effective campaign of two-dozen nonlethal bombings of German, Belgian, and other NATO targets.[78] Belgium went quiet, as before, and remained so, for many years.

Thus, a range of twentieth-century groups have been stalled or stopped cold in a few years. These include many secular ones, most of those communist. There are also several good right-wing terrorist examples.

I B: The known terror groups of short duration were not all total failures, however; some can claim limited achievements, if only when judged by their own lights, or the praise of their own community or prestigious mainstream partisans. It is reasonable to study the US Black Panthers in this way.[79] Colombia offers its own case of a militant organization that began with claims of virtue, degenerated into crime and terrorism, and came to an end after a few short years. The United Self-Defense Forces of Colombia (AUC) were an umbrella organization of peasant and middle-class militias that took shape to protect their communities from leftist insurgents. No government help was involved; indeed, AUC existed because of the absence of appropriate governmental effort. ELN and FARC, the Castroite insurgents, flourished for decades in rural Colombia before this challenger arose on the right. AUC leader Carlos Castaño saw explosive growth of his 1997 organization, which protected small farmers, defended some villages and towns, and actively sought out and attacked drug dealers and leftist terrorists. AUC would doubtless claim to have helped check the leftist insurgencies and contributed to their current marked decline. Their success is questionable, and of limited kinds. AUC methods too much mirrored the left's, including its drift into massive narco-trafficking. Before the year 2005, the group's leader had disappeared, mysteriously and permanently. And the group was swiftly demobilizing after successful negotiations on amnesty with the government. These talks, generous government terms, and the reassertion of proper powers from the national government of Alvaro Uribe in Bogota and its now-improved security forces add to the reasons AUC has vanished.[80]

Thus, our examination of terror groups yields few that are both short-lived and successful in limited ways. One is a leftist revolutionary and single-race organization in the

United States, while the other is a broad "preservationist" terrorist organization that flourished in Colombia.

I C: There are still fewer clear examples of terrorist movements of short duration that came to enjoy total success. Communism did win a violent triumph in Cuba, with remarkable swiftness; but most judge that success came far more from guerrilla war and political work than from terrorism.[81] If one leaves aside the Cuban case, there may be no short-lived classic terror organizations that succeeded so completely, in so brief a time. So we pass along to our second major rubric.

Midterm Life Spans

II A: The twentieth century's offerings under rubric two—medium-length terrorist campaigns—are numerous and varied. Some perish in exhaustion, be it physical, psychological, or organizational, and an early post–World War II example was the fatigue of Luis Taruc's Hukbalahaps (or Huks) in the Philippines. Their insurgency and also their flagrant terrorism[82] ran hard into many obstacles, especially Defense Secretary and later President Ramon Magsaysay. This government wore out its enemy with sophisticated grand strategy. Good political leadership enspirited the new democracy. Fine intelligence work captured a full politburo in Manila. A clever "free land" program seduced away some Huk cadres and demoralized others by answering their calls for "Land for the Landless." Well-trained, disciplined armed forces protected the Filipino people while hunting down terror cells. Eventually the rural leadership, under the labor activist-turned-communist Taruc, capitulated. The campaign ran from 1946 into 1955, a decade. Good leadership and good grand strategy defeated the Huks.[83]

In the Latin world of the 1960s through the 1980s were other forms of terrorism lasting eight to fifteen years until being totally defeated. Many important and compelling revolutionary terrorist organizations were crushed by governmental force. These included the Tupamaros[84] of Uruguay, who prompted a military coup, and the Montoneros of Argentina, whose cells were ground to pieces by government networks of intelligence, police, and soldiers. El Salvador offers a different kind of case study. FMLN, a front group of some five guerrilla groups, deeply engaged in nationwide terrorism and semiconventional battles against the military, was finally brought to an end in El Salvador. This did not occur because their demands were satisfied, as one strangely errant new study claims.[85] It was due to a combination of Salvadoran government and military resistance, enormous financial and intelligence help and military aid from the United States, the decline of Soviet bloc aid, and the close and skillful diplomatic engagement of neighboring and international states in a regional peace process. The latter included the United Nations and states such as the United States, but the most important actors were Mexico and Contadora countries.[86] This last factor was very important. Like the negotiated conclusion of IRA "Provo" violence in Northern Ireland, it suggests that at the right moment, negotiation may offer its opportunities, even with terrorist enemies.

Western Europeans also grappled with terrorism from the 1960s through the 1980s, of course. Another dozen campaigns of medium length by self-avowed "urban guerrillas" unfolded in cities and towns, but were doomed to defeat. The far left's fascinating failures included the Turkish People's Liberation Army (1969–1980); Portuguese of Popular Forces 25 April (1980–1986); German anarchists of the 2nd of June Movement (1971–1980); the

Baader-Meinhofs in Germany, whose main violence ran from about 1968 to 1977; Front Line, in Italy (1976–1981[87]); and Action Direct in France (1979–1987). The Italian left was torn apart by dissidents and *pentiti* ("repentants"), who, under prudent new laws, offered testaments against their former colleagues in exchange for light sentences for themselves.[88] But, in most cases, the European Marxist-Leninist organizations were slowly ground down by civilian law enforcement. TPLA was different; it was among the Turkish clandestine political forces to be forcibly suppressed after a 1980 military coup. The Army took power, defeated many terrorist groups, and gave it back to civilian authorities.

A few of these "rubric II" groups (eight to fifteen years of major violence) have a longer and less-crisp profile: they rose, fell, and yet still defy eradication. Peru's Sendero Luminoso has existed since the earliest 1970s and determined upon armed resistance in 1977, but did not openly attack until 1980. Thirteen years later, the gravest of blows reversed its rise toward national power. In September 1992, a tiny police intelligence unit located leader Abimael Guzman and made an arrest; he has since been locked up on an island under navy control. In practical terms, the Sendero Luminoso campaign ended there. But the insurgency had sunk deep roots, and a scattering of militants never left the field. As a hardened Maoist, Guzman would know the stories of the twentieth-century "comebacks" after jail or hardship: Adolf Hitler, "Long March" leader Mao Tse-Tung, Mahatma Gandhi, Nelsen Mandela, etc. So, while the self-described "Fourth Sword of Marxism" kept to his cell during the 1990s, a few remnants stumbled along the shining path of continuous revolution, enlivened by the obvious limitations of Peru's central government, and unchallenged by rivals on the left. In 2007 and then 2008, a few reporters stretched to insist that Sendero is reviving.[89] More conservatively, we argue that its ideological convictions have allowed it to fail without disappearing. Meanwhile, Shining Path's former leftist nemesis, the Túpac Amaru Revolutionary Movement (MRTA), has totally disappeared. It was weakened in the mid-1990s and decisively crushed by government security forces in 1997.

There are many "studies in defeat" for groups of midterm duration. All imaginable ideological categories are included: leftist, odd combinations of left and right, a religious cult, etc. Some of these groups are mostly urban in their focus, but the range includes many insurgencies as well.

II B: There are also examples of terrorist groups that arose, practiced violence for eight to fifteen years, and ceased operations with a feeling of considerable (but not total) success. Some of these may be found in the Eastern Mediterranean world of anti–British Empire organizations in Cyprus and the Jewish underground.

The National Organization of Cypriot Fighters (EOKA) was an unusual case of a post–World War II nationalist and ethnic Greek group that used terrorism and repudiated Marxism-Leninism. Remarkably independent, it lacked the kind of heavy external support and sanctuary to which some always ascribe insurgent success. The Cypriot Fighters were founded in 1951 by George Grivas; he arrived on the island three years later; April 1955 saw the opening of guerrilla war; the violence when combined with negotiations forced British troops to abandon Cyprus; independence came in 1960. This was, however, but a partial success. Grivas and his sophisticated organization were of the 80 percent on the island whose blood was Greek, not Turkish, and the revolutionaries dreamed of full unity with Greece, not a separate state. And so, a decade later, phase two of the struggle opened under the command of EOKA-B. Now the underground cells attacked indigenous Cypriots, took hostages, and raided armories in a renewed campaign to seize the whole island for unification with the mainland. George Grivas died of heart failure in 1974; attrition and jailing took further tolls on his organization. A December 1977 kidnapping of the Cypriot president's son in a plot to free colleagues from prison failed. The group announced dissolution in the next year.[90] Their legacy is thus mixed: a two-part campaign, separated by a decade of peace, left partial success—the expulsion of the British army and government, but not a new unification with Athens and Greece.

Several of the Jewish organizations fighting inside the British Mandate may also lay claim to a degree of success after mid-length campaigns. The achievement of an entirely new and free democratic state of Israel in 1948 appears in hindsight to some people to justify the actions of Irgun, Lehi, and others. In fact, their terrorism is no more redeemable than that of African National Congress/Spear of the Nation bombers, burners, and assassins whose efforts contributed to destroying apartheid in South Africa. The model for Jewish liberation fighters is no terrorist organization, but instead the Haganah, the mass organization that consistently and successfully resisted Arab, British, and Nazi rulers and deployed guerrilla attacks against their military assets. They were the militant Jews who most succeeded with war. But two further groups—both terrorist—helped destroy British authority over Palestine. Irgun Zvai Leumi (IZL, or Etzel) was founded by David Raziel in 1937, and was led after his death in 1941 by Menachem Begin. Irgun used terror against the Arab population as well as British targets. The latter included the King David Hotel (1946), which had both civil and military administrative functions; that attack killed ninety-one people and was later detailed in Begin's autobiography *The Revolt*.[91] A fanatical group broke away from Irgun in 1940, damning its truce with the British during years of war with the German Reich; Abraham Stern's gang was formally known as Lohame Herut Israel (LHI, or Lehi, or Lechi).[92] Their attacks on Jewish rivals mirror the inter-ethnic slaughters of a hundred of the twentieth-century's terror groups. The Stern Gang leadership moved to David Yassin in 1942 and the group continued killing: Jews, the British including Lord Moyne,[93] and, most revealingly, Sweden's Count Bernadotte whose very purpose was to negotiate peace in Palestine. Here, too, was a revealing terrorist pattern: the explicit war upon peacemakers.[94]

Several other terrorist groups might claim "limited success" after a campaign of eight to fifteen years' length. A most marginal case is the Armenian Secret Army for the Liberation of Armenia (ASALA), which killed two dozen Turkish officials abroad and left many more bloody spots around Western Europe, hitting hard as late as 1986. Its leader perished two years later. Soon thereafter the "Republic of Armenia" came into being. While this had mostly to do with the disappearance of Soviet power, it dramatically undercut perceived need for terrorism and brought relief to militant nationalists who had earlier waved the flag and the gun. Indeed, at times, violent substate groups are undermined by "political gifts." The sober and considered granting of semiautonomy to Bretons in France,[95] and Basques in France and Spain, turned many normal supporters against the use of violence against the innocent for larger political ends.

In slightly different light appears the Quebec Liberation Front. Founded in 1963, active by the next year, and soon wholly engaged in violence, they attracted French-speaking nationalists, anarchists, nihilists, and perhaps a few communists; these included several gifted propagandists. The group was never large but it was only shut down with great difficulty by Canadian authorities, as indicated above. Especially due to arrests, FLQ lost all its abilities by 1972. But its terrorists might argue that it had strengthened movement toward provincial self-determination at the expense of rule by Ottawa. Its general political effects reached far wider than its violent acts.

II C: The final parties to tier II are the more successful terrorists, whose eight- to fifteen-year campaigns brought them to power. The century's first success was doubtless the Bolsheviks, who achieved the near-impossible between 1905 and 1917, taking total power and immediately using it to terrorize and destroy their innumerable enemies on the left and the right. History's next example might be the more moderate National Liberation Front (FLN) of Algeria. Fatigued with years of squabbling between militants and reformers, the FLN sprang to life in late 1954, published a short powerful declaration to which they adhered closely, and took power in Algiers in 1962. These politicians, diplomats, guerrillas, and terrorists set the revolutionary standard for the post–World War II era. For example, their clever and violent methods of crushing Algerians opposed to them as "the sole legitimate voice" of nationalism would be aped by Palestinian militants under Yassir Arafat's leadership. They also exported the revolution to the Algerians in France, extracting funding, killing opponents, and undermining French desires to hold the Central Maghreb. The FLN is a brilliant example of how terrorism may end ... in success.

Central America offers the case the Nicaraguan Sandinista National Liberation Front (FSLN). While many neighboring revolutionaries failed, or slipped into dormancy, as in Guatemala, Honduras, or Mexico, the Sandinistas won and won completely. Founded by 1961,[96] at a time when the Cuban and Algerian FLN examples were heated inspirations, the Sandinistas were revolutionary but enjoyed broad popularity among frustrated farmers and other reformers. Soviet bloc provisioning and Cuban direction were of great help in shaping the group. For example, Carlos Fonseca Amador clarified his own allegiances authoring a book, *A Nicaraguan in Moscow*, that praised Soviet religious and press freedoms. His small organization was at the core of the Sandinistas. Other factions contributed the Ortega brothers, Tomas Borge Martinez, and Lenin Cerna-leaders and security experts who became famous during the war. Arguably their main period of violence is of midterm duration: 1963 to 1979. They slowly discredited the Somoza dictatorship and rattled the regime with terror attacks and strikes on the National Guard. Not long after the United States nervously withdrew support to the sitting government, the Sandinistas marched into Managua (July 1979). Powers of governance lasted eleven years, until they were given away in 1990. The Sandinistas dared to risk elections, and lost. But the turning screw of history kept on, and after years in the wilderness, somewhat less radical Sandinistas returned to power, winning elections in November 2006. Daniel Ortega is president, again.

Asian insurgencies on the Maoist model also demand attention—even when they do not get it from academics in terrorism studies. Let any observer skeptical about "whether terrorism ever works" study the cases of the Khmer Rouge and Communist Party of Nepal (Maoist) insurgencies. The former hacked its way into the capital in 1975 and ruled until expelled in late 1978 by a larger and stronger army—that of communist Vietnam. Comrade Prachanda's Nepalese Maoists also began slowly and with protracted war, by taking over swaths of countryside in the Great Helmsman's way: combining overt politics, clandestine organization, terrorism, and guerrilla war. Then, as Nepal's monarchy tilted in impotence, and reformists began calling out in Katmandu, the Communist Party of Nepal (Maoist), or CPN(M), cut a remarkable political deal that put Prachanda into the prime minister's chair in 2006. His promises to demobilize his thugs have only been partially kept, which means that if overt politicking ceases to meet the Party's needs, other options remain. No one need hurry in a protracted war.

Thus, a midterm lifespan does not signal defeat, necessarily. Religio-nationalist groups in this category have flourished and survived for many years and eked out gains of demonstrable kinds. Several secular leftist and revolutionary organizations using terrorism have similarly enjoyed limited success. Their will to survive, and their gains over time, indicate the truth in an old maxim about guerrilla war: that in some ways, merely to carry on fighting is to succeed.

Groups with Longevity

III A: The third and final tier is of organizations with great longevity—protracted campaigns by terrorist groups. Some were ultimately and thoroughly beaten. The international anarchists, dramatic actors of the last two decades of the nineteenth century, after 1920 all but ceased affecting the political world. Later came an ideological opposite but similar fate: the unbelievably long and entirely useless effort of Chin Peng and others of the Malayan Races Liberation Army to create a communist state ended formally with his surrender in 1989.

One might reasonably take the long view of a "war"—rather than study a given group's shorter "campaign"—when examining nationalist militants in Ireland, or in Puerto Rico. Puerto Rican nationalist attacks in the early 1950s, the latter 1970s, and the early 1980s all melted away as tactical successes had no real strategic results. Successively, the Puerto Rican Nationalist Party, the Armed Forces of National Liberation (FALN), and then Los Macheteros have won no important political change. The Commonwealth remains a commonwealth; polling data still show revolution or total independence to be a far-fetched idea; new recruiting is minuscule; no foreign powers have stepped in to aid the militants other than Cuba—now largely inactive in this respect.

The Tamil Tigers of LTTE lack roots so long, but they did begin as early as 1972.[97] They survived innumerable government campaigns and were only smashed in their "liberated zones" in early 2009. Anther communist group of very different and urban character enjoyed almost as long a lifespan, but was decidedly less lethal. Revolutionary Organization 17 November was made up of a handful of Greek Marxist-Leninists who operated in Athens for a quarter century. They attacked Greeks, Americans, and NATO personnel, sometimes using the same Colt pistol, and also targeted multinational corporations. They managed to do so year after year, never even suffering a single arrest. But the small size that made this evasion possible[98] also flagged N17's unpopularity and failure to recruit. Lack of numbers likewise determined that if all operations might be secure from police, there would only be very few operations. As the 2004 Athens Olympics approached, Greeks in government took a new attitude toward terrorists. A break for security forces came when a 17 November man failed in a bombing, wounded himself, and then talked. Immediately most of the small organization was arrested, and trials led to long sentences. The new group "Revolutionary Struggle" now seeks to revive leftist terrorism in Greece, but 17 November has come and gone.[99]

Thus, there are certain examples of fighting groups that devoted decades to their will to power and yet entirely failed. Those studied here are mostly "internationalists" of one sort or another, including anarchists and leftists. Two communist insurgent groups also manifest strong quotients of nationalism in their work. And, if one examined state terrorism sponsors, Libya's three-decade record would fit here—as a failure.[100] However, it is more common for a well-organized fighting group to achieve more over time, to create "liberated zones" or otherwise make permanent effects, which brings us to the next rubric.

III B: Terrorist groups of protracted duration that did or have achieved limited gains are many and richly varied.

If we chose to study the Provisional Irish Republic Army as a discrete entity, a guerrilla and terrorist organization with an intimate party affiliate, it began in a 1969 split with other Nationalists and ended its violence against unsuspecting civilians with the 1998 Good Friday Accord. That Irish Republican Army, so delimited, is a clear case of limited success. Militancy had of course cropped up often before the twentieth century, as when Napoleonic France aided Wolf Tone, and a few decades later when American citizens began contributing weapons and money to other insurrectionists in Ireland.[101] A periodically successful Irish fight began in 1916 and ran right through the twentieth century, manifesting guerrilla and/or terrorist variants. The IRA had some sleepy years in the twentieth century but came to life as the "Provos" in 1969 and 1970, fired with passion over civil rights, as well as nationalism, and a dash of Marxist-Leninism. A few British overreactions, and indeed the 1972 "Bloody Sunday" event, encouraged the hard men and drew in recruits. By the 1990s, many felt a kind of stasis; the Provos could neither win nor be beaten. Their leaders bent more to politics and sought to do less with terrorism. They negotiated with London, won limited concessions, and joined governance circles in the Stormont-based parliament in Ulster. There is no unification of Northern Ireland with the Eire republic, and the IRA Provos submitted to disarmament—or partially so. But on the other hand the Provos have seen comrades released from jails by the score; they operate openly, peaceably, and respectably; they have not surrendered their many foreign friends. And they can return to terrorism if they so decide. This could occur as a group effort, in theory, or, more likely, scattered individuals may choose to join extant splinter groups such as the Real IRA.

The irony in this is that Orangemen, too, can claim partial success from terrorist campaigns. And perhaps they should. Ulster Volunteer Force (which declared war on IRA in 1966) and Ulster Freedom Fighters (begun 1973) are as able as the PIRA/Provos' Gerry Adams and Martin McGuinness to see a "partial victory" in the status quo of the last decade. They fought below and above ground for decades, hurting as many Irish as English, but always securing prestige and precious political space in that tormented island. Unlike smaller killing squads (e.g., Red Hand Defenders), the UVF and UFF also work with political fronts, making them more significant as well as more morally credible. Now these major Loyalist groups have put down guns and taken up balloting; all their supporters, in English and Irish politics, may see the old terrorists sharing banal administrative duties and profound political responsibilities in a new parliamentary structure in the Stormont parliamentary building just outside Belfast. The Orangemen of illegal bands are "preservationist"[102] terrorists who have arguably helped keep the six counties under the British Crown; at least, few would dare tell them otherwise.

Twentieth-century history is crowded with candidates for this rubric of "protracted campaigns leading to limited success." American labor militants—a few of whom were terrorists—gradually won major concessions, first in wages and then organizational rights and later in benefits, and came to struggle pacifically and successfully in recent decades. The traditionalist and racist American Ku Klux Klan has atrophied drastically; once a mass movement, now but numerous cells, the KKK has never disappeared in a hundred and fifty years of influence. In Colombia, FARC and ELN are examples of rural insurgencies, widely using terror, that seem uneradicable and have endured for half a century. That mark may one day be met by India's Naxalites—Maoists who are in effect a shadow government in certain areas. Western Europe's ETA Basques have lasted exactly a half-century. France remains bedeviled by the Corsican National Liberation Front, which still lights up strings of bombs to keep alive hopes of withdrawal from metropolitan France and its system of district governance—as Algeria succeeded in doing in the insurgency ending in 1962. France is also troubled by being the Euro-home to the secular and ideologically vague People's Mujahideen of Iran (PMOI), also known as the People's Mujahideen al Khalq (MEK), which is still under veteran leaders' wings. Contained and disarmed on Iraqi territory and subject to US and Iraqi controls up through 2008, MEK still flourishes politically abroad. While this is especially true in France, MEK also enjoys friends in the halls of US and European national parliaments.

Certain Middle Eastern groups are marginal but unrepressed; these include the Popular Front for the Liberation of Palestine-General Command, a Syrian-supported terror outfit that has operated for decades with no one to control it but Israeli forces. Hezbollah has turned covert and overt organization and violence[103] into *de facto* political control over large swaths of Lebanon. Their success in national politics in Lebanon has been immense, as indicated by presence in political bodies and the national political life. The "mainstreaming" of such terrorists is a reproof to thinking that terrorism "has always failed and . . . will fail again," as one post-9/11 argument proclaimed. Much more narrowly, a think-tank report of 2008 about the fate of terrorists concludes that "Religious groups rarely achieve their objectives."[104] But even that more careful view is misleading—given the impressive if incomplete successes of such religious groups as Hezbollah and Hamas.

Thus, analysts may find innumerable cases in the range of moderately successful groups engaged in protracted struggle and terrorism. From the radical rightist and "preservationist" terror groups one may look to the left, and nationalist-leftist, and onward to religiously motivated politicos. The most successful have strategies that far exceed terrorist methods—combining these in a prudent and broad approach to power. Some may ultimately fail, but others appear likely to move to greater plateaus of success.

III C: Earlier pages and rubrics explored terrorist successes—e.g., Bolsheviks, the Algerian FLN, Greek-Cypriot EOKA, some Jewish groups, and Sandinistas—that achieved some or all of their strategic objectives after violent campaigns of medium duration. But there are as well a few groups of longer life that did come to triumph and take state power.

In South Africa, 1961 saw the creation of "The Spear of the Nation," forged to do bloody work for the African National Congress (ANC, founded 1912); this mid-century strategic choice followed years of indifferent political success; now ANC militants bombed energy companies, shopping centers, and other civilian targets. Later they commenced "necklacings": victims were bound, seated, and then burned, by means of placing an automobile tire around the torso, filling it with gasoline, and torching it off. This was apparently done to murder black rivals or dissidents more often than to white South Africans, an example of an old pattern—terrorism for discipline and control of "one's own." In retrospect, ANC terrorism led toward stunning electoral triumphs—not unlike the ways Palestinian terrorism has done so.

Yassir Arafat's Palestine Liberation Organization (PLO) was created in 1964. Like most revolutionaries, it aspired to match the fresh triumph of the FLN in Algeria. Fatah was the armed force the PLO created and shaped. After it came innumerable subgroups and splinters, which achieved a certain advantage in deniability and deception. But, except for Abu Nidal's gang,[105] which left the PLO only to hunt its former colleagues, the PLO splinter groups were generally helpful and useful to Arafat. He might support an Abu Abbas (of the Palestine Liberation Front) in one season, then hold him at arm's length later, and welcome him back in a new springtime. Skillful as an organizer, adequate as an orator, immovable as the controller of PLO businesses and income streams, Arafat won. It took three decades of his own blend of protracted war, yet he created a Palestine homeland. It may today be divided in civil war. But it is a statelet; Israel has departed and hopes to avoid unpleasant returns; foreign governments jostle one another to lead in supplying humanitarian aid to Palestinians under the control of the Palestine Authority; Hamas terrorist acts all rebound in favor of PA legitimacy and give the older more secular guard airs of empathy. Our Marshall Center is among the many mainstream locales where Palestine authority security officials are now schooled in countering terrorism.

Thus, PLO and Fatah and the ANC's Spear of the Nation are among the few cases in which long-term efforts including systematic terrorism have led eventually to strategic success.

An Afterword: Wither al Qaeda?

Al Qaeda falls within our rubric of real longevity and limited success (III B). This innovative, international, and powerful organization has taken body-blows without going down. It lost in Afghanistan and still found cover. It absorbed members of Egypt's battered al Jihad group at the end of the 1990s; in early 2007 it absorbed North Africans of the Salafist Group for Preaching and Combat; European converts and others have joined to offset losses. Many senior and mid-level leaders have been killed or captured, yet several of the newest leaders are from the ranks stupidly released from Guantanamo and other prisons.[106]

Certainly al Qaeda and its allies will never achieve their New Caliphate. But what matters is that they are fighting for it. No one should claim they have "failed" when top leaders with long experience and obvious charisma remain in the field (Osama bin Laden, Ayman Al Zawahiri, and Taliban partner Mullah Omar). Al Qaeda's terrorism has made impressions on the politics, public opinion, or defense policies of a hundred countries worldwide, as in influencing the US troop withdrawal from Saudi Arabia, bin Laden's birthplace. It accomplishes such things; holds up its intellectual, moral, political, and religious banners of attack; and protects many of its human and financial assets in the face of the largest manhunt in global history. To call al Qaeda a "failure" would be the most desperate form of false hopes. It is apparent that states, and the international community, have much to do before al Qaeda ends.

Extent of Terrorist Success

Defeated

Duration: Short (5 Years or Less)

Group	Main Violence
OAS (Org. of Secret Army) 1960–1962, No. Africa & W. Eur.	61–62
ELN (National Lib. Army) 1966–1967, Bolivia (Che)	67
ALN (National Liberating Action) 1968–1970, Sao Paulo, Brazil (Marighella)	68–70
SLA (Symbionese Lib. Army) 1972–1975, California	73–75
Front Line (Primea Linea) 1976–1982, Italy	76–81
VZJ (Free South Moluccan Youth Org.) 1975–1979, Netherlands	75–78
Hoffman Military Sports Group 1979–1981, Germany	80–81
The Order 1982–1984, Pacific N.W., USA	83–84
Communist Combatant Cells 1984–1985, Belgium	84–85

Duration: Midterm (8–15 Years)

Group	Main Violence
Huks (Hukbalahap) 1946–1955, Luzon, Philippines	48–54
Tupamaros 1962–1976, Uruguay	63–75
JVP (Janatha Vimukthi Permuna) (People's Lib. Front) 1967–1989, Sri Lanka	67–75
RAF (Red Army Faction) 1968–1992, Germany	68–77
The Weathermen 1969–1980, USA	69–75
Red Brigades 1970–1983, Italy	74–81
Montoneros 1970–1984, Argentina	70–77
M–19 (19th of April Movement) 1970–1989, Colombia	74–86
2nd of June Movement 1971–1980, Germany	71–78
Shining Path 1971– Peru	80–92
Aryan Nations 1974–2001, USA	84–99
FALN (Armed Forces of National Lib.) 1974–1985, Puerto Rico, US	75–83
MRTA (Tupac Amaru) 1975–1997, Peru	78–96
Los Macheteros (Machete Wielders) 1978–1986/88, Puerto Rico & USA	78–86
Action Direct 1979–1987, France	79–87
Popular Forces of 25 April 1980–1992, Portugal	80–86
FMLN 1980– El Salvador	80–90
The Order 1982–1985, USA	83–84
Aum Shinrikyo 1984–1995, Japan & Russia	88–95

Duration: Protracted (Decades)

Group	Main Violence
International Anarchists (lethal) 1866–1920s, Northern Hemisphere	1880–1920
Malayan Races Liberation Army & Chin Peng 1946–1988, Malaysia & Thai border	46–60
JRA (Japanese Red Army) 1969–2001, Japan, and Middle East	70–88
LTTE (Lib. Tigers of Tamil Eelam) 1972–2009, Sri Lanka	74–09
ANO (Abu Nidal Org. or Black June) 1974–2002, Middle East and world	74–94
Revy. Organization 17 November 1975–2003, Greece	75–02

Limited Gains

Duration: Short (5 Years or Less)	Main Violence	Duration: Midterm (8–15 Years)	Main Violence	Duration: Protracted (Decades)	Main Violence
Black Panthers 1966-1972, US	67-72	Irgun (Irgun Zvai Leumi) 1937-1948, Israel	37-48	KKK (Ku Klux Klan) 1866- USA (& Canada early 20th c.)	1866-
AUC (United Self-Def. Forces of Colombia) 1997-2005, Colombia	97-02	Lehi (Lohame Herut Israel/Stern Gang) 1940-1948, Israel	40-48	UVF (Ulster Volunteer Force) 1912- Northern Ireland	66-early 70s
		EOKA (Ntnl Org. of Cypriot Fighters) 1951-1960, Cyprus	54-59	ETA (Basque Homeland & Liberty) 1959- Spain (& French borderland)	62-
		FLQ (Quebecois Liberation Front) 1963-1972, Canada	66-70	ELN (National Lib. Army) 1964- Colombia	81-98
		ASALA (Secret Army for Lib. Armenia) 1975-1988, Lebanon & Europe	75-86	FARC (Revy. Armed Forces of Col.) 1966- Colombia	66-
		Hamas (Islamic Resistance Movement) 1987- Palestinian Territories & Israel	88-	IRA Provisionals 1916/69- UK and the Continent	69-98
		Taliban 1994- Pakistan & Afghanistan	94-01, 04-	NPA (New People's Army) 1969- Philippines	69-
				MEK / PMOI (People's Muj. Al Khalq) 1966/67- Iranians in exile	71-01
				PFLP-GC (Pop. Front for Lib. of Pstn General Command) 1967- Middle East & W. Europe	68-88
				Naxalites (Comm. Party of India/Maoist) 1969- India	75-
				UFF (Ulster Freedom Fighters) 1973- Northern Ireland	73-
				FLNC (Corsican National Lib. Front) 1976- Corsica & mainland France	73-
				Hezbollah (The Party of God) 1983- Lebanon	82/83-
				al Qaeda 1988- S.W. Asia & the world	98-

Strategic Success

Duration: Short (5 Years or Less)	Main Violence	Duration: Midterm (8–15 Years)	Main Violence	Duration: Protracted (Decades)	Main Violence
No group—with possible exception of M-26-7 (26th of July Movement), Cuba 1952/55-1959	58-59	Bolsheviks 1903-1917, Russia	05-17	ANC (African National Congress: Spear of the Nation, etc.) 1912/1961-	61-88
		FLN (National Lib. Front) 1954- Algeria, No. Africa, & France	54-62	FSLN (Sandinistas) 1961- Nicaragua	63-79
		Khmer Rouge 1951/61-1978, Cambodia	62-78	PLO: Fatah, Black Sept., etc. 1964- Palestinian Territories	65-
		Communist Party of Nepal (Maoist) 1990s-	96-05		

Dr. Christopher C. Harmon Dr. Harmon has long-held interests in the two subjects of this text: strategy and terrorism. His first book, coedited with low intensity conflict expert David Tucker, was *Statecraft and Power* (University Press of America, 1994), a work in honor of a teacher of strategy, Harold W. Rood. Harmon taught on the Strategy & Policy faculty of the Naval War College, Newport, RI, and then wrote and directed a strategy syllabus for 200 Marine majors, foreign allies, and US civilians at Command & Staff College, Quantico Virginia, where he later held Marine Corps University's Kim T. Adamson Chair of Insurgency and Terrorism (2005–2007). He is the author of two editions of the graduate-level textbook *Terrorism Today*—published by Frank Cass (2000) and Routledge (2007), as well as chapters on terrorism and counterterrorism for *Fanaticism and Conflict in the Modern Age* (2005) and The *American Military Tradition* (2007). Two of Dr. Harmon's articles have appeared in the journal *Vital Speeches*. The US State Department gave him a Distinguished Public Service Award. From March 2008 through September 2009, Dr. Harmon was executive director as well as curricula chief of the Marshall Center's Program on Terrorism & Security Studies; he is now Director of Studies.

Recommended Readings

Alterman, John B., Martha Crenshaw, Teresita Schaffer, and Paul Wilkinson. "How Terrorism Ends." United States Institute of Peace Special Report, 25 May 1999. http://www.usip.org/files/resources/sr990525.pdf

Crenshaw, Martha. "How Terrorism Declines." *Terrorism and Political Violence,* Vol. 3, No. 1 (Spring 1991), 69–87.

Crenshaw, Martha. "Why Violence Is Rejected or Renounced: A Case Study of Oppositional Terrorism." Ch. 9 in *A Natural History of Peace,* ed. Thomas Gregor (Nashville, TN: Vanderbilt University Press, 1996), 249–272.

Harmon, Christopher C. "How Al Qaeda May End." Lecture (host: James Phillips) & Backgrounder # 1760, The Heritage Foundation (19 May 2004), 1–13. www.heritage.org/Research/HomelandSecurity/bg1760.cfm

Harmon, Christopher C. "How Terror Groups End," web-cast lecture from The Woodrow Wilson Center, 20 March 2006. Hosts: Dr. Robert Litwak & Dr. Bruce Hoffman. Summary and event film: www.wilsoncenter.org/index.cfm?fuseaction=events.event_summary&event_id=1770...

Jensen, Richard Bach. "The International Campaign Against Anarchist Terrorism, 1880–1930s." *Terrorism and Political Violence*, Vol. 21, Issue 1 (January 2009), 89–109.

Kassimeris, George. "Last Act in a Violent Drama? The Trial of Greece's Revolutionary Organization 17 November," *Terrorism and Political Violence*, Vol. 18, No. 1 (March 2006), 137–157.

Ross, Jeffrey Ian, and Ted Robert Gurr. "Why Terrorism Subsides." *Comparative Politics*, Vol. 21, No. 4 (July 1989), 405–426.

US Dept. of State, "Rescission of Libya's Designation as a State Sponsor of Terrorism," "Significant Events in US Libyan Rapprochement," and other press releases of 15 May 2006. Available at http://libya.usembassy.gov

Notes

1. Scholars must recognize certain intellectual debts, and good scholars enjoy doing so. My debts are happily paid in this and earlier places, especially to Martha Crenshaw. One begins with her essay "How Terrorism Declines," in *Terrorism and Political Violence*, Vol. 3, No. 1 (Spring 1991), 69–87, and its admirable chart.

    There was a distinctive direction to my body of earlier work on this subject (e.g., many public presentations in 2004, a speech on Capitol Hill, a webcast from the Woodrow Wilson Center in Washington, DC, on 20 March 2006, a book chapter with Cambridge University Press early that year, etc.). It was to retrace researches I'd made over a previous quarter-century, present a half-dozen leading reasons for terrorist group decline, and then detail examples within each rubric. The present essay's approach is new, guided more by chronology, and my analysis profits from continued study of the individual named terror groups. Endnotes for Ch. 7 of my book *Terrorism Today*, 2nd ed. (London & New York: Routledge, 2007) indicate other resources I found worthy for study of how terrorist groups end.

2. The Dutchman's wooden shoe, or "sabot," made a sort of weapon if a laborer wanted to jam it into machinery at the workplace. "Sabotage" normally falls short of "terrorism," and its perpetrators sometimes intend avoiding human casualties, as do many practicing "eco-tage" on behalf of the wild world. One nineteenth-century American form of sabotage by laborers/militants is the activity of the "Molly McGuires," who damaged their own coal mines in eastern Pennsylvania from about 1862—until ten were hanged in 1877.

3. Joseph T. McCann, *Terrorism on American Soil: A Concise History of Plots and Perpetrators from the Famous to the Forgotten* (Boulder, CO: Sentient Publications, 2006), 33–40.

4. Labor histories by L. Adamic and G. W. Meaker are cited by Walter Laqueur, *The Age of Terrorism* 2nd ed. (Boston: Little, Brown & Co., 1987), 75.

5. Ibid.

6. From the Revolutionary Pamphlets, quoted by Mikkel Thorup, "The Anarchist and the Partisan: Two Types of Terror in the History of Irregular Warfare," *Terrorism and Political Violence*, Vol. 20, No. 3 (July 2008), 338. Peter Kropotkin's *Memoirs of a Revolutionist* are valuable for many reasons, including references to the role of police action (and capital punishment) in Russian suppression of its anarchists. The book was published in English in both the United Kingdom and the United States in 1899, appearing later in Russian.

7. There are occasional scholars' assertions that pre-WWI anarchists were not networked internationally. Perhaps not; who can argue that anarchists are well organized! Yet, there are levels of collusion and coordination in some sectors—just as anarchists today organize on the World Wide Web. The scattered indicators include these: The number of nineteenth- to early twentieth-century Italian anarchists operating across borders was very high. Entities such as study groups and newspapers fostered networks. Usually, perpetrators were students of the others' actions: even one of the most autonomous of all the anarchist murderers—a US-born, ethnic-Czech named Leon Czolgosz, who shot President William McKinley—carried in his wallet a folded news clipping about a recent anarchist murder elsewhere, and was careful to purchase the same make of revolver, the .32 caliber Iver Johnson, that an anarchist had used to shoot King Humbert I of Italy. McCann, *Terrorism on American Soil*, 27, ff.

8. The Kropotkin quotation from 1880 is again from Professor Thorup. Bakunin is quoted in 1869, in his *Principles of Revolution*, cited by W. Laqueur, 30.

9. Sometimes their exultations in the "liberating effects of violence" foreshadow Frantz Fanon, author of *The Wretched of the Earth*—but he would write and work as an insurgent for Algerian self-determination, not as an anarchist. All of Fanon's books help us understand modern terrorism, yet many post–September 11 academics barely know of him.

10. Barbara Tuchman, *The Proud Tower: A Portrait of the World Before the War*, 1890–1914 (New York: Scribner/Macmillan, 1966).

11. In my work of 2004–2007 I argued that not only terrorists—but even their doctrines—might be defeated in some times and places. A majority of communist terrorist groups failed. Anarchist violence alienated most workers, while police and other government forces turned against the movement, jailing the leaders, etc.; e.g., "How Al Qaeda May End," Backgrounder #1760, The Heritage Foundation (19 May 2004).

12. *Terrorism and Political Violence* is the journal leading this conversation on anarchism. Richard Bach Jensen made a fine and original presentation on "The United States, International Policing and the War against Anarchist Terrorism, 1900–1914," in Vol. 13, No. 1 (Spring, 2001), 15–46. The journal printed a useful and related article by Mikkel Thorup seven years later, and then a further Jensen essay in 2009, "The International Campaign Against Anarchist Terrorism, 1880–1930's," Vol. 21, Issue 1 (January 2009), 89–109. See as well Ersel Aydinli, Chair of the International Relations Department at Bilkent University, Ankara, "Before Jihadists There Were Anarchists: A Failed Case of Transnational Violence," *Studies in Conflict & Terrorism*, Vol. 31, No. 10 (October 2008), 903–923.

13. "For Jihadist, Read Anarchist: Repression Did Little to Stop Anarchist Violence. But Eventually the World Moved on and the Movement Withered," *The Economist*, 20 August 2005, 17–20. The authors' inquiry led them to such causal factors as the coming of World War I and the Russian Revolution—which surely played roles in the expiry of this movement. But they neglected US Supreme Court decisions on labor issues and other factors a magazine had no particular duty to cover.

14. Numerous anarchists' cases could be cited. Consider Sergei Gennadevich Nechaev, the young Russian author of the 1869 *Revolutionary Catechism*. He committed a murder in Moscow and fled to Geneva, but the Swiss extradited him back, and he died in Russian prison. Significant here are both the Swiss act of extradition and the Russian willingness to punish with a lengthy jail term. James Joll, *The Anarchists* (New York: The Universal Library, 1966), 93–96.

15. During the second term of the Reagan-Bush presidency, in the late 1980s, a US historian of Russia and the USSR took me aside after a speech to advise that, despite what many might think of communists, Lenin opposed terrorism. My own readings to that time, in primary sources and in Chapter 2 of Roberta Goren's *The Soviet Union and Terrorism* (London: George Allen & Unwin, 1984) had indicated that his view was predominant but errant. I thought of the irony: "simple" politicians such as Ronald Reagan were more correct than "sophisticated" academics on the question of Bolshevik support for terrorism.

16. This most useful definition of terrorism was proposed and used in publications by The Jonathan Institute, a think-tank, at the end of the 1970s.

17. See also Lenin's pamphlet *Where to Begin* of 1901, which explains that, when local revolutionary organizations are weak, the "individual attack" can be highly useful.

18. This is clear—but it was much debated at the end of the 1970s and the early 1980s. See for example the documents in Ra'anan, Uri, Robert Pfaltzgraff Jr., Richard H. Shultz, Ernst Halperin, and Igor Lukes, *Hydra of Carnage: The International Linkages of Terrorism and Other Low-Intensity Operations: The Witnesses Speak* (Lexington, MA: Lexington Books, 1986). There is considerable evidence in the books and other works of Ray Cline, Paul Henze, Michael Radu, and others.

19. East German support to the RAF was detailed early on by Jillian Becker, *Hitler's Children: The Story of the Baader-Meinhof Gang*, 2nd ed. (St. Albans & London: Granada Publishing Ltd., 1978), Chapter 9. Her brilliant volume never attained the full attention it deserved, and now seems almost forgotten, even during a revived interest in the RAF that peaked in 2008 with the new movie "The Baader Meinhof Complex." Years ago, a popular German newspaper also reported on East Berlin's subsidization of *Konkret*. And American journalist Claire Sterling wrote a book about these and similar linkages (see below, n. 48). She was often derided for unthinking anti-Communism. But as the wall came down, a wave of records followed to show how the Bloc had supported terrorists operating in Western Europe and other regions. These confirmations and revelations were widely reported, as in the *New York Times*, over a number of years. Thanks to the George C. Marshall Center and its translators, I have been able to obtain and study a 3 May 1979 example prepared in Berlin, Stasi document MfS - HA XX11, Nr. 18613, 16 pp. long in German, "INFORMATION on Activities by Representatives of the Palestinian Liberation Movement, in Conjunction with International Terrorists, to Involve the GDR in the Preparation of Acts of Violence in Western European Countries." That document discusses the free movement in Eastern Europe of Palestinians, their allies such as Carlos, and the Germans of RAF and 2nd of June Movement, and the Stasi's "goodwill and loyalty" shown to them.

20. Harvard University Press; ed. Stephane Courtois.

21. There are two good English-language accounts (known to me) of the precipitous fall of Nov. 17th. A gifted student at the Institute of World Politics in Washington, DC, aviation security expert Mr. Paris Michaels, wrote an unpublished 2003 paper for our course. George Kassimeris of the Univ. of Wolverhampton, England, published a detailed article, "Last Act in a Violent Drama? The Trial of Greece's Revolutionary Organization 17 November," in *Terrorism and Political Violence*, Vol. 18, No. 1 (March 2006), 137–157. The group's head of operations is quoted saying the group was finished as a terrorist organization yet could return in some other

form: "perhaps, in ten to fifteen years' time, a new generation of fighters for the people might re-launch the struggle." (153). It may be relevant that several Greek cities faced protracted rioting in late 2008, following a police shooting, and that since 2003 a terrorist group called Revolutionary Struggle has emerged.

22. I have often spoken in past lectures of the roles of Horst Herold and German police in the attrition of RAF cadre. Introducing "computer profiling" and diligence with detail allowed federal authorities to find, one by one, the RAF militants. As there were never more than a few dozen weapons-carrying members, arrests reduced the group to nothing. In recent years, nearly all members have been released from jail. The unrepentant Hans Christian Klar, guilty of 20 murders or attempted murders, won early release in late 2008, prompting debate in Germany and this comment by Bavarian justice minister Joachim Hermann: "Klar deserves no sympathy as long as he continues to show none for his victims." *Christian Science Monitor*, 22 Dec. 2008, and *BBC News*, 19 December 2008.

23. This appellation, often self-applied by the terrorists, was taken up by two scholars as a subtitle for their fine book: *Europe's Red Terrorists: The Fighting Communist Organizations*, by Yonah Alexander and Dennis Pluchinsky (London: Frank Cass, 1992). They include several post-1990 RAF documents, such as the aforementioned confession of failure dated 15 April 1992. 1998 occasioned yet another confession of failure from an RAF hand, so that year, too, appears in print sometimes as "the end of the Baader-Meinhof organization."

24. One careful listing of relevant regional and subregional offices and organizations is by Florina Cristiana (Cris) Matei, "Combating Terrorism and Organized Crime: South Eastern Europe Collective Approaches," in *Bilten Slovenske Vojske*, the journal of the Slovenian Armed Forces (Sept. 2008), 37–58.

25. In its first decades, the Lyon-based INTERPOL explicitly kept its distance from terrorism cases because its new authority might not be helped by political quarrels. But now INTERPOL handles terrorism acts more and more as they do other crimes. Also, governments' use of the agency's capacious data bases has dramatically expanded, for terrorism cases as well as others. Mr. Noble was unanimously elected to a second term of office in 2005 and came to Garmisch to address our Program on Terrorism and Security Studies on 23 May 2008.

26. Teaching case studies of counterinsurgency success long ago convinced me that defections are a superior metric for decline. When Colombia's Vice Minister of Defense Sergio Jaramillo wrote "Pourquot le Temps Joue Contre les FARC" for *Le Figaro*, 23 January 2008, he reported that 1,454 FARC members had quit in 2007, the double of the previous year. As this occurred in the context of much-enhanced skills and professionalism by the Colombian armed forces, I took it to be highly significant. A few months later, the Ingrid Betancourt hostage party was rescued in a Colombian special forces operation—another case in which years of negotiations failed but surgical force worked brilliantly.

27. Maoist China aided armed groups in Burma, Indonesia, Laos, Malaya, the Philippines, Thailand, and Vietnam, according to Quansheng Zhao, *Interpreting Chinese Foreign Policy: The Micro-Macro Linkage Approach* (Oxford: Oxford University Press, 1996), 55–56; available at http://books.google.de/books?id=tKmnESFGY8MC&pg=PA48&lpg=PA48&dq=cHINESE+support+to+revolutionaries&source=bl&ots=KmXYGUlmk2&sig=brvvnnvcMlzOlhRI 6ZjqoupAg8g&hl=de&ei=t0HYSuL4GoOJsAaXwdTyBg&sa=X&oi=book_result&ct= result&resnum=3&ved=0CBQQ6AEwAjge#v=onepage&q=cHINESE%20support%20to% 20revolutionaries&f=false. Aid may or may not include shipping arms. For example, I cannot document arms shipments by Beijing to the Filipino Huk communists or the New People's Army of a later generation.

28. Paul Henissart, *Wolves in the City: The Death of French Algeria* (London: Rupert Hart-Davis, 1971), 300–301.

29. Mike German, *Thinking Like a Terrorist: Insights of a Former FBI Undercover Agent* (Washington, DC: Potomac Books, 2007), 139–146. Now with the American Civil Liberties Union, Mr. German addressed our colloquium at Marine Corps University of April 2007 on "Terrorist Group Vulnerabilities."

30. Although this shooting (of a black state trooper) is missing in one comprehensive FBI booklet, the 30 June 1984 act is related in other sources, including Louis R. Mizell, Jr., *Target USA.:*

The Inside Story of the New Terrorist War (New York: John Wiley & Sons, 1998), 186–187. The perpetrator was scheduled to be executed on 19 April 1995, which apparently helped settle Timothy McVeigh on this date for bombing the federal building in Oklahoma City.

31. Mark S. Hamm, *Terrorism as Crime: From Oklahoma City to Al Qaeda and Beyond* (New York: New York University Press, 2007), 109–110.

32. *The Turner Diaries*, a 1978 novel by William L. Pierce (writing under the pseudonym Andrew MacDonald), is linked to at least five killings or nonlethal terrorist incidents of 1995–2006; see the 2nd edition of my book *Terrorism Today* (New York and London: Routledge, 2007), 18–19. Other incidents in the present text are documented by the Dept. of Justice/FBI publication *Terrorism in the United States: 1999: 30 years of Terrorism, A Special Retrospective Edition* (n.d. [Oct. 2001]), by Southern Poverty Law Center publications, and by media reports.

33. This answer reveals the difference between "pro-state" terrorism and right-wing terrorism. The former is exercised by agents or partisans of state power, but in the US case it was precisely federal power that was most active against the racists. Right-wing terrorism of the KKK sort was by substate actors who hated the federal government's intervention in southern American affairs.

34. Report circa 1984 of an earlier conversation, quoted in Morris Dees, *Gathering Storm: America's Militia Threat* (New York: HarperPerennial, 1996), 146.

35. This also happened in Cologne Germany. In September 2008, a few dozen rightists appeared to rally against "Islamisation and immigration invasion." Forty thousand counter-protestors swamped the scene, and the initial marchers literally fled. See Jess Smee, "'Anti-Islamisation' Event Abandoned After Protests," *The Irish Times,* September 20, 2008, available at http://www.irishtimes.com/newspaper/world/2008/0920/1221835126595.html, accessed 6 September 2009.

36. According to the Southern Poverty Law Center website, "SPLC civil suits would eventually result in judgments against forty-six individuals and nine major white supremacist organizations for their roles in hate crimes. Multimillion-dollar judgments against the United Klans of America and the neo-Nazi Aryan Nations effectively put those organizations out of business. Other suits halted harassment of Vietnamese fishermen in Texas by the Knights of the KKK and paramilitary training by the White Patriot Party in North Carolina." See http://www.splcenter.org/center/history/history.jsp, accessed 6 September 2009.

37. Europol, E.U. "Terrorism Situation and Trend Report" (The Hague: March, 2007), at www.europol.europa.eu, accessed in 2008.

38. Rachel Donadio, "Italy's Attacks on Migrants Fuel Debate on Racism," *The New York Times*, 12 October 2008.

39. Some analysts and writers relatively new to terrorism keep reporting the "news" that terror and organized crime have linkages. Perhaps they always have had such linkages, and for the reasons they do now. Certainly the pattern is very old and has often been described. A facilitator of the relationship, globalization, is also not new.

40. An indicator of this legacy of the Tupamaros outside their country is the testimony of Russell Little. This former terrorist admits to the enthusiasm his Symbionese Liberation Army in California had in the early 1970s for the Tupamaros and the movie they inspired *State of Siege*. Mr. Little mentions most of the factors I touched in the text above while speaking for the Robert Stone documentary film *Guerrilla: The Taking of Patty Hearst,* (Magnolia Pictures, 2005).

41. When freed from jail in the mid-1980s, Tupamaros leader Raul Sendic refounded his movement as a legitimate political party—the Movement of Popular Participation—and that too is part of how some terror groups end. On such groups as the Tupamaros, the best single source is Michael Radu and Vladimir Tismaneanu, *Latin American Revolutionaries: Groups, Goals, Methods* (Washington, DC: Pergamon-Brassey's, 1990).

42. The $60 million ransom came from the kidnapping of businessmen Juan and Jorge Born in September 1974. See Robert L. Scheina, *Latin America's Wars: The Age of the Professional Soldier, 1900–2001* (Dulles, VA: Brassey's, 2003), 299.

43. Of the chronicles of torture in Argentina, one thorough account in English is Paul H. Lewis, *Guerrillas and Generals: The "Dirty War" in Argentina* (Westport, CT: Praeger, 2002), e.g.,

150–159. The book was given to me by a gifted and humane military officer of that country who wished that others avoid his country's mistakes while waging the "global war on terror."

44. Paul Hockenos, *Joschka Fisher and the Making of the Berlin Republic* (Oxford: Oxford University Press, 2007).

45. Claire Sterling, *The Terror Network: The Secret War of International Terrorism* (New York: Henry Holt & Co., 1981), Chapter 2.

46. The impressive and deliberative way Italian democracy brought an end to terrorism has been remarkably understudied, despite bales of publications on that country's violence. A recent exception is the well-done Leonard Weinberg chapter "The Red Brigades." It does note that the antiterrorist police DIGOS probably used torture in a very few cases during the attempt to find kidnapped NATO General James Dozier and in its aftermath. *Democracy and Counterterrorism: Lessons from the Past*, eds. Robert Art and Louise Richardson (Washington, DC: US Institute of Peace Press, 2007); 49–56 are relevant.

47. No Italian leftist killings of the 1980s (after 1981) make the thirty-one-page chronicle of international terror incidents 1920–2007 by Ann E. Robertson, *Terrorism and Global Security* (New York: Facts on File, 2007). Detailed research by Donnatella della Porta is my main source: "Left Wing Terrorism in Italy," in *Terrorism in Context*, ed. Martha Crenshaw (University Park, PA: Pennsylvania State University Press, 1995). Certainly there have been leftist terrorist actions in Italy in the last ten years; two murders in 2002 and 2003 were claimed by a group calling itself "Red Brigades," prompting newspaper reports of a revival.

48. Martha Crenshaw is the scholar who has done far more than anyone to understand "How Terrorism Declines." The most significant way my ideas on the topic vary from hers is in judging that government counteraction is very important—often more so than internal factors.

49. I have yet to study Pierre Vallieres' introduction to the movement, *Qu'est-ce que le FLQ?* but read with profit his 1967/1968 aggressively titled prison memoir *White N------ of America: The Precocious Autobiography of a Quebec "Terrorist"* (New York: Monthly Review, 1968).

50. Elanor S. Wainstein, "The Cross and Laporte Kidnappings, Montreal, October 1970," RAND Corporation Report prepared for Department of State and Defense Advanced Research Projects Agency (R-1986/1-DOS/ARPA), February 1977.

51. One contribution to this Canadian case is Ted Robert Gurr, "Terrorism in Democracies," Chapter 6 in *Origins of Terrorism*, a superb book edited by Walter Reich (Washington, DC: Woodrow Wilson Center Press, 1998).

52. It is not surprising that Filiberto Ojeda Rios declined to "walk away" from terrorism when discovered in September 2005, or that the FBI had to use their weapons. In a previous arrest, this same terrorist had begun burning documents when agents knocked at his door; he then opened fire with a machine gun, blinding an FBI agent in the eye. Ojeda Rios was disarmed. Later he jumped bail.

53. When a country's justices system is corrupted or incompetent the effects on terrorist groups are doubtless exhilarating, or comic. A different problem are justice systems which are more generous to convicts than to the public on which convicts prey; this allows for short jail terms and releases a man onto the streets who may now be better-trained than ever (by others in jail) for future crime or terrorism.

54. If some four million live on the island of Puerto Rico, more than two million more now live in the rest of the United States—which helps explain the disparate locations of these terrorist attacks.

55. See "Timeline: ETA Attacks," *BBC News,* last updated 6 August 2009. Accessed 6 September 2009 at http://news.bbc.co.uk/2/hi/europe/545452.stm

56. "Paris and Madrid United Against Terrorism," *Le Figaro*, 11 Jan. 2008 (trans. CCH).

57. Notices of arrests of ETA leaders have come almost monthly from Madrid or Paris. Presumed leader Javier Lopez Pena was grabbed in France in mid-2008. Then in November came the arrest of "Cherokee," spelled "Txeroki" in Basque, the *nom de guerre* of Mikel de Garikoitz Aspiazu Rubina, alleged military chief. He and a reported lieutenant, Leire Lopez Zurrutuza are charged with conspiracy and arms offenses, although Txeroki is also suspected of murder— killing two undercover Spanish officers in France in Dec. 2007, reports the Agence France

Press; *Hurriyet* (Istanbul) in English, 22–23 November 2008. See also the story in *The Times* (London), 18 November 2008. Looking back now, one must remember the early observers of prescience who wrote on the declining power and prospects of ETA. E.g., no researcher's "How Terror Ends" subfile on Basque ETA should be without the Foreign Policy Research Institute article of 8 October 2004, "The End of ETA?" Author Michael Radu has been a reliable and forward-looking analyst of international terror groups for decades. Perhaps taking his lead, the *New York Times'* Renwick McLean followed on 20 December 2004 with a good dispatch from Madrid: "Bombings in Spain Are Seen as a Sign of Basque Group's Decline, Not Strength."

58. UK-US cooperation during the R. Reagan /M. Thatcher administrations was an earlier case of excellent bilateral cooperation—against the IRA Provos.

59. American writers, even in military journals, sometimes misrepresent Mao's concepts. From his writings of the 1920s and 1930s, and the historical work of Samuel Griffith, I see "phase one" warfare as the strategic defensive—characterized by political organization and guerrilla war (as well as terrorism, which Mao usually declines to mention). "Phase two" warfare is a strategic equilibrium in which the insurgency is strong enough to hold its ground, and in which guerrilla war continues, supplemented by positional and even conventional war elements. In "phase three," the insurgency has developed well politically and is battle-tested militarily, and commanders can use all manners of fighting that are appropriate, and especially conventional positional war. Mao's theory is too often treated skeptically, even by scholars; it well accounts for the progress and successful resolution of wars in China (1949) and Vietnam (1975). FARC and LTTE are thus groups that for many years were locked into "phase two" war with their respective enemies. For an effective use of Mao's theory to illuminate modern Islamist fighting, see Dr. Norman Cigar's introduction to *Abd Al-Aziz Al-Muqrin's A Practical Course for Guerrilla War: Al Qaida's Doctrine for Insurgency* (Dulles, VA: Potomac Books, 2008).

60. Apart from Sri Lankan progress on the ground, there were many sinkings of LTTE naval assets—that group being a rarity in having such fighting boats and suicide craft. *The Hindu* (India) reported that the army had the "LTTE Chief on the Run" on 27 December 2008. Press items point to attrition of the LTTE navy in 2008 and 2009; thanks to Larry Cosgriff for the steady stream of clippings. Somini Sengupta wrote the profile on the Sri Lankan minister for the *International Herald Tribune*, 22–23 November 2008; the paper is now the global edition of the *New York Times* and one angle of its interest was in Rajapaksa's status as a naturalized US citizen.

61. It remains important to learn the fate of certain second-tier leaders, especially "KP" or Kumaram Padmanathan, the logistics chief behind a global and skillful network of money and supplies. Fall of 2009 indicated he may be in custody at last. He has served the Tigers superbly, and almost as long as their supreme leader, and presumably remains in fighting trim. The leader's son, Charles Anthony Prabhakaran, until his death in May 2009, commanded the Tigers' nascent air force. Good short postmortems, summarizing LTTE's effects on the world of terrorism, have been written by Mia Bloom, "What the Tigers Taught Al Qaeda," *Washington Post*, 24 May 2009, and by Peter Leitner and Rajika Jayatilake, "Lessons from Sri Lanka," *Washington Times*, 22 June 2009. On the more historical side, the student of LTTE always does well with the detailed books of reporter M. R. Narayan Swamy.

62. One Sikh group took down a Canadian Air flight, killing 329 passengers, in June 1985. Perhaps a regional expert such as K.P.S. Gill, will one day detail how it was that international Sikh terror had so short a lifespan.

63. Ami Pedahzur, William Eubank, and Leonard Weinberg, "The War on Terrorism and the Decline of Terrorist Group Formation: A Research Note," *Terrorism and Political Violence*, Vol. 14 No. 3 (Autumn 2002), 141–147.

64. Of the several English-language books on Aum, the best on religion may be Ian Reader, *Religious Violence in Contemporary Japan: The Case of Aum Shinrikyo* (Richmond, Surrey, England: Curzon, 2000), e.g., 193–195.

65. Haruki Murakami, *Underground: The Tokyo Gas Attack and the Japanese Psyche* (New York: Vintage Books, 2001), trans. A. Birnbaum and P. Gabriel.

66. David E. Kaplan and Andrew Marshall, *The Cult at the End of the World: The Terrifying Story of the Aum Doomsday cult, from the Subways of Tokyo to the Nuclear Arsenals of Russia* (New York: Crown Publishers, 1996), 108–112.

67. A 16 April 2009 news item claims that jailed PKK leader Ocalan founded this new front; no date is given. When Kongra Gel was founded, much earlier, other names listed by the US State Dept. for the new entity included the Freedom and Democracy Congress of Kurdistan (KADEK), and the People's Congress of Kurdistan.

68. Richard Lloyd Parry, "Japan Poison Cult 'Hounded' by Police," *The Independent* (UK), 28 July 2002. Available at http://www.independent.co.uk/news/world/asia/japan-poison-cult-hounded-by-police-649680.html, accessed 6 September 2009.

69. Lt. Col. John Kane (USMC)—author of our chapter 3.6—has been of good help in tracking the cyber-side of Aum and of Aleph.

70. While events in 2008 seemed to instruct the national government in the dangers Hezbollah poses inside Lebanon, it has been striking to hear how apologetic have been many previous official statements. Twice I heard radio interviews in which the Lebanese Ambassador to the United States said nothing but good about Hezbollah and blamed the group's violence on the "Israeli occupation"—which with the exception of a couple of farms had ended years before. The government spokesmen were ignoring as well the policy ends of Hezbollah, which are contrary to those of democratic multiconfessional Lebanon, and the meddling roles of Iran, which Hezbollah itself counts as its mentor.

71. According to A. N. Pratt, posted to a Middle East diplomatic mission during early 2008, Iran gives Hamas some $120 million a year. Many others' past estimates of Iranian aid to Hezbollah have been as high.

72. See *Country Reports on Terrorism: 2007* (Washington, DC: Government Printing Office, April 2008), and past versions of this State Department annual—which has appeared for three decades. In certain recent years the report suffered from flaws in its statistics, which required correction in some cases. But I do not accept the implications suggested by resultant newspaper articles; I find the report in general an admirable compilation and a sound record of most events, highly useful to scholars, and less flawed than the terrorism coverage of many books and periodicals.

73. "The Covenant of the Islamic Resistance Movement," offered up to the "Name of the Most Merciful Allah," is dated 18 August 1988 and may be found on the website of The Avalon Project at Yale Law School, http://avalon.law.yale.edu/subject_menus/mideast.asp

74. In this chapter, when speaking of a group's lifespan, I treat its participation in violence of consequence to the state—so some periods of preparation and planning, of several years or even a decade (e.g., Sendero in the 1970s) may be excluded. So too might one exclude years of quiet, after violence (as when members of the Symbionese Liberation Army, having failed, hid underground, 1976–1999). So my chart shows dates for the group's existence, but others for the years of "main violence." Consistent with the PTSS approach, I include discussion of appropriate insurgent groups that systematically employ terror; neither this chapter nor this book is merely focused on small terrorist cells.

75. Janke, 23. The Hoffman group is so lost to history that even the US National Counterterrorism Center's annual desk diaries say nothing of the bombing on 26 September 1980. Yet its significance recurred in 2009 when the famous fall festival in Munich was again directly threatened by terrorists—of al Qaeda.

76. Radu and Tismaneanu, op. cit., 115–123.

77. Ibid., 115–123; Peter Janke, *Guerrilla and Terrorist Organizations: A World Directory and Bibliography* (New York: Simon & Schuster, 1983), 431–440.

78. Yonah Alexander and Dennis Pluchinsky, *Europe's Red Terrorists: The Fighting Communist Organizations* (London: Frank Cass, 1992), 148–150. Marine Corps University was honored to have both these scholars in our colloquium on "Terrorist Group Vulnerabilities" in Quantico, VA, 30 April 2007.

79. Are the Black Panthers a case of limited success? They emerged in 1966 and 1967 with aspirations to be a sort of armed wing of the civil rights movement. They expected status as a virtuous self-defense force, and carried weapons openly amidst claims to protect their communities and their race from the diffidence of a white majority and the aggressions of its white government. Their quotidian work included "survival activities" such as providing food and medical aid and schools in impoverished areas. Their other side was to be found in brutalizing critics, open calls to "Kill the Pigs" (police), and physical attacks on the establishment. The Panthers found themselves

very much out-gunned by police; many died at police hands; their supporters often claimed assassination. More (including "Defense Minister" Huey Newton) died committing crimes, or in battles with other black militants. Dozens were arrested and jailed for rape, drug-dealing, assault, etc., illustrating the criminality often typical of a political terror group. A few Panther notables fled abroad, to return years later, usually disillusioned by life in Cuba, or Algeria. Their organized political violence lasted but a half-decade, ending in 1971/1972. Some Panthers spent the next years folding peaceably into American political and social life, winning community and city elections, or devoting themselves to education. Some wrote memoirs. They had not fallen into indiscriminate killing of normal citizens; this set them apart, and helped make them a limited success in America. Panthers would doubtless claim to have helped the civil rights movement by using publicity, psychological shock, and the spectacle of openly bearing arms; they would say they advanced with force while other Black activists advanced related causes in more pacific, less controversial ways. There are many published memoires on these times—some by Panthers themselves—as well as Peter Collier and David Horowitz, *Destructive Generation: Second Thoughts about the '60s* (New York: Summit Books, 1990), 149 ff; Crenshaw, op. cit., 81.

80. US Dept. of State, *Country Reports on Terrorism: 2005* (Washington, D.C.: Government Printing Office, 2006), 141–142. The START database offers recent information but does not mention the disappearance of the AUC leader; National Consortium for the Study of Terrorism and Responses to Terrorism, accessed on 12 April 2009 at: www.start.umd.edu/start/data/tops/terrorist_organization

81. Dr. David Tucker is one of the very few American authors in recent years to document and discuss Castroite terrorism during the rise to power that ended in 1959—something older reports and US congressional hearings used to cover. Tucker details several incidents of hostage taking, etc., in a book drawing well on both his Defense Department and academic work: *Skirmishes at the Edge of Empire: The United States and International Terrorism* (Westport, CT: Praeger Publishers, 1997). My point that guerrilla war was far more important than terrorism is also why this essay does not attempt to include so massive a movement as the Chinese Communist Party's rise to state power in 1949.

82. One notable Huk attack devastated a military hospital and featured widespread murder of patients. That is a tactic even the most nihilistic terrorist groups avoid—although certain Chechens savaged a hospital.

83. By contrast, Malaysian Communists were pushed out without surrendering. Chin Peng and some remnants held out for decades in Thai border areas, quitting only with a treaty signed 2 December 1989.

84. The Tupamaros became fashionable; their kidnapping and political theater tactics excited widespread admiration on the militant left. One testament to this is Russell Little's words about his group the Symbionese Liberation Army (SLA, of California). He discusses their fascination with the group, the film "State of Siege," and says his own SLA literally took form from a discussion group on political films running in Berkeley; *Guerrilla,* op. cit.

85. "Politics and the FMLN in El Salvador," Chapter 4 in *How Terrorist Groups End: Lessons for Countering al Qa'ida* by Seth G. Jones and Martin C. Libicki (Santa Monica, CA: RAND, 2008). The notion that this Cuban-organized group of communists and self-proclaimed armed forces was mainly pushing for "reforms" and "for the transition to a democratic political regime" is comically naïve (p. 64). But after its defeats at phase two-style fighting, and then disarmament under various national and international pressures, FMLN did morph into a political party and compete in elections, often with a measure of success. A similar error occurs in Table A.1 in which the "goal" of the 2nd of June Movement in Germany is declared to be "policy change." They were anarchists, and later some joined the communist RAF.

86. Interview with Mr. Phil Peters of The Lexington Institute, Arlington, VA, 2006. Peters worked on Central American issues for many years in the office of James A Courter, a New Jersey congressman on the Armed Services Committee, and I also had the honor of employment there.

87. Donatella della Porta, "Left-Wing Terrorism in Italy," Chapter 4 in *Terrorism in Context*, ed. Martha Crenshaw (University Park, PA: Pennsylvania State University Press, 1995), 121.

88. Sources of interest on this include Richard Drake, *The Aldo Moro Murder Case* (Cambridge, MA: Harvard University Press, 1995), 259, ff.

89. See, for example, Frank Hyland, "Peru's Sendero Luminoso: From Maoism to Narco-Terrorism," *Jamestown Foundation Terrorism Monitor* Vol. 6, No. 23 (December 8, 2008). Available online at http://www.jamestown.org/programs/gta/single/?tx_ttnews[tt_news]=34237&tx_ ttnews[backPid]=167&no_cache=1, accessed 6 September 2009. The article states that ". . . SL's apparent resurgence may be viewed fairly as an integral part of a burgeoning wave of leftist ideology in Latin America" and "Concern over an SL comeback is well founded." But I think these reports overblown. As a November 2009 briefing at the Marshall Center by a Peruvian Lt.Col. indicates, the actual area of operations of Sendero today is miniscule and very isolated.

90. Janke, 7–10.

91. Menachem Begin, *The Revolt:Story of the Irgun*, 5th ed. by I.M. Greenburg, trans. Samuel Katz (Jerusalem: Steimatzky Agency Ltd., 1972). Doris Katz, *The Lady was a Terrorist: During Israel's War of Liberation* (New York: Shiloni Publishers, 1953).

92. Janke, 245–247, and the Jewish Virtual Library, accessed on the web on 20 December 2008.

93. Lord Moyne was a friend of Winston Churchill. After the 1944 murder, the prime minister made a scorching speech in the House of Commons, describing Jewish "terrorism" as evil and risking comparison to acts by Nazi terrorists. This was a principled political posture, the right one—however difficult it must have been for Churchill, well known to be a friend to the Jews since his earliest years in parliament.

94. There have been innumerable terrorist attacks upon those who would ameliorate social and economic problems, and often this is a strategy by the violent. Some of these are a pattern of anti–United Nations terrorism—e.g., today's visible al Qaeda hatreds of the United Nations. I've written on other such attacks in *Security Insights*, the first of a new series of policy papers from the Marshall Center: "The Assault on Aid Workers: A New Pattern in Terrorism," (January 2008).

95. For example, a Breton Liberation Front fought for independence in northern France from 1966 through 1978.

96. Authorities date the origin of FMLN differently; one sees 1958, 1960, 1961, etc.

97. A more common date of origin for the Tigers is 1976. This author chooses to begin when Velupillai Prabhakaran founded the Tamil New Tigers, 1972. An active terrorist and guerrilla in the next years, he refounded the Tigers as LTTE in 1976.

98. So long did N17 prosper that some began to whisper that the socialist governments of Greece did not care to arrest the terrorists, given the targets they were choosing. PTSS Adjunct Professor Keith Weston, once part of an official British contingent in Greece, disagrees. He believes the extremely small size of the group, and the blood connections many had as well, ensured secrecy.

99. The Kurdish PKK, the most beguiling of cases, may or may not deserve a place here in section III A. Once easily classified, this protracted insurgency has become an analytical challenge. Founded by Abdullah Ocalan in the mid-1970s, and ruled continuously by this charismatic leader, it was decapitated in February 1999 with his arrest and rendition. Kurdish violence all but disappeared for some four years. Ocalan's announcements from jail appeared to dissuade loyalists from terrorism, and no clear successor has appeared. The PKK appeared defeated. Then a shadow came over Turkey's accomplishment: violence by Kurdish militants of unclear loyalty slowly reappeared. The leader's son is an active militant, and new organizations that may or may not be well linked to the old have appeared and are fighting—in Turkey and from Iraq. There is, for example, the "Kurdish Freedom Falcons," which the US State Department initially reported on neutrally, and years later began referring to as a militant wing of the PKK. Today one might speak of a phoenix of Kurdish militancy. The US State Department, and the government of Turkey, see a new chapter in a <u>long</u> PKK life. Either of these different views may be defensible; a historian might well prefer the latter.

100. Ken Duncan, the PTSS program's expert on Middle Eastern states that sponsor terrorism, adds that Syria has been successful in its use—a contrast with Libya.

101. Jack Holland, *The American Connection: US Guns, Money, and Influence in Northern Ireland* (New York: Viking, 1987).

102. This unique term "preservationist" is from Bard O'Neill. The term "pro-state" terrorist is inferior because it is less exact; some right-wing groups want to preserve the cultural or political status quo, not necessarily the sitting government, with whose police they often quarrel.

103. Stephen Morris, an Australian scholar and former colleague at the Naval War College, propounded a very useful scheme for beginning study of an insurgent group—analyzing its performance in the overt political, the covert political, and the military realms. If we group terrorist violence in with the third category, the approach has much value for study of organizations such as Hezbollah and Hamas, and to lesser degrees al Qaeda.

104. The second source, described as more careful, is the aforementioned Jones/Libicki study dated 2008, which declares on p. xiv: "No religious group that has ended achieved victory since 1968."

105. The Abu Nidal Organization flourished for a quarter-century and killed some nine hundred people before expiring from combined causes. These culminated in the shooting of the leader in Iraq but included internecine violence in ANO, repudiation by other Palestinians, and a clever US effort in counterterrorism thus far described by almost no one in print; see the chapter on "History" in David Tucker, op. cit.

106. *ABC Radio News*, 24 January 2009 named a released terrorist who rejoined al Qaeda. These incidents have occurred perhaps once a year, during the very same years of popular European and American agitation for closure of the detention facility at Guantanamo Bay (on US-controlled land in Cuba).

Sebastian L. v. Gorka

International Cooperation as a Tool in Counterterrorism:

Super-Purple as a Weapon to Defeat the Nonrational Terrorist

In the decade following the fall of the Berlin Wall, the dissolution of the Warsaw Pact, and the collapse of the USSR, there followed a flurry of attempts at describing what the post–Cold War order would be. The lack of certainty was reflected in the variety of scenarios presented. Typically, in a fashion that reflected the rigidity of thought prevalent during the Cold War years, the first attempts concentrated on the identification of new poles to replace the dual superpower poles of the previous decades. Among the alternatives to the bipolar balance of the United States versus the USSR, were a unipolar order (United States alone), a tripolar order (United States, Europe, Japan), and various multipolar variations. Beyond these simplistic options, there developed more holistic and nuanced propositions. Perhaps the two most famous theories or visions were those of the conservative academic Francis Fukuyama and the doyen of nation-state security studies, Samuel P. Huntington. In the early nineties both attempted to give a new overarching appraisal of the coming geostrategic reality. Fukuyama ingeniously entitled his theory with the sufficiently provocative title *The End of History*. While obviously meant to be a controversial title, the thesis itself was less so. The argument essentially was that the twentieth century could be typified by the attempts of two extreme ideologies to destroy the "market democracy" model of state administration: Nazism and Communism. The fact that both were defeated[1] by the last decade of the century meant that democracy had been victorious and thus there was "no new history to write."[2]

Huntington's vision, as declared in his article and book *Clash of Civilizations*, was a far darker one. His prediction was that the age of conflicts between nation-states, or alliances of nation-states, would be replaced by an era of conflicts arising between cultures, or civilizations, or along the divides between them, a harking back to more medieval divisions. Wars in this new (or revisited old) age would be caused, or at least exacerbated, by poverty differentials between North and South, West and East, as well as by religious fundamentalism.[3]

Since their publication, these theories have prompted much criticism as well as comment. Perhaps most strikingly, their effect upon thinking relating to "hard security" issues was minimal. The question of what impact such theories would or should have—if proven valid—upon the exercise of national security was conspicuous by its absence. This in part has to do with the confusing nature of threat assessment in the period following 1990 and prior to September 2001.

The Cornucopia of Threats: A Challenge to Prioritization

Perhaps only after the fact did it become apparent to the national security community within the western community of "market democracies" that the Cold War had been an eminently workable international system. While the overarching threat—Mutually Assured Destruction (MAD)—was ultimate in scale, potentially ensuring for the annihilation of both East and West should World War III have happened, the fact was that the bloc-to-bloc arms race, perceived near parity, and the later developed system of arms negotiations and arms control regimes, together resulted in a system that was for the most part well balanced and predictable.[4] For those with responsibilities within the national security architectures of the western nations, the enemy and the related responsibilities were quite clear: (1) the USSR, its allies; (2) the prevention of WWIII (or, should that not be possible, preparation to win the "hot war"). The enemy(-ies) was a static nation-state, with easily identified points of gravity such as its capital, its industrial base, and its organs of security and defense. How to "take the Cold War" to these targets was relatively obvious, if not easy.

Beyond this overarching challenge, there was, of course, another national security–related task-set: terrorism. From the 1960s onwards countries such as the UK, Spain, Germany, and Italy, as well as several nations in Latin America, had to fight the scourge of political violence. However, here it is important to note that in comparison to the primary threat posed by the Soviet bloc, this enemy was in a fundamentally different class. Whichever group one cares to choose, be it the Baader-Meinhof Gang, Basque Fatherland and Liberty (ETA), or the Provisional Irish Republican Army (PIRA), while deadly, none had the capacity to strike a fatal blow against the government they were fighting, and thus they did not vitally endanger the given nation's existence as did the Soviet Union.

With the fall of the Iron Curtain, national security faced a new challenge. As the Soviet Union dissolved into several nations and the biggest, the Russian Federation, established normalized relations with the North Atlantic Treaty Organization (NATO) and would even become nominally an ally in later years,[5] other new or newly revitalized threats emerged to challenge western governments and concurrent domestic calls for a post–Cold War peace dividend. These threats ranged from the familiar, such as failed states, to the new and outré, such as information warfare and critical infrastructure defense. (See Table One.)

As the number and nature of the new panoply of threats and challenges grew and became more complicated, two obvious questions arose. The first was, given the limits to defense expenditure that exist in most democracies, how should governments now prioritize their national security investments and activities? Which of the enumerated threats should receive greater attention, where should limited public resources be invested so as to best protect the population and national interests? For many nations the answer was not clear. The second question had to do with capabilities.

In the European half of the Atlantic Alliance defense and security capabilities were very much shaped, understandably, with the scenario of WWIII in mind. The national war-planners and the multinational staffs at Supreme Headquarters Allied Powers Europe (SHAPE) in Belgium worked on the assumption that should conflict erupt the USSR and its satrapies would execute a massive land attack against the West through the Sibbesse Gap into West Germany and beyond, most likely using chemical weapons, before resorting to tactical nuclear weapons if necessary. It was NATO's *raison d'être* to ensure that the United States would respond to the overwhelming conventional advantage posed by the

Table One

Cold War Versus 1990s Threat Environments

Era	Threats
Cold War	USSR-Warsaw Pact / WWIII
	Terrorism
1990s	Terrorism
	Ethnic Conflict
	Mass Migration
	Proliferation of WMD (and related know-how)
	Organized Crime
	Resource Conflict
	Rogue States
	Failed States (peace support, nation-building)
	China
	Information Warfare, Critical Infrastructure Defense

2nd Red Army by bringing an intercontinental and intermediate nuclear response to such a land attack. Subsequently, the majority of forces in the European half of NATO were designed to fulfill a largely static territorial defense function, to act as a delaying force inhibiting the rapid invasion of Soviet forces until the transatlantic nuclear response was made. In layman's terms this meant that the armies of most western nations were replete with heavy, slow armor and anti-armor assets[6] fit for nation-on-nation conventional, or Clausewitzian war.

It soon became apparent that the appropriateness of such capabilities was limited in a new threat environment, which included the requirement that a nation be able to project its forces far further afield than its own national territory. As a result, very soon talk of a growing gap between US and European defense capabilities increased, given that the United States, thanks to its geography and the way in which it defined its global interests, had at its disposal a far more flexible and projectable force than any of its allies.

9/11: Clarity in Prioritization?

While the second problem was a factual one that could not be explained away, or would not disappear by itself, the first dilemma regarding prioritization was solved, at least according to some members of the Western Alliance, with the aircraft attacks aimed at civilians on one fall day in 2001.

Among professional students of political violence, there are few scholars who have been able to turn theoretical observations into policy-relevant products. Brian Jenkins, of the RAND Corporation, is one of them. One of his most famous observations—which has since become conventional wisdom within the field—was that "The terrorist doesn't want a lot of people dead. He wants a lot of people watching."[7] The inference, of course, is that the heart of terrorism is the desire to inculcate fear in a population and that in the modern age the media have become one of the most prized weapons of the terrorists, since they enable terrorists to further a message of fear to as wide an audience as possible. And in the era of regular hijackings, political assassinations, and high-exposure events such as the 1975 attack in Austria on the OPEC ministers, or the 1972 murder of members of the Israeli Olympic team in Munich, this adage was proven again and again. However, trends in the 1990s and 9/11 itself seem to point—at least for some observers—to a new, even more frightening trend.

The first observation regarding this new trend is a purely statistical one. Every year the US Department of State publishes a report on the previous year's terrorist attacks against American targets.[8] After the prose description of the year's events and those involved, each report contains a series of appendices detailing the names of terrorist groups and mathematical data related to the attacks. While the publication is admittedly not a comprehensive assessment of all terrorist activities in a given calendar year, focused as it is solely upon attacks executed against US interests, the changes identifiable over the twenty-four years that data have been collected have led to one clear conclusion being drawn. While the period since the end of the Cold War has seen a marked decrease in the frequency per year of successful attacks launched against the United States, the lethality of individual events has increased. In other words, more people are likely to die or be injured as the result of one single attack than would otherwise have been the case in previous (Cold War) years.

As a result of this trend, some commentators have extrapolated to conclude that Jenkins's famous observation no longer holds: While the size of audience was the driving factor in the past, now it is the extent of damage, the extent of killing that is more important[9] to the terrorist. We have moved from mass-audience terrorism to mass-casualty terrorism. This has led to the hypothesis that there now exist terrorists who simply wish to kill as many people as possible, and to this end they will attempt to acquire weapons of mass destruction (WMD). This nascent category of actor has been christened the hyper-terrorist.[10]

There is, however, one superficial problem with this hypothesis, and that derives from the nature of modern terrorism we have become acquainted with in the latter half of the twentieth century. If the hypothesis is to work, in this author's opinion a differentiation must be made between at least two fundamental types of terrorist.

Hyper-Terrorism and the Rational Versus the Nonrational Actor

One important common denominator among the vast majority of those substate actors that used political violence in previous decades was that the end-state they wished to achieve was at least theoretically possible. The classic terrorist groups, as typified by the PIRA and the Basque separatist group ETA, were predicated around clearly communicated demands for self-determination, or simply greater autonomy from the governing nation-state. As a result, while the concept of the counties of Northern Ireland being reunited with Eire, or the idea of a more independent Basque-land may have been anathema to the governments of London and Madrid, these were demands that could not be thought completely out of the question. Thus, differences between the given group and the relevant government were potentially resolvable via political means[11] and not just demands to be mitigated solely by exposing such groups to lethal force or interdiction by law enforcement authorities.

It is exactly by dint of the feasible nature of the end-state demanded that such groups should quite rightly be deemed *rational* or *pragmatic* in their strategy and behavior. It is also clear, therefore, why such groups never resorted to strategies or weapons that would result in truly mass casualties. The end-state to be achieved was a worldly, political one. The "game plan" was to achieve a political victory by forcing a capitulation of the government on a specific issue thanks to the majority of the public exerting (through fear) adequate pressure to change said policy. Any act that resulted in mass casualties, resorting to WMD technology, for example, would rationally and predictably result in two consequences: the loss of all potential support from the elements of the larger population that were sympathetic to the broader goals of the group; and justification for the government to use all means (even shoot-to-kill tactics) to eradicate the terrorist group once and for all. Thus, it would seem that *hyper-terrorism*—the desire of terrorists to obtain and use WMD capabilities—cannot apply to a rationally thinking substate actor who has a feasible (political) end-state in mind. But if hyper-terrorism is an extant phenomenon, then to whom does it apply?

Perhaps the clearest, most scientifically discrete candidate for designation as the modern age's first specimen of hyper-terrorism is Aum Shinrikyo. This organization is infamous as being the first non-state actor to use a chemical weapon successfully against civilians. In 1995, after years of experimenting with both chemical and biological agents,[12] the cult deployed a weak solution of sarin nerve agent on the Tokyo metro. We now know that the group had a very different end-state in mind from that witnessed in the case of "classic" pragmatic terrorist actors such as ETA or PIRA. Through a series of similar WMD attacks, the cult and its half-blind prophet-leader Shoko Asahara planned to take control of the government of Japan. Once it had established itself as the new government of Japan, the cult intended to unleash a global WMD campaign until it ruled the whole planet and could create a worldwide cultic religious state and then initiate End Times.[13] It is clear that such an end-state is not politically feasible and that there is no political solution possible that would bring the cult and its enemies to a possible negotiated compromise. The scenario driving this substate actor was not a worldly one, infused as it was with apocalyptic aspects, and thus we may make a distinction in this case and classify Aum as a nonrational, or transcendentally informed, terrorist group.[14]

The identification of whether or not a given terrorist group has such a worldview, one where compromise with the government is not just unimportant but impossible and where a transcendental "reality" informs the actions of the perpetrator is significant beyond solely the realm of theory. The question of whether or not we are dealing with a rational or nonrational actor[15] will have distinct implications upon what type of response government authorities can deploy. In the case of the former, the choice of tools is broad, ranging from military force and police action to secret or open negotiations and even third-party mediation or arbitration. If, however, the group is of the latter variety, then we are limited to two fundamental options: arresting or annihilating the terrorist group. Who the enemy is, therefore, dictates the modality of response.

Categorizing the Current Threat: Al Qaeda

It is clear that the 11 September 2001 attacks in New York, Washington, and Pennsylvania were designed to exact as many casualties as possible—and most interestingly as regards methodology, to do so without resorting at all to WMD technology. But the question remains: What were the end-state and specific demands of the group responsible for 9/11?

Here one needs to look at the communiqués and other items of propaganda disseminated by Osama bin Laden and high-ranking al Qaeda terrorists over the years.

In the beginning, before al Qaeda ("the Base") became well known in the intelligence and academic communities, Osama bin Laden had taken control of the Arab Service Bureau of which he had been a part and which had recruited and trained many of the foreign mujahedeen who had fought against the Soviet troops of occupation in Afghanistan.[16] At that time, the avowed aims of the new organization were clearly defined against the backdrop of a world seen in distinctly Huntingtonian and Manichean terms. For this fundamentalist fighter, by the early 1990s, having won the fight against the then "lead Satan" (the USSR), it was time to fight for oppressed Muslims everywhere and to take the fight to the, until then, secondary Satan: western civilization, led by the United States. The western world was and is seen by bin Laden as antithetical to his fundamentalist view of the Islamic faith, an affront to all that is good and holy and a force that through its soft power, capitalism and globalization, further weakens the hold of the Muslim system over its followers. The end-state depicted by the former mujahedeen is the re-creation of a caliphate, starting with the Middle East and Central Asia, but eventually spreading over the whole world as the West is systematically undermined over years and even decades through a campaign of attritional warfare that exploits the very aspects of the liberal democratic system of which its nations and leaders are so proud. In all this, since it is the standard-bearer of the liberal-democratic, capitalist model, and the source of most that is unholy, the United States stands as the primary "western" target.[17]

As a result of such pronouncements and based upon interviews[18] with captured or reformed members of the terrorist organization, one would be led understandably to the conclusion that al Qaeda fits quite neatly into the category of nonrational terrorist actor. No political resolution is even theoretically possible given the absolute and transcendentally informed nature of the desired state-of-affairs (a global caliphate) that al Qaeda wishes to achieve.

It should be noted, however, that since becoming a player on the world stage and after the more successful attacks that culminated in the events of 9/11, bin Laden has complicated matters by inserting other lower-level political demands into the broader palate of existing pronouncements. These have included the removal of US troops from the lands that contain the holiest of Muslim sites (such as Saudi Arabia) and, perhaps most pronounced, the demand made in the prerecorded video statement that was released on the invasion of Afghanistan in which bin Laden stated that there would no peace in the West, nor in America, until there existed a free and independent Palestine. Both of these are feasible demands open to a political approach that fits very nicely into the rational terrorist category. In fact, one of them has already occurred.

Subsequently we are left with the problem of how to classify the threat posed by al Qaeda's version of hyper-terrorism. In my opinion, the conflation of nonrational with rational elements, of political with transcendentally informed goals, may in fact be a deliberate ploy on behalf of the leaders of the organization to confuse us, "the enemy," or a crude attempt to forge tactical gains from among the consequences of strategic-level attacks. In any event, the higher-level nonrational demands, or end-state, overshadow the lower-level demands, and we can conclude that the group is fundamentally—from our point of view[19]—nonrational, or at worst and for practical purposes, a sui generis modification of this category.

Logically if we therefore decide that there does in fact exist a new type of threat, one whereby a nexus has been created between the desire to be a terrorist and the desire to cause as much damage as possible, that hyper-terrorism can exist only in the case of non-rational actors, the obvious question should be: Are we in possession of the requisite tools to fight this new form of political violence? As individual nations, based upon traditional nation-states structures and concepts we are not.

The Westphalian Inheritance

It is often far too easy to take for granted the system of governance and administration in which we live today. If one does not professionally study modern history, or the evolution of international law, one could be forgiven for thinking that the current system of independent nation-states has existed for much longer than it in fact has. Its evolution is quite recent, in historic terms. Most commentators consider the Peace of Westphalia (1648) as introducing the foundations for the creation in the West of a system in which the main actors were states, bodies with independent internal affairs—but which could ally with one another. In the Westphalian system, sovereignty would eventually become paramount.[20] Later, as this concept evolved and as the individual allegiances of the people shifted from local landowner and royal house to professional political elites defined around a national identity, the state would evolve further into the now-commonplace nation-state, with its fundamental aspects of citizenship and nationality.[21]

For our purposes, the most important side-effect of the founding and development of the nation-state as a way to run and define a territorial unit are the ramifications of this new locus of sovereignty on the practice of providing for security. While humans have been waging war for as long as territory and other forms of expropriable wealth have existed, the modern method for securing the nation-state resulted in a universal division of labor being replicated in practically every nation of the world.[22] The national security systems thus created were quite simply formed around a categorization of threats as being either external, internal, civilian, or military in nature. Since the threats were all relatively discrete in scientific terms (i.e., easily definable and differentiated), it was logical to make the responses reflect the given challenges. If the enemy state wishes to obtain sensitive information of a military nature, then "we" should have a capability to protect such information and to capture its agents. Likewise, if the enemy state intends an act of military aggression, then "we" must maintain a permanent capability to deter such an attack or to meet it head on with force, and so on. Of course, particular variations developed—nations that combined civilian and military counterintelligence into one body, for example—but on the whole, the majority of modern nation-states established a division of labor as described in Table Two.

In each case, as the nation-state evolved and solidified its structures, the internal architecture of national security was reinforced by the laws and constitutional measures that defined the responsibilities and specific missions of the given organs. As a means to preserve efficiency and to ensure against abuses of power and information, practically every state of the developed West would severely demarcate the spheres of authority of each national security body. Matters of military intelligence, for example, were to be the sole purview of the body (or bodies) expressly mandated to respond to this threat, and so on. In fact, any intentional or even inadvertent negation of this division of labor would, if found out, generally cause scandal and/or investigation.[23] This strict interpretation of missions

Table Two

The Inherited Architecture of Westphalian National Security

Type of Threat or National Security Task	Nation-State Institutional Response
External Military (Invasion)	Standing Professional Army
Internal Constitutional, Legal Disorder	Police Force
Theft of Military Secrets	Military Counterintelligence
Theft of Political, Economic Secrets	Civilian Counterintelligence
Enemy Military Intention/Capability	Military Intelligence
Enemy Intention of External Political Elite	Civilian Intelligence (Espionage)

and the resultant mirror-image response whereby the threat would be matched by a similar domestic body, would simply be further reinforced by the cut and dry, unequivocal threat environment presented by the Cold War.

Matching Threats to Capabilities in the Third Millennium

Whether or not one agrees with the still-influential theses cited earlier of *Clash of Civilizations* or *The End of History*, it seems clear that there has been at least one incontrovertible change in the geostrategic environment in which the developed countries of the West now find themselves: The Westphalian system's core presumptions no longer hold.

First, it may have become trite to say so, but that does not lessen the veracity of the statement that democracies do not wage war on one another. In fact, this tenet has in recent years been raised to the level of being a basic element of US foreign policy. Translated into more practical terms, it means that the countries of the western community of nations do not pose a threat to one another. This seems an uncontroversial statement since it is hard to envisage a classic nation-on-nation conflict involving the recognized tools of war erupting between Germany and the United States, or the United Kingdom and France. This fact is underpinned by the nature of new threats that have been identified in recent years, as enumerated in Table One.

While this statement seems perhaps obvious, its ramifications in practical terms are highly significant. As we have seen, the national security architecture universally established under the Westphalian system and reinforced by the Cold War was not a multifarious tool. It was originally designed exclusively to deal with external threats that were in the form of (enemy) nation-states. The ultimate purpose was to prevent or win an armed conflict against another country or group of countries, usually in relatively close physical proximity to one's own nation. Today, the transatlantic area is constituted by nations that do not hold grudges against one another that could reasonably lead to an armed conflict for territory or wealth. In fact, continental Europe is now for the most part represented by an institutional form of integration that represents the largest voluntarily unified market and trading bloc the world has ever seen.[24] Thus, both the NATO and EU communities consist of nations whose national defense and security structures are wholly out of step with the danger they actually face—dangers that are without borders, capitals, or nation-state-derived governments.

Managing the Disjunction:
Going "Super-Purple" and International

With the bombing campaign against Serbia in 1999 and the more recent invasion of Iraq in 2003, some commentators have stated that the whole Westphalian system has suffered a death blow. The sacrosanct nature of a country's sovereignty—irrespective of domestic events—was held previously to be the core operating tenet of the system. The idea that internal behavior deemed by one or more countries as going against the fundamental norms of human rights justifies military action by an otherwise unaffected party, or parties, is truly novel. However, it is important to note that this undermining of national sovereignty is very much limited to those states that can be classified as "failed" or "rogue" in nature. As a result we should posit that the principle of unadulterated sovereignty still applies in the community of developed market democracies.

Nevertheless, when it comes to ensuring the security of these nations, there is a clear disjunction. For centuries the tools of national security matched the threat. Today the threats operate in a milieu that is transnational and not limited by the shell of nation-state architecture. Our foe today moves in a world that is unrestricted by international convention, by physical borders, or the dictates of government. Yet, the successful members of the transatlantic community that won the Cold War inherited a tool box of means to provide for security that has not changed and is very much still bound to the architecture of the Westphalian nation-state. Armies and police forces still serve countries. They are funded out of national budgets and are controlled by national governments. While the enemy has moved to a higher plain of existence we have not and will likely never do so, since world governance is not something that is welcomed either by the majority of citizens who find their identity in the nation-state metier, nor by the entrenched stratum of politicians who would have everything to lose should their domestic authority be replaced by a higher transnational one.

As a result we must look elsewhere for a solution. If we recognize the fact that our internal national security and defense structures were inherited from another age and for another purpose, yet we are unable for various reasons—above all political—to create supranational solutions, then the only viable option is to radically reform our nation-state level instruments so as to make them more applicable to the new tasks at hand, to closer resemble the enemies of today. This means admitting the fact that the old division of labor is out-of-date and that we cannot justify the maintenance of hermetic seals between various agencies and forces. The internal barriers between the police force, the army, and various intelligence services must at least be in part dismantled so as to facilitate a modus operandi that is as flexible and as effective as that of our new enemies. This would result in the creation of "Super-Purple"[25] structures as flexible and hypermobile as the enemies they needed to neutralize. It would not even be too far-fetched to make the argument that many countries in the current geostrategic environment would be best served by a unitary body conglomerating all the skills of the various separate agencies and units into a new structure better suited to addressing threats like al Qaeda and transnational organized crime syndicates.[26] There even exists a national counterterrorism precedent for such a unified multiagency approach.[27] Such examples must be revisited and expanded internationally to follow the principle and vision laid out by Dr. Boaz Ganor (detailed later in this book).

Even so, the reality is that such a broad, sweeping reform and restructuring of the national security apparatus of the nations of the developed West will inevitably run into heavy resistance from all those who have an interest in maintaining existing structures and who do not see the necessity for change. Therefore, it is most likely the responsibility of the nongovernmental think-tank community to promote the initial discussion on how best to shape old capabilities to meet new threats and to convince as many members of the general public as possible that the topic should be placed on the political agenda of the various nations. For if we do not begin to discuss and then eventually effect change, the West will continue to suffer in a deadly game of "catch-up," as those unfettered by limits of the nation-state proceed to exact damage upon our countries and way of life.

In the meantime, the Marshall Center's Program on Terrorism and Security Studies represents the first and most successful example of the "Super-Purple" approach as applied to the creation of an international network of counterterrorism professionals. As the international and interdepartmental connections built through this program grow ever deeper and wider, it will become easier and easier to eventually institutionalize international jointness and thus take the fight most effectively to an enemy that already thinks and operates in the "Super-Purple" mode.

Dr. Sebastian L. v. Gorka Dr. Sebastian Gorka is an internationally recognized authority on issues of national security, terrorism, and democratization, having worked in government and the private and NGO sectors in Europe and the United States. A graduate of the University of London and Corvinus University, Budapest, he was Kokkalis Fellow at Harvard's John F. Kennedy School of Government and holds a Ph.D. in political science. He was the first Director of the Institute for Transitional Democracy and International Security, and also spent four years as Adjunct Professor for the PTSS program of the Marshal Center. Dr. Gorka has published in excess of 120 monographs, book chapters, and articles, many for the JANES Group of the UK and has appeared in the *Financial Times*, the BBC, CBS, CNN, Al Jazeera, REUTERS, the *Washington Post*, *EuroNews*, and *Newsweek*. Dr. Gorka advises and briefs the US Special Operations Command and NATO; recently he advised the Pentagon on Secretary Gates' draft guidance on strategic communications in the war on terrorism. Dr. Gorka is a frequent lecturer at institutions such as the FBI's International Law Enforcement Academy, USMA West Point, and the School of Advanced Military Studies, Fort Leavenworth. He teaches in the Irregular Warfare Department, College of International Security Affairs, National Defense University, Washington.

Recommended Readings

Aldis, Anne, and Graeme P. Herd. *The Ideological War on Terror: Worldwide Strategies for Counter-Terrorism*. London: Routledge, 2007.

Anderson, Sean K. and Stephen Sloan, *Historical Dictionary of Terrorism*. Lanham: Scarecrow Press, 2002.

Forest, James J. F., ed. *Influence Warfare*. Westport: Praeger Security International, 2009.

Gorka, Sebastian, and David Kilcullen. "Al Qaeda and US Strategic Communications." Meeting summary for Interagency Strategic Communication Fusion Team, 23 January 2009.

Harmon, Christopher C. "Public Diplomacy's Next Challenge," *Connections*, Vol. 7, No. 1 (Spring 2008), 141–153.

Jensen, Richard Bach. "The International Campaign Against Anarchist Terrorism, 1880-1930s." *Terrorism and Political Violence*, Vol. 21, No. 1 (January–March 2009), 89–109.

Kiras, James. *Special Operations and Strategy*. Abington: Routledge, 2006.

Laqueur, Walter. *The Age of Terrorism*. Boston: Little, Brown & Co., 1987.

Rennie, James. *The Operators—On the Streets with 14 Company*. London: Century, 1996.

Sookhdeo, Patrick. *Global Jihad*. McLean: Isaac Publishing, 2007.

Urban, Mark. *Big Boys' Rules—The SAS and the Secret Struggle against the IRA*. London: Faber and Faber, 1992.

Notes

1. Of course, there were and remain exceptions: communist regimes outside of the immediate vicinity of Europe, including North Korea, Cuba, Vietnam, and China.
2. Francis Fukuyama, *The End of History and the Last Man* (New York: Avon Books, 1992).
3. Samuel Huntington, *The Clash of Civilizations and the Remaking of World Order* (New York: Simon and Shuster, 1996).
4. Perhaps the two most obvious points at which the Cold War could have metastasized into a "hot war" were the Korean War of 1950 and the Cuban missile crisis of 1962. These represent just two events in a span of forty years, a ratio that underlines the fundamental stability of Cold War bipolarity.
5. This is especially true in formal terms with the creation of the Permanent NATO-Russia Joint Council (PJC) in 2001 and especially after President Putin's adroit manipulation of the post-9/11 situation in the White House.
6. The exceptions to this rule—those nations with more flexible armed forces that could be deployed well beyond the nation's own borders—were, of course, those countries that had had strong imperial histories and still retained quasi-colonial interests. Such countries include the United Kingdom, France, and Belgium.
7. Jenkins, Brian. *International Terrorism: A New Mode of Conflict*, Research Paper 48, California Seminar on Arms Control and Foreign Policy, Crescent Publications, Los Angeles, 1975. Near the end of the 1990s Mr. Jenkins publicly wrote that this theorum might be less and less true as the character of modern terrorism changed. He was correct—in both cases—in the editors' view.
8. For over two decades called *Patterns of Global Terrorism*, since 2004 this publication by the US Department of State is called *Country Reports on Terrorism*. Current and past reports are available at http://www.state.gov/s/ct/rls/crt/, accessed 11 September 2009.
9. In addition to the triple attacks of 9/11, which left almost three thousand dead, the other (somewhat lesser) examples of such hyper-terrorism include the attack on the Alfred P. Murrah Federal Building complex in Oklahoma City in 1995, which killed almost two hundred; the 2004 train bombings in Madrid, which killed nearly two hundred and injured more than a thousand; and the 2005 London subway attacks, which killed twelve and wounded almost two hundred.
10. François Heisbourg, *Europe and the Transformation of the World Order*, prepared for the IISS/CEPS European Security Forum, Brussels, November 5, 2001, available at http://www.eusec.org/heisbourg.htm, accessed 11 September 2009. Given that al Qaeda killed more people in 102 minutes on 9/11 than the PIRA did between 1968 and 1998, hyper-terrorism seems to be an incontravertible description of a new phenomenon.
11. It is interesting here to note that, in spite of strident statements in the 1980s by Margaret Thatcher's government that the British administration would never negotiate with terrorists, thanks to the various memoirs that have since then been published, we now know that such UK government–PIRA talks did in fact take place repeatedly well before the Good Friday Accords. For more information on negotiating with terrorists, see chapter 3.2 by James Wither.
12. Aum Shinrikyo even attempted biological attacks (unsuccessfully) prior to the Metro attack of 1995.

13. For an excellent discussion of the threat posed by terrorist use of WMD, see Richard A. Falkenrath, Robert D. Newman, and Bradley A. Thayer, *America's Achilles' Heel: Nuclear, Biological, and Chemical Terrorism and Covert Attack*, Cambridge, MIT Press, 1998, especially the case study on Aum. For a less specialized account of the sect see Robert J. Lifton's *Destroying the World to Save It: Aum Shinrikyo, Apocalyptic Violence, and the New Global Terrorism*, New York N.Y.: Henry Holt and Co., 1999.

14. Note that I am not using the word *irrational*, but *nonrational*, since there is a logic to the strategic thought of such a group, but it is one devoid of normal political cost-benefit analysis since it is transcendentally informed.

15. The provocative strategist Ralph Peters makes a similar distinction between the *practical* and *apocalyptic terrorist*, but unfortunately limits his discussion of the latter to Muslim extremists, such as Osama bin Laden, when in fact the group is larger and should rightly even include many non-Muslim and non-Arab groups, such as Aum Shinrikyo and potentially even Christian fundamentalists or other ethnically Caucasian groups such as the Branch Davidians. See Peters, *Beyond Terror: Strategy in a Changing World* (Mechanicsburg, PA: Stackpole Books 2002), especially Part I, "When Devils Walk the Earth"; and Sebestyén L. v. Gorka, "2000 AD: Boom Time in the Doom Market," *Jane's Intelligence Review*, January 2000.

16. See Sebastian Gorka, "Al Qaeda's Next Generation," in *Unmasking Terror*, Washington D.C.: Jamestown Foundation, 2004, pp. 49–51.

17. An excellent collection of al Qaeda statements was compiled by the former Foreign Broadcast Information Service (FBIS) and can be accessed by US government employees and contractors through the Open Source Center (which absorbed the FBIS) at https://www.opensource.gov/

18. For masterful analysis of the ideology behind al Qaeda pronouncements and the inherent weaknesses of its ideology, see Stephen Ulph: "The Weakness in the Ideology of Jihad," presentation made at the Westminister Institute, McLean, VA, 10 December 2009."

19. It is again important to note that the categorization of rational or nonrational refers to "our" point of view. There exists, undoubtedly, in the mindset of the Aum Shinrikyo or al Qaeda operator, a distinct logic all his or her own. The difference is whether or not the desired end-state is posited in reference to a transcendental reality. As a result one could also use, as I have, the labels "political" and "transcendental" terrorist.

20. In fact, it was the sacrosanct nature of sovereignty that lay behind the creation of the balance of power system so important to Europe in following centuries.

21. For a much lengthier and most influential discussion of the evolution of the nation-state, security, and international law, see the recent writings of Philip Bobbitt, especially his book *The Shield of Achilles: War, Peace and the Course of History* (New York: Alfred A. Knopf, 2002).

22. There are, of course, rare exceptions to the rule, such as Andorra or Costa Rica, but these all have in common either that they are too small to have their own armies or security services, or that they rely upon external and comprehensive guarantees of security (as in the case of Costa Rica and its treaty relationship with the United States).

23. One such example is when the CIA was accused during the Vietnam War of collecting information on American nationals in the United States—an activity that was mandated to the FBI.

24. For a discussion of the nature of the European Union and how its identity has fundamentally changed with the last rounds of enlargement this year, see the author's paper entitled "European Union Enlargement: Common Challenge or Internal Divide?" as presented to the German-American Fulbright Commission's Berlin Seminar: "Where Continents Meet," 20 March 2004. Available at http://www.fulbright-alumni.de/uploads/media/FRANKly15_2004.pdf, accessed January 2010.

25. "Purple" operations and structures are those that involve all the arms of military service, army, navy, air force, and marines. The US Department of Defense has been emphasizing the "Joint," or "Purple," mode for some years now, breaking down the technical as well as mental barriers to interoperability among the services. My proposal would take this approach and apply it across the whole national security structure, not just the armed forces. I am indebted to my good friend Keith Mines of the US State Department for christening my concept so aptly, "Purple"

referring to the slang for joint operations (arrived at when the service colors are mixed), and "Super-Purple" referring to interdepartmental and international jointness.

26. Lest the reader think I am making an argument here for states to follow the US model by creating their own Department of Homeland Security (DHS), I am not. The gargantuan DHS, which brings together over twenty agencies and two hundred thousand federal employees under one letterhead, is not a radical, new multidisciplinary approach, but represents just one more layer of bureaucracy that in its size and functioning reflects a distinctly Cold War approach as opposed to one that reflects the flexibility of, say, an al Qaeda.

27. In the bloodiest years of the PIRA's campaign against the UK government, the decision was taken to create a radically new unit that would take the fight to the most dangerous players. Variously called, 14 Intelligence Company, 14 Int., or "The Det," this formation employed units made up of local police officers, members of the Special Forces (SAS/SBS), and the intelligence services. 14 Company was very good at its job, overcoming the old divisions and obstacles to effective interagency cooperation. Unfortunately it was too good at its job, being responsible for the deaths of many IRA terrorists and doing so in a way that was unsanctioned in the broadest political sense of the word. As a result, the unit was disbanded. While information on this part of the PIRA/UK struggle is limited, some works have in recent years shed light on 14 Company. See, for example, Martin Dillon, *The Dirty War: Covert Strategies and Tactics Used in Political Conflicts* (New York: Routledge, 1999) and James Rennies, *The Operators— On the Streets with 14 Company* (London, Century, 1996).

Unit 2

Law, Force, and the Military Option

2.1

Dean L. Dwigans and Michael N. Schmitt

International Law and Counterterrorism

Since the tragic criminal attacks of 11 September 2001, the international legal regime governing the response by states to transnational terrorism has been a subject of intense scrutiny. In the twentieth century, transnational terrorism had generally been viewed as a subject almost exclusively in the domain of domestic criminal law regimes and international cooperative law enforcement arrangements. When states acted beyond that context—as, for instance, the United States did in conducting Operation El Dorado Canyon against terrorist bases and Libyan government facilities in response to an attack on Americans in Berlin—international condemnation followed.[1]

As the severity and frequency of transnational terrorism grew during the 1990s, the strict normative divide between responses based on law enforcement and those involving the use of military force began to break down. For instance, in 1998 the United States responded to terrorist attacks against its embassies in Tanzania and Kenya by launching cruise missile strikes against terrorist camps in Afghanistan and a pharmaceutical plant purportedly tied to terrorist activities in Sudan.[2] The former response met with *de minimus* objection, whereas the latter was criticized on the basis that the US strike had been mounted with insufficient evidence of a terrorism nexus to the facility (rather than on the fact of an attack in itself). This example of state practice, which is used to evaluate the existence of customary international law norms and the interpretation of treaty law, illustrates that by the 1990s states were increasingly comfortable with forceful counterterrorist options, although they still set a high evidentiary bar before operations could be mounted.

The relative acceptance of these US strikes foreshadowed international reactions to US and coalition operations in Afghanistan. Conducted in response to the 9/11 attacks, the international community actively supported Operation Enduring Freedom against the Taliban and al Qaeda as necessary and legally justified. Such a response signaled a dramatic paradigm shift in the prescriptive architecture governing counterterrorism. While law enforcement remains a key component of counterterrorist strategy, and although a thick web of cooperative law enforcement schemes exists to facilitate such efforts, robust military responses are now inarguably among the tools available to states in combating transnational terrorism.

Whether the response to international terrorism occurs primarily through domestic law enforcement (with international cooperation) or the use of military force, the *sine qua non* is strict compliance with the rule of law. Obviously, democracies are bound to respect the limits established by international and domestic law through the democratic process. However, quite aside from the moral argument, there is the reality that extralegal activities tend to undercut the international cooperation and domestic support that are required to fashion effective and efficient safeguards against terrorist activity.

This chapter surveys several of the key international legal issues that states crafting counterterrorist policies confront. Some issues have attracted particular controversy, which usually arises as a result of using military force to counter a threat that has traditionally been understood in the context of law enforcement. In light of terrorism's potential for devastating consequences, particularly when weapons of mass destruction may be involved, such a transition is sensible.

To some extent, a rebalancing of sorts—a rebalancing of the rights of society at large against those of individuals—has taken place. The former are essentially "security rights," whereas the latter are "civil liberties." Orderly societies typically favor civil liberties, which imply both well-defined laws and a thick web of procedural protections during criminal investigation, arrest, trial, and imposition of punishment. Favoring the protection of the individual requires society to assume greater risk vis-à-vis security; thus, typical civil liberties include strict evidentiary and procedural rules to preserve the integrity of the criminal process (including the requirement that arrest and search be based on probable cause), the exclusion of improperly obtained evidence, the presumption that all suspects are innocent with the state bearing the burden of proof, a requirement for reasonable and consistent sentences, and appellate review.

When the balance tips toward the security rights of society as a whole, law enforcement efforts may prove insufficient. After all, even a single error could lead to destruction far beyond that of 9/11. To respond to this greater threat, military force may be required. This chapter begins by looking at the international law governing the resort to military force as a tool against counterterrorism. It then turns to law enforcement, with particular emphasis on the cooperative legal regime. Ultimately, it concludes that the decision to use one or the other must be made on a case-by-case basis, although always in a manner consistent with the rule of law.

Counterterrorism and the *Jus ad Bellum*

The international law bearing on the use of military force—not in support of law enforcement, but rather as a core activity—can be subdivided into the *jus ad bellum* and the *jus in bello*. The former governs when it is that states may resort to force, typically with their military, in pursuit of their national interests. It governs such matters as self-defense, collective defense, using force pursuant to a Security Council mandate, and humanitarian intervention. By contrast, the latter, also labeled international humanitarian law, addresses issues of how that force may be applied once hostilities have begun. Thus, it addresses such matters as targeting norms and the rules governing detention during military operations. These complex and controversial *jus in bello* issues are not dealt with in this chapter.

In terms of the *jus ad bellum*, there are essentially two justifications for employing military force to combat terrorism. The first is action pursuant to a mandate by the Security Council under Chapter VII of the UN Charter. Article 39 of the Charter provides that the Security Council may determine that a particular situation amounts to a breach of the peace, act of aggression, or threat to the peace.[3] In this regard, the "threat to the peace" criterion is of particular import, for it enables the authorization of proactive measures in the face of a situation that has not yet matured into a breach of the peace or act of aggression, but that merely evidences the potential to do so. Once the Security Council recognizes that

---

UN Security Council Resolutions Mandating a Response to Terrorism Under Chapter VII

1. UNSCR 1267 (1999). Sanctions against the Taliban and al Qaeda.
2. UNSCR 1264 (1999). Response to violence in East Timor.
3. UNSCR 1368 (2001). Post-9/11 condemnation of attack and call to cooperate against terrorism.
4. UNSCR 1373 (2001). Broad response post-9/11 to prevent the movement, organization, and fund-raising activities of terrorist groups.
5. UNSCR 1377 (2001). Reinforced the need to cooperate and implement previous resolutions on terrorism.
6. UNSCR 1540 (2004). Imposed controls on nuclear, biological, and chemical weapons.

---

a particular situation has met the threshold Article 39 finding, it may mandate nonforceful actions under Article 41.[4] Should such actions prove unsuccessful, or should it be apparent that nonforceful measures would be unlikely to bear fruit; the Council may then authorize military action under Article 42.[5]

That terrorism may qualify as a *de jure* threat to, or breach of, the peace (as distinct from a *de facto* threat) under Article 39 is unquestionable. The Security Council has made just such a finding on repeated occasions. In particular, in Resolution 1368, adopted the day following the notorious terror attacks by al Qaeda against the United States, the Council so labeled international terrorism, a practice reaffirmed in numerous subsequent resolutions addressing the situation (see box above).[6] In November 2001 the Council likewise adopted a Resolution containing a ministerial-level declaration that styled international terrorism as "one of the most serious threats to international peace and security in the twenty-first century."[7] Indeed, it is now common practice for the Security Council to issue condemnatory resolutions in the aftermath of major terrorist attacks that typically cite them as threats to the peace.[8]

Despite such pronouncements, the Council has stopped short of authorizing the use of force against terrorists pursuant to Article 42. Rather, it has encouraged, and even required, international cooperation in combating terrorism,[9] and imposed sanctions on states deemed to have overtly or implicitly supported terrorist groups, for example, by offering them sanctuary.[10]

Nevertheless, the fact that terrorism has been labeled an Article 39 threat to peace leaves no room for doubt that the Council could legally mandate military action if it wished. That it has not merely indicates that it views the second legal ground for such action, self-defense, as usually sufficient in this regard.

The right of states to act militarily in self-defense is based in Article 51 of the UN Charter, which provides:

> Nothing in the present Charter shall impair the inherent right of individual or collective self-defense if an armed attack occurs against a Member of the United Nations, until

the Security Council has taken measures necessary to maintain international peace and security. Measures taken by Members in the exercise of this right of self-defense shall be immediately reported to the Security Council and shall not in any way affect the authority and responsibility of the Security Council under the present Charter to take at any time such action as it deems necessary in order to maintain or restore international peace and security.[11]

It is important to note that the right is deemed "inherent," thereby recognizing its independent and preexisting basis in customary international law.

Article 51, however, provides no elaboration of its terms, nor of the conditions precedent for acting in self-defense. Key in this regard is the phrase "armed attack." Prior to 9/11, it was generally understood that the right of self-defense applied to attacks by states, as distinct from criminal actions taken by nonstate actors such as terrorists. Indeed, when the United States launched Operation El Dorado Canyon in 1986, general condemnation followed—in part, on the basis that the attacks by terrorists in Berlin did not justify the violation of Libya's sovereignty. Critics believed the appropriate response was one of law enforcement. Although criticism of forceful military action against terrorists moderated over the ensuing years,[12] by 9/11 the general consensus was that the appropriate response to terrorism, whether domestic or transnational, was to be found in criminal law enforcement.

The international community quickly abandoned the apparent exclusivity of the law enforcement paradigm in the immediate aftermath of the 9/11 attacks. The following day the Security Council adopted Resolution 1368, which expressly referenced the inherent right to self-defense in the context of the attacks. What is normatively significant is that at the time there was no suggestion that they were tied to any state. Two weeks later, in Resolution 1373, the Council again referenced the right of self-defense, thereby eliminating the possibility that its Resolution 1368 citation of self-defense was but an emotive legal misstep in light of the previous day's events. Subsequent resolutions, including those adopted in the aftermath of the Coalition attacks against al Qaeda bases in Afghanistan, reaffirmed the stance. Moreover, regional organizations such as NATO and the Organization of American States relied on the collective self-defense provisions of their constitutive documents in offering assistance to the United States, while there were widespread offers of bilateral support on the basis of collective self-defense from around the world.[13] Thus, state practice and that of international organizations in the months after the 9/11 attacks appeared to signal the acceptance of the notion that the Article 51 right of self-defense now included armed attacks by nonstate actors, at least when said attacks resemble in scale and scope attacks by a state. The law enforcement paradigm had not been discarded; indeed, the attacks sparked the largest cooperative international law enforcement response in history. However, henceforth the law enforcement and use of force paradigms would coexist as simultaneous responses.

As to the conditions precedent to taking military action in self-defense, state practice and scholarly comment over decades have established that two exist. Recognized by the International Court of Justice in various cases, they comprise necessity and proportionality.[14] The former requires the exhaustion of reasonable alternatives (should any exist) to the use of force prior to acting in self-defense. The requirement has particular resonance in the case of counterterrorist operations, for the implication is that if law enforcement action, standing alone, will suffice to defeat or deter particular terrorist attacks, the use of force in self-defense (except in the case of an ongoing attack) would be prohibited.

With regard to necessity, it should also be noted that the criterion is not complied with unless a potential attacker has both the capability and the intention to conduct an attack. As an example, it is not enough for a neighboring state to possess arms capable of threatening a state proposing to act in self-defense. Before defensive action is permissible, the neighboring state must intend to use those arms. In the case of terrorism, terrorists may generally be presumed to harbor such an intent vis-à-vis states they are known to oppose.

The *jus ad bellum* requirement of proportionality limits defensive force to that required to defeat or deter particular armed attacks. The criterion does not require any equivalency of response in the sense that the defensive actions correspond in scale to those of the armed attack. Rather, they are measured by sufficiency. Less force than used in the armed attack may be sufficient or more force may be required than constituted the armed attack. The point is that compliance with the requirement is determined by reference to the degree of force needed to mount an effective defense.

A third criterion, albeit not mentioned by the International Court of Justice (it was not relevant to the cases), is that of imminency (also labeled immediacy). Derived from a nineteenth-century incident involving British forces crossing into the United States after rebels during the MacKenzie Rebellion (the Caroline case), imminency adds a temporal requirement for self-defense actions.[15] By the standard, a defensive action in anticipation of an attack (anticipatory self-defense) may not come too soon, while a response that follows an attack may not come too late, lest it be deemed retaliatory rather than defensive in nature. Traditionally, this criterion was judged in terms of temporal proximity to the attack. The underlying premise was that the more time preceding an anticipatory self-defense action, the greater the opportunity to resolve the matter peacefully; with regard to the response, the more quickly the return to nonforceful measures to resolve a situation, the better.

Such an emphasis on the objective time before and after an attack as the appropriate measurement of lawful response would be challenged in the case of terrorism. The dilemma is that, to be successful, terrorist attacks must be "surprise" attacks, for if the target becomes aware of an impending attack it can be easily foiled. To be meaningful, therefore, the criteria of imminency must be understood not in terms of temporal distance from the attack, but rather with regard to the opportunity the victim state has to act defensively. For instance, consider a case in which a state acquires credible evidence that a particular group is to mount an attack at some future time. Because terrorist operations are inherently surreptitious, mounting an immediate strike may represent the only opportunity the state has to effectively defend itself before the terrorists act. The question is not whether the defensive action is in close temporal proximity to the intended attack, but instead whether the defensive action occurs during the last viable window of opportunity the state has to defend itself.

Operation Enduring Freedom in Afghanistan constituted the first major counterterrorist operation widely accepted as lawful on the basis of the law of self-defense. It arguably met the criteria set forth above. States appeared to have settled the issue of whether Article 51 applies to attacks by nonstate actors through the widespread acceptance of the notion in the immediate aftermath of the 9/11 attacks. Although isolated small-scale terrorist attacks may not qualify as armed attacks in the sense of Article 51, and thus be entirely encompassed within the law enforcement paradigm, those that occurred on 9/11 were clearly of the scope and scale necessary to rise to the armed attack threshold.

With regard to the necessity criterion, the need to employ military force was apparent. Al Qaeda had launched attacks against US assets and by 2001 was already the target of substantial ongoing law enforcement and intelligence-gathering efforts. Yet, these efforts failed to predict or prevent the attacks of 9/11. It would have been unreasonable to assume that further law enforcement measures would alone have sufficed to foil subsequent attacks, which, in light of the organization's track record, were certain to be mounted. The necessity for military force was demonstrated by the fact that the post-9/11 law enforcement activities, even when conducted in conjunction with Operation Enduring Freedom, failed to end additional attacks.

Once the use of force is determined necessary, the criterion of proportionality must also be satisfied. While it is true that Operation Enduring Freedom resulted in the conquest of the country, ouster of its government, and more deaths than occurred during the 9/11 attacks, proportionality is measured against sufficiency of response in providing an effective defense. That the operation was not excessive is suggested by the fact that it did not completely eradicate the al Qaeda threat.[16]

Finally, Operation Enduring Freedom was mounted within a month of the 9/11 attacks. Given the distances involved and the difficulties of identifying and targeting al Qaeda forces in Afghanistan, the speed of the response was impressive. Since al Qaeda clearly represented a continuing threat, the situation met the imminency criterion.

Further, it may be argued that the 9/11 attacks were an aspect of an ongoing campaign against the United States that had commenced much earlier, certainly by the 1998 attacks against the US embassies in Tanzania and Kenya. Much as a military campaign is punctuated by tactical and operational pauses, so too may a terrorist campaign consist of distinct phases punctuated by breaks. In such cases, imminency is measured not by each individual attack, but rather by commencement and termination of the campaign as a whole. In this regard, it may be fairly objected that a campaign must be conducted by an identifiable, cohesive, organized armed group to be treated for immanency purposes as such. Whether the loosely structured al Qaeda network qualifies is debatable (an issue of no practical relevance as to Operation Enduring Freedom because the coalition response occurred soon after 9/11).

Counterterrorist operations such as Operation Enduring Freedom do raise a highly contentious legal issue, violation of the territorial integrity of the state where the terrorists are located. It is an established tenet of international law that a state's territory is generally inviolable.[17] However, certain exceptions exist when the principle needs to yield to other international concerns.[18] When rights clash in international law, as do the international law rights of self-defense and territorial integrity in this situation, the resolution that most fully accommodates the underlying purposes of each must be sought. In addition to rights, the relevant obligations of the respective parties have to be considered. It has long been settled that states have an obligation to ensure that their territory is not used to the detriment of other states, a norm directly relevant in the case of voluntarily (or involuntarily) providing terrorists sanctuary.

The best accommodation of these rights and obligations requires the victim state to request that the state where the terrorists are located police its territory—which is a firm duty of sovereignty. In the case of the Taliban, numerous pre-9/11 UN Security Council resolutions required the Taliban to put an end to terrorist activity on their territory; when that did not occur, sanctions were imposed. Following the attacks, the United States similarly demanded action from the Taliban, both publicly and through Pakistan, which maintained relations with the Taliban government and therefore served as a useful backchannel interlocutor. However, these requests were ignored.

Once the state in which the terrorists have harbored refuses to take steps to eradicate the threat, or when it simply chooses not to do so, the victim state may cross the border to conduct counterterrorist operations. However, because the right of the sanctuary state to territorial inviolability has only been temporarily suspended to accommodate the other state's right of self-defense, the victim state must do no more than necessary to defend itself and must withdraw from the territory of the other state immediately upon completion of the mission.

The Law Enforcement Response to Counterterrorism

Law enforcement must continue to evolve to meet the global dimensions of international terrorism. To establish jurisdiction over terrorists, conduct extraterritorial investigations, arrest suspects abroad, and prosecute offenders for their global activities requires in-depth international law enforcement cooperation. Terrorists are leveraging globalization to organize, plan, support, and conduct their attacks. Like classic criminals, terrorists are taking advantage of international commerce, the speed of international travel, and the ease of global communications via telephone and the internet to facilitate their operations. Law enforcement must be able to legally penetrate terrorist networks and eliminate "safe havens" for them, their assets, and evidence of their crimes—internationally.

This reality has led many nations to enter into international agreements to commit the parties to strengthen their domestic laws, ease multijurisdictional investigations, and enhance prosecutorial competence. Such agreements have been executed bilaterally, at the regional level, and internationally. In addition, the United Nations Security Council has approved key resolutions that apply to all United Nations member states. Once a treaty is signed and ratified, or upon issuance of a binding resolution by the Security Council, states become legally obligated to comply therewith. These instruments typically define terrorist acts for the purpose of the treaty, require domestic criminalization of said activities, establish criminal jurisdiction over the defined offenses, require state assistance in their investigation and prosecution, mandate prosecution (and prosecutorial cooperation), and serve as an extradition treaty. Key international treaties, as well as special committees established to facilitate and monitor their implementation, are set forth in the box on page 93.

In addition to international treaties, agreements instituted at the regional level also serve to facilitate cooperation. Regional agreements are particularly useful in addressing issues that are troublesome in a certain area or where regional cooperation is especially important (as in the transport of terrorist materials). Of course, the success of a particular treaty regime is limited to the strength and commitment of the regional organization itself. Key regional instruments on terrorism are listed in the box on page 95.

For certain forms of cooperation, a need exists for regimes of greater specificity in the investigation and prosecution of offenses. Agreements, commonly referred to as Mutual Legal Assistance Treaties,[19] can address a wide range of assistance; typical terms set out the power to take testimony or statements, compel the production of documents and records, locate potential witnesses, serve legal documents, issue search warrants, and seize

International Treaties on Terrorism

1. Convention on Offenses and Certain Other Acts Committed on Board Aircraft (Tokyo Convention, 1963). The Convention applies to acts committed on board an aircraft in flight. Its purpose is to protect the safety of the aircraft and passengers and to maintain order on board, and it gives authority to the crew to take necessary action.

2. Convention for the Suppression of Unlawful Seizure of Aircraft (Hague Convention, 1970). The Convention makes the act of unlawful seizure of aircraft an offense punishable by severe penalties. A State is obliged to prosecute or extradite the offender and return the passengers, crew, and aircraft without delay.

3. Convention for the Suppression of Unlawful Acts against the Safety of Civil Aviation (Montreal Convention, 1971). The Convention deals with acts other than those covered by the Tokyo and The Hague Conventions. The Montreal Convention defines a wide spectrum of unlawful acts against the safety of civil aviation, including aircraft sabotage, and makes these offenses punishable by severe penalties.

4. Convention on the Prevention and Punishment of Crimes against Internationally Protected Persons, including Diplomatic Agents (1973). The Convention applies to the crimes of murder, kidnapping, or attack on diplomatic agents and other "internationally protected persons," which includes Heads of State or Government, Ministers for Foreign Affairs, State officials, and representatives of some international organizations and their families. Parties are required to establish jurisdiction over the offenses described and prosecute or extradite offenders.

5. International Convention against the Taking of Hostages (1979). The Convention applies to acts of hostage-taking intended to compel some requirement prior to the release of the hostage. Each party is required to make offenses punishable by appropriate penalties, take all measures, and cooperate with each other to prevent hostage taking, prosecute or extradite offenders, and facilitate the return of any hostages.

6. Convention on the Physical Protection of Nuclear Material (1980). The Physical Protection Convention provides for the secure handling and transport of nuclear material. Parties are obliged to make punishable under their national law offenses with respect to nuclear material. Included are acts dealing with nuclear material that cause or threaten to cause death or serious injury or damage; theft or robbery of nuclear material; embezzlement or fraudulent obtaining of nuclear material; and demands for or threats to use nuclear material by any form of intimidation.

7. Protocol for the Suppression of Unlawful Acts of Violence at Airports Serving International Civil Aviation (1988). The Protocol adds to the definition of "offense" given in the Montreal Convention unlawful and intentional acts of

violence against persons at airports or acts that destroy or seriously damage airport facilities. Contracting States must prosecute or extradite offenders.

8. Convention for the Suppression of Unlawful Acts against the Safety of Maritime Navigation (1988). The Convention applies to offenses that threaten to endanger the safe navigation of a ship and obligates parties to establish jurisdiction over such offenses and prosecute or extradite offenders.

9. Protocol for the Suppression of Unlawful Acts against the Safety of Fixed Platforms Located on the Continental Shelf (1988). The Protocol applies to the offenses against a "fixed platform," defined as an artificial island, installation, or structure permanently attached to the seabed for the purpose of exploration or exploitation of resources or for other economic purposes, and obligates parties to establish jurisdiction over such offenses and prosecute or extradite offenders.

10. Convention on the Marking of Plastic Explosives for the Purpose of Detection (1991). The Convention requires parties to prohibit the manufacture or movement of unmarked plastic explosives in their territory.

11. International Convention for the Suppression of Terrorist Bombings (1997). The Convention establishes as an offense unlawful and intentional delivery of certain acts involving an explosive against a place of public use, government facility, public transportation system, or related infrastructure, with the intent to cause death or serious bodily injury, or extensive destruction likely to result in major economic loss, or commit such acts with a group of persons acting with a common purpose. The acts must involve certain international elements as defined by the Convention. Parties are required to establish jurisdiction over such offenses and prosecute or extradite offenders.

12. International Convention for the Suppression of the Financing of Terrorism (1999). The Convention makes it an offense to provide or collect funds that assist in carrying out certain listed acts intended to cause death or serious bodily injury to intimidate a population, or to compel a government or an international organization to do or abstain from doing any act, or commit such acts with a group of persons acting with a common purpose. The acts must involve certain international elements as defined by the Convention. Parties are required to establish jurisdiction over such offenses and prosecute or extradite offenders.

13. International Convention for the Suppression of Acts of Nuclear Terrorism (2005). The Convention applies to acts involving possession of radioactive material or a device with the intent to cause death or serious bodily injury or to cause substantial damage to property or to the environment. The Convention does not apply to the official activities of military forces, which are governed by international law, nor does it address the issue of the legality of the use of nuclear weapons by States. Parties are required to establish jurisdiction over such offenses and prosecute or extradite offenders.

United Nations Security Council Standing Committees on Terrorism

1. UNSCR 1267: Al Qaeda and Taliban Sanctions Committee
2. UNSCR 1373: Counter-Terrorism Committee
3. UNSCR 1540: 1540 Committee examines controls on nuclear, biological and chemical weapons
4. UNSCR 1566: 1566 Working Group examines terrorist activities, other than those designated by the Al Qaeda and Taliban Sanctions Committee.

Regional Treaties on Terrorism

1. Convention to Prevent and Punish Acts of Terrorism against Persons of International Significance (Organization of American States, 1971)
2. European Convention on the Suppression of Terrorism (Council of Europe, 1977; revised 2001)
3. SAARC Regional Convention on the Suppression of Terrorism (South Asian Association for Regional Cooperation, 1987)
4. Arab Convention on the Suppression of Terrorism (League of Arab States, 1998)
5. OAU Convention on the Prevention and Combating of Terrorism (Organization of African Unity, 1999)
6. Convention of the OIC on Combating International Terrorism (Organization of the Islamic Conference, 1999)
7. Treaty on Cooperation among the States Members of the CIS in Combating Terrorism (Commonwealth of Independent States, 1999)
8. European Union

   - Council Common Position 2001/931/CFSP of 27 December 2001 on the application of specific measures to combat terrorism

   - Council Regulation (EC) No. 2580/2001 of 27 December 2001 on specific restrictive measures directed against certain persons and entities with a view to combating terrorism

   - Council Decision 2003/48/JHA of 19 December 2002 on the exchange of information and cooperation concerning terrorist offenses.

---

assets. Without such agreements, these actions usually would require issuance of a judicial order, an often time-consuming process that is unavailable for some types of assistance.

Strengthening domestic laws and systems is the focus of the obligations imposed in the international agreements already discussed. Ultimately, their goal is to maximize jurisdiction in terrorism cases by ensuring that states that are party to the instruments have domestic legal mechanisms to establish jurisdiction over terrorist acts and those who commit them. It must be noted that there is no obligation on a state to actually exercise jurisdiction, for, under the legal notion of sovereignty, jurisdiction is a matter solely within the discretion of the sovereign state. Moreover, it is often the case that multiple states enjoy jurisdiction over a particular person or event ("concurrent jurisdiction").

Five principles undergird criminal jurisdiction in international law, principles that rely on a substantial link between the state and the persons or conduct over which jurisdiction is established.

1. Territorial Principle. Based on the concept of sovereignty, this principle permits the establishment and enforcement of criminal laws within a state's own territory. By it, a state has jurisdiction over all conduct occurring (and all persons engaging in said conduct) on its land, on or beneath its territorial sea, and in the airspace above national territory or the territorial sea. This principle recognizes that a state requires this power to fulfill the duties and obligations of statehood, including the obligation to ensure the rights and interests of other states are protected in its territory.

2. Nationality Principle. Every nation possesses the authority to establish and enforce criminal laws regarding their nationals and their nationals' conduct wherever located. This authority applies in a similar manner to vessels registered or corporations incorporated in a state. The principle recognizes that nationals owe allegiance to their nation, and that nations have an interest in and responsibility for their nationals, regardless of location. However, it is important to distinguish jurisdiction over a national outside a state's borders from actual custody of that national. Custody is necessary in order to physically exercise jurisdiction; obtaining custody requires the consent of the state where the individual is located.

3. Protective Principle. States may exercise jurisdiction regarding conduct outside their territories that threatens their security, so long as the conduct concerned is generally recognized as criminal by other nations. Examples include acts such as counterfeiting currency, falsifying passports or other official documents, espionage, and terrorism.

4. Universality Principle. States may exercise jurisdiction regarding conduct universally dangerous to all nations and their nationals, wherever it occurs and even in the absence of a link between the state and the persons or acts over which jurisdiction is exercised. Piracy, genocide, war crimes, and slave trading have classically been considered to be offenses subject to universal jurisdiction. In addition, various international treaties subject certain terrorist acts to universal jurisdiction.

5. Passive Personality Principle. Jurisdiction regarding conduct abroad that injures one of its nationals may be exercised on the basis of the passive personality principle. The use of this principle, previously rare, is gaining increased recognition in terrorism cases.[20]

Transfer of a suspect to a state that enjoys jurisdiction over the offense he is to be charged with, or to serve a sentence if already convicted, is known as extradition. Extradition usually occurs pursuant to a bilateral treaty that establishes a method for obtaining custody of the individual concerned.[21] In the absence of a specific bilateral treaty, domestic statutes or multilateral international terrorism treaties may serve as a basis for extradition.[22]

Consent by the state where the individual is located is essential (either through treaty or through ad hoc agreement) since that state enjoys sovereignty over its territory; thus, an extradition agreement resembles a prenegotiated consent to transfer with certain predetermined criteria to be met. A typical request is submitted formally through diplomatic channels and includes a copy of the charges, an explanation of those charges, an arrest warrant, and a detailed description of the facts and evidence.

All extradition agreements impose certain restrictions and prohibitions. Many prohibit the extradition of their own nationals. Some bar extradition if there is a belief that the individual will not receive a fair trial or that prosecution is motivated by race, religion, nationality, or ethnicity. It is common for extradition to be forbidden to a state with a death penalty for the offense unless there are express binding assurances that the death penalty will not be imposed. Extradition treaties typically specify the types of crimes for which extradition is permitted, and both the requesting and requested nation must consider the crime to be a serious offense. This doctrine of "dual criminality" usually applies to crimes punishable by one year or more in prison; lesser crimes are seldom extraditable. Military offenses may be rejected for extradition if not criminalized under ordinary criminal law. Further, once an individual has been extradited, he may not be tried for other crimes not listed in the original request, and re-extradition to a third country without the consent of the state originally granting the request is prohibited. Other concerns affecting extradition include whether: the prosecution will be carried out in an ordinary court; the requesting state has jurisdiction; the individual has already been tried for the same crimes (double jeopardy); the statute of limitations for the offense charged has expired; or the individual was found guilty without being present (in absentia prosecution).

Very significant in the case of terrorism is the common "political offense exception," which prohibits extradition for political crimes. Terrorism has motivated a sharp curtailment in the exception, and today crimes of violence such as hijacking, murder, and hostage-taking, even when motivated by political concerns, may not receive the protection of the political offense exception. On the other hand, political crimes where extraditions are rare include treason, espionage, sedition, and prohibited speech or worship.

Procedural obstacles include failure to provide sufficient evidence or to meet the level of proof required to support the request. Some states require requesting states to meet a very high burden of proof, such as the probable cause standard used in the United States, while others require less. For instance, the European Convention on Extradition requires virtually no evidentiary review.[23]

States may use methods other than extradition to obtain custody of an individual. These informal methods are based on the consent of the state in which the individual in question is located and often rely on the goodwill that may exist between the two countries. There may be nothing more than a request to turn the suspect over to the requesting state or to deport or expel the subject based on authority of domestic immigration laws. Informal methods may be attractive if the requested state fears creating political unrest, there is no applicable extradition treaty, the matter is urgent, or when extradition is likely to negatively impact relations between the requested and requesting state. Members of the European Union have adopted a streamlined procedure for transfer, a European Arrest Warrant. Since 2004 this warrant process has replaced traditional extradition between EU members. It dramatically simplifies matters by taking the process outside diplomatic channels. Additionally, EU member states may no longer refuse to extradite their own nationals.

In dealing with terrorism suspects, there have been some controversial cases involving transfer to a state for the purpose of interrogation. Such transfers are lawful if the interrogation is conducted in accordance with international law, especially human rights law. However, a state that transfers an individual to another country with the knowledge that that country will violate human rights standards will itself be responsible for any foreseeable violations. In this regard, the prohibition on torture is of particular relevance.[24]

Other alternatives, some nonconsensual, to extradition have also proven controversial. For example, suspects are sometimes intentionally lured to and arrested in a third nation where extradition is more likely. Similarly, the arrest may take place in international waters or airspace where consent of another state is not required. A well-known example is the case of Mr. Fawaz Yunis.[25] Yunis, who lived in Cyprus, was a suspect in the hijacking of an airliner carrying US nationals. Lured onto a yacht with the promise of a drug deal, Yunis was arrested by US law enforcement agents when the boat entered international waters. To avoid the jurisdiction of another sovereign, he was moved through international waters and airspace on US military ships and aircraft until reaching the United States. At federal trial, Yunis unsuccessfully protested the manner in which he was brought before the court; he was later convicted.

The most controversial alternative to extradition is forcible abduction of an individual from another state without its consent. Doing so is unlawful except under the rarest of circumstances[26] and could subject those involved to prosecution in the state where the abduction occurred. In many states, subsequent prosecution of those abducted will be affected due to the illegality of the method by which custody was obtained. Interestingly, in the United States a prosecution may still be possible as long as the circumstances of the arrest do not amount to a flagrant violation of the individual's human rights (the "Ker-Frisbie Doctrine"[27]).

Finally, law enforcement officials and prosecutors have long cooperated informally and formally in a variety of ways to assist each other within the confines of the law. Cooperation of this nature ranges from the very informal contacts, such as investigator-to-investigator sharing of tips in related cases, to the more formal systems set up under the treaties listed earlier.

Informal information exchange is especially useful in an environment where communication among terrorists and other criminals is global, instantaneous, and perishable. As a result, it is common for states to assign law enforcement officers abroad to serve as direct liaisons with foreign police officials. Often based out of their respective embassies, they do not, because of the concept of sovereignty, exercise traditional police powers, such as the power to arrest suspects. For the United States, special agents of the Federal Bureau of Investigation, Drug Enforcement Administration, and Immigration and Customs Enforcement serve in many US embassies.

To enhance informal cooperation on a wider scale, various international organizations have been established. INTERPOL, EUROPOL, and EUROJUST are the most prominent examples. INTERPOL is an intergovernmental organization formed in 1923 and based in Lyon, France.[28] It provides a secure police communications service and a range of databases to carry out its most important function of disseminating crime-related information to members. The primary purpose of the organization is to facilitate cross-border cooperation of police agencies. The INTERPOL system depends on the police communications network of member states; most states also have a representative in the Lyon headquarters. With regard to terrorism, an especially useful INTERPOL tool is a central list of suspected terrorists that includes information such as aliases, fingerprints, photographs, passport data, and other important information.

EUROPOL performs functions similar to INTERPOL, but within the European Union.[29] Its primary purpose is to facilitate operational police cooperation, especially with regard to collecting, exchanging, and analyzing information. Complementing EUROPOL is EUROJUST, an EU organization providing for cooperation between the judicial authorities of EU states in the investigation and prosecution of serious cross-border crimes, including terrorism and organized crime.[30] This network is instrumental in facilitating extradition and processing requests under mutual legal assistance treaties.

Conclusion

The past eight years have witnessed a sea change in the legal regime governing transnational terrorism and the response of states to it. Clearly, the response regime initiated by the United Nations Security Council in the aftermath of the terrorist attacks of 9/11 set the appropriate tone from the beginning. The Council demonstrated that from a legal perspective the terrorist threat was one shared by all member states. The result has been tolerance of the military option, the adoption of robust international agreements, and the establishment of formal and informal cooperative law enforcement systems. Without question, the emergence of new threats, such as cyber-terrorism, will continue to force reconsideration of the prevailing legal regime. In response, international law must prove more flexible, proactive, and relevant than in decades past. Whether it will do so remains to be seen.

Dean L. Dwigans Captain Dwigans is a career Judge Advocate in the U.S. Navy. Since his arrival at the George C. Marshall Center in Garmisch, Germany, in 2007, he has been a Professor of International Law, Navy Judge Advocate General International Law Chair, and Director of the Program in Advanced Security Studies. Captain Dwigans has had multiple assignments in Asia and Europe as a Navy prosecutor and legal advisor, and recently commanded the Navy's largest overseas prosecution office in the Pacific. In addition, Captain Dwigans was the senior Navy attorney in the National Security Agency, Office of General Counsel, and the Naval Criminal Investigative Service Headquarters where he was responsible for the worldwide oral and wire intercept program and the legal aspects of the foreign counterintelligence program. He also had multiple deployments on board an aircraft carrier to the Persian Gulf, and Pacific and Indian oceans, where he was the primary legal advisor and responsible for internal ship security. Captain Dwigans has an undergraduate business degree and Juris Doctor from Creighton University, and an LLM in international law from Georgetown University.

Michael N. Schmitt The Chair of Public International Law at Durham University Law School in the United Kingdom. Professor Schmitt previously served as Dean of the College of International and Security Studies at the Marshall Center and, from 2007 through 2008, was the Charles H. Stockton Visiting Chair of International Law at the United States Naval War College. In 2006, he was the Sir Ninian Stephen Visiting Scholar at Melbourne University and in 1997–98 was a visiting scholar at Yale Law School. The General Editor of the *Yearbook of International Humanitarian Law*, he serves on the editorial boards of the *International Review of the Red Cross*, *International Peacekeeping*, the *Journal of Military Ethics*,

The Journal of International Humanitarian Law Studies, Connections, and the International Humanitarian Law Series (Martinus Nijhoff). Professor Schmitt also serves on the advisory board of numerous organizations focusing on conflict studies and law. Before joining the Marshall Center, he served twenty years in the United States Air Force, specializing in operational and international law.

Recommended Readings

Ackerman, Bruce. *Before the Next Attack: Preserving Civil Liberties in an Age of Terrorism.* New Haven: Yale University Press, 2006.

Bianchi, Andrea, ed. *Enforcing International Law Norms Against Terrorism.* Oxford: Hart Pub., 2004.

Danner, Mark. *Torture and Truth: America, Abu Ghraib, and the War on Terror.* London: Granta Pub., 2004.

Duffy, Helen. *The "War on Terror" and the Framework of International Law.* Cambridge: Cambridge University Press, 2005.

Elagab, Omer, and Jeehan Elagab, eds. *International law Documents Relating to Terrorism.* London: Routledge, 3rd ed., 2007.

Fernandez-Sanchez, Pablo, ed. *International Legal Dimensions of Terrorism.* Leiden: Martinus Nijhoff/Brill, 2009.

Gearty, Conor A. *Essays on Human Rights and Terrorism: Comparative Approaches to Civil Liberties in Asia, the EU and North America.* London: Cameron May, 2008.

Greenberg, Karen J., and Joshua L. Dratel, eds. *The Torture Papers: The Road to Abu Ghraib.* Cambridge: Cambridge University Press, 2005.

Guiora, Amos, ed. *The Top Ten Global Justice Law Review Articles 2007.* Oxford: Oxford University Press, 2008.

Nanda, Ved P., ed. *Law in the War Against International Terrorism.* Ardsley: Transnational Publishers, 2005.

Ranstorp, Magnus, and Paul Wilkinson. *Terrorism and Human Rights.* London: Routledge, 2008.

Roberts, Adam. "Counter-terrorism, Armed Force and the Laws of War." *Survival,* Vol. 44, No. 1 (2002), 7–32.

Sambei, Arvinder, Anton du Plessis, and Martin Polaine. *Counter-terrorism Law and Practice: An International Handbook.* Oxford: Oxford University Press, 2009.

Saul, Ben. *Defining Terrorism in International Law.* Oxford: Oxford University Press, 2006.

Schmitt, Michael N. "Responding to Transnational Terrorism Under the Jus ad Bellum: A Normative Framework." *Naval Law Review,* No. 56 (2008), 1–42.

Schmitt, Michael N. "Targeted Killings in International Law: Law Enforcement, Self-Defense and Armed Conflict." In *International Humanitarian Law and Human Rights Law: Towards a New Merger in International Law.* Ed. Roberta Arnold and Noelle Quenivert, 525–554. Leiden: Martinus Nijhoff/Brill, 2008.

Schmitt, Michael N. "The United States Supreme Court and Detainees in the War on Terror." *Israel Yearbook on Human Rights,* No. 37 (2007), 33–84.

Schmitt, Michael N., and Gian Luca Beruto, eds. *Terrorism and International Law.* Italy: Edizioni Nagard, 2003.

Sparks, Thomas K., and Glenn M. Sulmasy, eds. *International Law Challenges: Homeland Security and Combating Terrorism.* Newport: Naval War College International Law Studies, 2006.

Tsang, Steve, ed. *Intelligence and Human Rights in the Era of Global Terrorism.* Westport: Praeger Security International, 2006.

Walter, Christian et al., eds. *Terrorism as a Challenge for National and International Law: Security Versus Liberty?* Berlin: Springer, 2004.

Whittaker, David J. *Counter-terrorism and Human Rights.* Harlow: Longman, 2009.

Notes

1. Germans, as well as Americans, were casualties of the La Belle Disco bombing. The United Nations General Assembly "condemned" the attack as "a violation of the Charter of the United Nations and of international law," G.A. Res. 41/38, 11, U.N. Doc. A/RES/41/38 (Nov. 20, 1986).
2. Operation Infinite Reach.
3. "The Security Council shall determine the existence of any threat to the peace, breach of the peace, or act of aggression and shall make recommendations, or decide what measures shall be taken in accordance with Articles 41 and 42, to maintain or restore international peace and security." Charter of the United Nations, "Chapter VII: Action with Respect to Threats to the Peace, Breaches of the Peace, and Acts of Aggression," Article 39.
4. "The Security Council may decide what measures not involving the use of armed force are to be employed to give effect to its decisions, and it may call upon the Members of the United Nations to apply such measures. These may include complete or partial interruption of economic relations and of rail, sea, air, postal, telegraphic, radio, and other means of communication, and the severance of diplomatic relations." Charter of the United Nations, "Chapter VII," Article 41.
5. "Should the Security Council consider that measures provided for in Article 41 would be inadequate or have proved to be inadequate, it may take such action by air, sea, or land forces as may be necessary to maintain or restore international peace and security. Such action may include demonstrations, blockade, and other operations by air, sea, or land forces of Members of the United Nations." Charter of the United Nations, "Chapter VII," Article 42.
6. The Council "unequivocally condemns in the strongest terms the horrifying terrorist attacks . . . and regards such acts, like any act of international terrorism, as a threat to international peace and security." S.C. Res. 1368, U.N. Doc. S/RES/1368 (12 September 2001). Also see UNSCR 1373, which encouraged international cooperation in the fight against terrorism. S.C. Res. 1373, U.N. Doc. S/RES/1373 (28 September 2001).
7. UNSCR 1377. It further declared terrorism "a challenge to all States and to all humanity."
8. See, for example, S.C. Res. 1438, U.N. Doc. S/RES/1438 (14 October 2002); S.C. Res. 1440, U.N. Doc. S/RES/1440 (24 October 2002); S.C. Res. 1450, U.N. Doc. S/RES/1450 (13 December 2002); S.C. Res. 1465, U.N. Doc. S/RES/1465 (13 February 2003); S.C. Res. 1516, U.N. Doc. S/RES/1516 (20 November 2003); S.C. Res. 1530, U.N. Doc. S/RES/1530 (11 March 2004); S.C. Res. 1611, U.N. Doc. S/RES/1611 (7 July 2005); S.C. Res. 1618, U.N. Doc. S/RES/1618 (4 August 2005).
9. In Resolution 1373, it obliged States to, *inter alia*, prevent the financing of terrorism; criminalize the collection of funds for terrorist purposes; freeze the financial assets of anyone who participates in, or facilitates, terrorism; and take any steps necessary to prevent terrorist acts, including passing early-warning information to other States. The Resolution additionally instructed States to "[r]efrain from providing any form of support, active or passive, to entities or persons involved in terrorist acts, including by suppressing recruitment of members of terrorist groups and eliminating the supply of weapons to terrorists"; "[d]eny safe haven to those who finance, plan, support, or commit terrorist acts, or provide safe havens; [p]revent those who finance, plan, facilitate or commit terrorist acts from using their respective territories for those purposes against other States or their citizens"; and "[e]nsure that any person who participates in the financing, planning, preparation or perpetration of terrorist acts or in supporting terrorist acts is brought to justice and ensure that, in addition to any other measures against them, such terrorist acts are established as serious criminal offences in domestic laws and regulations and that the punishment duly reflects the seriousness of such terrorist acts." S.C. Res. 1373, para. 2(e), U.N. Doc. S/RES/1373 (Sept. 28, 2001).
10. For instance, the Council directed nonforceful sanctions against both Libya and Sudan during the 1990s for their support of terrorism. S.C. Res. 748, U.N. Doc. S/RES/748 (31 March 1992) (Libya); S.C. Res. 1054, U.N. Doc. S/RES/1054 (29 April 1996) (Sudan).
11. Charter of the United Nations, "Chapter VII," Article 51.
12. E.g., in response to the US embassy bombings in Tanzania and Kenya.

13. See "The National and International Response to 9/11," The Heritage Foundation. Retrieved on 5 September 2009 from http://www.heritage.org/research/nationalsecurity/enemydetention/responseto9-11.cfm.
14. See, in particular, *Military and Paramilitary Activities in and Against Nicaragua* (Nicar. v. US), Merits, 1986 I.C.J. Rep. 14 (June 27), at para. 194; *Legality of the Threat or Use of Nuclear Weapons*, Advisory Opinion, 1996 I.C.J. 226, (July 8), at para. 41.
15. In the ensuing diplomatic exchange, Secretary of State Daniel Webster opined that "[There must be shown] a necessity of self-defense, instant, overwhelming, leaving no choice of means, and no moment for deliberation." 30 BRIT. FOREIGN ST. PAPERS 193 (1843), *reprinted in* Jennings, *The Caroline and McLeod Cases*, 32 AM. J. INT'L L. 82, 89 (1938).
16. Of course, the failure of measures taken in self-defense may be due less to sufficiency than to competency. In other words, a poorly executed operation that fails to meet defensive purposes does not excuse steps that, if executed in a reasonable fashion, would be disproportionate to the threat.
17. "All Members shall refrain in their international relations from the threat or use of force against the territorial integrity or political independence of any state, or in any other manner inconsistent with the Purposes of the United Nations." Charter of the United Nations, Article 2(4).
18. E.g., rescue of persons in territorial sea. UN Convention on the Law of the Sea (1982), Part II, Article 18.
19. The United States has Mutual Legal Assistance Treaties with over fifty countries. As an example, see the Treaty Between the Government of the United States of America and Ukraine on Mutual Legal Assistance in Criminal Matters, signed at Kiev on 22 July 1998 (Treaty Doc. 106-16).
20. 18 USC 2332 makes it a crime to kill or conspire to kill a US national outside of the United States.
21. For example, see the 1984 US-Italy Extradition Treaty, TIAS 10837
22. For example, the International Convention against the Taking of Hostages, Art. 10, *opened for signature* 17 December 1979, TIAS No. 11,081, 1316 UNTS 205
23. 13 December 1957, ETS No. 24,359 UNTS 273, Article 12.
24. Convention against Torture and Other Cruel, Inhuman or Degrading Treatment or Punishment, 10 December 1984, 1465 UNTS 85.
25. *United States v. Yunis*, 924 F.2d 1086 (D.C. Cir. 1991)
26. A possible argument could be made under the UN Charter, Art. 51.
27. *Frisbie v. Collins*, 342 US 519, 522, 72 S.Ct. 509, 511, 96 L.Ed. 541 (1952) (citing, inter alia, *Ker v. Illinois*, 119 US 436, 7 *1093 **136 S.Ct. 225, 30 L.Ed. 421 (1886)
28. For more information, see the INTERPOL website, www.interpol.int
29. For more information, see the EUROPOL website, www.europol.europa.eu
30. For more information, see the EUROJUST website, www.eurojust.europa.eu

Christopher C. Harmon

Illustrations of Discrete Uses of Force

An insurrection in the Philippine Islands in 1901 brought prominence to a talented but relatively inexperienced general of US Army volunteers: Frederick Funston. He demonstrated that good intelligence and deception were still as valuable as when the Chinese commander Sun Tzu called them the very essence of war some twenty-three hundred years before.[1]

Brigadier General Funston of the Army Reserves had just enough fighting experience with the nationalist guerrillas of Emilio Aguinaldo to know that jungle pursuit with baggage trains and field guns would be far less likely to yield success than sleight of hand. By capturing an enemy courier, and then deciphering the coded messages the man bore, American officers learned that the Filipino insurgents were in serious need of reinforcements—and were calling for them to assemble close to the hitherto-secret rebel headquarters. General Funston studied the matter and determined to oblige his foe. After much work with forgers, he sent out a faked dispatch that replied favorably to Aguinaldo's call. He then prepared his "reinforcements."

Philippine Scouts—that is, specially trained indigenous fighters on the American side[2]—were schooled carefully in the appearance, dress, weaponry, and methods of the rebel army. The culling and training process yielded eighty-one of these newly baptized "nationalists," who then made a long overland march to Aguinaldo's jungle lair in North Luzon. Funston solved the problem of how this unit would be commanded by accompanying them as a "prisoner," as did two other white US officers. Within a few hours of arrival, the false "relief force" had shot up Aguinaldo's personal guard and captured the man himself.[3] After that, the rebellion was easily defeated.

In the parlance of modern low-intensity conflict, this was a "pseudo-gang," created and used with unusual swiftness to "decapitate" an insurgency. Admirers of Homer's *Odyssey* would see a parallel between Funston's pseudo-gang, inserted into a movement to eviscerate it, and the wooden "gift" of a Trojan horse the Achaean Greeks built to get into Troy. Traditional students of war cannot but appreciate the boldness and guile of the US general's plans and his demonstration of personal leadership.

An equally fascinating Trojan horse appeared in the field in rural Colombia on 2 July 2008. Its shimmer caught the eyes of Revolutionary Armed Forces of Colombia (FARC) terrorists holding parliamentarian Ingrid Betancourt and numbers of helpless civilians unlawfully. Colombian army forces showed a cleverness that would have made Frederick Funston smile. They infiltrated the communications net of a regional FARC commander, won his confidence with false messages, and then set a trap. They sent a false order through now-accustomed channels, ordering the local FARC commander to assemble Betancourt and some other hostages for a heliborne-relocation.

But it was a fake. The FARC had made hostage releases in January and February 2008 and were thus accustomed to white helicopters with the Red Cross. The Colombian army played on this, and other aid flights by humanitarians, by sending in two "helos" painted white—though without any red cross.[4] Their flight crews were manifestly unmilitary, festooned with cameras, unruly hair, and even one Che Guevara tee shirt. FARC personnel loaded aboard their hostages and climbed in. Only as the aircraft lifted off were the communists overcome, without a single gunshot, by those they thought to be "aid workers." "Cesar," a thug who had personally abused Mrs. Betancourt for years in the jungle, found himself naked and bound on the steel flooring, flying into deserved captivity.[5]

Colombia's triumph underscored a pattern of psychological, political, and military progress yielding sharp gains against the insurgents in the previous two years. The revolutionaries had grown steadily over decades, enriching themselves with narco-wealth, enjoying training in at least one case in explosives by Irish Republican Army (IRA) Provisionals, and equipped with communications gear and weapons as good as what most states own. But Colombia's military, in both size and professionalism, was growing in the new millennium, and was enhanced by US training and assistance under "Plan Colombia." The years 2007 and 2008 yielded ever-better news from the field. Intelligence, skill levels, and attention to human rights all improved. The capture and killing of senior FARC operatives became frequent, and this was supplemented with a shocking pattern of defections—that supreme metric of an insurgency's decline. Ultimately it was military guile that saved the wan, gifted Betancourt and her fourteen fellows. High-level diplomacy had failed, for years. A French president had made an election campaign promise to see her released. Her natural appeal, a published autobiography, status as a member of Parliament, and dual French-Colombian citizenship combined to make her a central public focus in France. But all that did not win her release; her release came with a scheme by Colombian counterterrorists.

A Multitude of Such Success Stories

Although perhaps few have noticed, modern times have offered several dozen examples of ingenious, well-crafted forcible rejoinders to terrorist crimes. Dogged with South Moluccan terrorism beginning in 1970, the Dutch government developed negotiation strategies but also turned to their Marines, who brilliantly ended several hostage-barricade situations involving masses of civilians at a school and aboard a train. Germany did not break the Baader-Meinhof communists by installing a social welfare regime—they had already done that, beginning with Bismarck, and elaborated it in the 1950s and 1960s to a degree still striking to pure-market capitalism. It was arrest powers under German domestic law, and one decisive commando action by the border guards/special forces GSG-9 in 1977, that killed the spirit of Andreas Baader and the first generation of his Red Army Faction. It was not negotiation that ended Sendero Luminoso's long drive toward power in rural Peru—the Maoist fanatic Abimael Guzman was interested in victory, not peace talks. But a clever major in the Peruvian police ranks assembled enough intelligence on the whereabouts of this reclusive ideologue so as to capture him, without a shot. There followed the collapse of the elaborate communist machinery that had come to rule at least a third of Peru's countryside.[6]

These operations, effected during what most observers would call peacetime, highlight the need for counterterrorism professionalism to be resident in some capacity in the modern state. These successes in the discrete[7] use of force tend to showcase thorough training and technical capabilities, as well as a determination to outthink the terrorist and then outdo him in boldness when the right moment comes. The counterterrorist successes also occurred because of willingness by leaders (political and military) to take the calculated risks and send the technical experts into action. These permissions and decisions do not come easily; bureaucracies and leaders may often discover unending reasons to avoid such a choice. J. Q. Roberts instructs us in the following chapter that "capability" and "intelligence" must be deployed by "leadership" willing to engage with terrorism. Dr. Richard Shultz Jr.'s study of internal papers of the US Joint Staff in the Pentagon before 9/11 reveals how many grounds there are for reluctance, and how many times good men will prefer to pass, to play it safe.[8]

This chapter dwells in most cases on specially trained or elite forces, be they military, paramilitary, or police; space will not permit us to deal broadly with all types of forceful action, or all types of security forces, deployed against terrorists. There are indeed many. Most actions are routine and even banal; others—much more rare—are hyper-dramatic. An analyst could argue, for example, that uses of force fall into three categories: preventative, preemptive, and reactive. The first encompasses both routine and unexceptional uses of force to limit a problem, check an unsafe political movement, etc. Preemption takes place under pressure of time or imminent enemy terrorist action, using force to interrupt or defeat planned terrorist acts. The third type, the reactive, responds to a crime of terrorist violence quickly (e.g., action to pursue, capture, or kill hostage-takers, murderers of a politician, etc.). Another sound approach is the usual American military one of distinguishing antiterrorism measures from counterterrorist ones. The first includes improving security with better awareness, routine protective details, hardening of physical targets, or emplacement of an antiaircraft missile atop a center of government. Counterterrorism, by contrast, includes much more proactive options and operations, many of which take the struggle directly to the enemy: examples include removal or sabotage of an infamous terrorist website, sabotage of a weapons supply, rendition, or raids on terrorist encampments.

US security documents of 1984 through 1986 suggested a mild variant to this distinction when they began referring to "active" defense—by correct implication relegating to the category of "passive" most US practices up until the surprising April 1986 bombing of Libya.[9] That military raid proved unusual for the future, not just the past; it was no initiator of a trend; it was no precedent; the like of it would not be employed for another thirteen years (the Clinton administration's 1998 missile strikes on installations in the Sudan and Afghanistan). For the United States, as for nearly all governments around the globe, counterterrorism remained a law-enforcement problem. It was defined that way and treated that way. Only the rise of al Qaeda and its fierce *fatwahs* ignited discussion of a real "war" against terrorism. However analysts proceed, they find that counterterrorism forces do more work in peace, on the training grounds, and in the classrooms than they do in milieus featuring the bloody use of arms and violent shock. Preparation, intelligence collection and analysis, cultural and political awareness education, and other undramatic duties prevail. Or at least they did for most North Atlantic Treaty Organization members up to the start of hostilities in Afghanistan (October 2001) and Iraq (March 2003).

Reservations Against Using Force

There are evident and myriad reasons that democracies are disinclined to use force against terrorism—even when it comes from abroad. One, settlement of disputes by means other than arms, is, for many, at the heart of the democratic ideal. Two, terrorism is normally and should normally be a responsibility for police, experts in minimal use of force, not martial experts trained to kill. Thus, the elaborate "turnover" procedures are used twice in each case when a military unit assumes tactical control of a terrorist incident within most democratic societies—a very deliberate legal action suspends civil authority, and another takes it back as soon as possible. Three, excess is possible and even likely given how danger and violence can escalate. Use of excessive force concerns all citizens and may alienate many. Invariably, use of force brings lawsuits and recriminations. This is closely related to a fourth reason for reluctance to use force: legitimacy. Legitimacy is critical to civil government, and even a single excess in use of force has sometimes discredited years of good and normal law enforcement work and management of problems. Five, once heavy deployments of force, or use of force, delegitimate an elected government, these may serve the extreme minorities. Their propagandists are gratified; their militants feel vindicated and encouraged. Overall violence might increase, rather than be tamped down, by martial action.

Excesses of force, spurred by terrorism worries, have profoundly embarrassed many a good government in recent years. After 11 September 2001, for example, the United States worked hard to train and deploy sky marshals, rebuilding a program that began for good reasons and was let to dwindle away to mere tokenism. But in December 2005 an unarmed man, probably afflicted with schizophrenia or related mental illness, raced about on an aircraft and approach ramp until he was shot dead by skittish security forces. These edgy lawmen had apparently not learned from a tragedy five months earlier in the London "Tube." There, Metropolitan Police made lethal errors in identifying a suspect and misassessing his intentions. Piling on him in the subway tunnel, officers discharged five rounds into his head. The first of these stories, in the United States, has been forgotten; the second collected press attention for years, haunting the British public and policing establishment.[10]

If individuals may rattle police officers and more specialized counterterrorism experts, armed groups more easily do so. Religious and racial minority status is a guaranteed "stress enhancer." The long story of difficult relations between American police officers and black militants is replete with illustrations. These include the Black Panthers, leftists who armed themselves heavily and enunciated a doctrine of "defense of the black community" vis-à-vis predominantly white US urban policing forces. Many Panthers died in shoot-outs with police; some fled to Cuba or Algeria; others abandoned armed struggle. May 1985 brought crisis to Philadelphia, Pennsylvania, where a black activist group calling itself MOVE fortified a building and made of it a compound, collected arms, and acted belligerently toward the whole neighborhood. A disastrous operation by skill-free authorities saw the building burned and the city sued for damages.[11] The experience is doubtless not forgotten by authorities now observing al Fuqra. Jamaat al Fuqra is a black Muslim (Sunni) sect, founded by Sheik Mubarak Ali Jilani Hashemi[12] during a 1980 visit to New York City. There are at least several hundred members in the United States today, in as many as thirty-five encampments. Some send money to the sheik in Lahore, Pakistan; some travel to Pakistan for indoctrination or prayer. There are al Fuqra centers in Philadelphia, Baltimore, Tuscon, Denver, and even Canada; headquarters are said to be in Hancock, New York. The group's doctrine is to "purify Islam through violence," and in Colorado and other states al Fuqra "Soldiers of Allah" committed crimes, or even murder. One member was arrested in the mass-lethality terrorist plots that frightened New York City in 1993.[13] Yet, apparently, US authorities have taken little to no concrete action—perhaps because it has been some time since a sect member has been caught in violent acts. The bombing record of 1979 to 1990 has not been continued, for whatever reasons.[14]

Planned Inadequacy, Extremes of Restraint:
The US Sky Marshal Program

The Federal Air Marshal Service places armed experts aboard some flights with the mission to "detect, deter and defeat hostile acts."[15] The program was begun by President Richard Nixon and known as the Sky Marshal Program. So why were there no air marshals on any of the four flights hijacked on 9/11?

Air piracy began a few decades after air travel began. Skyjackings, often for political reasons, occurred as early as the late 1950s—Cuba was a favorite destination for US skyjackers.

Israel responded the earliest to air piracy, as El Al was one common tactical target of attackers, especially George Habash of the Popular Front for the Liberation of Palestine (PFLP). In 1970, when two Arabs seized a flight, Israeli guards shot one and arrested one. In 1972, security forces uniformed as aircraft maintenance crew retook a captured airliner, killing two PFLP terrorists and saving ninety-seven passengers in a complex, dangerous, and brilliant assault.

But the American program was doomed, always facing bureaucratic resistors, cost-cutters, and, occasionally, experts with dissident opinion.

The Federal Bureau of Investigation tried to kill the little program, according to the National Security Council's leading terrorism expert of the 1990s, Richard A. Clarke. "The Bureau was concerned that if an aircraft were hijacked, any Marshals on board would just get in the way of the FBI's Hostage Rescue Team [HRT], which was trained to seize a hijacked aircraft." But, rejoined Clarke, the aircraft would have to have landed first.[16] A marshal might conceivably help get the plane down safely. Certainly the plane would have to be landed safely and in a place assessable to the FBI before its HRT could do anything but negotiate over radios, and suicide artists would never open negotiations.

Other experts had their own considered reasons for opposing a serious air marshal program. Fears of a gunfight starting at 30,000 feet put off many who might be expected to approve the arming of pilots and marshals. Critics of the air marshal concept include a top Marine Corps expert, who held to his views even after 9/11.[17]

The result of all this careful argument, indolence, and saving of money was that no more than "a few dozen" marshals were deployed each day[18] on US carriers before 11 September 2001. The Federal Aviation Administration had (and the Transportation Safety Administration now uses) elaborate mental gymnastics to place the handful available on the most endangered air routes. But this would not be enough to deter terrorists' planning.

Citizens might imagine that everything has changed. But they may be wrong. If press reports are accurate, at best 5 percent of US aircraft are staffed by an armed officer or pilot. Pilots can now legally carry a gun, and some do. But silliness still survives. Hundreds of federal air marshal service agents work on the ground, in offices, as on the Joint Terrorism Task Force teams, and at airports. Few actually are in the air. Three years after 9/11, readers of the *Washington Times* learned that due to internal regulations, TSA marshals were held to strict dress and grooming codes that made them all look just like, well, air marshals.[19] In 2006, a directive by Mr. Dana Brown, Director of the Federal Air Marshal Service, relaxed this code covering appearances.[20]

Intelligence expert William Stephenson wrote in his 1977 book on the hijacking to Entebbe: "the public is far ahead of governments in wishing to arm against the new danger" of air piracy.[21] One suspects that if the public were offered the option of tripling the number of "covered" flights for an across-the-board passenger tax of ten dollars, they would overwhelmingly approve. But no one ever asks.

Hostage Rescues

Rescue operations are among the most challenging and intriguing of all forcible counterterrorist actions. They sometimes require something of the hitting power of a raid; they are as complicated as a rendition on a large scale. The dangers inherent in large-scale rescues are so evident that far more such operations have been conceived and planned than executed. Nonetheless, review of many cases of recent decades yields grounds for confidence: They may succeed, and there are basic principles of planning and action that help enhance the chances of success. A hostage rescue can become a counterterrorist triumph. Among the instructive cases are two air rescues—one forgotten, one better known: the Congo (Zaire) problem handled by Belgium and the United States (1964); and the Entebbe, Uganda, problem solved by Israel (1976).

"Dragon Rouge"[22] was as flamboyant as its name but now is rarely mentioned in contemporary accounts of counterterrorism. Four years after Congolese independence from Belgium, Simbas (lions) of the antigovernment Popular Army of Liberation (APL) led by General Nicholas Olenga initiated the problem in August 1964. This unfolded a thousand miles inland from the Atlantic Ocean, and alongside the Congo River, in the rebel capital of Stanleyville, now called Kisangani. Within the Democratic Republic of Congo these forces massacred some seventy Europeans and captured the US consulate, taking thirty American hostages. The case was burdened by colonial history and burned with race tensions too: the hostages, alive and dead, were white; the insurrectional APL was all black. And the hostage-barricade situation went protracted, lasting 111 days.

Belgium had the solemn duty to extract its countrymen. Just as important, it had the resolve to do so—despite the US ambassador's advice against a military operation. But ultimately the United States provided transport aircraft and pilots, and the small North Atlantic Treaty Organization country prepared a joint air-ground operation. All began 17 November with a flight of fourteen C-130 transports. They left Klein Brogel, Belgium, for Stanleyville by way of Moron, Spain; Las Palmas, Canary Islands; Ascension Island; and Kamina, Republic of Congo to drop 545 Belgian paratroopers at the airfield nearest Stanleyville with its captives. Operational secrecy was lost along the way, but the fighting power of the Belgians remained formidable, from a Congolese guerrilla's point of view. During all this, a ground force marched swiftly eastward through the Congo to link up with the Paras. The column moved at night, in the rain, amidst fighting; commander Frederick Van de Waele and a famed mercenary Michael Hoare had doubts about the progress and the prospects.

But by 26 November, Belgians were fighting their way, street by street, into Stanleyville. The rebels retreated slowly while massacring hostages—always a grave risk known to intervening forces. Some two thousand Europeans and other hostages were however saved; most were moved to the secured airport and flown away on 27 November. A wild parade in Brussels greeted returnees. Coached by President Lyndon Johnson, all US officials and air crew remained quiet—"in the background."[23] US silence included nothing of mercenary Mike Hoare and the "Wild Geese" whose expertise was central to saving innumerable hostages. Remarkably, only three Belgian soldiers died in the complex and extended operation; seven more were wounded. It was a stunning national success for the Belgians.

It was fully twelve years before a similar counterterrorist operation would unfold—but when it did, the parallels were striking. At Entebbe in 1976, Israel took a flight of air transports, over immense distances, landed in a most hostile environment, killed terrorists, rescued masses of hostages by air evacuation, and suffered precious few casualties. Boldness, speed, and skill were at a premium, and their successful combination was rewarded, and measured by historians, under such rubrics as risk-taking, public morale, and repudiation of the methods of terrorism.

PFLP air piracy occasioned the events. George Habash's team of four hijackers included people close to "Carlos the Jackal"; two were Euro-leftists, and two were Palestinians; all were to die in the operation.[24] The skyjackers set out on Air France flight 139 leaving Athens, Greece, already discolored by a reputation for laxity on air security. Taking control of the crew and plane, with its scores of Israelis and some 175 other hostages, the four-person gun team announced itself as the "Che Guevara Group" of the "Gaza Brigade" of the PFLP.[25] They had an ally on the ground in Idi Amin, coup-leader and now Ugandan head of government. His army shielded the party at Entebbe. Hostages were kept in the main hall of the terminal and were divided by race to accentuate the terror for the Jews. Unlike in the Congo, no one was executed—but that threat remained palpable.

Meanwhile in Israel a special air reconnaissance unit planned and built a mock-up of the hangar and rehearsed rescue concepts. The operation would require airplanes that could reach some 2,200 miles, action on ground held by a hostile army force, and safe loading and evacuation of lumbering jet aircraft with long runway requirements.

Israel accomplished all this with surprise and deception. They knew that Mr. Amin moved about in a black Mercedes and so acquired the same model. Once the first plane had landed, at the far end of a runway, this "VIP car" rolled down the transport's ramp and drove right up to the main hall. Some Ugandans did not react, and those who did were shot down. The surprise bought key moments and placed the first Israelis inside the main building quickly. From the C-130s flowed more men, overwhelming the confused indigenous force in the night. Three minutes after the Israelis landed, most of the terrorists were dead and nearly all hostages were secured. These included the Air France crew who heroically had turned aside the invitation to escape, staying with their passengers instead. Casualties included three hostages, and one soldier: terminal building assault force commander[26] Jonathan Netanyahu, brother of a future prime minister of Israel.

At Entebbe, so many citizens were rescued, and with such audacity, that it made for a strategic triumph. The nation was elated; the armed forces were vindicated in their dedication to readiness and intense training. Success pushed to the background certain earlier failures in countering terrorism—as at Ma'alot, where a school had been captured by Palestinian nihilists and retaken with great bloodshed. Entebbe seemed a kind of bookend to the gory Olympics in Munich; it competed a cycle in government learning. Now, governments might not merely take precautions, as against air piracy, they might promise to recapture "lost" civilians. Germany, for example, was supremely well prepared, and would prove it only one year later, retaking the Lufthansa jet hijacked to Mogadishu, Somalia, in October 1977.

Germany's readiness in 1977 was the result of the fallout from the Munich Olympics of 1972. The Games were a disaster in part because the modern German republic was deliberately decentralized by its creators, and no national special force could be called upon to deal with the well-armed and trained Palestinian terrorists. Bavarian police—earnest men untrained for such encounters—had to suffice. The messy legacy of Furstenfeldbruck Airport in September of 1972 was to be much more than lethal tragedy; it commenced creation of German counterterrorism capabilities, from the "nearly nonexistent" to among Europe's very best. The *Grenzschultzgruppe 9* (GSG-9) emerged under the command of Colonel Ulrich Wegener,[27] from the Border Police—it is deliberately not an army unit. Initially it worked with and learned from the British Special Air Service and other expert forces. Soon it would teach, as well; GSG-9 is one of the units the US Army studied before creating Delta Force, for example.

Andreas Baader and the Red Army Faction (RAF) coleader Gudrun Ensslin were in jail on 13 October 1977 when a Lufthansa Boeing was hijacked en route from Majorca to Frankfurt. The plan was a joint one by PFLP and RAF—the latter had advanced connections to Iraq and Lebanon, not just East Bloc states. The terrorists' mission had been to free RAF principals and other named convicts and political personalities. A fanatic and sadist named Zohair Akache, who had murdered top Yemenis and also operated in London, led the team of hijackers, and personally murdered pilot Jürgen Schumann. By the time GSG-9 had to act, it knew some of the details, for just months before the Border Police unit had worked out a kind of verbal code by which German pilots could pass along vital information.

If the terrorists had their Middle East connections, so too did the German government. When Lufthansa flight 181 landed in Somalia with its eighty-two passengers plus crew, local authorities proved willing to let German commandos follow. This was vital; Cyprus had shamefully rejected such a German request when the jet was stopped at Larnaca.[28] Twenty-eight handpicked GSG-9 men disgorged from a jet identical to the hijacked airliner and made a stealthy approach in the dark on the night of 17–18 October. With listening devices, they established the whereabouts of the four terrorists. They broke into the aircraft, deployed "flash-bang" grenades to stun, and shot the terrorists, killing three and wounding the fourth.

Deception was used at several levels. In communications, Bonn signaled that the RAF hostages in Stammheim would be released, so in Somalia, the terrorists were awaiting good news. Second, Somali Rangers performed well in an ancillary role on the ground at the airport, creating a timely distraction as the German GSG-9 made the critical move from their airliner to the hijacked plane. But the earlier effort to pass under the gunmen's noses in ground crew uniforms did not deceive. Arabs would have expected Somalis in ground crews, or perhaps British (who used to occupy Somalia); German accents disturbed them, and the team leader fired upon the fake "aircrew" with his pistol. Nor did all else in "Operation Feuerzauber" go perfectly. The assault team's ladders were too short. One airplane door resisted the experts' efforts to force it open for agonizing minutes. The German commandos also needed the help of sheer luck: Doorways inside the aircraft had been fitted with Semtex *plastique,* but it never detonated. And two grenades were deployed by terrorists, but aircraft seats largely absorbed their explosions.[29]

Impressive tactics that rendered all four terrorists immobile and a long operational reach yielded within one half-hour a strategic-level success that deserves study and restudy three decades later.[30] Many assume that the "Fall of the Wall" in 1990 killed the Red Army Faction. But the hopes of many in the RAF died on that much-earlier day, 18 October 1977. Suicides followed within hours inside Stammheim Prison near Stuttgart. Baader, Ensslin, and Jan Carl Raspe all took their own lives;[31] Ulrike Meinhof had already committed suicide a year earlier. A third generation of RAF would still operate in Germany, but without real success. They were all that remained to surrender after the communist states collapsed. The tenth of April 1992 is the date of the formal document in which these hold-outs for communism admitted they had no warm relations with the German proletariat, and their violent tricks were not strong enough to reach the average German.[32] The ill repute of the last of the Baader-Meinhofs makes a counterpoint to the wild popularity with which Colonel Wegener and his German police were received upon return from Somalia. The success of counterterrorist methods, skillfully deployed and ending in deaths of terrorists, not their captives, was a profound lesson. It effaced the shame of German politicians who had appeased terrorism, or failed to save hostage Hanns-Martin Schleyer.[33] The success also inspired Europe—the nascent counterterrorist forces had a valuable new lesson.

After 1977, GSG-9 went on to perform scores of further operations. Since 1996 its capabilities have been supplemented by the *Kommando Spezialkraft* (KSK), an army unit under the Special Forces Command. KSK is designed for operations beyond German borders, and has seen and done much in Afghanistan. GSG-9, while still focused primarily on German matters, has had much work to do in Iraq and conducted year-2008 operations in Sudan and off the Somali coast, where Berlin often felt need of the elite unit's skills at hostage rescue.[34]

More recent air pirates who ended in spectacular failure were well handled by France; a fifty-four hour drama ended in late 1994 in successful and forceful intervention on the ground in Marseilles. France was a country alleged to be "appeasing" terrorists in the 1980s. But France had since 1974 possessed other options, including a prepared police unit called the National Gendarmes Intervention Group (GIGN). The top operator of GIGN, then-Major Denis Favier,[35] had a brilliant reputation from schools and the field; he was fully ready to handle the provocations of the Armed Islamic Group, GIA, initially an armed wing of the political Front for Islamic Salvation.

The four GIA gunmen brazenly entered the Air France jet in Algiers dressed as uniformed security personnel.[36] False uniforms are now a classic deception technique of insurgents and terrorists alike. Their other actions were likewise scripted from past international terror incidents. They demanded the freeing of jailed colleagues. They used the black art of alternately terrorizing—and then reassuring—passengers. They executed two hostages early on to prove seriousness to potential negotiators. And they separated hostages by nationality (Algerians from non-Algerians) to enhance the effects of terror.[37]

Favier's GIGN flew out of its Satory base near Paris in an Airbus identical to the victim aircraft, and laid over to drill and rehearse "breaking and entering" schemes at Palma de Mallorcoa Spain. Barred from Algiers, they met up with Air France flight 8969 on an airstrip at Marignane Airport, a Marseilles suburb, where it touched down for fuel. "Attendants" (GIGN personnel in airline uniforms) serviced the plane, studying the hijackers up close and perhaps leaving listening devices. What they learned was yet more disturbing—the cockpit contained twenty sticks of dynamite; the terrorists' fuel demand was two and a half times what the scheduled flight on to Paris required; and their talk suggested they might blow up the plane. This would shower "The City of Light" with flaming wreckage. It all forecast the New York attacks of seven years later.[38] As negotiations continued and the terrorists demanded liftoff, GIGN was hidden nearby.

The French police unit moved in on three mobile staircases, standard airport equipment. Compelled to act in daylight, they knew their black "camouflage" gear offered no cover. When they broke the locks and forced the doors, they met "a wall of gunfire" from the terrorists. Fortunately the homemade grenades of GIA usually failed, while the commandos' stun grenades worked. After a firefight lasting seventeen minutes—or a quarter of an hour more than they could have wished—the gunmen were dead and most passengers safely descended on slides. GIGN suffered many wounds, but almost all the airline customers escaped with mental trauma, not physical damage.[39]

Prospects of "A Dutch Approach"

The final series of large-scale rescue operations to be discussed occurred in Holland. In the 1970s, the Netherlands faced hot criticism and occasionally violent tactics from separatists known as South Moluccans. The militants were Asian Dutch, living in Holland; at one time Holland had been their colonial ruler, and now, living in Holland, they sought official Dutch state intervention against the government of Indonesia.[40] They terrorized entirely innocent and somewhat unsuspecting ordinary Dutch citizens to advance this cause—an independent "Republic of the South Moluccas."[41] Here was an archetype of terrorism—the illicit use of violence, against the innocent, to reach a larger audience and affect the policy of another state. But they underestimated their opponent—as perhaps Islamist terrorists would later in Holland. The government in The Hague undertook a lengthy counterterrorist campaign that broke the will of the terrorists and yet well preserved the lives and liberties of Dutch citizens. "The Dutch Approach" came to be a term of art in Europe; it meant combining patience, resilience, and the attritional powers of protraction—with use of force only after nearly-endless negotiations. But it has almost been forgotten that, indeed, they would use force when compelled to do so.

The first important terrorist incident came in mid-1970 in Wassenaar, a suburb of The Hague, and at a predictable location: the embassy of Indonesia. A guard there was murdered in a successful seizure of the building; over thirty people were taken hostage by even more south Moluccans. Foreign Affairs Minister Joseph Luns rushed to the scene and personally negotiated—erring at one point by coming within shooting range of the hostage-takers. The event ended in surrender of the terrorists. Perhaps observers believed peace was restored, as the following years were mostly quiet. But if terrorism had failed, it had not been discredited or disavowed. And Ronald Janse of Utrecht University suggests this attack "shattered"[42] hopes of the Dutch government to liaise between the "Republic of South Moluccas" separatists and the government of Indonesia. And yet the Dutch government also had found that firmness and patience could be mixed in response to such a hostage-barricade situation.

From April 1974 through all of 1978 came the more intense and interlinked terrorist events that drove a change in the gentle Dutch temperament. Arson and other attacks were followed by a plot to kidnap the Dutch Queen, who had dared to speak for the independence of Suriname without doing the same for South Molucca. If anyone doubted there was now a severe threat to the state, this ended on 2 December 1975. Seven armed Moluccans boarded a train and, between Wijster and Beilen,[43] hijacked it and took hostages. As this drama unfolded, another terrorist group supported the action by overtaking the Indonesian consulate in Amsterdam. Protracted sieges followed on both sites. But there were steady diplomatic efforts, including work with Moluccan intermediaries, while the government stalled on actual concessions. All this yielded a calm result. The idea of the governmental "crisis center" for such an incident caught European eyes and would take hold on the continent. "The Dutch Approach" seemed to be sound—even if it could not bring back life to the train engineer and two hostages, all murdered.[44]

When the terrorists went to jail, Holland breathed a sigh of relief. But there were no far-reaching legal results or dramatic political effects. Prison sentences were stiffer than in the 1970 case in which Justice all but sheathed her sword; the newer batch of terrorists were given terms that were adequate without being onerous. The criminal code remained the main barrier to these new public crimes; the law was not revised despite some legislators who wanted new tools for opposing terrorism. As some officials saw a connection between the terrorism and legitimate grievances, the Dutch government did make efforts at dialogue with the Moluccan community. Certain elements of a grand strategy approach had thus begun to emerge, but without serious conviction on the question of force. The lessons of Munich 1972 were present. Holland began establishment of the *Bijzondere Bijstand Eenheid* (BBE) or Special Assistance Units, a company-size force for close combat, within their corps of Marines.[45] These were to prove vital when negotiations and patience were proving inadequate, as in a 1974 case of a prison insurrection led by a jailed Palestinian terrorist.

Unsatisfied that Holland would not make demands on Jakarta, South Moluccan terrorists unfolded another double operation on 23 May 1977. Fifty-four people became hostages in another train-jacking, this time near De Punt and Assen. After the nine terrorists released forty hostages, the rest settled into a lengthy siege. Not far away was the second target—a children's school. Clearly the Moluccans believed that forceful recapture at either site would now be beyond Dutch capabilities—for the same reason that, a decade later, separating western hostages in Beirut deterred attempts to storm any given imprisonment zone: Few governments are bold enough to "save" one group if it prompts murder at other sites. However, taking schoolchildren has its own unique risks—starting with loss of all public appeal. Palestinians had committed such a crime at Ma'alot only three years before, and some of the Moluccans had taken Palestinian training. The gunmen in the May 1977 crises also dealt in a smooth and practiced way with government negotiators, foiling their efforts. By killing no one, they did not trigger a forceful response. Many of the children fell ill and were released. But both sieges dragged along.

Royal Dutch Marines acquired a duplicate train and began rehearsing a "take down" on it at Gilze Rijen Air Force Base, close by. Day 20, or 11 June 1977, was portentous. At De Punt, combat swimmers and other reconnaissance assets approached the train from a proximate canal. They planted listening devices that provided good data on how the hostages were bearing up and where the nine captors slept or stood guard. Some forty to fifty Marines with night vision goggles made their own approach and hid themselves. British experts on scene coached the Marines on the use of stun grenades but the Dutch took another tactic: A flight of six combat jets suddenly dropped in just over the train. To this disorienting thunder[46] was added rifle fire from the sizeable ground force, and a forced entry of the cars with frame charges. Two-thirds of the terrorists died; there were eleven other casualties, few fatal. "It was a brilliant little operation . . . a nicely balanced mixture of psychology, force, and technology," commented Christopher Dobson and Ronald Payne, in one of their terrorism books[47] of those years. The nearby school at Bovensmilde was assaulted at the same time—just before 5 a.m. An armored personnel carrier went through a wall, and Royal Marines quickly subdued the groggy terrorists and freed hostages.

A last demonstration of South Moluccan terrorism was to come a year later, and it would confirm the rise of security forces and the decline of the prospects of hostage-takers in Holland. Three men of a self-described "Moluccan Suicide Squad" occupied the main government building of Assen, capital of Drenthe province, on 13 March 1978. Setting aside the obvious point that successful building seizures have usually involved more than three gunmen, these terrorists also showed ill appreciation for the effect of murdering a hostage. Such acts, often done early on, are intended to "show seriousness" about threats of greater harm. But to a much-provoked government it may signal the time for ending chatting on the phone. Counterterrorism's leading Dutch psychiatrist, D. Mulder, tried to manage the talks but the government stepped past him after a hostage was murdered. Even under "the Dutch Approach," negotiations and waiting can only go so far; now the baton passed to the special assistance unit of the Marines. They infiltrated the government building, and then stormed the hostage-holding area while an external force also assaulted. Barely one day after the standoff commenced, it was over. Five of sixty-nine hostages were wounded, but the three terrorists were captured, convicted, and destined for fifteen year sentences. Thus ended Moluccan terrorism within Holland. Sectarian fighting would still be known in Indonesia,[48] but the Dutch successfully defeated their indigenous problem.

Drama in Lima, 1996–1997

Peru provides a second country study for masterful resolution of a hostage barricade crisis. The Lima residence of the Japanese ambassador was taken over in 1996 by Tupac Amaru Revolutionary Movement (MRTA), the Castroite competitor for power in Peru's guerrilla underworld against a larger insurgency, the Maoists of Sendero Luminoso. Both groups used terror freely and fed off the drug trade. MRTA's usual targets were the government, the military, and multinational corporations. A classic treble motive for the present case, an official residence seizure, was freeing imprisoned comrades while garnering publicity in a stab at the Peruvian state. They were to fail—and in a more violent way than did Abimael Guzman, chief of Sendero, who a few years earlier had been quietly arrested and led to jail.

Tupac Amaru's second-generation leader Victor Polay Campos had been jailed, escaped, and been re-jailed. He and hundreds of comrades were hoping to win relief in the 1996 Japanese residence operation. Leader Nestor Cerpa and thirteen other MRTA males and females entered the grounds at a time when an embassy party had eight hundred dignitaries on hand, including the brother of the Peruvian president, the chief of the very police agency charged with antiterrorism, and senior military officers and politicians. MRTA knew these numbers were too great to manage and so, having enjoyed initial success and wide effect, gradually released groups of victims. Of course, each such release sought to make the terrorists appear reasonable, and each such release became a "media event"—given the scores of reporters and cameramen who took up positions in the conflict zone.

The formidable politician Alberto Fujimori was president and stood between the MRTA's ambitions and its chance of full success. Although he was involved directly in protracted negotiations, it later appeared he had no intention of making concessions, and used his time over the many months of siege to prepare an end to Tupac Amaru's presumptions. Strategic-level intelligence work included taking allies' advice and support; tactical preparations included smuggling in sophisticated devices that literally reached hostages' hands. For example, a microphone was embedded in a Bible, so that an imprisoned admiral[49] who paced about daily as if in prayerful reverie could murmur directly into the book, informing the government of precise details of the situation within the residence. Several electronic pagers were likewise smuggled in, and could transmit messages. Such tricks did not just boost morale and communicate vital information; they unquestionably saved many hostages' lives.

As intelligence work proceeded, so did military preparations. Peru built a mock-up of the residence, on a military base, and far from listening ears a joint armed force rehearsed rescue operations and tested controlled explosions. Years of work against guerrillas in rural and urban Peru had hardened the commandos, who included the country's gifted graduates of the US Navy's SEAL training. They were brought to a high pitch, both of skill and psychological intensity, before gathering in tunnels cut under the building for several dry runs. Above them, in the main hall of the official residence, an odd ritual had taken hold: Each day the hostage-takers played football for their exercise. This left too many terrorists together, in too dangerous a place, on too predictable a schedule.

On the 126th day of captivity for the eighty-plus hostages, Peru's commandos detonated C-4 charges under the building, killing six terrorists and paralyzing more with shock. In other tunnels, ninety commandos heard *Entrando al bravo* (Forward with Courage) and broke into the open to rush the various building entrances. As surviving terrorists ran to execute several high-value hostages, government forces hunted them down, all the while dealing with emplaced charges and rolling grenades—two of the terrorists' measures against counterattack. Admiral Luis Giampietri, who had trained many of these men, was one of the hostages they saved on 22 April 1997. He called his memoir *41 Seconds to Freedom* due to the swiftness of the commandos' entry. The innocents' freedom was purchased with the lives of two commandos, and the wounds of another seventeen. While Admiral Giampietri went on to be vice president of his country, the larger celebrity of the day, President Fujimori, fared badly, as did his intelligence chief Vladimir Montesinos. From prestigious perches, these two fell soon to corruption charges having to do with improper political influences. The year 2008 found Fujimori in exile in Japan, and Montesinos in jail—the same high-security prison that holds terrorists Victor Polay Campos and Abimael Guzman.

Are There "Principles" to Use of Force in Counterterrorism?

When Peru cracked open the building barricaded by MRTA, the government's explosives sounded the end of the small Castroite group. Its twenty-three-year run all but died on the spot, where property damage was so grave that remnants were bulldozed. The swift resolution of a complicated problem on that day in 1997 was another reminder of the realities: Forceful options must always be present when dealing with terrorism. The use of a clandestine agent, a police SWAT team, or even a military unit can in fact be decisive in certain cases. It is naïve to say otherwise, although more than a few have; those voices tend to depict resort to force as immoral, or as proof of policy failure, or as a stupid invitation to a worsening "spiral of violence." It need not be. Terrorism is by definition the use or threat of force in illegal ways, usually in peacetime; a legitimate democratic government cannot surrender its own force options in the face of such a challenge. Indeed, it may be an unwise governor whose only thought on the topic is that "Force can only be employed when every other option has been tried unsuccessfully." Such a posture is a blunder in strategy; announcing such a posture opens up a lengthy waiting period in which the terrorist group is invited to proceed in whatever ways it may choose.

So, if force may be advisable in some circumstances, how should governors and police officials and military leaders think about its exercise? This essay has not sought to address the many and involved strategic-level problems of policy, strategy, and law, or even to reprise the varieties of force that may suit a given problem. These might be portrayed as a continuum, in which, beginning with the least forceful means, the available elements include and are not limited to: antiterrorist training and posture; use of policing powers such as arrest; deployments for deterrence; patrols and other acts that garner intelligence and "show the flag" of local government and of powers; covert action such as sabotage of terrorist weapons stashes, equipment, or property; use of combat forces to displace large violent organizations and their training facilities and command structures; and war against a "repeat offender" state sponsor of terrorism. Instead, this essay restricts itself to dealing with specialized small forces, acting against terrorist units, at times when the counterterrorist country is not at war (actions in low-intensity conflict or peacetime).

Are there operational principles for using special units against terrorists? There may well be—however hard they are to lay down in print.[50] One of the more successful efforts to identify and describe principles for using special forces is the work of William McRaven. As a student at the Naval Post-Graduate School in Monterey, California, he grappled with what history seems to advise, based on famous special operations of the mid-twentieth century, such as Italy's manned torpedo attack in the harbor of Alexandria, Egypt, in December 1941; the German rescue of their ally Benito Mussolini two years later; the failed US effort to seize POWs from North Vietnamese hands at Son Tay; and the Israeli operation at Entebbe, Uganda.[51] McRaven's study added intellectual discipline and backbone to his many personal military experiences. As he rose in rank within the US Navy SEALS, McRaven's thoughts developed. His book *Spec Ops* describes the beau ideal as "A simple plan, carefully concealed, repeatedly executed with surprise, speed, and purpose." He enunciated six principles for this sort of controlled violence: Purpose, Simplicity, Repetition, Surprise, Speed, and Security.[52]

Purpose means a clear understanding of mission objectives, and a commitment to seeing them achieved, according to McRaven. Simplicity aims at plans and operations that do not bog down in the intricacies and frictions of large martial enterprises. Repetition means many tactical rehearsals, until operatives know their own roles cold and can also step in to other roles—if things go wrong, or if chance is an unkind mistress. Surprise, often hard to attain, is a powerful advantage—in the simple arrest of a perpetrator, as well as at all levels of war. Speed does not suit all aspects of counterterrorism, but during actual forcible operations it is frequently essential, as any expert at raids or rescues would attest. Security is about covering one's intentions and actions during the preparation phase, to bar the enemy from anticipating an impending move, or seeing it begin to unfold.

An analyst should notice what McRaven omits. One measure of that is the classic nine principles of war listed by historian J. F. C. Fuller and subsequently adapted by many armies as doctrine. "Mass" goes unmentioned by McRaven, not surprisingly. But also "missing" are the phrases "Unity of Command," "Maneuver," and "Economy of Force." *Spec Ops* may well embrace such military advantages in its own way. But unconventional war also may have, and deserve, many of its own principles. Carl von Clausewitz did not work to discover more than a few of these; his focus was elsewhere. Of the classical authors on war, Sun Tzu is perhaps the better teacher on our narrow topic; both terrorists and counterterrorists can learn much from study of the twenty-four-hundred-year-old *Art of War*.[53]

Emphasizing Intelligence and Initiative

The best list of possible principles of forcible counterterrorism must surely include intelligence. It is as important as surprise, and without intelligence there is no point in speed. While American military officers are prone to joke about "intel failures" dooming good missions, nearly all successful missions depend upon good intelligence—"intel successes."

Planning the Entebbe rescue in 1976 was hardly akin to planning the storming of beaches in Normandy in 1944, but in some respects the intelligence demands were similar. Lives would be saved or squandered by attention to details. How long is that landing strip, and will it be free of flood water, or barriers erected by a ground party? Will that roof support a landing, and if so, by how many men? What might be the subdivisions in the floor plan of building 2-B on map X? Are its walls of stone or the shoddiest of plaster and lathe? Thousands of such questions dwell in planners' minds, and all seem to demand answers, and many more important ones hover at higher levels of war. So, both for Normandy and Entebbe, intelligence experts went through procedures such as tracking down tourists' still photos and handheld movie film. This was indeed possible: Both beaches and airports are places human beings take many pictures; it was a matter of locating those, in large enough numbers, in short enough time, to create a composite view of detailed quality.

Little to nothing is perfect, especially in the field of intelligence. But to focus on setbacks is to forget how many extraordinary accomplishments there have been, placing the right information in the right hands at the right moment. In the Lima operation, intelligence assets' implanting of listening devices within the barricaded building allowed not merely listening, but transmission; security forces knew an amazing amount of what went on, month after month, on all floors of Japan's official residence. In the Philippine Army's pursuit of Abu Sayyaf, intelligence was able to introduce a device, or track a heat source, and thus follow a delivery right to an elusive leader of the terror group. The same intense offensive spirit was characteristic of the army troopers who relentlessly pursued the Abu Sayyaf cadre in the most difficult landscapes until most of the key figures had been eliminated. They killed the terrorists' commander in 1998 and then his brother and successor Khadaffy Janjalani in 2006; they captured or killed scores of other members in 2007;[54] since then, much less has been heard of this once-cocky ally of al Qaeda. Varieties of electronic intelligence were no doubt key to the Russian killing of Chechen Dzhokhar M. Dudayev in 1996, the assassination by Predator of an al Qaeda leader named Qaed Salim Sinan al-Harethi and confreres in a car on a road in Yemen in 2002, and the Jordanian-American tracking and killing of Abu Musab al-Zarqawi in Iraq in 2006.

Intelligence is also what allows for deception; without the former, the latter seems impossible to plan and to stage. Governments—not just terrorists—should be capable of trickery, if it leads to arrests and saves lives. Governments and negotiators have lied to bloody-handed gunmen about whether the plane has enough fuel, why a bus for the airport is not arriving for yet another hour, and many other unrealities. Part of Germany's success in the October 1977 operation in Somalia was in tricking the jailed RAF leaders in Stammheim into believing Bonn was negotiating with the skyjackers in place of planning the storming of the Lufthansa jet. Clear intelligence allowed a remarkable deception of a FARC leader in the rescue of Ingrid Betancourt and her comrades in July 2008. Innumerable messages passed, over the preceding days, and one false note in his delicate correspondence by the Colombian managers of the crisis—who were feigning status of another FARC commander—would have ruined the entire theater piece. The delicacy of such work, the prospect for disappointment, and the elaborate effort deception demands combine as a reason Carl von Clausewitz was reluctant to endorse deception.[55] But in counterterrorism, at least, it has often worked, and it should be employed more often than it is.

Intelligence has far wider purposes than the tactical, of course. It is needed for the patient "mapping of the human terrain" in fighting insurgents who freely use terror. This work is essential to, and related to, other efforts (by police, military intelligence, and military aid and contact organizations Americans call "civic action teams") to identify the terrorists and isolate them. In modern history, when counterinsurgent forces have failed at such granular mapping, they have often failed strategically as a result. Another strategic demand for good intelligence arises when governments contemplate negotiations. The apparent resolution of the Irish Republican Army case is but one indicator that negotiations may, in some cases, serve well as a counterterrorist strategy. But here it is vital to decide when to negotiate, and precisely with whom, and to be rather sure about such subjects as the morale of the organization, what weapons it has, or even its financial status. Nor should "talking to terrorists" preclude later using force against them.

As a recent study by Drs. Roy Godson and Richard Shultz Jr. has shown, where government focuses on "intelligence dominance" of the enemy and outperforms him in the human, electronic, video, and other realms of information gathering and management, it is possible to surprise, deceive, and defeat the terrorist organization.[56] Israeli and British campaigns over many years have conclusively proven that a state need not be the victim of the substate actor here. And in 2007–2008, as aging Baader-Meinhof jailbirds were singing for freedom or being freed, it was worth remembering that a police official, Mr. Horst Herold, had used manpower, patience, study, and revolutionary computer profiling to outwit them and, one by one, place them behind bars. Mr. Herold is now largely forgotten, but the German people enjoyed years of peace in part because of his years of effort.

The second change that might be made—if one were turning Admiral McRaven's list of principles of special operations into a list of counterterrorism operations principles—is adding "initiative." J. F. C. Fuller, and others since, have named "The Offensive" as a principle of war. They did so despite the relative strength of good defense (as established by Clausewitz) and the commensurate and evident abuse of offensive spiritedness in World War I's trench battles.

Willingness to take the offensive, or otherwise exercise initiative, is essential to effective counterterrorism for reasons special to that field. Perhaps no democratic society can afford to be endlessly in a state of war, without becoming a thing ugly to itself, or a marvel of an unwanted archetype—what Sparta was among ancient Greeks. For the same reason, a democratic society cannot enslave its citizens to a system of pervasive intrusion and intelligence gathering, citizen against citizen. There are limits to what security can justify and there are clear needs for liberty and privacy in civil society. Nor can a democratic society afford to lay about as terrorist groups build and then choose when and where to attack— that is strategic lunacy and neglects the first duty of good government—defense of the polity. But an alternative emerges. It is an alternative that is morally, legally, and politically defensible, and also quite practicable. Facing a violent enemy, democracy should deploy the intelligence resources necessary to firmly establish its capabilities and accurately identify its vulnerabilities and then move against it smartly.[57]

Just as grand strategy is about much more than force, "initiative" is not necessarily warlike. In negotiations with terrorists, initiative may be welcomed on all sides, or prove key to establishing a healthy agenda, or it might give a government the clear and deserved lead in public positioning vis-à-vis terrorist spokesmen. In US public diplomacy of 2002 and beyond, it is the very paucity of good initiatives that has made the policy so feeble.[58] In international and regional affairs, where a state cojoins with other states against international terrorism, executive initiatives at intelligence exchange and common policing methods, as well as legislative initiatives in rewriting of laws on material support to terrorism are among the many and urgent needs of the present. The point is that government gathers strength for its side and achieves dominance of hardened enemies by frequent renewal of effort and frequent initiative. This is required to carry and convince the polity, and keep morale strong among friendly forces, as surely as it is to keep the terrorist group off balance and ineffective.

After assassinations and bombings struck French and US personnel, embassies, and barracks in Lebanon in 1981–1983, the French government showed much spirit in approaching the United States about joint action against Hezbollah military targets in the Bekaa Valley. This was self-defense after the fact, more than aggressiveness, but it was a good idea. They went on with an air strike even though the United States oddly declined.[59] France then followed, within a few years, with a new legislative package that strongly enhanced the nation's ability to resist terrorism, especially domestically. As a following chapter by Raffenne and Clair shows, these events set Paris on a track of counterterrorism—for which it did not have a strong earlier reputation. Further reforms and continuing nonpartisan governmental moral resolution led to such strategies as preemptive arrests of terrorist conspirators. Not since 1996 has this oft-bloodied capital seen a major terror attack. Initiative in policing, judicial investigations, and intelligence have all contributed to a safer country. And while some European states seemed content to be suffering victims of Somali piracy of recent years, France twice deployed commandos to recapture sea-jacked vessels during 2008.[60] These modest uses of force remind others of the lesson in Thucydides that pirates are likely to rise or fall depending upon navies' work against them.

Rendition is another good example of initiative. When one state declines to extradite a terrorist to a requesting foreign state, sometimes the second state carries out a rendition. Normally this is a covert use of force to extract the terrorism suspect for trial—although on occasion the state of residence may quietly be glad to see an alien criminal go. France may have had Sudanese acquiescence when it rendered "Carlos the Jackal" to Paris. Cleverness and audacity characterized this French enterprise of August 1994. Ilich Ramirez Sanchez was the son of a noted Venezuelan communist, a terrorist operative, and an ally of George Habash's PFLP. He was snatched from Sudanese refuge[61] while under anesthesia for a medical procedure, it is said. Wanted for murdering two police officers in Paris and many other crimes, the once-invulnerable terrorist personality has since been in a French jail. In this case, as in the seizure of Adolf Eichmann by Israeli agents from a suburb of Buenos Aires in 1960, justice was done: A notorious criminal was caught and put on trial. That offers clear warnings to other terrorists and bears good and general effects. For example, a sovereign state that has feted or harbored international terrorists and endures even one rendition by a foreign counterpart may well think twice when, in the future, that state is asked to extradite an infamous political criminal. It is now largely forgotten that American-instigated renditions of drug dealers and terrorists were familiar, if unusual, in the decades before 9/11. US actions since then became muddled by charges of deportation to third countries and torture. This does not change the principle. Rendition is not necessarily a shameless attack on international law. When a well-known terrorist, on whom government holds a thick evidence file, would never come to trial and will not be extradited from safe haven, rendering the person for trail might be a forceful but reasonable response of an unusual sort.

A US strategic initiative that set international terrorism back was the late 2001 invasion of Afghanistan. Previously it was nearly impossible to find international security analysts arguing for such a course of action, though all knew of Osama bin Laden's presence there with many other "internationalists." Conventional wisdom was locked on the idea that the British Empire had failed in Afghanistan, and anyone who had forgotten should have been schooled again during the Soviets' later decade of misery there. Instead, the CIA and Department of Defense in Washington boldly assembled and implemented an effective plan that worked well with NATO forces but also many Afghan opponents of terrorism and Talibanism. They swept the country nearly clean in a few months, buying precious years for the elected government to get established and become effective, while locking up or killing hundreds of al Qaeda men and allies. Only after 2004 did insurgency begin to recover any strength.

It thus appears that certain principles for successful use of force in countering terrorism do emerge from analysis and from contemporary history. "Intelligence" and "Initiative" well deserve their place in considerations about whether and how to proceed with dangerous and politically charged instruments. This essay suggests that an optimal list of operational principles for good counterterrorism would be "Purpose, Intelligence, Initiative, Simplicity, Repetition, Speed, Surprise, and Security."

The last element refers to counterintelligence and maintaining operational security, not to a determination to protect all our security forces from harm. The latter is as impossible as it is desirable. Terrorism is a drive for power using means of violence. Therefore there is no way to prevent counterterrorism from being very dangerous. There are, however, good ways to protect civil society from terrorists, and some of them involve the use of force. This begins with attention to such obvious yet important needs as training in force protection and the placement of physical barriers in front of endangered public offices. It continues through the range of policing, martial, and covert operations in which assets are placed at risk for high national purposes and for which force may be needed. At the apex of such efforts— where challenges to martial art and science are most acute—are swift and effective special operations by highly trained personnel. Without such forces of intervention, carefully prepared and overseen by civil authorities, decent society is in danger from modern terrorism. By contrast, as a range of cases of the last decade manifests, having and using such forces well can render decisive victories against powerful terrorist groups and cells.[62]

Christopher C. Harmon has long-held interests in the two subjects of this text: strategy and terrorism. His first book, coedited with low-intensity conflict expert David Tucker, was *Statecraft and Power* (University Press of America, 1994), a work in honor of a teacher of strategy, Harold W. Rood. Harmon taught on the Strategy & Policy faculty of the Naval War College, Newport, Rhode Island, and then wrote and directed a strategy syllabus for 200 Marine majors, foreign allies, and US civilians at Command & Staff College, Quantico, Virginia, where he later held Marine Corps University's Kim T. Adamson Chair of Insurgency and Terrorism (2005–2007). He is the author of two editions of the graduate-level textbook *Terrorism Today*—published by Frank Cass (2000) and Routledge (2007), as well as chapters on terrorism and counterterrorism for *Fanaticism and Conflict in the Modern Age* (2005) and *The American Military Tradition* (2007). Two of Dr. Harmon's articles have appeared in the journal *Vital Speeches*. The US State Department gave him a Distinguished Public Service Award. From March 2008 through September 2009, Dr. Harmon was executive director as well as curricula chief of the Marshall Center's Program on Terrorism & Security Studies; he is now Director of Studies.

Recommended Readings

Courter, James A. (with CCH). "Protecting Our Citizens: When to Use Force Against Terrorists," *Policy Review*, Spring, 1986.

Dobson, Christopher, and Ronald Payne. *Counterattack: The West's Battle Against the Terrorists*. New York: Facts on File, 1982.

Erickson, Richard J. *Legitimate Use of Military Force Against State-Sponsored International Terrorism*. Maxwell Air Force Base, AL: Air University Press, 1989.

Jenkins, Brian M. "Embassies Under Siege: A Review of 48 Embassy Takeovers, 1971–1980." Santa Monica, CA: RAND, 1981.

Livingstone, Neil C., and Terrell E. Arnold. *Fighting Back:Winning the War Against Terrorism*. Lexington, MA: Lexington Books, 1984.

McRaven, William H. *Spec Ops:Case Studies in Special Operations Warfare: Theory and Practice*. Novato, CA: Presidio Press, 1996.

Mockaitis, Thomas Ross. *The British Experience in Counterinsurgency, 1919–1960*. PhD dissertation, University of Wisconsin, 1988. Ann Arbor, MI: UMI Dissertation Information services, 1990.

Netanyahu, Benjamin. *Fighting Terrorism:How Democracies Can Defeat Domestic and International Terrorism*. New York: Farrar, Straus, Giroux, 1995.

Schmitt, Michael. "Counter-Terrorism and the Use of Force in International Law." Garmisch, Germany: Marshall Center Papers No. 5, 2002.

Sun Tzu. *The Art of War*. Ed. Samuel B. Griffith. London: Oxford University Press, 1963.

Wilkinson, Paul. *Terrorism versus Democracy: The Liberal State Response*, 2nd ed. London: Routledge, 2006.

Notes

1. At differing points Sun Tzu praises deception or intelligence. "All warfare is based on deception." Invocations of intelligence include "[K]now the enemy and know yourself; in a hundred battles you will never be in peril," and a later reference to the conquering power of "foreknowledge." See pp. 66, 84, and 144 in *The Art of War*, trans. Samuel B. Griffith (Oxford: Oxford University Press [1963], 1971) 1st paperback ed. Yet another principle of war for Sun Tzu is speed: "Speed is the essence of war" (134).

2. Initially fighting as "Batson's Scouts," named for their enterprising US lieutenant, these excellent indigenous Filipino forces grew swiftly in numbers—to 5,500 by February 1901 after which they could enlist as "Philippine Scouts" in the US Army and its reserves. See Allan D. Marple, "The Philippine Scouts: A Case Study in the Use of Indigenous Soldiers, Northern Luzon, the Philippine Islands, 1899," unpublished thesis for the US Army Command & General Staff College (Fort Leavenworth, KS, 1983), available via the Combined Arms Research Library Digital Library, http://cgsc.cdmhost.com/cdm4/document.php?CISOROOT=/p4013coll2&CISOPTR=1711&REC=19, accessed 7 September 2009.

3. The brilliance of Funston's operation easily withstood a published critique by Aguinaldo himself, only to be largely obscured by current writers of history, who ignore it or make to it only passing references. There is a useful and somewhat awkward book by David Howard Bain, *Sitting in Darkness* (New York: Houghton Mifflin, 1984) devoted to the Funston vs. Aguinaldo story. Inquiries on the web may be well rewarded, as with Mark J. Denger's portrait of Funston as Medal of Honor recipient at "The California Military Museum," www.militarymuseum.org/funston.html, accessed 1 September 2008. The Museum of the Kansas National guard carries a long story at www.kansasguardmuseum.org/mohfunston.html. William F. Zornow wrote "Funston Captures Aguinaldo" for *American Heritage Magazine*, February 1958; http://skyways.lib.ks.us/museums/funston/capturea.html. All sites accessed 7 September 2009.

4. The Red Cross suggested the army's trick was illegal and that the famous Red Cross was used—a charge President Uribe admitted to only as it pertained to one nervous person's unauthorized tee shirt. See "Colombia Assailed for Using Red Cross Symbol in Hostage Rescue," *Associated Press*, 6 August 2008.

5. This story was covered extensively by the Associated Press and other international media on 3 July 2008. The French newspaper *Le Figaro* had attentive and detailed coverage of the FARC war in Colombia during 2007 and 2008, including a fine story on the counterinsurgents of Omega Force, 21 February 2008, and a guest editorial by the Colombian Vice Minister of Defense (Sergio Jaramillo) on 23 January 2008. *Le Figaro* on 7 July 2008 used the Trojan horse metaphor—doubtless not knowing that in a previous time and very different place Emilio Aguinaldo of the Philippines had also applied the metaphor to his own capture in the Philippines (see above). I thus have public sources for this Betancourt recapture story but also confirmed it with a Lieutenant Colonel in the country's Special Forces in an interview of July 2009.

6. Before 1992 the US State Department's admirable annual *Patterns of Global Terrorism* reported Sendero Luminoso's guerrilla strength as four to five thousand (men and many women). But not long after Guzman's capture in September 1992, the numbers dropped swiftly, and later fell into the low hundreds. There is thus great significance in the short life of the special police squad (formed within DINCOTE) by Major Benedicto Jimenez.

7. This well-chosen adjective is courtesy of James Wither, whose own essay also forms part of this book. The description "discrete uses of force" sets my case studies apart from the many other ways martial forces are used to deter, prevent, or punish terrorism and its sponsors.

8. Richard H. Shultz Jr. "Showstoppers: Nine Reasons Why We Never Sent Our Special Operations Forces After al Qaeda Before 9/11," *Weekly Standard*, Vol. 9, Issue 19 (January 2, 2004): 25–33.

9. Lt. Col. Richard J. Erickson, *Legitimate Use of Military Force Against State-Sponsored International Terrorism* (Maxwell Air Force Base, AL: Air University Press, July 1989), 6, 9, 10. The author has long appreciated this useful book, a gift from then-Lt. Col. Werner Hellmar, USMC.

10. "Terrorism: MET 'Has Not Learned' from Menzes' Death," *The Guardian*, 18 July 2008; *Sunday Times*, 29 June 2008; etc.

11. "Philadelphia, City Officials Ordered to Pay $1.5 Million in MOVE Case," CNN.com, 24 June 1996. Available at http://www.cnn.com/US/9606/24/move.vertict/, accessed 7 September 2009.

12. Gilani and Hashi are variants of the sheik's names.

13. For background on al-Fuqra, see "Terrorist Organization Profile: al-Fuqra," Terrorist Organization Profile Database, National Consortium for the Study of Terrorism and Responses to Terrorism (START), University of Maryland. Available at http://www.start.umd.edu/start/data/tops/terrorist_organization_profile.asp?id=3426, accessed 7 September 2009.

14. A recent disclosure is an al Fuqra training film showing training and killing exercises. Parts of this, and footage reportedly taken near Commerce and Jessup Georgia, were screened on *The Sean Hannity Show*, which also interviewed Martin Mawyer, an investigator of these "Muslims of America" encampments; 16 February 2009; www.foxnews.com/video2/video08.html?maven_referralObject=3625333&

15. See "Federal Air Marshal Service," U.S. Transportation Security Administration, http://www.tsa.gov/lawenforcement/programs/fams.shtm, accessed 7 September 2009.

16. Richard A. Clarke, *Against All Enemies: Inside America's War on Terror* (New York: Free Press, 2004), 131. See also Timothy Naftali, *Blind Spot: The Secret History of American Counterterrorism* (New York: Basic Books, 2005).

17. Interview at Command & Staff College, Quantico, VA, about 2003. One good argument against marshals, which I've not heard voiced, is that a capacious terror group with a serious approach to intelligence could place one or more persons within the organization; these would report steadily on the placement and use of agents, and deficiencies in the system.

18. Clarke, 28.

19. "Dressing Down the Air Marshals," *The Washington Times*, 12 December 2004. Available at http://www.washingtontimes.com/news/2004/dec/12/20041212-100604-9675r/?feat=article_related_stories, accessed 7 September 2009.

20. See "Dress Code Dropped for Undercover Air Marshals," ABCNews.com, 24 August 2006. Available at http://blogs.abcnews.com/theblotter/2006/08/dress_code_drop.html, accessed 7 September 2009. The link contains the full statement from Director Brown, who retired at the end of 2008.

21. William Stevenson was a top British agent during World War II. With material from Uri Dan, an Israeli journalist and associate of former Prime Minister Ariel Sharon, Stevenson wrote *90 Minutes at Entebbe* (New York: Bantam Books, 1976), 2.

22. The story is told in detail by Fred W. Wagoner, *Dragon Rouge: The Rescue of Hostages in the Congo* (Washington, DC: National Defense University, 1980).

23. President Johnson did not even mention this remarkable episode in his memoirs, *The Vantage Point*, according to Wagoner, but Hoare told his own story in *Congo Mercenary* (London: Robert Hale & Co., 1967).

24. Mr. Wilfred Bose, a Carlos associate, was among the skyjackers, but it is strangely difficult to name the leftist female involved, and most accounts avoid doing so. The book *90 Minutes at Entebbe* (op. cit.) identified her as Gabriele Krocher-Tiedemann. But accounts suggest that all four hijackers were killed, whereas Krocher-Tiedemann lived on, until capture in London years later. Jillian Becker, the RAF authority who wrote *Hitler's Children: The Story of the Baader-Meinhof Terrorist Gang* (Philadelphia, PA: J.P. Lippincott & Co., 1977) says the European woman at Entebbe was Italian, not a German, but gives no name. Her second edition states that the woman shot at Entebbe by Israelis was a German named Halimeh, later commemorated as "Martyr Halimeh" by the RAF (Herts, London, and New York: Granada Publishing Ltd., 1978), 348.

25. Mark Ensalaco, *Middle Eastern Terrorism: From Black September to September 11* (Philadelphia: University of Pennsylvania Press, 2008), 96.

26. According to A. N. Pratt, and William McRaven, the mission commander was Brigadier General Dan Shomron (d. February 2008). Also on the ground was *Sayeret Matkal*, the reconnaissance unit of General Headquarters of the IDF, which handled the recapture of the air terminal and its hostages; its action was led by Jonathan Netanyahu, who died of a wound there.

27. In the early 1980s, at a London symposium, Wegener looked back to 1972: "First, there was the lack of an intelligence organization especially designed to combat terrorism, which is absolutely necessary. We know that today, but at the time there were no special units with unconventional, highly trained and selected personnel highly motivated by their mission, and there was a lack of equipment and weapons and an absence of tactical concepts." Quoted by Christopher Dobson and Ronald Payne, *Counterattack: The West's Battle Against the Terrorists* (New York: Facts on File, Inc., 1982), 95. During the 1980s Dobson and Payne collaborated on this and several other very good terrorism books.

28. J. Paul de B. Taillon, *Hijacking and Hostages: Government Responses to Terrorism* (Westport, CT: Praeger, 2002); see Chapter 3.

29. Taillon, as well as Dobson and Payne, op. cit., 98. Both volumes offer good analyses of this superb "Operation Feuerzauber."

30. Instead it is little referred to, and was all but ignored in the lengthy German film *The Baader-Meinhof Komplex* (Magnolia Pictures, 2008).

31. A fourth RAF member, Irmgard Moller, was found with stab wounds in her chest but survived; Becker, *Hitler's Children*, 2nd ed., 352.

32. Yonah Alexander and Dennis Pluchinsky, *Europe's Red Terrorists: The Fighting Communist Organizations* (London: Frank Cass, 1992), 85–89.

33. Schleyer was kidnapped in September 1977, five weeks before the Lufthansa hijacking to Mogadishu. He was murdered, and his body was found in Mulhouse, France, just west of the German border.

34. Here the author appreciates information offered on current German operations by Marshall Center professors Jay Le Beau and A.N. Pratt. In "German Elite Troop Abandons Plan to Free Pirate Hostages," *Der Spiegel* (4 May 2009) detailed a GSG-9 deployment that never became an engagement, in a Somali hijacking case. Website SpecialOperations.Com mentions a June 1994 arrest of RAF man, Wolfgang Grams, and a July 1994 seizure of a hijacker of a KLM flight. In the second case, the gunman was reportedly subdued without a shot—which is not apparently true in the RAF case of a month earlier, http://www.specialoperations.com/Foreign/Germany/GSG9.htm accessed 7 September 2009.

35. Favier has been promoted to general as of 1 June 2008; "Secret Defense," a blog of the French daily *Liberation*, posting of 5 June 2008 (see http://www.specialoperations.com/Foreign/Germany/GSG9.htm). At GIGN training grounds he has kindly received several PTSS classes from Garmisch.

36. A witness suggested the hijackers looked like uniformed police, with badges. *Time* magazine, in an interesting and careful article, reported blue "Air Algeria" uniforms, badges, arms, and claims of being a security team; Thomas Sancton, "Algeria: Anatomy of a Hijack," *Time*, 9 January 1995, available at http://www.time.com/time/magazine/article/0,9171,982288-1,00.html, accessed 7 September 2009.

37. Such terrorist psychological operations were in evidence during the June 1985 hijacking of the TWA 847 airliner and recalled previous such actions. I investigated this problem with Rep. James A. Courter, "The TWA Case: Terrorists Put in Practice What They Learned," *Christian Science Monitor*, 24 July 1985.

38. Few American security professionals appeared to study this 1994 suicide airliner operation or suggest what it meant for the future. An exception, Colonel A. N. Pratt was teaching the case study at the George C. Marshall European Center for Security Studies in 1999. Much noted, but only later, was one warning in a 1999 Library of Congress report (ed. Rex Hudson) that "Suicide bomber(s) belonging to al Qaeda's Martyrdom Battalion could crash-land an aircraft packed with high explosives (C-4 and Semtex) into the Pentagon, the headquarters of the Central Intelligence Agency (CIA), or the White House. Ramzi Yousef had planned to do this against the CIA headquarters." *The Sociology and Psychology of Terrorism: Who Becomes a Terrorist and Why?*," U.S. Library of Congress, September 1999, republished under the subtitle (Guilford, CT: Lyons Press), 15. See also "Terror from the Sky" by Rohan Gunaratna, who in 2001 was one of the world's few experts on al Qaeda; his article on past terrorist air operations appeared 24 September 2001 on the Jane's website; a nonsubscriber extract is available at http://www.janes.com/security/international_security/news/jir/jir010924_1_n.shtml, accessed 7 September 2009.

39. Several vivid films of the rescue exist, including a brief passage in a documentary the GIGN has made about their own activities entitled "GIGN: Au Coeur de L'Action," JLO Presse (2006), courtesy of Lt. General Jean-Paul Raffenne of the French Marines. Another recent and general depiction of the police unit is "Plongee au Coeur des Secrets du GIGN," by Christophe Cornevin, *Le Figaro*, 10 October 2008, available at http://www.lefigaro.fr/actualite-france/2008/10/10/01016-20081010ARTFIG00569-plongee-au-cur-des-secrets-du-gign-.php, accessed 7 September 2009. There are good details and photos in "Air France 8969," an account on the GIGN section of Italian-language website *Corpi d'elite.net*, available at http://corpidelite.info/AIR%20FRANCE.html, accessed 7 September 2009.

40. In religious terms, this matched members of a minority Christian community against a similarly Christian government, with the aim of forcing a Muslim government (Indonesia) to yield to Christian Moluccan separatists.

41. On 25 April 1950 on the island of Ambon, a Declaration of Independence proclaimed a new "Republic of the South Moluccas," to separate from East Indonesia and the Republic of the United States of Indonesia. Indonesian troops retook the area in seven months, and in 1963 arrested President Christian Soumokil, executed in Djakarta in 1966. Valentine Herman and Rob van der Laan Bouma, "Nationalists without a Nation: South Moluccan Terrorism in the Netherlands," in *Terrorism: A Challenge to the State*, ed. Juliet Lodge (New York: St. Martin's Press, 1981).

42. Ronald Janse, "Fighting Terrorism in the Netherlands: A Historical Perspective," *Utrecht Law Review*, Vol. 1, No. 1 (Sept. 2005), 60.

43. Not Beilan, with an "A." "Beilen" is often misspelled in English-language accounts of the incidents, and their chronologies for these attacks often err. For example, Leroy Thompson's *The Rescuers: The World's Top Anti-Terrorist Units* is a vigorous and detail-filled little book (Boulder, CO: Paladin Press, 1986) but its dates on incidents in Holland are not reliable.

44. Another hostage died when leaping out a window at the consulate. The siege of the train lasted twelve days, and that at the embassy a few days longer. Martijn Rasser, "The Dutch Response to Moluccan Terrorism, 1970–1978," *Studies in Conflict & Terrorism*, Vol. 28, No. 6 (November 2005), 485.

45. The author thanks Dr. M. J. de Weger, a civil expert on defense for the Dutch government, for his critique of a draft of these paragraphs. He adds that snipers and members of the national gendarmerie Marechaussee also played an important role in several of thse crises. Recent information on Holland's range of special forces can be found on the website of the National Coordinator for Counterterrorism, as at http://english.nctb.nl/

46. One investigator has noted that given the train's subdivision into many walled cars, the use of F 104 "Starfighter" engines was more efficient than trying to deploy stun grenades in all the cars; Thompson, *The Rescuers*, 29–30. This Dutch tactic was a superior example of the principle of surprise in the use of force.

47. Dobson and Payne, *Counterattack*, 117.

48. For example, at the turn of the millennium there were three years of sectarian fighting between Christian and Muslim communities in the Moluccans; factions signed a peace accord in mid-February 2002, according to John Haseman of *Jane's Defense Weekly*, web posting of 14 February 2002.

49. While I've seen film and still pictures of the Peruvian CT assault, my best source for these details is the book by Admiral Luis Giampietri, *41 Seconds to Freedom: An Insider's Account of the Lima Hostage Crisis, 1996–97* (New York: Presidio Press, 2007); coauthors were Bill Salisbury and Lorena Ausejo. The Admiral had been in charge of suppressing an earlier prison insurrection by jailed communist terrorists, an explosive fact never known to his MRTA captors. During the 1996–97 crisis, he managed to lead resistance forces from within, emerging a hero.

50. Carl von Clausewitz, *On War*, ed. and trans. Michael Howard and Peter Paret (Princeton, NJ: Princeton University Press, 1984), 202–203; 562–563. Carl von Clausewitz was among the many thinkers to wrestle with the concept of "principles of war." He assembled a list for one royal student, which later appeared as a short book. But when writing *On War* over many subsequent years, he resisted creating such lists and occasionally ridiculed the concept. He devoted great care to more normal forms of prose, leaving it to the reader to deduce principles from the work.

51. William H. McRaven, *Spec Ops: Case Studies in Special Operations Warfare: Theory and Practice* (Novato, CA: Presidio Press, 1996). Thanks to Matthew Karres for recommending this fine reading.

52. Ibid. Admiral McRaven later commanded US Special Operations Forces in Europe, and now all Joint Special Operations Forces of the US Navy. He might dislike my re-ordering of his list; his book lists, in this order: simplicity, security, repetition, surprise, speed, and purpose. This paragraph of my text, and that following, depend heavily upon McRaven's work in Chapter 1 of *Spec Ops*. For a newer American study by civilian experts, it is easy to recommend David

Tucker and Christopher J. Lamb, *United States Special Operations Forces* (New York: Columbia University Press, 2007).

53. After 11 September 2001 I was a guest at a school where a question from a military officer in the audience was about what to study to prepare the mind for the years to come in the struggle with al Qaeda. My answer was Sun Tzu's *The Art of War*. A decade of lecturing on the book had left me convinced that, while Clausewitz is deeper, Sun Tzu may be the preferred source for studying terrorism and counterterrorism. *On War* is a work of genius with wide applicability to many human affairs, and it offers a chapter on "The People in Arms," useful for students of insurgency and politics. But it would be a stretch to deduce from Clausewitz many "principles" for counterterrorism.

54. One roster of Filipino successes against Abu Sayyaf is in the US State Department's annual, *Country Reports on Terrorism: 2007* (Washington, DC: Government Printing Office, 2008). Doubts persist about whether Khadaffy Janjalani perished; for example, reports accessed in May 2009 in databases of START, the National Consortium for the Study of Terrorism and Responses to Terrorism, themselves conflict on this. But the Philippine Army has announced with certitude that this terrorist is dead, and published reports link that conviction to US DNA testing.

55. Clausewitz, *on War,* pp. 202–203; 562–563.

56. Richard H. Shultz, Jr. and Roy Godson, "Intelligence Dominance: A Better Way Forward in Iraq," *Weekly Standard*, Vol. 11, Issue 43 (31 July 2006): 22–26.

57. In some cases, preemption of known violent threats, skillfully done, is more responsible than awaiting disaster. Some Americans, for example, are critical of the George W. Bush doctrine of preemption—which probably was applied in error in the case of Iraq. On the other hand, one can only regret the previous US administration's years of failure to preempt the growing threat of al Qaeda, which declared war on the United States in 1996 and 1998.

58. Among recent articles on the problem, see Sebastian Gorka and David Kilcullen, "Al Qaeda and US Strategic Communications," The Interagency Strategic Communication Fusion Team, 23 January 2009; and Christopher C. Harmon, "Public Diplomacy's Next Challenge," *Connections* (Spring, 2008), 141–153.

59. See, for example, David C. Martin and John Wolcott, *Best Laid Plans* (New York: Harper and Row, 1988), a respected book. The United States would disappoint another ally about twelve years later. After Egyptian President Hosni Mubarak was targeted by snipers during a visit to Addis Ababa in 1995, Egypt reportedly sought US help against the terrorist camps in Sudan, which had made the plot possible. Apparently the United States declined. I raised the question with one intelligence officer and regional expert, who opposed any such action against the camps in Sudan. Yet Osama bin Laden was in Sudan, and his other camps there were playing a role in international terrorism of the 1990s, to include a major plot against New York City. The UN Security Council imposed counterterrorist sanctions on Sudan in resolutions 1044, 1054, and 1070.

60. *Le Monde*, 16 September 2008 (Cubic Translation Services); *Le Figaro*, 13 & 14 April 2009; *International Herald Tribune*.

61. Roland Jacquard and Dominique Nasplezes, *Carlos: Le Dossier Secret* (Paris: Jean Picollec, 1997). John Follain, *Jackal: The Complete Story of the Legendary Terrorist, Carlos the Jackal* (New York: Arcade Publishing, 1998), Chapter 12. Sudan may have had foreknowledge of the French operation or allowed it, given the world's increasing notice of bin Laden's residence in Khartoum, and the heavy-handed Islamist character of governance by such personages as Hassan al Turabi.

62. When Iran shamelessly broke international law by occupying the US embassy and took scores of hostages in 1979, only inadequate measures were taken in reply. Presidential candidate Ronald Reagan made apparent his intent to do business differently, and upon his election there was a near-instant "breakthrough" and the hostages were released. Reagan welcomed back fifty-two Americans with words that democratic states do well to keep in mind: "We hear it said that we live in an era of limits to our powers. Well, let it also be understood, there are limits to our patience."

James Q. Roberts

Building a National Counterterrorism Capability:

A Primer for Operators and Policymakers Alike

This chapter describes the diverse considerations governments should take into account as they seek to build or improve a national counterterrorism capability. For the purposes of this discussion, conducting a successful hostage rescue operation will serve as the benchmark for a competent counterterrorism capability. Although terrorists armed with a weapon of mass destruction and seeking to leverage that weapon (or weapons) to blackmail a government present perhaps the most difficult decision for politicians as they consider the employment of their counterterrorism forces, we can be thankful that such a scenario has not yet occurred.

Rather than address such a theoretical challenge, this chapter will focus on counter terror hostage rescue operations. Recent history is replete with many case studies of both successes and failures in these operations, from which lessons learned may be drawn. These also serve to highlight the key challenges for the three elements involved in any hostage rescue decision; the counterterrorism force, the intelligence structures supporting the rescue, and the politicians who must decide whether or not to launch the operation.

Despite a decrease in the appeal of hostage-taking operations in apparent favor of suicide body, car, and truck bombs, terrorists still can get major mileage out of hostage taking. The most recent example is the attacks on luxury hotels by Lashkar e-Tayyiba–trained Muslim extremists in Mumbai during November 2008.

To have decent odds for the conduct of a successful hostage rescue, there are three components of any government that must come together to form an alliance of shared capabilities, risk analysis, and political resolve. First, the government beset with a hostage-taking situation must possess a trained hostage rescue force—the hammer. Second, an intelligence capability must be able to provide adequate details about the hostage crisis to enable a reasonable chance of a successful rescue—the eyes. Third, political leaders must have confidence in both the rescue force and the intelligence underpinning the operation. Politicians, the brain, must muster the political will to close the crisis by launching an operation—and suffer the consequences, good or bad.

I refer to these three components—hammer, eyes, brain—as the "Iron Triangle" of counterterrorism decision making. In most governments, the three components (where they exist) live in separate worlds, that is, separate ministries, different values, divergent concepts of risk and degrees of risk aversion, different skill sets, different understandings of the political environment.

All too frequently, they come together only at the moment of crisis. However, for a successful rescue they must coalesce into a competent political-military whole—like a skilled carpenter, striking a nail with a hammer, on the first swing, without denting the wood below. This chapter argues that such coordination requires practice, practice, practice.

The Rescue Force—the Hammer

The first component of the Iron Triangle is the rescue force itself. History shows us that successful rescues almost always have been executed by a specialized hostage rescue force. Whether the force is a military, police, or gendarmerie organization is not of critical importance. What is absolutely crucial are the skill sets the force possesses, and its readiness. The key skills combine outstanding physical and mental toughness, an unparalleled sense of mission and duty, and a set of lethal and nonlethal capabilities, which is ever evolving and can be brought to bear with speed, force, and surgical precision.

To find the "right cut of cloth" for their operators almost all hostage rescue units begin with an assessment and selection process. In this phase the unit is building its initial cadre or looking for new members to fill losses or make the force more robust. An initial records screening is conducted to establish that the candidate possesses the requisite intellect, performance record, and physical abilities, and can obtain the necessary security clearances. Next, a typical assessment and selection process involves a series of physical, mental, and psychological tests, usually putting the candidates under significant and unexpected stress in an effort to weed out the weak of heart, or mind, or will. This process is usually several days to several weeks in length and is often conducted in an isolated and uncomfortable environment.

The stress period allows the unit to observe behaviors such as individual performance, teamwork, competition among candidates, ethical decision making under stress, and the effects of fatigue, weather extremes, and sleep deprivation on candidates' physical and mental capabilities. Some units also test for preexisting skills such as photography, martial arts, marksmanship, demonstrated leadership, mountaineering, or experience in urban operations. Almost all conduct basic and advanced physical fitness tests, and swimming examinations in difficult conditions. A few also test for irrational fears such as claustrophobia or acrophobia.

A detailed physical examination and some degree of psychological assessment frequently round out the assessment phase. Finally, many units conduct some type of interview with the candidate during which leaders try to get a final measure of the candidate. If he or she is deemed to possess "what it takes," an offer to join the unit may be extended on the spot or in a follow-up contact.

The training phase is next. Operators habitually undergo extensive training regimens to further develop their individual and team skills. Honing physical conditioning and exercising mental toughness are standard fare. So are martial arts and other one-on-one, and team-on-team, hand-to-hand combat exercises. Marksmanship forms the cornerstone of most individual and unit skills, with many units firing thousands of rounds per member per month in both range and shooting house environments.

Close quarters combat experts and snipers evolve into their own specialty worlds, yet regularly interact in coordinated training scenarios to ensure both skills can be orchestrated to produce the desired results. Many units conduct street craft training to ensure that members can operate unobtrusively in diverse urban environments. Military hostage rescue units also train in a wide variety of natural terrain environments—mountains, deserts, and jungles are the norm. Both civilian and military units usually have parachute and water/underwater capabilities as well.

Individual training gives way to team training as the new operators develop. Team training leverages the individual skills and brings them to bear in a variety of situations. Most units train for hostage rescue operations in urban static (building) scenarios, land mobile scenarios (cars, busses, trains), water environments (ships and oil platforms), and aircraft scenarios. Each of these requires different skills, equipment, tactics, techniques, and procedures. Command and control for each may also require adaptation or special communications equipment.

Counterterrorism units often serve as test beds for developmental equipment or emerging technologies—body armor, scopes and other targeting devices, specialized team communications gear, long-range observation and photography equipment and techniques, explosives and shaped charges, medical advances, robotics, and others.

Finally, readiness, alert status, and emergency transportation arrangements round out the force requirements. Most units maintain some portion of their force in a high readiness state, usually expressed in the number of hours required to assemble an initial force and have it ready for transport. Many ensure they possess or have access to vehicles, boats, or aircraft to ensure quick deployment, either throughout their country or for the more global powers around the world.

The most common practice is to divide the entire force into three subordinate units, each "on watch" for a period of a few weeks. Of the two elements not on stand-by, one is usually in a team training phase, preparing for its "watch period" while the third has just finished its "watch" and is conducting leaves, training, or developing individual skills.

After a year or two of training and development these units begin to exhibit a personality all of their own. The unit's traits most often include a spirit of independence, a certain degree of secrecy, a sense of invulnerability or invincibility, and an elite mentality that sets them apart from peers. Operators and their commanders tend to be tough, uncompromising, competent, brusque, and edgy.

Long hours of training and standing ready also result in a collective impatience for operational opportunities in "the real world." These attributes form both the strength and the weakness of counterterrorism units around the globe. As one senior commander of such units was fond of saying, "We must not confuse enthusiasm with capability."

The Intelligence and Investigative Unit—the Eyes

The second component of the Iron Triangle is the intelligence and investigative capability that a nation can bring to bear on the hostage crisis. These scenarios typically present a multifaceted intelligence and investigative challenge. At what one might call the strategic level, of key concern from the outset are the identity and agenda of the hostage-takers. Are the hostages being held for political reasons? Or is this a kidnapping-for-ransom scenario? Do the hostage-takers represent a domestic or foreign terrorist organization? Does the organization have a track record? Do they rely on internal or external support? Are they state supported, or state sponsored? Are the local media sympathetic to their cause? If this is not their first adventure at hostage taking, what is the previous track record? How lethal have their actions been in the past? And what are their tactical and/or strategic demands in the current crisis?

As a general consideration, if the terrorists are foreigners, national intelligence organizations may have the lead; if they represent a domestic group, then law enforcement and other domestic agencies may be better suited to develop the strategic intelligence picture for both the counterterrorist force and the political leadership. If the terrorists are threatening to kill the hostages in the near term, then the pressure to develop this strategic picture must run in parallel with the development of the tactical intelligence picture. A quick rudimentary tactical picture is always required to enable an emergency assault by the hostage rescue force, should that become the only option to save the remaining hostages.

If the terrorists are foreign, another key intelligence question is whether this represents a state-sponsored attack. If state sponsorship is suspected, or can be proven, then national responses can be structured very differently than if the group is a foreign non-state actor without known or discernible links to any foreign government. In the event of the former, all tools of state power can be used to pressure the sponsor. However, in the latter, the tool box is far more constrained and must more directly address the hostage-takers and their (often shadowy) non-state actor organization.

Nevertheless, for a successful rescue, detailed intelligence and information about the tactical situation are essential. At the top of the list is the number of hostages. Within the hostage group are there women, children, elderly, or others who might be released on humanitarian grounds? What are the nationalities of the hostages? If the terrorists make no initial demands, can some intent be determined based on these biographical aspects of the pool of hostages? Can negotiators gain the release of some of the hostages based on knowledge of the hostage population?

Next are the details about the terrorists. How many? What ages and sexes? Which ethnic, cultural, religious backgrounds? Armed with what? Is there a suicide bomber's device involved? Are there small arms only? Or do the terrorists have grenades, other explosives, tear gas or other chemicals, rocket-propelled grenades, or other heavy weapons? What other equipment did they bring to the crisis, such as body armor, gas masks, or video or audio monitoring equipment? What is the chain of command, and who is the commander? Does he or she have a track record from former terrorist operations? What languages are they using? Is chain of command respected among the terrorists? What indications are there of military training? Do they have communications with an outside force or support base? Do they have contact with the media?

Next the hostage rescue force needs details about the specific location and whether the terrorists envisage moving with all or a portion of the hostages. To the extent possible all details about the physical site where the hostages are being held must be obtained to enable planning by the hostage rescue force.

These include details about the construction of the building from top to bottom, with particular emphasis on the floor plans where the hostages are being held; numbers and locations of windows and doors; building support systems such as heating, ventilating, air conditioning, and associated duct work; water and sewerage plans; elevators; internal furnishings; food sources (snack bars, restaurants, kitchens, food storage facilities); parking garages; basements; and the like.

As these tactical details are being collected, the intelligence unit must also develop exact locations for the terrorists and the hostages. Knowing how many, and where, the terrorists are at any given moment is one of the most valuable elements of information that can be provided to the hostage rescue force. It is highly desirable to obtain long duration, constant, concealed observation of the crisis site and to employ multiple audio and video means to augment that observation.

This durable observation task is often initiated by or turned over to the tactical hostage rescue unit preparing the assault. Most such units have skilled sniper/observers who can monitor the crisis site and keep the tactical commander fully informed about activities therein. Bringing the entire intelligence and observation picture together into an all-source real-time view of all aspects of the crisis is perhaps the single most important contribution of the intelligence component.

This picture needs to be provided to the tactical commander of the hostage rescue force in a constant stream for situational awareness. Some political leaders may also want such details about the state of play, in order to better assess their options and the viability of any proposed rescue operation. This situational awareness may also determine the necessity of launching an emergency assault, in particular, should the terrorists begin to systematically kill the hostages.

Investigative and intelligence skills needed to accomplish these tasks are beyond the skill levels of many standard domestic police or civilian or military foreign intelligence units. Nations must determine how best to develop and maintain such capabilities. In many instances there are legal or constitutional prohibitions against combining investigative and intelligence skills or organizations. Whatever the challenges, obtaining timely intelligence of this specificity is a *sine qua non* for successful hostage rescue operations.

The intelligence and investigative units capable of these tasks, if they exist at all, tend to have some quirks of their own. First, they will be secretive in the extreme. Second, they will likely consistently underplay their capabilities, for fear of not being able to produce when needed. Third, like almost all intelligence organizations, they will likely caveat their information with great care. Fourth, they probably will be comfortable with the uncertainty of the unknown. Fifth, they will shun any media, and often even any political, attention.

These qualities can make a poor mix with the psychological profile of the hostage rescue force and its leaders. The first obstacle to overcome is the issue of trust. The intelligence professionals will tend to see the operators as "a bunch of cowboys," while the operators will see the intelligence types as timid, evasive, shifty, and potentially unreliable. Since the prestige of the hostage rescue unit, and in fact, the success of the operation, will rely heavily on the accuracy and timeliness of the intelligence, it is essential to close this gap in trust. The question is how? There are two well-proven methods.

The first is to develop a habitual relationship between the operators and the collectors. This typically involves conducting frequent exercises that stress the capabilities of both elements. Over time each begins to learn the strengths and weaknesses of the other, and each becomes more tolerant of the personality quirks of the other. The unit commanders develop an appreciation of "the possible" for each element, and trust can be developed with a concerted, long-term effort. It is clear, however, that the first time the two units encounter each other must not be at the moment of crisis. The exigencies of a real crisis will stress even the best of strong relationships—the teams must know each other well, long before they get to the field of strife.

The second model is to build a tactical intelligence capability inside the hostage rescue unit. Such a solution helps to establish the habitual relationship and to build teamwork among the components. The downsides are that this approach is expensive, and there may be significant legal hurdles to overcome, depending on the charter and authorities of the ministry from which the hostage rescue force comes. Additionally, interagency jealousies may doom the effort as the intelligence and investigative bureaus become aware that the operators are building their own capabilities. In some countries there may be budget authority considerations, especially when it comes to the purchase of particularly sensitive intelligence-related audio or video monitoring gear. Finally, the downside of this approach is that a counterterrorism unit commander is already stretched thin to keep his assault force on razor's edge—ready and trained to go at a moment's notice. Keeping these intelligence and investigative types at the top of their game simultaneously may be too much to ask.

Success, however, requires that these two components be fully compatible and well trained together, like the eyes and the hands of our carpenter referred to earlier.

The National Political Leadership—the Brains

The national political leadership is the ultimate authority that must decide whether or not to launch a hostage rescue operation. Those authorities are charged, first and foremost, with the protection of their populations. The taking of hostages is a direct and irrefutable challenge to the security of their citizens. Policymakers cannot avoid coming to grips with their responsibilities when confronted with the stark choices terrorist hostage scenarios present. The lives of the hostages swing in the balance, based on the outcomes of their decisions. Successful rescues reinforce the moral authority of political leaders, while failed ones, particularly in democratic regimes, have caused governments to fall.

I refer to these leaders as the "brain" of the Iron Triangle, not out of deference to any (possible?) superior intellect, but because it is they who are charged with this decision, as is the brain of the carpenter, using the "eyes" to guide the "hammer" to strike the nail with precision and finesse. But this "brain" operates in a very different world from the other two components of the Iron Triangle.

Politicians are products of an entirely different culture than either the hostage rescue force operators, or the intelligence collection and analysis experts we have addressed so far. For politicians, decisions are best delayed for as long as possible, and when one must be made, a compromise or trade-off is usually the preferred course of action. This is why hostage taking creates such political pressure. It places politicians between three bad choices, each of which they would prefer to avoid.

Essentially, political leadership is faced with three options in a hostage situation: (1) acquiesce to the demands of the terrorists in hopes the hostages will be released, their lives spared; (2) refuse to meet the terrorists' demands and perhaps see the hostages killed either one by one, or as a group; or (3) launch a hostage rescue attempt in the hopes of rescuing the hostages while killing or arresting the terrorists. Because for most politicians the decision "not to decide now" is considered a legitimate decision, launching a hostage rescue effort is usually their last choice, often by default. But waiting too long can create risks for the possible success of any rescue operation, and it places the initiative in the hands of the terrorists.

Given their culture of "deal making," many politicians would prefer to meet, or partially meet, the demands of the terrorists, and hope for the release of the hostages. There are many cases where this tactic has resulted in short-term gains, particularly in kidnapping for ransom cases, where hostage-takers have been paid off. But true terrorist attacks present additional pressures on the government—first, their political demands are unlikely to be able to be met, and second, the political dimension of capitulating to their threat of violence will undermine the legitimacy of that government in the eyes of its population. Third, the terrorists may go back on their promises, either increasing their demands or killing some or all of the hostages anyway. Capitulating to demands will also likely result in future terrorists trying the same tactic for similar or different causes.

In the long run, giving in to terrorists' demands only serves to strengthen the terrorists' hand, while weakening the government's. This essential equation should be reviewed with policymakers in advance, so that, should a crisis occur, the "brains" will understand the challenge their propensity for "deal making" presents in their role as protectors of their populations. In many nations the tendency for deal making is countered by policy pronouncements such as "we don't negotiate with terrorists" or other such political edicts. These pronouncements notwithstanding, most nations do negotiate with terrorists, especially hostage-takers. There are two legitimate reasons for this, both tactical.

First, skilled negotiators may be able to gain the release of some number of the hostages. Most frequent are agreements to release women and children. There may be other groups in the hostage population (based on race, religion, or other factors) that negotiators may be able to convince the terrorists to release. Every hostage freed by negotiations is one less requiring to be rescued, and one less potential hostage casualty. These freed hostages can also provide key information about conditions inside the crisis site and can answer many of the key questions to which the rescue force requires answers. Negotiators may also be able to develop a sense of rapport with the hostage-takers, which can come in useful later on. Sometimes this sense of rapport coupled with time to wear down the terrorists' resolve can result in the hostage-takers "giving up."

But should a rescue attempt become inevitable, a relationship between negotiators and the terrorists can be played to excellent advantage by the rescue force. This is the second reason why it is important to negotiate during the crisis. Negotiations can be used to modify the terrorists' behavior or their disposition, adjust the fidelity of the crisis intelligence, and optimize the timing of any eventual operation.

Deciding who should be the negotiators, and how to integrate them into the three structures we have discussed, is another key decision governments must make. In some instances, the negotiators are an integral part of the hostage rescue force—sometimes even the force commander takes on this role. In other models, negotiators come from the investigative or intelligence units. Some nations may rely on "profilers" or psychologists to perform these tasks. Finally, some political leaders may want to control the negotiations and frame the discussions with the terrorists at their level. Whichever model is selected, practicing negotiations as an integral part of the government's hostage rescue capability is another key relationship that must be developed over time and on a basis of trust, by all parties—hammer, eyes, and brain. Negotiators could be considered as the other hand of the carpenter, placing the nail in just the right spot, fully coordinated by the eyes and the brain, and thus optimizing the effectiveness of the strike by the hammer.

Building a Governmental Counterterrorism Team

This next section provides some advice to policymakers on how to assemble and exercise the components of a national counterterrorism hostage rescue capability. A sense of trust and shared values, or at least a cognizance of the key differences between the components, is a basic starting point. Setting out national rules of the road is another. Finally, exercising the components under a variety of scenarios is also necessary.

First, establish a national policy framework. Governments should develop an agreed national policy on combating terrorism. One element of that policy should be on handling hostage crises. The policy should be an interagency consensus document, well known to the rescue force, the intelligence apparatus, and the political leadership. It should be an enduring document that reflects the core values of the society, and it must differentiate between terrorism and other forms of political violence. It should also establish a balance between the responsibility of the government for combating terrorism and its responsibility to ensure the basic freedoms of its citizens. This is particularly important when it comes to subjects such as domestic intelligence and surveillance and the collection and retention of personal data on citizens, immigrants, and visitors.

Second, develop a national strategy for combating terrorism. Such a document would assign roles and missions to agencies involved in the many facets of a full-spectrum campaign, with timelines and coordinating instructions. Key components might include:

Diplomacy

Intelligence

Law enforcement

Customs

Border control

Finance

Information

Agriculture

Health

Emergency services

Military

Others, as appropriate

Third, create a national-level interagency working group for combating terrorism. Depending on the structure of the government involved, this group can be chaired either by a representative of the office of the chief executive—president, National Security Council, prime minister—or by a lead agency such as the Ministry of Interior for domestic terrorist events, or the Ministry of Foreign Affairs for events involving foreign or international terrorists. This working group should assemble all of the ministries involved in the nation's combating terrorism strategy and meet regularly to address threats and assess vulnerabilities.

The group should develop plans to defend critical infrastructure and other national resources against terrorist attacks, respond to terrorist events with force when appropriate, and manage the consequences of a terrorist attack. Particular attention should be given to events involving attacks at multiple locations, attacks on critical infrastructure nodes or capabilities, and attacks involving weapons of mass destruction. It may be appropriate to create a subgroup devoted to disrupting terrorist financing, another focused on countering the informational or ideological aspects of terrorism, and other subgroups as necessary. Both functional and regional structures should be considered. Another concept might be to organize around key terrorist groups active in the nation or region concerned.

The combating terrorism working group should meet regularly, ideally once a week or once every two weeks. The intent of the group is to ensure that all agencies concerned are kept abreast of threats and capabilities, and to build a sense of teamwork and shared responsibility over time. Furthermore, the group must be ready to provide focused expert advice to the government, in the event of a crisis. The requirement for the national foreign intelligence and domestic law enforcement communities to provide a consolidated, complete, and current threat picture to the group, and the agencies involved, is an absolute necessity for the development of coherent responses.

Fourth, exercise the team at multiple levels. The top level is the head of state or head of government, and the ministers represented in the combating terrorism working group. Since the top political authorities will be making the ultimate decisions to launch a counterterrorism operation, it is essential that they become exposed to, and ideally familiar with, both the rules of this game and the capabilities of their players.

Since their time is precious, an optimal way to engage them is to conduct "tabletop games." These typically propose a scenario, with a series of "moves"—by both the terrorists and the government. As the players work through the moves, they are exposed to the tactical, strategic, and political risks and results of their decisions—both good and bad. Such learning can take place over a short period, three to five hours—but can be invaluable in exposing the most senior members of the government to the challenges they would face in a real situation. The key is to develop a scenario that is seen as feasible by the players, which involves "moves" that highlight the choices to be made, and to have a facilitator who can gain the respect of all. To avoid embarrassment of any players, individuals should be briefed in advance on the design of the game, their general roles, and the roles, capabilities, and limitations of their ministry, so they can be comfortable during the play.

The next level of exercises or games should involve the members of the national interministerial working group. The group's exercises should be similar to the tabletop exercises discussed earlier, but conducted in more detail, with more moves, and over a longer period of time—perhaps twelve to twenty-four hours. These games should be conducted in two formats. First, the game should be played only within the working group. This will familiarize the players with their roles and responsibilities, and with each other. Once the inter-ministerial process has been "debugged," then the group should move on to the second format.

This format should bring the tactical players—operators, collectors, and negotiators—together with the working group policymakers. They also should participate in two types of exercises. The first would be what the military would call a "command post exercise." This would exercise roles and missions, inter-ministerial coordination, and decision making, based on a tactical scenario in which the leaders of the intelligence and operational units would play roles, but no troops would be deployed. Such an exercise might last from one to several days. One goal should be to demonstrate the effects fatigue will have on both the government officials and the terrorists, as the crisis drags on.

The second level of exercise would be a "field training exercise" in military parlance. This would be similar to the foregoing "command post exercise" but would involve the deployment and employment of all the forces involved. It will also require the fielding of a group of "terrorists" and a group of "hostages." The terrorist role players often come from within the operational and/or intelligence units involved. Before the exercise they are pulled aside, sworn to secrecy, and prepared for their roles in the game. For hostage role players it is usually best to choose government personnel with no experience in the counterterrorism business. Not knowing what to expect is an integral part of the hostage experience, and neither the terrorists nor the government forces are sure what the hostages may do next. This unpredictability is a key wild card in each of these games, but it adds a degree of reality and free play that is invaluable.

The full "field training exercise" should unfold over several days to a week, and may involve all aspects of the operation, testing the deployment, intelligence picture development, emergency and deliberate assault capabilities, hostage-handling techniques, and post-operations forensics aspects of a counterterrorism mission. Such an exercise requires a detailed scenario, experienced exercise controllers, an appropriate venue, and a good process to conduct debriefings of all involved in order to capture "lessons learned."

Although such a series of games and exercises is an expensive and time-consuming endeavor, it will pay big dividends when it comes time to execute an operation "for real." These exercises and games provide all involved with a sense of purpose. They highlight capabilities and vulnerabilities across all forces involved and can be used to allocate resources for investment in areas needing improvement. They also develop familiarity between the many components—hammer, eyes, brain—and thereby increase trust and confidence among these key players.

The intent of all of these preparations is to bring the elements of the Iron Triangle together at multiple levels, in multiple scenarios, in advance of any actual operation. Bringing them together will forge bonds of friendship and trust. These will be critically important if and when a real rescue operation is needed.

For the senior policymakers such a regimen can serve two purposes. The first is to bring the Iron Triangle together to enhance the chances for a successful rescue operation. On a more political level, the preparations can be used to demonstrate to a skeptical parliament (or public) that the government is taking terrorism seriously, and has taken appropriate steps to ensure all ministries are as prepared as can be, in the event of an actual terrorist hostage crisis. More skeptically, in the event a crisis occurs and an assault fails, these preparations can serve as a form of "political insurance" to counter the inevitable charges of unpreparedness, clumsiness, or intelligence failure from national or international political opponents.

The final ingredient for a successful operation is one over which we have no control. A rescue force that is only marginally capable, but enjoys a large dose of luck, will likely achieve results far superior to one with outstanding skills, but bad luck. It may seem fickle or inappropriate to speak of luck in such a context, but long years of experience demonstrate the crucial role played by this uncontrollable variable. Operators and policymakers alike must recognize that once they cast the dice by launching an operation, skill will only take them so far. Although any operational commander worthy of the title will seek to convince the policymaker he or she can prevail, in all likelihood, Lady Luck will have the last word. Pray that she will be on your side.

Conclusion

This chapter has described the ingredients for a competent counterterrorism force and a governmental structure to support the employment of that force. It is intended to serve as a "cookbook" for operators, intelligence personnel, negotiators, and policymakers at several levels of government. Developing such a set of capabilities is an expensive and time-consuming enterprise. It will require a long-term political commitment at many levels of government, development of an inter-ministerial approach, allocation of resources to all components of the team, and constant exercising and adaptation, particularly in light of the rapidly evolving terrorist threat.

Nevertheless, building such a national capability should be near the top of every government's agenda. Given the breadth and scope of terrorist acts in today's world, to be without such tools when terrorists do attack is to fail to uphold one of the most basic bargains between governments and their citizens—the requirement to provide an environment safe and secure from terrorists—to the extent practicable.

James Q. Roberts is Principal Director, Special Operations Capabilities, in the Office of the Assistant Secretary of Defense for Special Operations/Low-intensity Conflict and Interdependent Capabilities. A former Special Forces officer, Mr. Roberts has held many senior government positions, including: Principal Director to the Deputy Assistant Secretary of Defense (Policy & Missions) in the Office of the Assistant Secretary of Defense, Special Advisor of the United States to the European Union, Principal Director of Special Operations and Combating Terrorism for the Office of the Secretary of Defense, and Acting Deputy Assistant Secretary of Defense for Special Operations and Combating Terrorism. He was a Deputy Director of the Marshall Center from 2006 until assuming his current counterterrorism post.

Recommended Readings

Alexander, Yonah, ed. *Counterterrorism Strategies: Successes and Failures of Six Nations.* Washington, DC: Potomac Books, 2006.

Corum, James S., and Wray R. Johnson. *Airpower in Small Wars: Fighting Insurgents and Terrorists.* Lawrence, KA: University of Kansas Press, 2003.

Clarke, Richard A. *Against All Enemies: Inside America's War on Terror.* New York: Free Press, 2004.

Giampietri, Luis. *41 Seconds to Freedom: An Insider's Account of the Lima Hostage Crisis, 1996–97.* New York: Ballantine Books, 2007.

"Countering the Terrorist Threat," Section III in *Terrorism and Counterterrorism: Understanding the New Security Environment: Readings & Interpretations.* Howard, Russell D., and Reid L. Sawyer, eds. Revised and updated. Guilford, CT: McGraw-Hill, 2002, 310–501.

"National and Local Responses to the Threat," Section III in *Homeland Security and Terrorism: Readings and Interpretations.* Howard, Russell D., James J. F. Forrest, and Joanne C. Moore, eds. New York: McGraw-Hill, 2006, 27–322.

Christopher G. Cavoli

The Contribution of Counterinsurgency to a Strategy to Combat Global Terrorism

Insurgency and terrorism are not identical phenomena. It follows that counterterrorism and counterinsurgency are also not the same thing. Nevertheless, the two endeavors frequently overlap, and responses to one can greatly affect the other. Properly conducted, stability operations—a growing component of counterinsurgency operations—can and must aid in countering terrorist groups.

Relationships Between Terrorism and Insurgency

Insurgency is a ". . . struggle between a non-ruling group and the ruling authorities in which the non-ruling group consciously uses political resources . . . and violence to destroy, reformulate, or sustain the basis of legitimacy of one or more aspects of politics."[1] That is, insurgency is a type of struggle that includes both violent and nonviolent means of action. Terrorism, on the other hand, is a form of political warfare, a tactic ". . . in which violence is directed primarily against noncombatants (usually unarmed civilians) rather than operational military and police forces or economic assets."[2]

These definitions also help to define the groups who wage them. When an organization uses the tactic of terrorism as its primary method of pursuing its goals—that is, when the group's basic strategy is to employ terrorism—the group can be labeled a terrorist organization. But it need not be pursuing those goals as part of a larger insurgency. For example, Aum Shinrikyo conducted or prepared a significant number of sophisticated terrorist attacks on unarmed Japanese civilians during the mid-1990s. But while they used terroristic methods, the group's goals were more cultish and religious than political in nature.[3] Attacks aimed at the Japanese state were not intended to revise the forms of governance but the policies that the group felt obstructed its achievement of religious and self-interested goals. On the other hand, a terrorist group can have insurgent aims, but the size and scope of its activities never become large enough and wide enough to escape definition by their most prominent tactic. For example, Italy's large Red Brigades and the tiny Symbionese Liberation Army in the United States both considered themselves vanguards of a social and political revolution, but the scale of their activities and the breadth of the groups' appeal never approached a level where they might be considered insurgents; they were terrorists.

Conversely, insurgent groups need not be terrorists at all. Although an insurgency could certainly include the use of terroristic methods, many rely mainly on a combination of propaganda and guerrilla activity that is aimed mostly at government forces or assets, not unarmed civilians. The anti-Somoza Sandinista insurgency of 1970s and 1980s Nicaragua, for example, seems to have eschewed terrorism as a basic strategic approach, despite the Sandinistas' well-known and documented human rights violations, cases of assassination, etc. There are further cases of insurgencies that adopt guerrilla fighting but reject the purposeful killing or maiming of civilians as a fundamental strategy.[4]

Terrorist groups, then, are not necessarily insurgents, and insurgent groups are not necessarily terrorists. This is true despite the common practice of besieged governments to label all opponents as terrorists. This practice is destructive for two reasons. First, by inaccurately labeling a group, a government confirms the lack of comprehension its opponent seeks to impute to it. Second, by confusing opponents' methods with their ends, it muddies the waters exactly when clarity is most needed. It is necessary, then, to see how and when terrorism and insurgency overlap.

Many insurgents use terrorism, of course. Iraqi insurgents fighting against the US-led coalition in 2004–2008 routinely targeted civilians. And sometimes, the insurgent group uses terror methods to an extent that almost comes to define the character of the entire group. The activities of the Provisional Irish Republican Army so frequently included terrorism that to this day one may categorize the group as insurgent, or terrorist, or both. Likewise, Palestinian fighters in the Second Intifada have used urban guerrilla warfare and terrorism in equal measure to accomplish their aims. When an insurgency turns to terrorism (illegitimate violence), it then can be rightfully called an illegitimate and terrorist group.

Building on the foregoing discussion, it is possible to identify four possible permutations of the intersection of terrorism and insurgency. Each interaction suggests a strategy to counter it. First, there are terrorists who do not pursue insurgent goals. This group requires a pure counterterrorism strategy, discussed elsewhere in this volume. Second, there are insurgencies that are not terrorist. Such groups require a counterinsurgency strategy, a topic discussed at length in a large and growing body of literature.[5] Third, there are terrorist groups that exist to pursue an insurgent goal. And fourth, there are insurgents who use terrorist tactics.

Insurgents who use terrorist techniques pose a fairly simple case. For them, terrorism is one of the varieties of violent and nonviolent tools they use to further their insurgency. They use terrorism to: befuddle the government's forces; attack the credibility of the government by demonstrating its impotence; provoke government forces into overreactions that will alienate the population; galvanize the support of the population; coerce the population; intimidate government agents and collaborators; and create a sense of chaos and disorder that will amplify the effects of future action.

For an insurgent group, then, terrorism is an act of armed propaganda that, when correctly executed, increases the chances of success for other activities that may bring about the group's political goal. When insurgent groups do use terrorism, they do so in an effort to prolong or accelerate the insurgency, not in an attempt to change the character of the group. It is a rare insurgency, indeed, that seeks to morph into a terrorist group; examples escape the imagination.

When insurgents seek to use terrorism, they can take two paths. First, they can develop an internal capability for terrorism and do the operations "in house." Palestinians of Abu Nidal and Colombians of FARC supply examples of groups of the 1980s that used terror as a method of internal discipline, as well as external attack. Alternatively, insurgents can seek outside help, inviting the operations of existing terrorist groups to complement their strategies. In either case, though, this is a strategy of expansion through adoption of new methods.

Terrorists with an insurgent agenda seek to use terrorism to catalyze social change, just like any other insurgency, but lack the ability or intention to pursue this goal by means other than terrorism. Typically, these groups find themselves in a position of political and military weakness that is so pronounced they cannot even move directly to traditional guerilla activity. Therefore, their chief goal becomes growing the movement until it can become an insurgency. This usually happens in two ways. First, the terrorist group can seek to use terrorism to raise consciousness of its cause, and to draw recruits and support by demonstrating its power and the fecklessness of the government. In effect, the group grows the insurgency from the inside out. Alternatively, a terrorist group can seek to ally itself with an existing insurgency, or with a series of insurgencies, and try to co-opt them to its effort—as al Qaeda sought to affect the Taliban. That is, the group can seek to grow into an insurgency from the outside in. In reality, of course, most terrorist groups that seek an insurgent agenda use a combination of the inside-out and the outside-in techniques, attempting both to foment new insurgencies and to adopt existing ones. But in all cases, theirs is a strategy of merger and adoption.[6]

Going further, we can define four categories of interaction between insurgent and terrorist groups. First, some insurgent groups seek to use terrorist methods and develop that capability on their own. Second, some insurgent groups seek terrorist capabilities, and look to recruit them from external terrorist groups. Third, some terrorist groups seek to develop into full-blown insurgent movements, and do so by trying to grow their movements independently. Fourth, some terrorist groups seek to develop into insurgency, and do so by establishing a series of alliances and mergers with insurgent groups.

The first of these scenarios requires a counterterror strategy to defeat it. That is, the insurgent group must be prevented from acquiring and employing terrorist capabilities. However, unlike previous cases discussed elsewhere in this volume, in this case the counterterror strategy has to be closely nested inside a counterinsurgency strategy, lest the inevitable kinetic actions of the former nullify the nonkinetic efforts necessary in the latter. We will return in a moment to this question of "doing no harm," but first must examine more closely the last three groups, in which terrorist and insurgent groups create symbiotic relationships that can be particularly difficult to stop.

Two current and useful examples that illustrate these three phenomena can be found in Algeria and the border regions of Pakistan-Afghanistan.

In the late 1990s, the Salafist Group for Preaching and Combat (GSPC) was founded to conduct an insurgency in North Africa with a local aim: to replace the government of Algeria with an Islamic emirate. Its goals appealed directly to a population disaffected with the regime in Algiers and attracted to the group's vow to avoid the civilian casualties that characterized recent operations of the Armed Islamic Group (GIA), from which the GSPC had split because of the former group's increasingly indiscriminate brutality.[7] However, government operations (which themselves invited complaints about human rights violations) reduced the power of the GSPC and circumscribed its operations significantly.[8] By 2003, the group was reeling; as a result, it turned to terrorism and hit a "soft" target of thirty-two European tourists, whom they took for ransom.[9] The effect was twofold. Understandably listed by the United States as a "terrorist group," the GSPC headed more and more into the realm of terrorism, and sought a way to jump-start these operational capabilities; they began to seek outside help. The second effect was that the GSPC was noticed by al Qaeda as an opportunity for expansion.[10]

Al Qaeda is well known as a terrorist group, but has sought to use its actions to catalyze a global Salafist insurgency.[11] Its modus operandi has been to use its terrorist acts to attract attention to its cause and to establish itself as the vanguard of a broader movement. Then, the group seeks out local insurgencies that might be sympathetic to the al Qaeda cause. Relying on the reputation it has established through its terrorist acts, al Qaeda then, essentially, trades support to the local insurgency in turn for its loyalty. Al Qaeda provides the local insurgency specialty expertise, funding, ideological support, and an overall context for the insurgency. In turn, the local insurgency provides manpower, moral support, and a grounding of practical grievances for al Qaeda to link to its own more abstruse agenda.

In Algeria, al Qaeda began to provide financing and technical information to the GSPC, enhancing the latter's capabilities and contributing to the shift in its operational methodology. Al Qaeda endorsed GSPC's local agenda, and in the process co-opted the agenda into its own; the Algerian fight was now claimable—and claimed—as part of the international jihad. In turn, the GSPC willingly gave al Qaeda what it really wanted: GSPC endorsed al Qaeda's vision of a global caliphate, and announced that its own struggle was no longer local, but a part of a greater cause.[12]

Both groups won. The strategy of mutual cooptation and merger gave GSPC stronger capabilities that had been lacking within its insurgency, and gave al Qaeda the opportunity to claim a more significant, insurgent agenda.

At around the same time, al Qaeda was also expanding in a different part of the world. Deprived of a safe haven by the US-led intervention in Afghanistan in late 2001, al Qaeda needed to reestablish a level of control over western Pakistan in order to reestablish itself there. The surest way to do this was to weaken government control over the Federally Administered Tribal Areas and the corresponding border portions of Afghanistan. In these areas, the longtime relationship between al Qaeda and local tribes facilitated a new understanding. Al Qaeda would support a recrudescence of the Taliban's fight in Afghanistan, and the Taliban would in turn support al Qaeda's global agenda. This is a bigger change than would seem on the surface. Previously, the Taliban had sympathized with and condoned al Qaeda's agenda, but had not had significant global aspirations of its own and had a mixed feeling at best toward the non-Afghans who were brought in by the terrorist group; the Taliban was a Pashtun grouping with strictly Afghan-oriented goals, and maintaining popular support or acquiescence was sometimes difficult while harboring the ambitious Arabs. Now, however, needing to reestablish itself in Afghanistan, the Taliban welcomed al Qaeda's declaration that the Taliban cause was part of its global jihad; in turn, the Taliban stirred with supra-local ambitions.[13] This merger was more significant than the previous host-guest relationship that the two groups had shared. Whereas previously, the Taliban tolerated with mixed emotions al Qaeda's presence and the endorsement it implied, now they adopted both.[14] Likewise, al Qaeda began to dig itself into the local agenda of the Taliban, contributing to the anti-Kabul fight even in areas like Nuristan, where it had previously benefited from a relatively stable situation that did not invite scrutiny.[15] The relationship became symbiotic. The Taliban gained al Qaeda status, financing, and fighting and terror expertise and tied al Qaeda to its local agenda. Al Qaeda gained another front in its global jihad, as well as the direct benefit of continued haven.

In this triple example, we can see a general pattern for how terror and insurgent groups establish their symbiosis. Terrorist groups present their ideology as an overarching narrative that explains local grievances, justifies reactions to them, and then claims those actions as contributions to their causes. In effect, terrorist groups say, "See what those guys are doing? That's part of our struggle, too!" In turn, local insurgent groups accept (or even, as in the example of the GSPC, seek out) these affiliations in order to further their own aims. The local group thereby empowers its efforts, and the terrorist group expands its ambitions into insurgency. This symbiotic relationship requires special care to combat.

Counterinsurgency in the Face of a Symbiotic Relationship

Counterinsurgency efforts can make a major contribution to a counterterror strategy by preventing the salutary effects on the terrorist group that would be gained by merging with local insurgencies. Essentially, by countering insurgencies thoughtfully, a force can deprive the terrorists of the opportunity to capitalize on local grievances and co-opt the resulting movements to their cause.

When terrorist and insurgent groups seek to conflate their causes and aggregate their power, the primary strategy to be employed against a symbiotic terror-insurgency must be a strategy of disaggregation.[16] That is, a counterinsurgency strategy must be developed that will deprive the terrorists of grist for their propaganda mill, disprove terrorist groups' claims that local insurgencies are their own, and prevent local insurgents from reaching out to and adopting the goals of terror groups in an effort to enhance their own causes.

There are basic areas in which counterinsurgency forces must take efforts in order to disaggregate terrorist and insurgent aims and methods. The necessary approaches and efforts are neither linear nor sequential; rather they are intertwined and mutually reinforcing.

The counterinsurgent force must have a direct counterterror strategy to prevent the galvanizing attacks that allow the terrorists to focus the minds of the people. One of the chief goals of any insurgency is to discredit the government's ability to protect itself, its infrastructure, and the population. Spectacular events that undermine the government's claim to legitimacy through competence serve this purpose. The attacks can be in the form of guerrilla warfare, as was the case in Iraq when insurgents cut off the main road from Baghdad International Airport to the coalition headquarters for much of 2005 and 2006. Or the attacks can be nearly conventional, as in the Tet Offensive of 1968 in Vietnam. These two examples also illustrate that the attacks need not be successful at the operational level in order to achieve their goals. It is often sufficient merely to demonstrate the capability to conduct the attacks. However, attacks of this nature are costly, both in terms of potential losses and in terms of the materiel, expertise, and human capital necessary to stage them. A cheaper approach is to use terrorist style attacks on soft targets, which is often why insurgent groups turn to terrorism. This means a counterterror strategy, or at least an anti-terror strategy, is normally necessary in a counterinsurgency.

A counterterror strategy must, of course, include definitive efforts to defend relevant targets against enemy attacks, as well as to discern and dismantle the terrorists' infrastructure of leadership and materiel. But this is not enough; the counterterror strategy must also include an effort to minimize the popular support for the terrorists among the populace. In a counterinsurgency, this effort (referred to broadly in the United States as Countering

Ideological Support for Terrorism, or CIST) is specifically designed to counter the terrorists' goal to conflate their own ideology and goals with the goals of the insurgency and to counter the insurgents' willingness to do the same. It is an effort to prevent terrorist groups from benefiting from the popular support that insurgents seek.

Properly conceived, a counterinsurgency strategy must be viewed not as a military effort but as a persuasive effort.[17] That is, a counterinsurgency must be designed to persuade the population to eschew the enemy and its goals, and to support the government. The implications of this formulation are important: It means that a counterinsurgency consists of everything a force says and does, and how they say and do it. Similarly, a CIST effort conducted within the context of a counterinsurgency must also be a campaign of persuasion; thus, it will consist of everything the force says and does and how they say and do it—as well as what is not done or said. Understood in this holistic fashion, it becomes clear that CIST is a basic task of any counterinsurgency; that task drives the spirit and conduct of the counterinsurgency in fundamental ways. Properly conducted, a counterinsurgency will have a CIST effect that will isolate the insurgency from potential linkages to other insurgencies and terrorist groups, and will allow the insurgency to be dealt with alone.

A counterinsurgency-based CIST campaign must follow the imperative to "do no harm."[18] That is, a counterinsurgency force must never conduct itself in such a manner that it confirms the enemy narrative that seeks to conflate the insurgency's goals with the terror group's. This concept can have as many practical expressions as there are insurgencies in the world; however, for the sake of clarity and relevance we will limit ourselves to examples that apply generally in the cases of insurgency and terrorism in the Muslim world that occupy much current thought and effort.

Counterinsurgency forces must not ever appear to be occupation forces, nor the puppets of occupation forces. A common claim of both terror and insurgent groups in current conflicts is that external forces are alien bodies, unwelcome, and intent only upon subjugation of the peoples native to the country in which the operations take place. Actions, words, or implications that fulfill this accusation "prove" a basic claim of both terror and insurgent groups, and thus drive them together conceptually. Examples of "doing harm" in this regard can include but are not limited to: acting outside the bounds of the country's laws or formal agreements with the country; publicly flouting minor laws such as traffic rules or employment practices; using or appropriating lands and real estate in a way that does not accord with the country's customs and law; engaging in business practices that seem designed to move money, either indigenous or externally provided, out of the country rather than into it; directing and dictating to indigenous institutions and agencies, rather than consulting with and aiding them. It does not take the reader very long to conclude that these principles must apply equally at the strategic, operational, and tactical levels.

Counterinsurgency forces must also be careful not to operate in a manner that conflicts with the culture and religion of the affected population. It is a common claim of both insurgent and terrorist groups that counterinsurgency forces are alien entities, and that dealing with them will irreparably harm the society of the population, as well as the souls of those individuals who make it up. Doing things or saying things that seem to prove this point merely paves the way for the merger of terror and insurgent groups. "Doing harm" in this regard is an especially common mistake in current conflicts. Examples of religious mistakes include: infringing during operations upon religious customs and locations, such as prayer time, religious festivals, and mosques; proselytizing, publicly conducting non-Muslim religious activities, and displaying non-Muslim iconography and symbols; seeming to profess any sort of atheism; and promoting secular values, institutions, and programs without explaining how they are accommodated by Islam. Cultural mistakes are more difficult to generalize about, for the obvious reason that cultures vary greatly and locally. However, it is safe to say that CIST efforts can be set back by: interacting untowardly with local women; operating in a fashion that ignores traditional power structures, such as tribal leadership; and applying economic principles that ignore traditional allocation of resources and wealth.

Perhaps most obviously, counterinsurgency forces must seek to "do no harm" in the most literal sense—by avoiding causing damage to people or things not fully associated with the insurgency. The killing of any person, in any culture, carries with it significant social, economic, moral, and legal implications. More to the point, it also carries with it an emotional charge that is hard to defray. It is certainly hard to imagine winning the loyalty of a population unnecessarily or carelessly depleted by the killing of civilians or damage of their property. Doing so confirms in the most visceral way the propaganda of the terrorists and insurgents alike; it must be avoided.

This leads to another basic principle that must govern counterinsurgencies that seek a CIST effect: The actions and words of the counterinsurgents must not confirm the enemy's narrative or justify the enemy's claims.

The first and most obvious conclusion to draw from this principle is covered by the edict to "do no harm": the counterinsurgents' operations must not gratuitously provide grist for the mill of enemy propaganda. But the principle goes beyond this concept of avoiding trouble; it is also necessary to take active measures to disprove the enemy's narrative. How exactly to do so depends on the particular propagandistic attempts being made by terror groups. This effort will include the need to counter a variety of open lies and disinformation about the conduct of government forces. An example might be false allegations of rape. It is obviously not enough to not rape people; it is also necessary to take active steps to deny that rape has occurred. There are two basic categories of active measures to be taken to disprove enemy propaganda: one's own propaganda, and actions to display behavior that counters the propaganda. In the example of false claims of rape, it is critical to publicly and effectively communicate a convincing denial to the population. It is also critical to stage a public communication campaign that informs the people, for example, of the great care taken by government forces when dealing with local women. Finally, in this example, it is necessary to act in a way that denies any credibility to such claims in the first place: operating in an open and transparent manner; ensuring that women are dealt with only in the presence of other women; using female agents to handle female detainees; and medically evacuating a woman only with a male family escort. These are all proactive behaviors that can avert the opportunity for the enemy to make specious claims about a force's behavior toward local women. By avoiding and actively combating such misleading propaganda through words and deeds, the counterinsurgency force can minimize the terrorists' appeal to the population.

A further principle of effective counterinsurgency is to create or maintain splits between terrorist groups and their potential allies in the insurgency: the counterinsurgency strategy must focus on the aspects of the local insurgency's appeal that do not coincide with the terrorists' wider agenda. If the first two principles consisted of ways to prevent the attempts of terrorists to conflate their movement with an insurgency, this principle and the next focus on how to actively disaggregate the enemy's overlap with the insurgency. This is essentially the beginning of a wedge-driving strategy, in which the government force discerns what the terrorists' goals are; what the insurgency's goals are; how they overlap; and how they do not. Then, the counterinsurgency force adopts propaganda activity and operational activity that stress the divergence among those goals. For example, in Iraq in 2005 and 2006, the coalition learned that differences were appearing among the terrorists in Zarqawi's al Qaeda in Iraq (AQI), which sought to conflate itself with the domestic insurgency. The main divergence between Zarqawi's group and the domestic movement was that the local insurgency was just that—local. The majority of fighters sought only control of their towns or districts, or at most Iraq itself. AQI, to them, had been only a means to get there. With AQI's alliance with al Qaeda in 2005, the group began to pursue coalition forces and sectarian targets that were not necessarily of primary interest to local insurgents; and in any case, effectively promoted the insurgency's shift from a national one to a sectarian civil war. This gave the coalition the opportunity to court Shiites by stressing the fundamental difference their religion created between them and AQI and al Qaeda. It also gave the opportunity to court Sunnis by emphasizing the nationalist aspect of their agendas, which had little to do with AQI's goals. Coming through 2006 and 2007, the coalition's counterinsurgency continued to stress the "underlap" between the agendas of local insurgents and globalist terrorists; the coalition-favored Shia political movements in the south; promoted and supported a Shia head of government; protected resolutely Shia rights to worship publicly; largely reversed the de-Baathification campaign that had disenfranchised the Sunni; promoted Sunni "reconciliation councils" that took effective control of Sunni towns; and, perhaps most famously, created local militias that would protect their "homes" from "foreign terrorists."[19] This strategy of disaggregation refocused the local insurgency on its own concerns, versus AQI's, and consequently stopped and reversed what had threatened to be a signal example of the symbiosis between local insurgents and globalist terrorists.

The final principle to be emphasized is that to counter ideological support for terrorism, counterinsurgency must appeal to the values of the local people involved. This aspect of the counterinsurgency is an active measure and is not unrelated to the previous principles. When one stresses the "underlap" between terrorist campaigns and insurgencies, it is most profitable, obviously, to focus on differences in the areas the local population holds most dear. Usually, these are local, cultural preferences and are often strongest in rural or traditional societies. In the border regions of eastern Afghanistan, for example, the otherwise extremely pious Pashtun population expresses its religion with significant local modification. For instance, bride price and the method of its establishment vary greatly between Kunar and Nuristan—both conservative Muslim populations, but each with distinct social traditions. It is difficult for a globalist Islamist terror group to make a tent big enough to include both of these traditions without contradiction. And since the topic at hand is of fundamental importance to the societies in question—bride price being a basic instrument of social control—it is a topic that stokes passions when contradictions arise. A counterinsurgency strategy would do well to emphasize such differences in order to effectively counter terrorist efforts to co-opt local insurgencies in an effort to grow their movement. Implementing this principle, or any of the others discussed, requires significant understanding of an area and its culture. The study necessary to gain this understanding usually must happen *in situ*, so a force is left with a paradox: The efforts it takes while learning what efforts it should take may unnecessarily complicate appropriate future efforts. The earlier principle of "doing no harm" applies especially during this period.

In general, we also see that all of the foregoing principles interact in a complex and reflexive fashion; they are not necessarily sequential, and sometimes are even iterative. An anecdote may help to illustrate how these principles can be applied and how they interact.

Conducting COIN with a CIST Effect in Northeastern Afghanistan

In the summer of 2006, 1st Battalion of the 32nd Infantry from the US 10th Mountain Division was assigned the mission to pacify and bring under government control a small town in south-central Nuristan called Aranas.[20] Aranas sat, geographically and conceptually, at the nexus of local insurgent groups and more globally minded terrorists. The original inhabitants of Aranas were native sons of Nuristan and were proud of their history of resistance to government rule; for a variety of social and economic reasons, their town and valley were the starting point of a number of rebellions, to include *inter alia*, the first rebellion against the communist government of Kabul in 1979. Theirs was a classic local counterinsurgency, based on social, cultural, political, and economic grievances; although quiescent in the 1990s, it was starting to flare again in connection with Nuristan's post-Taliban recognition as a province, which implied the reciprocal loyalty of the people to Kabul. The town itself was located in a very remote mountainous area, but one that uniquely managed also to afford rapid foot and vehicle access to Pakistan for those who knew the way and could claim safe passage. As a result, it was an amenable area for Pakistan-based terrorists to hide.

After 2002, when Pakistan finally bowed to US pressure and outlawed the Kashmiri separatist group Lashkar e Tayyiba (LeT), those terrorists required a new safe haven outside Pakistan. Having also lost, at least temporarily, Pakistan's support for the Kashmiri cause, the group also needed a *raison d'être*. LeT sought both relevance and a haven in northeastern Afghanistan, where Nuristan represented the western end of a natural geographical and cultural line of drift connecting Kashmir, the Northern Territories of Pakistan, and Afghanistan. LeT needed to expand into a new area; and that area had an extant insurgency. A strategy of cooption and merger was obvious.

LeT came into Nuristan on a vector established long ago by the *Panjpiris*, a group of radical clerics from the Deobandi school who sought to strengthen the Islamization of Nuristan—which had been converted, after all, only a hundred years previously. The *Panjpiris* came to many towns in Nuristan in the 1950s and 1960s, and established themselves as holy men and guests. Then, they began to pronounce self-serving *fatwahs* that enabled the clerics to establish themselves in towns; for example, they lowered bride prices wherever they could, and then despite their indigence, married into townships, thus establishing a base of support. The LeT shared the *Panjpiris'* radical interpretations of Islam, and used the consequent affinity as a way to get into the villages.

Once in Aranas, LeT leaders tried to conflate their religious *jihad* with the local insurgents' political, cultural, and economic resistance to Kabul. The arrangement became profitable to both sides: LeT received a safe haven, access to new recruits, and a cause to employ them while they waited for Kashmir to reopen as a front for their activity; the local insurgents got expertise, money, and moral support for their continued resistance against Kabul. The population, meanwhile, was subjected to crude propaganda that offended their most basic values, and attempted to justify the alliance of their "own" insurgents with this outside group. They were told that Kabul was godless and had only two mosques; that Americans dictated to the government, hated Muslims, and prevented proper worship; furthermore, that Americans raped women and had been known to eat Muslim babies. The situation meant that any counterinsurgency strategy to bring the town into a loyal relationship with the government would necessarily involve a CIST element that disaggregated the enemy into his natural components, and then split those elements apart in order to deal with them separately.

The alliance between the locals and the terrorists was convenient, but flawed. Too many basic differences were papered over, and this provided the American battalion and their Afghan partners with opportunities.

Upon first arrival in the town, the coalition force understood that learning and discerning the details of the situation were of paramount importance and that during this learning period they would be very vulnerable to making mistakes. It became a key goal, then, to avoid "doing any harm." The coalition force was kept small—fewer than fifty personnel, despite the fact that the town was more than twenty-five kilometers from the nearest supporting coalition base. The force resolutely declined to engage in any violent activities, or to "solve" any of the problems that were brought to them; they limited their activity to reconnaissance, and to endless discussions with locals in town. As they avoided making big mistakes that would confirm in the people's mind the LeT's propaganda, they also took active steps to further undermine the false message. The force donated money to refurbish portions of the town's main mosque; created a small but visible area where the Afghan soldiers prayed daily (augmented on a couple of memorable and powerful occasions by a temporarily assigned US Muslim soldier); and eagerly pushed the Afghan company commander, himself a mullah, to the forefront in all dealings with the town. The men made themselves visible in the town with no body armor and no helmets, to ensure that they did not appear as the "evil" outsiders LeT claimed them to be. And, over time, it even became obvious to the people that the coalition force was not "eating babies" either.

Having begun to disprove the crudest of the LeT's propaganda, the coalition force began to seek the "underlap" between LeT's agenda and methodology and the insurgents'. By focusing on this, they would seek to pull apart the alliance and hoped to do so completely non-kinetically.

The greatest divergence between the two groups lay in the management of the town. The townspeople were supremely practical (as previously noted, their grievances with Kabul were almost all material), and they wanted nothing to limit their ability to secure and control the town's materiel welfare. The *mujahedin* insurgents were sons of the town and knew that the townspeople would only tolerate the alliance with the terrorists if the terrorists remained aloof from the town's politics, and never brought fighting into the town. Understanding this, the coalition carefully but quickly began to push management decisions onto the town's elders: Where should we house the coalition force? Would you like a road? Where should the road run? Would you rather have a school or a clinic? We will make you a school, but where? And, who will be the teacher? The members of LeT hidden among the population desired intensely to get involved in the decision making in order to prevent the coalition's delivery of these offers, since each of them promised to weaken the LeT's bond with the population and its insurgency by appealing to the population's material desires—which the coalition could fulfill much better than the LeT. But the population sensed LeT's desire to get involved in the decision making, and this reminded them that the terrorists were outsiders. Furthermore, the population understood that the LeT wanted to get involved in order to prevent the delivery of physical goods and services, and were thus made to understand that the LeT prioritized their own goals over the material, political, and cultural welfare of the people—which were, of course, the primary concerns of the population.

The actions of the coalition polarized the locals and LeT. Their behavior disproved the grossest propaganda of the enemy. And the sudden rush of management and leadership decisions purposefully foisted upon the townspeople by the coalition accentuated the differences between the LeT's goals and the population's, leaving the insurgents to choose between the two; understanding that their natural allies must be the latter, the insurgents chose the population. In short order the population and the insurgents tacitly "sided" with the coalition against the LeT, ceased their cooperation, and expelled the bulk of the terrorists from the town. While this left the coalition to contend with the insurgency, at least the conflict was insulated from exacerbation by a merger with external terrorists; the more local grievances of the insurgents could be conventionally dealt with, and more easily, absent the polarizing effects of a terrorist movement.

The LeT, left with few options, decided to fight. They adopted an overtly hostile posture and attacked coalition forces openly. This had two effects. First, it exposed the LeT members to the greater firepower of the US troops, who killed them in short order. Second, because the coalition forces were among the townspeople, it caused the LeT to bring fighting into the town. This was the final straw. The local townspeople thereafter insisted that the insurgency break any ties to the LeT. Bereft of that external support, and largely swayed by the efforts the coalition took to disprove early LeT narratives, the insurgents mainly laid down their arms and joined the new political life of the town.

Conclusion

Although terrorism and insurgency are not the same phenomena, they are closely related and sometimes seek to merge. In these cases, the efforts of counterinsurgency and counterterrorism must work in complementary fashion. Counterinsurgency operations must have the effect of countering the appeal of the terrorist group, in order to avert the merger of the two. This requires the counterinsurgent force to disprove enemy propaganda; to appeal to the values of local populations; to disaggregate the goals and methods of the insurgents and the terrorists; and to stress those aspects of each group's agenda and modus operandi that are dissimilar, so as to sow discord where the enemy seeks to produce an alliance. Operating in this way requires, perhaps, a degree of subtlety, and certainly a measure of knowledge. Careful study and understanding of a situation are necessary before such a holistic approach can be made. But, indeed, it is only intelligence and understanding that will win any conflict that has its roots in the desires and aspirations of a people.

Christopher G. Cavoli Colonel Cavoli is a career Infantry officer who has served in a wide variety of operational billets in airborne and light infantry units throughout Europe, Asia, and the United States. He is also a qualified Foreign Area Officer, with specialization in Russia and Eurasia. Colonel Cavoli's staff experience includes service as a Politico-Military Planner for Russia on the Joint Staff/J5, and as the Deputy Executive Assistant for the Chairman of the Joint Chiefs of Staff. His operational assignments include command at several levels, in both peacetime and combat. Colonel Cavoli currently commands the 3rd Infantry Brigade Combat Team of the 1st Armored Division. He previously commanded the 1st Battalion, 32nd Infantry of the 10th Mountain Division, with which he deployed to Afghanistan for sixteen months; the battalion's area of responsibility included Nangarhar, Nuristan, Laghman, and Kunar Provinces. Colonel Cavoli holds degrees from Princeton and Yale Universities.

Recommended Readings

Kilcullen, David. "Countering Global Insurgency," *Small Wars Journal,* 30 November 2004. Available at www.smallwarsjournal.com/documents/kilcullen.pdf, accessed 10 September 2009.

Kilcullen, David. *The Accidental Guerrilla: Fighting Small Wars in the Midst of a Big One.* Oxford: Oxford University Press, 2009.

McMillan, Joseph, and Cavoli, Christopher. "Countering Global Terrorism," Ch. 2 of *Strategic Challenges: America's Global Security Agenda*, Stephen J. Flanagan and James A. Schear, eds. Dulles, VA: Potomac Books, 2008, 20–60.

Myers, Richard B. *Eyes on the Horizon: Serving on the Front Lines of National Security*, Ch. 12, "The Enduring Threat." New York: Simon and Schuster, 2009.

Tierney Jr., John J. *Chasing Ghosts: Unconventional Warfare in American History*. Washington, DC: Potomac Books, 2006.

United States Army and United States Marine Corps. *Joint Field Manual, FM 3–24: Counterinsurgency.* Washington DC: US Army, December 2006.

Notes

1. Bard E. O'Neill, *Insurgency and Terrorism: Inside Modern Revolutionary Warfare* (Dulles, VA: Brassey's, 1990), 13.
2. O'Neill, 24.
3. Holley, David, "Cult Attracted Many Followers—And Notoriety," *Los Angeles Times*, 23 March 1995; available at http://articles.latimes.com/1995-03-23/news/mn-46249_1_aum-supreme-truth, accessed 10 September 2009.
4. Robert Asprey details dozens of insurgencies in his classic compendium, *War in the Shadows: The Guerrilla in History* (New York: William Morrow, 1994), and throughout the work makes a distinction between terrorism and guerrilla fighting, which he views as two potentially but not necessarily complementary tactics available to insurgents. Bard O'Neill picks up on this distinction, and points out that although guerrilla fighting and terrorism are "the most common" combination of insurgent groups that mix tactics, it is neither a necessary nor a universal combination; see Bard O'Neill, *Insurgency and Terrorism: Inside Modern Revolutionary Warfare*, 2nd ed. (Dulles, VA; Potomac Books, 2005), 33–36. O'Neill also points out that disputes about using terrorism as a tactic are a frequent cause of discord and disunity in insurgent organizations (p. 131).
5. The body of counterinsurgency literature has grown quickly with the renewed focus brought to the topic by the wars in Afghanistan and Iraq. Since John Nagl's work in *Learning to Eat Soup with a Knife: Counterinsurgency Lessons from Malaya and Vietnam* (Chicago: University of Chicago Press, 2005), the number of high-quality books, monographs, and

online publications devoted to population-centric counterinsurgency has flourished. See for example, David Kilcullen's "Twenty-Eight Articles: Fundamentals of Company-Level Counterinsurgency," *Small Wars Journal*, March 2006, available at http://smallwarsjournal. com/documents/28articles.pdf, accessed 10 September 2009; this is an echo of a T. E. Lawrence article. See as well Kalev Sepp, "Best Practices in Counterinsurgency," *Military Review*, May–June 2005, 8–12; Daniel Marston and Carter Malkasian, *Counterinsurgency in Modern Warfare* (Oxford: Osprey Publishing, 2008); *The Small Wars Journal* (http://smallwarsjournal.com/); and, of course, the United States Army's and United States Marine Corps' joint field manual, *FM 3-24: Counterinsurgency* (Washington DC: US Army, December 2006).

6. This sort of growth pattern is reflected in most theories of insurgency warfare. For example, Maoist doctrine called for a progression through three phases, the "strategic defensive," "equilibrium," and "strategic offensive" (see Mao Tse-Tung, "Strategy in China's Revolutionary War," *Selected Military Writings of Mao Tse-Tung* (Peking: Foreign Language Press, 1967), 210–219. The defensive phase required mobilization of the peasantry and preparation for the second phase, both of which required a significant degree of violence, in practice including terrorist acts. The aggregation of that activity into a larger insurgency movement, and its succession of more conventional forms of war, was a conscious part of Mao's strategy to move from guerrilla warfare to mobile warfare to conventional "positional" warfare (Mao, 246–248).

7. Lianne Kennedy Boudali, *The GSPC: Newest Franchise in Al Q'Aeda's Global Jihad* (West Point: The Combating Terrorism Center, April 2007), 1–3, accessed at http://www.dtic.mil/cgi-bin/GetTRDoc?AD=ADA466539&Location=U2&doc=GetTRDoc.pdf on 10 September 2009.

8. Michael Knights, "Algerian Operations Compress Islamist Insurgency," *Jane's Islamic Affairs Analyst*, 1 December 2003; http://search.janes.com/Search/documentView.do?docId=/content1/janesdata/mags/jir/history/jir2003/jir07781.htm@current&pageSelected=allJanes&keyword=GSPC&backPath=http://search.janes.com/Search&Prod_Name=JIR&, accessed 1 June 2009.

9. BBC, "Profile: Algeria's Salafist Group," 14 May 2003; http://news.bbc.co.uk/2/hi/africa/3027621.stm, accessed 10 September 2009.

10. "Is Al Q'Aeda/GSPC Alliance Spin?," *Jane's Terrorism and Security Monitor*, 15 November 2006; http://search.janes.com/Search/documentView.do?docId=/content1/janesdata/mags/jtsm/history/jtsm2006/jtsm5025.htm@current&pageSelected=allJanes&keyword=gspc&backPath=http://search.janes.com/Search&Prod_Name=JTSM&, accessed 1 June 2009. See also Boudali, *The GSPC: Newest Franchise in Al Q'Aeda's Global Jihad*, especially 5–6.

11. This phenomenon has been explored increasingly in recent years. See David Kilcullen's "Countering a Global Insurgency," *Small Wars Journal*, 30 November 2004; www.smallwarsjournal.com/documents/kilcullen.pdf, accessed 10 September 2009. See also Joseph McMillan and Christopher Cavoli, "Countering Global Terrorism," Chapter 2 of *Strategic Challenges: America's Global Security Agenda*, Stephen J. Flanagan and James A. Schear, eds. (Dulles, VA: Potomac Books, 2008), 20–60.

12. Regarding the underlying logic, see BBC, "Algerian Group Backs al Q'aeda," 23 October 2003; http://news.bbc.co.uk/2/hi/africa/3207363.stm, accessed 10 September 2009. With regard to the formal merger, see "Algerian Salafists Adopt al Q'aeda Brand," *Jane's Terrorism and Security Monitor*, 14 February 2007, http://search.janes.com/Search/documentView.do?docId=/content1/janesdata/mags/jtsm/history/jtsm2007/jtsm5053.htm@current&pageSelected=allJanes&keyword=gspc&backPath=http://search.janes.com/Search&Prod_Name=JTSM&, accessed 1 June 2009.

13. Antonio Giustozzi provides an excellent description of the increasingly global vision of the Taliban in his book, *Koran, Kalashnikov, and Laptop: The Neo-Taliban Insurgency in Afghanistan* (New York: Columbia University Press, 2007).

14. Giustozzi; see especially section 4.11 on pp. 136–139.

15. The author received a very full, if somewhat subjective, description of this process from Tamim Nuristani, Governor of Nuristan, during a lengthy personal interview on the evenings of 17 and 18 May 2007, at the governor's residence just south of Pashki, Nuristan.

16. See Kilcullen, and Cavoli & McMillan.
17. Frank Kitson, *Bunch of Five* (London: Faber and Faber, 1977), 282.
18. US Marine Corps General James Mattis began to paraphrase the Hippocratic Oath when he commanded the First Marine Division in Iraq in 2004 and 2005, telling his men that their first responsibility in a counterinsurgency was to "do no harm" to the people or the counterinsurgency effort. See James Mattis, "Letter To All Hands," 23 March 2004; http://faculty.washington.edu/ sidles/ISH/Mattis_message.pdf, accessed 10 September 2009.
19. The historiography of this period is still emerging, but Tom Ricks provides a good description and analysis in *The Gamble: General David Petraeus and the American Military Adventure in Iraq, 2006–2008* (New York: Penguin, 2009). For a good contemporaneous account of the arming of militias, see Greg Bruno, "The Role of the 'Sons of Iraq' in Improving Security," *Washington Post*, 28 April 2008; http://www.washingtonpost.com/wp-dyn/content/ article/2008/04/28/AR2008042801120.html, accessed 10 September 2009.
20. The author commanded 1-32 Infantry during this period, and the details of this story come from his personal recollections, field notes, correspondence with his former subordinates, and the battalion's combat record.

Unit 3

Instruments of National Power

David Litt and Mary Ann Peters

Diplomacy:

The First Weapon Against the Terrorist

An ambassador is an honest man sent to lie abroad for the good of his country.

Sir Henry Wotton
Seventeenth-century British diplomat

A diplomat is a person who can tell you to go to hell in such a way that you actually look forward to the trip.

Caskie Stinnett
Twentieth-century American humorist

What Is Diplomacy?

Diplomacy clearly has its detractors and its cartoonists. Caricatures of diplomats frequenting cocktail parties, dressed in effete garb, engaged in meaningless chit-chat, are popular, especially in circles that favor "persuasive" force over "useless" talk. Movies relentlessly lampoon embassy officials as craven, crass bureaucrats—especially in comparison to the soldier or desperate private citizen who appear on the screen in stark heroic contrast to the reputedly feckless diplomat.

Much of this disillusionment with diplomacy can be traced to the cataclysm of World War I, for which the secret diplomacy of the nineteenth century was at least partly to blame. In the interwar years, the failures of the League of Nations and European efforts to restrain Germany further tarnished the reputation of diplomacy as a means of avoiding conflict or resolving international problems. Writing in 1972, historian Barbara Tuchman captured the spirit of what she called a "deep-seated American distrust" of diplomacy. "Diplomacy means all the wicked devices of the old world, spheres of influence, balances of power, secret treaties, triple alliances, and, during the interwar period, appeasement of Fascism."[1]

Modern diplomacy has evolved since the period that inspired this disdain. In the years following World War II the practice of diplomacy stretched beyond its traditional boundaries of bilateral state-to-state political, economic, and security relations. With the explosion in the number of new nations (from only 51 UN signatories in 1945 to more than 190 members today) and the establishment of the UN family of agencies, multilateral diplomacy became the preferred means for grappling with international scientific challenges like the environment; social and legal issues like human rights, narcotics, and international criminality; and health issues like flu pandemic, smallpox, and malaria.

In addition to dozens of new international and multilateral organizations, we now have other new players on the international stage, most notably nongovernmental organizations (NGOs), such as Oxfam or the International Committee of the Red Cross, and powerful multinational corporations. CNN and other news networks have added urgency to the conduct of diplomacy by delivering analyses and images of world events directly to the world citizenry, forcing diplomats more comfortable with deliberation and discretion to make decisions quickly and in the spotlight.

Today, a more accurate and dispassionate definition of diplomacy comes from British historian G. R. Berridge:

> Diplomacy . . . is a major ingredient of power. Its chief purpose is to enable states to secure the objectives of their foreign policies without resort to force, propaganda or law. It follows that diplomacy consists of communication between officials designed to promote foreign policy either by formal agreement or tacit adjustment.[2]

Against this backdrop, we propose to examine how diplomacy can be used to combat the scourge of international terrorism.

At first blush there seems to be a contradiction between the peaceful nature of diplomacy and the violence of terrorism. The main tools of diplomacy are persuasion and negotiation. How can such tools be of any use against terrorists who are prepared to kill and maim large numbers of innocent people? Unlike military force or law enforcement, diplomacy is usually not directed at the terrorists themselves but rather aims to influence the actions states take to combat terrorism, and to remove popular support for terrorists and extremist organizations. Diplomacy is the means we have to persuade countries to join forces against terrorism, and to find ways to assist them in doing that. No one nation can defeat international terrorism on its own. Neither can any one nation be certain of its ability to prevent a catastrophic attack by terrorists on its own soil.

While a universally-accepted definition of terrorism remains elusive,[3] what distinguishes terrorism from other crime is the political nature of the terrorist acts. As Michael Sheehan wrote in *Attacking Terrorism*, "The centrality of diplomacy in a counterterrorism strategy derives from the fact that international terrorism by definition is a political act."[4] It is true that today's global terrorists do not have traditional territorial or constitutional goals, like those of the Irish Republican Army (IRA) or Basque Fatherland and Liberty (ETA). However, the terrorist acts perpetrated by the new breed of global terrorists are emphatically political in that they take place within the arena of power and policy. Moreover, some terror organizations like Lashkar e Tayyiba (LeT), the Liberation Tigers of Tamil Eelam (LTTE), and Kurdistan Workers' Party (PKK) maintain territorial objectives; in short, terrorism, of whatever kind, entails political consequences for governments. That is why diplomacy must have a central role in combating terrorism.[5]

Bilateral Diplomacy

What tools, then, do diplomats employ to counter the growth, impact, and viability of terrorism? The most common vehicle for the diplomat is bilateral diplomacy, using influence based on the relationship between two nation-states. Bilateral diplomacy is the appropriate vehicle for seeking to influence a country to take action against terrorists on its soil, or against those elements inside one country that support terrorists and terrorist organizations somewhere else. Through bilateral diplomacy, countries negotiate extradition agreements and other arrangements to enable law enforcement agencies to act against international terrorists. Capacity-building assistance programs that train and equip law enforcement agencies may be a useful tool in bolstering another nation's willingness and ability to take action against terrorists. The United States has a number of such programs that are implemented through bilateral diplomatic channels, including the Antiterrorism Assistance Program (ATA)[6] and the Terrorism Interdiction Program (TIP).[7]

Bilateral diplomacy can also be used to help to make the territory of a nation inhospitable to terrorists over the long term. Here diplomacy partners with its sister tool of national security policy, development. In the United States, the three "Ds"—defense, diplomacy, and development—are increasingly interlinked as instruments of national power. As such, they are very effective in the counterterrorism struggle. Violent extremists and terrorists hide within all nations; however, they take greater risks and pay higher penalties in states enjoying greater transparency, broader empowerment of citizens, and legal systems that enforce accountability. Conversely, they thrive in nations characterized by corruption and violence; terrorist organizations have greater freedom to train, recruit, equip, and finance themselves in such weak and vulnerable states. Terrorists therefore tend to burrow into such failed or failing states. In weak states, diplomacy tends to have a tougher time in finding solutions, as diplomatic representation is likely to be infrequent and ineffectual, as it has been in Somalia, for example. A particular challenge is posed by what are commonly known as "ungoverned spaces" in countries that are not state sponsors of terrorism. The vulnerable area is not under the effective control of the legitimate government of the nation in question.[8] Parts of Yemen, Afghanistan, and Pakistan would qualify under that definition. Clearly extremism, violence, and terror find safe harbor in all of these environments, irrespective of the will of the host government. Of course, terrorists also find sanctuary in states that tolerate or even encourage terrorist activity. The United States, Canada, the European Union, and others maintain formal lists of state sponsors of terrorism, and direct much of their counterterrorism diplomacy toward isolating those states.

The first line of offense in combating terrorism in weak states or in undergoverned spaces may be to assist the legitimate government to extend central government authority and services across the entire territory of the state. This may first require deliberate and extraordinary efforts to establish effective diplomatic presence, including that of development agencies, with appropriate levels of risk management and force protection. These bilateral relationships can then work with the host government to implement extensive assistance programs aimed at undermining the so-called root causes of terrorism.

Yemen is an excellent example of a nation facing, as of this writing, at least three direct threats to its stability and security, including a chronic socioeconomic crisis, domestic insurgencies in the north and south, and the presence of violent extremist groups like al Qaeda. Yemen will continue to depend on training and other forms of security assistance from its bilateral partners, including the United States, to meet the immediate threat from al Qaeda. Equally important, the country will require significant assistance in improving the capacity, transparency, and reach of the central government. Diplomatic and development initiatives must spearhead efforts to assist the Yemeni government in improving the provision of basic services and the rule of law, which have as their end goal improving the government's legitimacy in the eyes of local leaders and the general population. In turn, Yemen's ability to resist the growth of terrorist organizations should improve.

There is a vigorous debate over the relationship between poverty and terrorism. Poverty cannot be said to cause terrorism, and in fact, individual terrorists often come from relatively comfortable backgrounds. Nevertheless, poverty and unemployment can breed hopelessness and despair, which in turn generate resentment and frustration that can be exploited by extremist and terrorist groups. These groups fill the economic and social gaps that government leaves vacant, and appear as alternatives to legitimately constituted government. Effective economic development assistance, therefore, particularly if aimed at creating jobs for young people, needed infrastructure, and new economic activity, can be another valuable bilateral tool to undermine terrorism.

In addition to assistance efforts aimed directly at economic problems, bilateral programs in good governance may also be effective over the long term in expanding the rule of law in all of its manifestations (e.g., criminal investigations, judicial process, and humane incarceration and punishment); supporting broad political participation; and advocating transparency and accountability, including in a free and viable media. Partner nations might advocate and support all of these programs through diplomacy and development, as part of a bilateral diplomatic relationship.

No less important than addressing root causes is the role of diplomacy in building political will to combat terrorism. In the immediate aftermath of the 9/11 attacks, the United States sought to create a broad political coalition against terrorism. On 12 September 2001, US diplomats in virtually every country in the world were instructed by the Department of State to request the support of the host nation for international efforts to defeat al Qaeda. Although the problem of terrorism is global and the solutions require multilateral action, the first steps had to be taken bilaterally. As Anthony Cordesman has emphasized, it is a myth that cooperation is the natural basis for international action.[9] International cooperation does not simply arise but has to be built on the basis of a web of bilateral relationships and shared interests, reinforced and codified through negotiations.

Diplomacy can also help change the attitude of a neighboring country that serves as a safe haven for terrorists. For many years Basque terrorists active in ETA were able to avoid capture and prosecution in Spain by crossing the border into France. Beginning in the 1990s Spanish diplomatic efforts, coupled with an improved human rights climate, led to active French cooperation against ETA terrorists. An agreement signed at the Spain-France Bilateral Summit in January 2008 further enhanced bilateral cooperation against ETA terrorism; several high-level ETA terrorists were arrested in France during 2008.

Even where there is no cross-border problem, diplomatic efforts can bolster the political will within a particular country for domestic actions to combat terrorism. Counterterrorism programs have to compete for resources with other desirable government programs, such as education and health care. Since catastrophic or even significant terrorist events are infrequent, there is a risk that counterterrorism activities can slip down on a government's list of priorities. Diplomatic intervention can help ensure that terrorism remains at the top of the agenda, strengthen the political will to combat terrorism, and ensure that counterterrorism efforts have a priority claim on the resources of governments. This is particularly the case whenever terrorist activities are of greater concern in one of the two states. More difficult still is persuading a reluctant government to take action against individuals and organizations under its jurisdiction that are providing financial, logistical, and even political support to violent extremist entities that do not appear to pose a direct and immediate domestic threat to the nation in question.

Persistent diplomatic pressure can, in fact, pay off, especially by capitalizing on tactical errors that terrorist groups sometimes make. For many years the United States had pressed Saudi Arabia to take more effective actions against sources of terrorism emanating from the kingdom. These diplomatic efforts gained significant traction when terrorists targeted Saudi facilities and residences beginning in 2003. In addition to ramping up its own security force counterterror efforts, the Saudi government established a joint task force with the United States to investigate terrorist financing and took extensive actions to take control over mosques and charitable organizations suspected of having terrorist ties.[10]

A very specific type of bilateral diplomacy is defense diplomacy, the peacetime cooperative use of armed forces and related infrastructure as a tool of foreign and security policy. During the Cold War, defense policies were designed to deter strategic adversaries, establish favorable spheres of influence, and support "friendly" regimes, regardless of whether they were democratic or repressive. As used today, defense diplomacy builds cooperative relationships, even with former or potential enemies; promotes democratic civilian control, liberal democracy, good governance, and respect for human rights; and develops a partner nation's capacity to contribute to peacekeeping or peace enforcement operations. All of these efforts go a long way to rendering a nation infertile ground for terrorist and extremist infection. This is particularly true in Latin America, where the symbiotic relationship between terrorist organizations and narcotics cartels is well known and widespread. US Special Operations Forces, for example, have been assisting in training and exercising with Colombian forces, among others in Latin America, in counterterrorism and counter narcotics tactics, techniques, and procedures in addition to the broader policy objectives listed above.[11]

Bilateral diplomacy also has a role in helping develop a nation's security forces against threats from other states, including those who would use terrorist proxies, as well as those neighbors who might protect terrorist groups. This, along with support by security forces for protecting host government, diplomatic, and development workers in difficult areas, completes the "3D" partnership in states vulnerable to extremist and terrorist violence.

Multilateral Diplomacy

If bilateral diplomacy can have effective results in the counterterrorism fight, then multilateral diplomacy can amplify those successes. Like bilateral diplomacy, multilateral diplomacy has a variety of instruments at its disposal. Multilateral diplomacy normally takes place in permanent international organizations, such as the Organization for Security and Cooperation in Europe, the European Union, the North Atlantic Treaty Organization, and the African Union, and especially in the United Nations and its broad family of agencies. A critical advantage of multilateral diplomacy is that treaties negotiated in international bodies and ratified by a sufficient number of member states have the force of international law. The thirteen international terrorism conventions[12] are testimony to the commitment of the international community to addressing this issue collaboratively. Persuading nations to ratify these conventions is an objective of ongoing multilateral and bilateral diplomacy by those nations that are already parties to them. Additionally, all nations are required under the UN Charter to take any action mandated by the UN Security Council. For instance, UN Security Council Resolution (UNSCR) 1373, passed on 28 September 2001, requires all states to criminalize al Qaeda financial activities and to freeze its financial assets. It would be almost impossible to negotiate this level of international obligation through bilateral channels.

While most multilateral diplomacy takes place in permanent organizations, another effective tool for generating international action against terrorism is the convening of ad hoc multilateral conferences, such as the Madrid Middle East Peace Conference (1991) and the Bonn Conference on Afghanistan (2001). While multilateral conferences do not always produce all of the desired results despite removing some of the underlying causes of terrorism (such as the 1999 Rambouillet Conference on Kosovo),[13] they are generally highly visible events that may create momentum for international action against dissatisfied extremists and other desperate actors who choose terrorism to carry on their fight.

A third device of multilateral diplomacy is the role of a credible, respected international intermediary or special representative. Such emissaries have been used primarily for conflict resolution in the past (e.g., former Finnish President Martti Ahtisaari in Kosovo; Nigerian diplomat Ibrahim Gambari in Myanmar) but can also be effective in addressing terrorist-related issues. For instance, German Public Prosecutor Detlev Mehlis was brought in to head the original UN commission investigating the 2005 assassination of Lebanese Prime Minister Rafik Hariri. Here we should also note the diplomatic leadership role that Costa Rican President Oscar Arias Sánchez played in 1987 to resurrect the prospects for peace among the five Central American states following the demise of the Contadora Process—itself a multilateral but flawed initiative. Arias was awarded the 1987 Nobel Peace Prize for his plan. The possible diplomatic advantages of an outside intermediary include objectivity, patience, and the renewed attention to the conflict by outside powers capable of supporting the eventual settlement.

Multilateral diplomacy has coercive power at its disposal as well. Diplomatic pressure is a common coercive but nonviolent tool. The power of nation-states expressing a unanimous position on international policy, especially when it comes from the UN Security Council, has significant, even if not universally effective, impact on transgressor nations. Among the levers that international institutions have at their disposal to enforce compliance with the international will are expulsion from the organization, international support for the offender's victim (e.g., Kuwait in the wake of Iraq's 1990 invasion), the establishment of international tribunals to bring to trial individuals accused of violations of international law, and imposition of economic sanctions.

Economic sanctions (which can be either a bilateral or a multilateral diplomatic tool, but are most effective when multilateral) are a coercive instrument designed to bring about a change of behavior on the part of the target state, organization, or individual. In counterterrorism efforts, the target may not be the terrorist group itself, but a nation that is seen as supporting terrorists or terrorist organizations. International sanctions, however, have also been directed against terrorist individuals and non-state organizations like al Qaeda and the Taliban.

Much analysis has been devoted to the question of whether international sanctions work. In 1996 (during the so-called decade of sanctions), the United Nations concluded after an exhaustive study: " . . . an effectively implemented regime of collective Security Council sanctions can operate as a useful international policy tool in a graduated response to threats to international peace and security."[14] The record of sanctions in changing the policies of target states or organizations is decidedly mixed.[15] Nevertheless, because of a natural reluctance to use force except as a last resort, sanctions are likely to remain a tool of multilateral coercion and may be effective if well designed.

How are effective sanctions regimes constructed? First, there must be a strong international consensus on clear, realistic objectives. Sanctions should enjoy full international compliance, especially by neighboring states and regional organizations. The administration of the sanctions regime should be well resourced and run by proactive sanctions committees, including effective monitoring and implementation activities. Studies have shown that a comprehensive, rigorously enforced sanctions regime is much more effective than some half-hearted effort with limited, unenforced measures. Clearly, sanctions have no chance at all in the total absence of credible enforcement and concerted international co-operation. Sanctions should be appropriately aimed, especially those designed to dry up terrorist financing; financial sanctions are more effective if targeted against designated individuals, organizations, and decision-making elites. Finally, although unilateral sanctions regimes are generally less effective, they do have a political impact on the targeted nation. If that nation values normal relations with the states imposing sanctions, then resolution of the offensive behavior, including supporting terrorism, can lead to lifting of sanctions—as was the case with Libya.

The Libyan example merits closer attention because sanctions played an important role in a complex interaction of national wills and economic forces. The United States first designated Libya as a state sponsor of terrorism in 1979, and levied a series of layered sanctions over the next few years in response to Libya's growing radical and violent behavior. The bombing of the La Belle Discotheque in Germany in 1986, by Libyan agents, ratcheted tension upward substantially, and resulted in a series of increasing pressure against Libya, including US bomb strikes on Tripoli and Benghazi. A few years later, allegedly in response to that American bombing campaign, Libyan agents blew up Pan American flight 103 (1988), and French flight UTA 772 (1989).[16]

After several years of intense investigations and relentless public outcry, French and US investigators respectively issued arrest warrants for Libyan suspects in these attacks. The United Nations demonstrated international support for the victims by passing UNSCR 731 in January 1992 calling on the Libyan government to surrender the suspects. When Libya failed to meet that condition, the UN levied its first set of sanctions with the passage of UNSCR 748 in March 1992, and added additional ones the following year with UNSCR 883. After additional years of political wrangling, the US and UK in 1998 proposed a compromise to Libya: turn over the suspects to a trial in the Netherlands run by a Scottish court. The UN followed quickly with a resolution offering to suspend sanctions if Libya complied, or impose further actions if it did not (UNSCR 1192). The following year Libya complied and UN sanctions were suspended. UN sanctions were fully lifted in 2003 after Libya accepted responsibility for the PanAm 103 bombing and renounced terrorism. While not acknowledging a role in the UTA bombing, Libya increased compensation to the victims, a move sufficient to avoid a French veto of the UN sanctions removal.[17] All US sanctions were finally removed in 2004.

What role did sanctions play in Libya's ultimate decision to comply? In 2003 Dr. Meghan O'Sullivan produced a thorough and excellent analysis of the impact of sanctions on Libya.[18] Her conclusions were that the combination of effective UN and US sanctions, together with prevailing economic and political conditions in the 1990s, were decisive factors in Muammar Qaddafi's turnaround and submission to the United States and the United Nations. None of these factors alone might have been sufficient, but together they imposed on Libya unpleasant economic choices and excessive financial costs as the government scrambled to avoid a downward spiraling economy under intense international pressure. Moreover, the sanctions effectively reinforced in the minds of most governments around the world a negative image of Libya, amplified international wariness about getting involved with the Libyan government, and helped marginalize Qaddafi's influence. Once sanctions were lifted, the reversal in Libya's economic misfortunes was swift, as was its reintegration into the community of nations as a constructive player. BBC diplomatic correspondent Jonathan Marcus was quoted as saying, "If diplomats wrote fairy tales, this would probably be one."[19]

Multilateral diplomacy can also be used to establish new international norms—both values and rules—that isolate terrorists and those that support them. Creating new international norms reduces the credibility of terrorists by identifying them as murderers and sociopaths, thereby making it less acceptable to give them money or sanctuary, and constraining countries to identify themselves with the international consensus against terrorism or risk being labeled as pariahs. In a message delivered to the International Counter-Terrorism Conference in Riyadh in 2005, former UN Secretary-General Kofi Annan declared, "All states must make clear that no cause whatsoever justifies the targeting of civilians and noncombatants,"[20] a clear repudiation of the old saw that "one man's terrorist is another man's freedom fighter." As the Secretary-General is the world's premier international diplomat, such a statement on terrorism had to reflect not only his views but an international consensus reached through diplomacy. In effect, Annan's statement represented the codification of a new norm that delinked terrorism from the purported goals of any terrorist group.

What are some of the advantages of multilateral diplomacy as opposed to bilateral diplomacy in the fight against terrorism? Strength in numbers is probably the most prominent advantage, as outcomes represent international consensus, which adds legitimacy and pressure. As noted above, formal international agreements or treaties are legally and often morally binding. Additionally, when willing nations all agree on goals and priorities, they can combine resources toward common objectives, as in the Libya case. The multilateral environment can also improve the chances for compromise and constructive solutions, because it can provide a forum to air grievances, which in turn undermines the self-proclaimed legitimacy of violent extremist groups, who must have the loyalty of disaffected populations in order to survive. Turkey, Iraq, and the United States have engaged in trilateral talks over several years to resolve peacefully security and cooperation issues, especially regarding the Kurdish populations in Turkey and Iraq, in order to deal a decisive blow to PKK terrorism. Finally, smaller countries that might have less influence or little to contribute in their normal bilateral relationships can contribute valuable and constructive ideas on countering terrorism in a multilateral forum.

Of course, there are also disadvantages to the multilateral process. Because so many actors are involved, results are usually slow in coming and immediate action is highly unlikely. Moreover, since full consensus is a desirable goal, a powerful minority of countries might effectively resist unanimity. Conversely, a weak or ambivalent majority might be unable to avoid a consensus on issues that a few influential and persistent players might table. Success in a multilateral forum depends at least on the presence of certain critical players, who might therefore choose not to attend, or do so at an insufficient level of representation, so as to stymie the purpose of the multilateral intervention. Unlike bilateral diplomacy, multilateral diplomacy tends to take place in the public eye; for this reason, propaganda and histrionics might dominate proceedings. There is an inevitable tendency to focus on process (venues, membership, procedures), not substance; miscommunications multiply when many interlocutors are involved, including through the inefficiencies of language interpretation; and finally, after all of that, the ultimate outcome is likely to be much more diluted than the most committed participants would like.[21]

Mediation

Diplomatic mediation by a third party is a frequent tool in conflict resolution, including in conflicts that involve terrorist activity. The outside party should have either substantial credibility as an objective outsider or the ability to provide incentives and guarantees to the parties to the dispute.

Norway is an example of a small nation that on more than one occasion has used its good offices to try to resolve issues of terrorism involving nations outside of its own traditional bilateral engagements. Most people are by now aware of its secret, back-channel efforts in the early 1990s to promote dialogue between Israel and the Palestinians. More instructive, perhaps, for this chapter is Norway's experience in facilitating negotiations between the government of Sri Lanka and the separatist terror group Liberation Tigers of Tamil Eelam (LTTE), with the assistance of other Nordic countries and international sanctions. This example demonstrates some of the limits of diplomacy in wrestling with terrorism in a civil war or insurgency scenario.[22]

Norway first announced its attempts to initiate direct talks between the Sri Lankan government and the LTTE rebels in early 2000, after a couple of years of exploratory diplomacy by Norwegian diplomats. The high-water mark of Norway's efforts occurred in February 2002 when, after nearly twenty years of fighting, the parties agreed to an extended ceasefire and the initiation of direct talks. A key feature of the agreement was the establishment of a small Sri Lanka Monitoring Mission (SLMM), comprised of representatives from five Nordic nations, whose tasks were to monitor the ceasefire and investigate any violations. The SLMM was an excellent tool, but critically flawed, since it lacked any enforcement mechanism to impose accountability on any party violating the ceasefire. Six rounds of peace talks took place from September 2002 to March 2003, but they failed to make any progress. Essentially, neither side trusted the other. Both sides engaged in significant ceasefire violations, and even disputed what the ceasefire agreement required. A few serious shooting incidents off the coast and some inept missteps by Norwegian aid donors combined to reinforce the mistrust. The Norwegian negotiators tried to reactivate talks, and even managed to organize meetings in Geneva to discuss terms for a future agenda, but by this time neither party evidenced very much good faith.

From 2003 onward, the credibility of Norway—still the only game in town—sank in its facilitation efforts, as Sinhalese elites and government officials accused Oslo of being "pro-Tiger," due simply to its continuing direct contacts with the LTTE. Moreover, some saw Norway growing increasingly "disengaged" during this period. While this generated some criticism, the fact remained that any efforts that Oslo made, even to generate "talks about resurrecting talks," fell on deaf ears, as neither side was seriously interested in talking peace. Another motivation for Norwegian distance at the time might have been to counter any notion that either party could cynically manipulate them at will.

An additional blow to diplomacy came in the LTTE's retaliation against the EU members of the SLMM in 2006, following the EU's declaration of the LTTE as a terrorist organization. Only Norway and Iceland—non-EU members—remained, effectively gutting what had already been an underresourced effort. This might have been an LTTE ploy to claim to support the SLMM on the one hand, while at the same time running a sword through it with the other. Although Norway reengaged at that point, it was by then probably too late, as both sides were *de facto* back at war, while paying only lip service to the ceasefire. Any potential donor influence over the parties to resume talks had always been unbalanced: Toward the government, they had only the "carrot" of financial largesse and the "stick" of public embarrassment. Neither had any impact on the LTTE, since most donors refused to deal with them, and while the EU declaration of it as a terrorist organization was meaningful, in practice it failed to bring the LTTE back to the negotiation table.

The history of diplomatic engagement to resolve this conflict reveals miscommunications and misperceptions on all sides, which fed deep-seated resentments. Norway justifiably prided itself on a track record of peaceful resolution of conflicts, its focus on human rights and democratic ideals, and its recognition of the need for patience. In the end, however, their efforts became irrelevant with the resumption of war. Moreover, many on the Sri Lankan side came to doubt Norway's bona fides, especially in light of persistent LTTE violence, despite Norway's open channels to it.

At the same time, many governments, international organizations, and NGOs condemned Sri Lankan government violence against the Tamils, which was echoed loudly by the considerable Tamil diaspora around the world. This in turn helped undermine Colombo's confidence in the policies of some of its allies, to include the United States and Canada, further exacerbating tensions among the actors.

Of key importance was the failure in the early days to create a strong and effective institution for bringing ceasefire violators to account under the pressure of world opinion and to use the promise or withdrawal of foreign aid and humanitarian development—ironically, Norway was the world's leading proponent and practitioner of providing substantial development assistance globally—as an incentive system for progress. Negotiators, donor communities, and other interested parties are limited in offering to non-state actors the incentives that they can readily provide to nation-state authorities. Non-state actors are also less responsive to "sticks," particularly if they can easily ratchet up the terrorist activity.

The final lesson from the Sri Lankan case is the difficulty of playing the role of a diplomatic broker during a civil war in which terrorism is a principal weapon. Diplomats have tools to deal with the political issues and conventional warfare, but are hamstrung in addressing terrorists. Their facilitator role implies talking directly to unsavory actors, without guarantees of influencing their behavior. Some legitimate authorities refuse to accept that fact. The general public often attaches a stigma to such dialogue, which also leads to claims of bias, as we have clearly seen in Sri Lanka.[23]

In short, diplomacy requires much greater flexibility in dealing with non-state actors and creativity in devising incentives and disincentives when working with rebels or insurgents who use terrorist tactics. Some of this entails improving outdated laws and regulations against dealing with terrorists, and some of it lies in developing innovative diplomats and negotiators. "Track two" diplomacy, described below, might be one tool that addresses some of these shortcomings.

Additional lessons on diplomatic mediation in conflicts involving terrorism can be drawn from the role of the United States in the Northern Ireland peace process, which led to the Good Friday Accord signed in 1998 and to subsequent agreements that further codified political arrangements in Northern Ireland. A primary goal of the peace process was an end to the terrorist violence by the IRA and (to a lesser extent) by loyalist paramilitary groups. As one scholar notes, "The extraordinary case of the Northern Ireland peace process is a rare example of terrorism being dramatically reduced, indeed almost extinguished, by means of a ceasefire followed by a comprehensive political agreement and a gradual movement towards establishing a power-sharing arrangement."[24]

The history of the Northern Ireland conflict is long and contentious. For our purposes it is sufficient to note that the modern IRA (also called the Provisional IRA, or "Provos") began a terrorist campaign after 1969 to force British security forces to leave Northern Ireland, which remained part of the United Kingdom when Ireland was partitioned in 1921. By August of 1994, when the IRA declared a ceasefire, "The Troubles" in Northern Ireland had taken more than three thousand lives.[25] The IRA ceasefire, which was followed by ceasefires by the loyalist paramilitary groups, provided the impetus for an active US role in mediating the conflict.

The difficulties of entering into dialogue or negotiation with terrorist organizations are examined in depth in Chapter 3.2 by James Wither. In the case of Northern Ireland, while there was no doubt that key leaders of the IRA's political wing, Sinn Fein, were also leaders of the paramilitary organization, the fiction that the two organizations were separate made it easier for the state actors—primarily the United Kingdom and the Republic of Ireland, but also the United States—to engage with terrorists and their representatives.

Unlike Norway's role in Sri Lanka, the US role in the Northern Ireland peace process was not one of an outside power with little stake in the conflict. On the contrary, the moral and financial support provided to the IRA by Irish Americans made the United States a player in the peace process but also created mistrust of the United States among unionists. Nevertheless, the Clinton administration was able to mediate credibly among all parties thanks to its strong bilateral diplomatic relationship (often described as the "special relationship") with the United Kingdom and a deliberate effort to incorporate unionist perspectives into the dialogue. From 1994 to 1998, the Clinton administration was engaged in continuous bilateral diplomatic contact with both the United Kingdom and the Republic of Ireland. These diplomatic exchanges underpinned the peace process and enhanced US credibility with the parties to the conflict. The willingness of President Clinton himself and National Security Advisors Tony Lake and Sandy Berger to devote substantial time and effort to the process was also critical to its eventual success.[26] A third decisive factor was the appointment of former Senator George Mitchell as US special envoy for the Northern Ireland peace process. By all accounts, Senator Mitchell's patient and creative diplomacy was critical to the achievement of the Good Friday Accord.

The thorniest issue in the Northern Ireland peace process was "decommissioning" of paramilitary (mainly IRA) weapons. This is likely to be a central issue in any negotiation with a well-organized terrorist group. The IRA was unwilling to lay down its arms in advance of a negotiated agreement, and the unionists were loath to negotiate under the implicit threat of a return to terrorist violence. The 1996 Report of the International Body on Arms Decommissioning chaired by Senator Mitchell called for an unequivocal commitment by all parties to "democratic and exclusively peaceful means" of resolving the conflict but it did not insist that the IRA decommission prior to entering talks.[27] While this formula did not give the hoped-for impetus to the talks (in fact, the IRA broke the ceasefire shortly after the report was issued and did not restore it for 17 months), the International Body's artful compromise provided the foundation for an eventual settlement. Decommissioning was completed in 2005.[28]

Richard Haass, who succeeded George Mitchell as US envoy for the Northern Ireland peace process, summarized the lessons of the Northern Ireland diplomatic intervention process in a commencement address at Hamilton College in May 2007. Haass said, "First, diplomacy is a policy tool, not a favor to the other side. We must get past the idea that negotiations constitute a reward. Second, we must avoid undue emphasis on preconditions. What matters in a negotiation is not where you start but where you end."[29]

Public Diplomacy

The most underutilized but most effective diplomatic tool available to a nation is public diplomacy. Public diplomacy is the art of diplomatic persuasion directed not at governments but at members of the public, often at elites and opinion-makers with the goal of influencing public attitudes. Public diplomacy differs from traditional diplomacy not just in its audience but in the nature of the message. The messages delivered through public diplomacy are liable to be much less direct than the specific requests or demarches passed between embassies and foreign ministries in a bilateral diplomatic context. The goal of public diplomacy is often to change mind-sets rather than to affect policy on a particular issue.

Public diplomacy can be conducted either in person (for example, through speeches at meetings or conferences) or through the public media. In the counterterrorism struggle, informing publics about efforts by governing authorities or international donors to improve the lives of citizens, and unmasking the insidious nature of terrorist organizations, go a long way to provide hope to citizens, lend legitimacy to deserving governments, and combat efforts of extremists and fanatics to sway public opinion toward helping them conduct violence.

In many ways, the globalized broadcast media are *the* principal battlefield of our adversaries in the terrorism fight. We are in a struggle with those adversaries on that battlefield, and we are not winning. In the twenty-first century, the media are more than just a vehicle; the media have become actors in diplomacy, not just reporters of events. Extremist and terrorist organizations recognize the enormous value in generating coverage of their violent operations and fanatical ideologies as a recruiting and marketing tool. They utilize the latest and most effective cinema techniques in order to appeal to their audiences—especially young, malleable males who become recruits, disgruntled citizenries who provide haven for extremists, and panic-prone western publics who might become more sympathetic to policies that confirm extremists' portraits of western "hypocrisy."

Violent extremist organizations know that many global news organizations will broadcast their products immediately and very effectively. This "fast-breaking" news complicates a government's ability to take the initiative in managing public perceptions and implementing appropriate policies. Today's media, especially television, gravitate toward drama; "news" borders on entertainment, adorned by not-so-subtle advocacy. Sophisticated broadcasters also use persuasive techniques to enhance the impact of their message and raise its dramatic effect in visuals for the audience. The use of "B-roll," or file footage, illustrates the script that an anchor or reporter is reading, but it is not completely a photographic capture of the event being discussed. Sometimes the desired, subliminal impression is that the visuals represent what actually happened during the event reported. Many TV journalists also employ dramatic narrative styles that are designed to incite an emotional response on the part of the viewer. We should not, however, ascribe responsibility only to the journalist or reporter in the field. The media organization's hierarchy decides the structure, content, and priorities of news programming. The organization's editorial staff is responsible to corporate interests, sponsors' sensitivities, and the demands of their perceived audience.

In view of this discouraging state of affairs, governments should redouble their efforts to engage in effective public diplomacy through and with the media. Just as terrorists do, diplomats must use the media smartly to affect perceptions of their own nation's intentions, behavior, and policies. At the same time, public diplomacy can undermine the superficial appeal of extremist groups and expose the side of terrorist groups that they do not wish revealed.

To accomplish this, the diplomats must first know and understand the target audience. Knowing what messages motivate and inspire the audience, as well as what antagonizes them, is critical to having the desired impact. Such positive themes might include yearning for justice, a brighter economic future, or safety in the neighborhood. Conversely, an in-your-face informational monologue might arouse negative feelings in certain cultures that the speaker is arrogant and patronizing—rendering any meaningful content irrelevant. This approach should obviously be avoided. One of the authors of this chapter sought to reach out to Muslim clerics in Bangladesh in the wake of 9/11 through a series of meetings with Muslim imams. The purpose was twofold: to introduce the clerics to US-funded development assistance projects in their villages and to highlight certain common values, such as religious faith and commitment to justice.

Second, it is critical to understand what media the intended audience pays attention to. Is a traditional face-to-face gathering around a tribal leader the means of conveying information credibly? Do TV talk shows or weekly "reality" programs attract viewers that governments need to reach? Does the target audience surf the internet or gain its information from blogs and websites? Each of these venues calls for a different public diplomacy construct. Diplomats are most comfortable with the first venue, direct contact with local elites. We need to improve, however, our capabilities on TV—which requires education and training on how to use this medium more effectively. Our adversaries, however, are increasingly using the third environment, cyberspace, as the dominant medium for disseminating their messages of extremism and terror, including for the purposes of recruitment, training, and marketing. Some search engines generate results on the first few pages for terrorist or extremist websites that tend to display enticing, provocative, or attractive information. Casual "surfers" rarely venture beyond those, especially people prone to their appeal. It would be very valuable in the struggle against terrorist propaganda to have readier access to legitimate and credible websites critical of extremists and terrorists. Governments and moderate civil society alike should devote more time to understanding this medium and becoming adept at utilizing its capacities.

Finally, it is vital to understand whom the audience views as the trustworthy messengers. Does it respect an elder statesman, a religious leader, or a cultural or sports icon? How subtle or how direct should the messenger be in order to appeal most effectively to the audience? What cinematic or broadcast techniques might enhance the credibility of the message and messenger? Some have argued that America's public diplomacy campaigns after 9/11 squandered international support by ignoring the key differences between what appealed to a domestic audience and what appealed to an international one. President Bush's "telephone diplomacy" was not as effective as a more personal approach with some nations, and the constant drumbeat of administration spokespersons on Sunday talk shows appealed to an American viewership, but not necessarily an international one.[30]

The focus in Washington since 9/11 has arguably been on crafting the US message, as if there were a one-size-fits-all approach to countering the ideological appeal of terrorism. That appeal, where it exists, reflects complex political, economic, and social factors that must be taken into account to craft a sophisticated, empathetic, and country-specific public diplomacy strategy. Finally, in utilizing public diplomacy to communicate with foreign publics, it is wise to take into account that communication involves listening as well as speaking. In recognition of the importance of this fact, the Marshall Center has sponsored a project over the past several years to engage representatives of more than 60 countries in collaborative research and sharing actual practical experiences in delegitimizing ideological support for terrorism. The conference forums have encouraged dialogue among policy and military/counterterrorism professionals, academics, and theologians from both western nations and nations with predominantly Muslim populations. These exchanges have contributed to defining mutually acceptable terminology and best practices for addressing the sources of violent extremism. The research findings have underscored the importance of adjusting messages for differing local contexts that can only be achieved by willingness to seek out the perspectives and recommendations of those most familiar with unique cultural circumstances.[31]

Track Two Diplomacy

The fifth type of diplomacy that may be useful in combating terrorism is known as "track two diplomacy,"[32] or diplomacy conducted outside official diplomatic channels. Track two or second-track diplomacy is:

> . . . broadly defined as the bringing together of professionals, opinion leaders or other currently or potentially influential individuals from communities in conflict, without official representative status, to work together to understand better the dynamics underlying the conflict and how its transformation from violence (or potential violence) to a collaborative process of peace building and sustainable development might be promoted.[33]

Track two diplomacy may be the tool required in long-standing conflicts where the adversarial parties have invested much in their apparently irreconcilable public positions. One of its key advantages is that it is low key and out of the public eye. In the context of counterterrorism, track two initiatives may be appropriate when it is useful to engage the terrorist or extremist organization but politically impossible for governments to do so officially. In this regard, track two diplomacy could be a valuable tool in national reconciliation efforts in insurgency environments, during which terrorism has played a large role, such as in Iraq, Sri Lanka, Afghanistan, or the Palestinian-Israeli conflict. A track two process is designed to allow the participants to be nonjudgmental, noncoercive, and nonthreatening to each other. It may be conducted by private parties, such as NGOs, scholars, or clerics, or it can be conducted by people closer to, but not in, the government, such as retired diplomats. Track two discussions endeavor to "humanize" all of the parties, no matter what terrible deeds the participant organizations might have committed. With that in mind, the discussants can freely explore and inject new ideas into the conversation. The process usually involves sharing perceptions rather than negotiating "positions." The gradual outcome of this process is to reduce tensions and slowly create public support for solutions. If successful in setting the conditions for commitment to a peaceful outcome, track two diplomacy can be valuable in preventing backsliding once a formal resolution is under way and agreements are in place.

The disadvantages, of course, are that this kind of diplomatic effort is long term and requires infinite patience. It can be morally distasteful to engage with violent opponents, even when the engagement is through unofficial channels. And since track two diplomacy is divorced from governments, it rarely impacts "track one," or official diplomatic negotiations, directly, and indeed often does not deal with the formal conflict per se. Therefore, it is not a substitute for traditional diplomacy in most cases. In the Middle East, for instance, numerous track two efforts have been under way for years; however, they have rarely advanced formal diplomatic negotiations in any significant way. On the other hand, the Catholic Community of Sant'Egidio is credited with facilitating an end to the civil war in Mozambique with an agreement signed in 1992.[34]

Conclusion

The skillful use of diplomacy—bilateral, multilateral, mediation, public diplomacy, track two, or a blend of these tools—is indispensable in the fight against terrorism. The use of force internationally is limited under international law and is in any case costly, dangerous, and uncertain. Diplomacy therefore should be seen as the first and preferred policy instrument for countering international terrorism.

Diplomacy is not only preferable to the use of force, but it also has a track record of success in countering terrorism. Bilateral programs to strengthen weak states and reestablish central control over undergoverned spaces effectively "drain the swamp" where terrorists train and hide. Bilateral diplomacy also helps to gird political will to take courageous stands against terrorists and their supporters. A strong international consensus against terrorism underpins military and law enforcement counterterrorism efforts. New international norms decrease tacit support for terrorist tactics among publics and reduce their ability to attract recruits and money. Properly constructed sanctions regimes can have an effective impact on terrorist organizations and individuals and those who support them. Diplomatic mediation can create momentum for a negotiated end to terrorist violence. Public diplomacy shapes public attitudes about the efforts of the government and their supporters, as well as the true nature of the extremists and terrorists trying to subvert the local, regional, or international order. Occasional use of track two diplomacy can engage extremist groups that may be ready to eschew terrorist tactics and mitigate sociopolitical tensions that extremists exploit. Nations need the full arsenal of diplomatic instruments to confine and limit the threat of transnational extremist terrorist organizations to minimize the need for the use of force.

David C. Litt Ambassador Litt is currently Executive Director of the Center for Stabilization and Economic Reconstruction at the Institute for Defense & Business, a nonprofit executive education institute in Chapel Hill, North Carolina. He served for 34 years as a career US diplomat, specializing in the Middle East and Southwest Asia. He was US Ambassador to the United Arab Emirates (1995–1998) and Consul General in Dubai ten years prior. Among his other assignments, Ambassador Litt was Political Advisor to US Central Command and to Special Operations Command (1998–2004); the Director of the Office of Northern Gulf Affairs (Iran and Iraq) at the State Department; and economic/commercial officer in Kabul, Afghanistan, in the late 1970s. In 2005–2006 he was the third-ranking officer at the US Embassy in Baghdad, Iraq, serving as liaison between the Embassy and the Multi-National Forces-Iraq. Prior to retirement from the government in 2008, he was the Associate Director for International Liaison at the George C. Marshall European Center for Security Studies. David Litt received a bachelor's degree from the UNC–Chapel Hill in 1971 and a master's from the Johns Hopkins School of Advanced International Studies in 1973.

Mary Ann Peters Ambassador Peters is the fourth Provost of the Naval War College. From 2003 to September 2008 she served as Dean of Academics of the College of International and Security Studies, and Associate Director for International Liaison, at the George C. Marshall Center. Ambassador Peters spent more than 30 years as a career diplomat with the US Department of State. From 2000 to 2003 she was US Ambassador to Bangladesh. Her other assignments included Deputy Chief of Mission at the US Embassy in Ottawa, Director for European and Canadian Affairs at the National Security Council, Deputy Assistant Secretary of State for European and Canadian Affairs, Deputy Chief of Mission in Sofia Bulgaria, and Economic Counselor in Moscow. The Ambassador holds a B.A. degree from Santa Clara University and a master's in International Studies from the School of Advanced International Studies at The Johns Hopkins University.

Recommended Readings

Banks, William C., Renee de Nevers, and Mitchel B. Wallerstein, "International Cooperation," in *Combating Terrorism: Strategies and Approaches.* Washington, DC: CQ Press, 2008, 232–267.

Berridge, G. R. *Diplomacy: Theory and Practice*, 3rd ed. New York: Palgrave, 2005.

Freeman, Chas W. *Arts of Power: Statecraft and Diplomacy.* Washington, DC: United States Institute of Peace Press, 1997.

Lauren, Paul Gordon, Gordon A. Craig, and Alexander L. George. *Force and Statecraft: Diplomatic Challenges of Our Time.* New York: Oxford University Press, 2007.

O'Sullivan, Meghan L. *Shrewd Sanctions: Statecraft and State Sponsors of Terrorism.* Washington, DC: Brookings Institution Press, 2003.

Pillar, Paul R. *Terrorism and U.S. Foreign Policy.* Washington: Brookings Institution Press, 2003.

Satloff, Robert. *The Battle of Ideas in the War on Terror: Essays on U.S. Public Diplomacy in the Middle East.* Washington, DC: Washington Institute for Near East Policy, 2004.

Sheehan, Michael. "Diplomacy," Ch. 4 in *Attacking Terrorism: Elements of a Grand Strategy*, Audrey Kurth Cronin and James M. Ludes, eds. Washington, DC: Georgetown University Press, 2004.

Slavik, Hannah. *Intercultural Communication and Diplomacy.* Geneva: DiploFoundation, 2004.

Notes

1. Barbara W. Tuchman, "If Mao Had Come to Washington: An Essay in Alternatives," *Foreign Affairs* (October 1972), 60.
2. G. R. Berridge, *Diplomacy: Theory and Practice*, 3rd ed. (New York: Palgrave, 2005), 1.
3. The thirteen international conventions against terrorism—see note 12—deliberately avoid defining it, focusing instead on the offenses terrorists commit. There is a workable definition of a terrorist offense in the 2002 treaty on countering terror financing.
4. Michael Sheehan, "Diplomacy," in *Attacking Terrorism: Elements of a Grand Strategy*, ed. Audrey Kurth Cronin and James M. Ludes (Washington: Georgetown University Press, 2004), 97–114.
5. For additional perspective on the role of diplomacy in countering terrorism, see Paul R. Pillar, *Terrorism and U.S. Foreign Policy* (Washington: Brookings Institution Press, 2003), 73–79.
6. "Antiterrorism Assistance Program," US Department of State Under Secretay for Management, Bureau of Diplomatic Security, http://www.state.gov/m/ds/terrorism/c8583.htm, accessed 13 September 2009.
7. "Program Assessment: Terrorism Interdiction Program," ExpectMore.gov, http://www.whitehouse.gov/omb/expectmore/summary/10001110.2004.html, accessed 13 September 2009.
8. Therefore, a more appropriate term might be "undergoverned spaces," since some form of governance—usually tribal—almost always exists.
9. Anthony H. Cordesman, *International Cooperation in Counter-Terrorism: Making the Myth a Reality*, Center for Strategic and International Studies, 2005.
10. Christopher M. Blanchard and Alfred B. Prados, "Saudi Arabia: Terrorist Financing Issues," Congressional Research Service (CRS) Report for Congress (RL32499), updated 14 September 2007, http://www.fas.org/sgp/crs/mideast/RL32499.pdf, accessed 13 September 2009.
11. John M. Collins, *Special Operations Forces: An Assessment* (Washington, DC: National Defense University Press, 1994), 88–89.
12. The thirteen conventions include five from the UN—Convention on the Prevention and Punishment of Crimes against Internationally Protected Persons, including Diplomatic Agents (1973); International Convention against the Taking of Hostages (1979); International Convention for the Suppression of Terrorist Bombings (1997); International Convention for the Suppression of the Financing of Terrorism (1999); and Convention for the Suppression of Acts of Nuclear Terrorism (2005)—and eight with other depositories—Convention on Offences and Certain Other Acts Committed on Board Aircraft (1963); Convention for the Suppression of Unlawful Seizure of Aircraft (1970); Convention for the Suppression of Unlawful Acts against the Safety of Civil Aviation (1971); Convention on the Physical Protection of Nuclear Material (1980); Protocol on the Suppression of Unlawful Acts of Violence at Airports Serving International Civil Aviation (1988); Convention for the Suppression of Unlawful Acts against the Safety of Maritime Navigation (1988); Protocol for the Suppression of Unlawful Acts against the Safety of Fixed Platforms Located on the Continental Shelf (1988); and Convention on the Marking of Plastic Explosives for the Purpose of Detection (1991).
13. Ignacio Ramonet, "A Fine Mess," *Le Monde Diplomatique*, http://mondediplo.com/1999/05/01leader, accessed 13 September 2009.
14. "Statement on Sanctions," Informal Open Ended Working Group on an Agenda for Peace, Sub Group on the "Question of United National Imposed Sanctions," United Nations General Assembly, 10 July 1996, http://www.globalpolicy.org/index.php?option=com_content&view=article&id=41719&catid=2002, accessed 13 September 2009.

15. For a thorough discussion of UN sanctions during the 1990s, see David Cortright and George A. Lopez, *The Sanctions Decade: Assessing UN Strategies in the 1990s* (Boulder, CO: Lynne Rienner Publishers, 2000).

16. For a useful overview of US-Libya relations and related incidents, see "Background Note: Libya," US Department of State, Bureau of Near Eastern Affairs, March 2009, http://www.state.gov/r/pa/ei/bgn/5425.htm, accessed 12 September 2009.

17. Felicity Barringer, "Libya Admits Culpability in Crash of Pan Am Plane," *The New York Times*, 16 August 2003, available at http://www.nytimes.com/2003/08/16/international/middleeast/16NATI.html, accessed 12 September 2009.

18. Meghan L. O'Sullivan, "Limiting Libya," in *Shrewd Sanctions: Statecraft and State Sponsors of Terrorism* (Washington, DC: Brookings Institution Press, 2003), 173ff.

19. Eric Weiner, "U.S. Finds Diplomatic Success with Libya," National Public Radio, 24 July 2007, http://www.npr.org/templates/story/story.php?storyId=12208070, accessed 13 September 2009.

20. "Terrorism Threat to All Civilized Countries, Anathema to All Faiths, Says Secretary-General in Message to Riyadh Counter-Terrorism Conference," United Nations Press Release (SG/SM/9708), 2 July 2005, available at http://www.un.org/News/Press/docs/2005/sgsm9708.doc.htm, accessed 12 September 2009.

21. Berridge, "Multilateral Diplomacy," in *Diplomacy: Theory and Practice*, 146–164.

22. C. Christine Fair, "Sri Lanka's Drift Back into War: European Peace Mission Fights for Its Very Survival," *Journal of International Peace Operations*, Vol. 2, No. 3 (November–December 2006), http://peaceops.com/web/images/pdf/journal_2006_1112.pdf, accessed 12 September 2009. This article informs the Sri Lanka case found over the next several paragraphs.

23. Ambassador Teresita Schaffer, who was US Ambassador to Sri Lanka from 1992 to 1995 and spent more than 30 years in the Foreign Service, principally in South Asia, in an e-mail message to author, 21 May 2009.

24. Paul Wilkinson, "How Significant was International Influence in the Northern Ireland Peace Process?" in *Combating Terrorism in Northern Ireland*, ed. James Dingley (New York: Routledge, 2009), 245.

25. "1994: IRA Declares 'Complete' Ceasefire," BBC News, 31 August 1994, available at http://news.bbc.co.uk/onthisday/hi/dates/stories/august/31/newsid_3605000/3605348.stm, accessed 12 September 2009.

26. For a description of President Clinton's visit to Northern Ireland in 1995, see Trevor Birney and Julian O'Neill, *When the President Calls* (Derry: Guildhall Press, 1997).

27. The full text of the Report of the International Body on Arms Decommissioning (22 January 1996) is available on the University of Ulster CAIN website at http://cain.ulst.ac.uk/events/peace/docs/gm24196.htm, accessed 13 September 2009.

28. "IRA 'Has Destroyed All Its Arms'," BBC News, 26 September 2005, available at http://news.bbc.co.uk/2/hi/uk_news/northern_ireland/4283444.stm, accessed 12 September 2009.

29. Richard Haass, "Diplomacy in Today's World," commencement address at Hamilton College (NY), 20 May 2007, https://secure.www.cfr.org/publication/13436/diplomacy_in_todays_world.html, accessed 13 September 2009.

30. R.S. Zaharna, "Asymmetry of Cultural Styles and the Unintended Consequences of Crisis Public Diplomacy," in *Intercultural Communication and Diplomacy*, ed. Hannah Slavik (Geneva: DiploFoundation, 2004), 133ff.

31. See the Partnership for Peace Consortium's two-volume issue on "Countering Ideological Support for Extremism: Challenges and Implications," *Connections: The Quarterly Journal*, Vol. V, Nos. 3 and 4 (Winter 2006); Sharyl Cross, John C. Reppert, and James K. Wither, "Advancing International Cooperation in Countering Ideological Support for Terrorism: Toward Building a Comprehensive Strategy," Conference Summary Report for the George C. Marshall European Center for Security Studies (Garmisch-Partenkirchen, Germany) and Centre for Excellence, Defence Against Terrorism (Ankara, Turkey), November 2007; and John C. Reppert, Sharyl Cross, James K. Wither, John J. LeBeau, and Alberto Cervone,

"Exploring Military Dimensions in Countering Ideological Support for Terrorism," Conference Summary Report for the George C. Marshall European Center for Security Studies (Garmisch-Partenkirchen, Germany) and the Center for High Defense Studies (Rome, Italy), September 2008.

32. See Montville and William D. Davidson, "Foreign Policy According to Freud," Foreign Policy, Vol. 45 (Winter 1981–1982): 145–157, available at http://www.foreignpolicy.com/Ning/archive/archive/045/6.PDF, accessed 13 September 2009.

33. John Davies and Edward Kaufman, eds., in *Second Track/Citizens' Diplomacy: Concepts and Techniques for Conflict Transformation* (Lanham, MD: Rowman and Littlefield, 2002), 2.

34. Andrea Bartoli, "Mediating Peace in Mozambique: The Role of the Community of Sant'Egidio," in *Herding Cats: Multiparty Mediation in a Complex World*, ed. Chester A. Crocker, Fen Osler Hampson, and Pamela R. Aall (Washington, DC: United States Institute of Peace Press, 1999), 245–274.

James K. Wither

Engaging Reconcilables:

Dialogue and Negotiation as Counterterrorism Strategies

The long-established norm is that legitimate governments do not talk to terrorists. Russian Federation President Vladimir Putin ruled out dialogue with Chechen rebels before launching the second Chechen War in 1999; Turkish Prime Minister Recep Tayyip Erdogan has declared that his government will never sit at the negotiating table with representatives of the Kurdistan Workers Party (PKK); and former US President George W. Bush proclaimed at the height of his "war on terror," "No nation can negotiate with terrorists. For there is no way to make peace with those whose only goal is death."[1]

In fact, governments *do* talk to terrorists. The proscription against such engagement is notable for the large number of exceptions to the general rule. European colonial powers, for example, frequently negotiated with the leaders of national liberation movements they had previously condemned as terrorists. The British government opened dialogue with the leadership of the Provisional Irish Republican Army (PIRA) long before the group eschewed violence and US officials negotiated with tribal leaders in Al Anbar province in Iraq despite their involvement in an ongoing insurgency against American forces. Despite its official stance, even President Putin's government held secret talks with Chechen rebel representatives in 2001.[2] Notwithstanding public statements, government officials, intelligence officers, and members of the security forces commonly open channels of communication with terrorist groups even while actively seeking to eradicate them. Initially these contacts are usually secret to avoid the political embarrassment of disclosure or failure. Engagement through dialogue has sometimes created the conditions for formal negotiations that, as in South Africa, Northern Ireland, El Salvador, Nicaragua, and Indonesia, have brought about the peaceful resolution of long-standing internal armed conflicts.

This chapter examines the option of talking to terrorists. It analyzes the potential advantages and risks of such engagement and addresses the questions of who to talk to, when to talk, how to talk, and what to talk about; it also attempts to draw lessons from the experience of negotiations with terrorist groups throughout the world. The final section assesses the extent to which productive dialogue can be established with contemporary terrorist groups that frequently lack the clear chain of command and internal discipline of the so-called traditional, nationalist-separatist movements.

The focus here is on dialogue and negotiation with terrorist groups as an element of a comprehensive counterterrorism strategy. Although law enforcement agencies have to talk with terrorists during the hostage crises that are a perennial feature of terrorist campaigns, negotiating with hostage-takers is not a subject covered here. Such negotiations, though critical to save lives, are not normally a strategic counterterrorist activity.[3] The conflict resolution process referred to as "track two diplomacy" can play a role in bringing a long-running conflict to a close; most notably it helped promote understanding and build trust between different ethnic groups in South Africa at the end of the apartheid era.[4] Track two activities are part of a package of confidence-building measures that can be employed to try to heal societies divided by conflict, but because such initiatives do not involve direct engagement with terrorists, they are not addressed in this chapter.

An important distinction needs to be made between the terms "dialogue" and "negotiations" in the context of talking to terrorists. Although the media tend to portray all engagement with terrorist groups as negotiations, this is misleading and contributes to the overall reluctance of governments to be open about such activity. Negotiation is normally a formal process intended to create options to bring about the resolution of a conflict. It invariably involves concessions and compromises by both governments and terrorist groups. Conversely, dialogue is usually informal, often covert, with no fixed agenda or commitments. Dialogue with terrorists almost always precedes negotiations; an exchange of views and information can take place for many years before the start of a recognized peace process. Even if the prospect of a negotiated settlement is far away, dialogue may help conflicting parties develop mutual understanding, buy time, and possibly set limits to violence.

Talking to Terrorists: Expedient or Foolhardy?

A RAND Corporation study of 648 terrorist groups between 1968 and 2006 concluded that military force was the primary cause of the end of a terrorist campaign in only 7 percent of cases, whereas the transition to a nonviolent political process took place in 43 percent of the examples reviewed.[5] There is no question that military force has a role to play in counterterrorism campaigns, particularly if a terrorist group grows in size to the point where it can mount an insurgency. However, the RAND statistics starkly illustrate the limitations of a counterterrorist strategy based predominantly on a kinetic approach. During G. W. Bush's first administration, the use of military force was the most obvious international manifestation of America's determination to root out terrorism, with the campaigns in Afghanistan in 2001 and, less plausibly, against Iraq in 2003 portrayed as preventive operations in a war on terror. The phrase "war on terror" itself arguably influenced a tendency to frame the problem in military terms, although there was far from universal acceptance of the notion that America was at war against terrorism, not least because it gave terrorist groups a standing as military antagonists that they did not merit.

The historical record suggests that it is difficult, especially for democratic states, to defeat extremist groups that enjoy a measure of popular support by military or law enforcement means alone, unless governments are ready to tolerate widespread human rights abuses by their security forces and risk the loss of core societal and constitutional values. If a government is unable or unwilling to crush a terrorist group by brute force, it will be forced to contemplate some form of political engagement. As the perception grew that America was not winning the war on terror, analysts argued for more sophisticated strategic thinking and emphasized non-kinetic counterterrorism measures, including possible engagement with terrorist groups that did not directly threaten the United States.[6]

Much of the rhetoric of the now superseded "war on terror" portrayed an enemy that was uncompromising and extreme. Such a stance made any kind of engagement morally indefensible and limited the range of options available to officials campaigning against terrorism. Analyst Brian Michael Jenkins has described such a situation, where dialogue and negotiations with terrorists are ruled out as a matter of principle, as "an ideological trap."[7] This trap can prevent talks with the more moderate elements within a terrorist organization and leave the terrorists with no alternative but armed struggle. Arguably it was Russia's refusal to countenance negotiations with Muslim rebels in Chechnya in the 1990s that allowed a basically nationalist-separatist resistance movement to fall under the influence of Wahhabi jihadists from 2000 onwards. The case of Hamas provides a particularly good example of this danger as a potential opportunity for substantive dialogue was lost after the movement's electoral victory in January 2006. Neither the western powers nor Israel would enter talks with Hamas leaders in the Palestinian Authority, although some were on record as supporting a two-state Israeli-Palestinian solution or a long-term truce (*hudna*) with Israel. The Saudi government attempted unsuccessfully to persuade western governments to engage in dialogue, Foreign Minister Prince Saud al Faisal making the obvious point that "If we don't talk to them, how do we convince them they should change their attitude towards peace?"[8] Former US President Jimmy Carter expressed similar sentiments during his controversial meetings with Hamas's leaders in spring 2008. Unfortunately the prospects for peace between Israel and the Palestinians remain as distant as ever. Hamas remains committed to the violent overthrow of Israel, and US policy continues to proscribe engagement with Hamas unless the group first ceases violence and recognizes the state of Israel.

The Hamas case also provides a reminder that dialogue and negotiations with terrorists may be better than the alternatives. Sir Winston Churchill may have popularized the declaration that "It is better to jaw-jaw than to war-war." Skeptics can justifiably argue that truces and ceasefires are sometimes exploited by terrorist groups to recuperate and rearm rather than search for peace, but dialogue can save lives by limiting terrorist and security force violence for extended periods. Although the Good Friday Agreement was signed in Northern Ireland in 1998, the peace process was not formally completed until 2007. The intervening years involved hard bargaining by all interested parties, but the level of PIRA and Protestant paramilitary terrorist activity in Northern Ireland was negligible. While most talks with terrorists fail, it is notable that internal conflicts often end on terms that were on the table for government and terrorist negotiators decades earlier. Such was the situation in Northern Ireland and it is arguably still the case in the Middle East. Notwithstanding changing military and political realities, Israeli Prime Minister Ehud Barak commented after the failure of talks with Yasser Arafat in 2000 that the two sides "will sit down once more to the same geography, the same demography, the same problems."[9]

From a counterterrorism perspective, "jaw-jaw" can sometimes weaken terrorist organizations in a way that "war-war" has failed to do. A conciliatory response by a government may weaken the cohesion of a terrorist group. The Liberation Tigers of Tamil Eelam (LTTE) in Sri Lanka are a case in point. LTTE's combat capability was significantly damaged when Colonel Karuna, with his Eastern Tamil fighters, left the organization in 2004. Karuna's claims include this one: that his defection resulted from the LTTE leadership's unwillingness to address the peace process with the Sri Lankan government following the ceasefire agreement of 2002.[10] Even if talks do not advance the prospects for peace, they may offer an intelligence windfall for a government's counter terrrorism campaign. Dialogue can help security officials assess terrorists' motives, their capabilities, and the caliber of their leadership and organization. Analyst Louise Richardson has argued that years of behind-the-scenes discussion between government officials and terrorists in Northern Ireland provided invaluable insights that facilitated the agreement in 1998, which effectively ended PIRA's terrorist activities.[11]

Some have argued that terrorism itself is best understood as a form of coercive dialogue, characterized by rhetoric and reciprocal acts of violence between the terrorists and a targeted government.[12] In such a situation, talking and listening to terrorists may move a brutal dialogue in a more peaceful and productive direction and halt what international negotiations expert P. Terence Hopmann has identified as a "vicious spiral" of violence.[13] Hoffman argues that escalating conflict reduces people's capacity to analyze problems in a sophisticated manner, which leads to ever more simplified and stereotypical arguments on both sides that in turn nourish further violence. This is particularly true in the case of terrorism because the term itself triggers an emotional reaction. This can obscure the possibility of compromise and make the rational analysis of cause and effect especially difficult.

Despite the case for engagement, it is hardly surprising that governments are often reluctant to open discourse with terrorists. As a monopoly of the legal use of force is a basic characteristic of a nation-state, violent extremists undermine a government's sovereignty and credibility. More broadly they also challenge the entire modern nation-state-based international system. Engagement with terrorists creates ethical and legal dilemmas. It legitimizes violence and betrays fundamental values by rewarding individuals who have rejected the rules and norms of international society. Talking to terrorists means setting aside their record of violence and extremist ideology in the interests of political pragmatism. This is particularly difficult if, as is normally the case, a terrorist movement has already been described by government officials as uniquely evil and irreconcilable. A policy of engagement poses considerable political risks as it may be perceived by the general public and the terrorists themselves as appeasement and weakness. Opposition parties can be quick to condemn dialogue in such terms as did the Partido Popular in Spain following talks between the Socialist government and ETA in 2006. Fragile democracies with weak governments are particularly vulnerable when they seek to accommodate a terrorist movement. Hezbollah, for example, has successfully entered politics in Lebanon without abandoning its radicalism and has achieved veto power over Lebanese government decisions.

Terrorists often cynically take advantage of talks or ceasefires to buy time. The LTTE and the Revolutionary Armed Forces of Colombia (FARC) in Colombia are just two examples of groups that have exploited such temporary lulls in fighting to regroup and rearm for their next offensive. In 1998 the Colombian government granted FARC a territorial safe haven as a confidence-building measure to facilitate peace talks. The terrorist group used this opportunity to rebuild its fighting capacity with impunity. Flagrant breaches of the so-called peace process eventually led the Colombian government to break off the talks and order the army to reoccupy the FARC enclave in 2002.[14] Recent calls by the FARC leadership for a political resolution of their 44-year-old war have been motivated by the military successes of the Colombian security forces rather than national or international mediation and negotiation efforts.

In an international context, talking to terrorists risks damaging relations with allied states and potentially can undermine coalitions against terrorism. Repeated calls by British officials for negotiations with the Taliban initially caused considerable disquiet in government circles in both Washington and Kabul. Likewise, the United Kingdom's decision to engage directly with political leaders of Hezbollah in 2009 angered President Obama's administration, which regards both the political and military wings of Hezbollah as integrated parts of a terrorist organization.[15] Terrorist groups will naturally seek opportunities to divide their opponents. Osama bin Laden's 2004 offer of a truce to Europe appeared to open the possibility of engagement, but should properly be interpreted as an attempt to separate countries supporting the coalition against al Qaeda.

It has become a truism to state that no two counterterrorist campaigns are the same. As every conflict is different, there is no one dialogue and negotiations template that can be conveniently applied in every situation. The sheer variety of terrorist organizations alone makes generic approaches to engagement difficult. Nevertheless, an increasing number of analysts have attempted to identify success factors, patterns of behavior, and best practices when it comes to talking to terrorists.

Talking to Terrorists: Who, When, How, and What?

Engagement should not be viewed as an alternative to law enforcement and military measures, but rather as a complementary part of an overall strategy. Martha Crenshaw, for example, has identified negotiations as one of the tools that a government can use in response to terrorism, along with what she refers to as "deterrence," "criminal justice," and "enhanced defense."[16] Obviously the suggestion that democratic governments should recognize the potential of engagement as a tool of counterterrorism predates the events of 9/11, although since these attacks, a growing number of scholars have addressed the subject, analyzing potential risks and benefits and offering guidance to governments contemplating such talks.[17]

Arguably the first issue to consider is with whom to talk. Negotiations specialist William Zartman classifies terrorist groups into three categories: terrorists who actively seek negotiations as part of their strategy; absolutists whose ideology, objectives, and methods allow for no compromise; and other groups that he labels rather inelegantly as "conditional absolute terrorists."[18] Terrorists in this latter category do not actively seek to negotiate, but have something tangible about which to bargain, such as territory or autonomy, even if their methods, in particular the use of suicide attacks, categorize them as extreme. For his part, Zartman advocates engagement with these groups, as the leadership or at least a part of the membership may be reconcilable if offered the possibility of real progress toward their objectives.[19] Al Qaeda and its affiliates appear too extreme for meaningful dialogue as their ideology alone places them in the irreconcilable category. Osama bin Laden's mentor, Abdullah Azzam, famously ruled out talks in his oft-quoted slogan: "The rifle and *jihad* alone; no negotiations, no conferences, no dialogues."[20] Bin Laden himself is also on record as scorning Muslims who seek to negotiate rather than fight the "crusaders." Nevertheless, some analysts have not ruled out dialogue with even the most ideologically committed terrorists.[21] Scholar Mohammad-Mahmoud Ould Mohamedou caused controversy in 2005 when he argued that al Qaeda's political goals should be distinguished from its religious rhetoric and proposed direct engagement by the United States to address the movement's stated grievances.[22]

A terrorist group's goals are not the only factor to be considered. The organization's leadership and structure are also critical issues. Terrorist analyst Peter Neumann stresses that a group's leadership must offer the prospect of being good negotiating partners in the sense of having tangible political objectives, a willingness to limit violence, and an ability to maintain discipline among the movement's foot soldiers.[23] Jonathan Powell, former UK Prime Minister Tony Blair's chief negotiator in Northern Ireland, also emphasizes the importance of strong and consistent leadership, not just of the terrorist group, but of all parties in the negotiation process.[24] A charismatic and respected individual can help to build trust and garner internal and international support for a peace process, although figures of the stature of Nelson Mandela, who led the African National Congress (ANC) in South Africa, remain rare. Tough leaders with a long-term perspective may be particularly important to minimize the effect of the hardcore terrorist "spoilers" who will normally seek to disrupt peace talks by temporarily escalating the level of violence.[25] Governments must take into account the impact of so-called spoilers before contemplating engagement with terrorist groups, not least because the prospect of peace talks can prompt radical elements opposed to the process to take over the movement. British dialogue with the Official IRA in the early 1970s, for example, facilitated the rise of the more intransigent "Provisionals," which removed any early prospect of peace.

Talks are facilitated when a terrorist organization is sufficiently mature to have an established political wing. This permits government officials and mediators to open dialogue with terrorist leaders who are one step removed from direct participation in violence. It may also require a government to grant the political wing of a terrorist movement formal, legal recognition, a step that governments may be reluctant to contemplate given the fact that military and political wings are often well integrated. The British government legalized Sinn Fein, the political wing of the PIRA, as early as 1974, but the South African regime only reluctantly legalized the ANC in 1990 in order to facilitate a negotiated end to apartheid. In the case of terrorist groups that have formal or informal state sponsorship, diplomatic efforts, including negotiations, are often best aimed at the governments of the countries in question. Pakistan, Saudi Arabia, Iran, and Syria are among states that have been accused of allowing terrorist groups to organize or operate on their territory. Prior to 9/11 the US government negotiated unsuccessfully with the Taliban regime in Afghanistan to expel al Qaeda. However, in 2001 it had more success in talks with Pakistan, ending the government's tacit support for both the Taliban and al Qaeda by offering economic incentives, such as the removal of sanctions set up in response to Pakistan's nuclear program.[26]

Analysts are deeply divided on the subject of when to talk to terrorists. Respected terrorism scholar, Paul Wilkinson argued back in the 1970s that liberal democratic states must take a consistently hard line against terrorists and their supporters, one that ruled out any "political negotiations or conferences with groups or movements engaged in, or aiding and supporting terrorism."[27] More recently Harvard law professor Alan Dershowitz has condemned the tendency of governments to reward acts of terrorism with negotiations and concessions. He argues that punishment and incapacitation are more appropriate responses.[28] Conversely, some analysts maintain that governments should always keep the prospect of dialogue open at any stage of a conflict because only engagement can promote alternatives to violence.[29] However, the most common perspective on talks acknowledges that governments must be circumspect in their relations with terrorist groups, but such caution should not preclude dialogue and negotiations when these offer opportunities to limit violence or advance a peace process. Commentators frequently refer to some sort of strategic turning point or "hurting stalemate" as being a ripe moment for dialogue. Such a situation arises in a protracted conflict when terrorist leaders or government security forces begin to question the continued utility of violence as the primary means of achieving their objectives and both sides sense the support of their constituents ebbing away.[30]

A perceived stalemate and war weariness in the theater of conflict are not necessarily the only significant factors. Changes in the international environment can help to create conditions that make talks more fruitful. The withdrawal of US and Soviet material and ideological support for proxy governments and terrorist groups in the early 1990s helped facilitate United Nations' (UN) mediation to end protracted, internal armed conflicts in Latin America and sub-Saharan Africa. Likewise, America's single-minded focus against terrorism after 9/11 added further impetus to peace negotiations in regions as diverse as Northern Ireland and the Philippines.

British diplomats Jonathan Powell and Michael Ancram, who both negotiated with PIRA, stress the need to avoid setting preconditions, such as a permanent cessation of violence, before engagement begins.[31] Both acknowledge that an agreement to end violence will be necessary before exploratory dialogue can turn into formal peace negotiations, but the Northern Ireland experience suggests that governments have to handle this issue delicately as undefeated terrorist groups are unlikely to enter peace negotiations if an agreement to end violence is interpreted as surrender. The Northern Ireland case is by no means unique. Former Taliban Foreign Minister Wakil Ahmed Muttawakil has publicly called for talks between the Afghan government and Taliban without preconditions;[32] earlier attempts by the Afghan government to court reconcilable Taliban members were not helped by President Karzai's insistence at the time that fighters first lay down their weapons, disavow armed insurrection, and accept the presence of foreign troops.

Talking to terrorists is often characterized by a mixture of dissimulation and posturing on all sides. Initial contacts between governments and terrorists tend to be covert, although both sides may make formal declarations, conduct media interviews, or use trusted intermediaries to signal a willingness to seek dialogue and possible accommodation.[33] Governments normally try to avoid potential political embarrassment by eschewing direct talks between government officials and terrorist leaders, at least in the early stages of a bargaining process. Contacts are often made through trusted, discrete neutral parties, like the Catholic priest Alex Reid or US Senator George Mitchell in the Northern Ireland context or even mavericks such as Michael Semple, employed by the European Union as a "political officer" to seek reconciliation with Afghan Taliban.[34] Sometimes go-betweens remain nameless, such as "Mr. Hezbollah," a German intelligence agent who has apparently acted as a mediator between Israel and Hezbollah.[35] On the government's side the use of domestic or foreign intelligence officials acting covertly allows plausible deniability and therefore carries less political risk than formal official contact. In another German example, the media recently revealed that the German foreign intelligence service had held secret, although ultimately unsuccessful, talks with the Taliban in 2005.[36]

It is often assumed that government officials or a mediator acting on their behalf make the initial offer of dialogue, but Scheffler has argued that extremists are often keener to seek talks than the governments that oppose them. Apart from tactical benefits, such as time to reorganize and better treatment for their prisoners in government jails, engagement offers the opportunity to gain recognition as a legitimate party to the conflict and strengthens the movement's leadership against competing extremist splinter groups.[37] Naturally terrorists can be especially concerned about their personal fate. The leadership of the Lord's Resistance Army (LRA) in Uganda, for example, has demanded immunity from prosecution in return for peace, although arrest warrants issued by the International Criminal Court (ICC) in 2005 on account of the group's widespread human rights abuses make such a concession unlikely.

As in any conflict resolution process, third-party mediation is often essential to avoid the emotional and often fruitless exchanges that can otherwise occur between embittered protagonists. Recently, the Saudi government has played a low-key but essential role in hosting and encouraging talks between representatives of the Afghan government and Taliban insurgents. Friendly neutral governments sometimes have to facilitate talks over extended periods of time, as the Malaysian government has done in the protracted and often problematic negotiations between the Moro Islamic Liberation Front (MILF) and the Republic of the Philippines government since 1997. Similarly, representatives of the Organization of the Islamic Conference (OIC) have mediated talks with another, older Muslim group in the Philippines, the Moro National Liberation Front (MNLF). There are also nongovernmental organizations (NGOs) that specialize in mediation in intrastate conflicts. The Swiss-based Centre for Humanitarian Dialogue (CHD), founded in 1999, has been involved in facilitating back-channel dialogue and negotiations with rebel leaders and the Indonesian government in Aceh, between the Nepalese government and Maoist insurgents, and in assisting the Spanish government's ceasefire talks with Basque Fatherland and Liberty(ETA).[38] Similarly, a British-based organization called Conflicts Forum has attempted to serve as an interlocutor between militant Islamist groups and the West.[39]

Mediators can use their professional skills and impartial status to help parties in a conflict see the opportunities presented by dialogue. However, mediators are by no means "soft" on terrorism. As Norwegian Foreign Minister and experienced international mediator Jonas Gahr Store maintains: "Engaging . . . does not mean lowering requirements. It can be a means to set yardsticks, hold interlocutors accountable, and probe their thinking while surrendering nothing."[40] Professional mediators, unlike most politicians, can work on a conflict for years and build up a level of trust and knowledge. They can also facilitate the negotiating process by training negotiating team members, using techniques to encourage productive dialogue, such as "brainstorming," and by drafting "strawman" agreements. Mediators will sometimes use deadlines to help force the pace of talks, although if deadlines are breached too frequently both the mediators and the negotiating process itself can lose credibility. On occasion, senior statesmen can play a significant, personal mediation role. President Clinton, for example, hosted negotiators, engaged directly in the Good Friday Peace Agreement talks, and helped to keep the whole Northern Ireland peace process on track following the Omagh bombing by dissident Republicans in August 1998.[41]

As the Omagh attack illustrated, those opposed to negotiations will often attempt to use terror to disrupt a peace process. Leaders can find themselves unable or unwilling to pursue talks in the face of violence that damages both their authority as negotiators and public support for the process. In view of this problem, Matthew Levitt has advocated what he terms the "preemptive insulation of the negotiating process" through the prior agreement of a crisis-response mechanism including continuing direct communication channels at the political and working levels to sustain negotiations.[42] Jonathan Powell expresses similar, if less formal, sentiments about the need to insulate negotiations from the impact of violent setbacks. Based on his experience in Northern Ireland, Powell stresses the importance of persistence, the need to maintain contacts with other parties throughout crisis periods, and above all the acceptance of short-term "political pain" in order to allow dialogue to continue.[43]

Initial contacts and exploratory dialogue are normally conducted without fixed agendas and commitments. Such engagement may lead nowhere or can promote mutual understanding and allow areas of possible compromise to be explored. In September 2008, for example, Saudi officials hosted a meeting in Mecca between envoys of President Karzai and allies of the Taliban. Typically, both sides denied that the meeting involved peace negotiations, but some sources at the conference felt that the talks might constitute a prelude to more formal engagement.[44] Exploratory dialogue can sometimes set limits to violence, establishing actual or tacit rules of engagement. Both ETA and PIRA agreed to provide coded warnings to the security forces in order to allow civilians to be evacuated when explosives were used against economic or infrastructure targets. Incidentally, such agreements also helped to minimize the unnecessary disruption to public life caused by bomb hoaxes. A notable example of setting limits to violence was a tacit agreement between Israel and Hezbollah in the 1990s, whereby Hezbollah refrained from firing rockets at Israeli settlements, while Israel agreed to stop shelling Lebanese villages.[45] Hamas has reputedly offered Israel a similar deal, agreeing to restrict its operations to purely military targets if Israel similarly refrains from attacking civilians.[46]

The Challenge of Moving from Dialogue to Negotiations

The first stage in moving from dialogue to negotiations is normally a ceasefire. However, turning a ceasefire into a political process involving a permanent cessation of violence is a fraught and difficult process, and in practice most ceasefires collapse. In recent years, promising ceasefires between governments and terrorist groups in Spain, Sri Lanka, Palestine, and the Philippines have broken down into mutual recriminations and renewed violence. Often ceasefires break down because peace talks cannot abate long-standing fear, mistrust, and suspicion on both sides, even when joint negotiated gains appear possible. The conduct of negotiations is often assumed to be an essentially rational process, which reflects the dominant influence of the Harvard Negotiation Project (HNP) interest-based bargaining school.[47] However, scholars in the negotiation field, in particular HNP founder Roger Fisher, now recognize the role that embedded emotions play in derailing even the most productive talks. Fisher's recently published sequel to his renowned book *Getting to Yes* tacitly acknowledges the limitations of the rational, interest-based negotiating method. The book *Beyond Reason* focuses on the emotions that negotiators must anticipate, manage, and even use productively to minimize the chances of failure.[48] The training of conflict resolution mediators and negotiators increasingly reflects this potentially valuable approach.

If a ceasefire holds, dialogue may progress to formal negotiations for a political settlement. At this stage, the verbal ambiguities acceptable to give early impetus to talks have to be replaced by formal commitments. Naturally, it is at this stage that talks are most likely to fail. Most experts maintain that a terrorist group must commit to a permanent cessation of violence in return for government concessions.[49] A permanent ceasefire provides political momentum toward conflict resolution. It builds trust, maintains government credibility, and helps commit terrorist leaders to peaceful solutions. The blame for the breakdown of negotiations frequently falls on terrorist splinter groups or rogue elements in the security forces that deliberately use violence to disrupt peace talks. However, often it is the government side that is unable to deliver its side of the bargain. There has to be broad, cross-party political support for a peace process, but political will or public support for compromise may be lacking. Dissident government ministers and opposition party politicians can act as spoilers in their own right, as the recent history of talks with ETA in Spain demonstrates. Sometimes, as in Sri Lanka, there is no political consensus for a negotiated settlement. Elsewhere there have been legal or constitutional barriers to agreement. In October 2008 the Philippines' Supreme Court rejected as unconstitutional a Malaysian-brokered peace agreement between the government and the MILF that would have granted the Moros additional territory and autonomy in Mindanao.[50]

Among the most difficult problems to resolve in the last phase of negotiations are the issues of disarmament and amnesty. Disarmament signifies the end of armed conflict and the acceptance of the continuation of a struggle by peaceful political means. But terrorist groups that believe that their armed struggle is far from lost tend to be unwilling to disarm before the end of peace negotiations, not least because such an act suggests surrender and exacerbates problems keeping hard-liners committed to the peace process. Prime Minister Major's insistence on PIRA decommissioning before exploratory dialogue could progress to formal talks bedeviled attempts to move the Northern Ireland peace process forward in the 1990s. Major's successor, Tony Blair, adopted a more flexible approach, dropping disarmament preconditions, accepting "progressive decommissioning," and introducing independent verification. Even so the issue of PIRA decommissioning remained an intractable problem for mediators and negotiators until the final agreement in May 2007.[51] In the case of the negotiated settlement that ended the conflict between the government and the Farabundo Marti National Liberation Front (FMLN) in El Salvador, disarmament only took place after the signing of the peace accord in January 1992. Demobilization of the guerrillas and government armed forces took place under UN supervision between February and October 1992 but was marked by continuing suspicion and mistrust on both sides.[52]

Amnesties are another critical and controversial issue. Allowing terrorists convicted of murder and members of the security forces who may have committed atrocities to go free can be hard to sell to the public on all sides of a civil conflict. Nevertheless, some sort of amnesty is needed to cement a peace deal and may be essential to dissuade dissident elements from a terrorist group or the security forces from continuing violence. In South Africa an amnesty for ANC fighters and members of the apartheid government security forces was discussed throughout the extended period of peace negotiations, but only finally resolved with the establishment of the Truth and Reconciliation Commission by the first post-apartheid government in 1995. With some success President Abdelaziz Bouteflika of Algeria was able to implement an amnesty in 2005 for remaining combatants from the civil war. This amnesty sought to isolate the terrorists of al Qaeda in the Islamic Maghreb (AQIM) group, who refused any accommodation with "apostates," from the majority of Islamist militants who were prepared to contemplate a compromise deal with the Algerian government.[53]

Prospects for Dialogue with Contemporary Terrorists

The foregoing discussion suggests that engagement is most likely to be successful when a terrorist group has realizable political objectives, is prepared to limit violence, and has strong and disciplined leadership. Reconcilable terrorists tend to be the traditional nationalist-separatist or other special interest groups with specific political, economic, and social grievances. These groups are by no means anachronisms. For example, Basque and Corsican separatists continue their decades-old violent struggles for independence. Despite the failure of negotiations so far, some sort of compromise with the Spanish and French governments, respectively, remains a likely outcome of their campaigns. The Movement for the Emancipation of the Niger Delta (MEND) in Nigeria fights against economic deprivation, government corruption, and environmental degradation by targeting foreign oil company operations in the Niger Delta. As a terrorist organization, MEND has clearly articulated grievances, is highly organized, and exploits hostage taking for ransom rather than murder. Violence is largely directed at members of the security forces rather than civilians. Talks between MEND and the Nigerian government in 2006 collapsed, but clearly demonstrated the potential for a negotiated settlement.[54]

Unfortunately, many contemporary terrorist groups tend to be more extreme in their objectives, more violent in their methods, and more loosely organized than ETA or MEND. Millenarian terrorist cults or lone fanatics in the Timothy McVeigh mold offer the most unlikely prospects for engagement. The Japanese group Aum Shinrikyo provides the best recent example of millenarian terrorism. This cult mounted the sarin gas attack on the Tokyo subway system in 1995, an act of terrorism intended to hasten the end of the world as Aum Shinrikyo members believed contemporary society was irretrievably corrupted and unjust. Such single-minded fanaticism does not lend itself to accommodation and compromise. Thankfully, millenarian terrorists have little hope of garnering public support for their activities, and strenuous law enforcement measures can be employed to suppress them. In the future, however, these groups and indeed "super-empowered" individuals may pose more of a threat as the diffusion of biotechnology, radiological, chemical, and advanced tactical weapons is likely to furnish them with ever greater lethality.[55]

An all-embracing ideology offers a potent justification for acts of violence. Ideology equips terrorists with a set of principles, a system of values, or a proposal for an ideal society. Adherents can claim that their brand of terrorism is perpetrated for the good of humanity in the longer term. Such zealots make unlikely negotiating partners as their commitment to universalistic, utopian ideologies is normally coupled with contempt for alternative political or religious systems and beliefs. As Peter Sederberg acknowledges, conflict regulation is only possible if both parties "recognize the necessity of each other's existence."[56] During the Cold War western Europe was plagued by social revolutionary, Marxist-Leninist-inspired terrorist groups such as the Red Army Faction and the Red Brigades. By the 1990s, effective law enforcement, terrorist "burnout," and the lack of popular support had led to the failure of all of these terrorist campaigns. Negotiations were not a factor in government counterterrorism strategies because there were no common interests to identify and address with these extremists, although authorities did leave open the prospect of dialogue, reconciliation, and resettlement into civilian life for those terrorists prepared to defect and repent their crimes. In Italy, this program proved highly effective in helping to break the back of the Red Brigades in the early 1980s.[57] Recently, in two very different theatres, the Colombian and Saudi governments have had some success in convincing terrorists to abandon their violent campaigns through similar approaches. The Colombian government's amnesty legislation, the 2005 Peace and Justice Law, helped to persuade the Guevarist Revolutionary Army (ERG) to disband in 2008. Individual terrorists were offered minimal prison sentences and training programs for reinsertion into civilian life, which proved preferable alternatives to probable death at the hands of the security forces.[58] Since 2004 Saudi Arabia has made rehabilitation a major feature of its counterterrorism strategy. Detained violent extremists are given religious and psychological counseling to persuade them to renounce terrorist ideologies. Repentant terrorists who complete the program are offered social, educational, and financial support to reintegrate into society.[59] Similar programs intended to demobilize terrorists are increasing in popularity and have been adopted or trialed in Algeria, Egypt, Jordan, Yemen, Singapore, Indonesia, and Malaysia.

Radical Islamism has replaced revolutionary Marxist-Leninism as the most prevalent terrorist ideology. Writing in 1988, Bruce Hoffman noted that religiously inspired terrorists were more likely to view their struggle in totalistic terms than those motivated by secular ideologies because they considered violence a sacramental act and therefore resisted utilitarian considerations in their political decision making.[60] Whereas revolutionary groups of the Cold War era were quite prepared to use ruthless violence to achieve their objectives, indiscriminate assaults on civilians were rare. Preferred victims were politicians, police, industrialists, or other symbols of capitalism. In contrast, much Islamist terrorism has been characterized by attacks intended to cause mass civilian casualties, justified by the perpetrators on ideological grounds. Osama bin Laden has stated on a number of occasions that all American civilians are legitimate targets, being guilty of crimes against Muslims merely by association with their government. Al Qaeda's chief ideologue, Ayman al Zawahiri, made similar comments about British citizens after the "7/7" bombings in London in 2005.[61]

There appears little prospect of conciliation with absolutists, but not all religiously motivated groups are so extreme. Arguably the potential for fruitful engagement with Islamists fighting to achieve regional political objectives, rather than al Qaeda's universalistic goals, have been relatively neglected by western governments. Although militant Islamists usually share a religious agenda along with an antipathy to Israel and the United States, they differ in their objectives and methods. Many, including Hezbollah and the MILF, have no ambition to create a new caliphate or wage implacable war against infidels. As was the case with communist-inspired movements formed to fight military occupation or colonial rule in the twentieth century, strategic objectives often trump ideological purity. British scholar Tarak Barkawi has described campaigns by Islamist terrorist groups as a "hybrid form of anti-colonial resistance,"[62] essentially a continuation of a historical struggle by the Islamic world to resist western military, economic, and cultural expansion. Similarly, American analyst R. A. Pape has argued that Islamist suicidal terrorism is best understood as a strategy to attain the independence of Muslim people, property, and way of life from foreign influence and control rather than a response to religious ideology.[63] Muslim insurgencies in Mindanao in the Philippines and southern Thailand are examples of secessionist campaigns that have remained largely separate from the *jihadist* terrorism of al Qaeda's regional affiliate Jemaah Islamiyah (JI).[64] Nor have religious zeal and martyrdom been the primary motivations of Chechen suicide bombers despite the spread of Wahhabist thinking after 2000.[65]

Unlike the most extreme Islamist groups, Hezbollah and Hamas emphasize local political grievances rather than a universalistic ideology and both have joined the democratic political process. These factors alone differentiate them from al Qaeda. Hezbollah leader Hassan Nasrallah is on record as condemning the 9/11 attacks and the sectarian atrocities committed by former al Qaeda leader al Zarqawi.[66] As a sophisticated and highly disciplined organization with strong and respected leadership, Hezbollah arguably meets many of the criteria for a viable negotiating partner discussed earlier. Opportunities to isolate the most extreme Islamists, physically, morally, and ideologically have potentially been lost because of a tendency for western governments to lump together local Islamist groups with al Qaeda. The Islamic Courts Union (ICU) in Somalia is a case in point. The ICU brought temporary peace to the country in 2006 and, although a fundamentalist Muslim movement, its spokesmen rejected links with al Qaeda and sought engagement with western states. However, such initiatives were rejected by the US government, and an American-backed invasion by Ethiopia ended the prospects for stability. Since 2007 Somalia has descended into worse chaos and violence, while virulently anti-western jihadist groups like al Shabab have largely supplanted the more moderate ICU.[67] Islamist ideology may not lend itself easily to compromise and reconciliation, but selective engagement may help to accelerate the growing backlash among even radical Muslims against the excessive brutality of some al Qaeda–affiliated terrorist groups. An increasing number of reports suggest that Muslim clerics, former terrorist supporters and influential spokesmen in Egypt, Jordan, Saudi Arabia, Indonesia, and elsewhere are challenging Osama bin Laden's religious credentials and al Qaeda's justification for violence against noncombatants.[68] In Anbar Province in Iraq, growing hostility to the movement's methods and ideology promoted accommodation between local leaders, formerly allied to al Qaeda, and the US military. Negotiations led to joint action by the military and tribal militias that virtually eradicated terrorism in the province.

The extreme violence of many contemporary terrorist groups makes it harder for governments to contemplate dialogue; the public are likely to find talks with mass murderers hard to stomach. It used to be a cliché that terrorists wanted a few people dead, but a lot of people watching. However, since the 1980s, there has been a growing trend toward attacks designed to create the maximum number of civilian casualties. In part, this is a direct result of the use of suicide bombers by groups such as LTTE and Hamas. Suicide terrorism has proved more effective than traditional tactics for causing mass casualties, garnering extra publicity and establishing a terrorist group's credibility in the eyes of its constituents.[69] In Afghanistan, for example, suicide terrorism was not used during the war against Soviet occupation in the 1980s, only being introduced recently as a tactic by the Taliban and al Qaeda. The increase in mass casualty attacks on civilians is not only the result of suicide terrorism. In March 2004, an al Qaeda-affiliated group bombed commuter trains in Madrid, killing 191 and wounding over 1,600 people, an attack that contrasted starkly with the relative restraint of the long-running ETA separatist campaign. In another notable example of the contrast between so-called "traditional terrorists" and "new" or "absolutist" terrorists,[70] the radical Islamists affiliated to Lashkar e Tayyiba that attacked Mumbai in November 2008 took hostages for tactical purposes rather than using them to negotiate ransoms or publicize their cause. Nor are mass casualty attacks only a Muslim phenomenon; secular terrorists are also responsible for a general trend toward greater extremes of violence. One such group, the national-separatist United Liberation Front of Assam, recently appears to have switched its targeting from oil and gas pipelines and depots to indiscriminate car bombings in urban areas.[71]

In a protracted campaign, splinter groups frequently break away from parent terrorist organizations in response to changing operational circumstances. As these terrorists tend to be the more radical elements, they have often complicated or even stymied efforts to find peace. In Northern Ireland, for example, the Real and Continuity IRA groups attempted to derail the peace process launched by the Good Friday Agreement in 1998. However, in the case of the majority of terrorist groups that emerged during the 1960s and 1970s, a dominant faction was usually able to maintain overall political and military control of the movement. This provided a leadership focus for governments seeking dialogue. From the mid-1970s the Palestinian Liberation Organization (PLO) provided such a focus for the Palestinian movement, despite the plethora of terrorist splinter groups engaged in attacks against Israel. By contrast, contemporary terrorism is increasingly perpetrated by loose networks that range from local to global, often with differing and sometimes obscure objectives—a development that makes productive engagement especially difficult. As the insurgency in Iraq has illustrated, boundaries are blurred between insurgents fighting for local autonomy, criminals seeking self-enrichment, and terrorists engaged in global *jihad*. In late 2008, groups still opposing US policy in Iraq included the Political Council for Iraqi Resistance, the Islamic Front for Iraqi Resistance, the al-Mujahidin Army, the Islamic Army in Iraq, the Sa'd Bin-Abi-Waqqas Army, the Supreme Command for Jihad and Liberation, and Hamas-Iraq.[72] The South Thailand case demonstrates the difficulty of negotiating with loosely networked terrorists rather than a group with a declared political leadership. Since 2004 efforts by the Thai government to establish dialogue with militant separatists have been frustrated by the insurgents' apparent lack of structure and recognized chain of command.[73] As al Qaeda assumes more of an ideological, motivational, and propaganda role, its operations have increasingly been assumed by small autonomous cells and individuals. In Europe this has led to the emergence of small, informal, home-grown terrorist networks. Membership is often based on groups of friends who appear well integrated into the host country, are information technology adept, but have little regular contact with other groups or cells. These amorphous micro-actors are both difficult to detect and counter and are also unfeasible negotiating partners. The authorities have no recognized leadership or organization with which to establish contact, even in the unlikely event that sufficient common interests exist to provide a basis for meaningful dialogue.

Conclusions

Dialogue and negotiations need not be seen as alternatives to other counterterrorism measures; rather they may be options to consider as part of an integrated government strategy. Engagement with terrorists can form an element in a comprehensive approach in which repressive and conciliatory measures are weighted according to operational, political, and international circumstances. Engagement is undoubtedly risky and, as this chapter has illustrated, burdened with practical difficulties. It is all too easy in democracies for the general public and political opposition to accuse a government of appeasement for talking to extremists who are murdering their citizens, especially in an era of mass casualty terrorism. Talks often end in failure and sometimes political embarrassment, especially when terrorists exploit periods of dialogue to recover and rearm ready for renewed violence. It is therefore tempting to negotiate only when a terrorist group is already "on the ropes" as a result of military or police operations. As discussed above, the problem is compounded by the networked character and ideology of many contemporary terrorist groups. Without tangible objectives, defined leadership, and internal organizational discipline, it is hard to start and maintain a dialogue, let alone negotiate a peace deal. Traditional nationalist-separatist terrorist organizations offered better prospects for negotiation than contemporary, religiously motivated terrorists, who believe that they are fulfilling an immutable divine plan and despise their opponents.

Nevertheless, all counterterrorism strategies have to be judged on their merits, and no potentially productive approach should necessarily be ruled out. Engagement can help isolate and marginalize the most violent extremists and offer more moderate elements within a terrorist movement the opportunity to end an armed struggle and seek change through peaceful, legitimate political activity. Some terrorist campaigns have ended in this way, with amnesties and rehabilitation for the rank and file and, in a few cases, even respected elder statesmen status for former terrorist leaders. However, political leaders have to be prepared to talk to their enemies and take risks for peace. Only through dialogue is it possible to identify common interests, explore possible compromises, and build trust. If extreme positions rule out the prospect of any meaningful negotiations, whether to limit violence or begin a search for peace, then at least engagement can help the authorities to better understand the character of their enemy and the nature of the threat. Conflict resolution is usually a protracted process, but it cannot begin at all without a willingness to talk. If strong leadership is needed to fight terrorism, arguably even greater courage and determination are required to pursue the negotiated resolution that might provide the only basis for a lasting peace.

James K. Wither Professor of National Security Studies and Director of the Fellows Programs at the George C. Marshall European Center for Security Studies, James Wither has been a member of the faculty since 2000. He is a retired British Army officer and former researcher in twentieth-century warfare at the Imperial War Museum, London. Professor Wither lectures on warfare, negotiations, and other security issues in Garmisch and abroad for the Marshall Center, while remaining a regular member of the teaching faculty for its Program on Terrorism and Security Studies. His research and writing interests include terrorism, contemporary warfare, and Anglo-American relations, and his recent articles have appeared in the journals *Parameters, European Security, Studies in Conflict and Terrorism,* and *Small Wars and Insurgencies.*

Recommended Readings

Alterman, John B., Martha Crenshaw et al. "How Terrorism Ends," United States Institute of Peace Special Report, 25 May 1999.

Ancram, Michael. "Dancing with Wolves: The Importance of Talking to Your Enemies," *Middle East Policy,* Vol. 14, No. 2 (Summer 2007): 22–30.

Byman, Daniel. "The Decision to Begin Talks with Terrorists: Lessons for Policymakers," *Studies in Conflict and Terrorism,* Vol. 29, No. 5 (June 2006): 403–414.

Fisher, Roger, and Daniel Shapiro. *Beyond Reason: Using Emotions as You Negotiate.* New York: Viking Penguin, 2005.

Levitt, Matthew. *Negotiating Under Fire: Preserving Peace Talks in the Face of Terror Attacks.* Lanham, MD: Rowan & Littlefield, 2008.

Neumann, Peter R. "Negotiating with Terrorists," *Foreign Affairs,* Vol. 86, No. 1 (January–February 2007): 128–134.

Powell, Jonathan. *Great Hatred, Little Room: Making Peace in Northern Ireland.* London: Bodley Head, 2008.

Sederberg, Peter C. "Conciliation as Counter-Terrorist Strategy," *Journal of Peace Research,* Vol. 32, No. 3 (August 1995): 295–312.

Spector, Bertram I. "Negotiating with Villains Revisited: Research Note," *International Negotiation,* Vol. 8, No. 3 (2003): 443–450.

Wither, James K. "Selective Engagement with Islamist Terrorists: Exploring the Prospects," *Studies in Conflict and Terrorism,* Vol. 32, No. 1 (January 2009): 18–35.

Notes

1. "President to Send Secretary Powell to Middle East," President George W. Bush Remarks to Press, 4 April 2002. http://georgewbush-whitehouse.archives.gov/news/releases/2002/04/20020404-1.html, accessed 18 September 2009.

2. Audrey Kurth Cronin, "Russia and Chechnya" in *Democracy and Counterterrorism: Lessons from the Past,* Robert J. Art and Louise Richardson, eds. (Washington, DC: USIP Press Books, 2007), 398.

3. Hostage crises do not always have only a tactical impact. The seizure of the Japanese embassy in Lima by the Tupac Amaru Revolutionary Movement (MRTA) in 1996–1997 effectively ended the terrorists group's campaign. All fourteen MRTA terrorists were killed when Peruvian Special Forces stormed the embassy in April 1997.

4. See, for example, Daniel Lieberfeld, "Evaluating the Contributions of Track-Two Diplomacy to Conflict Termination in South Africa, 1984–90," *Journal of Peace Research,* Vol. 39, No. 2 (May 2002): 355–372.

5. Seth G. Jones and Martin C. Libicki, *How Terrorist Groups End: Lessons for Countering al Qa'ida* (Santa Monica: RAND Corporation, 2008), 18–19. Other reasons for the end of terrorist groups were law enforcement action (40 percent) and victory (10 percent).

6. See, for example, David J. Kilcullen, "Countering Global Insurgency," *The Journal of Strategic Studies* Vol. 28, No. 4 (August 2005): 597–617; Ian Shapiro, *Containment: Rebuilding a Strategy against Global Terror* (Princeton, NJ: Princeton University Press, 2007); and Walter Russell Meade, *Power, Terror, Peace and War: American Grand Strategy in a World at Risk* (New York: Alfred A. Knopf, 2004).

7. Brian Michael Jenkins lecture to the Program in Terrorism and Security Studies, George C. Marshall European Center for Security Studies, 25 January 2008.

8. "Saudis Tell Bush Not to Isolate Hamas," *Jerusalem Post,* 18 May 2006, available at http://www.jpost.com/servlet/Satellite?pagename=JPost/JPArticle/ShowFull&cid=1145961366094, accessed 18 September 2009. See also Gabrielle Rifkind, "What Lies Beneath Hamas' Rhetoric: What the West Needs to Hear" *Oxford Research Group,* March 2006. Available from: http://www.oxfordresearchgroup.org.uk/publications/briefing_papers/hamas.php, accessed 18 September 2009.

9. Quoted in Madeline Albright, *Madam Secretary: A Memoir* (London: Macmillan, 2003), 498.

10. Roland Buerk, "A Date with a Renegade Rebel Tiger," *BBC News,* 4 April 2007, available at http://news.bbc.co.uk/2/hi/south_asia/6524869.stm, accessed 18 September 2009; and Emily

Wax, "Without Me, They Couldn't Win the War," *The Washington Post,* 11 February 2009, available at http://news.bbc.co.uk/2/hi/south_asia/6524869.stm, accessed 18 September 2009.

11. Louise Richardson, "Britain and the IRA" in *Democracy and Counterterrorism,* op cit, 95–96.

12. Anne Speckhard and Khapta Akhmedova, "Talking to Terrorists," *Journal of Psychohistory* (Fall 2005), available at http://www.uwmc.uwc.edu/alumni/news_items/speckhard/talking_to_%20terrorists.pdf, accessed 18 September 2009.

13. P. Terence Hopmann, *The Negotiation Process and the Resolution of International Conflicts* (Columbia, SC: University of South Carolina Press, 1998), 126–127.

14. "Colombian army moves against rebels," *BBC News,* 21 February 2002, available at http://news.bbc.co.uk/2/hi/americas/1832060.stm, accessed 18 September 2009.

15. Tom Baldwin and Catherine Philp, "America angered by Britain's 'secret' talks with Hezbollah," *The Times,* 14 March 2009, available at http://www.timesonline.co.uk/tol/news/world/us_and_americas/article5904412.ece, accessed 18 September 2009.

16. John B. Alterman, Martha Crenshaw et al., "How Terrorism Ends," United States Institute of Peace Special Report, 25 May 1999, 2–3.

17 See, for example, Peter C. Sederberg, "Conciliation as Counter-Terrorist Strategy," *Journal of Peace Research,* Vol. 32, No. 3 (August 1995), 295–312. Among more recent relevant works are: Peter R. Neumann, "Negotiating with Terrorists," *Foreign Affairs,* Vol. 86, No. 1 (January–February 2007), 128–134; Daniel Byman, "The Decision to Begin Talks with Terrorists: Lessons for Policymakers," Studies in *Conflict and Terrorism,* Vol. 29, No. 5 (June 2006), 403–414; Thomas Scheffler, "Negotiating with Extremists: Why, When and How?" *Dialogue with the Islamic World* (Berlin: Auswärtiges Amt), 13 April 2005; Deborah Goodwin, "A Poison Chalice?: Negotiating with Extremists," Conference Paper, "Analysing Conflict and Its Resolution," Institute of Mathematics and Its Applications, Oxford, UK, 28–30 June 2004, available at http://www.ima.org.uk/conflict/papers/Goodwin.pdf, accessed 18 September 2009; Bertram I. Spector, "Negotiating with Villains Revisited: Research Note," *International Negotiation* Vol. 8, No. 3 (2003): 613–621; I. William Zartman, "Negotiating with Terrorists," *International Negotiation,* Vol. 8, No. 3 (2003): 443–450; and James K. Wither, "Selective Engagement with Islamist Terrorists: Exploring the Prospects," *Studies in Conflict and Terrorism,* Vol. 32, No. 1 (January 2009): 18–35.

18. Editors of the present volume suspect that the arcane terminology employed by Prof. Zartman on this one point is not nearly as useful as the language of our author Prof. Wither, whose lectures and writings are lucid.

19. Zartman, op. cit., 446–447.

20. Lawrence Wright, *The Looming Tower: Al-Qaeda and the Road to 9/11* (New York: Alfred A Knopf, 2007), 95.

21. See for example: Scheffler, op. cit.; Goodwin, op. cit.; and Ram Manikkalingham and Pablo Policzer, "Engaging Al Qaeda? Armed Groups, Information and Coercion," paper presented at the Canadian Political Science Association Conference, 29 May–1 June 2007, available at http://www.cpsa-acsp.ca/papers-2007/Policzer.pdf, accessed 18 September 2009.

22. Mohammad-Mahmoud Ould Mohamedou, "Non-Linearity of Engagement: Transnational Armed Groups, International Law, and the Conflict between al Qaeda and the United States," Program on Humanitarian Policy and Conflict Research, Harvard University, July 2005, 17–25, available at http://www.hpcr.org/pdfs/Non-Linearity_of_Engagement.pdf, accessed 18 September 2009. See also Ram Manikkalingham Policzer, op. cit. Officials of the Norwegian and Swiss governments have also advocated talks with al Qaeda.

23. Neumann, op. cit.

24. Jonathan Powell, *Great Hatred, Little Room: Making Peace in Northern Ireland* (London: Bodley Head, 2008), 309–332.

25. A detailed analysis of the impact of "spoilers" on peace processes in the 1990s is provided in Stephen John Stedman, "Spoiler Problems in Peace Processes," *International Security,* Vol. 22, No. 2 (Fall 1997): 5–53.

26. Richard E. Hayes et al. "Negotiating the Non-Negotiable: Dealing with Absolutist Terrorists," *International Negotiation,* Vol. 8, No. 3 (2003): 458–461.

27. Paul Wilkinson, *Terrorism and the Liberal State* (Hoboken, NJ: John Wiley, 1977), 128. Wilkinson has taken a softer line in more recent publications. See, for example, his paper in Alterman et al. Ancram, Michael, "Dancing with Wolves: The Importance of Talking to Your Enemies," *Middle East Policy,* Vol. 14, No. 2 (Summer 2007): 22–30. Alterman, op. cit, 5.

28. Alan M. Dershowitz, *Why Terrorism Works: Understanding the Threat, Responding to the Challenge* (New Haven: Yale University Press, 2002), 27.

29. See, for example, Goodwin, op. cit., 24 and Scheffler, op. cit.

30. See, for example, Newman, op. cit., 132–133; Scheffler, op. cit., 37; and I. William Zartman, "The Timing of Peace Initiatives: Hurting Stalemates and Ripe Moments," *Global Review of Ethnopolitics,* Vol. 1, No. 1 (September 2001): 8–12.

31. Powell, op. cit., and Michael Ancram, "Dancing with Wolves: The Importance of Talking to Your Enemies," *Middle East Policy,* Vol. 14, No. 2 (Summer 2007): 22–30.

32. "Taliban May Give Up Al-Qaeda, Ex-Minister Says," *Reuters,* 15 October 2008, available at http://in.reuters.com/article/southAsiaNews/idINIndia-35984620081015, accessed 18 September 2009.

33. This process is described concisely in Byman, op. cit., 404–405.

34. Stephen Gray, "'Lawrence of Afghanistan' and the Lost Chance to Win Over Taliban Fighters," The *Sunday Times,* 29 March 2009, available at http://entertainment.timesonline.co.uk/tol/arts_and_entertainment/books/article5992800.ece, accessed 18 September 2009.

35. Georg Mascolo and Holger Stark, "German Mediates Between Israel and the Shiite Militants," *Der Spiegel Online,* 23 October 2006, available at http://www.spiegel.de/international/spiegel/0,1518,444128,00.html, accessed 18 September 2009.

36. "Report Says German Secret Service Held Talks with Taliban," *Deutsche Welle,* 20 August 2007, available at http://www.dw-world.de/dw/article/0,,2745686,00.html, accessed 18 September 2009.

37. Scheffler, op. cit., 2.

38. See "About Mediation," Centre for Humanitarian Dialogue, available at http://www.hdcentre.org/mediation, accessed 16 September 2009.

39. Conflicts Forum website, http://conflictsforum.org, accessed 16 September 2009.

40. Paraphrased in Roger Cohen, "Scandinavia's Scarred Mr. Dialogue," *The New York Times,* 14 July 2008, available at http://www.nytimes.com/2008/07/14/opinion/14cohen.html, accessed 18 September 2009.

41. Alistair Campbell and Richard Stott, eds., *The Blair Years: Extracts from the Alistair Campbell Diaries* (London: Arrow Books, 2008), 296–297 and 319–321.

42. See presentation by Matthew Levitt, "Negotiating Under Fire: Preserving Peace Talks in the Face of Terror Attacks," Washington Institute for Near East Policy, 3 October 2008, available at http://www.washingtoninstitute.org/templateC07.php?CID=429, accessed 18 September 2009.

43. Powell, op. cit.

44. "Are Theological Tensions Distancing Taliban from Al-Qaeda?" *Radio Free Europe/Radio Liberty,* 26 October 2008, available at http://www.rferl.org/content/Are_Theological_Tensions_Distancing_Taliban_From_Al_Qaeda/1332904.html, accessed 18 September 2009; and "Afghanistan: The Taliban's Break with Al Qaeda," *STRATFOR Global Intelligence,* 7 October 2008, available at http://www.stratfor.com/analysis/20081006_afghanistan_talibans_break_al_qaeda, accessed 18 September 2009.

45. Daniel Byman, "Israel and the Lebanese Hizballah" in Robert J. Art and Louise Richardson, op. cit., 320.

46. "Meshaal Offers Military Deal with Israel," *The News International,* 1 April 2008. The Israeli authorities have been justifiably skeptical about this offer as it would severely constrain military operations against Hamas fighters.

47. Harvard Negotiation Project team members have acted as advisers in many negotiations between governments and terrorists, including the El Salvador government and the FMLN; the Sandinistas and Contras in Nicaragua; and the South African government and the ANC.

48. Roger Fisher and Daniel Shapiro, *Beyond Reason: Using Emotions as You Negotiate* (New York: Viking Penguin, 2005).

49. See for example: Crenshaw op. cit., 3 and Neumann, 130.

50. Jonathan Adams, "Philippine court ruling deals blow to peace agreement with Muslim militants," *Christian Science Monitor,* 16 October 2008, available at http://www.csmonitor.com/2008/1016/p99s01-duts.html, accessed 17 September 2009.

51. For illustration of the difficulties of decommissioning, see Powell, op. cit., 203 and 245–247.

52. Edward J. Laurance and William H. Godnick, "Weapons Collection in Central America: El Salvador and Guatemala," chapter contribution for the Bonn International Center for Conversion, January 2000, 5–9, available at http://sand.miis.edu/research/2000/jan2000/bicc_elsgua.pdf, accessed 18 September 2009.

53. "Nationalist Embrace Co-opts Algerian Islamism," *Jane's Islamic Affairs Analyst,* 1 November 2006.

54. Taylor Michelle Hazelton, *The Movement for the Emancipation of the Niger Delta,* unpublished research paper prepared for Bruce Hoffman, August 2008.

55. See, for example, National Intelligence Council, "Global Trends 2025: A Transformed World," NIC 2008-003 (Washington, DC: Government Printing Office, November 2008), available at: www.dni.gov/nic/NIC_2025_project.html, accessed 18 September 2009.

56. Sederberg, op. cit., 306.

57. Leonard Weinberg, "The Red Brigades" in *Democracy and Counterterrorism,* op. cit., 53.

58. Jeremy McDermott, "Columbia Seeks Rebels' Surrender," *BBC News Europe,* 27 August 2008, available at http://news.bbc.co.uk/2/low/europe/7582292.stm, accessed 18 September 2009.

59. Christopher Boucek, "Saudi Arabia's 'Soft' Counterterrorism Strategy," *Carnegie Papers,* No. 97 (September 2008), Carnegie Endowment for International Peace Middle East Program.

60. Bruce Hoffman, "The Contrasting Ethical Foundations of Terrorism in the 1980s," *RAND Paper* P 7416 (January 1988), 14–15.

61. Dan Murphy, "In a broadcast on Thursday, Al Qaeda's Ayman al-Zawahiri blamed Tony Blair for the 7/7 attacks" *The Christian Science Monitor,* 5 August 2005.

62. Tarak Barkawi, "On the Pedagogy of Small Wars," *International Affairs,* Vol. 80, No. 1 (January 2004): 9–37.

63. Robert A. Pape, "The Strategic Logic of Suicide Terrorism," *American Political Science Quarterly,* Vol. 97, No. 3 (August 2003): 20–32.

64. See, for example, International Crisis Group, "Southern Thailand: Insurgency, not Jihad," *Asia Report* No. 98, 18 May 2005, available at http://www.crisisgroup.org/home/index.cfm?id=3436, accessed 18 September 2009.

65. Robert W. Kurz and Charles K. Bartles, "Chechen Suicide Bombers," *The Journal of Slavic Military Studies,* Vol. 20, No. 4 (October 2007): 529–547.

66. See comments by Nasrallah quoted in the *Middle East Media Research Institute (MEMRI)* Special Dispatch Series, No. 867, 22 February 2005, available at http://memri.org/bin/opener.cgi?Page=archive&ID=SP86705, accessed 18 September 2009; and Robin Wright, "Inside the Mind of Hezbollah" *Washington Post,* 16 July 2006, available at http://memri.org/bin/opener.cgi?Page=archive&ID=SP86705, accessed 18 September 2009.

67. See Craig Timberg, "Somali Militias Decry Terrorists," *Washington Post,* 16 June 2006, available at http://www.washingtonpost.com/wp-dyn/content/article/2006/06/15/AR2006061502086.html, accessed 18 September 2009; "Somalis Wary of 'Bin Laden' Tape," *BBC News,* 2 July 2006, available at http://news.bbc.co.uk/2/hi/africa/5138888.stm, accessed 18 September 2009; Daveed Gartenstein-Ross and Kyle Dabruzzi, "Jihad's New Leaders" *Middle East Quarterly* (Summer 2007), available at http://www.meforum.org/1710/jihads-new-leaders, accessed 18 September 2009; and Martin Fletcher, "How the War on Terror pushed Somalia into the Arms of Al Qaeda," *The Times,* 18 November 2008, available at http://www.timesonline.co.uk/tol/comment/columnists/guest_contributors/article5175525.ece, accessed 18 September 2009.

68. See, for example, Peter Wehner, "Al-Qaeda Is Losing the War of Minds," *Financial Times,* 5 March 2008; Frank Gardner, "Al-Qaeda Faces Islamist Backlash," *BBC News Online,* 7 August 2008, available at http://news.bbc.co.uk/2/hi/south_asia/7546322.stm, accessed 18 September 2009; Simon Scott Plummer, "Muslims Reject al-Qaeda and Osama bin Laden,"

Daily Telegraph 26 September 2008, available at http://www.telegraph.co.uk/comment/personal-view/3562403/Muslims-reject-al-Qaeda-and-Osama-bin-Laden.html, accessed 18 September 2009; and "Turning Their Backs on Jihad," *Der Spiegel,* 14 July 2008, available at http://www.spiegel.de/international/world/0,1518,565750,00.html, accessed 18 September 2009.

69. Rollie Lal and Brian A. Jackson, "Change and Continuity in Terrorism Revisited: Terrorist Tactics, 1980–2005," *MIPT Terrorism Annual 2006* (Oklahoma City: Memorial Institute for the Prevention of Terrorism, 2006), 16–17, available at http://www.terrorisminfo.mipt.org/pdf/2006-MIPT-Terrorism-Annual.pdf, accessed 18 September 2009.

70. Richard E. Hayes, Stacey R. Kaminiski, and Steven M. Beres, "Negotiating the Non-Negotiable: Dealing with Absolutist Terrorists," *International Negotiation,* Vol. 8, No. 3 (2003): 451–467. The authors acknowledge that they are "unhappy" with the phrase "traditional terrorists" but use it to distinguish "new" or "absolutist" terrorists from other groups.

71. Subir Bhaumik, "Deadly Blasts Rock Indian State," *BBC News Online,* 30 October 2008, available at http://news.bbc.co.uk/2/hi/south_asia/7699105.stm, accessed 18 September 2009.

72. "Iraq Insurgent Groups Oppose SOFA, Differ on Course of Action," Open Source Center Report, 29 October 2008, available to US government employees and contractors at www.opensource.gov.

73. International Crisis Group, "Thailand: Political Turmoil and the Southern Insurgency," Asia Briefing No. 80, 28 August 2008, 10, available at http://www.crisisgroup.org/home/index.cfm?id=5640, accessed 18 September 2009.

John J. Le Beau

Intelligence and Counterterrorism:

Examining the Critical Tools of Secrecy and Cooperation

The welfare of the people is the ultimate law. (Salus Populi Suprema Est Lex)

Cicero

Acting with precision and professionalism, western military forces succeed in capturing a known, active, key member of a sophisticated and security-conscious terrorist network. Over time, the captors are able to persuade the terrorist to cooperate with them. The detention of the terrorist is not disclosed to the outside world. The now-compliant detainee is secretly directed by his captors to maintain contact with his network of terrorist comrades, and he agrees to do so. While in custody, the captive terrorist communicates with active terror cell members but is, in fact, working from a script produced by those detaining him. Subtly and effectively employing subterfuge and his own intimate knowledge of the terrorists' own clandestine communications system, the "turned" terrorist eventually proves instrumental in identifying and locating a chain of other terror group members, who are subsequently captured or killed by the authorities in a series of strikes. So effective is the turncoat in concealing from his former compatriots his deceit and treachery that he is actually promoted within the terrorist infrastructure for his loyal and high-risk services. Ultimately, as he is viewed as a person above suspicion in terrorist circles, the agent is even able to arrange for his western masters to locate and capture the very head of the terrorist organization himself.

The summary of events related above could well describe the relatively recent application of what are recognizably intelligence and deception methods against al Qaeda cells in Iraq or the Taliban in Afghanistan, but it does not. The episode noted in fact transpired in Algeria during 1957. The western forces referred to were French. This enterprising and ambitious intelligence operation involving the recruitment and focused direction of a human collaborator was conducted under the direction of Colonel Marcel Bigeard, at the time the legendary commander of the elite Third Colonial Parachute Regiment. The intelligence operation employed an Algerian human asset named Gandriche Hacene, alias Zerrouk. Hacene's undercover services as an intelligence tool of the French crippled the National Liberation Front (FLN) infrastructure in Algiers and eventually resulted in the capture by French forces of FLN senior leader Yacef Saadi. The damage did not stop there. Saadi, in his turn, subsequently betrayed the whereabouts of his own second in command. "Double agents, not torture, had provided the intelligence necessary for the capture of two major

FLN leaders. Meanwhile, the terrorist network in Algiers had ceased to exist."[1] This carefully constructed operation was perhaps less dramatic than the fiercely pitched battles that took place between battalions of French troops and large FLN bands in the Atlas Mountains. But the use of a captive in an intelligence-driven operation also enjoyed more lasting impact.

To consider a more contemporary but equally important episode in counterterrorism annals, covert intelligence activity and robust cooperation between at least two intelligence services led to the capture and imprisonment of one of the most high-profile and lethal terrorist planners of all time, Khalid Sheikh Mohammed (KSM), usually described as the operational architect of the 9/11 attacks on the United States. George Tenet, Director of Central Intelligence (DCI) at the time of Mohammed's capture, commented that "By early 2002, we believed that KSM, like much of the al Qaeda leadership, was hiding in the teeming cities of Pakistan. To find him, CIA ran elaborate human intelligence operations."[2] Tenet further observes that CIA worked extremely closely with host-country Pakistani security officials to successfully track and capture Mohammed in his safe house. As was the case with the captured Algerian FLN terrorist acquired by the French decades earlier, Mohammed in custody was induced (in this instance through the application of admittedly coercive measures) to provide detailed and accurate information that subsequently led to the detention of several other al Qaeda terrorists. Tenet's own description of this intelligence "cascade effect" merits recounting.

> Through hard work, each success cascaded into others. . . . For example, the same day that KSM was captured, a senior Al Qaida financial operator by the name of Majid Kahn was also taken into custody. In interrogation, KSM told us that Majid Khan had recently provided fifty thousand dollars to operatives working for a major Al Qaida figure in Southeast Asia known as "Hambali." When confronted with this allegation, Khan confirmed it and said he gave the money to someone named Zubair, and he provided the man's phone number. Before long, Zubair was in custody and provided fragmentary information that led us to capture another senior Hambali associate. . . . That person provided information that led to the capture of Hambali in Thailand.[3]

Absent the initial, above-noted painstaking work of intelligence collection operations, the al Qaeda terror organization would not have suffered the severe damage that it did as a result of this string of arrests, detentions, and interrogations. The rigorous application of intelligence methods was the key element in the apprehension of Khalid Sheikh Mohammed as it also was in the capture or killing of numerous al Qaeda operatives before and after this episode, and the prevention of a number of al Qaeda terrorist plots in various stages of planning and preparation. Given the circumstances, it is difficult to conceive that the use of conventional military tools would have led to the capture of a key al Qaeda terrorist. Diplomatic activity with the government of Pakistan would also, more than likely, have been wholly ineffective in this instance. Rather, the acquisition and exploitation of detailed intelligence, coupled with close intelligence cooperation between the security services of the United States and Pakistan (and doubtless including a pinch of luck as well), ultimately placed the elusive Khalid Sheikh Mohammed in the hands of his CIA interrogators. As was the case with the Algerian Gandriche Hacene decades before, the application of intelligence operational methods had reaped significant dividends for counterterrorism authorities.

The Intelligence Tool

It has often been asserted in recent times that terrorism, at its core, is not primarily a military phenomenon, and that seeking to apply purely or even mainly military means and techniques to fight terrorism is unlikely to enjoy real or lasting success. As one military officer recognized over a decade ago, "Terrorism is not fundamentally a military problem; it is a political, social and economic problem. A military, by its nature, is not suitably structured, trained or equipped to defeat terrorism."[4] To be sure, there may be a role, real or perceived, for the employment of armed forces to guard against or react to terrorist attacks (recall the presence of uniformed military personnel in US airports and other public places following 9/11 and in Mumbai following the November 2008 attacks in that city) in areas that are not war zones, but conventional militaries are historically poorly organized to ferret out and surgically counter small, covert, and inherently secretive terrorist groups. Conventional armed forces are most often structured to effectively confront and deal with other conventional armed forces although, with proper training, some have proven effective in countering unconventional forces as well. This is most evident in arenas that we call "war zones," with Iraq (since 2003) and Afghanistan (since 2001) providing illustrative examples. Unconventional military units, on the other hand, often cooperating with intelligence organizations, have a much better record of counterterrorism success. However, the broad use of conventional military forces to deal with terrorists is generally inappropriate in areas that are not recognizably active zones of combat. Simply put, conventional military means can often be the wrong tool drawn from the counterterrorism toolbox.

Military force can be and has been highly effective in eliminating a known, observed enemy. Conventional military force alone, however, is essentially useless against a foe it cannot "fix" or even identify, such as an anonymous, invisible network of small, dispersed moving parts. Intelligence agencies are in many instances well equipped to deal with precisely this sort of challenge. While intelligence agencies are pledged to protect the civil societies that terrorists attack, it is not an inconsiderable advantage that intelligence agencies, for their own purposes, regularly employ many of the operational methods and techniques used by terrorist organizations, or at least methods that are similar. Operating from essentially the same sheet of music as the terrorists, in a sense, permits intelligence officers to inherently understand the strengths and vulnerabilities of terrorist methods of operation. Indeed, as we shall explore, intelligence agencies in some respects architecturally mirror their terrorist opponents and operate in the same environment, both physically and psychologically.

Historically, espionage techniques have been directed at nation-states, by nation-states, an activity that continues unabated to this day. However, the record since at least 2001 strongly suggests that intelligence activity has time and again proven significantly effective in uncovering and countering the plans and actions of terrorist organizations and in degrading terrorist capabilities.[5] This chapter will argue for the criticality and perhaps even the primacy of intelligence as an effective and indispensable tool both in the context of an overarching national counterterrorism strategy and in counterterrorist activities at a tactical level. Intelligence bodies and agencies and, arguably to a somewhat lesser degree, law enforcement organizations (recognizing that in some countries there is no real distinction between the two) are well structured and equipped by training, method of operation, and internal culture to attack and defeat terrorist groups, whether national or international in nature. To understand why this is so, it is prudent to first survey some of the common characteristics of terrorist groups.

The Covert World

At their core, terrorist organizations are clandestine bodies. They are clandestine in their structure, in their recruitment activities, in their membership, and in their manner of operation. Of their nature, terrorist organizations are illegal in the countries they have targeted for operations and, accordingly, like criminals everywhere, terrorists dutifully seek to avoid the attention and the reach of legal authorities. To accomplish this, the true identities of terrorist group members are routinely kept secret, and pseudonyms, sometimes multiple, are often employed to enhance security. Forged or purloined passports, false or altered documents such as birth certificates, and other items are routinely employed by terrorists to protect the true identity of members. As well, enormous effort is often expended in achieving and maintaining a high level of operational security, including the use of safe houses, impersonal means of communications such as post boxes, encrypted messages, and so on.

Additionally, sophisticated terrorist groups often purposefully employ a highly compartmentalized cellular structure precisely to avoid detection by the authorities and to cauterize the amount of damage to the overall organization if one individual or cellular unit is ever compromised. Although the particulars vary from one terrorist group to another, and from country to country, terrorist cells always contain a limited number of personnel who operate tightly together and who possess only basic information on the identities and plans of the larger organization to which they have pledged allegiance. The cellular structure used by al Qaeda in Iraq is illustrative. As an al Qaeda operative explained, "I know our men, of which there are about ten. And I know one leader of another cell nearby. We both report to a leader who commands five of our groups. . . . I know there is someone above him. But I only know the names of my men and two [other] men: the one above me and [another cell commander based nearby]."[6] The same sort of security compartmentation appears to have been employed in 2008 by the Lashkar e Tayyiba (LeT) terrorist team that trained in Pakistan to carry out the multi-target assault on Mumbai.[7]

While intelligence agencies are, of course, not criminal entities as their activities are officially (if confidentially) sanctioned, monitored, and legally controlled by their respective governments, they do engage in activities and operate in venues that routinely bring them into contact with criminal elements. To a considerable degree, the activities and operational methods of intelligence organs often mirror the manner in which terrorists themselves operate. To use one example, intelligence operations officers, like terrorists, regularly employ false identities or aliases in their work. Many intelligence organizations actually produce high-quality false passports and travel documents to move their undercover operatives internationally without coming to the attention of the authorities. By a combination of instinct and training, intelligence case officers, like their terrorist opponents, will look for the vulnerabilities in customs checks, airport security, passport control, and similar mechanisms.

Also like terrorists and criminal elements, intelligence officers will, when required, rent or otherwise acquire safe houses (often in alias) and establish nonofficial cover entities to facilitate their activities or to launder either the origin or the true destination of operational funds. In some cases, like terrorists or criminals, intelligence case officers will carry concealed weapons and use encrypted communications devices. As well, intelligence officers will often ply the venal with payments of cash or goods in exchange for privileged information or the provision of operational services. Intelligence agencies will engage in surveillance and countersurveillance, covert photography, phone-tapping, and other elements of what is widely referred to as intelligence operational "tradecraft." Due to their routine engagement in these and other activities, intelligence operators instinctively recognize and understand many aspects of the covert world that the terrorist inhabits; both dwell in the same ecosphere. This shared environment arguably better positions intelligence officers to identify and exploit terrorist vulnerabilities than might be the case with traditional military officers, diplomats, or other public officials (any of whom can be assigned counterterrorism responsibilities). By understanding in considerable detail the challenges that terrorists face in their quotidian activities, the intelligence officer is, to some extent, able to think like a terrorist—in itself a valuable counterterrorism tool.

The employment of intelligence methods as counterterrorist tools is by no means a recent development and certainly not a development restricted to application against international jihadist terror networks such as al Qaeda or the Islamic Jihad Union. The United Kingdom's long and violent struggle against the Irish Republican Army (IRA) in South Armagh and elsewhere in Northern Ireland, for example, was importantly conducted by military intelligence units, the Royal Ulster Constabulary (RUC) and the British internal intelligence service, MI5. The methods employed to identify, capture, or kill IRA members and to disrupt or prevent planned terrorist acts (not only bombings but also lethal sniper attacks) present a veritable catalogue of applied intelligence tools. These include the installation and use of hidden microphones or "bugs" to overhear conspirative conversations; the assessing, recruitment, and "turning" of human reporting sources within and on the margins of the IRA; covert, professional physical surveillance of suspected and known terrorists; telephone call tracing; and other traditional means of espionage and intelligence gathering. An especially creative method was known as "jarking," which involved "the placing of tiny tracking devices on weapons in arms caches so their movements can be followed."[8] Many of the methods utilized against the IRA, in turn, would have been quite familiar to the French military intelligence and associated entities trying to crush the Algerian FLN in the late 1950s. These collection methods and procedures would also be immediately recognizable to professional intelligence operations officers engaged in counterterrorist operations in Pakistan, Morocco, Spain, Colombia, or any South American country experiencing an active terrorist problem.

What type of intelligence is of the most utility against a terrorist target? There is considerable evidence that "police-type" information has been extremely useful in locating and neutralizing terrorist cells and individuals. This means that the fine, verifiable details are critical—accurate street addresses, taped conversations of intentions, dates of planned attacks or clandestine meetings, license plate numbers of vehicles being used by terrorists, recent photographs of a target individual or location, other identifying information. This was surely the type of granular information instrumental in the CIA's capture of Khalid Sheikh Mohammed, Abu Zubaydah, and other al Qaeda luminaries. Unlike law enforcement, however, intelligence agencies do not primarily want this type of information to build a legal court case against a terrorist. Rather than having prosecution as an end goal, intelligence agencies actively exploit this information for an operational end—a raid on an occupied safe house, a recruitment approach to a potentially disgruntled terrorist, a rendition, or a targeted killing. To be sure, more strategic information on a terror organization's hierarchy and "wiring diagram" structure, or its historical background and ideology can be very useful. But investigative details are more immediately exploitable and more likely to prevent a terrorist attack.

Intelligence as a counterterrorist tool has certainly been employed frequently and with demonstrable success in the twenty-first century, sometimes with high-profile results. This was the case with France and Spain acting in concert against the Basque separatist group Basque Fatherland and Freedom (ETA), by Pakistani security forces (even if without overwhelming enthusiasm) against the LeT and Taliban elements, by the United States against al Qaeda, and by the United Kingdom against various jihadist terror cells of both foreign and domestic pedigree. Following the highly publicized 2008 LeT assault on several sites in Mumbai, for example, Pakistani forces raided LeT training camps in that country, capturing a number of leading terrorists. "'This is an intelligence-led operation against banned militant outfits and organizations,' the military said in a statement last night. 'There have been arrests and investigations are going on.'"[9] In this as in many other cases, the careful assembling and vetting of detailed intelligence have served as the necessary precursors to a military action.

Understanding the Target

A longstanding and fundamental requirement of intelligence organizations everywhere has been to collect sensitive information that another organization desires to protect. Thus, traditional espionage (including but by no means restricted to the employment of spies, the key component of "human intelligence") has been a key intelligence activity on behalf of royal courts, dictatorships, democracies, and other forms of government for several centuries. Indeed, references to recognizable espionage activity can be found as far back as the Old Testament and the writings of Sun Tzu. The record to date suggests as well that the collection of sensitive, protected information is just as important a pursuit against non-state terrorist organizations as it is against nation-states. Al Qaeda, ETA, or Jemaah Islamiyah desire to protect information on their capabilities, plans, and intentions every bit as much as does a recognized country.

Intelligence agencies that have been given a counterterrorism mission by their governments will often employ an array of methods designed to penetrate the barricade of secrecy that a terrorist group erects to conceal its operations. In an intelligence operation against a terrorist organization, the acquisition and analysis of information are not restricted to snippets of detail provided by a network of human assets (spies). Open-source information—unclassified, available information—can be of notable counterterrorist utility as well. Birth records and death certificates, family tree information, schooling, marriage and travel records, seemingly banal articles from local newspapers or electronic media can all be of service to intelligence organizations trying to build a picture of a terrorist organization's hierarchy, membership, size, or geographical center and reach.

It should be noted in this regard that in 2005, the US Director of National Intelligence (DNI) established an Open Source Center (OSC), to be administered by the CIA and charged specifically with the analysis of open-source information—a recognition of the utility of unclassified information.[10] Tellingly, this major initiative took place at a time when the US intelligence community was tasked with counterterrorism as its first priority. Although this initiative to some extent retooled an earlier open-source government organization, the Foreign Broadcasting and Information Service , OSC has been accorded much more attention and emphasis as a counterterrorism resource for intelligence analysts.

Ideally, in the intelligence world, open-source information will be merged with protected information obtained from covert sources and methods (human intelligence, signal intelligence, and photographic intelligence, for example), the aggregate providing the counterterrorism intelligence analyst with a detailed, textured, and constantly updated picture of a particular terrorist organization, its plans and capabilities. The resulting "all-source intelligence," as it is sometimes called, is in its optimal form the key to unlocking the door that conceals a terrorist group.

Actionable Intelligence

Intelligence services are on some occasions called upon by policymakers not only to provide timely and accurate information on terrorist membership, plans, intentions, and capabilities, but to take an additional step and proactively prevent terrorist attacks, disrupt or destroy terrorist infrastructure, and kill or capture identified terrorists. This is clearly the tasking that the CIA was given in the aftermath of (and, in a more cautious and nuanced manner, prior to) the September 2001 attacks.[11] Intelligence agency activities specifically designed to damage or disrupt terrorist interests have, in the early twenty-first century, become a subject of considerable, lively international public and policy debate. Indeed, a lexicon of controversial counterterrorist tactics designed to elicit actionable intelligence has emerged: extraordinary renditions, black flights, secret prisons, ghost detainees, aggressive interrogation. All of these tactics, if journalistic accounts are to be credited, involve, at their core, the work of intelligence agencies. Notable as well, at least in passing, is the fact that techniques such as extraordinary renditions and aggressive interrogation are largely restricted to the counterterrorist components of intelligence agencies. These methods of operating were generally not employed against more conventional targets during, say, the Cold War.

In a sense, select intelligence agencies today are being asked to perform two separate but related services. First, they are to acquire privileged (as well as open-source) information and provide finished analysis on a terrorist target to inform decision makers, but also to inform the intelligence agencies themselves. Second, intelligence agencies are to use the information they acquire as the basis to act directly against a terrorist target (be it network, cell, or individual). The available record suggests a number of instances where intelligence agencies have used intelligence material they have collected as a fulcrum for physical counterterrorist action. Intelligence acquired (via surveillance operations and covert photography) by French Directorate of Territorial Security (DST) intelligence operatives was utilized in the successful rendition from Sudan of the notorious Venezuelan terrorist Ilich Ramirez Sanchez, also popularly known as Carlos the Jackal. Similar is the case of Aimal Kasi, responsible for murdering two CIA officers and wounding three others in a 1993 assault outside CIA headquarters in Virginia. After a four-year effort, Kasi was tracked to Pakistan, enticed to a controlled location through a complex and creative intelligence operation, and rendered to the United States by a joint CIA-FBI team.[12] More recently, although officially unconfirmed, press reporting alleges that al Qaeda terrorist Abu al-Harithi was targeted and killed in an intelligence agency lethal operation based on information assembled by the United States and, possibly, Yemeni intelligence. Additionally, United Kingdom intelligence and law enforcement agencies working in unison have on several documented occasions disrupted plots ("Operation Crevice" being a high-profile case in point) and arrested suspected terrorists based primarily on details that the services have clandestinely collected and assembled.[13] It might be said that the requirement for actionable intelligence moves the intelligence operations officer from being purely a collector of secrets to being, in some instances, a jailer, interrogator, paramilitary, or strike force member.

Intelligence Sharing and Cooperation: The Antithesis of Traditional Intelligence Work

Historically, intelligence agencies jealously guard their secrets and restrict access to the sensitive information that they have covertly acquired by various means. As Cardinal Richelieu declared, "secrecy is the first essential in affairs of the state." Protecting information has for centuries been one of the important tasks and arguably the primal instinct of the professional intelligence officer. This venerable imperative to restrict the distribution of intelligence on a "need to know" basis has importantly eroded in the years since 2001. The international threat posed by stateless, transnational terrorist networks has impelled many intelligence services around the globe, to one degree or another, to find a way to share sensitive information with their partners in other countries, both to build a solid understanding of terrorist group structure and membership and to disrupt their plans and operations.

The sharing of sensitive information on terrorist targets has been demonstrated to be a highly important force multiplier in the struggle against terrorist groups and networks—as recently attested to by the US Director of the CIA and the DNI, and the last German Minister of the Interior, Wolfgang Schaeuble, among other high-profile individuals with counterterrorist responsibilities. Indeed, then-Minister Schaeuble explicitly underlined the criticality of sharing intelligence during a 2007 interview: "We are literally vitally dependent on cooperation with other intelligence agencies, especially the Americans. Otherwise, I wouldn't be able to bear the responsibility for the security of this country as interior minister."[14] Three twenty-first century examples of intelligence sharing and cooperation between and among services merit consideration in this regard:

- The "Liquid Bomb Plot" targeting several transatlantic airliners from Heathrow Airport in 2006 with binary chemical explosives was prevented mainly by intelligence information exchanges and by the launching of the largest surveillance operation ever mounted in the history of the United Kingdom. Intelligence sharing among services involved, at a minimum, security agencies in the United Kingdom, the United States, and Pakistan. Despite some operational disagreements on when to move to prevent the planned attack, this close intelligence cooperation arguably saved thousands of lives.

- The disruption of an ambitious, multi-target terrorist plot in Germany in late 2007 was solely prevented by extremely close intelligence cooperation between the intelligence agencies of Germany and the United States (code-named "Operation Alberich" by German authorities). As one news outlet reported, "American assistance in uncovering the terrorist plot last week to attack U.S. and German targets in Germany was 'vital,' according to a German official familiar with the investigation. . . . 'US intelligence was of utmost importance,' said the official. . . ."[15] Absent muscular intelligence cooperation, this attack, involving low-profile German-born converts to radical Islam, might very well have succeeded in inflicting several hundreds of casualties, using approximately ten times the amount of explosives employed in the Madrid train bombings of 2004.

- Active terrorist planning by a geographically dispersed al Qaeda-associated network linked by the internet was ended by robust, real-time cooperation between intelligence services in Denmark, Bosnia-Herzegovina, Canada, the United States, and the United Kingdom. Shared telephone tap and other sensitive information appears to have prevented at least one imminent suicide bombing and other planned operations. Importantly, this multilateral cooperative effort also put an end to the exploits of Younis Tsouli (using the moniker "Irhabi007"), an internet wizard praised by Abu Musab Zarqawi.[16]

Despite such real and publicly advertised successes, it bears mention that problems in intelligence sharing still appear to persist. As the experienced Spanish counterterrorist magistrate Baltasar Garzon remarked, "There is an enormous amount of information but much of it gets lost because of failure to cooperate. There is a lack of communication, a lack of coordination and a lack of broad vision."[17] In some instances, political considerations or policy-level sensitivities have resulted in an inability of intelligence services from different countries to cooperate effectively, even if they share an intense interest in the same terrorist target, as was the case between the United Kingdom and Pakistan in 2008 concerning Mumbai.[18] In other instances, concern for the protection of information has caused some intelligence agencies, even two agencies of the same government, to withhold intelligence on a common terrorist target from one another. This appears to have been the case between the United Kingdom's Government Communication Headquarters (GCHQ, a signal intelligence agency) and Special Branch in 1998. Both organizations were actively engaged against the IRA, but a lack of transparency with intelligence may have contributed to a massive terrorist bomb successfully detonating in Omagh, Northern Ireland, killing twenty-nine people.[19] We will examine some of the reasons inhibiting better cooperation as well as how communication, coordination, and intelligence sharing might be improved among partners in the counterterrorist struggle. Although there will sometimes be disagreement between agencies on some intelligence methods employed by various countries—harsh methods of interrogation such as "water-boarding" or sleep deprivation, for example—there are surely other areas where cooperation can be strengthened.

Tools of the Trade

A number of intelligence methods that have been employed against terrorist targets over the years can be readily identified. The intelligence tools or methods of operation outlined below have been widely applied internationally by a variety of intelligence and law enforcement services confronting the terrorist target. Some of the more common counter-terrorist methods include the following:

Surveillance: This can broadly refer either to physical surveillance or to technical surveillance operations. In a counterterrorism context, surveillance would involve discreetly observing the routines and travel of a suspected or known terrorist to determine his activities and connections. Usually, surveillance can be accomplished through the deployment of teams of operatives or through employing technical means of coverage such as CCTV cameras. Surveillance has paid dividends against terrorist cells. A combination of physical surveillance and technical surveillance uncovered the ammonia nitrate plot (codenamed "Operation Crevice" by British authorities) in the United Kingdom in 2004 and established a connection between terrorists from separate cells.

Robust and Real-Time Liaison: The Heathrow liquid bomb plot, briefly considered above, appears to have involved continual formal interaction and fast-paced exchange of detailed information between multiple intelligence services internationally. At a minimum, this close intelligence liaison effort involved the security services from the United Kingdom, Pakistan, and the United States, according to available press and open-source reporting. Although most intelligence liaison arrangements are not publicly acknowledged, there is a considerable body of reporting to suggest that there are currently active intelligence liaison arrangements under way in virtually all regions of the world affected by terrorism, including Europe, North America, Asia, and Africa. Some of these liaison arrangements are purely bilateral affairs, while others, such as the episodes cited above, are clearly multilateral in nature. Although difficult to prove empirically as liaison relationships are generally secret, anecdotal information indicates that the number and scale of standing intelligence arrangements specifically targeted on terrorism (and not restricted to jihadist targets) have been on the rise since 2001. In December 2008, for example, French antiterrorism police arrested the suspected military head of ETA in the village of Gerde, along with two of his associates. "French police moved in on the three men after receiving a tip-off from domestic intelligence services. Spanish police later detained three people in connection with the arrests in France, Spanish media said."[20] The timing of the events in the two countries indicates the existence of a close, real-time liaison arrangement. A formal liaison arrangement provides the necessary structure for operational exchanges between the intelligence services of different countries.

Link or Network Analysis: The meticulous, detailed cataloguing and exploitation of the connections—links—between terrorist individuals, sympathizers, front organizations, and cells is a methodology widely employed in intelligence and law enforcement circles, from the Balkans to the United States. These links in the terrorist chain can incorporate details such as bank account information, suspicious telephone numbers, addresses of suspected and known safe houses or other meeting venues, aliases associated with an individual terrorist, biographic details, etc. These fragments of information can be graphically displayed and regularly updated as additional information becomes available. Link analysis permits disparate pieces of information to be brought together to help develop a more comprehensive and comprehensible picture of a terrorist group. Link analysis methodology can also be employed to determine the relative importance of a particular terrorist, based, for example, on how many other terrorist individuals are "linked" to him via intercepted communications, surveilled personal visits, and similar quantifiable items. The resulting chart of links is a graphic exposition of a terrorist organization, which can be of considerable value at both the strategic and the tactical counterterrorism level. At its most useful, link analysis can identify critical terrorist nodes and suggest which parts of a terrorist network might be the most vulnerable to disruption or other forms of attack by counterterrorist forces. In other words, link analysis can serve as a basis for action against a terrorist entity.

Concentric Circles of Recruitment: While not impossible, it may be extremely difficult for intelligence officers to meet, develop, and recruit a human reporting source in the hard inner circle of a terrorist organization. In the case of al Qaeda, this would refer to people close to Osama bin Laden, Ayman al-Zawahiri, or their intimate paladins, or, perhaps, to cite an example with more pedigree, any of the active terrorists in the Baader-Meinhof group that operated in Germany in the 1970s and 1980s. It is often far more realistic and operationally secure for an intelligence service to gain access to individuals on the margins that are not key players, or even active terrorists, but who, individually, might nonetheless be privy to useful, exploitable tactical information. In the aggregate, information from a collection of such sources can prove extremely valuable. These circles of individuals on the margins of a terror group can include relatives, near or distant, former neighbors, school friends, former teachers or religious counselors, and so on. Any of these people can be targeted for recruitment by an intelligence service. In some instances, such individuals can be effectively employed not only to passively provide information to their covert intelligence handlers, but, if they are willing or subject to inducement, they can be tasked to attempt to make direct contact (under one pretext or another) with terrorists or other persons of operational interest. Such active operations are not absent considerable risk, of course, and these risks must be carefully weighed by intelligence organizations in their operational planning.

Joint Direct Operations: A counterterrorist operation engaged in by two or more intelligence services acting in concert against a commonly agreed-upon terrorist target is a long and significant step beyond the simple exchange of intelligence information, however robust that exchange might be. At an absolute minimum, joint intelligence operations require a common operational planning effort and real operational burden-sharing, such as the pooling of personnel, materiel, and capabilities, and perhaps the common handling or debriefing of human sources. For example, in a theoretical joint antiterrorist intelligence operation involving the United Kingdom and Pakistan, the United Kingdom might bring to the table its highly sophisticated and far-reaching signals intercept and decryption capability while the Pakistani Inter-Services Intelligence (ISI) harnesses an active, clandestine network of very low-tech but extremely useful local, ethnic human assets in a geographical area where terrorists are known to be present. Both sides profit from such an arrangement as their shared resources are greater than either partner's purely unilateral capabilities. Joint operational efforts are in this sense a true force multiplier.

Joint operations are frequently complex affairs and are not cost free, however, and they do require a significant investment in terms of coordination, attention, and transparency on the part of the services involved. This is not always an easy fit for intelligence agencies that are of their nature secretive and charged with protecting their unilateral sources of information and methods of operation. To be effective, joint operations would seem to demand the following from participating agencies:

- Policy-level agreement on the parameters of operational cooperation. The "rules of the road" for all sides engaged in joint intelligence ventures need to be understood from the start, before a joint operation gets under way, to avoid problems at a later date. For example, one government might insist to another that, due to the particular requirements of its domestic laws, its officers will not be permitted to participate in an operation designed to kill terrorists, but only to track and capture them. Restrictions such as this need to be understood and agreed to by all parties before operational resources are expended.

- Willingness to compromise. No single partner in a joint antiterrorist intelligence operation will always get its own way. There may, for example, be considerable disagreement between joint operations partners on when to shut down a terrorist cell or how long to permit a terrorist plot to proceed (in hopes of acquiring more intelligence); such important issues simply have to be worked out to mutual satisfaction. Precisely this sort of issue occupied United States and British intelligence partners in the Heathrow liquid bomb plot case. Joint operations of this sort require an understanding that all partners to the joint intelligence venture have equal status; the operation is not a "big brother, little brother" arrangement.

- Exposing technical capabilities. Working intimately with another intelligence service on a counterterrorist operation can easily result in the exposure of unilateral technical capabilities (such as decryption)—and, perhaps just as importantly, technical limitations—to the members of other services involved in the joint effort.

Nonetheless, despite the real costs or challenges involved, the record to date suggests that joint operations can be a highly effective weapon against terrorist targets, especially against disciplined international terrorist organizations that enjoy a wide geographical reach and presence and that operate without any regard for national borders. Such organizations (al Qaeda is a classic example) can have a presence that is spread across several countries or regions and can be extremely difficult for a single national intelligence organization to collect on or act against with success, underlining the value of engaging other intelligence services in a common effort.

One illustrative episode detailed in the press is the joint French-German-US operation launched via a covert facility named "Alliance Base" in Paris against Christian Ganczarski, an al Qaeda operative and German citizen (of Polish extraction, who converted to Islam) formerly active in Europe.[21] Ganczarski was tied by German communications intercepts to the suicide bombing of a historic synagogue in Djerba, Tunisia, which caused several western tourist fatalities. For legal reasons and despite the compelling evidence, Ganczarski could not be prosecuted by German authorities for his alleged role in the attack. A well-crafted and intricate joint intelligence operation involving several "Alliance Base" participating intelligence services subsequently led to Ganczarski's capture, trial, and conviction. The Ganczarski case was a clear example of a single service—in this instance, the German external intelligence agency Bundesnachtrichtendienst (BND), or Federal Intelligence Service—being unable to neutralize a known terrorist on its own, and as an alternative calling on the pooled resources of partners to devise an effective operational response. Joint operational cooperation between "Alliance Base" members served as a tangible force multiplier permitting measurable success.

Intelligence and Counterterrorism: Lessons Learned and Signposts to the Future

There are a number of general lessons that can be drawn from our examination of how intelligence has fared against the terrorist target over the decades and particularly in the period since a variety of intelligence agencies, including those in the United States, were instructed to take on counterterrorism as a primary mission since 2001. Although not a set of immutable, concrete principles, the role intelligence has played as a counterterrorism tool suggests that we can infer some lessons.

The utility of counterterrorism intelligence is directly dependent on the level of detail of the information acquired. Tactically granular, timely, nitty-gritty "police-type" pieces of information are especially valuable and often can be readily and effectively exploited to damage terrorist interests.

"Old school" intelligence techniques, such as carefully conducted surveillance and clandestine photography or filming, though time and resource intensive, can produce real results in tracking down terrorists and breaking up ongoing terrorist operations.

Intelligence sharing between domestic intelligence organizations and between the intelligence agencies of different countries expands both the capabilities and the plinth of knowledge of all the services involved in such an arrangement. The record is clear that liaison arrangements, despite the occasional difficulties, make practical counterterrorism sense.

Active, imaginative joint operations conducted on a bilateral or multilateral basis permit intelligence agencies to transcend national boundaries and extend their operational reach. Joint operations can succeed where a unilateral operation would almost certainly fail. The evidence is strong that joint operations have proven especially useful in combating international terrorist networks.

Intelligence officers involved in counterterrorism may well be called on to engage in activities beyond those associated with traditional espionage and intelligence collection. Operations officers (either working independently or in tandem with law enforcement or military establishments) will sometimes be called upon to serve as captors, aggressive interrogators, paramilitaries, or killers of identified terrorists.

The policy-driven requirement for actionable intelligence is unlikely to disappear in the foreseeable future. Fairly or not, the intelligence agencies of major or at-risk states will be held responsible to disrupt and prevent terrorist attacks against their respective states and to take active terrorists out of circulation. This imperative, in turn, places a premium on operational risk-taking and creativity by intelligence agencies.

The nature of intelligence training (both initial and mid-career) may in the future need to undergo significant change to better equip officers to address the special requirements of counterterrorist intelligence gathering. Skills (including language skills) other than those valued during the Cold War will need to be nurtured. This holds true for both the analytical and the operational intelligence disciplines.

Intelligence officers (from the analytical as well as the operational disciplines) would be well advised to be conversant with state-of-the-art commercial, public-sector technological developments, and items that can be purchased and employed by terrorist organizations. Ideally, to stay ahead of the terrorists, intelligence officers should be familiar with next generation technology before it becomes commercially available.

What seems certain is that the importance of professional intelligence activity as a key counterterrorism tool will not diminish in the foreseeable future. Indeed, to the extent that terrorist organizations become increasingly clever and sophisticated in their ability to harness commercial technology to better conceal their membership, intentions, and activities, the more critical intelligence work will become. The first essential step in confronting a clandestine terrorist organization is to accurately identify that organization and to develop a detailed picture of its inner workings, strengths, weaknesses, and capabilities. This task puts a premium on collecting, collating, and analyzing the pieces of information that the terrorists seek to protect. Without developing an intelligence capability to effectively and continually perform this task, any counterterrorist strategy will be blind and thus unlikely to succeed.

Although perhaps less certain than the continuing need to use intelligence to disrupt terrorist conspiracies, it is nonetheless very likely that select intelligence agencies will in future (as at present) be tasked by decision makers to conduct aggressive counterterrorist activity using their own resources. Although actions like covert, small-scale paramilitary raids, targeted killings, extraordinary renditions, deception operations, unorthodox interrogations, and other controversial counterterrorism initiatives might conceivably be given to military organizations to conduct, this seems unlikely. These activities—conducted in times of peace and in sovereign countries—will often have an extra-judicial dimension. Militaries are structured for overt, not covert, missions. Similarly, unless the end goal of a counterterrorist disruptive action is to bring the terrorist to trial, law enforcement agencies are generally not permitted to engage in actions that arguably have more to do with breaking laws than with enforcing them. The inherently clandestine nature of counterterrorist actions conducted beyond a country's own borders, and the desire for "plausible deniability" buttress the argument for keeping intelligence organizations as the prime mover in counterterrorist operations of this sort.

To be sure, the "rules of the road" for the type of counterterrorist activities that intelligence agencies are sanctioned to conduct may well change in the future, depending on the preferences of policymakers and the rulings of judicial authorities. Many countries might not permit coercion as an acceptable counterterrorist interrogation technique, but other imaginative techniques might be discovered to be highly effective in eliciting information from detained terrorists, and these new techniques could well be employed following judicial review. This is to say that the manner in which counterterrorist activity is conducted by the intelligence organs of various states is apt to change to greater or lesser degree in the future, but this is perhaps best seen as part of the dynamics of the always evolving terrorist-counterterrorist struggle. Although proactive counterterrorist methods may change, it remains likely that intelligence agencies will be the primary practitioners of these methods a decade from now.

In sum, there appear to be few practical alternatives to the robust use of intelligence organizations to confront terrorism in the twenty-first century. As intelligence agencies absorb "lessons learned" from their past counterterrorism activities, they are likely to become more proficient in understanding and tackling terrorist groups. As well, as long as international terrorist organizations continue to pose a threat to the established order, we are almost certain to see an increase in the amount of counterterrorist cooperation and information sharing among the intelligence services of various countries. Looked at another way, it is difficult to imagine a future where the degree of intelligence cooperation against international terrorism diminishes. Technology represents another challenge for intelligence organizations with a counterterrorist mission. A number of terrorist groups have proven adept at employing cutting-edge commercial technology to securely communicate and coordinate their activities. Terrorist use of encryption to protect the content of messages has become commonplace and standard practice in the twenty-first century. We should expect that committed terrorists will continue to seek out ways to employ emerging commercial technological developments to their operational advantage. This means that intelligence collection, if it is to remain effective, will require skill and agility in order to defeat the array of technological tools that terrorist groups bring into play.

Intelligence operations, collection, and analysis will undoubtedly continue to be key elements in disabling clandestine terrorist networks. Intelligence is no silver bullet, however. Intelligence collection can provide bad information, poorly sourced information, the wrong information, or insufficient information. Even if the right information is collected, intelligence analysis can draw the wrong conclusions. Further, intelligence agency operations aimed at disrupting terrorist plots or incapacitating terrorist members can go wrong, and on occasion will. Intelligence operations have always been high-risk enterprises. But, as in the cases of Gandreche Hacene and Amir Kasi, intelligence operations can also achieve considerable results in diminishing terrorist capabilities. This, in turn, is a not inconsiderable virtue.

The hidden world of intelligence and terrorism:
Are there similarities in activities that both sides perform in a covert environment?

TERRORIST GROUP	INTELLIGENCE AGENCY
hostage-taking/kidnapping	extraordinary rendition
targeted killing (e.g., B. Bhutto)	targeted killing (e.g., al-Harithi)
covert financing, money laundering	covert financing, cover firms
recruitment	recruitment
(persuasive, manipulative, coercive)	(persuasive, manipulative, coercive)
clandestine organization	clandestine organization
use of alias identities	use of alias identities

John J. Le Beau Dr. Le Beau is Professor of Strategy and Security at the Marshall Center, a director of studies for the Senior Executive Seminar, and a regular faculty member on the Program on Terrorism and Security Studies. Dr. Le Beau also chairs the Partnership for Peace Consortium's Combating Terrorism Working Group, which enjoys a broad international membership. A former senior operations officer in the US Central Intelligence Agency, he retired in 2005 after a career spent on assignment outside of the United States, including locations experiencing active terrorism. His intelligence duties included assignments as chief of an operational facility in Europe engaged in counterterrorist and counterproliferation operations, operational chief for an intelligence collection program directed at transnational issues, and a counterinsurgency officer in an active conflict area. In addition to several classified intelligence assessments for the United States intelligence community, Dr. Le Beau has authored articles and papers on the topics of international terrorism and insurgency. Dr. Le Beau is a contributing editor of the Marshall Center *PTSS Daily* online. His novel *Collision of Evil* is about international terrorism. Dr. Le Beau lectures on terrorism, intelligence, and security topics internationally, including in Afghanistan, Algeria, Bosnia, Germany, Georgia, Macedonia, Turkey, and the United States.

Recommended Readings

Coll, Steve. *Ghost Wars: The Secret History of the CIA, Afghanistan, and Bin Laden, from the Soviet Invasion to September 10, 2001*. New York: Penguin Press, 2004.

Central Intelligence Agency website. www.cia.gov (contains regularly updated articles and information on various aspects of intelligence activity and analysis).

George, Roger Z., and Robert D. Kline. *Intelligence and the National Security Strategist: Enduring Issues and Challenges*. Lanham, MD: Rowman & Littlefield Publishers, 2006.

Kessler, Ronald. *The Terrorist Watch: Inside the Desperate Race to Stop the Next Attack*. New York: Three Rivers Press, 2008.

National Commission on Terrorist Attacks Upon the United States. *The 9/11 Commission Report*. New York: W.W. Norton & Co., 2004.

Tenet, George. *At the Center of the Storm: My Years at the CIA*. New York: HarperCollins, 2007.

Notes

1. Anton Menning, "Counterinsurgency in the Battle of Casbah," *Small Wars Journal*, Vol. 6 (October 2006): 28–38, available at http://smallwarsjournal.com/documents/swjvol6.pdf, accessed 19 September 2009.
2. George Tenet, *At the Center of the Storm: My Years at the CIA* (New York: Harper Collins, 2007), 251.
3. Ibid, 254.
4. LTC Stephen Gotowicki (US Army), "Middle East Terrorism: New Form of Warfare or Mission Impossible?" *Military Review*, May–June, 1997.
5. For accuracy, it should be noted that the CIA's Counter Terrorism Center (CTC) has a long pedigree; it was actually founded in the 1980s by veteran operations officer Duane "Dewey" Clarridge, but was smaller in scale and importance to the policymaker than it has become since 2001. For further information on the origins of the CTC, see Duane R. Clarridge, *A Spy for All Seasons: My Life in the CIA* (New York: Scribner, 1997).
6. UPI, "Leader of Terror Cell Reveals Data on Command Structure," *Washington Times*, 8 December 2003, available at http://www.washingtontimes.com/news/2003/dec/08/20031208-111942-6488r/, accessed 19 September 2009.

7. Geeta Anand, Matthew Rosenberg, Yaroslav Trofimov, and Zahid Hussain, "India Names Mumbai Mastermind," *Wall Street Journal*, 3 December, 2008, available at http://online.wsj .com/article/SB122823715860872789.html, accessed 19 September 2009.

8. Toby Harnden, *Bandit Country: The IRA and South Armagh* (London: Coronet Books, 1999), 262.

9. Jeremy Page, "Pakistan Refuses to Extradite Mumbai Terrorists," *The Times*, 9 December 2008, available at http://www.timesonline.co.uk/tol/news/world/asia/article5311366.ece, accessed 19 September 2009.

10. Office of the Director of National Intelligence (ODNI), "ODNI Announces Establishment of the Open Source Center," 8 November, 2005, available at http://www.dni.gov/press_ releases/20051108_release.htm, accessed 19 September 2009.

11. For detailed accounts of CIA taskings on al Qaeda, see Steve Coll, *Ghost Wars: The Secret History of the CIA, Afghanistan, and Bin Laden, from the Soviet Invasion to September 10, 2001* (New York: Penguin Press, 2004), and Gary Schroen, *First In: An Insider's Account of How the CIA Spearheaded the War on Terror in Afghanistan* (New York: Presidio Press/ Ballantine Books, 2005).

12. Central Intelligence Agency, "A Look Back . . . Murder at CIA's Front Gate," available at https://www.cia.gov/news-information/featured-story-archive/murder-at-cia.html, accessed 30 April, 2009. For additional details, see also Coll, *Ghost Wars*, 374–375.

13. For a brief summary of Operation Crevice, see "Timeline: Operation Crevice," BBC News, 30 April 2007, available at http://news.bbc.co.uk/2/hi/uk_news/6207348.stm, accessed 20 September 2009.

14. "We Could Be Struck at Any Time: Interview with German Interior Minister Wolfgang Schäuble," 9 July 2007, available at http://www.spiegel.de/international/germany/0,1518, 493364-2,00.html, accessed 19 September 2009. Germany's government reformed in November 2009 following elections, and Herr Schauble became Finance Minister.

15. Andrew Purvis, "U.S. Helped Nab German Suspects," *Time*, 14 September 2007, available at http://www.time.com/time/world/article/0,8599,1661985,00.html, accessed 19 September 2009.

16. See Sebastian Rotella, "World Wide Web of Terrorist Plotting," *Los Angeles Times*, 16 April 2007, available at http://articles.latimes.com/2007/apr/16/world/fg-net16, accessed 11 May 2009.

17. Quoted in the *International Herald Tribune*, 22 March 2004; see Michael Taarnby, "Recruitment of Islamist Terrorists in Europe: Trends and Perspectives," Research Report funded by the Danish Ministry of Justice, 14 January 2005, 51, available at http://www.investigativeproject .org/documents/testimony/58.pdf, accessed 20 September 2009.

18. Jeremy Page, "Pakistan Rejects UK Request to Question Mumbai Terror Suspects," *The Times*, 16 December 2008, available at http://www.timesonline.co.uk/tol/news/world/asia/ article5348499.ece, accessed 19 September 2009.

19. John Ware, "The Words That Might Have Saved Omagh," *Daily Telegraph*, 13 September 2008, available at http://www.telegraph.co.uk/news/uknews/northernireland/2911310/The-words-that-might-have-saved-Omagh.html, accessed 19 September 2009.

20. Charles Sicurani, "French Police Arrest Suspected New ETA Military Chief," Agence France-Presse, 9 December 2008, available at http://www.france24.com/en/20081209-french-police-arrest-suspected-new-eta-military-chief-0, accessed 19 September 2009. For more on Franco-Spanish cooperation against ETA in the border region, see also "Paris and Madrid Unite Against Terrorism," *Le Figaro*, 11 January 2008.

21. Dana Priest, "Help from France Key in Covert Operations" *Washington Post*, 3 July 2005, available at http://www.washingtonpost.com/wp-dyn/content/article/2005/07/02/ AR2005070201361.html, accessed 19 September 2009. See also Lorenzo Vidino, *Al Qaeda in Europe: The New Battleground of International Jihad* (Amherst, NY: Prometheus Books, 2006), 29–30 and 163–164.

3.4

Celina B. Realuyo

Following the Terrorist Money Trail

Money is the lifeblood of terrorist operations. Today, we're asking the world to stop payment.

President George W. Bush, 24 September 2001[1]

In combating terrorism, the international community must employ all the instruments of national power to disrupt, dismantle, and deter terrorist groups. These instruments include diplomatic, military, intelligence, information, law enforcement, economic, and financial capabilities that can be applied singularly, or in combination, to counter international security threats, including terrorism. These countermeasures have been successfully leveraged at the local, national, and international levels to combat terrorist networks around the globe. This chapter will focus on the financial front of the war on terrorism and demonstrate how "following the money trail" enhances governments' efforts to identify, root out, and defeat terrorists and their financiers. We will begin with an overview of how terrorist groups raise and move their money. Subsequently, strategies to combat terrorist financing through law enforcement and intelligence operations, public designations, international cooperation, and capacity building programs will be examined. A case study of Indonesia's response to the tragic October 2002 Bali bombings will demonstrate how counterterrorism measures, including those to address terrorist financing, have been developed and applied successfully to combat terrorism. We will conclude with a review of the progress made to combat terrorist financing and underscore the challenges that remain in this arena.

Methods of Terrorist Financing

Financing is essential for any organization and its activities, and terrorist networks are no different. Terrorist activities can be categorized into operational and support activities. Operational activities include surveillance and reconnaissance, rehearsal, final preparations, and the actual attack. Support activities entail propaganda, recruitment, fund-raising, procurement, transportation and travel, safe havens, multiple identities, communications, and training. All of these activities require financing. While the actual cost of a terrorist attack can be merely in the thousands of dollars, developing and sustaining a terrorist network require millions of dollars. So how do terrorist groups raise and move their money?

Over the years, terrorist groups have relied on a broad spectrum of methods to fund their networks and operations. While money laundering involves disguising funds obtained through illicit activities, terrorist financing does not always involve "dirty money," receiving funding from state and individual sponsors; and this presents more challenges for the counterterrorism community. The tragic attacks of September 2001 brought to light how al Qaeda exploited the international financial system to fund its preparations for and execution of the attacks. In response to 9/11, the international public and private sectors instituted more stringent controls over the traditional banking sector to combat terrorist financing and money laundering. However, over the years, we have observed that terrorist groups have turned to various funding sources and methods to circumvent this increased oversight of the banking sector. Let us examine some of the mechanisms beyond traditional banking abused by terrorist networks.

NGOs/Charities. Terrorists may be attracted to charities and nongovernmental organizations (NGOs) to raise and move their assets because of the industry's nontransparent nature. According to the Financial Action Task Force (FATF) on Money Laundering's *Report on Money Laundering Typologies 2002–2003*, some charities have served as a cover for moving funds to support terrorist activities, usually on an international basis, in addition to serving as a direct source of income.[2] For example, according to the US Department of Justice, the Global Relief Foundation, an Illinois-based charity, sent more than 90 percent of its donations abroad and had connections to and provided support and assistance to individuals associated with Osama bin Laden, the al Qaeda network, and other known terrorist groups.[3] Similarly, the Department of Justice asserts that the Illinois-based Benevolence International Foundation moved charitable contributions fraudulently solicited from donors in the United States to locations abroad to support terrorist activities, as the foundation had offices worldwide through which it could facilitate the global movements of its funds.[4] While legitimate charities promote noble social and economic causes, the lack of regulation and oversight of the sector, as well as the international nature of charitable work, make this sector vulnerable to abuse by terrorist networks.

Cash Couriers. Moving large amounts of currency, through bulk cash smuggling or cash couriers, is an attractive terrorist financing mechanism since US dollars are accepted as an international currency and are readily convertible. There is no traceable paper trail, no third party involved, and the terrorist has total control of the movement of that money by using cash couriers. However, this is a more risky method of moving funds for terrorists. There is the risk of a courier stealing the money, of informants within the network, and of border searches or government inquiries that could compromise the network or mission. In the United States, bulk cash smuggling is a money laundering and terrorist financing technique designed to bypass financial transparency reporting requirements. The currency is often smuggled into or out of the United States concealed in personal effects or shipping containers, or it is transported in bulk across the border via vehicle, vessel, or aircraft. According to the Federal Bureau of Investigation (FBI), "some of the September 11 hijackers allegedly used bulk cash smuggling as another method to transfer funds."[5] In response to the 9/11 events, US Customs initiated an outbound-currency operation, Operation Oasis, to refocus its efforts to target twenty-three identified nations involved in money laundering. Between October 2001 and August 2003, the Department of Homeland Security (DHS) Immigration and Customs Enforcement seized more than $28 million in bulk cash.[6] While some of the cases were linked to terrorism, DHS officials were unable to determine the precise number and the extent to which these cases were involved in terrorist financing. In the war in Iraq, bulk cash smuggling has been used by al Qaeda in Iraq to fund their operations and foreign fighters, facilitated by the lack of border control.[7]

Alternative Remittance Systems. Terrorist organizations use a type of alternative remittance system or informal banking system, sometimes known as *hawala*, to move their assets, due to the system's nontransparent and liquid nature. A remittance is a transfer of money by a foreign worker to his/her home country. An informal banking system is one in which money is received for the purpose of making that sum, or an equivalent value, payable to a third party in another geographic location. Such transfers generally take place outside of the conventional banking system through nonbank money services, businesses, or other, unregulated and undocumented, business entities. Traditionally, expatriates—traders and immigrant laborers—use informal banking systems to send money home from or to countries lacking formal and secure banking systems. These informal systems are still used by immigrant ethnic populations in the United States and Europe due to their high efficiency and low costs. Such systems are based on trust and the extensive use of connections, such as family relationships or regional affiliations. In Afghanistan and Somalia, the al Barakaat informal banking system reportedly moved funds for al Qaeda.[8] In the more recent case of the November 2008 siege of Mumbai, the perpetrators of Pakistani origin are believed to have relied on *hawala* transactions to fund this operation.[9] Informal banking systems remain challenging to safeguard against money laundering and terrorist financing.

Strategies to Combat Terrorist Financing

Terrorist networks use an array of means and methods to raise and move their money. In order to combat terrorist financing, counterterrorism officials have had to devise comprehensive strategies to identify, interdict, and isolate terrorists and their financiers. According to the 9/11 Commission, "after the September attacks, the highest-level US government officials publicly declared that the fight against al Qaeda financing was as critical as the fight against al Qaeda itself. It has been presented as one of the keys to success in the fight against terrorism: if we choke off the terrorists' money, we limit their ability to conduct mass casualty attacks."[11] To this end, counterterrorism finance (CTF) strategies intended to detect, disrupt, and deter the funding of terrorist networks are based on the following four lines of operation:

1. Law enforcement and intelligence operations
2. Public designations and asset freezes
3. International standards set to counter terrorist financing
4. Capacity building programs[12]

CTF Law Enforcement and Intelligence Operations

"Following the money trail" has greatly enhanced law enforcement and intelligence operations against terror networks. How, when, where, and from/to whom money has been trans-

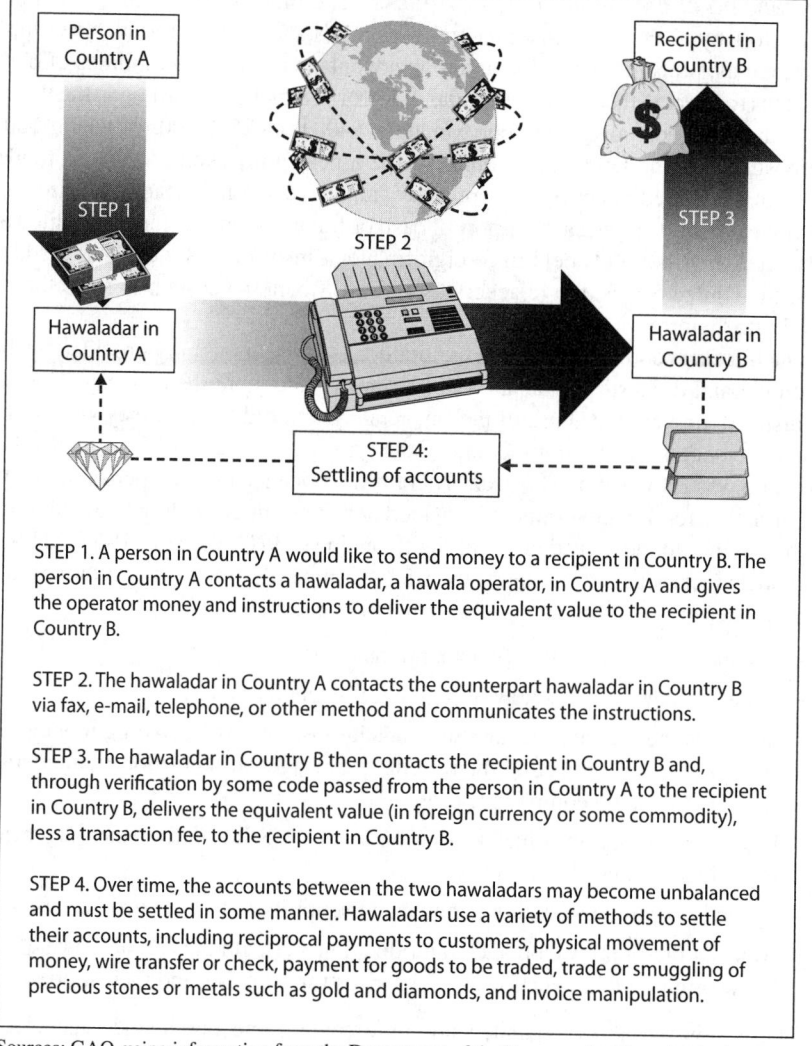

STEP 1. A person in Country A would like to send money to a recipient in Country B. The person in Country A contacts a hawaladar, a hawala operator, in Country A and gives the operator money and instructions to deliver the equivalent value to the recipient in Country B.

STEP 2. The hawaladar in Country A contacts the counterpart hawaladar in Country B via fax, e-mail, telephone, or other method and communicates the instructions.

STEP 3. The hawaladar in Country B then contacts the recipient in Country B and, through verification by some code passed from the person in Country A to the recipient in Country B, delivers the equivalent value (in foreign currency or some commodity), less a transaction fee, to the recipient in Country B.

STEP 4. Over time, the accounts between the two hawaladars may become unbalanced and must be settled in some manner. Hawaladars use a variety of methods to settle their accounts, including reciprocal payments to customers, physical movement of money, wire transfer or check, payment for goods to be traded, trade or smuggling of precious stones or metals such as gold and diamonds, and invoice manipulation.

Sources: GAO, using information from the Department of the Treasury, the Financial Action Task Force on Money Laundering (FATF), Interpol, U.S. law enforcement, and other experts.

ferred are reliable data points that counterterrorism officials use to map out and identify terrorist groups, their facilitators, and their activities. In many cases, financial intelligence and forensics are determining factors in developing and prosecuting cases of terrorism and material support of terrorism. Unlike confidential informants and witnesses for the prosecution, the money trail presents clear evidence of a financial connection or link between two or more parties.

The Financing of the September 11 Attacks. The financial blueprint of the multiple-aircraft effort by al Qaeda is instrumental for understanding how the nineteen hijackers lived among us, prepared their plot, and took advantage of the vulnerabilities of our security systems to execute the most spectacular of terrorist attacks. According to the 9/11 Commission, that plot cost al Qaeda approximately $400,000–$500,000, of which $300,000 was deposited into the US bank accounts of the nineteen hijackers. Al Qaeda funded the hijackers in the United States by three primary and unexceptional means: (1) wire transfers from overseas, (2) the physical transport of cash or travelers' checks into the United States, and (3) accessing the funds held in foreign financial institutions by debit or credit cards. Once in the United States, the hijackers used the US banking system to store their funds and facilitate their transactions.[13]

The hijackers and their financial facilitators used the anonymity provided by the vast international and domestic financial system to move and store their money. The existing mechanisms to prevent the abuse of the financial system did not fail; they were just never designed to detect or disrupt transactions of the type that financed 9/11. Virtually all of the plot funding was provided by al Qaeda. There is no evidence that any person in the United States, or in any foreign government, provided any substantial funding to the hijackers.[14]

In response to the investigation of the financing of 9/11, the USA PATRIOT Act was enacted on 26 October 2001 to expand the US government's tool kit in anti-money laundering and counterterrorism financing. This legislative package:

- Enhances transparency in financial transactions
- Protects international gateways to the US financial system
- Increases the vigilance of all our financial institutions (including money services and businesses) subjecting them to the more rigorous anti-money laundering and terrorist financing compliance programs
- Facilitates critical information sharing among US law enforcement agencies that investigate financial crimes
- Amends existing legislation to enhance the ability to freeze terrorist assets
- Amends the Immigration and Naturalization Act with the creation of the Terrorist Exclusion List that denies or revokes visas for terrorists and their supporters[15]

These new measures expanded law enforcement and intelligence agencies' abilities and authorities to "follow the money trail" to pursue terrorism cases. The successful prosecution of US citizen Jose Padilla, better known as the "Dirty Bomber," and his co-defendants relied heavily on evidence of terrorist financing and the provision of material support. In August 2007, the jury found the defendants guilty of being part of a North American support cell designed to send money, physical assets, and *mujahedin* recruits to overseas *jihad* conflicts.[16]

Public Designations and Asset Freezes

The US government has sought to stem the flow of financial resources to terror groups for decades through various designation programs. The first of these efforts aimed at state sponsors of terrorism. To target these actors, a provision of the Export Administration Act of 1979 (Section 6j) authorized the Secretary of State to designate states who provide funding to terrorists or terrorist organizations as state sponsors of terrorism.[17] Past designations of this kind have triggered a variety of sanctions, including restrictions on US foreign assistance, a ban of defense exports and sales, control over exports for dual-use items, and miscellaneous financial and other restrictions, including a denial of foreign tax credits for income earned in designated terrorist-sponsoring states.[18]

By the mid-1990s, intelligence reports had indicated that terror groups were seeking financial independence by using front companies and charities to obtain funding. The William J. Clinton administration drafted legislation to make it illegal to provide material support for specific acts of terrorism or for foreign terrorist organizations (FTOs). Enacted as the Antiterrorism and Effective Death Penalty Act of 1996, this legislation specifically criminalized not only financial contributions, but also the provision of financial services to groups designated as FTOs by the Secretary of State.[19] In January 1995, at about the same time the legislation was introduced in Congress, the Clinton administration issued Executive Order (E.O.) 12947 to freeze the assets of twelve terrorist groups (ten Palestinian and two Jewish) that threatened the use of violence to thwart the Middle East Peace process. This was pursuant to the authorities of the International Emergency Economic Powers Act.[20]

One of President George W. Bush's first initiatives after 11 September 2001 aimed directly at the financial front of the war on terrorism. On 24 September 2001 he declared, "We will starve the terrorists of funding, turn them against each other, rout them out of their safe hiding places, and bring them to justice."[21] A day prior to this statement, the president issued E.O. 13224 to designate and block the assets of organizations and individuals linked to terrorism. By this order, President Bush declared a national emergency to deal with the "unusual and extraordinary threat to the national security, foreign policy, and economy of the United States," posed by grave acts of terrorism and threats of terrorism, and the continuing and immediate threat of further attacks on US nationals or the United States.[22]

The new Executive Order broadened the Treasury, Justice, and State Departments' mandates to designate individuals and entities (not only foreign terrorist organizations) as material supporters of terrorism. Since 2001, designations of terrorist financiers by the Treasury, State, and Justice Departments have been used to disrupt terrorist networks by blocking their assets and deterring would-be terrorist supporters from providing financial resources to terrorist groups, pursuant to E.O. 13224. According to the Government Accountability Office (GAO), "the US has taken an active role in developing and implementing international standards to combat terrorist financing through the United Nations conventions and resolutions and Financial Action Task Force recommendations on money laundering and terrorist financing," and in promoting international cooperation.[23]

International Cooperation

Since terrorism presents a transnational threat, governments cannot solely rely on national responses to effectively combat this security concern. International cooperation on all fronts, including the financial front, is essential to defeat terrorism. For decades, under the auspices of the United Nations, international standards have been devised and adopted in response to various acts and methods of terrorism (airline and maritime hijackings, piracy, use of explosives, etc.). There are thirteen UN conventions and protocols against terrorism, yet no single universally adopted definition of terrorism. Since 11 September 2001, international cooperation and coordination on counterterrorism financing have progressed dramatically at the national, regional, and multilateral levels. In addition to the United Nations, the FATF responded to the 9/11 attacks by expanding its mission beyond anti-money laundering and devoting its energy and expertise to combat terrorist financing. The FATF issued Nine Special Recommendations on Terrorist Financing (see the box on p. 217) and called on all countries to adopt and implement these measures.

The FATF and member nations attempt to identify emerging methods and trends in money laundering and terrorist financing and to devise regulations and best practices to counter these new methods. International cooperation has contributed to successful cases against terror networks operating in multiple jurisdictions thanks to CTF measures put into place. The international standards set and adopted by the public and private sectors around the world have safeguarded international financial systems and created formidable barriers and challenges for terrorists and their financiers.

Building Capacity to Combat Terrorist Financing

Counterterrorism finance assistance programs are aimed at "build[ing] sustainable, dynamic anti-money laundering and counterterrorist finance regimes that adhere to international standards and implement effective programs in the legal, financial regulatory, financial intelligence, law enforcement, prosecutorial, and international cooperation fields," according to Gerald Feierstein, former State Department Deputy Coordinator for Counterterrorism Programs and Plans. He told the US House of Representatives in 2006 that "improving the capability of our partner nations to combat terrorist financing significantly enhances our own ability to detect and isolate terrorist financiers and to 'follow the money' to where it links global terrorists and their support networks."[25]

To successfully combat terrorist financing, governments must develop an effective counterterrorist finance regime based on five basic elements described below.[26]

I. Legal Framework to Criminalize Terrorist Financing

Each country should dispose of a legal framework that criminalizes terrorist financing and money laundering. This allows countries to comply with international standards pursuant to UN Security Council Resolution 1373[27] and the Financial Action Task Force Special Recommendations on Terrorist Financing.

II. Financial Regulatory Supervision to Protect the Integrity of the Banking System

Each country should develop a financial regulatory framework that vigilantly supervises the financial services sector. Additionally, the financial services sector must develop and employ strict anti-money laundering and counterterrorism finance compliance measures that ensure that their employees "know their customer" and file suspicious transaction reports that may indicate money laundering and terrorist financing activities.

FATF Nine Special Recommendations on Terrorist Financing[24]

I. Ratification and implementation of UN instruments

Each country should take immediate steps to ratify and to implement fully the 1999 United Nations International Convention for the Suppression of the Financing of Terrorism.

Countries should also immediately implement the United Nations resolutions relating to the prevention and suppression of the financing of terrorist acts, particularly United Nations Security Council Resolution 1373.

II. Criminalizing the financing of terrorism and associated money laundering

Each country should criminalize the financing of terrorism, terrorist acts, and terrorist organizations. Countries should ensure that such offences are designated as money laundering predicate offences.

III. Freezing and confiscating terrorist assets

Each country should implement measures to freeze without delay funds or other assets of terrorists, those who finance terrorism and terrorist organizations in accordance with the United Nations resolutions relating to the prevention and suppression of the financing of terrorist acts.

Each country should also adopt and implement measures, including legislative ones, which would enable the competent authorities to seize and confiscate property that is the proceeds of, or used in, or intended or allocated for use in, the financing of terrorism, terrorist acts, or terrorist organizations.

IV. Reporting suspicious transactions related to terrorism

If financial institutions, or other businesses or entities subject to anti-money laundering obligations, suspect or have reasonable grounds to suspect that funds are linked or related to, or are to be used for terrorism, terrorist acts, or by terrorist organizations, they should be required to report promptly their suspicions to the competent authorities.

V. International cooperation

Each country should afford another country, on the basis of a treaty, arrangement, or other mechanism for mutual legal assistance or information exchange, the greatest possible measure of assistance in connection with criminal, civil enforcement, and administrative investigations, inquiries, and proceedings relating to the financing of terrorism, terrorist acts, and terrorist organizations. Countries should also take all possible measures to ensure that they do not provide safe havens for individuals charged with the financing of terrorism, terrorist acts, or terrorist organizations, and should have procedures in place to extradite, where possible, such individuals.

VI. Alternative remittance

Each country should take measures to ensure that persons or legal entities, including agents, that provide a service for the transmission of money or value, including transmission through an informal money or value transfer system or network, should be licensed or registered and subject to all the FATF Recommendations that apply to banks and non-bank financial institutions. Each country should ensure that persons or legal entities that carry out this service illegally are subject to administrative, civil, or criminal sanctions.

VII. Wire transfers

Countries should take measures to require financial institutions, including money remitters, to include accurate and meaningful originator information (name, address, and account number) on funds transfers and related messages that are sent, and the information should remain with the transfer or related message through the payment chain.

Countries should take measures to ensure that financial institutions, including money remitters, conduct enhanced scrutiny of and monitor for suspicious activity fund transfers that do not contain complete originator information (name, address, and account number).

VIII. Nonprofit organizations

Countries should review the adequacy of laws and regulations that relate to entities that can be abused for the financing of terrorism. Nonprofit organizations are particularly vulnerable, and countries should ensure that they cannot be misused: by terrorist organizations posing as legitimate entities; to exploit legitimate entities as conduits for terrorist financing, including for the purpose of escaping asset freezing measures; and to conceal or obscure the clandestine diversion of funds intended for legitimate purposes to terrorist organizations.

IX. Cash couriers

Countries should have measures in place to detect the physical cross-border transportation of currency and bearer negotiable instruments, including a declaration system or other disclosure obligation.

Countries should ensure that their competent authorities have the legal authority to stop or restrain currency or bearer negotiable instruments that are suspected to be related to terrorist financing or money laundering, or that are falsely declared or disclosed.

Countries should ensure that effective, proportionate, and dissuasive sanctions are available to deal with persons who make false declaration(s) or disclosure(s). In cases where the currency or bearer negotiable instruments are related to terrorist financing or money laundering, countries should also adopt measures, including legislative ones consistent with Recommendation 3 and Special Recommendation III, which would enable the confiscation of such currency or instruments.

III. Financial Intelligence Unit as the Link Between the Private and Public Sectors

Each country should set up a financial intelligence unit charged with collecting, analyzing, and disseminating suspicious transaction reports submitted by the private sector associated with financial transactions. An effective financial intelligence unit leverages well-trained analysts, equipment, information technology platforms, and specialized analytical software to meet its mission to develop and refer relevant evidence of financial crime cases (including terrorist financing cases) to law enforcement authorities.

IV. Law Enforcement Investigations to Track Down Terrorist Financiers

Each country should develop specialized financial crime units within their law enforcement agencies. These units may reside in different law enforcement agencies but must possess the deep technical skills necessary to follow financial forensics and develop financial crimes cases that include terrorist financing. Oftentimes, these financial crime units follow the money trail of terrorist groups and greatly complement counterterrorism investigations.

V. Judicial/Prosecutorial Process to Bring Terrorist Financiers to Justice

Finally, each country should possess a well-developed judicial system capable of bringing terrorist financiers to justice. An effective regime would employ well-trained prosecutors who are able to "follow the money trail" and make their case to the judges and magistrates.

Impact of CTF Programs

Despite some interagency growing pains, these counterterrorism finance programs have made a remarkable difference in partner nations' abilities to combat terrorist financing.[28] Relative to the inherent challenges of the fight against international terrorist financing, US CTF strategy, based on law enforcement and intelligence investigations, public designations, and foreign assistance programs has been very effective over the past seven years. In December 2005, the 9/11 Commission gave an "A−" grade to the US government's vigorous effort against terrorist financing for winning the support of key countries in tackling the issue.[29] In particular, CTF capacity building programs have enhanced countries' ability to "follow the money," from drafting legislation to criminalize terrorist financing, to creating financial intelligence units, to organizing specialized law enforcement task forces and cash courier training. Law enforcement and intelligence officials believe that these CTF measures have significantly reduced al Qaeda and its affiliates' funding. Several experts, including those associated with the 9/11 Commission, are convinced that al Qaeda is having a difficult time raising funds and that the terror group has had to cut back significantly on its expenditures.[30] Such funding is instrumental for recruiting, training, planning, and executing terrorist operations.

Case Study: Counterterrorism Capacity Building in Indonesia[31]

Background. On 12 October 2002, Indonesia experienced the largest and most deadly terrorist attack since 9/11 anywhere in the world: a bombing at a popular night spot for foreign tourists on the island of Bali. Since the terrorist group Jemaah Islamiyah (JI) perpetrated these murders, and subsequent attacks in the capital, Indonesia has endeavored with its international partners to strengthen its defenses. The United States and other allies employed several instruments of national power to deliver foreign assistance programs to Indonesia to counter the terrorist threat from JI in Southeast Asia. From direct law enforcement training to broader judicial assistance, the international community came together to help Indonesia rapidly develop its capacity to fight terrorist activity.

At the time, Washington considered the Bali attacks another manifestation of the global threat of terrorism. The US government emphasized the importance of assisting Indonesia with the Bali investigations and coordinated interagency efforts to deliver such assistance in a timely and effective fashion. Washington developed and executed a comprehensive strategy in support of Indonesia's counterterrorism efforts. In this case, US antiterrorism assistance and counterterrorism finance programs directly empowered Indonesian counterterrorism professionals to confront the threat from JI.

Immediate Response: Arresting Those Responsible

The Bali bombings began at 11:05 p.m. on 12 October 2002, when an explosive device was electronically detonated inside a crowded bar in the heart of the island resort's entertainment district. Seconds later, as victims ran from the site of the first explosion, a minivan packed with explosives detonated nearby. Terrorists had strategically targeted young tourists at popular nightspots, leaving 202 people dead, including 88 Australians, 38 Indonesians, and seven Americans. The devastating attack on innocent civilians was compounded by dramatic economic consequences for Indonesia. The terrorist operation, which cost about $35,000 to execute, shattered Bali's tourist industry, leading to losses estimated in the millions of dollars. In the aftermath, Indonesia, unprepared to counter the growing dangers posed by terrorist groups alone, eagerly met a coalition of countries willing and able to provide extensive guidance and assistance in counterterrorism.[32]

With the aid of the United States and other international allies, Indonesia quickly launched a credible and professional law enforcement campaign to investigate and capture the terrorists responsible for the attack. Australian and US law enforcement experts rapidly deployed to Indonesia to assist with the various aspects of the Bali bombing investigation. Ultimately, from identifying the victims to "following the money trail" using ATM receipts, the Indonesian authorities investigated the attack and arrested most of the Jemaah Islamiyah members involved in the Bali operation. As a result of coordinated law enforcement assistance, in areas such as forensics, and preparing sound evidentiary packages, Indonesian judicial authorities have successfully prosecuted the Bali bombing perpetrators.[33]

Longer-Term Counterterrorism Capacity Building in Indonesia

Following the 2002 Bali bombings, the Indonesian government sought to strengthen its overall capacity to prevent future terrorist attacks. A specialized counterterrorism unit within the Indonesian National Police, known as Special Detachment 88 (SD-88), was established in Jakarta and was trained and mentored by US law enforcement and Australian

National Police counterparts.[34] Indonesia also developed and improved the Indonesian National Police's (INP) capacity to investigate and prevent terrorist crimes that included Crisis Response Team (CRT) and Explosive Incident Countermeasure (EIC) training.[35] As "following the money trail" was considered an important aspect of countering JI, officers with financial forensic and counterterrorism finance expertise have been incorporated in these specialized CT units. With such instruction and interdisciplinary skills, Indonesian counterterrorism forces have become more effective in disrupting plots and rooting out terror cells linked to JI. In November 2005, SD-88 located Indonesia's most wanted terrorist, Azahari bin Husin, who was linked to the Bali and Jakarta bombings. SD-88 planned and executed a successful assault on Azahari's stronghold, killing him and securing valuable intelligence to help prevent other attacks.[36] Since its inception, according to State Department testimony, "Detachment 88 has been instrumental in the apprehension or elimination of more than 425 terrorists. In 2007, they and other police units arrested more than 30 terrorists and killed several others, including top JI leaders Abu Dujana and Zarkasih."[37]

On the judicial front, Indonesia's attorney general staffed the long-awaited Terrorism and Transnational Crime Task Force in July 2006, which had been designed by US and Indonesian judicial experts to oversee counterterrorism trials nationwide and develop a cadre of special terrorism prosecutors. Task Force members immediately began to take on over a dozen counterterrorism cases. The Task Force won several high-profile convictions and is prosecuting a dozen members of JI's military unit who were arrested in March and June 2007 raids in central Java, including two key figures—Zarkasih, the JI military leader, and his deputy, Dujana.[38]

On the financial front, the Indonesian government, with foreign assistance, also dedicated significant resources to protecting its financial system from abuses by terrorists. Indonesia has made substantial progress in reinforcing its ability to combat terrorist financing and money laundering in the five key areas for an effective counterterrorist financing regime as outlined below.

1. **Legal Framework.** Successful prosecution of terrorists relies on a strong legal framework, and the United States and its partners have assisted Indonesia in developing strong anti-money laundering/CTF laws. Since July 2002, the United States has been training Indonesian and other Southeast Asian judicial authorities in drafting and amending legislation that would enable them to adopt the UN conventions related to terrorism and comply with UN Security Council Resolution 1373 to criminalize terrorist financing and money laundering. In the past, Indonesia had a weak track record in countering financial crimes; in 2001, it was added to the Financial Action Task Force list of Non-Cooperating Countries and Territories (NCCT) of money laundering concern, which affects investor confidence in listed countries. However, in September 2003, technical assistance from a US interagency team helped Indonesia adequately amend its anti-money laundering legislation to meet international standards and avoid further FATF sanctions.[39] As a result of this legislative progress, FATF removed Indonesia from the NCCT list in February 2005.[40]

2. **Financial/Regulatory.** Central banks are instrumental in monitoring and suspending money flows to terrorist groups. Indonesia has been working with the Asian

Development Bank and other international donors to modernize its financial sector. In October 2003, Indonesian central bankers participated in a financial regulatory workshop on how to combat terrorist financing and money laundering and how to detect suspicious activities in private banks.[41] The training led Bank Indonesia to later devise and build out a compliance audit program for AML/CTF and plan to conduct full on-site supervision and examination of banks.

3. **Financial Intelligence Unit (FIU).** Bali's remote location and inadequate preparedness for a large-scale attack meant that national and international law enforcement agents could not rely solely on crime scene evidence to track and apprehend the responsible terrorists. One of the most powerful investigative tools in the Bali bombings was the analysis of communication and financial transactions between JI members. Working closely with Australia's financial intelligence unit, US officials assisted in developing the Indonesian FIU. Washington conducted a one-week training seminar entitled "Basic Analysis and Suspicious Transaction Reporting" for FIU personnel and other government officials responsible for combating money laundering and terrorist financing. Through a grant from USAID to procure essential information technology equipment, the United States directly assisted Indonesia's FIU in bringing its electronic reporting system online in October 2003 to collect suspicious transaction reports from the private sector. With this assistance from the United States and Australia, Indonesia's FIU passed a milestone in June 2004 when it officially became a member of the Egmont Group of FIUs[42]—the international body that promotes financial intelligence sharing.[43] Financial intelligence, according to a former Treasury Department official, has played an important role in individual operations, such as the investigation that led to the capture of Hambali, Jemaah Islamiyah's operations chief who masterminded the 2002 Bali bombings.[44]

4. **Law Enforcement.** In January 2004, the FBI Terrorist Financing Operations Section conducted training courses for sixty-nine Indonesian National Police and other officials responsible for combating money laundering and terrorist financing. In an attempt to foster interagency cooperation in terrorist financing cases, participants included personnel from the Indonesian National Police SD-88 counterterrorism unit, financial crimes unit, and financial intelligence unit. As a result of this training, Indonesian law enforcement authorities have initiated over thirty money laundering investigations, two-thirds of which have been referred to the Attorney General's office.[45]

5. **Prosecutorial/Judicial Process.** The US Department of Justice's Overseas Prosecutorial Development Assistance and Training division (OPDAT) has assigned a resident legal advisor in Jakarta to work with the host government in applying the new counterterrorism and anti-money laundering legislation. The resident legal advisor assisted with the passage and application of mutual legal assistance legislation.[46]

Lessons Learned

Through law enforcement operations and public designations, Indonesia responded quickly to the Bali bombings and made significant strides in rooting out the JI cell responsible for the attacks. Training and capacity building provided by the US government and other international donors have significantly augmented Indonesia's ability to prevent and respond to terrorist financing and international terrorism. From law enforcement programs to a comprehensive overhaul of financial and legal structures, Indonesia has benefited extensively from the continuing assistance of its allies, and it serves as a positive example of international capacity building efforts. The case of Indonesia demonstrates how Indonesia and its allies were able to work together to build counterterrorism capacity to confront Jemaah Islamiyah.[47] Washington and other world capitals dedicated and deployed technical expertise drawn from across the disciplines (law enforcement, financial, judicial experts) that enabled Indonesia to work toward defeating terrorist groups such as JI.[48]

Conclusion

For nine years the international security community has newly focused on addressing the threat of terrorism and on disrupting, defeating, and deterring terror networks. Governments at the national, regional, and international levels have devoted considerable resources to these counterterrorism efforts, including to the financial front of the war on terror. So, how successful have these counterterrorism finance measures been in combating terrorism? Very successful, according to former US Director of National Intelligence Michael McConnell. In February 2008, he commented that "over the past 12–18 months, the intelligence community notices that al Qaeda and its affiliated groups have had difficulty in raising funds and sustaining themselves."[49] Post-9/11, we have witnessed governments around the globe establish and reinforce more robust counterterrorism finance regimes. These actions have hampered the ability of terrorist groups to raise and move money to such an extent that they are resorting to more risky methods of terrorist financing such as cash couriers, alternative remittance systems, charities, and front companies. The nexus between terrorism and crime is of growing concern to international security experts as terrorist groups have partnered with criminal organizations or turned to engaging directly in criminal activities to finance and support their networks' operational and support requirements.

Since financing is the lifeblood of terrorist networks, depriving terrorists of funding constrains their operating environment and ability to plan and execute deadly attacks. This is the objective of counterterrorism finance strategy. The four lines of operation—(1) law enforcement and intelligence operations, (2) public designations and asset freezes, (3) international cooperation, and (4) CTF capacity building—enhance each country's and the international community's ability to combat terrorist financing. There has been greater appreciation for the importance of "following the money trail" and financial intelligence to track down terrorist groups and their enablers. Although it is impossible to stem the flow of funds to terror networks completely, counterterrorism finance measures serve as a disruptive tool, intelligence resource, and deterrent by becoming an integral part of broader counterterrorism policies. There has been significant progress made on the financial front of the war on terrorism; however, the international community must remain ever vigilant and responsive as terrorist groups and their financiers devise new means and methods of raising and moving funds for their murderous plots and attacks.

Celina B. Realuyo Ms. Realuyo is President of CBR Global Advisors. As Assistant Professor of Counterterrorism (2007–2010) at the National Defense University, Celina Realuyo educated US and foreign military and civilian leaders through her "Combating Terrorism: Strategies and Policies," "Terrorism and Crime," and "Globalization and National Security" courses. Formerly a private banker, Ms. Realuyo served as the US Department of State's Director of Counterterrorism Finance Programs from 2002 to 2006. Under her stewardship, the United States delivered technical assistance to twenty countries, training over 1,800 foreign counterparts, and her team received an "A−" from the *9/11 Commission* for combating terrorist financing. An earlier career as a US diplomat saw assignments in Madrid, Panama, and the US Mission to NATO and in Washington at posts including the National Security Council's White House situation room. Realuyo holds an M.B.A. from Harvard Business School, an M.A. in International Relations from Johns Hopkins University School of Advanced International Studies (SAIS), and a B.S. in Foreign Service from Georgetown University. She is a member of the Council on Foreign Relations and the Professional Risk Managers International Association. Ms. Realuyo has traveled to over fifty countries and speaks French and Spanish fluently.

Recommended Readings

Biersteker, Thomas J., and Sue E. Eckert, eds. *Countering the Financing of Terrorism.* New York: Routledge, 2008.

Giraldo, Jeanne K. and Harold A. Trinkunas, eds. *Terrorism financing and State Responses: A Comparative Perspective.* Stanford: Stanford University Press, 2007.

Levitt, Matthew, and Michael Jacobson. "The Money Trail: Finding, Following, and Freezing Terrorist Finances," The Washington Institute for Near East Policy, Policy Focus #89, November 2008. Available at http://www.washingtoninstitute.org/templateC04.php?CID=302

Naim, Moises. *Illicit: How Smugglers, Traffickers and Copycats Are Hijacking the Global Economy.* New York: Doubleday, 2005. Ch. 7, "The Money Washers."

Roth, John et al. *National Commission on Terrorist Attacks Upon the United States: Monograph on Terrorist Financing.* Washington, DC, 2004. Available at http://www.9-11commission.gov/staff_statements/index.htm

US Government Accountability Office. *Terrorist Financing: Better Strategic Planning Needed to Coordinate US Efforts to Deliver Counter-Terrorism Financing Training and Technical Assistance Abroad.* Washington, DC: Government Printing Office, October 2005. Available at http://www.gao.gov/new.items/d0619.pdf

US Government Accountability Office. *Terrorist Financing: US Agencies Should Systematically Assess Terrorists' Use of Alternative Financing Mechanisms.* Washington, DC: Government Printing Office, November 2003. Available at http://www.gao.gov/new.items/d04163.pdf

Zarate, Juan. "Winning the War on Terror: Marking Success and Confronting Challenges." Prepared remarks presented at the Washington Institute for Near East Policy, 23 April 2008. Available at http://www.washingtoninstitute.org/templateC07.php?CID=393

Notes

1. President George W. Bush, "President Freezes Terrorist Assets," White House Press Briefing, 24 September 2001, available at http://georgewbush-whitehouse.archives.gov/news/releases/2001/09/20010924-4.html, accessed 9 September 2009.

2. Financial Action Task Force on Money Laundering, *Report on Money Laundering Typologies, 2002–2003*, 14 February 2003, available at http://www.fatf-gafi.org/dataoecd/29/33/34037958 .pdf, accessed 19 September 2009.

3. *Global Relief Foundation vs. Paul O'Neill, et al.*, 207 F. Sup. 2d 779, US District Court, Northern District of Illinois, Eastern Division, 11 June 2002.

4. *United States of America vs. Enaam M. Arnaout, Case No. 02CR892,* US District Court, Northern District of Illinois, Eastern Division, April 2002.

5. US Government Accountability Office, *Terrorist Financing: US Agencies Should Systematically Assess Terrorists' Use of Alternative Financing Mechanisms*, Washington, DC: Government Printing Office, November 2003, available at http://www.gao.gov/new.items/d04163.pdf.

6. Ibid.

7. Rohan Gunaratna, "The Evolution of Al Qaeda," in *Countering the Financing of Terrorism*, edited by Thomas J. Biersteker and Sue E. Eckert (New York: Routledge, 2008), 58–59.

8. According to the US Department of Justice, al Barakaat operated a hybrid hawala in which its informal system interconnected with the formal banking system. Since al Barakaat used financial institutions, law enforcement was able to discover the transactions to Somalia by analyzing Suspicious Activity Reports generated by the banks pursuant to the Bank Secrecy Act of 1970.

9. Doug Farah, "A Bit More on Dawood Ibrabim and Why He Matters," DouglasFarah.com, 11 December 2008, available at http://www.douglasfarah.com/article/429/a-bit-more-on-dawood-ibrahim-and-why-he-matters.com, accessed 19 September 2009.

10. According to US Department of Justice, al Barakaat operated a hybrid hawala in which its informal system interconnected with the formal banking system. Because al Barakaat also used financial institutions, law enforcement was able to discover the transactions to Somalia by analyzing Suspicious Activity Reports generated by the banks pursuant to their obligations under the 1970 Bank Secrecy Act [Pub. L. No. 91-508, 84 Stat. 1114 (1970) (codified as amended in 12 U.S.C. §§ 1829(b), 1951–1959 (2000); 31 U.S.C. §§ 5311–5330 (2000)].

11. John Roth et al., *National Commission on Terrorist Attacks Upon the United States: Monograph on Terrorist Financing,* (Washington, DC, 2004), available at http://www.9-11commission .gov/staff_statements/index.htm, accessed 19 September 2009.

12. US Government Accountability Office, *Terrorist Financing: Better Strategic Planning Needed to Coordinate US Efforts to Deliver Counter-Terrorism Financing Training and Technical Assistance* (Washington, DC: Government Printing Office, 2005), available at http://www.gao .gov/new.items/d0619.pdf, accessed 19 September 2009.

13. National Commission on Terrorist Attacks Upon the United States, "Outline of the 9/11 Plot: Staff Statement No. 16," June 2004, 11–12, available at http://www.9-11commission.gov/ staff_statements/staff_statement_16.pdf, accessed 19 September 2009.

14. Roth, op. cit., 1–16.

15. For an overview of the USA PATRIOT Act, see Charles Doyle, "The USA PATRIOT Act: A Sketch," CRS Report for Congress RS21203, 18 April 2002, available at http://fas.org/irp/crs/ RS21203.pdf, accessed 19 September 2009.

16. Abby Goodnough, "Jose Padilla Convicted on All Counts in Terror Trial," *The New York Times*, 16 August 2007, available at http://www.nytimes.com/2007/08/16/us/16cnd-padilla.html, accessed 19 September 2009.

17. 50 USC. App. 2401 ET. seq.

18. U.S. Department of State, "State Sponsors of Terrorism," available at http://www.state.gov/s/ ct/c14151.htm, accessed 19 September 2009. Also see "Testimony of Juan Carlos Zarate, Assistant Secretary, Terrorist Financing and Financial Crimes," US Department of Treasury, Before the House Financial Services Subcommittees on Domestic and International Monetary Policy, Trade and Technology and Oversight and Investigations, 30 September 2004, available at http://www.treas.gov/press/releases/js1971.htm, accessed 19 September 2009.

19. Charles Doyle, "Antiterrorism and Effective Death Penalty Act of 1996: A Summary," Congressional Research Service American Law Division, 3 June 1996, available at http://www .fas.org/irp/crs/96-499.htm, accessed 19 September 2009.

20. (50 USC. 1701 et seq.)(IEEPA), the National Emergencies Act (50 USC. 1601 et seq.), and section 5 of the United Nations Participation Act of 1945, as amended (22 USC. 287c) (UNPA), and sec. 301 of Title 3, US Code.

21. President George W. Bush, "President Freezes Terrorist Assets," White House Press Briefing, 24 September 2001, op. cit.

22. President George W. Bush, "Executive Order on Terrorist Financing," White House Press Office, 24 September 2001, available at http://georgewbush-whitehouse.archives.gov/news/releases/2001/09/20010924-1.html, accessed 19 September 2009.

23. US Government Accountability Office, *Terrorist Financing: Better Strategic Planning Needed to Coordinate US Efforts to Deliver Counter-Terrorism Financing Training and Technical Abroad,* 2–3.

24. "9 Special Recommendations on Terrorist Financing," Financial Action Task Force (FATF), available at http://www.fatf-gafi.org/document/9/0,3343,en_32250379_32236920_34032073_1_1_1_1,00.html, accessed 19 September 2009.

25. US House of Representatives, Financial Services Committee, Subcommittee on Oversight and Investigations, "Counter-Terrorism Financing Foreign Training and Assistance: Progress Since 9/11," 109th Congress, 2nd Session, 6 April 2006, available at http://financialservices.house.gov/media/pdf/109-84.pdf, accessed 19 September 2009.

26. Celina Realuyo, "Building a Counterterrorist Finance Regime," US Department of State Bureau of International Information Programs, *E-Journal USA: Economic Perspectives,* Vol. 9, No. 3 (September 2004): 10–13, available at http://guangzhou.usembassy-china.org.cn/uploads/images/tlZ5ybS8T9PYsu730CyKsA/ijee0904.pdf, accessed 19 September 2009.

27. Adopted in late September 2001, the resolution calls on UN members to share intelligence relating to terrorist activities and attempts to restrict terrorist financing activities. UNSCR 1373 is binding on all member states.

28. From author's interviews with Department of State, Office of the Coordinator for Counterterrorism program managers on 22 February 2008.

29. 9/11 Public Discourse Project, *Final Report on 9/11 Commission Recommendations,* 5 December 2005, p. 5, available at http://www.9-11pdp.org/press/2005-12-05_report.pdf, accessed 19 September 2009.

30. Roth et al., op cit., 10.

31. Much of this case study is drawn from a previous work by the author. See Celina Realuyo and Scott Stapleton, "Response to Bali: An International Success Story," US Department of State Bureau of International Information Programs *E-Journal USA: Economic Perspectives,* 14–17.

32. Ibid., 14.

33. Ibid., 14–15.

34. Ibid., 15.

35. US Department of State, "The Antiterrorism Assistance Program: Report to Congress for Fiscal Year 2005," available at http://www.state.gov/documents/organization/75780.pdf, accessed 19 September 2009.

36. US Department of State Bureau of Resource Management, "Strategic Goal 2: Counterterrorism," *FY 2006 Performance and Accountability Highlights,* available at http://www.state.gov/s/d/rm/rls/perfrpt/2006hlts/html/79818.htm, accessed 19 September 2009.

37. Gina K. Abercrombie-Winstanley, Deputy Coordinator for Counterterrorism, testimony to the House Committee on Oversight and Government Reform, Subcommittee on National Security and Foreign Affairs, 4 June 2008, available at http://nationalsecurity.oversight.house.gov/documents/20080604115139.pdf, accessed 19 September 2009.

38. US Department of State, Office of the Coordinator for Counterterrorism, "Chapter 2—Country Reports: East Asia and Pacific Overview," *Country Reports on Terrorism,* 30 April 2008, available at http://www.state.gov/s/ct/rls/crt/2007/103706.htm, accessed 19 September 2009.

39. Realuyo and Stapleton, op. cit., 15–16.

40. Berita Sebelumnya, "RI Removed from Money Laundering List," *Jakarta Post,* 12 February 2005.

41. Realuyo and Stapleton, op. cit., 16.
42. Realuyo and Stapleton, op. cit., 16–17.
43. See http://www.egmontgroup.org/ for more information.
44. Michael Jacobson, "Extremism's Deep Pockets: The Growing Challenge of Fighting Terrorist Financing," *The Politic* (Yale University), 17 February 2008, available at http://www.washingtoninstitute.org/templateC06.php?CID=1134, accessed 19 September 2009.
45. Realuyo and Stapleton, op. cit., 17.
46. Realuyo and Stapleton, op. cit., 17.
47. Realuyo and Stapleton, op. cit., 17.
48. More background available from the Australian Government Department of Foreign Affairs and Trade, "Indonesia Country Brief," June 2008, available at http://www.indo.ausaid.gov.au/projects/counterterrorism.html, accessed 19 September 2009; and AUSAID in Indonesia, "Counter-Terrorism Capacity Building Initiative," available at http://www.indo.ausaid.gov.au/projects/counterterrorism.html, accessed 19 September 2009. Australia has a strong historic interest in Indonesia, which it considers to be part of its "back yard." Bali is a major tourist destination for Australians and New Zealanders, somewhat comparable to the Caribbean for Americans and Canadians. In an informal arrangement discussed with S/CT officials to make joint resources go further, Australia and New Zealand generally have taken the lead in assisting South Pacific nations in law enforcement and counterterrorism issues. Coordination takes place through regular meetings and at the embassy level. Australia and Indonesia have also taken the lead in promoting regional counterterrorism cooperation, including by jointly hosting the Sub-Regional Ministerial Conference on Counter-Terrorism in Jakarta in March 2007. That meeting provided impetus for closer regional counterterrorism cooperation and led to agreement on priorities for future CT action in Southeast Asia.
49. US House of Representatives, "Hearing of the House Permanent Select Committee on Intelligence: Annual Worldwide Threat Assessment," 7 February 2008, 16–18, available at www.dni.gov/testimonies/20080207_transcript.pdf, accessed 19 September 2009.

3.5

Patrick Sookhdeo

Ideas Matter:

How to Undermine the Extremist Ideology Behind al Qaeda

Wars of subversion and counter subversion are fought, in the last resort, in the minds of the people.[1]

Frank Kitson

The struggle with revolutionary Islam will only be won when the West begins to methodically analyze the ideological religion that empowers it and forms its basis.[2]

Stephen P. Lambert

Introduction

The *9/11 Commission Report* concluded that the ultimate requirement for eliminating the danger posed by al Qaeda is "prevailing in the longer term over the ideology that gives rise to Islamist terrorism."[3] This statement rightly pinpoints the fact that it is the ideology promoted by Osama bin Laden and his associates that holds together the impressively disparate, multiethnic movement that is al Qaeda, a movement described by one expert as "the ideological organization par excellence."[4]

International terrorism perpetrated by Muslims is a symptom of a deeper malaise.[5] It is a weapon in the hands of an ideological movement that has specific doctrines and goals. Insurgency and criminality are merely expressions of a political war of ideas carried on in numerous fields, such as psychology, communication, economics, etc. While experts might argue over whether terrorism is a criminal activity or a military act of war, they often forget that it is an ideological war with much wider implications. Active terrorism is but an end product of the greater ideological movement that sustains it and manipulates it to further the goals of reshaping the world in that movement's own image.

Indeed, the ideological battle is in many ways more important than the physical battle. It is easier to defeat radical Islamist jihadists than to defeat their Islamist ideology. Ideology is what gathers resources and recruits new fighters to replace those who have been eliminated. Defeat the ideology and the terrorism-inspiring movement withers and dies.[6]

Some experts tend to minimize the importance of religion and ideology in contemporary Islamic terrorism. Marc Sageman, for instance, while presenting a good analysis of its decentralized network, debunking the various popular suggestions regarding its "root causes" and stressing the importance of personal links in its recruitment strategy, seems

228

to denigrate religion and ideology as its motivating forces. As a result he offers solutions, such as criminalizing terrorism, that are merely tactics and not a strategy to win the war against it.[7]

Ideology is al Qaeda's main strength and center of gravity. It is linked to classical Islamic doctrine and therefore appeals to a wide Muslim constituency. This enables it to recover from tactical defeats and constantly renew its personnel, resources, and moral authority. It is important to try and discover its linked critical vulnerability, which could then be exploited to achieve its ultimate defeat.[8]

'Abd Al-'Aziz Al-Muqrin was al Qaeda's leader in the Arabian Peninsula until his death in 2004. His posthumous manual, *A Practical Course for Guerrilla War*, provides many insights into the organization's strategic thinking and operations. In the introduction to an English translation of the work, Norman Cigar writes:

> The Islamic framework used in this book is not just a cosmetic or marketing factor. The Islamic basis for legitimacy is embedded throughout the text, with recourse to the Koran, Sunna, and religious scholars, as one might expect originating from an organization that views itself as the champion of genuine Islam. . . . Islamic principles, however controversial the Islamists' interpretation of these may be, provide the moral compass for Al-Muqrin and inform his view of *jihad*.[9]

This task will not be easy for western strategists, as the western worldview assumes an uninhibited exchange of ideas. Ideologies, theories, and the wildest of hypotheses and speculations can be given free rein in a society based firmly on freedom of belief and freedom of speech. A corollary of this is the ease with which many westerners can abandon former beliefs or guiding principles and move on to embrace new ones. This process causes little or no anguish, let alone a crisis of identity, in a culture of free discussion and debate. But in Islamic culture, individuals are more firmly wedded to their ideologies and beliefs and to their history.

E. M. Forster perceptively illustrates this contrast in a conversation between his fictional characters in *A Passage to India*, the British Mr. Fielding and the Muslim Dr. Aziz. Fielding describes his approach to life by saying, "I travel light." Aziz thinks to himself,

> So this was why Mr. Fielding and the others were so fearless! They had nothing to lose. But he [Aziz] himself was rooted in society and Islam. He belonged to a tradition which bound him, and he had brought children into the world, the society of the future. Though he lived so vaguely in this flimsy bungalow, nevertheless he was placed, placed.[10]

From this perspective, altering the ideology of a Muslim can be considerably more challenging than altering the ideology of a westerner. For Muslims, Islam is not merely a personal faith, but a total way of life; an all-encompassing religious, social, and political system; a worldview, civilization, and culture. This worldview and way of thinking is based on the model of Muhammad, the Islamic source scriptures, and the history of the early Islamic state, which is seen as paradigmatic by most Muslims.

Contemporary Islam is a complex faith consisting of a variety of often conflicting theological, sectarian, ethnic, linguistic, and cultural movements and elements. Muslim sources include a rich variety of views, giving scope for many selective readings and interpretations. Doctrine and its application are colored by local culture and tribal traditions. Such a complex entity cannot be neatly pigeonholed as "peaceful" or "violent." Rather, it embraces both extremes at one and the same time: Both are integral parts of Islam. The real question is: Which interpretations are favored by the dominant movements within contemporary Islam?

The Ideology of Islamism

International terrorism carried out by Muslims in the name of Islam and Islamic causes is a small visible part of a much larger ideological movement known as "Islamism" (and also called "political" or "fundamentalist" Islam). "Islamism" is an umbrella term for a wide variety of contemporary religious-political, ideological, global, transnational, and extremist movements, including al Qaeda. These movements and their discourses are committed to Islam as a political ideology, a totalitarian system and way of life, and a viable alternative to western secular ideologies.[11] They operate across all areas of human society and all over the world, and have defined grievances and goals.[12]

Muslim weakness, humiliation, and shame at the hands of the hegemonic West are the main grievances expounded by Islamists, and these resonate with the general dissatisfaction in the Muslim world with the existing order. The restoration of Muslim power and glory is therefore one of Islamism's main goals.[13] The best known ideologue of the Muslim Brotherhood in Egypt, Sayyid Qutb, defined the goal of Islamism as:

> The restoration of Islamic life in an Islamic society governed by the Islamic creed and the Islamic conception as well as by the Islamic *sharia* and the Islamic system (*nizam*).[14]

While we must distinguish between Islamists and the majority of ordinary peaceful Muslims, we must also recognize the deep roots of Islamism in classical and traditional Islam. It is its link to the sources of Islam and its early history that maintains Islamism's vitality and enables it to propagate itself and gain recruits and resources wherever Muslims are found.

Among the variety of Islamic concepts, a strand of radicalism and violence is inherent in much of traditional Muslim theology, ideology, and history. Like the others, it is based on passages in the Muslim source texts (Koran, *Hadith*, *Sira*), on Muhammad's example, and on early Muslim history.[15] The distinguished scholar of Islam, Bernard Lewis, noted that:

> From the earliest times, the reported events of Islamic history, supported by the precepts of Islamic tradition and law, reflect two distinct and indeed contradictory principles. The one we have called authoritarian and quietist; the other might be called radical and activist . . . the radical activist tradition is also old and deep-rooted, and is acquiring new significance in our day, with the emergence of the idea of an Islamic Revolution, and of leaders and movements devoted to its accomplishment. . . . The exponents of both traditions naturally looked to the life and teachings of the Prophet for guidance and inspiration; both concentrated their attention on the political actions which the prophet found necessary to undertake in order to accomplish his religious mission.[16]

Because the Islamic source texts of Koran and *Hadith* contain many passages encouraging violence, intolerance, and contempt for non-Muslims, they have provided a powerful motivation and justification in all ages for some Muslims seeking to further the power of Islam by aggression and violence. As the well-known Egyptian scholar Nasr Hamid Abu Zayd has noted:

> If we follow the rules of interpretation developed from the classical "science of Koranic interpretation," it is not possible to condemn terrorism in religious terms. It remains completely true to the classical rules in its evolution of sanctity for its own justification. This is where the secret of its theological strength lies.[17]

Some more peaceful forms of contemporary Islam, in trying to present Islam as a religion of peace and tolerance, seek to spiritualize the violence found in Islamic source texts and call for a reform of traditional Islam and a reinterpretation of its source scriptures. A number of Muslim scholars have used a variety of hermeneutical stratagems to offer alternative readings of the key passages.[18] But throughout history the presence of these passages at the very core of the Islamic holy books has provided a basis for aggressive attitudes among Muslims. And the dominant groups within contemporary Islam are those that base their positions on traditional and mainly literalist readings of the sacred source texts and on the paradigmatic model of Muhammad and of early Muslim history. These groups include the Islamists, who endorse and expand upon these normative, radical themes within classical Islam.

As Ehsan Masood, former editor of the Muslim journal *Q-News* and project director for the Gateway Trust in Woking,[19] explains,

> The Koran is taught across the Muslim world (including in Britain) as a set of eternal truths with little reference to its historical context. . . . Unless the Koran is read in context, neither Bin Laden nor the BNP [the British National Party, a far-right political party in the UK] is wrong when claiming that Islam glorifies violence.[20]

Thus, Islamists demand a return to the sacred source texts of Islam, interpreted literally. This return, however, brings them face to face with Muhammad's setting up of a political state system under Islamic law (bent on expansion and world dominion), fighting his enemies, and dealing severely, sometimes brutally, with opponents of his political and spiritual authority. Also, of the revered first four caliphs, three were assassinated, and all their reigns were attended by great violence that included wars of Islamic expansion and civil strife within the Islamic community. Much of the future development of Islam was a response to this early stage of violence in the paradigmatic community, which has provided models for radical groups throughout Muslim history.

So Islamists are committed to purifying society from un-Islamic practices and teachings, and to the establishment of an ideal Islamic state modeled on the teachings of Muhammad, the Rashidun (the four Rightly Guided Caliphs), and Muhammad's Companions: a unified worldwide "Islamic state" (*khilafa*, or caliphate), in which *sharia* is the basis and sole source of all legislation.[21] Islamist movements are devoted to the pursuit of the Islamization of the entire social and political system of their societies, their states, the whole Muslim world, and ultimately the entire globe.[22] Islamization involves the bringing of everything under God's sovereignty, rule, and law, as revealed in a literalist interpretation of the Islamic scriptures—its integration within a total Islamic system in which implementation of *sharia* is the crucial element. Islamists aim to transform Muslim society and acquire political power in the state so as to set up true Islamic states under *sharia.*

Islamists are united in their pan-Islamic view of the global *umma*[23] as the locus of their loyalty. They reject modern states as temporary evils that will give way to their utopian global Islamic state under *sharia*. Islamists reject western cultural, political, and economic systems as corrupting and detrimental to the Muslim world. They hold that these systems were forcibly imposed by the imperial and colonial powers and that they must be rejected and replaced.

In their ideological emphasis on the state, Islamists are sharply distinct even from traditionalist Muslims. In Islamism the state is seen as the main instrument for implementing the Islamist vision of a God-pleasing society under sharia and as the guarantor of its survival. Because Islamists perceive the modern state as the most efficient tool for establishing their vision, they concentrate their efforts, everywhere and at all times, on capturing the state, its centers of power, and its instruments of violence, either legally within the democratic framework, or violently by revolution or coup d'état.[24]

So, Islamists such as al Qaeda are radical in their contemporary application of the Islamic source scriptures, extremist in their methods, and exclusivist in their views of competing ideologies.[25] Their radicalism is expressed in their commitment to achieving a thorough reordering of society in order to bring it in line with their ideal vision of what they believe Islamic scripture demands, and in their efforts to that end. Their extremism is reflected in their readiness for sacrifice and their willingness to engage in aggressive action in pursuit of their goals. This includes saving individuals and adding them to alternative, pure, Islamist societies, erecting walls of separation to protect the community from the pollution of the outside world, entering the democratic process in order to influence society and majority culture so as to effect constitutional changes in line with Islamist ideology, and legitimizing violence in order to take over power in the state and impose reforms from above. Their exclusivism is seen in their rejection of other Islamic streams as syncretistic and deviationist, and their conviction that Islamism is the only valid expression of authentic, pure, and true Islam. Radicalism, extremism, and exclusivism imply a degree of intensity and a commitment to political activism and/or the legitimization of violence.

Islamists have revived the classical concept of *jihad*, including its violent military aspect (*jihad* of the sword). In their view, *jihad* is a permanent state of war between the Islamic state and the non-Muslim world, waged on all fronts and in all spheres. This twofold division of the world is defined in classical Islam as the House of Islam (*Dar al-Islam*), where Islam holds power, and—significantly—the House of War (*Dar al-Harb*), where non-Muslims have power. The latter name expresses the Islamist view that *jihad* must be waged until *Dar al-Harb* becomes *Dar al-Islam*. As the Syrian Muslim scholar Majid Khadduri explains:

> The universalism of Islam, in its all-embracing creed, is imposed on the believers as a continuous process of warfare, psychological and political, if not strictly military. . . . The Jihad, accordingly, may be stated as a doctrine of <u>a permanent state of war</u>, not continuous fighting. [emphasis added][26]

The Pakistani Brigadier S. K. Malik has a similar view of *jihad*:

> <u>*Jihad* is a continuous and never-ending struggle</u> waged on all fronts including political, economic, social, psychological, domestic, moral and spiritual to attain the objectives of policy. [emphasis added][27]

Linked to *jihad* is the idea of the staged development of the Islamic movement, as prefigured by Muhammad's paradigm: his so-called *hijra* from Mecca to Medina in AD 622. In the first stage of his mission Muhammad lived in his hometown of Mecca and preached his new monotheistic message there. Most Meccans rejected his teaching, however, and their growing hostility led to violent persecution of the small band of Muslims. In that context of weakness he was bidden to preach and warn peacefully, with patience and forbearance. Following his migration to Medina, whose inhabitants were more amenable to his message, he became much more aggressive in his pronouncements and actions against his opponents. This *hijra* is understood as his temporary separation from a hostile environment in order to consolidate his community's strength and eventually to return in power to destroy the evil system and establish God's rule by force of arms.

In the first stage of Islamic development (weakness) the use of force is not allowed. After migration to a safe place, the second stage (organization and growth) allows for some defensive action. The final stage (strength) includes an aggressive return to the original territory to conquer and impose Islam on all opponents. While Islamic gradualists see themselves in the first two stages and as preparing for the final stage, radicals claim they are already in the final stage, basing their view on the command to fight all infidels until the end of time.

Radicals diverge from the gradualist mainstream in justifying the immediate use of force to achieve their aims. They reinterpret traditional concepts and ancient classical Muslim paradigms to justify indiscriminate violence against all perceived enemies, both Muslims and non-Muslims. Islamists also interpret separation in the second stage to include separation from evil and heretical teachings and systems, and many have set up their own independent movements and institutions.

The borderline between mainline gradualist Islamists and the violent radicals is not clear-cut and defined, but flexible and permeable in both directions. While there is agreement on ultimate goals, there is constant argument over how best to achieve them.

Modern Islamism emerged as a branch of the Islamic reform movement of the nineteenth century. But since the 1970s it has been becoming dominant in both the Muslim street and the Muslim power centers, empowered by generous funding from Muslim oil wealth. Islamism has succeeded in gaining acceptance of its tenets in most Muslim states and societies, while its operatives have largely taken control of many important Muslim institutions and organizations, and hold powerful positions in politics and the military.

It is also important to realize that there is a linkage between the universal Islamist agenda and local and regional aspects and concerns. Islamists are masters at manipulating local Muslim grievances to further their own global ideology. One of the most potent and universally felt of these grievances is the Palestinian issue; another is Kashmir—but virtually every area of the globe yields its own grievance over power or territory, whether contemporary or in the never-to-be-forgotten past.

So the war against Islamist terrorism is a war of ideas, ideologies, and worldviews. It is important to clarify, however, that it is not a "war on Islam," as Islamists are quick to label it. Islamists have "politicised Islam and religionised politics."[28] While the Islamist concept of *jihad* is rooted in Islamic classical doctrine, it goes beyond it, taking an extreme position that rejects the limits imposed by the classical *ulama* (learned Islamic scholars). In this sense it is a modern and postmodern phenomenon that draws on Islamicized Fascist, Marxist, and anarchist concepts to complement its Islamic core.

The Ideology of al Qaeda

Al Qaeda bears the hallmarks of a typical revolutionary movement on an international scale.[29] It presents itself as a protest on behalf of the poor and oppressed, a liberation movement seeking to free Muslim lands from the post-colonial influence of the West and from the rule of insufficiently Islamic Muslims. As in so many revolutionary movements, violence is glorified as a means of purification. Talk of revolution, liberation, the oppressed, and violence as a purifying element is part of a pattern of messages propounded by modern, totalitarian, Islamist ideologues such as Sayyid Qutb (1906–1966), Hassan al Banna (1906–1949), Abu'l A'la Mawdudi (1903–1979), and Ali Shariati (1933–1977). These served as bin Laden's ideological predecessors.

Al Qaeda belongs to the radical wing of Islamism known as Salafi-Jihadism, which has two main ideological sources:

Muslim Brotherhood ideology as promulgated by Sayyid Qutb, the main ideologue of the Muslim Brotherhood in the 1950s and 1960s. Qutb taught that the greatest crisis in the contemporary world is the return of humanity to the immoral and corrupt paganism of the pre-Islamic age of ignorance (*jahiliyya*) and the concurrent dethroning of God from his rightful sovereignty and rule (*hakimiyya*). *Jahiliyya* is not only the historical, pre-Islamic era of paganism; it is an ever-present condition of denying God's rule, usurping his authority, and living by human laws that engender oppression. *Jahiliyya* is always evil in whatever form it manifests itself, always seeking to crush true Islam.

Qutb claimed that the first step toward Islamic renewal was the judging of all societies, institutions, and regimes by the criterion of their adherence to the doctrine of God's sovereignty, as revealed by their implementation of sharia and their repudiation of western-influenced legal systems. All those that did not fulfill this criterion were to be excommunicated (*takfir*) and denounced as *jahili*. Jihad "by force" (*bil saif*) had to be used to annihilate *jahili* regimes and replace them by true Muslim ones.[30] Qutb denounced all western societies, whether Christian, Jewish, or Communist, as well as all contemporary Muslim societies as *jahili*, making them into legitimate targets of active *jihad*; he asserted that no truly Islamic state existed in the world in his day.

Qutb's reinterpretation of *jahiliyya* and *takfir* unsheathed a tempting weapon for radicals—the pronouncement of all rival groups and individuals as infidels *(kuffar)*—thus paving the way for indiscriminate terror. All radical movements have used the concepts of *jahiliyya* and *takfir* to legitimize their actions. They are willing to denounce as *kuffar* whole societies (including Muslim ones) and regimes as well as individuals. Radical movements claim that gradualist attempts at reform are un-Koranic, and view most regimes in Muslim countries as in a state of *jahiliyya*. For contemporary radicals, however, modern *jahiliyya* is far worse than that of the pre-Islamic era as it includes the rejection of the message of Islam. "It is not a *jahiliyya* of ignorance, but a *jahiliyya* of conscious rejection."[31]

Wahhabi-Salafi ideology. Wahhabi Islam is the dominant form of state Islam in Saudi Arabia. It is linked to Salafism, which rejects the schools of law and later developments in Islam and demands a return to the early model of Muhammad, his Companions (the *salaf*), and their followers. Salafis limit religious authority to the Koran and *Hadith* interpreted in a literalist manner. In recent decades, Wahhabi Islam has become part of cultural Islam, and according to Muslim scholar Khaled M. Abu al-Fadl, is now the dominant school of Islamic thought:

> The Wahhabi school of thought, empowered by its newfound wealth, was easily accom-modated by the anti-intellectual and ahistorical trends of the late 1970s and 1980s. In fact, I believe it is fair to say that by the 1990s Wahhabism had become the dominant system of thought in the Muslim world.[32]

While many Salafis adhere to the traditional injunction of obedience to all Muslim rulers, even unjust ones, they are deeply hostile to any suggestion of the reform and reinterpretation of Islam. Wahhabi Salafism has supported most radical Muslim groups around the world, thus increasing their power and escalating their slide into terrorism. The more radical Salafis, the Salafi-Jihadis, arose in opposition to the traditionalists following the preaching of Abu Muhammad Al-Maqdisi from 1992 onward, which emphasized the need to overthrow "impious" regimes through violent means. They accept the concept of labeling other Muslims as infidels (the practice of *takfir*), as taught and practiced by the founder of Wahhabism, Muhammad ibn 'Abd al-Wahhab (1703–1792), and the waging of active *jihad* against them. They also emphasize the doctrine of universal loyalty among true Muslims and an openly active hatred of all non-Muslims, expressed in a permanent battle against them (*al-wala' wal-bara'*), until they submit to Islam, either by converting or by accepting minority *dhimmi* status.[33]

Al Qaeda thus integrates Salafi-Wahhabi teachings with Qutbist doctrines. It uses a mixture of reinterpreted traditional concepts such as *jahiliyya* (neo-paganism), *takfir* (ex-communication), *jihad* (holy struggle), and *istishhad* (martyrdom) to justify terrorism, in-discriminate violence, and suicide bomb attacks. While classical Islam carefully delimited the contexts in which these concepts could be invoked, al Qaeda has developed a variety of interpretations, based on ancient precedents of early Muslim groups and contemporary *fatwas* by a variety of *ulama*, to defend and promote its strategy.

Al Qaeda follows 'Abdullah 'Azzam, bin Laden's mentor, in glorifying *jihad* as one of the main pillars of Islam and as the solution to all problems faced by Muslims in the present world order. *Jihad* is both offensive and defensive and is God's method of estab-lishing Islam in the world.[34] According to 'Azzam,

> We are terrorists. Every Muslim must be a terrorist. Terrorism is an obligation as dem-onstrated in the Koran and the Sunna. Allah Most High said: "Muster against them [infidels] all the men and cavalry at your command, so that you may strike terror into the heart of your enemy and Allah's enemy" [Q. 8:60] Thus terrorism is a [religious] obligation. And the Messenger of Allah is the first terrorist and the first menace.[35]

Al Qaeda divides the world into two incompatible camps, one of true Islam (God's camp) and the other of infidelity (Satan's camp). As we have seen, this division origi-nated in the classical Islamic categories of *Dar al-Islam* and *Dar al-Harb*; they are not an Islamist innovation. There is a permanent war between the two camps, and there are no neutrals or innocents. On the one hand is the camp of world Christianity allied to Zionist Jewry and led by the United States, Great Britain, and Israel; on the other hand is the Mus-lim world.[36] The conspiracy led by America, Great Britain, and Israel is the great enemy, an infidel Crusader-Jewish alliance under the cover of the United Nations fighting against

Islam.[37] So al Qaeda's various elements are united by their hatred of the West (especially the United States), as well as of the "illegitimate" regimes in Muslim states. Bin Laden repeats the doctrine of obligatory perpetual hostility to infidels, with whom there can be no coexistence.[38]

Al Qaeda ideology is utopian, sharing with communism a worldview that Rosenau calls an "unprogramatic simplicity": a vague utopian dream of a future paradise to be achieved through revolutionary violence and sacrifice, but lacking detailed specifics on the basic issues of governance, the structure of the state, and the political system. As communism called for the dictatorship of the proletariat, so al Qaeda calls for the reestablishment of the caliphate. Both visions, however, lack specific and basic details of implementation. Al Qaeda ideology ignores fundamental questions of governance, of how political decisions would be made and of how the state should be structured. It offers a vague image of a future paradise to be achieved "through armed struggle, discipline, and revolutionary rigor," but offers no concrete plans of how to implement it. This is one of the weaknesses of the radical Islamist project.[39]

The ultimate, inflexible goal of al Qaeda is the achievement of complete victory over all infidel powers, within and without the Muslim world, and the establishment of a pan-Islamic caliphate throughout the world. This strategic goal is considered so self-evident that it needs no discussion. No half-solutions or bargaining are permitted. Steps along the way include the overthrow of regimes it deems non-Islamic and the expulsion of westerners and non-Muslims from Muslim countries. A main aim is the expulsion of US forces from Muslim lands, especially Afghanistan, Iraq, Saudi Arabia, and the Gulf. The United States is seen as the primary enemy of Islam at this time. The end of all western influence in the Muslim world and the destruction of Israel are further aims, as is the support of all *jihad* groups around the world including in Chechnya, Bosnia, Eritrea, Algeria, Sudan, Somalia, Indonesia, Thailand, and the Philippines. Bin Laden claims it is the duty of every Muslim to fight for the establishment of Islamic states in all areas that have ever been under Muslim control at any time in history.

One important tactic used by al Qaeda (and most Islamist groups) is the practice of dissimulation (*taqiyya*): the use of different discourses aimed at different audiences. To the West and to potential recruits it uses the language of grievances and reciprocity. The West has repeatedly attacked, invaded, humiliated, and oppressed Muslim lands and people, so terrorism is simply a legitimate defensive Muslim reaction to western aggression. To its own constituency, it teaches the doctrine of eternal enmity and war against all infidels until they convert to Islam or submit to its rule. This includes the doctrine of aggressive, offensive *jihad* aimed at spreading Islamic dominion over the whole world.[40]

In the view of some commentators, bin Laden is a *khariji*[41] Muslim, a heretic, a non-Muslim, and a criminal. There is an increasing reluctance to admit that he is a Muslim, who affirms the Islamic creed (the normal test of a Muslim), and is in no way a heretic or infidel. By and large bin Laden adheres to the classical teachings of Islam, as formulated by the *ulama* in the early centuries, although sometimes he steps beyond their boundaries, for example in setting aside the classical principle that *jihad* may be declared only by a caliph. Bin Laden's Islamist ideology is in reality little more than classical Islamic doctrine interpreted along Islamist Qutbist and Salafist lines. Denial of this fact has serious and dangerous consequences in that his ideology is virtually impossible to undermine if its true nature is not recognized.

It is difficult for Muslims, even moderate Muslims, to classify bin Laden and other Islamist radicals as heretics. Even if they are very judgmental toward non-Muslims, in traditional Islam, it is forbidden to judge other Muslims simply by their actions. It is their inner intent that is important. Muslims may be misguided and mistaken in their actions, but so long as they accept the main witness and creed of Islam, they remain Muslims, and no one may say that they cannot attain Paradise. Ultimately, only God may judge them, on judgment day. It is for this reason that Muslim scholars always conclude their contributions with "And Allah knows best."

Of course, many radical Muslims refuse to criticize bin Laden not for this reason, but because they support him. Some of them see him as a modern Saladin who will restore Islam to its former glory. On the other hand, some Muslims do want to speak out against him and al Qaeda, but they are afraid to do so. The claim of the moderate British Muslim scholar and convert to Islam, Abdal Hakim Murad, that bin Laden's indiscriminate violence is heretical is therefore exceptional.[42]

In an unexpected development in 2008, a senior Islamist cleric, Sayyid Imam al-Sharif, published a book attacking al Qaeda. Al-Sharif is a longtime associate of bin Laden's lieutenant Ayman al-Zawahiri, but he is currently in prison in Egypt, and from there he had already written a critique of contemporary jihadism. His new book accuses al-Zawahiri and bin Laden of apostasy and compares them to the *Dajjal* or antichrist. He claims that al Qaeda has founded a heretical school of jurisprudence for the single purpose of justifying their own actions. Although al-Zawahiri claims to believe that al-Sharif is writing under duress, he considers the latter's arguments worthy of detailed response. The clash may indicate the beginning of a fault line within al Qaeda itself on the organization's practice of *jihad*.[43]

Trends in Western Counterterrorist Efforts

The recent tendency of western governments and security services to marginalize the fight against terrorism and counter only its most violent aspects may be doing no more than gaining time. The idea is to placate Muslim societies worldwide and Muslims in the West so as to ensure security and peaceful relations, which are especially important in an age of increased western dependence on Muslim oil and gas resources. It is also hoped that Muslim states will be valuable allies in any potential confrontation with a resurgent Russia or a belligerent China. Language is adapted to lessen any perceived provocation of Muslims, as in the claims that "Islam is a religion of peace," "There are no Islamic terrorists," and "Islam has nothing to do with terrorism."

A paper written by American counterterrorism experts recommended that westerners cease using the word *jihad* to denote the main doctrine of the radical Islamic groups, and the word *mujahedin* to denote their members. It also recommended not using the term "caliphate" to denote their ultimate goal of a worldwide Islamic state under sharia.[44] A US Homeland Security memo dealing with the strategic use of terminology in counterterrorism recommended that US government officials avoid using theological terms in describing al Qaeda, so as to deny it any religious legitimacy.[45]

These word plays may be tactically useful in promoting social cohesion, but if used as a basis for counterterrorism strategy they will eventually backfire. The totalitarian Islamist ideological camp will continue quietly but inexorably to further its control of Muslim states and societies, while infiltrating western centers of power—political, cultural, and economic—under the veil afforded it by western media, academia, and governments.

Suggestions that radical Islamists should be called "un-Islamic extremists" so as not to encourage their sense of pride as the vanguard of true Islam are potentially dangerous, because they blur the true identity of the enemy.[46] Nor should opposition to Islamism be constrained by the alleged danger of ordinary Muslims, failing to understand the difference between Islam and Islamists, and thus feeling accused, resentful, and alienated. Ordinary Muslims need to be reminded of the affinity between Islamism and classical Islam and to unite in denouncing it and drawing a clear line between Islamists and themselves.[47] Otherwise Islamism is granted legitimacy by western governments and media, and ordinary Muslims are left defenseless against its persuasion.

Attempts at defending Islam against charges that it is linked to violence and to nefarious schemes are also dangerous. Advocates of this approach argue that accusations of a linkage between Islam and violence implicitly label all Muslims in the West as potential terrorists. Such allegations are depicted as emanating from the extreme right (xenophobic, neo-Fascist, and racist) and thus unworthy of serious deliberation. But the claim that those concerned about Islamist ideology necessarily see Islam itself and all Muslims as a threat is demonstrably inaccurate.[48] Acceptance of it by government and the security services would again deflect their focus from the real source of danger, which is allowing Islamists to continue advancing their program.

Western academic apologetics for Islamic *jihad*, which spiritualize it and downplay its nature as an imperative grounded in Muhammad's example and commands, tend to conceal the real intentions of Islamists and dull perceptions of the threat posed by their commitment to the goal of Islamic hegemony by all means. An example of this problem is a US government website that used to include a dictionary of Islamic terminology that stated, "jihad should not be confused with Holy War, [which] does not exist in Islam."[49]

While tactical imperatives may require some negotiation with Islamists, the belief of some in the West that Islamist movements are committed to democracy, tolerance, and peace are without foundation. Democracy appears to be simply one tactical path among many that Islamists follow toward the goal of political power, which they pursue in order to impose the Islamist version of the totalitarian Islamic state under the rule of sharia.

I suggest that advocates of all these views and approaches have not taken full and proper account of the ideology of Islamism described above. This ideology reveals that Islamist extremists are enemies of western civilization and combine the worst elements of totalitarian ideological movements:

> The theocratic intolerance of the inquisition, the fifth-column potential of revolutionary Communism, the implacable racialism of the Nazis, and the readiness of each to deny justice, human rights and life itself to any perceived adversary.[50]

The ideology demonstrates that Islamism has a specific doctrine:

> Aiming as it does to impose extreme theocratic rule upon the existing Muslim world, and eventually beyond its borders. The views and values of extreme theocracies are implacably opposed to those of a West currently engaged—whether realizing it or not—in fighting to preserve its own civilization.[51]

The ideology indicates that Islamism is deceptive: classical and well-established rules of *jihad* include the claim that "war is deceit" and that dissimulation and breaking of treaties are part of the Islamic arsenal.[52] Western analysts must understand this principle, which is seen by Islamists as religiously legitimated in times of war.

These trends also reflect an implicit denial of the Islamist threat. But the reality of this can readily be seen in any region or state falling under Islamist dominion: Iran, Sudan, Afghanistan under the Taliban, and Gaza under Hamas, among others. The consistent Islamist drive for the Islamization of the state is clearly seen in such countries as Pakistan and Egypt.

The limiting of counterterrorism to the military, judicial, and criminal spheres, moreover, fails to recognize the reality of the ideological universe of Islamism, its roots in certain aspects of classical Islam, and its global claims to hegemony in all spheres of human existence and in all geographical regions. More recently, there have been those who realize the importance of facing up to the ideological basis of Islamist terrorism and who suggest an ideological campaign based on lessons from the Cold War against communism. They emphasize the concepts of political warfare, strategic influence, psychological operations, and propaganda that were used in the Cold War while searching for better terms to apply in the campaign against Islamist ideology, terms that will capture the essence of the main objective: "prevailing in the longer term over the ideology that gives rise to Islamist terrorism."[53]

With reference to Al-Muqrin's *A Practical Course for Guerrilla War*, Norman Cigar writes:

> Al-Muqrin's work also reminds us that we have to accept the enemy as he is, not as we would like to see him in conformance with some theoretical constructs, and that we cannot impose our vision on how an enemy should think or act.[54]

How to Undermine the Islamists' Ideology

Islamists recognize that the long-term war of ideas is the ultimate battleground. Theirs is a multifaceted *jihad*, being waged on many fronts: economic, political, diplomatic, intellectual, ideological, and military. Therefore, the strategy to undermine Islamist ideology must be equally comprehensive and must think equally long term.

Undermining the extremist ideology of Islamism in general and of al Qaeda in particular is the only strategy that offers hope of a permanent solution to the threat of Islamist terrorism. For this it is essential to have an awareness of and a willingness to face the legitimacy that Islamist ideology derives from classical Islamic theology. It is important carefully to study and analyze Islamist ideology, history, and practice, and the reasons for its wide appeal to ordinary Muslims. It is necessary to recognize the success with which

Islamists have embedded their message into mainstream Islam and the sophistication of their use of propaganda and media.

Islamism must be discredited as an ideology that dehumanizes its adherents, a totalitarian, political, utopian ideology detrimental to all Muslims, and an ideology that denies the dignity of all humanity—an ideology of death. It is necessary to expose the weakness of Islamist ideas (including the view that Islam is under attack from the West) and broadcast Islamist failures, crimes, and brutalities. To delegitimize the Islamists, it is vital that "all who need to resist them be made aware of what they believe, declare and intend to do." This approach will isolate Islamists and might subvert some of their more moderate elements.[55]

Islamism's ability to project its ideology to the wider world must also be restricted. This policy will involve cutting off the sources of its financial, social, and political support. Simultaneously, the content of its message can be made less effective by dividing and diluting its ideology. But the most fundamental way in which Islamist ideology can be undermined is by replacing it with a counter-ideology.

In order to discredit Islamism and undermine al Qaeda, it is vital to "win hearts and minds" in the Muslim world. A main indicator of success in the counter-ideology campaign is when Muslims themselves take up the theme. The influence of non-Muslims is of a necessity rather limited. The possibility of successful persuasion on a wide scale lies in the hands of Muslims themselves. This is recognized by Michael Hayden, former director of the CIA, who has spoken of the need for authentic (i.e., Islamic) voices in the war of ideas.

> Even today, as we speak, in New York City, one of the most prominent voices in Islam, King Abdullah of Saudi Arabia, the keeper of the two holy places, is right now sponsoring and attending an international symposium on religious tolerance. I've always said that the civilized world will win this fight when we win the war of ideas. And so these developments are very, very promising. And I should underscore, this conflict of ideas requires authentic voices. And in the world as we find it, in this conflict as we find it, authentic voices are Islamic voices. And what I've just referred to are Islamic voices speaking out against Al Qaeda.[56]

The mobilization of alternative anti-Islamist ideologies within Islam should focus on its progressive, liberal, and secularist elements. This strategy may take decades to yield substantive results. It must be handled with great care, as too much overt non-Muslim support may be damaging. Credible allies within Islam could include Sufi movements[57] (so long as they are peaceful) and liberal reform-oriented individuals or groups. It will include the encouragement, support, and funding of such Muslim movements, organizations, NGOs, and political parties, helping them become a powerful force within global Islam. It will involve the encouragement and active support of individual writers, scholars, journalists, and other anti-Islamist intellectuals in the Muslim world. Some Muslim intellectuals are already mounting sophisticated attacks on radical Islamism, and these should be given a wider hearing across the Islamic world. Friendly regimes should be under pressure to give them the political space to develop and the freedom to impact the popular discourse and the political process, including access to the mass media.[58]

Friendly Muslim governments can be encouraged to develop sophisticated methods to combat the ideological justifications for Islamist terrorism. Good examples are the recent publication of the book *The Exposure*, written by Sayyid Imam al-Sharif (also known as Dr. Fadl), the former leader of Egyptian Islamic Jihad, which refutes jihadi violence;[59] and the Saudi rehabilitation programs designed to encourage jihadi supporters and sympathizers to renounce violence, including aftercare programs to prevent them falling back and to reintegrate them into Saudi society.[60]

In certain geographical contexts it may be that progressive and liberal Muslims are nonexistent; in these cases the best alternatives would be carefully selected traditionalists or tribal groups that harbor resentment against the Islamists.

The kind of ideologies to look for and support are those that aim to liberalize Islamic teaching on *jihad, sharia*, and the relationship of religion and state. They should reject a literal interpretation of the Islamic sources, especially on the subjects of *jihad*, the caliphate, and non-Muslims. They should weaken the authority of the *Hadith*, and interpret violent passages in the Koran and *Hadith* as normative only in their immediate historical contexts and therefore not applicable today. Such ideologies should support the view of Muhammad as a fallible human who sinned in the violent episodes of his life and reject the classical view that his example is to be emulated in every detail by Muslims in every age. Ideologies of this kind spiritualize the Islamic teaching on *jihad*, seeing it as a moral battle against personal sin; they explicitly deny the validity of military and violent aspects of *jihad* for today, and support the separation between state and religion.

It is notable that in the Amman Message of 2004 the Muslim *ulama* rejected *takfir* as a tool for use against other Muslims.[61] This could, in theory, be a first step toward the rejection by Muslim scholars of violence against all people. At that point the concept of violent *jihad* would be consigned to history. Such signals of hope should be welcomed and further progress encouraged.

A pitfall to avoid when mobilizing alternative ideologies is support for seemingly moderate Islamists. As we have seen, there is no hard and fast boundary between gradualist Islamists and radical Islamists: The former can easily evolve into the latter. They share the same goals, and ultimately the gradualists cannot but support the radicals. Gradualists often work by seeking to undermine governments' antiterrorism activities. Some western governments have already inadvertently strengthened the radical cause by courting Islamists whom they thought were "moderates." Therefore, support for "moderate Islamists" should be avoided, even if it seems to promise short-term benefits.

The campaign ought carefully to study and analyze the radicalization process in Muslim societies that recruits many into the Islamist (not just the terrorist) fold and devise effective measures to counter it.

In order to cut off sources of financial, social, and political support to al Qaeda and thus reduce its ability to spread its own ideology, it will be necessary to find long-term solutions to some of the local issues that fuel resentment and a sense of grievance. These can be dealt with effectively only by supporting good governance, including anticorruption drives, establishing development work and social-welfare services among poor and marginalized communities, finding political solutions to ongoing ethnic and national disputes, and in general "winning hearts and minds." In practical terms this approach involves support for infrastructure development, economic development, and social welfare projects by allied Muslim states and moderate/secular NGOs to counter the success of Islamist social welfare provision. The aim must be to prevent Islamist groups, including al Qaeda, from being an alternative source of services.

This part of the strategy must not be misunderstood to imply that Islamist terrorism is merely a product of socioeconomic problems. This common view ignores the vital driving force of religious ideology and the undeniable fact that wealthy, middle-class, and well-educated (even apparently westernized) Muslims are often drawn to terrorism. Bin Laden himself is hardly poor or illiterate.

These tactics must be applied differently in different parts of the world. Ungovernable regions and failed states that can serve as potential safe havens for Islamists need to be carefully monitored to see what action is possible. Al Qaeda's constant search for new safe havens in which to build new bases for terrorism, whether in Somalia, the Sahel, Yemen, Pakistan, the Far East, or any other unstable part of the world, must be energetically frustrated.[62] But pro-western, secular Muslim states should be encouraged and strengthened. Any Muslim region in danger of destabilization, failure, and conflict should be helped toward stability. Liberal and secular parties should be empowered wherever they are in the Muslim world.

At the same time as a counter-ideology is promoted and Islamist support cut off, the Islamist ideology can be weakened by dividing and diluting it. This strategy will require infiltration of al Qaeda and similar Islamist terrorist groups, and the exploiting of rivalries and ideological disputes among the Islamists themselves. Some elements may be considered reconcilable, and these should be engaged with, whereas those deemed irreconcilable should be neutralized. This is the classic counterterrorism double-I, double-N strategy (identify, isolate, neutralize, and negotiate)[63] applied to the wider sphere of al Qaeda and global Islamism. Islamists must be identified wherever they are and in whatever form they masquerade. Most importantly, they must be isolated from ordinary Muslims and prevented from penetrating their institutions and western centers of power, as well as from broadcasting their propaganda in all its forms. Finally, as they weaken, negotiation might be helpful in separating those willing to get out in order to gain the best deal they can. Negotiations must always be held from a position of strength, however, so as to manipulate fissures and create division among the Islamists.[64]

An important goal is to counter Islamist control and exploitation of the many modern media and communication channels while developing sophisticated, flexible, efficient, and targeted communications strategies to challenge Islamist assertions about ideology, Islam, and US policies.[65] As Julian Lewis asks, "Where is the Western response to the extensive output of the [Islamist] message via the Arab media and the internet?"[66] Islamists must be neutralized by measures that deny them any propaganda victories and popular sympathy in the West. This is an expensive but vital tactic.

Effective counterpropaganda and psychological operations in the Muslim world can also help expose Islamist duplicity and double-talk. It should discredit individual Islamist leaders, showing the barbarity of their actions, the duplicity of their communications, and the flaws in their ideological arguments as compared with those of alternative ideologies. According to Lewis, "Systematic use against one's opponents of their own words, promises and predictions has always been a most effective propaganda tool."[67] Where possible, censorship—for example, by shutting down the servers that carry the Islamists' message—should be employed.

At the same time the active war on Islamist terrorism must not be forgotten; "[t]he military must protect the population from terrorists and insurgents, deny jihadists freedom of movement, and isolate insurgents from the population."[68] Effective counterterrorism will involve cooperation between many different security forces and governments.

It is also important to realize that western public sympathy for terrorist causes, expressed in the claim that terror is the only weapon of the "oppressed" and of the "wretched of the earth," who have no other choice, serves only to legitimize their immoral and criminal acts and to strengthen their cause. All western groups, individuals, and movements that support and sustain Islamist discourse and power must be delegitimized. This is important in politics, the media, and the academic world, where radical Islamism has found allies and apologists in the West. For example, the socialist former mayor of London, Ken Livingstone, has given his support to some Islamist organizations in the United Kingdom, such as the Muslim Association of Britain (MAB), which represents the Muslim Brotherhood, and to Yusuf al-Qaradawi, the popular Sunni sheikh alleged to be the Muslim Brotherhood's spiritual leader.

To defang the main grievances of Muslims worldwide, the West must invest resources and pressure in finding a peaceful negotiated solution to the Palestine and Kashmir problems.

Conclusion

The war against the ideology that drives al Qaeda and similar radical Islamist jihadi groups is of necessity a long and many-sided one. The search for quick fixes, for easy methods, for compromise and appeasement serves only to strengthen the extremists. The ideological war of ideas must be waged with great firmness so as to contain and then reverse the impact of Islamism on Muslim societies worldwide. Defining the enemy is imperative: Islamist movements and their ideology, including the Muslim Brotherhood, Jama'at-i-Islami, Ahl-i-Hadith, Salafism, and radical Deobandis must be identified as such alongside the jihadi, takfiri, and Salafi-Jihadi organizations. As in the Cold War against communism, the West must be willing to mobilize its resources to discredit and weaken its ideological adversary. It is important to set up a multifaceted network of counterterrorist and counter-ideological institutions that will study Islamism and devise and implement methods to discredit and destroy it.

A main aim should be the gaining of allies within the Muslim world. These can then be resourced and empowered to resist the Islamist ideology from within by developing and disseminating alternative, peaceful, Muslim ideologies and spiritual interpretations that ring true to Muslims and might convince many. They include progressive Muslims of the secular and the liberal kind who accept the separation of religion from the state, and see the need radically to change traditional, orthodox Islam in such a way as to place liberal humanistic values at its very core. This indirect method is likely to be far more fruitful than direct argument addressed by non-Muslims to Muslims. While non-Muslims may hope to win some minds, it is unrealistic to think that they can win many hearts as well; only Muslims can win the hearts of Muslims.

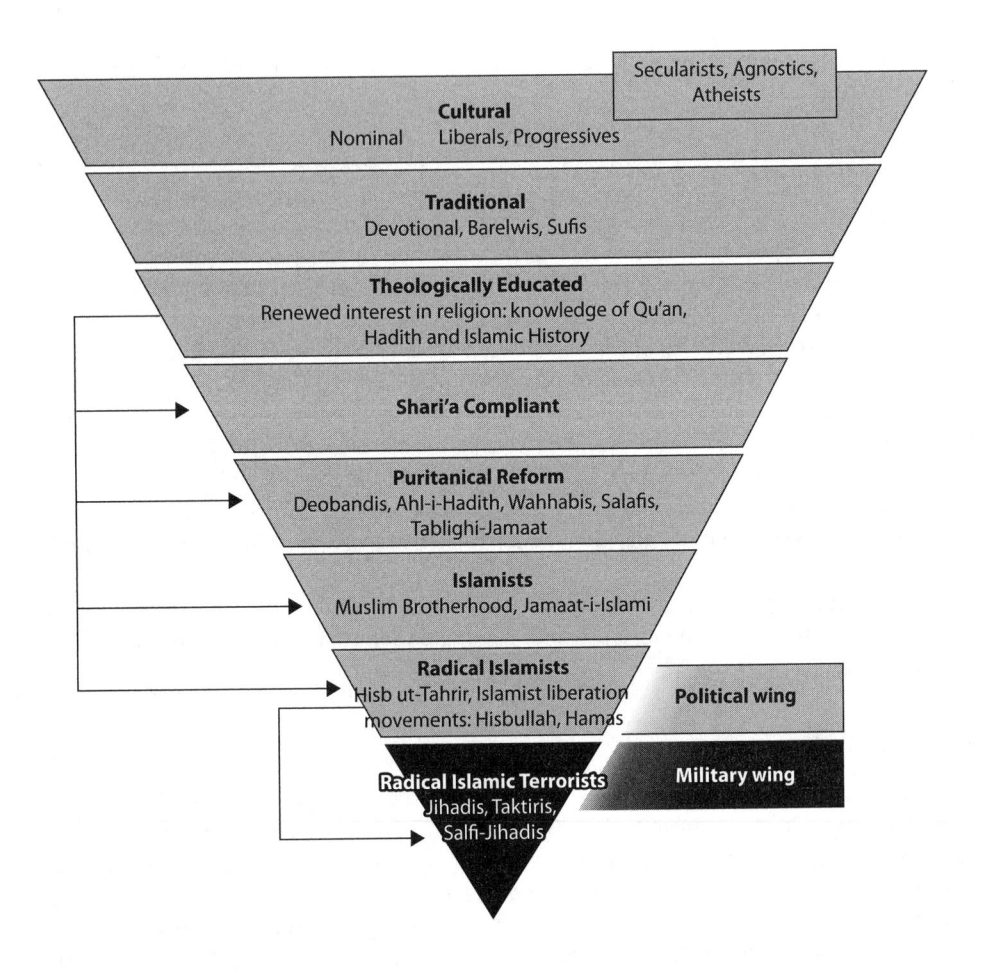

A rejection by Muslims of the radical, violent stream of Islam that is based on the literal interpretation of its sources ought to be a main goal of western counterterrorist efforts. But in order to achieve this, the West must first understand the differences within the Muslim community, and how individual Muslims become radicalized.

The Muslim community can be viewed (see diagram above) as an inverted pyramid of eight sections (with a small and semidetached group of secularists, agnostics, and atheists, who hardly merit the designation "Muslim"). In the uppermost bar are cultural Muslims, whose identity is Muslim but who do not practice many of the duties of Islam. In the point of the pyramid are the radical Islamic terrorists, who include al Qaeda and other Salafi-jihadis; these act as the military wing of the radical Islamists in the bar immediately above, who operate in the political sphere. Between these two are various other kinds of Muslims, whose adherence to the Islamist ideology that we have described in this chapter is greater the further down the pyramid they appear. An individual Muslim moves downward from his original position as he becomes educated in his faith and later radicalized by the various Islamist ideologies, ending in the terrorist groups at the bottom.

The most common movements are shown by the arrows. The Islamist ideology is implicit in some aspects of Muslim theology and sharia, such as the integration of religion and politics, the rule of sharia over the whole of life, the priority of loyalty to the global *umma*, and the centrality of *jihad*. Therefore, anyone in the third bar (theologically educated) or the fourth (*sharia* compliant) is liable to move further down. When those in the fifth bar (puritanical reform) press their reformist agenda to its extremes, they move to the sixth bar (Islamists), and when Islamists do the same with their political agenda, they move to the seventh (radical Islamists). From there they may be transferred to the military wing. So once Muslims are educated in Islamic theology, they begin to experience a dynamic that drives them toward radicalism and even violence, and although most of them resist this to a greater or lesser extent, some do not and eventually become terrorists. (It is true that theologically educated Muslims may also move to the bar above, but this change is relatively unusual.)

A Muslim who is being radicalized normally moves toward the point of the pyramid by stages. Dr. Tawfik Hamid, who was indoctrinated and radicalized as a medical student in Cairo under the influence of Ayman al-Zawahiri, has described this process.[69] Hamid began as a cultural Muslim, who believed in the central doctrines of Islam and affirmed its practices but did not himself practice his faith consistently. Through a process of theological instruction (the purpose of which was "to make the individual into a living Koran"), he became much more fully convinced of the tenets of Islamic theology and the need to be faithful to it. He was then introduced to *sharia* and encouraged to order his life according to it, and he began to fulfill its duties, accepting both its attitude to non-Muslims and the principle of *jihad*. Finally, he embraced Islamist ideology in its radical and violent form. Thus, he made a complete journey from the upper bar of the cultural Muslim to the point of the violent jihadist. (He has since renounced Islamism altogether.)

It should be noted, however, that the process is not always gradual. Some individuals have become terrorists very quickly, jumping over one or more of the upper bars to the point. The incidence of this rapid transformation is higher among converts to Islam and people of more limited intellectual ability. It often takes place not by means of instruction but as a response to specific grievances.

It might seem obvious that the key transition points from one bar to another must be guarded very carefully, and that western governments, security agencies, law enforcement bodies, and other institutions should avoid pushing Muslims further down the diagram toward an Islamist ideology. In fact, however, it is often argued that young people are being radicalized because they do not know Islam. On this view, Muslims who have a full and proper understanding of their faith and of *sharia* will be able to resist the attractions of Islamism. As a result, many western counterterrorist approaches have been directed to strengthening and encouraging Muslims in their faith, for example, by the funding of madrassas.

These approaches are likely to be counterproductive. It is sometimes assumed by western leaders that any religion, fully and rightly understood, must be inherently peaceable. But Islam does not tend to make its followers peaceable, and educating them in Islamic theology and *sharia* may well push some of them not only into the third and fourth bars, but through them to the lower levels. Islam is after all the religion of submission to God's revelation through Muhammad and at its very core lies the duty of following Muhammad's paradigmatic model (*sunna*), which includes aggression, violence, and *jihad*. It follows that Islam should never be promoted as a means of counterterrorism.

Instead a twofold approach is required to arrest the drift toward radicalism. First, a suffocation strategy must be developed, whereby the flow of individuals toward the point of the pyramid is choked and eventually cut off. But second, to change the metaphor, the toxin of violent jihadism within the Islamic community must be combated directly by the introduction of an antitoxin. This should partly take the form of a counter-ideology, such as that outlined above. But it should also include the concepts of peace, love, and forgiveness, in opposition to those of violence, hatred, and resentment. It is by these means that the ideology of al Qaeda, and of the Islamism that it represents, may best be effectively confronted and finally defeated.

Patrick Sookhdeo Dr. Sookhdeo gained his Ph.D. from London University's School of Oriental and African Studies. He also holds a D.D. from Western Seminary, Oregon, for work on pluralism, as well as a D.D. from Nashotah House, Wisconsin, for work on human rights and religious freedom. A regular lecturer for the George C. Marshall Center, Patrick Sookhdeo also teaches and advises at the Defence Academy of the United Kingdom, Cranfield University's Resilience Centre, the Royal Military College of Science, the Security Institute of the United Kingdom, and several US military commands. He is involved in pre-deployment training for UK armed forces and serves as advisor to the Permanent Joint Headquarters UK. Between 2007 and 2010, Dr. Sookhdeo has been a Cultural Advisor to British and/or international coalition forces in Iraq and regions of Afghanistan: Basra, Kabul, and Kandahar. Dr. Sookhdeo has written or edited numerous articles and books including *Understanding Islamist Terrorism* (2009), *Global Jihad* (2007), *Faith, Power and Territory: A Handbook of British Islam* (2008), *Understanding Sharia Finance* (2008) and *Freedom to Believe: Challenging Islam's Apostasy Law* (2009). In 1990, he was awarded the Templeton Prize, and in 2001, the Coventry Cathedral International Prize for Peace and Reconciliation.

Recommended Readings

Abou El Fadl, Khaled M. *And God Knows the Soldiers: The Authoritative and the Authoritarian in Islamic Discourses.* Revised edition. Lanham, MD: University Press of America, 2001.

Ahmad, Mumtaz. "Islamic Fundamentalism in South Asia: The Jamaat-i-Islami and the Tablighi Jamaat." In *Fundamentalisms Observed*, edited by Martin E. Marty and R. Scott Appleby. Chicago: University of Chicago Press, 1991.

'Azzam, 'Abdullah. *Defence of the Muslim Lands.* London: Ahle Sunnah Wal Jama'at, n.d.

Bergen, Peter, and Laurence Footer. "Defeating the Attempted Global Jihadist Insurgency: Forty Steps for the Next President to Pursue Against al Qaeda, Like-Minded Groups, Unhelpful State Actors, and Radicalized Sympathizers." *The ANNALS of the American Academy of Political and Social Science*, Vol. 618, No. 1 (2008): 232–247.

Boucek, Christopher. "Counter-Terrorism from Within: Assessing Saudi Arabia's Religious Rehabilitation and Disengagement Programme." *RUSI Journal*, Vol. 153, No. 6 (December 2008).

Davis, Jacquelyn K., and Charles M. Perry. "Rethinking the War on Terror, Developing a Strategy to Counter Extremist Ideologies: A Workshop Report." March 2007. Organized for U.S. Central Command (CENTCOM) with the support of The Defense Threat Reduction Agency (DTRA) under contract HDTRA1-06-F-0054.

Esposito, John L. *The Islamic Threat: Myth or Reality?* New York: Oxford University Press, 1992.

Guazzone, Laura. "Islamism and Islamists in the Contemporary Arab World." In *The Islamist Dilemma: The Political Role of Islamist Movements in the Contemporary Arab World*, edited by Laura Guazzone. Reading, UK: Ithaca Press, 1995.

Hamid, Tawfik. *Inside Jihad: Understanding and Confronting Radical Islam*. Self-published, 2008.

Khadduri, Majid. *War and Peace in the Law of Islam*. Baltimore, MD: Johns Hopkins University Press, 1955.

bin Laden, Osama. "Declaration of War Against the Americans Occupying the Land of the Two Holy Places." Formerly published at http://www.azzam.com/html/body_declaration.html, accessed 10 July 2002.

bin Laden, Osama. "Moderate Islam is a Prostration to the West." In *The Al Qaeda Reader*, edited by Raymond Ibrahim. New York: Doubleday, 2007.

Lewis, Bernard. *The Political Language of Islam*. Chicago and London: University of Chicago Press, 1988.

Malik, Brigadier S. K. *The Quranic Concept of War*. Lahore, Pakistan: Associated Printers, 1979.

al-Maqdisi, Abu Muhammad 'Asim. *Millat Ibrahim and the Calling of the Prophets and Messengers*. English trans. 2nd ed. London: At-Tibyan Publications, n.d.

Qutb, Sayyid. *Milestones (Ma'alim fil Tariq)*. English trans. Indianapolis: American Trust Publications, 1990.

Qutb, Sayyid. "Social Justice in Islam." In *Sayyid Qutb and Islamic Activism: A Translation and Critical Analysis of Social Justice in Islam*, edited by William Shepard. Leiden: E. J. Brill, 1966.

Rosenau, William. "Waging the 'War of Ideas.'" In *The McGraw-Hill Homeland Security Handbook*, edited by David Kamien. Columbus, OH: McGraw-Hill, 2005.

Satloff, Robert. *The Battle of Ideas in the War on Terror: Essays on U.S. Public Diplomacy in the Middle East*. Washington, D.C.: The Washington Institute for Near East Policy, 2004.

Shamaa, Mohammed Abu. "Former Al Qaeda Ideologue Exposes Al Zawahiri." *Asharq Alawsat*, November 19, 2008. Available at http://www.asharqalawsat.com/english/news.asp?section=3&id=14775, accessed 21 January 2009.

Strawson, John. "Encountering Islamic Law." Paper presented at the Critical Legal Conference, New College, Oxford, UK, 9–12 September 1993.

Streusand, Douglas E., and Harry D. Tunnell IV, "Choosing Words Carefully: Language to Help Fight Islamic Terrorism," *IOSphere*, Joint Information Operations Center, Fall 2006. Available at http://www.au.af.mil/info-ops/iosphere/06fall/iosphere_fall06_tunnell.pdf, accessed 12 May 2009.

The Terrorism Research Centre. "Usamah Bin-Laden, the Destruction of the Base." Interview with Usama bin-Laden conducted by Jamal Isma'il, aired 10 June 1999. Formerly published at http://www.terrorism.com/terrorism/BinLadinTranscript.shtm (accessed 10 July 2002).

Tibi, Bassam. "Countering Ideological Terrorism." *Defence Against Terrorism Review*, Vol. 1, No. 1 (Spring 2008).

Zaid, Nasr Hamid Abu. "Brutality and Civilisation—Violence and Terrorism?" In *War, Repression, Terrorism, Political Violence and Civilisation in Western and Muslim Societies*, edited by Jochen Hippler, 301–329. Stuttgart: Institut fur Auslandsbeziehungen/ Institute for Foreign Cultural Relations, 2006.

Notes

1. Frank Kitson, *Low Intensity Operations: Subversion, Insurgency, and Peacekeeping* (London: Faber and Faber, 1971), 78, quoted in William Rosenau, "Waging the 'War of Ideas,'" in *The McGraw-Hill Homeland Security Handbook*, ed. David Kamien (Columbus, OH: McGraw-Hill, 2005), 1131–1148.

2. Stephen P. Lambert, *Y: The Sources of Islamic Revolutionary Conduct* (Washington, DC: Center for Strategic Intelligence Research, Joint Military Intelligence College, 2005), 171. Available at http://www.dia.mil/college/pubs/pdf/5674.pdf, accessed 21 September 2009.

3. National Commission on Terrorist Attacks Upon the United States, *The 9/11 Commission Report,* Official Government Edition (Washington, D.C.: U.S. Printing Office, 2004), 363. Available at http://www.gpoaccess.gov/911/, accessed 21 September 2009.

4. Michael Doran, "The Pragmatic Fanaticism of al Qaeda: An Anatomy of Extremism in the Middle East," *Political Science Quarterly*, Vol. 117, No. 2 (Summer 2002): 187.

5. The deeper malaise is the confusion within the Islamic world as to its relationship with modernity and its inability to adapt to the fast changes taking place in the world. It includes the indecision as to whether Islam is willing to accept a peaceful role, or aspire (in the traditional classic mode) to reconstruct its "lost glory" and achieve dominance and hegemony in world affairs.

6. Fred Burton and Scott Stewart, "Al Qaeda and the Tale of Two Battlespaces," Stratfor Global Intelligence, 1 October 2008, available at http://www.stratfor.com/weekly/20081001_al_qaeda_and_tale_two_battlespaces, accessed 20 January 2009.

7. Marc Sageman, *Leaderless Jihad: Terror Networks in the Twenty-First Century* (Philadelphia: University of Pennsylvania Press, 2008). See also book review by Robert R. Reilly, "Thinking Like A Terrorist," *Claremont Review of Books*, Spring 2009, 31–33, available at http://www.claremont.org/publications/crb/id.1619/article_detail.asp, accessed 21 September 2009.

8. On the relationship between Center of Gravity and Critical Vulnerability, see: Joe Strange and Richard Iron, "Understanding Centers of Gravity and Critical Vulnerabilities, Part 2: The CG-CC-CR-CV Construct: A Useful Tool to Understand and Analyze the Relationship Between Centers of Gravity and Their Critical Vulnerabilities," available at http://www.au.af.mil/au/awc/awcgate/usmc/cog2.pdf, accessed 12 May 2009.

9. Norman Cigar, *Al-Qa'ida's Doctrine for Insurgency: 'Abd Al-'Aziz Al-Muqrin's 'A Practical Course for Guerrilla War'* (Dulles, VA: Potomac Books, 2008), 35.

10. E. M. Forster, *A Passage to India* (Orlando FLA: Harcourt, 1924; repr. Borders. 1989), Ch. xi, 131. The repetition of the last word is in the original.

11. Mumtaz Ahmad, "Islamic Fundamentalism in South Asia: The Jamaat-i-Islami and the Tablighi Jamaat," in *Fundamentalisms Observed*, edited by Martin E. Marty and R. Scott Appleby (Chicago: University of Chicago Press, 1991), 507.

12. Jacquelyn K. Davis and Charles M. Perry, "Rethinking the War on Terror, Developing a Strategy to Counter Extremist Ideologies: A Workshop Report," March 2007, organized for U.S. Central Command (CENTCOM) with the support of the Defense Threat Reduction Agency (DTRA) under contract HDTRA1-06-F-0054.

13. Gabriel Ben-Dor, "The Uniqueness of Islamic Fundamentalism," in *Religious Radicalism in the Greater Middle East*, edited by Bruce Maddy-Weitzman and Efraim Inbar (London: Frank Cass, 1997), 241.

14. Sayyid Qutb, "Social Justice in Islam," in *Sayyid Qutb and Islamic Activism: A Translation and Critical Analysis of Social Justice in Islam*, edited by William Shepard (Leiden, the Netherlands: E. J. Brill, 1966), 277.

15. Both Muslims and many westerners, Christian and secular, accuse Christianity of being a violent religion intent on propagating itself and gaining dominance in the world through war and persecution. The Crusades, the inquisition, and the colonial period are offered as examples. This presumed equivalence of Christianity and Islam in their use of violence serves the apologetic purposes of Islamists, and the accusations against Christianity are widely disseminated, thus appearing to justify Islamic violence (while concurrently suppressing the historical fact of Islamic violence). The difference between both religions in their attitudes to violence, is, however, found in their sacred source texts and the persons and teachings of their founders. Christians have frequently in their long history departed from Christ's teachings and perpetrated cruelties against Jews, Muslims, and heretics. When returning to their source scriptures, however, they come face to face with the person of Christ and the gospel of love and reconciliation he preached, as well as his supreme example of service, suffering, and nonviolence. When Muslims return to their original sources, they meet Muhammad, the Koran, and the example of Muhammad's words and deeds (recorded in the *hadith*), which are considered as perfect in every way and to be followed by all Muslims at all times. Following

the doctrine of abrogation, the later aggressive and warlike verses of the Koran given in Medina are accepted by most as valid for today, while the more peaceful Meccan verses are viewed as superseded and abrogated. Islam has set up Muhammad as the supreme example in every aspect of his words and actions, and so has included his use of violence as part of its binding paradigm. This is the real cause of the contradictions so prevalent in Islamic societies and Islamic history, especially on issues relating to *jihad*, the treatment of women, and the contempt shown to non-Muslims.

16. Bernard Lewis, *The Political Language of Islam* (Chicago: University of Chicago Press, 1988), 92.

17. Nasr Hamid Abu Zaid, "Brutality and Civilisation—Violence and Terrorism?" in *War, Repression, Terrorism, Political Violence and Civilisation in Western and Muslim Societies*, edited by Jochen Hippler (Stuttgart: Institut fur Auslandsbeziehungen/Institute for Foreign Cultural Relations, 2006), 301–329. Available via the Transnational Institute at http://www.tni.org/detail_page.phtml?page=archives_hippler_politicalviolence, accessed 21 September 2009.

18. There are a variety of such voices, but they still form a small minority within the Islamic world. Many of these Muslims live in exile in the West because of repression in their home countries. Nasr Hamid Abu Zaid (now in the Netherlands), Ziauddin Sardar and Ehsan Masood (in the United Kingdom), Bassam Tibi (in Germany), and the Malaysian "Sisters in Islam" are examples. In Indonesia the former President Abdurrahman Wahid (Gus Dur) and Ulil Abshar-Abdalla of the Liberal Islam Network could be included.

19. The Gateway Trust is a British educational charity aiming at encouraging the publication, in English and other European languages, of the works of nonfiction writers from Arab-speaking and predominantly Muslim countries. For more information, see www.gatewaytrust.org, accessed 21 September 2009.

20. Ehsan Masood, "A Muslim Journey," *Prospect Magazine*, Issue 113 (28 August 2005), available at http://www.prospectmagazine.co.uk/2005/08/amuslimjourney/, accessed 21 September 2009.

21. Gabriel Ben-Dor, op. cit., 241; John L. Esposito, *The Islamic Threat: Myth or Reality?* (New York: Oxford University Press, 1992), 22–23.

22. Abdel Salam Sidahmed and Anoushiravan Ehteshami, eds., *Islamic Fundamentalism* (Boulder, CO: Westview Press, 1996), 1.

23. The *umma* is the the universal Muslim community based on shared Islamic faith and the implementation of Islamic law (*sharia*). It is a transnational community that transcends ethnic, racial, linguistic, and national identities, and it demonstrates the essential unity of Muslims in diverse geographical and cultural settings.

24. Laura Guazzone, "Islamism and Islamists in the Contemporary Arab World," in *The Islamist Dilemma: The Political Role of Islamist Movements in the Contemporary Arab World*, edited by Laura Guazzone (Reading, UK: Ithaca Press, 1995), 10–12.

25. Gabriel Ben-Dor, op. cit., 239–240; see also: Gabriel Almond, Emmanuel Sivan and R. Scott Appleby, "Fundamentalism: Genus and Species," in *Fundamentalisms Comprehended*, edited by Martin E. Marty and R. Scott Appleby (Chicago: University of Chicago Press, 1995), 405.

26. Majid Khadduri, *War and Peace in the Law of Islam* (Baltimore, MD: John Hopkins Press, 1955), 64.

27. S. K. Malik, *The Quranic Concept of War* (Lahore, Pakistan: Associated Printers, 1979), 54.

28. Bassam Tibi, "Countering Ideological Terrorism," *Defence Against Terrorism Review*, Vol. 1, No. 1 (Spring 2008): 101–136. Available at http://www.coedat.nato.int/datr.htm, accessed 21 September 2009.

29. William Rosenau, op. cit., 1131–1148.

30. Sayyid Qutb, *Milestones (Ma'alim fil Tariq)*, English trans. (Indianapolis: American Trust Publications, 1990), 5–10, 15–17, 45–50, 64–68, 91–92, 101, 123.

31. John Strawson, "Encountering Islamic Law" (paper presented at the Critical Legal Conference, New College, Oxford, UK, 9–12 September 1993). Available at http://www.uel.ac.uk/law/research/publications/islamiclaw.htm, accessed 21 September 2009.

32. Khaled M. Abou El Fadl, *And God Knows the Soldiers: The Authoritative and the Authoritarian in Islamic Discourses*, revised edition (Lanham, MD: University Press of America, 2001), 6.

33. Abu Muhammad 'Asim Al-Maqdisi, *Millat Ibrahim and the Calling of the Prophets and Messengers*, English trans., 2nd ed. (London: At-Tibyan Publications, n.d.), 9, 19, 35–39, 45–46, 52, 57–58. Al-Maqdisi tries to prove that the hostility to infidels is a basic part of Islam, instituted early on in the Meccan stage of weakness, based on the example of Abraham in Q. 60: 4, and valid for all times. *Dhimmi* status was accorded to Jews and Christians (considered to be "people of the book") who surrendered to Muslim political dominance and were accorded a tolerated but subservient, humiliating, and second-rate position in the Islamic state.

34. 'Abdullah 'Azzam, *Defence of the Muslim Lands* (London: Ahle Sunnah Wal Jama'at, n.d.), 4–6.

35. 'Abdullah 'Azzam, quoted in Raymond Ibrahim, "An Analysis of Al-Qa'ida's Worldview: Reciprocal Treatment or Religious Obligation?" *Middle East Review of International Affairs (MERIA)* , Vol. 12, No. 3 (September 2008), 13. Available at http://www.meriajournal.com/en/asp/journal/2008/december/ibrahim/index.asp, accessed 21 September 2009. The application of the word "terrorist" to one's self in the quotation should not be deemed shocking, or even rare. Despite what some academics have written, many terrorists of secular or religious ideologies have freely admitted to terrorist strategies and/or use of the word for themselves; examples are in "Introduction to the Second Edition," Christopher C. Harmon, *Terrorism Today* (London & New York: Routledge, 2007), 1–5.

36. The Terrorism Research Centre, "Osama bin Laden, the Destruction of the Base" (interview with Osama bin Laden conducted by Jamal Isma'il, aired 10 June 1999), formerly published at http://www.terrorism.com/terrorism/BinLadinTranscript.shtm, accessed 10 July 2002; no longer available.

37. Osama bin Laden, "Declaration of War Against the Americans Occupying the Land of the Two Holy Places," formerly published at http://www.azzzam.com/html/body_declaration.html, accessed 10 July 2002; no longer available.

38. Osama bin Laden, "Moderate Islam Is a Prostration to the West," in *The Al Qaeda Reader*, edited by Raymond Ibrahim (New York: Doubleday, 2007), 43.

39. William Rosenau, op. cit., 1131–1148.

40. Raymond Ibrahim, "An Analysis of Al-Qa'ida's Worldview: Reciprocal Treatment or Religious Obligation?" op. cit., 8.

41. The Kharijis were an early Islamic sect that rebelled against both Sunni and Shia regimes and doctrines of leadership and that used *takfir* to define other Muslims as heretics and apostates who were to be fought by *jihad*.

42. Abdal-Hakim Murad, "Bin Laden's Violence Is a Heresy Against Islam," Islam for Today, available at http://www.islamfortoday.com/murad04.htm, accessed 15 January 2008.

43. For background on Sayyid Imam al-Sharif, his book, and al-Zawahiri's response, see Lawrence Wright, "The Rebellion Within," *The New Yorker*, 2 June 2008, available at http://www.newyorker.com/reporting/2008/06/02/080602fa_fact_wright?currentPage=all, accessed 21 September 2009.

44. Douglas E. Streusand and Harry D. Tunnell IV, "Choosing Words Carefully: Language to Help Fight Islamic Terrorism," *IOSphere*, Joint Information Operations Center, Fall 2006, available at http://www.au.af.mil/info-ops/iosphere/06fall/iosphere_fall06_tunnell.pdf, accessed 12 May 2009.

45. "Terminology to Define the Terrorists: Recommendations from American Muslims," US Department of Homeland Security, Office for Civil Rights and Civil Liberties, January 2008, available at http://www.dhs.gov/xabout/structure/gc_1212591972165.shtm, accessed 21 September 2009.

46. Julian Lewis, "Double-I, Double-N: A Framework for Counter-Insurgency," *RUSI Journal*, Vol. 153, No. 1 (February 2008), 36–40.

47. Quilliam Foundation, "Pulling Together to Defeat Terror," available at http://www.quilliamfoundation.org/images/stories/pdfs/pulling-together-to-defeat-terror.pdf, accessed 10 November 2008.

48. Toby Archer, "Countering the 'counter-jihad'," *RUSI Monitor* (15 August 2008).

49. Quoted in Robert Satloff, *The Battle of Ideas in the War on Terror: Essays on U.S. Public Diplomacy in the Middle East* (Washington, DC: The Washington Institute for Near East Policy, 2004), 25.

50. Julian Lewis, op. cit., 36–40. The present volume's editors note that, unlike Mr. Lewis, many experts on Islamism do not characterize it as racist; instead, some see a universalism in the appeal of this ideology.

51. Ibid.

52. Raymond Ibrahim, "Islam's War Doctrines Ignored," Middle East Strategy at Harvard Blog, 29 May 2008, available at http://blogs.law.harvard.edu/mesh/2008/05/islams_war_doctrines_ignored/, accessed 7 November 2008.

53. William Rosenau, op. cit., 1131–1148.

54. Cigar, op. cit., 56.

55. Julian Lewis, op. cit., 36–40.

56. Michael Hayden, "Transcript of Director's Remarks at the Atlantic Council," 13 November 2008, available at https://www.cia.gov/news-information/speeches-testimony/speeches-testimony-archive-2008/directors-remarks-at-the-atlantic-council.html, accessed 21 January 2009.

57. Sufism is the mystical stream within Islam, which lays stress on a spiritual loving union with God rather than on strict adherence to Islamic law.

58. William Rosenau, op. cit., 1131–1148.

59. Mohammed Abu Shamaa, "Former Al Qaeda Ideologue Exposes Al Zawahiri," *Asharq Alawsat*, 19 November 2008, available at http://www.asharqalawsat.com/english/news.asp?section=3&id=14775, accessed 21 January 2009.

60. Christopher Boucek, "Counter-Terrorism from Within: Assessing Saudi Arabia's Religious Rehabilitation and Disengagement Programme," *RUSI Journal*, Vol. 153, No. 6 (December 2008), 60–65.

61. See the Official Website of the Amman Message, www.ammanmessage.com, accessed 21 September 2009.

62. Peter Bergen and Laurence Footer, "Defeating the Attempted Global Jihadist Insurgency: Forty Steps for the Next President to Pursue against al Qaeda, Like-Minded Groups, Unhelpful State Actors, and Radicalized Sympathizers," *The ANNALS of the American Academy of Political and Social Science*, Vol. 618, No. 1 (2008), 232–247.

63. Julian Lewis, op. cit., 36–40.

64. Ibid.

65. Jacquelyn K. Davis and Charles M. Perry, op. cit.

66. Julian Lewis, op. cit., 36–40.

67. Ibid.

68. Peter Bergen and Laurence Footer, op. cit., 232–247.

69. Personal interview with the author, Virginia, 17 January 2009; see also Tawfik Hamid, *Inside Jihad: Understanding and Confronting Radical Islam*, self-published, March 2008, 15–51.

John J. Kane

Virtual Terrain, Lethal Potential:

Toward Achieving Security in an Ungoverned Domain

Although the terrain discussed in this chapter and activities conducted therein are in the virtual world, the danger posed to all of us is very real. Therefore, the battleground discussed should not be confused with the fantasy world that computer gamers use, for it is a real combat zone with real casualties and potentially deadly consequences.

From the perspective of a military officer, the author has witnessed the application of computer automation since the very inception of its implementation at the tactical level in American combat units (in the early 1980s). With this implementation has come a steadily increasing dependency upon the smooth functioning of cyber operations for the support of the structures and processes critical to national security, from the lowest tactical level of military ground operations up to the highest levels of government.[1]

Heavy dependence creates vulnerabilities that, combined with stated and implied terrorist intent, result in a case for serious and concerted counteraction on a global scale. This author suggests that the likelihood of a devastating attack in cyberspace, whether it comes in the form of asymmetric warfare against a state by a non-state group, or in the form of unrestricted warfare by one or more nation-states against another, is present and increasing. In particular, a cyber attack against critical infrastructure, either singularly or more likely in close coordination with various possible forms of physical attack and mass media manipulation, has the potential to bring down governments and create a human catastrophe.

The purpose of this chapter is to illustrate the nature of the cyber domain and the threat therein; to draw parallels between the physical and cyber worlds regarding criminal/terrorist action; to illuminate the very real potential for impact on our security that terrorists can have in this lightly patrolled area of operations; and, finally, to offer recommendations on cyber counterterror action to mitigate such a threat.

The Terrain: What Is Cyberspace?

John Perry Barlow, an activist from the American West, saw the internet as more than a computer network but rather something he called an "electronic frontier." Consequently, he founded an organization called the Electronic Frontier Foundation. Of it, he writes:

> Imagine discovering a continent so vast that it may have no end to its dimensions. Imagine a new world with more resources than all our future greed might exhaust, more opportunities than there will ever be entrepreneurs enough to exploit, and a peculiar kind of real estate that expands with development. Imagine a place where trespassers

leave no footprints, where goods can be stolen infinite number of times and yet remain in the possession of their original owners, where business you never heard of can own the history of your personal affairs.[2]

In a very perceptive view of the nature of cyberspace and the threats that would emerge within it, he presciently states the following in *Crime and Puzzlement*:

Cyberspace, in its present condition, has a lot in common with the 19th Century [American] west. It is vast, unmapped, culturally and legally ambiguous . . , hard to get around in, and up for grabs. Large institutions already claim to own the place, but most of the actual natives are solitary and independent, sometimes to the point of sociopathy. It is, of course, a perfect breeding ground for both outlaws and new ideas about liberty.[3]

The last line of Barlow's statement is all too true, since the internet has become a breeding ground for outlaws in the years since the dawn of the information age. But what exactly is cyberspace from the standpoint of a counterterror practitioner? The US National Military Strategy for Cyberspace Operations emphasizes that cyberspace is not merely the internet, but a "domain characterized by the use of electronics and the electromagnetic spectrum to store, modify, and exchange data via networked systems and associated physical infrastructures."[4]

Is cyberspace important? If so, great efforts may be warranted in protecting and policing it. Modern societies, particularly the more globally interconnected, whether powerful or not, are greatly and increasingly dependent upon the use of cyberspace. Whether one examines statistics associated with industry, the economy, banking, military, or governance structures, this fact is clear. Critical areas include global data processing infrastructure, the internet, media used by digital communications technologies, satellites and all that they facilitate, and the unfettered use of various devices utilizing the electromagnetic spectrum, such as cell phones, garage door openers, radio waves, and television signals.

Perhaps of greatest concern is the fact that cyberspace is often the node of control for our critical infrastructure—dams, train networks, air traffic control systems, power grids, water purification systems, satellites, etc. Most, if not all, of these processes have been made more efficient through the use of advanced technology, but how vulnerable have we become to those who can manipulate and control cyberspace? We must ensure that control of this vital domain is not dominated by a tyrant; that the free world is not held hostage by a relative few who could threaten catastrophic disruption through their actions in cyberspace.

As one example of a process that has become highly digitalized and efficient but also perhaps more fragile, consider the concept of "just-in-time supply." According to the United Parcel Service, "the basic premise is to have just the right amount of inventory, whether raw materials or finished goods, available to meet the demands of your production process and the demands of your end customers. No more, no less."[5] It eliminates the need for large volumes of storage space, increases efficiency, and reduces the risk of waste, but it also makes the process more fragile and vulnerable to disruption if the supply is interrupted or if databases containing supply requirements or computer systems controlling ordering processes are corrupted.[6]

Process enhancements utilizing computerized, interconnected, globalized technology and communications likely make those processes an order of magnitude more efficient, but they also become more fragile. The question then concerns mitigation or what some refer to as "graceful degradation"—once processes are computerized, are the previously used manual processes retained as a backup, or, once automated, have they typically passed a point of no return beyond which a loss of automation capability results in chaos and total loss of the process in question?

A 2005 Italian study of interdependent infrastructures included the following conclusions:

- "Welfare of population depends on many technological infrastructures such as energy distribution, telecommunications, water supply networks, transportation, etc.

- Rapid change in organizational, operational and technical structures due to the wide spread of information and communications technologies results in an increased level of interdependency.

- This phenomenon represents a new and very dangerous vulnerability. Due to the coupling among the different infrastructures, an accidental or malicious failure in one of them may easily spread across, amplifying its negative consequences. . . ."[7]

Globalization has unintended security consequences. Results of a survey seem to suggest a connection between the amount of hacking attacks experienced by certain businesses and the amount of outsourcing of the coding of their software. In April 2008, TechWorld reported that 90 percent of businesses that reported being the recipients of hacking attacks had outsourced at least 40 percent of their applications, and that companies that outsource the coding of their computer software applications typically have little or no visibility into the coding behaviors of their subcontractors.[8]

Charles Perrow cites Peter Neumann, an expert in the subject of computer fallibility, as saying that "Events that can happen accidentally can be caused intentionally, and events caused intentionally can happen accidentally."[9] A common problem that has characterized the information age involves systems of a critical and/or sensitive nature, originally designed as stand-alone systems having become connected to the internet in order to facilitate remote access to maximize efficiency and decrease the manpower necessary to supervise these systems. Unwittingly, however, these efforts in the interest of efficiency have resulted in increased vulnerability, as critical systems have been made accessible to manipulation by anyone with the requisite computer skills.

This is clearly an example of the "coupling resulting in dangerous vulnerabilities" of which the authors of the Italian study cited above speak.[10] In some cases, this coupling is done by necessity and with forethought, and in other cases, it is likely a result of well-meaning engineers and administrators seeking efficiencies. Perrow states, "Not only are all of our critical infrastructures connected to the internet, but they are interconnected themselves. Thus an operating system failure or intentional penetration can interact in unexpected or even mysterious ways with seemingly unrelated parts of the infrastructure."[11]

A good example of this occurred on 7 March 2008. An American software contractor was tasked with installing a software update on the business network at a nuclear power plant in the US state of Georgia. The business and operations computer networks were connected to each other so that chemical and diagnostic data could be monitored through the business computer terminal. According to a report by the Nuclear Regulatory Commission, the update caused the business computer to reboot, which resulted in a reset of data in the facility's primary control system, which was then interpreted by the control system as a problem with the cooling reservoirs, triggering an automatic shutdown and subsequent emergency actions. The report concludes that the event "illustrates the unintended consequences that could occur when business information technology systems interconnect with industrial control systems without adequate design considerations."[12]

To summarize this section on cyber dependency, the domain of cyberspace is worthy of serious scrutiny since society is becoming increasingly dependent on networked automation and communications processes. The resultant interconnectedness of various life-sustaining, commercial, and security systems has created vulnerabilities that can be exploited by those with criminal/terrorist intent. In order to assess current vulnerabilities to this domain, one has only to observe the success with which cyber criminals operate, examine the stated and implied intent of certain terrorist groups and the ways that criminals and terrorists cooperate, and extrapolate into a likely terrorist plan of cyber action. The potential damage that can be done is significant, and calls for a robust cyber counterterrorist plan of action.

The Threats: Cyber Crime

Cyber crime is popular, and the US Federal Bureau of Investigation (FBI) Internet Crime Complaint Center lists the reasons for the ease of online crime:

- Ability to communicate with numerous potential victims simultaneously
- Anonymity
- Global area of influence
- Minimal cost
- Ease of production: false ID, spoofed sites, e-mail, spam
- Lucrative[13]

Considering that in the physical world, criminals and terrorists use the same basic weapons (handguns, rifles, explosives, grenades, car bombs, etc.), albeit with different motives, it seems reasonable to suggest that criminals and terrorists would use common weapons in cyberspace as well. A quick survey of the arsenal available to the cyber terrorist would yield such weapons as worms, viruses, denial of service attacks, Trojans, robot computer networks, spoofing, phishing, morphing, etc., as well as the images and music of skillfully produced videos. Malicious software, imbedded in the computers of unsuspecting citizens, causes their computers to be controllable remotely by others. Unknown to the legitimate owners, their computers carry out tasks of a criminal nature, their actions synchronized with dozens, hundreds, or even thousands of other similarly controlled "robot" computers, acting as part of a "robot net" or "botnet," a surprisingly powerful entity in cyberspace at the hands of criminals. Symantec Corporation estimates that as of the end of 2008 there were over 9 million bot-infected computers and that, "With such a large number of bots available to attackers, it is likely that many would be used to generate profit."[14]

Botnets can be used to send spam, steal credit card information, or focus attacks on certain targeted websites.

Because of the efficiency of cyber crime and the demonstrated tendency of terror groups to use cyberspace for their own objectives, there is good reason to believe that terrorist groups use cyber crime to raise money. The Heritage Foundation, a Washington-based think-tank, reports: "Many Islamic charitable organizations allow users to make a *zakat* contribution online. Some terrorist organizations use front companies and charitable organizations under their control to receive such donations."[15] After six years of research, Gabriel Weimann—a senior fellow at the United States Institute of Peace and professor of communication at Haifa University in Israel—established that terrorist groups use the internet to raise funds. He notes, "Al Qaeda, for instance, has always depended heavily on donations, and its global fund-raising network is dependent upon a foundation of charities, non-governmental organizations, and other financial institutions that use websites and internet-based chat rooms and forums."[16]

Info-war and Related Phenomena

For the purposes of exploring virtual terrain, several phenomena that exist outside of cyber crime, but are neither crime nor terrorism, should be briefly addressed. These involve the actions of individuals and states using the global reach and anonymity of cyberspace to express opinions, influence others, and impose the will of an individual, a group, or a state upon other individuals, groups, and states. They include cyber hooliganism, cyber vigilantism, and cyber espionage, as well as citizen journalism, sympathy protests, and electronic civil disobedience. This writer would suggest that information warfare involves actions of a generally hostile nature conducted in cyberspace to advance national or non-state group interests, but that do not contain the basic elements normally associated with terrorism: violence or the threat thereof directed against civilians to induce fear for a political purpose.

Info-war events clearly illustrate the asymmetric power of cyberspace, the predilection of people to act in their own self-interest using whatever tools are available (particularly since they are usually able to retain plausible deniability), and the importance of strategic communication. These last concepts of national interest and strategic communication play powerfully in the hands of terrorists as well, and it is in this context that they will be discussed further under the heading of cyber terror.

Two examples of individual activists show the new trend. Mr. Aaron Weisburd is founder of the internet Haganah (Hebrew for "defense") and in his own words is engaged in a "global, non-governmental, ad-hoc intelligence network" that goes after extremist Islamist websites, particularly al Qaeda websites. He claims to have shut down 600 to 1,000 of these websites and turned over volumes of actionable information to authorities. His activities are controversial, partially because he often takes direct action to shut sites down without coordinating with law enforcement. Shannen Rossmiller, a Montana judge, housewife, and mother, on her own initiative and without being compensated, spent seven years after 11 September 2001 in undercover cyber war against radical Islamists. Having taught herself Arabic, her modus operandi consisted of operating in their chat rooms, assuming over two dozen different extremist personas, gaining their confidence, listening to their plans, and then turning them over to the FBI. According to one report, she has provided intelligence to support well over 200 cases of espionage and terrorism. An early 2009 report indicates that she will shift her focus to training a "cyber corps" of operatives who will follow her lead in ensnaring terrorists online.

As can be seen from the previous examples, groups as well as nation-states have found good use for the internet and cyberspace to advance their agendas and interests, whatever they may be, in a wide variety of ways. We now turn to the subject of cyber terror.

Info-War Illustrations

- During the Kosovo Campaign in 1999, while NATO was conducting a bombing campaign against Serbia, Belgrade conducted actions in cyberspace against NATO websites. A group called the Beograd Hackers was attacking various sites by replacing them with pro-Serbian propaganda messages, and unidentified individuals were sending viruses to administrators of the NATO website. Russian or Serbian hackers were suspected of launching simultaneous hacking attacks on the US White House website. Some reports claim that the US conducted a computer network attack on Serbia in order to defeat their air defense system during the bombing campaign and that other information operations were also conducted against Serbia.[17]

- In late April and early May 2007, a massive cyber attack was conducted against the government of Estonia after a dispute arose over Russian reactions to the relocation of a Soviet-era statue of a WWII Soviet soldier. Attacks seemed to originate from the Russian Federation, although the Russian government vehemently denied directing the attacks, suggesting that they were the actions of nationalistic individuals.[18]

- In April 2008, the Radio Free Europe/Radio Liberty (RFE/RL) Belarus operation was the target of a distributed denial of service attack, which quickly spread to RFE/RL websites in Kosovo, Azerbaijan, Russia, Tajikistan, and others. RFE/RL was covering a large protest by the opposition party in Belarus calling attention to the 22nd anniversary of the Chernobyl disaster. The date of the attack was also the one-year anniversary of the cyber attack on Estonia.[19]

- In June 2008, hackers plastered Soviet symbols and profanity on more than 300 Lithuanian websites two weeks after the Lithuanian Official Ethics Commission voted to ban such symbols, which included the Soviet hammer and sickle and five-pointed star. Lithuanian authorities stopped short of accusing Russia, however.[20]

- In July and August 2008, the Georgian government experienced a barrage of attacks against a large number of its websites during the prelude to and during hostilities over the separatist regions of South Ossetia and Abkhazia. Cyber security experts tracked the activity back to three servers based in Russia. The South Ossetia Hack Crew took responsibility for juxtaposing images of Hitler next to images of Georgian president Saakashvili in similar poses to those in the pictures of Hitler.[21] According to another report, cyber security researchers in the United States tracked anti-Georgian cyber action back to servers known to be controlled by a St. Petersburg criminal organization called the Russian Business Network (RBN). The researchers are said to have watched the servers being staged before the attack and then activated shortly before the commencement of Russian airstrikes.[22] Yet another reporter claims that during the conflict he followed online instructions that led him, within one hour, to gain the capability of attacking Georgian government sites and also the websites of states supporting Georgia.[23]

• In November 2008, a series of reports appeared regarding problems with cyber security and hacking attacks against the World Bank and International Monetary Fund's (IMF) computer system. The IMF computer system, which contains highly sensitive global financial data regarding central bank balances and currency payments, is said to have experienced hacking attacks over the previous several months.[24]

Cyber Terror

Ahmad Kamal of the UN Institute for Training and Research provides a workable definition of cyber terror: "Terrorism in cyber-space is generally understood to mean unlawful attacks and threats of attack against computers, networks, and the government or its people in furtherance of political or social objectives. To qualify as cyber-terrorism, an attack should result in violence against persons or property, or at least cause enough harm to generate fear."[25]

Dorothy Denning of the Naval Postgraduate School seems to agree: "The attack should be sufficiently destructive or disruptive to generate fear comparable to that from physical acts of terrorism. Attacks that lead to death or bodily injury, extended power outages, plane crashes, water contamination, or major economic losses would be examples."[26]

This writer would suggest that cyber terrorism is the use or threat of harm to innocents for a political or ideological purpose through the deliberate and unlawful use of, interference with, manipulation of, corruption of, or destruction of their cyber infrastructure and/or the information stored or processed therein.

The most successful terrorist groups recognize the great potential of cyberspace to advance their cause and have been planning diligently to such effect. In September 2006, a website called Electronic Jihad attracted attention; it was described by the Jamestown Foundation as a group of cyber *jihadis* with the aim to help organize an electronic jihad against websites that insult Islam and Islamic sacred figures.[27] Dr. E. Alshech explains the objectives of Electronic Jihad: "assisting Islam by attacking Web sites that slander Islam or launch attacks against Islamic Web sites, or by attacking Web sites that interfere with the goal of rendering Islam supreme (e.g., Christian Web sites) . . . avenging the death of Muslim martyrs and the suffering of Muslims worldwide (including imprisoned jihad-fighters);

inflicting damage on the Western economy; affecting the morale of the West; and even bringing about the total collapse of the West. . . ."[28]

Kamal explains that the concept is anything but random:

> . . . electronic jihad is a form of cyber warfare with ideological underpinnings and defined goals which manifests in well-coordinated cyberattacks . . . they mean to position themselves as a formidable electronic attack force which is capable of inflicting severe damage—greater even than the damage caused by conventional terrorist attacks.[29]

Terrorists have enjoyed physical sanctuary in places such as the Tri-Border Area of South America, the Federally Administered Tribal Areas (FATA) of Pakistan, or the mountains of Afghanistan. Whether their physical sanctuary is still reasonably secure, or whether it is threatened by military or law enforcement action, terrorists have gravitated to cyberspace where they enjoy certain advantages.

Magnus Ranstorp, Director of the Centre for Asymmetric Threat Studies of the Swedish National Defense College, sees cyberspace as being of such great value to a range of terrorist activities that he describes this phenomenon as a "university of *jihad*":

> In many ways, the virtual world has become the principal vehicle through which terrorist organizations communicate with their own clandestine members, reach a broad audience of real and potential sympathizers, publish propaganda and wage a skillful auxiliary psychological warfare campaign to amplify violence on the ground . . . cyberspace has created a virtual university of *jihad* with advice available anytime to any militant.[30]

Some have even argued that al Qaeda has become the first terrorist movement in history to migrate from physical space to cyberspace. But what is the great attraction to cyberspace? The answer is similar advantages to those we spoke of when discussing cyber crime:[31]

- Anonymity
- Diverse targets
- Low risk of detection
- Low risk of personal injury
- Low investment
- Operate from any location
- Few resources needed

If one recalls the motivations for asymmetric warfare, it becomes apparent that the tools and the battlespace are abundantly available in cyberspace. One expansive case of terrorist recruiting, planning, training, and inciting in cyberspace will illustrate:

Younis Tsouli, otherwise known as "Irhabi007," was a Moroccan living in London. Tsouli helped enable al Qaeda to reconstitute itself in cyberspace after its eviction from Afghanistan in 2002. He posted militant videos from Iraq on the Web, including the beheading of businessman Nicholas Berg in spring 2004, and was commended by an aide to Abu Musab al Zarqawi in October 2004 for his service to al Qaeda in Iraq. In addition to functioning as a media executor for Zarqawi, Tsouli began recruiting fighters and assisting them in traveling to Iraq for jihad. Among Tsouli's many contacts were Mirsad Bekta-sevic, a Bosnian living in Sweden also known online as "Maximus"; six teenagers living in Denmark who were of Palestinian, Moroccan, Turkish, and Bosnian ancestry; Syed Haris Ahmed, a Pakistani-American, and Ehsanul Islam Sadequee, a Bangladeshi-American, both living in Atlanta; Abdul Basit Abu-Lifa, a Palestinian-Dane; Bajro Ikanovic and Amir Bajric, both Bosnians; and seventeen other suspects in Toronto. Most were complicit in the planning of attacks in various locations and in supporting al Qaeda operations in Iraq. Many of the contacts were initiated and nurtured over the internet and demonstrate how the internet has become a virtual training camp as well as a facilitator of terrorist recruiting, planning, reconnaissance, funding, logistics, and other activities.[32]

Radicalization and Recruitment

Inciting violence is a legally tricky subject for many states because it involves questions about freedom of expression and freedom of the press. Cyberspace is an excellent venue through which one can reach a maximum number of receptive people in a short period of time.

One case of this is Malika El Aroud, widow of the killer of Ahmed Shah Massoud (the Afghan leader murdered two days before 11 September 2001). This resident of Bel-gium and self-described female holy warrior saw "incitement to jihad" as her mission in life. Specifically, the objectives of her web-work were shaming Muslim men to conduct violent jihad; encouraging Muslim women to participate in some way in holy war; distrib-uting extremist material; and supporting pro-al Qaeda websites. She is known to express her extreme message in French under the name "Um Obeyda." Some analysts believe she was responsible for a measurable increase in female suicide bombers in 2007 and 2008. Arrested and convicted in Switzerland in December of 2007 along with her new husband Moez Garsalloui for allegedly operating pro-al Qaeda websites, her sentence was later suspended.[33] El Aroud was arrested again a year later in Belgium in December 2008 with thirteen others on suspicion of planning to conduct a terrorist attack on the EU Summit, which was held in Belgium a few days later.[34]

Another inciter, Omar Bakri Mohammed, a Muslim cleric who was banned from living in the United Kingdom in 2005, continued to proselytize extremism on the internet from his home in Lebanon as well as via video teleconference and telephone to the United Kingdom. Bakri was the founder of a radical group called "al-Muhajiroun," which was outlawed in the United Kingdom.[35]

Cases like El-Aroud and Bakri cause some to question the relevance of anti-terror legislation. Although the European Union agreed in April 2008 to impose tighter laws on incitement and to establish an "early-warning system" on stolen explosives and detonators, actual implementation of such measures requires discussion in the parliaments of the vari-ous states, and possibly the adjustment of already existing legislation in order to apply such measures on a practical level.[36]

The internet also lends itself well to "narrowcasting," the tailored targeting of specific population groups. Al Qaeda uses flashy, pulsating, entertaining videos to attract young Muslim adolescents in the West. By cleverly targeting an age group for whom the concept of belonging to a group is particularly important, among a population often marginalized within their nation, al Qaeda hopes to radicalize the greatest number possible.

Terrorists are often supported, wittingly or unwittingly, by criminal groups that are co-opted for a price. The advantages to terrorists are obvious. Established criminal support systems (supply, access, documents, transportation, etc.) facilitate terrorist purposes and obviate the necessity to establish their own support networks, which may attract the attention of law enforcement authorities. The use of criminal networks as subcontractors may mean that they can be compartmentalized more efficiently, and then detached when their usefulness has ended without ever having received intimate knowledge about the workings of the terror group. It also may mean that the terrorist group is not required to expand its membership in order to handle the specialized work that needs to be done. This crime-terror nexus exists in the virtual world as well. The ease of online crime facilitates and fuels terror groups. Fund-raising in particular, either through identity theft or through receipt of donations to bogus charities, is particularly lucrative for those who know how to manipulate the tools of cyberspace. The British *Daily Telegraph* asserts that terrorists are using online gambling to launder money.[37] The virtual world facilitates not only fund-raising but serves as an alternate remittance system, allowing funds to be transferred as required.

Mitchell Silber and Arvin Bhatt of the New York Police Department researched and wrote a widely admired study entitled *Radicalization in the West*. They highlight a continuum of action online that contributes to and accelerates the radicalization process of susceptible individuals, resulting ultimately in violent action in the furtherance of al Qaeda goals either in the West or in the "lands of *jihad*." According to Silber and Bhatt, "The internet plays an important role during the radicalization process. As individuals progress through the various stages, their use of the internet evolves as well."[38] They identify three basic phases during which the subject is gradually drawn into an increasingly extreme mindset:

- A self-identification phase, during which the internet serves as a source of information and venue to meet other seekers online;

- An indoctrination phase, during which the subject spends time in extremist websites and chat rooms with like-minded individuals from around the globe available any time of the day or night who can both reinforce and legitimize the extreme ideas being proposed—the internet effectively becomes a "virtual 'echo chamber'," in the words of the NYPD;

- The final stage is the so-called jihadization phase, during which the subject is challenged to act on these new beliefs. At that point, the internet conveniently becomes a training resource for such subjects as weapons, targeting, bomb-making, and the logistics of moving to the physical battlefield.[39]

We have seen how cyberspace is used by terrorist groups for various purposes such as recruiting, fund-raising, indoctrinating, inciting, training, planning, organizing, information collection, and so forth. These numerous activities have certain ends, and a report by the US Congressional Research Service offers a concise list of terrorist objectives in cyberspace, which is worth serious consideration by counterterrorist practitioners:[40]

- Loss of Integrity—the accuracy of information cannot be trusted

- Loss of Availability—the data are not there when needed

- Loss of Confidentiality—the data have been compromised to enemies or competitors
- Physical Destruction—information systems create actual physical harm

Protection of Critical Infrastructure

The destruction of critical infrastructure could cause a loss of life, either incidental to the destruction of the targeted infrastructure, or as a result of the domino-like action of one infrastructural system after another failing due to the combined results of successive failures. If the incapacitation of critical infrastructure were orchestrated to occur in synchronization with a kinetic attack, emergency services could be delayed or defeated, ultimately resulting in a lack of confidence in the government and a consequent loss of control. Hostile manipulation of the news media could further complicate the ability of governmental authorities to regain control.

Theoretically, cyber terrorists could cause destruction of critical infrastructure if they acquired access to and successfully manipulated the Supervisory Control and Data Acquisition (SCADA) software, which is the software that regulates the functioning of infrastructural systems such as oil and gas pipelines, water treatment and distribution systems, electrical grids, power generation and transmission systems, dams, air traffic control systems, chemical plants, trains, factories servicing major corporations, satellites, and the like. Power grid experts, for example, have noted the incidence of SCADA software being accessible through the internet, and have under test conditions been able to severely disrupt operation via remote computers. The US Department of Homeland Security has identified this problem as a major vulnerability.[41]

Cyberspace is currently rather lightly patrolled and ungoverned. We know from hard experience that ungoverned physical areas such as the Tri-Border Area of South America, the FATA of Pakistan, and failing states such as Somalia and others are breeding grounds and safe havens for criminals, terrorists, and tyrants—and they are also often places in which nation-states conduct overt and covert operations amid all the confusion based on their perceived national interests in those areas. Similarly, cyberspace is a vast ungoverned area in which criminals and terrorists thrive, and over which the community of nations must get control, and soon.

Emerging Trends

There are some terrorist groups who specifically profess an interest in and capability for conducting cyber attacks. Though al Qaeda is well known for maximizing use of the internet to further its cause and encourage radicalization of people around the globe, Aum Shinrikyo (renamed "Aleph" in 2000) view themselves as a "cyber cult." The so-called "doomsday cult" that attacked the Tokyo subway system with nerve gas on 20 March 1995 remain under surveillance in Japan under the new name; and a declassified CIA report indicates that Aum "is the terrorist group that places the highest level of importance on developing cyber skills." Surprisingly, the report also indicates that the group still "derives millions of dollars a year from computer retailing."[42] Previous to its nerve gas attack, Aum Shinrikyo had produced and sold computers and software. Sales of its software may have gone to as many as ninety government bodies and private firms, including the Japanese defense agency, which had to delay implementation of a major computer system after it was determined that some of the software used was developed by the cult. Other ministries having ordered Aum software were the Education, Construction, and Telecommunications ministries. Some reports indicated that members of the cult "were operating five software companies and conducted sales activities covering 500 major companies by offering large discounts." Earlier reports indicate that Aum was involved in the sale of software to Japanese police, which facilitated the tracking of police and emergency vehicles around the country. It is unclear whether investigations have been able to establish that the cult does not continue to have access to police or other systems in Japan through "peculiarities" such as "trap doors" and "Trojans" they may have built into the software they sold to various agencies.[43,44] This problem harkens back to the survey previously discussed that indicated a significant percentage of businesses who outsourced the coding of their software had a high incidence of hacking problems. It seems likely that a terrorist group producing software can naturally be expected to code the software in such a way as to allow themselves remote access to the clients' systems.

"Unlimited war" and "unrestricted warfare" are concepts previously associated more with the Cold War and "mutually assured destruction." But lately, certain states and non-state actors, especially those with a messianic or extremist religious motivation, seem to find these notions of warfare to be compelling. Al Qaeda, for example, almost never offers any willingness to negotiate, but is intent on destroying western civilization based on their perception of the will of God and would do so by any means. As previously stated, an effective means of warfare and vulnerability for most states is warfare through cyberspace, and the concept of unrestricted warfare in cyberspace is worthy of note. The Chinese military has strongly advocated the concept of conducting an unrestricted brand of asymmetric warfare featuring what it describes as "new concept weapons" such as financial warfare, computer hacking, and information warfare capabilities to disrupt economic, military, and governance structures. It is a holistic approach to imposing the will of one entity upon another. Consider the following quotes from a book written by two Chinese military officers appropriately entitled *Unrestricted Warfare*:

> As we see it, a single man-made stock-market crash, a single computer virus invasion, or a single rumor or scandal that results in a fluctuation in the enemy country's exchange rates or exposes the leaders of an enemy country on the Internet, all can be included in the ranks of new-concept weapons.[45]

> If the attacking side secretly musters large amounts of capital without the enemy nation being aware of this at all and launches a sneak attack against its financial markets, then after causing a financial crisis, buries a computer virus and hacker detachment in the opponent's computer system in advance, while at the same time carrying out a network attack against the enemy so that the civilian electricity network, traffic dispatching network, financial transaction network, telephone communications network, and mass media network are completely paralyzed, this will cause the enemy nation to fall into social panic, street riots, and a political crisis.[46]

Though expressed articulately by the Chinese Army, this holistic approach to warfare, if adopted by terrorists, is a threat to be taken very seriously indeed.

Electromagnetic terrorism is the use of an electromagnetic pulse to destroy computer circuitry for a terrorist motive. During the Soviet era as well as today, a threat scenario outlines the possibility of an intercontinental ballistic missile being detonated over a western city, generating a High-Altitude Electromagnetic Pulse (known as HEMP) and effectively destroying all unshielded circuitry. The result would be a breakdown of various critical systems and accompanying mass confusion. A current adaptation involves the potential use of a smaller, less capable electromagnetic pulse generator or high-power microwave that could be delivered by man or by vehicle to a location close enough to a target to destroy or severely disable it. The target could be a power station, financial center, transportation hub, or other critical infrastructure.[47]

Virtual reality (VR) technology, featuring three-dimensional user-generated content, is becoming an important "place" in which to be able to operate proficiently. VR is increasingly the location of significant and influential forces affecting the flow of vital information of all kinds, such as finance, demographics, various special-interest communities, and simulations of all sorts, including military, homeland security, and terrorist training simulations. These simulations are increasingly sophisticated, featuring avatars—or computer-generated people controlled by real people—who can interact with other avatars on a variety of subjects. According to the US Congressional Research Service, China, for example is actually building a virtual world with infrastructure that will support 75 million simultaneous users.[48]

As the physical world becomes more intertwined with and dependent upon operations in the virtual world, mastery of VR technology and freedom of action in the virtual world will become more significant and more critical to national security. In order to counter cyber terror, it therefore becomes increasingly important to develop the ability to operate proficiently on the cyber terrain, to use the tools and weapons of cyberspace, and to be capable of keeping cyberspace free and safe for all to use.

The Response: Cyber Counterterrorism

> . . . cyber-security should be a primary objective for our governments. This is not only a matter of economic crime but also of national security. It is time for this issue to come out of the realm of a few specialists and be debated at political level, as it implies a new approach to the way in which we conceive international relations, the relationship between states and private individuals and the threat of terrorism.

Council of Europe, Parliamentary Assembly, 27 June 2007[49]

Cyber security should indeed be a primary objective for governments. Over time it appears that the virtual world will, for all practical purposes, become "real" due to the gravity of the actions and commerce there, the criticality of the communications pathways existing in cyberspace, and the very real impact that they have in the physical world. Free nations cannot afford to relinquish control of this vital domain to criminals, terrorists, and tyrants. It is critical, therefore, that the international community makes a concerted effort to set cyber defense and cyber counterterrorism as a top priority.

Because cyberspace (like terrorism) has no boundaries, the solution for cyber counterterror must be a comprehensive, global, cooperative effort that encompasses measures

A Glossary of Cyber Weapons

Anti-forensics—technical methods of "cleaning" a computer, designed to remove evidence of wrongdoing such as browser history, cookies, recent documents, certain files and programs, etc.

Backdoor—a method of gaining access to a normally secure location on a computer. Sometimes known as a trap door, it may be purposely built into a system during development to facilitate legitimate maintenance, or for criminal purposes.

Botnets—a network of robot computers directed to work in a synchronous manner for any number of illegitimate purposes.

Denial of Service Attacks—a means of attack in which network service is disrupted or denied by overwhelming the system with multiple repeated requests, which causes the system to slow or crash.

Distributed Denial of Service—a denial of service attack conducted by a number of different computers focused at the same attack point simultaneously.

Keyloggers—a software program or hardware device that collects information on keyboard keystrokes for the purpose of gaining information on passwords, credit card numbers, and other personal or security information.

Hacking—breaking through computer security for a wide variety of possible reasons.

Hiding Data—software designed to scramble or make innocuous the presence of certain data such as files, audio or video, by scrambling (encrypting) it or embedding it in other media such as a photograph (steganography).

Phishing—the use of spoofed e-mail and websites designed to deceive internet users into divulging sensitive information.

Robot—also called a "zombie," a computer controlled surreptitiously by someone other than the legitimate owner for a number of possible illegitimate purposes.

Spoofing—a method of attack by which the attacker creates a reputable-looking website that causes the victim to provide security information to the attacker.

Spyware—software that surreptitiously embeds itself in the target computer and is designed to collect and report information back to some location to gain an advantage for the purpose of sales, espionage, intelligence gathering, or illicit activity.

Trojans—malicious files masquerading as harmless software upgrades, programs, help files, screen savers, pornography, etc., which upon opening by the user run a program in the background that may have a variety of harmful purposes.

Virus/Worm—executable programs that affect or attach themselves to another executable program for the purpose of doing harm to files and other data, by deleting, modifying, corrupting, or distributing it.

Wireless Surveillance—software programs that allow the monitoring and possibly recording of network traffic, often passively from a remote location.

and policies to defend individuals and their personal computers; standards and procedures for the software industry; encouragement of truly innovative technical developments; updates for legal systems both domestic and at the international level; creation of cooperative structures that enhance the abilities of states to take rapid, effective, cross-boundary action; new thinking in terms of strategic communication and public diplomacy; and the development of revolutionary capabilities and organizations in defense departments that enable not only cyber defense but offensive cyber combat against terrorists.

What follow are some thoughts and suggestions regarding measures in the categories mentioned above. Some are already in place to an extent in some nations, particularly in those with a denser and more highly developed cyber infrastructure and therefore greater cyber dependency. Other suggestions are concepts that have as yet not been well developed as far as the author is aware. This writer proposes to examine possible responses to cyber counterterrorism by category, beginning with responses of a technical character. These will be followed by those that fall into categories of a legal, structural, rehearsal, strategic, and finally offensive character.

Technical

Solve the Cyber Anonymity Problem. In this writer's view, anonymity is the single most important challenge that, if resolved, would significantly mitigate the problems of both cyber crime and cyber terror. The international community must spare no effort to develop the ability to determine the physical location of servers, computers, and operators that initiate various types of illegal cyber action. The removal of anonymity in cyberspace is essential to ensuring that cyber criminals and terrorists as well as hostile nation-states can reliably be assigned responsibility for their actions in cyberspace. Criminals, con artists, terrorists, tyrants, and nation-states currently act with impunity in cyberspace, committing burglary, theft, sabotage, conspiracy, blackmail, and espionage, to name just a few crimes. Although some capabilities do exist, law enforcement authorities are hard-pressed to determine the identities and locations of the computers and servers involved in these crimes and to associate them with human suspects. Due to current technological limitations, states engaging in espionage against other states have a high level of deniability when accusations are leveled at them. China especially, but also Russia, is frequently accused of harboring cyber criminals, of conducting cyber espionage, and even of launching cyber warfare.[50] For the above reasons, the state of anarchy in cyberspace is unacceptably high. There is probably no action that would have a greater impact on the success of cyber crime-fighting and cyber counterterrorist efforts than the solving of the anonymity problem in cyberspace. The efforts that should be expended, therefore, in solving this problem should be of a global nature, maintaining a highly focused sense of urgency appropriate to the tremendous potential good that such a breakthrough would represent.

Ensure Use of Security Software. In addition to the many harmful effects the ubiquity of cyber crime has on the economies of states and confidence therein, cyber crime is known to fuel terrorist groups. Therefore, the combating of cyber crime at the individual personal computer (PC) level will contribute in no small way to the combating of terrorists and their actions in cyber space. Consequently, every individual computer should have a well-defined minimum level of effective security protection. Government and industry should consider creating arrangements by which high-quality, reliable cyber security software can be issued to all computer users and kept updated free of charge. An unprotected PC is a liability not only to the individual owner but to the entire world because of the danger of that computer becoming co-opted into a robot network (botnet) and harnessed with thousands of other computers to commit cyber crime on a wide scale. Because of the specialization of cyber criminals and the availability of such things as "botnets for hire," terrorist groups can have this powerful tool for a price to facilitate and magnify their actions. Perrow refers to a study by the American Enterprise Institute (AEI)–Brookings Joint Center for Regulatory Studies that advocates the concept of mandatory insurance for computer operations, priced in accordance with the amount and reliability of the security software a user or company has.[51]

Minimize Time Online. In order to decrease the possibility of computers becoming part of a botnet, phished[52] for personal identification, banking and credit card information, or otherwise manipulated by cyber criminals, a standard practice should be established in which computers are always off-line by default unless their interaction with the internet is specifically required, and then for only as long as required. Disconnection from the internet should not be dependent on individuals remembering to do so, but should occur automatically, just as power-save measures are implemented after a period of inactivity and when the user logs off. The risk of criminal or terrorist manipulation of PCs is at least as important as the depletion of battery power, after all. An automatic scan for and elimination of malware (to include the elimination of spyware) should occur immediately upon disconnection, and malware characteristics recorded for reporting cyber-forensics to authorities upon reconnection. This could have the effect of making individual computers unavailable to robot nets for a significant percentage of the day or night. It would also allow them to act as malware reporters as a matter of routine. While this would not have significant effect in the case of systems requiring continuous connection with the internet, the fact remains that when computers are off-line, they are not immediately available to criminal use (even if they are infected). The likelihood that malware will be created to surreptitiously reconnect machines to the internet should naturally be anticipated, and measures should be taken to defeat this attempt. Perhaps one possible measure is a hardware ergonomic reconfiguration that makes physical disconnection of the computer from the internet simple and easily accessible for all users. In general, significant scrutiny should be paid across all levels of cyber infrastructure to reducing the amount of time that computers must be connected to the internet.

Diversify Software, Reduce Complexity, and Increase Modularity. In *The Next Catastrophe,* Perrow makes an excellent case for redundancy and diversification as a means of reducing vulnerability to catastrophic system failure, either due to accidental or criminal/terrorist action. Some of his major points are that the creator of Windows is effectively a monopoly, which results in a lack of motivation to ensure reliability and security and software products that are both not of a sufficiently modular design (which would facilitate rapid and lower-cost maintenance and repair) and overly complex (due to business decisions related to a desire to maintain proprietary software in order to "lock in" the customer). "Complexity is the enemy of both reliability and security," he points out.[53] Because of the ubiquity of Microsoft—used across all key industries worldwide and often "controlling" critical infrastructure—Perrow suggests that an open-source concept should be encouraged, particularly through large organizations (such as the federal government of the United States). This would encourage competition among software vendors and, more importantly for cyber counterterrorism (CT), lessen the chances that a virus or other malicious action would be successful in disabling systems across an entire industry or worse, across several industries. He gives an example. The state of Massachusetts, which

> . . . standardized desktop applications on OpenDocument, an open-source format that is not supported by Microsoft Office. About 50,000 desktop PCs will be required at least to save their documents in the open-source format. . . . OpenDocument-based products will cost the state about $5 million, in contrast to the $50 million for Office 12. . . . In Massachusetts, a department might choose to use word-processing products such as OpenOffice and variants of it from companies including Sun Microsystems, IBM, and Novell. It is an example of how large customers could bring about deconcentration in an industry.[54]

Include "Intrusion Tolerance" Technology in Cyber Defense Plans. Cyber security practitioners utilize a strategy common in other types of security fields known as a "defense in depth." This defensive concept acknowledges that no one security measure can be assumed to be impenetrable; therefore, multiple layers of security are implemented. In addition to passive preventive measures in cyberspace such as firewalls, and active defensive measures such as security scans, a basic philosophical shift is necessary in the business of cyber security in which a realistic assumption is made that intrusions will occur no matter how good the passive defensive barrier is. The question that follows, then, is how to best contain the intrusion once it occurs. George Mason University is developing a technology called "self-cleansing intrusion tolerance"[55] in which the server in contact with the internet is rotated off-line periodically for "cleaning," while another server is rotated online to contact with the internet. Rotation occurs whether or not an intrusion takes place, effectively reducing exposure time to possible attacks. This technology, in combination with the minimizing of online time, could significantly reduce the opportunity "window" in which malicious cyber action could take place.

Maximize Use of Reporting Software to Benefit Law Enforcement Efforts. Good intelligence is also key to a successful defense, and there are technical processes that can assist in gathering information. Cooperation between software developers and law enforcement practitioners can be very effective. Microsoft, for example, shares data gathered from user feedback regarding their Malicious Software Removal Tool with law enforcement authorities.[56] Referred to as "botnet" intelligence, the data collected from approximately 450 million computer users is the cyber equivalent of tips from the public on criminal activity and gives law enforcement authorities an idea of the nature, frequency, and location of the problem. Similar tools are the Symantec Phish Report Network, which claims to be "an extensive antifraud community where members contribute and receive fraudulent Web site addresses for alerting and blocking attacks across a broad range of solutions."[57] This company's semiannual Security Threat Reports advertise use of the "Symantec Probe Network, a system of over two million decoy accounts in more than 30 countries, [which] attracts email from around the world to gauge global spam and phishing activity."[58] These are only representative examples of cyber-activity data collection tools. Cyber counterterrorists must use the speed and analytical tools afforded by the power of automation and the global nature of cyberspace to rapidly collect and analyze information about the threat in order to bring to bear a combination of available tools in a timely manner to mitigate or eliminate it.

Legal

Continue to Update and Reinforce the Legal Framework. All terror acts are criminal acts, and therefore all acts of cyber terror should be acts of cyber crime. International law must adjust for the realities of cyber attacks; update the definitions of "armed attack," "act of war," etc.; and continue to be relevant in questions of law in the unique context of cyberspace. For example, was the cyber attack on Estonia in 2007 an attack on NATO? What kind, and by whom? Did the cyber attacks on Georgia in 2008 accompanying the physical attack by Russia constitute an act of war? Does it fall into the category of armed attack as recognized by international law? Development of law regarding incitement on the internet is another important endeavor, and one that would be a significant tool for cyber counterterrorist practitioners. In April 2008, European Union ministers agreed to enact new legislation that would "ensure that terrorist-linked offences include . . . public provocation to commit a terrorist offence, recruitment for terrorism, training for terrorism." They also agreed to establish an "early warning system on stolen explosives and detonators by the end of the year," as well as a "European Bomb Data System."[59] It is perhaps not too far-fetched to think of websites as being much like military bases; of malicious software as analogous to hunter-killer teams; of spyware like reconnaissance elements; of firewalls like obstacles and fortifications; and so on. It is a virtual world, but there is potential for real damage in the physical world.

Structural

Continue to Create Regional, National, and Subnational Cyber CT Centers and Encourage Information Sharing. Structures help states pool their resources into common and cooperative endeavors, encourage collaboration in highly technical areas of research, and also act as symbols of resolve against the threat. The Cooperative Cyber Defence Center of Excellence has been established in Tallinn, Estonia, with a vision "to become a primary source of expertise for NATO in cooperative cyber defense-related matters."[60] NATO has accepted this Estonian offer, and in May 2008 seven NATO members signed an agreement to fund the center's cyber research entity. The new partners included Estonia, Latvia, Lithuania, Germany, Italy, Spain, and Slovakia, with the United States and others in observer status. The formal opening occurred in 2009.[61]

A regional cyber defense and research center in Selangor, Malaysia, is the headquarters for an organization called the International Multilateral Partnership Against Cyber-Terrorism (IMPACT),[62] which has been described as a "kind of Center for Disease Control for cyber security."[63] It will provide both a forum and communications means for the coordination of an international response to cyber attacks, particularly regarding civilian networks. Malaysia considers this to be a global (rather than regional) cyber CT center for the purpose of providing "an emergency response to high-tech attacks on economies and trading systems around the world." The Malaysian initiative may be funded by member governments as well as donations.[64]

The Middle East Media Research Institute (MEMRI) is advertised as an independent, nonpartisan, nonprofit organization that explores the Middle East through the region's media.[65] It publishes analysis and translation, including material from extremist websites and the messages and images being pushed therein.

The Search for International Terrorist Entities (SITE) Intelligence Group monitors terrorist websites, translates the messages, and shares with intelligence agencies. The SITE website features a range of services, including a monitoring service, web portal, forensic analysis, and customized reports on cyber terror.[66]

Certain cyber security measures, organizations, and programs of the United States of America might prove useful as examples upon which further CT programs might be modeled:

- The National Infrastructure Protection Plan facilitates coordination between the federal government and the civilian community, which owns 85 percent of America's critical infrastructure regarding the defense of the nation's critical infrastructure.

- The National Asset Database, created by the Office of Infrastructure Protection in the Department of Homeland Security (DHS), comprises 77,000 assets. It is said to be characterized "not as a list of critical assets, but rather as a national asset inventory providing the 'universe' from which various lists of critical assets are produced."[67] DHS is also said to have developed a subset of approximately 600 assets, which might be considered to be "critical." The database has been the subject of political debate since it inevitably drives funding decisions.[68]

- The US Federal Bureau of Investigation (FBI) created a cyber division, which has a fourfold mission: to stop the spread of malicious code, to protect children from online exploitation, to counter the theft of intellectual property, and to defeat organized crime organizations who conduct internet fraud.[69] The FBI cyber division's operations include the following:

  - The FBI's Internet Crime Complaint Center (IC3) is a "clearinghouse for triaging cyber crime complaints." Citizens who encounter cyber crime can call the Bureau's hotline and receive assistance. The FBI conducts analysis and research, working with a variety of law enforcement agencies and private-sector organizations.

  - The FBI Cyber Division's Cyber Action Teams (CATS) are "small, highly trained teams of FBI agents, analysts, and computer forensics and malicious code experts who travel the world on a moment's notice to respond to fast-moving cyber threats."

  - The FBI Computer Crimes Task Forces handle various cyber-related cases such as those involving computer scams, online child predators, and analysis of suspect computers.[70]

  - The US Computer and Emergency Readiness Team (US-CERT) is a 24-hour command center watching and providing warnings regarding the US federal government's cyber infrastructure.[71] It is a partnership between the Department of Homeland Security, other public agencies, and private entities. One significant effort under way by US-CERT and Homeland Security is the EINSTEIN

Program, which is an early warning system that would alert authorities to attacks against the infrastructure of the United States. It is an "automated process for collecting and sharing security information" and will improve the government's ability to analyze threat information.[72] The Joint Task Force concept has worked well in the past, and involves the teaming of federal agencies for information sharing, coordination, and training.

Adequately Fund Cyber CT Efforts. All good security measures tend to be costly, and the cyber CT effort is no different. Cyber CT deserves high ranking on international security priorities, if it is to be effective.

Rehearsal

Periodically Conduct Realistic Readiness Exercises. While exercises can be expensive, they can also provide tremendous insights into areas in which the state's plans and procedures are adequate and the international community's coordination is strong, as well as areas in which more emphasis is required. Developing a plan is useful, but if developed in a vacuum without sharing information and expectations with higher, subordinate, and lateral organizations, or if the plan simply sits on a shelf and is never exercised, then the shortfalls will only become apparent when the plan is exercised in time of emergency. It is better to work out the kinks when the stakes are not so high.[73] Improved simulations technology can mitigate exercise costs and facilitate increasingly realistic exercises. Multiple participants may be involved from their own places of business despite widely dispersed physical locations. Clear objectives must be set; some of the various possibilities are: identification of future planning and process improvements; exercise of the cyber response organizations of public and private agencies, associations, and corporations within a region or across multiple regions and even states; and enhancement of the development of various skills required of military commanders and civilian leaders.[74]

Global/Strategic

Project via Cyberspace a Unified, Coherent "Strategic Communications" Message. The world needs to understand what counterterrorism practitioners are trying to do, why and how they are trying to do it, and how citizens can help. The message should address and effectively refute extremist ideas and claims, offering a better message. The following points are key to the development of the message:

- Draw in the news media; give them the cyber CT story.
- Use the power and skills of the entertainment industry to tell the real story.
- Rapidly and articulately refute extremist accusations.
- Explain all contentious actions that take on a strategic character.
- Prepare effective arguments against extremists' actions.
- Create regional indications and warning centers to head off problems; act regionally and publicize success.

Take a Holistic Approach to Cyber CT and Refute the Terrorists' Message. Professors Weimann and von Knop use the concept of "noise" in communications theory to arrive at the notion that strategic communications planning must include elements of both hard (coercive) power such as hacking, and soft (attractive) power such as psychological operations (PSYOPS).[75] They cite Joseph Nye in *The Power of Persuasion* as saying that "soft power does not increase relative power on the hard side, but it does make hard power more acceptable, lowering the costs of exercising such power."[76] The team argues that "the answer to terrorist use of the internet lies not in censorship of the internet, but in a more sophisticated and complicated strategy."[77] They propose that understanding the communication process that terrorists and extremists use, and identifying the targets of their message, will present opportunities for disruption of this process.

It is this writer's opinion that hard and soft power are both necessary in the cyber CT fight. The replacing of an extremist idea with a better idea, well articulated and attractively packaged, can change minds and hearts, and may seriously inhibit recruiting by the terror group. But, in the shorter term, it might well be necessary to shut down terrorist activities in cyberspace—if the intelligence value from monitoring their activity is not great. Further, and as previously mentioned, if the technical capability were developed to determine the location and identity of the terrorist, direct action, either by police or military, against the individual might well be possible and warranted.

There has been much material written about terrorist networks—how they meet each other, how they communicate, how they recruit, how they operate, etc. John Arquilla and David Ronfeldt, in their book *Networks and Netwars* (2000), make the observation that "all networks that have been built for waging netwar may be analyzed in terms of a common analytic framework. There are five levels of theory and practice that matter: the technological, social, narrative, organizational, and doctrinal levels. A netwar actor must get all five right to be fully effective."[78] This holistic approach to modern warfare is in agreement with the Chinese way of thinking as articulated in *Unrestricted Warfare*: "Regardless of whether the war was 3,000 years ago or at the end of the 20th century, it seems that all of the victories display one common phenomenon: the winner is the one who combined well."[79]

Offensive

Offensive Measures: The Best Defense Is a Strong Offense. Cyber CT practitioners must have the capability to prevail over criminal or terrorist forces in cyberspace by denying their attempts to control or to otherwise use for their own illegal purposes the free and legal flow of information throughout cyberspace. Law enforcement authorities need software that fights and eliminates malicious software, releases computers that have been ensnared in so-called robot networks, monitors illegal activity, and destroys or otherwise shuts down illegal websites. This may well include the creation of "good botnets," which dissemble or otherwise defeat their criminal or terrorist counterparts.

Conduct Undercover Police Work in Terrorist Chat Rooms. The actions of such cyber vigilantes as Shannen Rossmiller and Aaron Weisburd have already been discussed as a phenomenon of information warfare and initiative counterespionage, but vigilantes should not have led our cyber CT fight. Further, independent action by such individuals can disrupt the plans of law enforcement authorities and play into criminal hands. Investing in formal training by cyber CT practitioners to selected government operatives who will become part of a coordinated law enforcement "cyber-corps" is a worthy endeavor and potentially very effective tool.

Create Cyber Forces That Are Capable of Conducting Offensive Cyber Combat. The free world must develop not only a robust cyber defense capability but an agile, effective offensive cyber combat capability. The US National Military Strategy for Cyberspace Operations defines cyberspace as a "domain characterized by the use of electronics and the electromagnetic spectrum to store, modify, and exchange data via networked systems and associated physical infrastructures."[80] The US Air Force's doctrine suggests that cyberspace is considered a domain in which to achieve freedom of action to ensure security. It must be governed, controlled, and patrolled by the forces of good order, security, and rule of law. This offensive capability would ideally include the ability to detect, deny, pursue, and destroy the websites, malicious software, and other cyber agents, and also the computer hardware of those with criminal and terrorist intent. In so doing, one must assemble sufficient evidence of wrongdoing to allow prosecution of the criminals or terrorists involved. The United States has taken various actions in order to build a force capable of maintaining freedom of action in such a domain.

The head of the Joint Functional Component Command for Network Warfare (JFCC-WF) is also the Director of the National Security Agency. JFCC-WF facilitates coordination with other organizations in both defensive and offensive information warfare. Major supporting commands include the Defense Information Systems Agency and the Joint Task Force for Global Network Operations, which defends the nation's worldwide information networks.[81]

The United States Air Force had designated the 8th Air Force at Barksdale Air Force Base in Louisiana as the "Cyber Command," and this provisional organization conducted such groundbreaking work as defining roles and missions, identifying required capabilities, and writing doctrine. Originally the command was to have been responsible for the security of the whole nation's cyber infrastructure, but the concept has devolved. In late 2007 outside of Barksdale Air Force Base, construction began on a civilian equivalent to the USAF Cyber Command, a Cyber Innovation Center, according to reports. Ultimately, the USAF decided to establish a numbered Air Force for Cyber Operations under Space Command rather than creating another major command.[82]

Other US armed forces have been developing their own cyber capabilities: the Naval Network Warfare Command (NETWARCOM) is located in Norfolk, Virginia, and is the US Navy's lead cyber agency, while the US Army's Training and Doctrine Command (TRADOC) has created a new office called the TRADOC Project Office for Gaming, and according to reports, has also set up a task force with the mission of countering the theft of sensitive information by hackers breaking into defense contractors' networks. The organization is called the Defense Industrial Base Cyber-Security Task Force, and is tasked with the mission of protecting US Army weapon systems by ensuring sensitive data associated with the systems are not stolen during the procurement and development process.[83]

The US Congress has ordered the Defense Advanced Research Projects Agency (DARPA) to create a "National Cyber Range." This was included in a $30 billion US government effort. It would be able to "replicate realistic human behavior on nodes" to include but not be limited to interacting with authentication systems.[84] Virtual reality technology and operations in virtual reality should be a large part of this effort.

Nations with National Caveats Against Physical Combat Could Conduct Cyber Combat. Under the category of "Offensive Cyber CT," those several states of NATO and the EU and elsewhere, which find themselves hampered in their efforts at offensive global CT by national caveats against physical combat, could and should develop a capability to wage offensive warfare in cyberspace in support of liberty and the rule of law.

Develop Multi-use Micro-bot Attack Swarms. In coordination with a technological solution that removes the anonymity of cyberspace, micro-robot technology should be leveraged to develop the capability of delivering micro-bugs, aerial platforms the size of insects or smaller. These might be launched by means such as unmanned aerial vehicles (UAVs) or manned aircraft to detect the origin of certain types of signature electromagnetic transmissions consistent with specific target computers, detect certain words or names associated with terrorism, and determine the location of cyber terrorists and their computer hardware. The robot "bugs" could listen for certain sounds, detect certain frequencies or even smells, and collect data or pictures. Others perhaps could enter and destroy computer infrastructure.[85]

Conclusions

It seems to this writer that an analogy could be drawn between the security crisis presented to civilization by cyber terror and a time in the early twentieth century at the advent of air power, when defenders who had been masters at fortifications, obstacles, and ground combat found themselves in the position of seeing these defensive tools rendered seemingly irrelevant by a technological innovation called the airplane. Our predecessors in the business of national security had to work furiously to develop ways of defending our borders from men and machines that could fly over them. Over time, technological and organizational solutions to this problem were developed that were and continue to be both defensive as well as offensive in character. Ultimately, the invention of the aircraft did not make borders irrelevant, but a significant effort, technological and organizational, defensive and offensive, was required to mitigate the threat.

Now the world finds itself in a less dramatic but strategically similar situation, in which borders seem to have evaporated again in the face of the reality that is cyberspace and cyber terror, leaving civilization vulnerable to malicious attacks, to harmful ideologies, to manipulation of news media, and to disruption of commerce and communications and control systems. It is this writer's sense that, as was the case in the last century, the situation is manageable but concerted action is required—action in the form of technological innovation, structural reorganization, updates to domestic and international law, unified strategic narrative, and the development of defensive as well as offensive forces capable of cyber combat.

By way of summary, the following conclusions are the result of the arguments articulated in this chapter:

- Cyberspace continues to be an ungoverned area. No state truly has control over it, the rule of law cannot currently be enforced in it, and perpetrators of crimes within it cannot usually be identified with much certainty. Like physically ungoverned areas, cyberspace is a breeding ground and sanctuary for criminals, spies, and terrorists.

- Every citizen who owns a computer must take responsibility for the security of cyberspace, and provide conscientious support to efforts to maintain its free and legal use. It is essential, however, for citizens to coordinate with law enforcement authorities in order to ensure that their actions do not work at cross purposes.

- The anonymity with which illegal actors can function is an especially difficult problem. This issue must be technologically overcome so that cyber criminals, cyber spies, and cyber terrorists cannot hide or act with impunity. No expense should be spared to acquire this capability as soon as humanly possible.

- A serious, concerted effort must be sustained by the international community as well as within the individual states to update laws so that they are effective in the apprehension of cyber criminals and terrorists, and relevant and responsive to the foreseeable future threats to law and order in cyberspace. Much progress has been made in the last several years, but more work is necessary.

- States must set as a high priority the creation, delivery, and maintenance of a unified, articulate, effective strategic message opposing the virulent and extremist ideologies being spread by terrorists in cyberspace. All available tools of the entertainment industry, psychology expertise, audiovisual technology, religious authorities, and public diplomacy should be combined to present a message of life and liberty that is attractive enough to draw all but the most radicalized away from the current messages of terror and death.

- The free world must have the capability to protect and patrol the domain of cyberspace, like that which we use to protect the free and legal use of the sea and the air. Responsible states should be able to prosecute cyber terrorism, and even take offensive action against those who would deprive the global community of the use of cyberspace.

John J. Kane Lieutenant Colonel Kane is a 28-year veteran of the United States Marine Corps with extensive operational experience in Marine Aviation and as a Foreign Area Officer specializing in the Former Soviet Union. Service in Marine aviation included operational billets in the Far East, United States, Europe, and the Middle East. Staff tours include Executive Officer of a Stinger Missile Battalion, Operations Officer of an Air Control Group, Director of Battlestaff Operations for an Aircraft Wing, and Future Operations Officer, Aviation Combat Element, II MEF, in Iraq. As a Foreign Area Officer Colonel Kane served as a POW/MIA investigator in Russia, as an Arms Control Team Leader for conventional forces in Europe, and as Marine Corps Attache, US Embassy Moscow. For three years John Kane was Deputy Course Director, Program on Terrorism and Security Studies, George C. Marshall Center. He researched and lectured on cyber terrorism, also creating and leading the first experts panel on cyber terror for the Marshall Center. Colonel Kane currently serves with the Center for Advanced Operational Culture Learning, Marine Corps Training & Education Command. A graduate of the US Naval Academy, he holds a master's degree from Norwich University.

Recommended Readings

Arquilla, John, and David Ronfeldt, eds. *Networks and Netwars: The Future of Terror, Crime, and Militancy.* Santa Monica, CA: Rand Corporation, 2001.

Bakier, Abdul Hameed. "New Website Incites Electronic Jihad," *Jamestown Foundation Terrorism Focus,* Vol. 3, No. 38 (3 October 2006). Available at http://www.jamestown.org/single/?no_cache=1&tx_ttnews%5Btt_news%5D=918, accessed 28 May 2009.

Carafano, James Jay, and Richard Weitz. "Combating Enemies Online: State-Sponsored and Terrorist Use of the Internet," *Heritage Foundation Backgrounder,* No. 2105 (8 February 2008). Available at http://www.heritage.org/research/nationalsecurity/upload/bg_2105.pdf, accessed 22 September 2009.

Chairman of the Joint Chiefs of Staff. "The National Military Strategy for Cyberspace Operations," December 2006. Available at http://www.dod.mil/pubs/foi/ojcs/07-F-2105doc1.pdf, accessed 25 May 2009.

Denning, Dorthy E. "Is Cyber Terror Next?" Social Science Research Council, *After Sept. 11: Perspectives from the Social Sciences,* 1 November 2001. Available at http://www.ssrc.org/sept11/essays/denning.htm, accessed 27 May 2009.

Liang, Qiao, and Wang Xiangsui. *Unrestricted Warfare.* Beijing, China: PLA Literature and Arts Publishing House, 1999.

Perrow, Charles. *The Next Catastrophe: Reducing Our Vulnerabilities to Natural, Industrial and Terrorist Disasters.* Princeton, NJ: Princeton University Press, 2007.

Rollins, John, and Clay Wilson. "Terrorist Capabilities for Cyberattack: Overview and Policy Issues," Congressional Research Service RL33123 (22 January 2007). Available at www.fas.org/sgp/crs/terror/RL33123.pdf, accessed 29 May 2009.

Weimann, Gabriel. "www.terror.net: How Modern Terrorism Uses the Internet," *United States Institute of Peace Special Report* No. 116 (March 2004). Available at http://www.usip.org/files/resources/sr116.pdf, accessed 22 September 2009.

Wilson, Clay. "Avatars, Virtual Reality Technology and the U.S. Military: Emerging Policy Issues," Congressional Research Service RS 22857 (9 April 2008). Available at http://fas.org/sgp/crs/natsec/RS22857.pdf, accessed 22 September 2009.

Notes

1. As an example, in 2005, the writer had the honor of being responsible for the tasking of all Marine Corps aircraft in Iraq, an extremely complex process made possible at an acceptable level of efficiency only through heavy dependence upon computer processing operations.
2. John Perry Barlow's words of 1981, as quoted in John Gerstner, "Cyber Cowboy: An Interview with John Perry Barlow (Internet Expert)," *Communication World* (November 1995).
3. John Perry Barlow, *Crime and Puzzlement: Desperados of the DataSphere* (Electronic Frontier Foundation, 1990), available at http://w2.eff.org/Misc/Publications/John_Perry_Barlow/HTML/crime_and_puzzlement_1.html, accessed 22 September 2009.
4. Chairman of the Joint Chiefs of Staff, "The National Military Strategy for Cyberspace Operations," December 2006, ix, available at http://www.dod.mil/pubs/foi/ojcs/07-F-2105doc1.pdf, accessed 25 May 2009.
5. Chris Larson, "A Just-In-Time Supply Chain? Achieving Just-In-Time Operational Objectives Requires the Coordination of Production Planning, Sourcing, and Logistics," United Parcel Service (UPS) Supply Chain Solutions, White Paper, 2005, available from http://www.ups-scs.com/solutions/white_papers/wp_JIT.pdf, 2005, Internet, accessed 25 May 2009.
6. Yossi Sheffi and James B. Rice Jr., "A Supply Chain View of the Resilient Enterprise," *MIT Sloan Management Review,* 15 October 2005, available at http://sloanreview.mit.edu/the-magazine/articles/2005/fall/47110/a-supply-chain-view-of-the-resilient-enterprise/, accessed 25 May 2009. Author's note: After the 11 September 2001 attacks, the US government

closed land borders and halted incoming and outgoing flights. As a result, the Ford Motor Company, which adheres to the JIT supply method, had to idle certain assembly lines as it waited for components that normally arrive by truck from Mexico and Canada. Similarly, supplies for Toyota's assembly process suffered delays as they waited to enter US airports from Germany. If such circumstances can cause serious disruption, what is possible should those acting with extreme malice attempt to do harm to a state's industry?

7. Stefano Panzieri, Roberto Setola, and Giovanni Ulivi, "An Approach to Model Complex Interdependent Infrastructures," Paper Presented to the 16th International Federation of Accountants (IFAC) World Congress in Prague, July 2005, available at http://www.nt.ntnu.no/users/skoge/prost/proceedings/ifac2005/Fullpapers/02774.pdf, accessed 22 September 2009. ICT stands for "information and communication technologies."

8. John E. Dunn, "Outsourcing Blamed for Rising Security Woes," *TechWorld*, 8 April 2008, available at http://www.techworld.com/news/index.cfm?newsID=11922&printerfriendly=1, accessed 25 May 2009.

9. Charles Perrow, *The Next Catastrophe: Reducing Our Vulnerabilities to Natural, Industrial and Terrorist Disasters* (Princeton, NJ: Princeton University Press, 2007), 250.

10. Panzieri et al.

11. Ibid, 257.

12. Brian Krebs, "Cyber Incident Blamed for Nuclear Power Plant Shutdown," *Washington Post*, 5 June 2008, available at http://www.washingtonpost.com/wp-dyn/content/article/2008/06/05/AR2008060501958.html, accessed 22 September 2009.

13. See FBI Internet Crime Complaint Center website, www.ic3.gov, accessed 24 September 2009.

14. Symantec, *Symantec Global Internet Security Threat Report*, 90.

15. James Jay Carafano and Richard Weitz, "Combating Enemies Online: State-Sponsored and Terrorist Use of the Internet," *Heritage Foundation Backgrounder* No. 2105 (8 February 2008): 3, available at http://www.heritage.org/research/nationalsecurity/upload/bg_2105.pdf, accessed 22 September 2009.

16. Gabriel Weimann, "www.terror.net: How Modern Terrorism Uses the Internet," United States Institute of Peace Special Report No. 116 (March 2004): 7, available at http://www.usip.org/files/resources/sr116.pdf, accessed 22 September 2009.

17. Chris Nuttall, "Kosovo Info Warfare Spreads," BBC News, 1 April 1999, available at http://news.bbc.co.uk/1/hi/sci/tech/308788.stm; accessed 18 January 2009; see also Bob Brewin, "Kosovo Ushered in Cyberwar," *Federal Computer Week*, 27 September 1999, available at http://fcw.com/articles/1999/09/27/kosovo-ushered-in-cyberwar.aspx?sc_lang=en, accessed 22 September 2009.

18. Ian Traynor, "Russia Accused of Unleashing Cyberwar to Disable Estonia," *The Guardian*, 17 May 2007, available at http://www.guardian.co.uk/world/2007/may/17/topstories3.russia, accessed 18 January 2009.

19. "RFE/RL Websites Hit by Mass Cyberattack," Radio Free Europe/Radio Liberty, 28 April 2008, available at http://www.rferl.org/content/article/1109642.html, accessed 26 May 2009.

20. "Hackers Place Soviet Symbols on Hundreds of Websites," *Baltic Times*, 30 June 2008, available at http://www.alfa.lt/straipsnis/c78573, accessed 18 January 2009.

21. Thomas Claburn, "Under Cyberattack, Georgia Finds 'Bullet-Proof' Hosting with Google and Elsewhere," *Information Week*, 12 August 2008, available at http://www.informationweek.com/news/security/attacks/showArticle.jhtml?articleID=210002702, accessed 26 May 2009.

22. John Markoff, "Before the Gunfire, Cyberattacks," *The New York Times*, 12 August 2008, available at http://www.nytimes.com/2008/08/13/technology/13cyber.html, accessed on 26 May 2009.

23. Evgeny Morozov, "An Army of Ones and Zeroes: How I Became a Soldier in the Georgia-Russia Cyberwar," *Slate*, 14 August 2008, available at http://www.slate.com/id/2197514/, accessed on 26 May 2009.

24. Richard Behar, "Exclusive: Cyber-Hackers Break into IMF Computer System," Fox News, 14 November 2008, available at http://www.foxnews.com/story/0,2933,452348,00.html, accessed 26 May 2009.

25. Ahmad Kamal, *The Law of Cyberspace: An Invitation to the Table of Negotiations* (New York: United Nations Institute for Training and Research, 2006), available at http://www.un.int/kamal/thelawofcyberspace, accessed 22 September 2009.

26. Dorothy E. Denning, "Is Cyber Terror Next?" Social Science Research Council, *After Sept. 11: Perspectives from the Social Sciences*, 1 November 2001, available at http://www.ssrc.org/sept11/essays/denning.htm, accessed 27 May 2009.

27. Abdul Hameed Bakier, "New Website Incites Electronic Jihad," *Jamestown Foundation Terrorism Focus*, Vol. 3, No. 38 (3 October 2006), available at http://www.jamestown.org/single/?no_cache=1&tx_ttnews%5Btt_news%5D=918, accessed 28 May 2009.

28. E. Alshech, "Cyberspace as a Combat Zone: The Phenomenon of Electronic Jihad," Middle East Media Research Institute, *Inquiry & Analysis*, No. 329 (27 February 2007), available from http://www.memri.org/bin/opener.cgi?ID=IA32907, accessed 17 January 2009.

29. Kamal, op. cit.

30. Magnus Ranstorp, "The Virtual Sanctuary of Al-Qaeda and Terrorism in an Age of Globalization," in *International Relations and Security in the Digital Age*, Johan Eriksson and Giampiero Giacomello, eds. (London: Routledge, 2007). Dr. Ranstorp is formerly the research director of the Centre for the Study of Terrorism and Political Violence at St. Andrews University in Scotland, and a prolific writer.

31. US Army DCSINT Handbook No. 1.02 "Cyber Operations and Terrorism," TRADOC, 2005.

32. Sebastian Rotella, "A World Wide Web of Terrorist Plotting," *Los Angeles Times*, 16 April 2007, available at http://articles.latimes.com/2007/apr/16/world/fg-net16, accessed 22 September 2009.

33. Elaine Sciolino and Souad Mekhennet, "Al Qaeda Warrior Uses Internet to Rally Women," *The New York Times*, 28 May 2008, available at http://www.nytimes.com/2008/05/28/world/europe/28terror.html, accessed 18 January 2009.

34. "Belgian Police Arrest 'al Qaeda Legend'," CNN.com, 11 December 2008, available at http://edition.cnn.com/2008/WORLD/europe/12/11/belgium.terror.arrests/index.html, accessed 22 September 2009.

35. Mark White, "Banned Cleric Preaching to Brits," Sky News, 13 December 2008, available at http://www.investigativeproject.org/ext/1891, accessed 16 January 2009.

36. Oana Lungescu, "EU Tightens Anti-Terrorism Laws," BBC News, 18 April 2008, available at http://news.bbc.co.uk/2/hi/europe/7355446.stm, accessed 18 January 2009.

37. Thomas Harding, "Terrorists Launder Cash Through Online Gambling," *Daily Telegraph*, 1 January 2009, available at http://www.telegraph.co.uk/scienceandtechnology/technology/4060727/Terrorists-launder-cash-through-on-line-gambling.html, accessed 28 May 2009.

38. Mitchell D. Silber and Arvin Bhatt, *Radicalization in the West: The Homegrown Threat* (New York: New York City Police Department, 2007), 37, available at http://www.nypdshield.org/public/SiteFiles/documents/NYPD_Report-Radicalization_in_the_West.pdf, accessed 24 September 2009.

39. Ibid.

40. John Rollins and Clay Wilson, "Terrorist Capabilities for Cyberattack: Overview and Policy Issues," Congressional Research Service RL33123 (22 January 2007), available at www.fas.org/sgp/crs/terror/RL33123.pdf, accessed 29 May 2009.

41. As an example, see Jeanne Meserve, "Staged Cyber Attack Reveals Vulnerability in Power Grid," CNN.com, 26 September 2007, available at http://edition.cnn.com/2007/US/09/26/power.at.risk/index.html, accessed 22 September 2009.

42. The CIA's unclassified responses to questions posed on 6 February 2002 by the Senate Select Committee on Intelligence in a letter dated 8 April 2002 includes the following under "The Threat of Cyber Terrorism": "Aleph, formerly known as Aum Shinrikyo is the terrorist group that places the highest level of importance on developing cyber skills. These could be applied to cyber attacks against the US. This group identifies itself as a cyber cult and derives millions of dollars a year from computer retailing." Letter available at http://www.fas.org/irp/congress/2002_hr/020602cia.html, accessed 22 September 22, 2009.

43. Dorothy Denning provides the fascinating and alarming details in her essay "Is Cyber Terror Next?" (op. cit.): "In March 2000, Japan's Metropolitan Police Department reported that a software system they had procured to track 150 police vehicles, including unmarked cars, had been developed by the Aum Shinryko cult, the same group that gassed the Tokyo subway in 1995, killing 12 people and injuring 6,000 more. At the time of the discovery, the cult had received classified tracking data on 115 vehicles. Further, the cult had developed software for at least 80 Japanese firms and 10 government agencies. They had worked as subcontractors to other firms, making it almost impossible for the organizations to know who was developing the software. As subcontractors, the cult could have installed Trojan horses to launch or facilitate cyber terrorist attacks at a later date."

44. "Japan's Computers Hit by Cult Fears," BBC News, 1 March 2000, available at http://news .bbc.co.uk/1/hi/world/asia-pacific/662172.stm, accessed 29 May 2009.

45. Qiao Liang and Wang Xiangsui, *Unrestricted Warfare* (Beijing, China: PLA Literature and Arts Publishing House, 1999), 25.

46. Ibid., 145.

47. R. Montano et al., "On the Response and Immunity of Electric Power Infrastructures Against IEMI—Current Swedish Initiatives," Electromagnetic Compatibility and 19th International Zurich Symposium on Electromagnetic Compatibility, 19–23 May 2008, 510–513.

48. Clay Wilson, "Avatars, Virtual Reality Technology and the U.S. Military: Emerging Policy Issues," Congressional Research Service RS 22857 (9 April 2008), available at http://fas .org/sgp/crs/natsec/RS22857.pdf, accessed 22 September 2009. Some observers note that any country that succeeds in dominating the VR market may also set the technical standards for the rest of the world, and may also own and operate the VR servers that give them unique access to information about future global financial transactions, transportation, shipping, and business communications that may rely on virtual worlds.

49. Council of Europe Parliamentary Assembly Opinion Document No. 11335, "How to Prevent Cybercrime Against State Institutions in Member and Observer States?" 27 June 2007, available at http://assembly.coe.int/Documents/WorkingDocs/Doc07/EDOC11335.pdf, accessed 18 January 2009.

50. Murad Ahmed and Laura Dixon, "Russia and China accused of Harboring Cybercriminals," *Times Online*, 9 December 2008, available at http://technology.timesonline.co.uk/tol/news/ tech_and_web/article5312323.ece, accessed 22 September 2009.

51. Perrow, 270.

52. As our glossary indicates, "phishing" is the use of spoofed e-mail and websites designed to deceive internet users into divulging sensitive information.

53. Perrow, 260.

54. Ibid, 268.

55. Kelly Jackson Higgins, "New Intrusion Tolerance Technology Treats Attacks as Inevitable," *DarkReading*, 12 May 2008, available at http://www.darkreading.com/security/management/ showArticle.jhtml?articleID=211201079.

56. Robert McMillan, "Microsoft Botnet-hunting Tool Helps Bust Hackers," IDG News Service, 29 April 2008, available via PC World at http://www.pcworld.com/businesscenter/article/145257/ microsoft_botnethunting_tool_helps_bust_hackers.html, accessed 22 September 2009.

57. See Symantec, "Phish Report Network," available at http://www.phishreport.net/, accessed 27 September 2009.

58. Symantec, *Symantec Global Internet Security Threat Report*, Vol. XIV, April 2009, available at http://eval.symantec.com/mktginfo/enterprise/white_papers/b-whitepaper_internet_ security_threat_report_xiv_04-2009.en-us.pdf.

59. "EU to Punish Incitement to Terrorism on Internet," Reuters, 18 April 2008, available at http://www.reuters.com/article/technologyNews/idUSL1889698320080418?feedType=RSS& feedName=technologyNews&pageNumber=1&virtualBrandChannel=0, accessed 31 May 2009.

60. See the Cooperative Cyber Defence Center of Excellence website, http://www.ccdcoe.org/, accessed 27 September 2009.

61. "NATO Allies Sign Agreement on Cyber Defense Center," Associated Press International, 14 May 2008.

62. See International Multilateral Partnership Against Cyber Terror website, http://www.impact-alliance.org/, accessed 27 September 2009.

63. Ars Technica, "New International Group to Become the CDC of Cyber Security," 14 May 2008, available at http://arstechnica.com/new.ars/port/20080514-new-international-group-to-become-the-cdc-of-cyber-security.ars, accessed 18 January 2009.

64. "IT Chiefs Warn of Cyber-Terrorism Threat," Agence France-Presse, 20 May 2008, available at http://afp.google.com/article/ALeqM5h_fadPsFriHf8FGka-wUNdLsm0tQ, accessed September 24, 2009.

65. See the Middle East Media Research Institute website, http://www.memri.org/, accessed 27 September 2009.

66. See SITE Intelligence Group website, www.siteintelgroup.com, accessed 27 September 2009.

67. John Moteff, "Critical Infrastructure: The National Asset Database," CRS Report for Congress RL33648, updated 16 July 2007, 2, available at http://ftp.fas.org/sgp/crs/homesec/RL33648.pdf, accessed 27 September 2009.

68. Incidentally, Germany and the United Kingdom do not publish a database of critical infrastructure, considering that it would prove to be a targeting tool for terrorists.

69. See FBI Cyber Investigations website, http://www.fbi.gov/cyberinvest/cyberhome.htm, accessed 24 September 2009.

70. Ibid.

71. See United States Computer Emergency Readiness Team (CERT) website, available at http://www.us-cert.gov/, accessed 31 May 2009.

72. Ibid.

73. Some of the cyber security exercises conducted by the United States follow:
    ELIGIBLE RECEIVER was a classified exercise in which the National Security Agency acted as aggressor against the Pentagon. Conducted in 1997 with commercially available hardware and software, the attacks were successful in disrupting Department of Defense computer systems, denying services, reading and changing or deleting e-mails, and disrupting phone services. This no-notice exercise resulted in the discovery and exploitation of serious weaknesses in the security of the DoD's cyber infrastructure. (Global Security, "Eligible Receiver," available at http://www.globalsecurity.org/military/ops/eligible-receiver.htm, accessed 24 September 2009.)
    CYBER STORM I was designed to exercise communication, incident response policies, and operational procedures in response to various cyber incidents, and to identify future planning and process improvements. Conducted in February 2006, the exercise simulated a large-scale cyber campaign affecting and disrupting multiple critical infrastructure elements, primarily within the energy, IT, and transportation sectors, and secondarily within telecommunications. Cyber Storm simultaneously exercised the cyber response organizations of over 100 public and private agencies, associations, and corporations in over 60 locations and five countries. (Department of Homeland Security National Cyber Security Devision, "Cyber Storm Exercise Report," 12 September 2006, available at http://www.dhs.gov/xlibrary/assets/prep_cyberstormreport_sep06.pdf, accessed 24 September 2009.)
    CYBER STORM II "simulated a coordinated cyber attack on information technology, communications, chemical, and transportation systems and assets. It simulated a crash of the US and international telephone system which in turn caused problems for top level domains such as .com, .net and .gov. Crisis managers had to identify, evaluate and respond to more than 1,800 malware incidents. These included botnet, phishing, and denial of service attacks. Some were 'white noise.' These were relatively harmless events designed to mask or confuse more serious attacks on the systems." The week-long cyber-security exercise was conducted in March 2008; Cyber Storm III is scheduled for early 2010. (Ian Grant, "Cyber Storm II Exercise Reveals Security Preparedness," *Computer Weekly.com*, 18 March 2008, available at http://www.computerweekly.com/Articles/2008/03/18/229909/cyber-storm-2-exercise-reveals-security-preparedness.htm, accessed 24 September 2009.)

NOBLE RESOLVE 08 was a planned virtual reality exercise advertised to use intricate computer-based models and long-distance virtual connections to provide the environment for participants to make decisions and work together as they would in case of a real crisis. See also: http://www.jfcom.mil/newslink/storyarchive/2008/pa011608.htm

74. **URBAN RESOLVE** was a "distributed training simulation" conducted in 2006 by the US Joint Forces Command, Joint Experimentation Directorate. The exercise used virtual world technology to enhance development of various skills required of joint force commanders for warfighting operations in an urban terrain. According to the *Defense Industry Daily*, "USJFCOM Joint Futures Lab executive director Dave Ozolek said the experiment is enabling the command to get inside two concepts: First, how does the US military operate in the new urban environment? Because 'That's where the fight is, that's where the enemy is, that where the center of gravity for the whole operation is.' It's more than the classic MOUT [Military Operations in Urban Terrain] because '. . . the environment is not only terrain, it's infrastructure, it's culture, it's governance, it's rule of law, it's legality, food, water, fire and safety and all of those things that make up a complex environment of a city.' This feeds into the second concept: operations to stabilize the situation in a city, and then transition to local control." ("Urban Resolve 2015 Hopes to Provide Window into Urban Combat Future," *Defense Industry Daily*, 25 October 2006, available at http://www.defenseindustrydaily.com/urban-resolve-2015-hopes-to-provide-window-into-urban-combat-future-02745/, accessed 24 September 2009.)

75. Gabriel Weimann and Katharina von Knop, "Applying the Notion of Noise to Countering Online Terrorism," *Studies in Conflict & Terrorism*, Vol. 31, Issue 10 (October 2008), 891.

76. Ibid.

77. Ibid., 899.

78. John Arquilla and David Ronfeldt, eds., *Networks and Netwars: The Future of Terror, Crime, and Militancy* (Santa Monica, CA: Rand Corporation, 2001), x.

79. Liang and Xiangsui, 140.

80. Chairman of the Joint Chiefs of Staff, "The National Military Strategy for Cyberspace Operations," page IX, available at http://www.dod.mil/pubs/foi/ojcs/07-F-2105doc1.pdf

81. See US Strategic Command, "Functional Components," available at http://www.stratcom.mil/functional_components/, accessed 27 September 2009.

82. The decision by the Air Force leadership seems to have been based on both political and organizational difficulties associated with taking over responsibility for the nation's cyber protection. See Bob Brewin, "Air Force Suspends Cyber Command Program," NextGov.com, 12 August 2008, available at http://www.nextgov.com/nextgov/ng_20080812_7995.php; accessed 31 May 2009; and "Plan B for Cyber Innovation Center," KTBS 3 Online (Shreveport, LA), 15 May 2009, available at http://www.ktbs.com/news/plan-b-for-cyber-innovation-center, accessed 31 May 2009.

83. Shaun Waterman, "Army Defense Task Force Targeting Hackers," *Washington Times*, 27 October 2008, available at http://www.washingtontimes.com/news/2008/oct/27/army-defense-task-force-targeting-hackers/, accessed 24 September 2009.

84. Noah Schachtman, "Pentagon Wants Cyberwar Range to 'Replicate Human Behavior and Frailties'," *Wired Magazine Danger Room*, 6 May 2008, available at http://www.wired.com/dangerroom/2008/05/the-pentagons-w/, accessed 31 May 2009.

85. Homeland Security Newswire, "USAF Looks for More Discriminating UAVs," 22 June 2009, available at http://homelandsecuritynewswire.com/usaf-looks-more-discriminating-uavs, accessed January 2010.

3.7

Mark Trevelyan

The Media and the Terrorist:

Is There a "Right" Way to Cover Political Violence?

Acts of terrorism are inherently dramatic. They arouse strong feelings. They challenge governments and invade the lives of ordinary people, bringing death and destruction sometimes on such a scale as to destabilize countries and shock the entire world.

They are, in short, big news. The 11 September 2001 airplane attacks and the series of events they set in motion—including the launch of the "war on terror," which was used to justify the invasions of Afghanistan and Iraq—changed the course of history, dominated the presidency of George W. Bush, and provided the international media with the biggest news story of the early years of the twenty-first century.

Media coverage of terrorism matters. Terrorism is a means of sending a message, and the media provide the channel by which that message is carried, beyond the immediate victims, to reach a mass audience. Killing and destroying are the means the terrorist uses to "speak" to the government and to citizens, seeking to spread fear and destroy their resolve. The power of the message is amplified by the scale of death and carnage, and by the mode of attack. In the case of a suicide bomber, for example, the intended message goes roughly as follows: "I am prepared to die for my beliefs. You are facing an enemy who is so committed to his cause that you have no chance of defeating him." In the words of Sir Richard Dearlove, former head of Britain's foreign intelligence service, MI6: "Terrorism is an extreme act of political communication."[1]

This immediately confronts the media with a dilemma: How can they report on terrorism without amplifying the terrorists' message? If they report what the terrorists are saying, are they abetting them, even doing their work for them? Depending on how and what they report, media are in a position to provide many of the things that terrorists seek, including publicity, an understanding of their cause, legitimacy, and the maximizing of panic and fear.[2]

Coverage that hypes up the drama of terrorist violence may have the effect of heightening public anxiety. An account in a British news magazine of attacks on Mumbai, India, which killed more than 150 people in November 2008, was critical of news media for precisely this reason: "The terror instilled by the attacks was somehow deepened by the news coverage, with its melodramatic music, its repetition of rumours and supposition, and its sheer ghoulish relentlessness."[3]

Even responsible media that recognize the pitfalls of rumor, hype, and ghoulishness may feel themselves obliged to supply their readers and viewers with blanket coverage of events so dramatic and compelling that they find they simply cannot afford to ignore them.

During the seventeen-day hijack of TWA flight 847 in June 1985—which had 104 Americans and 49 others on board—a study of coverage in the *Washington Post, New York Times*, and *Los Angeles Times* found that stories on the crisis dominated all three newspapers, featuring on 31, 28, and 23 percent, respectively, of the pages in their main news sections throughout the entire episode.[4] Television coverage was proportionately even more intensive: the US networks ABC, CBS, and NBC devoted, respectively, 68, 62, and 63 percent of their airtime to the crisis. In a study, Dutch academic Alex Schmid argued that extensive media coverage of the plight of the hostages' distraught families had "increased the price" of the captives in a way that placed overwhelming pressure on the US and Israeli governments to do a deal. The Islamic Jihad group had demanded the release of 776 Shiite prisoners from Israeli jails, and its demands were eventually met almost in full: 756 were freed, in return for 39 hostages. "The media's profuse exposure of the hostage families and their grief thereby played into the hands of the terrorists," Schmid argued.[5]

A Symbiotic Relationship?

It is common among experts on terrorism to speak of a relationship of symbiosis—mutual dependence—between terrorists and the media: According to this argument, the terrorists need media coverage to advance their cause, while the media need the drama of terrorist attacks to fill their pages and news broadcasts, thereby maximizing their audience and their profits.

Britain's Paul Wilkinson argues that the relationship between terrorists and the mass media tends inevitably to become symbiotic once terrorist violence is under way. In a 1997 article, he cited the example of the seizure and massacre of Israeli athletes by the Palestinian Black September movement at the Munich Olympic Games a quarter of a century earlier, which was relayed to an estimated worldwide television audience of over five hundred million (a fraction of the number that would have access to coverage of such an event today). Terrorists, Wilkinson wrote:

> . . . want to appear on prime time TV to obtain not only massive, possibly world-wide, publicity but also the aura of legitimisation that such media attention gains for them in the eyes of their own followers and sympathisers. For the mass media organisations the coverage of terrorism, especially prolonged incidents such as hijackings and hostage situations, provides an endless source of sensational and visually compelling news stories capable of boosting audience/readership figures.[6]

Other leading academics such as Walter Laqueur have gone even further:

> It has been said that journalists are terrorists' best friends, because they are willing to give terrorist operations maximum exposure. This is not to say that journalists as a group are sympathetic to terrorists, although it may appear so. It simply means that violence is news, whereas peace and harmony are not. The terrorists need the media, and the media find in terrorism all the ingredients of an exciting story. Their attitude towards terrorism has run the gamut from exaggerated respect to sycophancy (such as calling a terrorist a freedom fighter, an activist, a patriot, a militant or a revolutionary). Media coverage has supplied constant grist to the terrorist mill; it has magnified the

political importance of many terrorist acts out of all proportion. In some cases it has even been responsible for the murder of innocents and obstructed complicated rescue missions. The media cannot ignore terrorism, but society would certainly be better off if the media were not driven by sensationalism.[7]

However, the idea that terrorism requires the participation of the mass media ignores the fact that terrorism existed long before the modern communications era. To assert that the media are somehow allies of the terrorist is to overlook the valuable role in society that responsible coverage can play. It provides a vital channel through which the authorities can counter terrorist propaganda, rally society against the threat, and enlist the participation of the public, for example, by telling people how to behave in an emergency and step up their vigilance in case of further attacks. By investigating the motivations of the perpetrators and critically examining their stated aims and beliefs, the media can also help society to answer one of the biggest and most basic questions that terrorist atrocities raise: "Why did they do this to us?" Raising the level of understanding of terrorism by both the populace and the decision makers is an important first step toward helping a society to formulate an effective counterterrorism response.

The idea, moreover, that the media depend on terrorists to supply them with fodder for maximizing profits is not only grotesque but wrong. First, the staple diet of the popular media in many western countries is based far more on celebrities, sex, show business, and sports—readers and viewers would quickly tire of a relentless diet of stories on terrorism. Second, it is worth noting that coverage of the "war on terrorism"—as defined by President George W. Bush to include the military campaigns in Afghanistan and Iraq—has cost media organizations heavily, in terms of both the financial outlay and the number of journalists killed.

Even among academics, the "symbiotic relationship" between terrorists and journalists is a matter of dispute. French sociologist Michel Wieviorka argued that the attitude of terrorists toward the media ranged from pure indifference to cases where they come to view the media themselves as enemies.[8] William Biernatzki, writing in 2002, noted that:

> One could as easily say that government officials and insurgent terrorists are in some kind of symbiotic relationship, the officials using the terrorist threat in one way or another to strengthen their own hold on power, and the terrorists referring to officials' wrongdoing to justify their own violent acts. In fact, the interrelationships among media, terrorists and government are extremely complex and multivalent.[9]

"Oxygen of Publicity"

A case study in these interrelationships—and how they can go wrong—was the British government's attempt to suppress media coverage of the militant republican movement in Northern Ireland in the late 1980s and early 1990s. At the height of the British government's struggle against the Irish Republic Army (IRA), only nine months after it had narrowly failed to blow her up in a bomb attack on a hotel, Prime Minister Margaret Thatcher made a famous speech:

> For newspapers and television, acts of terrorism inevitably make good copy and compelling viewing. The hijacker and the terrorist thrive on publicity: without it, their

activities and their influence are sharply curtailed. There is a fearful progression, which the terrorists exploit to the full. They see how acts of violence and horror dominate the newspaper columns and television screens of the free world. They see how that coverage creates a natural wave of sympathy for the victims and pressure to end their plight no matter what the consequence. And the terrorists exploit it. Violence and atrocity command attention. We must not play into their hands. . . .We must try to find ways to starve the terrorist and the hijacker of the oxygen of publicity on which they depend.[10]

Thatcher was infuriated by the media attention being given to the IRA and its political wing, Sinn Fein. In her determination to "starve the terrorists of oxygen," she introduced restrictions that prevented groups believed to support terrorism from broadcasting directly on the airwaves. The main target was Sinn Fein, but the law failed to achieve what Thatcher had hoped. Media got around it by conducting interviews with Sinn Fein leader Gerry Adams and then paying actors to read out his words. Not only did she fail to stop him getting his message across, but she handed him a publicity coup and made him look like an underdog, the victim of an unfair ban on free speech. The attempt to gag him was widely ridiculed; nevertheless, the broadcast ban on Sinn Fein lasted from 1988 until the IRA declared a ceasefire in 1994.

If censorship failed to silence the IRA's voice decades ago, it would stand even less chance today. Al Qaeda's message is out there, on thousands of websites around the world. As of 2008, one Israeli research institute was monitoring 5,800 militant sites.[11] Some of the best-known al Qaeda-linked forums, including one that in 2007 published a guide on how to kidnap Americans,[12] are hosted by Web service providers in the United States. But under US freedom of speech laws there is no way of shutting them down. Security and law enforcement professionals might not even want to, as they provide a window on the jihadists' world and an easy way of monitoring the enemy's propaganda. Even if they were closed down, they would pop up somewhere else. These websites carry regular statements from al Qaeda leaders but also from lesser known and more shadowy figures.

Media considering whether to report such statements need to ask themselves whether they are gratuitously supplying al Qaeda with the "oxygen of publicity" or whether the content can justifiably be seen as news. When Osama bin Laden made his first video appearance for nearly three years in September 2007, it made news largely because it disproved persistent speculation he was dead or gravely ill. Likewise, bin Laden's periodic offers of various types of truce or accommodation with western countries have been worth reporting because they provide a glimpse of al Qaeda's tactical thinking and purported openness to making deals, although they have always been roundly rejected by the target governments. Many other statements by al Qaeda figures have amounted to pure propaganda, without news value, and have correspondingly attracted little or no coverage. That is the way it should be. Responsible media do not routinely give air time to al Qaeda, but only when it makes major pronouncements that tell us something new about its thinking and strategy. Moreover, it is only by identifying and exposing the arguments of bin Laden—notably his core narrative that Islam is the target of a western crusade of persecution—that the media can help its audience understand the phenomenon of al Qaeda. Societies need to know their enemy and what they are up against. You have to hear what your adversary is saying in order to argue back.

Drawing the Line

Of course, there are limits to what the media should say or show: As responsible actors with a duty to society, they must not endanger life by divulging information that could compromise a counterterrorism operation such as a hostage rescue. Likewise it would be wrong to broadcast a bin Laden message that might contain coded instructions to al Qaeda members to carry out attacks; in fact, though, US officials have made clear they do not believe his statements contain such signals.

It would also be abhorrent and wrong to show the public footage of atrocities such as the murder of hostages who have been forced to plead for their lives before being beheaded. First, such material goes way beyond the limits of "acceptable violence" that broadcasters can show their viewers, and could deeply traumatize those who watch it. Second, screening it would only serve the purpose of groups like al Qaeda by spreading the fear and terror that they crave. In practice, however, such footage has been posted directly on the internet by insurgent groups. The emergence of the World Wide Web has made terrorists less dependent than before on the traditional media because it offers them publishing and broadcast channels of their own to reach many millions of people.

According to Manuel R. Torres Soriano, writing in 2008: "For the first time in history, cyberspace allows for there to be direct communication between a terrorist and his 'public.'"[13]

Codes of Practice

Faced with the challenges of reporting on terrorism, media organizations have put in place codes of practice for journalists. The BBC offers the following guidance on reporting of "terror":

> We must report acts of terror quickly, accurately, fully and responsibly. Our credibility is undermined by the careless use of words which carry emotional or value judgements. The word "terrorist" itself can be a barrier rather than an aid to understanding. We should try to avoid the term, without attribution. We should let other people characterise while we report the facts as we know them. . . .
>
> We should convey to our audience the full consequences of the act by describing what happened. We should use words which specifically describe the perpetrator such as "bomber," "attacker," "gunman," "kidnapper," "insurgent," and "militant." Our responsibility is to remain objective and report in ways that enable our audiences to make their own assessments about who is doing what to whom.[14]

Reuters' policy goes further, telling journalists not to refer to specific events as terrorism or to use the word "terrorist" to describe specific individuals, groups, or events. This international news agency tells its journalists:

> Report the subjects of news stories objectively, their actions, identity and background. Aim for a dispassionate use of language so that individuals, organisations and governments can make their own judgment on the basis of facts.[15]

Such guidelines do not imply that the media concerned deny the existence of terrorism. They represent, rather, a recognition that "terrorist" and "terrorism" are emotive, value-laden terms. For media that strive for neutrality in their worldwide reporting, it is necessary to remain objective in describing even the most repugnant acts. These policies also reflect the view that using the terrorist label in even one instance would invite pressure from governments, lobby groups, and other parties all over the world to apply it in other cases that are far less clear-cut. As the BBC guidance states:

> Some will argue that certain events are so evidently acts of terror (and, therefore, perpetrated by "terrorists") that those descriptions are reasonable, and non-judgemental. However, the language we choose to use in reporting one incident cannot be considered in isolation from our reporting of other stories. So to use the word in incidents which we may consider obvious creates difficulties for less clear-cut incidents.[16]

The guidelines go on to quote a former editor of BBC World Service News, David Spaull, writing in 1988:

> Accepting that there are some actions which most people would recognise as a terrorist act—the hand grenade thrown into a crèche, the airport queue machine-gunned—we should still avoid the word. In the first place, our audience is as perceptive as we are, and can make up their own minds without being provided with labels. In the second place, there are actions which are not quite so clearly terrorism and we should not be forced into the position of having to make value judgements on each event.[17]

There is another argument against the use of the "T-word" in media coverage—namely, that it designates the group concerned as being beyond the pale, tending to preclude the possibility of any negotiation or narrowing of differences. The phrase "one man's terrorist is another man's freedom fighter" is a cliché. But Menachem Begin of Israel, Yasser Arafat of the Palestine Liberation Organization, and Nelson Mandela of the African National Congress were all members of organizations that were labeled terrorist by their opponents, and they all went on to win the Nobel Peace Prize. Those who today are branded terrorists may be the very people we will need to engage and potentially negotiate with tomorrow, however loathsome that idea might seem.

Media Choices

Reporting on governments' counterterrorism methods can present the media with difficult choices. In November 2005, Dana Priest of the *Washington Post* broke the following story, which made headlines around the world.

> The CIA has been hiding and interrogating some of its most important al Qaeda captives at a Soviet-era compound in Eastern Europe, according to US and foreign officials familiar with the arrangement. . . .[18]

The article went on:

> The secret facility is part of a covert prison system set up by the CIA nearly four years ago that at various times has included sites in eight countries, including Thailand, Afghanistan and several democracies in Eastern Europe, as well as a small center at the Guantanamo Bay prison in Cuba, according to current and former intelligence officials and diplomats from three continents.[19]

This was a "scoop" for the newspaper. Interestingly, however, the *Post* chose to withhold from readers some of the information it had gathered:

> *The Washington Post* is not publishing the names of the Eastern European countries involved in the covert program, at the request of senior US officials. They argued that the disclosure might disrupt counterterrorism efforts in those countries and elsewhere and could make them targets of possible terrorist retaliation.[20]

It is possible to argue against the line the newspaper took. Critics might say that the *Post* owed it to its readers—both in America and in the countries that allegedly hosted the secret prisons—to reveal the full details of what it knew. Was this an example of censorship, or self-censorship? Do citizens of democracies not have the right to know what policies their governments are pursuing in their name? Or is censorship justified in order to safeguard counterterrorism efforts and protect the countries involved against al Qaeda retaliation? In purely journalistic terms, the newspaper also ran the risk that other media might reveal the names of the countries concerned, and the *Post* might then be scooped on its own story. Whether or not one agrees with the newspaper's decision, this was clearly an example of a media organization examining its conscience and responsibly weighing the impact that its coverage was likely to have.

A second example, also from the United States, showed a major newspaper taking a different decision: rejecting a request from the authorities not to publish sensitive information on security grounds. In mid-2006, the *New York Times* and *Los Angeles Times* revealed a previously secret US program in which authorities were tapping into records of an international banking consortium, the Society for Worldwide Interbank Financial Telecommunications (SWIFT), to examine customer transactions. The US administration was furious over the disclosure, saying it gave away important secrets about the fight against terrorism financing. Even at the *New York Times* itself, opinion was divided. The newspaper's reader representative initially supported the article. But he wrote several months later that he had been wrong to do so, because the program was not illegal under US law and there was no evidence people's private data had actually been misused.

In a column, the editors of the *Los Angeles Times* and *New York Times*, Dean Baquet and Bill Keller, defended the decision with an argument that encapsulates how many media see their role in relation to governments: "Our job, especially in times like these, is to bring our readers information that will enable them to judge how well their elected leaders are fighting on their behalf and at what price."[21] Such cases illustrate the inherent tension between the role of the media and that of the state and its counterterrorism authorities. The tension is at its most acute when media are covering a terrorist operation that is actually under way.

Paul Wilkinson, in the paper cited earlier, writes, "It is important to emphasize that the objectives and concerns of the law enforcement agencies in terrorist situations are not only at variance with the aims of the media: they are intrinsically in conflict with them."[22] He cites two examples of "media irresponsibility" in covering counterterrorism operations: the TV filming of British SAS commandos rappelling down the walls of the Iranian embassy to rescue hostages held there during a 1980 siege; and the intrusive media presence that prevented commandos from mounting a rescue operation at Larnaca airport in Cyprus during the 1988 hijacking of a Kuwaiti airliner by Hezbollah.

Such examples contain an obvious lesson for governments, armies, and the police: They need to impose a media blackout on filming of counterterrorism operations in situations such as sieges and hijacks. Few would argue with the logic of such a measure. Likewise, it makes sense for authorities to refrain from giving a "blow-by-blow commentary" on running investigations, although they need to release at least basic levels of information to reassure the public. In the aftermath of the July 2005 suicide bombings in London, the Metropolitan Police addressed this issue by convening news briefings at which it read out statements but declined to take questions afterwards. This tactic enabled senior officers to address the clamor for information but avoid being placed in a situation where they might appear evasive or ill-informed by having to answer a multitude of questions with "No comment" or "We don't know."

Journalist Jonathan Foreman, writing on the 2008 Mumbai attacks, highlighted the problems of issuing either no information—leaving journalistic speculation to fill the vacuum—or too much conflicting information from competing sources:

> These attacks have already been going on for more than a day and a half, and as they draw on, unresolved, rumor seems to grow more powerful, fed by TV anchors who need to say something even when there is nothing new to report. . . . It doesn't help that there is no central command post briefing the press. The police, the army, the commandos that flew down from Delhi, the naval commandos and the state government have all been giving briefings both on and off the record. There is apparently a bureaucratic imperative for all of them to seem important or in charge.[23]

Handling the Media

Countries and intelligence services vary in their approaches to briefing the media. In Germany, for example, the agencies at state and federal levels have press officers who are available to all journalists, and the federal heads of domestic and foreign intelligence give news conferences at least once a year. This relative openness is a deliberate attempt at accountability in a country that for historical reasons is conscious of the need to subject its intelligence services to democratic control. In Britain, the MI5 and MI6 agencies have never held news conferences, and speak only to a small number of approved reporters specializing in security matters. The British approach has, nevertheless, evolved considerably in the past few years and it is clear the agencies are now convinced that they need to have a relationship with the media in order to get their side of the story across. In 2007, a major terrorism trial in Britain featured evidence that MI5 had encountered two of the July 2005 suicide bombers more than a year before their attacks, as part of surveillance of a different group of plotters.[24] MI5 was well aware that this news would provoke strong criticism in the media, who would demand to know whether the suicide bombers could have been stopped if leads from the earlier investigation had been followed up. The agency prepared its response well in advance, briefed reporters, and published information on its website explaining why the eventual suicide bombers had been peripheral to the original investigation.[25] The result was that the media were able to write the story with a much better understanding of the background, and MI5 was able publicly to defend its actions—although it was not successful in avoiding criticism altogether.

This example shows how even a secret state organization may have an interest in briefing the media. Such contacts may serve to trumpet successes or, as in this case, to defend against criticism. Invariably information is given under strict conditions, agreed upon in advance, so that media know exactly what may be reported and to whom it may be attributed (e.g., "a security source").

To Talk or Not to Talk?

Authorization to brief the media is, in this reporter's experience, usually confined to one or two designated spokespersons within an intelligence organization. The individual counterterrorism officer may therefore be taking a calculated risk in deciding to speak to a journalist. Several factors may make this risk worthwhile. First, it may be possible to correct false information or wrong impressions, defend against criticism, counterbalance terrorist propaganda, and highlight CT successes with the aim of ensuring that these are fairly and positively portrayed in media coverage, damaging the enemy. Second, it may be possible to learn valuable information from a well-informed reporter. Journalists have some advantages over intelligence operatives, in that they may openly approach both parties to a conflict in search of information, rather than being forced to operate under cover. The best reporters therefore enjoy a vantage point that gives them both useful intelligence and a deeper analytical understanding of the dynamics of the conflict. In the relationship between the reporter and the CT professional, neither party will fully reveal his hand. But they may be able to enter—cautiously at first, and then more readily as trust develops—into a kind of transaction, exchanging information in such a way that each side benefits. This "two-way street" of information is at the heart of the reporter's work in all spheres of journalism, not just the counterterrorism field.

Military or counterterrorism officials dealing individually with the media would also be well advised to agree in advance on the ground rules. Misunderstandings can arise when either the source, or the journalist, or both have failed to be sufficiently clear about the basis on which the conversation is taking place. The terms "off the record," "on background," "on deep background," etc., may be used by different people to mean different things. For both sides, therefore, it is good practice to check. For the source, that means asking the journalist: What are you planning to do with this material? For the journalist, it means asking: Can I quote you, and on what basis? It is nearly always possible to come up with a formula that preserves the anonymity of the source while giving the reader an idea of how the journalist got the information. For the reporter, sourcing is a vital part of a news story that can significantly boost its authority and credibility. To write that a story is based on conversations with government sources, law enforcement, and counterterrorism officials gives it far more impact than to convey the information unsourced or to use vague formulations like "It is understood that. . . ."

It is also worth noting that journalists have a strong incentive to respect the confidentiality of their sources and to report accurately what they say. A journalist who betrays or "burns" a source guarantees that the person will never speak to him or her again.

Conclusion

This chapter argues against the often-held view that terrorists and the media are inevitably in a symbiotic relationship. It also acknowledges the real danger that sensational and irresponsible reporting can help terrorists to achieve their objectives. The challenge for the media is to avoid falling into that trap.

The media are naturally drawn to cover terrorism as a subject that is inherently dramatic, involves conflict, and throws up many wider issues for societies: religion, immigration, race relations, human rights, and the balance between security and freedom. Journalists and their readers and viewers are also fascinated by the secretive world of the military and the security services, a world that for the most part is closed to them apart from tantalizing glimpses.

There are in fact several parallels between the roles of security correspondents and counterterrorism officials. Both are in the business of acquiring sources and persuading them to pass on information. Both have to sift through large volumes of material and make judgment calls about what is important and what can safely be ignored. Both have to distinguish between reliable data and deliberately misleading information, and to be on guard against attempts to manipulate or dupe them.

The sort of information that interests security officials is also of huge potential interest to journalists and readers—information about terrorist groups, threat levels, and specific plots and investigations. But this is where the tension between the press and the authorities becomes apparent. The need for operational secrecy means counterterrorism officials can tell journalists only a fraction, if anything, of what they know. The job of the security correspondent can be a frustrating one, trying to piece together fragmentary pieces of information in search of an elusive bigger picture.

The inherent tension in this relationship can lead to frustration on both sides. "Are you with us or against us?" one official demanded of me during a vigorous question-and-answer session after I lectured on "Media and Terrorism" at the George C. Marshall European Center for Security Studies in February 2008. The question is understandable, but it slightly misses the point about the role of the press. It is not the job of independent media to act as cheerleaders for governments, but to report as objectively as they can on the course of events. One of the most valuable services the press has performed in the course of the "war on terror" is to investigate flaws and abuses—the Abu Ghraib scandal, CIA rendition and secret prisons, the use of "waterboarding," or the tapping of Americans' phones without judicial warrants. That in turn has brought pressure on the US administration to adapt and improve its counterterrorism methods. The media would be failing in its task if it did not critically examine government policies from the point of view of both their moral justification and their practical effectiveness.

To whom, then, is the journalist ultimately responsible?[26] First and foremost, to readers, listeners, or viewers, who collectively represent society as a whole. The journalist enjoys a privileged position, with special access to protagonists and decision makers, and has a duty to ask the questions that ordinary people want answered. A journalist should never be a mere mouthpiece for the government or for the terrorists. He or she should critically report the words and actions of both sides, subjecting them to critical analysis and exposing what is false, duplicitous, brutal, murderous, or otherwise threatening to society and its freedoms. The journalist's social duty includes the responsibility not to report information that could make society more vulnerable to attack or help terrorists to plan operations or resist capture. When Britain's top counterterrorism police officer walked into the Prime Minister's Downing Street office in April 2009 carrying documents—clearly visible through photographers' lenses—that set out plans for a major counterterrorism operation, no journalist published the details. But the fact of the officer's failure of judgment was—rightly—widely reported, and led to his resignation the next day.[27]

As trained professionals fulfilling an important role in society, the media must expect criticism when they get things wrong. They must also, when reporting on matters of national security, submit to certain restrictions. Reporters "embedded" with troops in Iraq or Afghanistan, for example, may be privy to secrets that they cannot reveal because to do so would compromise operations against insurgents. This is plain common sense. There are, however, less clear-cut cases—like the *Washington Post* and *New York Times* cases previously discussed—where the case for censorship or self-censorship is much more complex and nuanced.

At the same 2008 lecture already mentioned, a professor suggested to CT professionals that they think of the media as a gun on the table between the terrorist and the counterterrorist: whoever grabs it first can take advantage of a powerful weapon. That is an intriguing image, but it should also be remembered that most journalists are skeptics, and their worst fear is to be duped or exploited. Even as they seek the insights of the security experts, reporters are—or should be—questioning their agenda and wondering if they are being manipulated. This natural suspicion has if anything increased in light of recent experience, notably the fatally flawed intelligence-based case advanced by US and British leaders for invading Iraq to seize Saddam Hussein's alleged weapons of mass destruction. In the past few years, media have also become more cautious about relying on single, anonymous intelligence sources and will normally look for corroboration from at least two, and preferably more.

Remembering the characterization of terrorism as "an extreme act of political communication," it follows that the worst thing journalists can do is to exaggerate the threat and make the terrorists' message louder. That serves only to deepen people's fear and sharpen the divisions in society the militants can then exploit further. That way, the media simply play into their hands.

On the other hand, we make a mistake if we play down the threat and accuse the military and security establishment of hyping it up to keep themselves in business and guarantee their budgets. A former counterterrorism specialist at the State Department, Larry C. Johnson, wrote in the *New York Times* on 10 July 2001:

> Judging from news reports and the portrayal of villains in our popular entertainment, Americans are bedevilled by fantasies about terrorism. They seem to believe that terrorism is the greatest threat to the United States and that it is becoming more widespread and lethal. They are likely to think that the United States is the most popular target of terrorists. And they almost certainly have the impression that extremist Islamic groups cause most terrorism. None of these beliefs are based in fact.[28]

Ironically, Johnson said part of the blame for inflating the terrorist threat could be assigned "to 24-hour broadcast news operations too eager to find a dramatic story line in the events of the day and to pundits who repeat myths while ignoring clear empirical data."[29] Nine weeks later, al Qaeda struck the United States, killing nearly three thousand people.

The media walk a fine line, then, between exaggerating and underplaying the threat of terrorist violence. At their worst, they may fall into the trap of becoming the terrorists' mouthpiece. At their best, they strip away the romantic "freedom fighter" image and portray the brutal reality of terrorism and its appalling consequences. They alert the public to the dangers and help people understand the causes of terrorism by providing a forum for education and debate.

The media are often criticized, and sometimes rightly, over their coverage of terrorism. But for all their flaws, they perform on balance a positive role. Terrorists seek to exploit free speech and the media in the same way they try to exploit many of the rights and freedoms we enjoy, for the purposes of subverting those very rights and freedoms. That does not mean we should respond to the terrorist challenge by curbing the media and encroaching on free speech. That would be to hand the terrorists an important victory.

As societies confront the threat of terrorism, the media carry an important responsibility. Terrorism cannot be beaten by law enforcement or military force alone, and the "war on terror" is not really a war: It is a contest between different ideologies and views of the world. You cannot defeat an idea on a battlefield. The way to conquer it is by force of argument and force of example, by showing that one's values and way of life are superior to those of the enemy who seeks to destroy them. And it is through the twenty-first-century global media that the competition between democratic societies and al Qaeda will partly be played out.

The CT officer needs, at the very least, to understand the role of the media in this battle of ideas. He or she should prepare for the possibility of encounters with the press and be ready with an individual media strategy for dealing with these. One simple option is to shun journalists altogether. A harder but potentially more productive approach is to engage with the reporter, take careful soundings, and find out whether there is something to be gained for both sides from such a relationship. The prizes are useful information and an opportunity to use the media as a weapon against the terrorist. By exchanging a passive stance for a proactive one, the thoughtful counterterrorism professional has potentially much to gain.

Mark Trevelyan Born in Manchester, England, Mark Trevelyan joined Reuters as a trainee journalist in 1986 after graduating from Oxford University with a first-class honors degree in French and Russian. He has reported from more than thirty-five countries, with postings in London, Brussels, Warsaw, Moscow, Berlin, and Wellington, New Zealand. Between 2003 and 2008, he held the position of Security Correspondent, Europe, Middle East, and Africa, writing on terrorism and counterterrorism and running a team of reporters spread across Reuters' network of bureaus. Among other stories, he reported on the March 2004 attacks on Madrid, the July 2005 London bombings, the Hamburg trials of suspected 9/11 plotters, the Alexander Litvinenko poisoning case, and the US military's counterterrorism initiatives in Africa. His work has appeared in many of the world's leading newspapers and on their websites, and he contributed chapters to the

Reuters books on 9/11 and on Iraq. He is now working as a political and general news editor for Reuters and lives with his family near London. Mr. Trevelyan has lectured several times on media coverage of terrorism for the PTSS program at the Marshall Center.

Recommended Readings

Bergen, Peter L. *Holy War, Inc.: Inside the Secret World of Osama bin Laden*. New York: The Free Press/ Simon and Shuster, 2001.

Borowitz, Albert. *Terrorism for Self-Glorification: The Herostratos Syndrome*. Kent, OH: Kent State University Press, 2005.

Coll, Steve. *The Bin Ladens: An Arabian Family in the American Century*. New York: Penguin Press, 2008.

Fouda, Yosri, and Nick Fielding. *Masterminds of Terror: The Truth Behind the Most Devastating Terrorist Attack the World Has Ever Seen*. Edinburgh: Mainstream Publishing, 2003.

Laqueur, Walter. *No End to War: Terrorism in the Twenty-First Century*. London: Continuum, 2003.

Livingstone, W. D. "Terrorism and the Media Revolution," Ch. 15 in *Fighting Back: Winning the War Against Terrorism*, edited by Neil C. Livingstone and Terrell E. Arnold. Lexington, MA: Lexington books, 1984.

Miller, Abraham H., ed. *Terrorism, the Media, and the Law*. Ardsley, NY: Transnational Publishers, 1982.

Nacos, Brigitte L. *Mass-Mediated Terrorism: The Central Role of the Media in Terrorism and Counterterrorism*. Lanham, MD: Rowman and Littlefield Publishers, 2002.

Townshend, Charles. *Terrorism: A Very Short Introduction*. Oxford: Oxford University Press, 2002.

Notes

1. Sir Richard Dearlove, speech at award ceremony for Global Security Challenge, London, November 2007.
2. See Raphael F. Perl, "Terrorism, the Media and the Government: Perspectives, Trends, and Options for Policymakers," *CRS Issue Brief*, 22 October 1997, available at http://www.fas.org/irp/crs/crs-terror.htm, accessed 1 June 2009.
3. Jonathan Foreman, "Four Days of Terror in Mumbai," *Standpoint*, Issue 8 (January 2009), available at http://www.standpointmag.co.uk/four-days-of-terror-in-mumbai-january-09, accessed 25 September 2009.
4. Brigitte Nacos, David P. Fan and John T. Young, "Terrorism and the Print Media: The 1985 TWA Hostage Crisis," in *Essential Readings on Political Terrorism: Analyses of Problems and Prospects for the 21st Century*, edited by Harvey W. Kushner. New York: Gordian Knot Books, 2002.
5. Alex P. Schmid, "Terrorism and the Media: The Ethics of Publicity," *Terrorism and Political Violence*, Vol. 1, Issue 4 (October 1989), 555.
6. Paul Wilkinson, "The Media and Terrorism: A Reassessment," *Terrorism and Political Violence*, Vol. 9, No. 2 (Summer 1997), 51–64.
7. Walter Laqueur, *The New Terrorism. Fanaticism and the Arms of Mass Destruction*. UK version. London: Phoenix Press, 2001, 44.
8. Michel Wieviorka, *The Making of Terrorism*. Chicago: University of Chicago Press, 1993, 43–45; Wilkinson 1997 challenges Wieviorka's argument.
9. William E. Biernatzki, "Terrorism and Mass Media," *Communication Research Trends*, Vol. 21, No. 1 (2002), available at http://cscc.scu.edu/html/trends/v21/v21_1.pdf, accessed 1 June 2009.
10. Margaret Thatcher, speech to American Bar Association, London, 15 July 1985, available at http://www.margaretthatcher.org/speeches/displaydocument.asp?docid=106096, accessed 1 June 2009.

11. Alexandra Zawadil, "Governments Struggle as Militants Refine Web Tactics," *Reuters*, 16 November 2007, available at http://www.reuters.com/article/internetNews/idUSL1656842 820071116?pageNumber=2&sp=true, accessed 1 June 2009.

12. Middle East Media Research Institute (MEMRI), "Online Islamist Forum Hosted in Texas Posts Guide for Kidnapping Americans," *MEMRI Special Dispatch*, No. 1680 (15 August 2007), available at http://memri.org/bin/latestnews.cgi?ID=SD168007, accessed 1 June 2009.

13. Manuel R. Torres Soriano, "Terrorism and the Mass Media After Al Qaeda: A Change of Course?" *Athena Intelligence Journal*, Vol. 3, No 2 (1 April 2008), available at http://www .isn.ethz.ch/isn/Digital-Library/Publications/Detail/?ots591=0C54E3B3-1E9C-BE1E-2C24-A6A8C7060233&lng=en&id=55237, accessed 25 September 2009.

14. BBC, "Guidance: Terrorism, Use of Language When Reporting: Introduction," *BBC Editorial Guidelines*, available at www.bbc.co.uk/guidelines/editorialguidelines/advice/terrorismlanguage/index.shtml, accessed 1 June 2009.

15. Reuters, "Terrorism," *Reuters Style Guide*, available at http://handbook.reuters.com/index .php/T#terrorism, accessed 25 September 2009.

16. BBC, "Guidance: Terrorism, Use of Language When Reporting: Our Approach," *BBC Editorial Guidelines*, available at http://www.bbc.co.uk/guidelines/editorialguidelines/advice/terrorismlanguage/ourapproach.shtml, accessed 1 June 2009.

17. Ibid.

18. Dana Priest, "CIA Holds Terror Suspects in Secret Prisons," *Washington Post*, 2 November 2005, http://www.washingtonpost.com/wp-dyn/content/article/2005/11/01/AR2005110101644.html, accessed 1 June 2009.

19. Priest, 2005.

20. Priest, 2005.

21. Dean Baquet and Bill Keller, "When Do We Publish a Secret?" *New York Times*, 1 July 2006, available at http://www.nytimes.com/2006/07/01/opinion/01keller.html, accessed 1 June 2009.

22. Wilkinson, 1997.

23. Foreman, 2008.

24. Ian Cobain, Richard Norton-Taylor, and Jeevan Vasagar, "MI5 Decided to Stop Watching Two Suicide Bombers," *The Guardian*, 1 May 2007, available at http://www.guardian.co.uk/uk/2007/may/01/terrorism.politics2, accessed 25 September 2009.

25. See, for example, "Rumours and Reality: Facts Behind the Myths," MI5 website, available at http://www.mi5.gov.uk/output/news/rumours-and-reality-facts-behind-the-myths.html, accessed 25 September 2009.

26. This book's editors believe that a journalist should also consider her or his responsibilities as "a citizen."

27. See Karla Adam, "Britain's Top Counterterrorism Officer Resigns After Security Blunder," *Washington Post*, 10 April 2009, available at http://www.washingtonpost.com/wp-dyn/content/article/2009/04/09/AR2009040900467.html, accessed 25 September 2009.

28. Larry C. Johnson, "The Declining Terrorist Threat," *New York Times*, 10 July 2001, available at http://www.nytimes.com/2001/07/10/opinion/the-declining-terrorist-threat.html, accessed 25 September 2009.

29. Ibid.

John L. Clarke

Managing Counterterrorism Crises

"Terror" and "crisis" are words that seem inextricably linked. Successful attacks by terrorists, and often even partially successful or interdicted attacks, almost inevitably result in crises for national governments. The manner in which governments deal with these crises can often determine their success or failure.

Crises brought about by terrorist actions can be among the most difficult for governments to manage effectively. Since terror attacks are deliberately designed to induce terror, the panic that may result from such an attack can result in a crisis of significant, even existential, dimensions. In addition, terrorist attacks are almost always designed to provoke an overreaction on the part of the government. In the heat of a crisis, rhetoric may be extreme and calls for revenge strong. Crises involving terrorist attacks differ in this respect from other kinds of crises, in that they are likely to elicit strong reactions from the public, including demands for revenge. Leaders must always guard against playing into the hands of terrorists who welcome such reactions.

The attacks in November 2008 in Mumbai, India, demonstrate the exquisite dilemma that often confronts leaders after a terrorist attack: respond with force against those one supposes perpetrated the act and risk provoking more violence; or act in a restrained manner and run the risk of being accused of failing to respond. The public, through the media, will demand action; leaders must understand the consequences of such action.[1]

Therefore, the ability to effectively manage crises and the consequences of such crises is a fundamental function of government at all levels—local, provincial, and national. This chapter will examine the fundamentals of crisis management, with a view toward assisting the reader in helping to prepare his or her organization for successful management of crises, be they of terrorist origin or other sources.[2]

Crises are inevitable and therefore must be anticipated and planned for. While the precise nature of a crisis may not be always easy to predict, it should be clear that crisis management plans and procedures must be developed that are useful through a full range of contingencies. These plans are most valuable for the processes they establish and the lacunae they uncover than for their content alone.

Overview of Crisis Management

Crisis management consists of three elements: organization, procedures, and arrangements. They are designed to accomplish two objectives simultaneously: to gain control of the crisis in the present and to shape its future course. The goal of crisis management is to return to a more normal state of affairs as soon as possible at the least possible cost in terms of lives, property, and lost economic activity.[3] In order to accomplish these objectives and this goal, a crisis management process must be thought of as a cycle, with the continuous addition of new information adding complexity to each iteration of the cycle.

This chapter will consider each of the three elements in turn, in order to identify the proper crisis management tools for terrorism-induced crises. Given the lack of resources in most countries, the right solution for any state faced with a serious terrorism threat is to develop solutions that function in both terrorist scenarios and other kinds of crisis situations as well.[4]

By organizations, we mean the appropriate political and professional institutions designed to facilitate the acquisition of information and for assembling the right players in crisis environments, as well as those designed to manage the consequences of terror acts. This includes ensuring we have the organizational structure appropriate to the form of government and that, in a crisis, the responsibilities of each component of government are clear.

By procedures, we mean developing, exercising, and, when necessary, executing the proper and appropriate sets of rules and policies for a given crisis. Operational and contingency plans, particularly for likely events, are included in this construct. Procedures include the broad range of crisis action preparations and plans established in advance of a crisis.

By arrangements, we mean identifying and codifying the appropriate relationships to other ministries and agencies, as well as partners and contacts in advance of a crisis so that a smooth crisis management process can be executed. Arrangements will also include links to organizations about the national levels, such as international organizations, and subnational elements, such as nongovernmental organizations (NGOs). Links are critical in ensuring that crisis management coordination goes smoothly and must be established in advance. Once a crisis has begun, it is too late to begin establishing new links.

A final element is leadership. Terrorism-induced crises put a premium on effective leadership—the ability to not only make the right decisions and bring the government together, but to do so in a manner that inspires confidence. Leadership is more than management, in that it has political aspects. Leadership in crises, particularly terrorist-induced crises, is essentially political in nature, and can have important political repercussions. Failure in such crises can result in the loss of political power.[5] The three elements we speak of must be brought together in an effective manner, in order to achieve the goals of crisis management efficiently.

In addition to identifying the right organization, procedures, and arrangements, this chapter will examine the fundamentals of successful crisis management, with a view toward identifying the essential elements of success.

Characteristics of Terrorism Crises

There is no standard, widely accepted definition of crisis. But there are some key elements that figure importantly in crises and that we may consider as the characteristics of crises. These characteristics are: threat, urgency, uncertainty, intensity, and surprise.[6]

While these characteristics are not always present in all crises, nearly all crises caused by acts of terrorism usually exhibit them. Terror attacks preceded by intelligence indicators, or even those telegraphed by the perpetrators, seem to feature most, if not all, of these characteristics. Further, while a terror attack may feature these characteristics, they may be present in varying degrees, depending on the nature of the incident.

Terrorist attacks most commonly occur as a surprise; while general indicators of terrorist activity may be known to authorities, and attention to indicators is a full-time affair, the attacks themselves usually come without precise warning.[7] Terrorist attacks, even those that fail, threaten important values, in that they target noncombatants. A terrorist attack–induced crisis is a very intense period, causing a spike in emotions and fear—the objective of every terrorist attack. Frequently, they are surrounded by uncertainty as to the cause and perpetrator, and as to whether more attacks will occur, which can hamper crisis response operations. Most importantly from a crisis management perspective, they demand an urgent response.[8]

Of equal importance with regard to surprise are the second- and third-order effects of terrorist attacks. While crises brought about by natural disasters usually have predictable effects upon critical infrastructure (even if the degree varies with the nature of the event), this is often difficult to anticipate in the case of terrorist attacks. Because the target and the method of the attacks, as well as the timing, are most often a surprise, the follow-on effects are likely to be unanticipated as well. These second- and third-order effects are often highly scenario-dependant and difficult to plan for.

By way of an example of this phenomenon, consider the second-order effects of the London Underground attacks of July 2005. Because the attacks occurred at the height of the morning rush hour, London was full of commuters. The attacks, in part because there were multiple detonations, caused the London transit authority to shut down all underground and bus lines until it could be sure that no other bombs were in place. This meant, however, that millions of commuters had no way to get home that night. Crisis managers were confronted with the dilemma of what to do with millions of commuters stuck in London.[9]

The threat characteristic indicates that the terror attack is designed to cause damage to priority values, interests, or goals. Of course, the terrorist's perception of these priorities may differ from that of key decision makers or the public at large. Nevertheless, by design, terrorist attacks are intended to damage or destroy a target of actual or symbolic value.

Uncertainty is a key characteristic of terrorist-induced crises. Often, there is doubt about the nature of the attack, or even if it is an attack, as opposed to an industrial accident of natural catastrophe, such as an outbreak of disease. Crisis managers must operate under the presumption that much of the information they have at the outset will prove to be incomplete, or even wrong.

In addition, there is likely to be considerable uncertainty regarding the proximate cause of the attack and who the perpetrators are. Decision makers must guard against making assumptions regarding these issues, which may prove embarrassing or even damaging later.

The attacks in Madrid in March 2004 and London in July 2005 illustrate this dilemma. There was considerable uncertainty as to the identity of the perpetrators in Madrid, which ultimately caused the ruling party to lose the national election; and in London, there was confusion as to the nature of the incident for at least an hour after the first bomb exploded. Many in the London Transit headquarters thought the problem was an electrical failure in the underground system; this uncertainty was resolved only when the fourth bomb exploded above ground in a bus.[10]

Urgency and intensity are often relative in crises. But a terrorist attack, because of the other characteristics, often generates a dynamic of its own with regard to these two characteristics. Attacks are often accompanied by a strong feeling that something must be done—now. This emotion often drives crisis managers to take actions that may be viewed as ill-considered in retrospect but seem justified in the heat of the moment. Particularly in states with no long or recent experience with terrorism, the sense of urgency may seem overwhelming, as was the case with the United States in the aftermath of the 11 September 2001 attacks.[11]

Toward a Definition

By way of a working definition, we may say that a crisis as a result of a terrorist attack poses a serious threat to vital or important national values or interests and comes as a surprise with little verifiable information, leaving little time to respond. But it is important to understand that not every difficult situation is a crisis. Nor is every conflict a crisis, just as not every crisis is also a conflict. We must guard against allowing the term "crisis" to be used too liberally, lest it lose its utility to describe an extraordinary incident. In particular, the tendency of the media to ascribe crisis to events that do not significantly differ from routine events is common.

The fact of the matter is that many attacks perpetrated by terrorists ought not to rise to the level of a national crisis. Many low-effect attacks (an attack on a government building with low casualties) differ little from endemic criminal attacks in many countries. That many of these attacks seem to be politically motivated allows the media to put them in a category that can force the hand of government, requiring officials to initiate crisis management procedures, even if the actual effects of these attacks are far from damaging to vital national interests.[12]

This is particularly true in the world of near-instantaneous communication in which we live and work. All too frequently, the media are liable to take a difficult or unusual situation and raise it to the level of a crisis even if the government has knowledge of and control over the events. It must be recognized that the pace and direction of a crisis change constantly, with new information entering the cycle continuously. This makes the task of controlling the future course of a crisis so difficult. By way of example, the global financial crisis that began in September 2008 has taken an extraordinary number of twists and turns as it has progressed. While terror-induced crises tend to be more discrete, focusing on a single event, it must nevertheless be recognized that surprise and uncertainty will accompany the entire crisis management process.

Finally, it is useful to consider the differences and similarities in the management of terrorism crises with other types of events that may also trigger a crisis management reaction. Increasingly, the term "all-hazards" is being used to describe events that may require a serious national-level response. These events may include natural phenomena, such as earthquakes and cyclones, and other human-made or unintentional events, such as industrial accidents involving toxic or hazardous materials. Crisis managers are increasingly recognizing that, from an efficiency perspective, preparation for and execution of crisis management are, at base, not fundamentally different for terrorism and other all-hazards events and that an exclusive focus on terrorism can be counterproductive.[13]

Causes of Terrorism Crises

The perpetration of a terrorist act almost always precipitates a national-level crisis. Such attacks, many spectacular in nature, are usually so shocking that governments must shift rapidly to manage the resulting crisis. Other attacks, such as those involving a single death or a small bomb, often do not rise to the level of a true national crisis.

Thus, we must distinguish between those attacks that rise to the level warranting crisis management response and those that do not. Often, in a state inured to terror attacks, many small-scale attacks do not warrant an emergency response. India, for example, has suffered a large number of terrorist attacks over the past decade, but only a handful, such as the Mumbai attack of November 2008, have risen to the level of a national crisis.

Moreover, a crisis may also come about as a result of a specific threat or proclamation by a terrorist group, which may or may not precede an attack. Likewise, while the great majority of terror attacks involve physical violence, some do not. Cyber attacks on important financial networks, for example, would fall into this category.[14] Thus, a terror incident that leads to a crisis may not necessarily involve an attack. It may be enough for terrorists to threaten an attack and for the media to report such a threat to be a catalyst for the government to manage the event as if it were a crisis. Indeed, the successful interdiction of an attack may cause, through fear, changes in habit by the public, thus resulting in a crisis.

Equally important, some events may be attributed to terrorists but are, in fact, accidental or natural in origin. An explosion at a chemical factory may be initially attributed to terrorists, particularly if there is a well-known threat of terrorism, but the incident might actually be the result of an industrial accident. In a similar vein, a terrorist attack may go unnoticed or unappreciated as a terror incident for a substantial period of time. Indeed, an attack using a biological agent, such as anthrax, might not be viewed as an attack until the incubation period has passed and a significant number of those infected have presented themselves to treatment facilities.[15] Thus, miscommunication and misperception may often render more difficult the ability of governments to respond in a timely manner or even to avoid a crisis situation. Failure to correctly understand the nature of the event is an ever-present danger.

In terror events, governments will usually have to undertake serious and often large-scale measures to manage the incipient crisis. Often, these very measures may precipitate or exacerbate a crisis. A misinformed and ill-thought-out pronouncement may result in a panicked reaction by the public. Clearly, governments wish to avoid such occurrences, but they are also obligated to keep the public informed, thus creating an excruciating dilemma: what to tell the public and when to tell them.

The Fundamentals of Terrorism Crisis Management

Management of terrorism-induced crises has a simple goal: to control the events at hand and shape the future course of those events. It should be evident that governments, even the most powerful, are likely to be unable to prevent some measure of crisis if confronted with a serious attack with significant levels of casualties.[16] Therefore, confronted with a legitimate threat of possible terrorist acts, governments must accept a certain degree of inevitability and plan for such attacks. Such plans must be predicated on a realistic assessment of risk, in terms of what assets are critical and vulnerable to attack.[17]

The crisis management process follows a six-step process: preparation, prevention, response, mitigation, resolution, and recovery. These steps are discussed in detail in this section, but it is important to remember that with each step the goal is to control the current situation and manage the pace and direction of future events.

Ensuring timely and adequate preparedness is a hugely difficult task under the best of conditions. Many efforts will be seen in the aftermath of an attack to have been "wrong," in that preparations were not adequate for the attack that occurred. Planning officials quite naturally focus on the most recent attacks, while sophisticated terrorists are not likely to repeat an attack in the same way. Hence, officials are likely to again be surprised by the next attack.

Since it must be assumed that potential attackers will have some knowledge of a government's preparations and thus will make appropriate adjustments to target selection and method of attack, the element of surprise, already mentioned, is an important element to acknowledge during crisis management planning. No level of preparation, as distinguished from prevention, will be equal to all manners of attack.

Given that terrorist attacks are but one kind of event that may require a crisis management response, most governments are well advised to undertake an "all-hazards" approach to crisis management planning. Such an approach recognizes that terrorist attacks and other catastrophic events, such as industrial accidents, severe weather phenomena, such as cyclones, and other natural catastrophes, such as earthquakes and tidal waves, share a number of the characteristics mentioned in this chapter.

The US Department of Homeland Security (DHS), created in the aftermath of the terror attacks of 2001 and with a specific, indeed almost exclusive, focus on terror, found itself ill-equipped to manage the crisis thrust upon it by Hurricane Katrina in August 2005. In particular, the Federal Emergency Management Agency (FEMA)—which became part of the DHS in 2003—was widely criticized for its slow and uneven response to the disaster. Part of the problem was the federal nature of the US governmental system, which placed primary responsibility on the states, such as Louisiana, to respond first. But the fact that the primary focus of the DHS was on terrorism rendered it somewhat less capable of responding to other disasters. This debacle brought about a major change in orientation of the department toward an all-hazards focus.[18]

Therefore, it makes sense to ensure that crisis management planning is not limited to potential terrorist events, but has applicability across a broad range of events. Doing so will ensure that crisis management assets, such as crisis communications equipment, logistics capabilities, and emergency medical assistance, are available when needed. Indeed, given the increasing frequency of severe weather phenomena and other natural hazards, as well as the potential of catastrophic effects of industrial accidents in metropolitan areas, governments must take steps to prepare adequately for all likely events.

Of course, the best and most efficient means of managing crises is to prevent them in the first place. This is, of course, not always possible. Crisis prevention, the second step in the process, is a subject that has been dealt with elsewhere in terms of the steps taken to prevent terrorist attacks. But the return on investment for prevention measures for almost all kinds of crises is often significant.

Assuming that preparations have been adequate, once a crisis occurs, planners must take action to mitigate and remediate the effects of the crisis. Moreover, they must proactively take control of the crisis—and be seen to be taking control. This last point is key: It is not enough to take action, but this action must be visible to the public. They will seek reassurance and will expect demonstrative action—even if such action later proves to be mistaken or less than ideal. This demonstration of action is of particular importance in terrorism crises, as the public may believe that multiple or follow-on attacks may be planned or under way—as was the case in Madrid and London. Thus, a clear demonstration of authority and control will serve to assure the public that the government has the situation well in hand.

The final phase of the crisis management process is focused on the effort to resolve the crisis and return to normalcy. This includes the steps taken to remediate and attenuate the effects of a crisis. Often, the term "consequence management" is used to describe this phase of the crisis management process. Consequence management is predominantly an emergency management function and includes measures to protect public health and safety, restore essential government services, and provide emergency relief to government, businesses, and individuals affected by an act of terrorism.[19]

Consequence management often begins with and runs conterminously with other crisis management steps. Even as leaders are struggling to understand and control events, emergency response organizations are usually already beginning to undertake consequence management operations. Therefore, it is essential to recognize that managing the operations of these groups may pose a unique challenge, particularly if the terrorist attack has employed a weapon of mass destruction or disruption.

Inevitably, mistakes will be made in the crisis management process. Events will be misinterpreted, information will be miscommunicated, and directives will be misunderstood. It is therefore essential that leaders recognize the inherent frailty of the crisis management process and make every effort to demonstrate confidence in their decisions and to lend credibility to their actions. This issue will be addressed later in this chapter.

Finally, crisis managers must bear in mind the manner in which their actions will be perceived. The media and the public will be hungry for guidance, and crisis managers will be anxious to avoid panic. The manner in which information is presented in this environment can be as important as the information itself. Therefore, crisis managers will want to ensure that they portray themselves in a confident way and that their words and actions enhance their credibility. Confidence and credibility are hugely important assets in a crisis, but can be fragile and ephemeral—and damaged irreparably by a single wrong word or action.[20]

Organizing for Crisis Management

The management of national crises is, in the final analysis, a political task. Irrespective of the organizational and institutional preparations, political leaders will be held to account for success or failure of crisis management. Therefore, political leaders must guard against the notion that crisis management can safely be left to professional crisis managers. That is a recipe for failure and one of the key lessons learned by the US government in the aftermath of the Katrina debacle, in which the federal government relied on FEMA to manage the crisis, rather than allowing it to focus on its traditional consequence management role.

That said, the organizational framework found within government must be sound. This section addresses the principal considerations for ensuring that governments at all levels possess the institutional capacity for managing the full range of potential crises with which they may be confronted. Governments are generally organized to effect the transactional business of managing the provision of services to the population on a routine basis. The advent of a crisis, particularly a serious terrorist event, is likely to severely tax the instruments government has established for these routine purposes. Yet it is unrealistic to develop an institutional crisis management solution and expect that it can operate independent of the rest of government in time of crisis. Clearly, leaders must rely on solutions that leverage existing organizational elements in an adaptive manner that is equal to the crisis management task at hand. This means, among other things, inculcating a crisis management mindset in existing governmental organizations so that they are capable of adapting to new circumstances.

Indeed, the notion that a specialized crisis management agency can perform these functions without recourse to other government assets has been proven to be mistaken. As a practical matter, crisis management organizations, such as the US Federal Emergency Management Agency or the Russian Ministry for Civil Defense, Emergencies, and Elimination of Consequences of Natural Disasters (EMERCOM), do not manage crises—they mange the <u>consequences</u> of crises. As noted above, crises are managed by political leaders. Organizations like FEMA coordinate the response and oversee such efforts as the provision of humanitarian aid or emergency housing, but they do not manage the crisis.[21] This is because they are government agencies composed of technocrats, as opposed to political decision-making bodies. They are designed to carry out the decisions and priorities of the political leadership.

Therefore, the key task in organizing government for crisis management is to develop the procedures for close cooperation among all elements within the government. This is often best accomplished by the establishment of an interministerial or interagency process. Such interministerial groups are the preferred means of ensuring all relevant government agencies are fully engaged in the task, and often provide the best means for ensuring that information is shared by the key players. In the United States, this coordinating role is played by the Homeland Security Council (HSC). The HSC is responsible to the president for coordinating the interagency process on homeland security matters. Recently, the HSC was made part of an expanded National Security Council, which is now responsible for both domestic and international security. A common staff now supports both the National and Homeland Security Council.

Within the interministerial institutional framework, a clear delineation of responsibilities is essential. Most governments that employ successful crisis management systems employ a variant of the US lead agency approach. This method clearly assigns responsibility for crisis management to one ministry or agency and assigns all others to assist or support that lead agency.[22]

Depending on the nature of the crisis, the lead agency may be one with functional area responsibilities, such as the ministry of agriculture for terrorist acts against the food supply system, the ministry of health for pandemic disease, or one with broader antiterrorism responsibilities, such as the ministry of internal security. Defining responsibilities in this manner ensures that all players understand the required working relationships. This approach to government organization is often employed across the full range of government responsibilities, but it is particularly important in crises. A terrorist attack, particularly one involving a weapon of mass destruction, may leave little time to create a coherent government response. It is thus imperative that a functioning lead agency process be in place, so that there is a clear understanding of who is in charge and that the supporting-to-supported relationships are clearly delineated.

Along with creating the interministerial system, governments must also create key linkages to other crisis management elements. These include other levels of government, such as provincial and city, and to NGOs involved in emergency management, such as the Red Cross. Linkages may also include neighboring governments, particularly as many types of crises can spread across borders and require a coordinated international response. Likewise, contacts with the media in advance of a crisis can be important, as they can create an air of familiarity and credibility that can be of great utility when a crisis strikes. These contacts also provide an opportunity to educate the media on key aspects of government organization and crisis management planning, so they are able to report in a more knowledgeable and professional manner.

In addition to the right organizational framework, attention should be paid to establishing the appropriate legal framework as well. While crises, especially terrorism crises, can create an occasional need for extralegal responses, this should always be the exception, not the rule. Empowering crisis management organizations within a tested legal framework can be of great use in the post-crisis phase, when challenges to responses can be expected. The employment of military forces, which may be critical in terrorism crises involving the use of weapons of mass destruction, may run afoul of important prohibitions on the role of military forces in domestic contingencies. Likewise, in many federal systems, there are important issues regarding the division of power and responsibility between the national and regional or provincial levels of government. In some government systems, the lower level of government may be constitutionally entitled to make decisions regarding the employment of national-level assets, while in others, the employment of federal-level assets brings with it political control.[23]

Crisis management arrangements should also include mechanisms for early warning. Increasingly, governments have come to rely on a variety of nongovernmental early warning sources, such as news television (CNN, BBC, etc.) and internet sources to complement government intelligence sources. Such channels of information often report on developing situations more quickly than government agencies. Of course, this can also work to the disadvantage of decision makers, as the credibility of many of these sources may be suspect.

Planning for Crisis Management

Successful crisis management requires rules. By this we mean the set of procedures that guide decision making and action in crises; commonly, we think of crisis action plans, which are developed and maintained by most governments. However, the complexity and instantaneity of contemporary crises mandate a broader approach. Because contemporary crises often lack well-defined beginnings and especially endings, crisis action plans must be viewed as an iterative continuum. To be effective, crisis planning must address not only actions taken during a crisis, but also pre-crisis preparation and post-crisis consequence management; they must also include procedures for exercising actions in advance and for inculcating a mindset for crisis management.

Frequently, governments rely on contingency plans for managing terrorism crises. It is incumbent on governments to develop plans for those kinds of crises that can reasonably be anticipated, such as earthquakes or storms. Terrorism crises, because of their unpredictable nature, often mandate a slightly different approach. While contingency plans are needed, they must be adaptive in nature. Moreover, such plans must strike a delicate balance between planning for the worst case, which normally entails a significant amount of resources, to planning that is too lean, which allows for too much risk. However, in the resource constrained environment in which most government planning is conducted, risk management is essential.

The great difficulty with risk management is that it is subject to failure. This sounds trite, but it is often a huge problem for government. Public appetite for risk often hovers around zero. Political leaders find it difficult to explain that, in many instances, risks must be taken. This is particularly acute with regard to terrorist threats, as it will affect the liberty/security balance. Protecting against all possible threats will inevitably result in a diminution of liberty. Politically, it is toxic to say in public that some risks must be taken with regard to terrorist threats. If terrorists are able to exploit a government's plans due to gaps created by ineffective risk management, this exploitation will always be difficult to explain or de-emphasize to the public after the fact. But planners must accept that this is the essential nature of risk management, and that complete protection against a thinking enemy is an illusion under any scenario.[24]

Terrorism crisis action plans must focus on post-attack rather than attack phase events. Unlike crises that can readily be planned for, a terrorist attack will confront decision makers with an act that has already been committed and for which the consequences are becoming apparent. Seldom do terrorist attacks exceed several hours, but the post-attack consequences phase may go on for days. While governments may well stand accused of failing to prevent an attack, they are even more likely to be criticized for their response to an attack should it be perceived as a failure.

Doubts, Desires, and Delusions: Decision Making in Crises

Crises put a great premium on the ability of leaders to make good decisions. A wrong decision can result in catastrophe, with war or the fall of a government being among the most extreme of possible outcomes. Crises, particularly those caused by terrorist events, put great pressure on leaders to make decisions with celerity under conditions of great uncertainty, and often with public opinion at a fever pitch, demanding that something be done.[25] Under these circumstances, it is little wonder that information can be misunderstood or intentions subject to misperception. An attack involving a weapon of mass destruction or great loss of life and property will often set up an ineluctable process leading to a forceful reaction, if the perpetrators can be identified. In many instances, this is the terrorist's desire: an overreaction on the part of the government.

There are a number of obstacles to good decision making that will confront leaders in the aftermath of an attack. Humans tend to acquire and process information in ways that can cause decision makers to render bad decisions, a tendency exacerbated by a crisis. We tend to rely heavily on preexisting frames of reference built from previous experience and knowledge to help us process information quickly and efficiently. Unfortunately, these frames of reference, which are known as (mental) images, can cause decision makers to misinterpret the situation and render a wrong decision.[26]

Decision makers will unconsciously engage a broad range of cognitive and motivational devices to help them evaluate information. Phenomena such as cognitive dissonance, perceptual satisficing, and defensive avoidance are often used to describe these subconscious devices. We use cognitive dissonance, for example, in a subconscious way to explain away information that does not conform to our beliefs or understanding. Perceptual satisficing often means that we settle on the minimal amount of change necessary, consistent with our images. Defensive avoidance can cause us to disregard information not consistent with our decisions. These phenomena can inhibit rational decision making in everyday life, and their effect on crisis decision making can be pernicious. They can cause decision makers to see what they *expect* to see and see what they *want* to see, resulting in poor decision making.

We often subconsciously make new information conform to images we already have formed. These cognitive obstacles to decision making may result in a kind of cognitive consistency that may be inaccurate or even irrational. As a result, we may dismiss information that does not conform, or find devices that help us explain away information that does not correspond with our established mental images. Our preformed images about particular terrorist threats may blind us to other threats. For example, our aviation-related concerns prior to 11 September 2001 were hijacking and hostage situations, not airplanes used as flying bombs. These images lie at the center of the "failure of imagination" charge often levied at the US government.[27] Thus, in a crisis, we will often see what we expect to see.[28]

Similarly, our doubts and desires play a significant role in decision making, often preventing us from objectively evaluating information. Decision makers are strongly influenced by these factors to maintain a stable decision environment with their values intact. These motivational obstacles may render them blind to new information that challenges these desires. Decision makers may be motivated, for domestic political reasons, to believe that an attack has been perpetrated by one extremist group, even as the evidence mounts that another may be involved. In the case of the United States, authorities may have been focused on domestic terrorists as a result of the Oklahoma City bombing of 1995, and thus failed to appreciate the accumulation of indicators that there were other threats, just as the UK government was long focused on threats emanating from the IRA, not Islamist extremist groups. In a terrorist crisis, the desire to avoid hard choices is likely to be influenced in this way: Decision makers may not see things properly because they do not want to see them.[29]

To illustrate these dilemmas, consider the Spanish government's reaction to the March 2004 railway bombings. The conservative government knew that the Socialists would, if elected, reverse their policy on Iraq. In the run-up to the election (held three days after the attack), there was concern that an attack would be made in an effort to influence the election. The government was therefore very sensitive to the threat of Islamic fundamentalist terrorism, which would seek to influence this decision against the government.[30] When the attacks occurred, however, the first reaction of the government was to blame the Basque ETA terrorist organization. After all, there was no history of fundamentalist terrorism in Spain, whereas attacks by ETA were common. Thus, they expected ETA to be responsible. At the same time, because the attack took place only days before the elections, the government knew that it could adversely affect its electoral chances. An attack laid at ETA's feet would be far less controversial than a fundamentalist attack. Therefore, even as the evidence mounted that ETA was not responsible, the government clung to its assertion that ETA was behind the attack; it wanted ETA to be responsible. The consequences are well known: The majority of politically active Spaniards lost confidence in the ruling government and voted it out of office. Upon assuming power, the new Socialist government quickly began to withdraw Spanish troops from Iraq, resulting in what might reasonably be called a major victory for the terrorists.[31]

Such cognitive and motivational obstacles abound in every decision we make, particularly so when time is of the essence, as in a crisis. Therefore, decision makers must guard against such traps and ensure that, to the extent possible, decisions are made on the basis of verifiable fact. They must resist the temptation to act impetuously, and make every attempt to consider the possible unintended consequences of their decisions.

Managing Crisis Communications

Communicating government policies to the public is always a challenging task that is made more difficult by crises. The media will always be present in a crisis—and the public will form views on the crisis in large measure in response to how it is portrayed by the media. It is therefore incumbent on the government to recognize this relationship and to work toward establishing a partnership that serves the public's need for information in time of crisis. The partnership is often very finely tuned—a government misstatement may be magnified and repeated by the media, resulting in unintended consequences. Governments must always be careful to balance information with security and must always be cognizant of the danger of inciting panic through the clumsy or inadvertent release of information.

Information management poses a number of hard decisions for crisis managers both in the pre-crisis preparation phase and during the actual attack itself. Leaders are always challenged to balance informing the public about threats and running the risk of losing credibility when nothing happens, or worse, creating a panic. If insufficient information is provided to the public, leaders are likely to be blamed for failing to inform the public. Likewise, there are security considerations relevant to public information. When leaders announce information on potential terrorist operations in order to inform the public, they are also informing potential attackers of the extent of knowledge about their plans. It is not a coincidence that the public does not know exactly how many terrorist plots have been disrupted—nor should they. The notion of full public disclosure of all threats is unrealistic and dangerous.

The characteristics of terrorist crises put a premium on communicating with the public. Surprise, urgency, and intensity combine to ensure a volatile environment and a public hungry for information and guidance. Into this febrile mix, decision makers are thrust, armed with little more than great uncertainty about the facts, inadequate preparation for such endeavors, and a media pressing relentlessly forward with information that may be largely uncorroborated. It is a tenet of crisis decision making that the first reports are almost always wrong to some degree, but constant repetition by the media gives unwarranted credibility to them.

In this environment there are some key considerations. First, in a world of near-instantaneous communication, it is essential to report your own bad news. Bad news does not get better with time and will almost always be unearthed by the media, which are likely to get at least part of it wrong. Reporting the bad news directly allows the government to put it in perspective and to accentuate any actions the government is taking to mitigate the effects of terrorist action. Doing so will enable the government to at least stay even with, if not a bit ahead of, the news cycle. In a crisis, governments must be wary of spending their time reacting to inaccurate or incomplete news reports.

Second, the integrity and reputation of the government are often at stake, and public information gaffes can have a devastating impact even after the crisis has passed. Government statements run the risk of being repeated *ad nauseum* by the media and becoming the accepted wisdom on government actions during the crisis. Recovering from such gaffes can be difficult, if not impossible.

Third, with regard to terrorist attacks, the media cannot be expected to be knowledgeable about terrorist methods or intentions. Likewise, they are generally not knowledgeable about government crisis means and consequence management operations. Therefore, it is incumbent upon crisis managers to ensure that media representatives receive extensive background information in order to ensure the quality of what they report. Generally, governments have a good story to tell regarding their actions in a crisis and need a receptive media in order to tell it. Crisis managers must vigorously challenge errant media reports, lest they become received wisdom.

Finally, avoid speculation about matters related to the attack. While numbers of casualties and degree of property loss may be evident, it behooves government spokespersons to limit their statements to what is known and to avoid speculating about the cause of the attack or the responsibility for the attack. Governments should focus on the actions they are taking to ameliorate the effects of the attack and what they are doing to prevent further attacks.

The media will be an ever-present factor in crises, particularly crises involving terrorist attacks. It is therefore incumbent upon governments to recognize that their success or failure will often be viewed by the public through the prism of media coverage. Recognizing the essential role that the media play in the success or failure of crisis management is the first step to succeeding in managing this delicate relationship.

Exercises and Lessons Learned

A final consideration for crisis managers concerns the value of exercising the crisis management system. Such exercises can prove crucial to determining any evident flaws in the organization, the institutional links, and the arrangements for crisis management. It is during exercises that such flaws can be determined and corrective action taken. Exercises are also very useful for inculcating a culture of preparedness in the organization and for educating the organization, particularly new members, regarding the procedures.

It is vitally important that senior government officials personally take part in these exercises, if only on an occasional basis. As noted, crisis management is a responsibility for elected officials and they should be knowledgeable of their responsibilities in a crisis. Their participation may also serve to inspire others in the organization to take their own crisis management responsibilities seriously. Exercises also provide opportunities for establishing the linkages so critical in successful crisis management. Once a crisis hits, it is too late to start building such linkages. They must be established and exercised in advance of the event. Thus, it is important to invite not only representatives of all the ministries with roles in crises, but also external players, such as NGOs and the media, to ensure that their capabilities and contributions are taken into consideration.

Likewise, plans should provide for a mechanism for gathering and institutionalizing lessons learned. Institutionalizing this process is often a key difference between successful and unsuccessful crisis management organizations. The ability to learn from one's own mistakes and those of others is an important asset. One should never pay for the same lesson twice!

Conclusion

Crises are inevitable. Even in countries without a significant history of terrorism, the possibility that they may be affected by a terrorist incident has grown in recent years. Managing security crises certainly ranks among the most challenging tasks of government. Particularly with regard to terrorist crises, not only can governments fail, but large numbers of people may be killed, many more injured, and infrastructure wrecked. States may overreact and may be plunged into war. The seriousness of these consequences mandates that governments take a disciplined and consequent approach to managing these events. This chapter has attempted to demonstrate the consequences of failure to develop and use the right framework for crisis management.

Effective management of terrorism crises is, in the final analysis, a question of leadership. Elected leaders must recognize their role in the process and embrace the requirements that it imposes. Crises are managed by political leaders, while government organizations, in cooperation with NGOs and private industry, manage the consequences of these crises. This distinction is key to understanding the process of terrorist incident crisis management.

Preparation for effective crisis management means getting the framework right. This means ensuring that the organization, the institutions, and arrangements are the right ones for a given state in a given situation. It also means recognizing that these elements are not fixed and will always be in need of revision and reform. Quality crisis management is a process, not an end-product.

John L. Clarke Dr. John Clarke is Professor of Leadership, Management, and Defense Planning at the Marshall Center and directs the center's Seminar on Transatlantic Civil Security. An expert on military forces and their roles in homeland security, he has developed numerous courses on crisis management and stability operations, and developed scenario-based exercises and simulations. He recently led a major research project on European Approaches to Homeland Security and edited the book *Armies in Homeland Security: American and European Perspectives*. Dr. Clarke's graduate degrees include a *Doktorat* in political science from the University of Salzburg, a *Brévet* from the Ecole Supérieure de Guerre in Paris, and an M.A. from the University of Southern California; he was a post-doctoral fellow at Harvard University and an Olmsted Scholar. Jack Clarke was a Special Forces officer and held senior politico-military positions during a US Army career spanning a quarter-century and has led projects in fifty countries. Dr. Clarke is a frequent contributor to German and Austrian radio and television.

His articles appear in such publications as *EuroFuture, Survival, Defense News, Magazine der Bundeswehr, European Security, Homeland Security, Homeland Defense,* and *Journal of Homeland Security.*

Recommended Readings

Clarke, John, ed. *Armies in Homeland Security: American and European Perspectives.* Washington, DC: National Defense University Press, 2006.

Grey, Michael R., and Kenneth R. Spaeth. *The Bioterrorism Sourcebook.* New York: McGraw-Hill, 2006.

Howard, Russell D., James J. F. Forest, and Joanne C. Moore (eds). *Homeland Security and Terrorism: Readings and Interpretations.* New York: McGraw-Hill, 2005.

Maniscalco, Paul, and Hank Christen. *Terrorism Response: A Field Guide for Law Enforcement.* Upper Saddle River, NJ: Prentice Hall, 2002.

Memorial Institute for the Prevention of Terrorism: http://www.start.umd.edu/gtd/

National Consortium for the Study of Terrorism and Responses to Terrorism, "Global Terrorism Database:" http://www.mipt.org/terrorism-resource-guide

Sauter, Mark, and James Jay Carafano. *Homeland Security.* New York: McGraw-Hill, 2005.

Notes

1. The Indian government's response has been criticized for being both ineffective and lacking in vigor. But a forceful response could be highly dangerous in the explosive cauldron of South Asia. After all, a response with force is likely to have been the terrorists' aim. See Damien McElroy, "Mumbai Attacks: Foreign Governments Criticize India's Response," *Daily Telegraph*, 28 November 2008, available at http://www.telegraph.co.uk/news/worldnews/asia/india/3533279/Mumbai-attacks-foreign-governments-criticise-Indias-response.html, accessed January 2009.

2. This chapter focuses on preparation for and response to acts of terror; but the fundamental principles discussed here are of use in a range of contingencies, not just terrorism attacks.

3. The term "crisis management" will be used, in the context of this chapter, to refer to formal organizational responses to exceptional circumstances, as opposed to *ad hoc* responses.

4. There are a number of works that set forth models for crisis management at both the national and the private venture level of analysis. See, *inter alia*, the Thales Corporation research paper entitled *Crisis Management Models and Timelines*, available at http://www.thalesresearch.com/Portals/0/TRT060601.pdf, accessed October 2009.

5. For a fuller discussion of the political leadership aspects of crisis management, see A. Boin, P. T. Hart, E. Stern, and B. Sundelius, "The Politics of Crisis Management: Public Leadership Under Pressure," *Journal of Contingencies and Crisis Management*, Vol. 15, Issue 3 (September 2007), 168–169.

6. For a survey of definitions of crisis, see "Crisis—Modern Concepts of Crisis, Contemporary Definition and Usage, Bibliography," available at http://science.jrank.org/pages/7604/Crisis.html, accessed January 2009.

7. Unlike terrorist attacks perpetrated by the Irish Republican Army in the 1980s and 1990s, in which telephonic warnings were often given in advance to minimize casualties, contemporary terrorists seldom offer such warnings. See David Sharrock, "'IRA Is Not So Ruthless and Always Gives Bomb Warnings'," *Daily Telegraph*, 19 September 2001, available at http://www.telegraph.co.uk/news/uknews/1340995/IRA-is-not-so-ruthless-and-always-gives-bomb-warnings.html, accessed January 2009.

8. Richard Betts, *Surprise Attack: Lessons for Defense Planning* (Washington, DC: The Brookings Institution Press, 1982).

9. See "Special Reports: In Depth: London Attacks," a compilation of coverage from BBC News, last updated 8 July 2008, available at http://news.bbc.co.uk/2/hi/in_depth/uk/2005/london_explosions/default.stm, accessed January 2009.

10. As noted, uncertainty regarding the incident prevailed for the first hour, as the archaic London underground system is prone to such electrical failures. See "Hazmat/CBRN Incident: London's King Cross Station," *Fire Engineering*, available to subscribers at http://www.fireengineering.com/login/index.html;jsessionid=755FEB37B09B555A156E95AD90D5F9B6?articleType=Prt, accessed January 2009.

11. Despite the spate of terror attacks against US targets in the 1990s (World Trade Tower 1993, Oklahoma City 1995, and numerous attacks against US targets in Africa), the attacks of 11 September 2001 seemed a complete surprise to many, both inside and outside the government. See Daniel Byman, "Strategic Surprise and the September 11 Attacks," *Annual Review of Political Science*, Vol. 8 (June 2005), 145–170.

12. Many examples of media hype with regard to crises exist. This has been particularly the case with the financial crisis of 2008. See, *inter alia*, Howard S. Katz, "Media Hype," GoldSeek.com, 1 December 2008, available at http://news.goldseek.com/GoldSeek/1228141440.php, accessed January 2009.

13. The all-hazards construct has gained in popularity over the last decade in both the United States and Europe. The Hurricane Katrina event demonstrated that the Department of Homeland Security's focus on terrorism events was insufficient to deal with other hazards. See, for example, the US Government Accountability Office, *Homeland Security: DHS Effort to Enhance First Responders' All-Hazards Capabilities Continue to Evolve* (Washington, DC: GAO, July 2005), available at http://www.gao.gov/new.items/d05652.pdf, accessed January 2009.

14. Cyber attacks have figured prominently in the news. Estonia suffered a significant denial-of-service attack in April and May 2007 and the US Department of Defense suffered a malware attack in November 2008. See Ian Traynor, "Russia accused of unleashing cyberwar to disable Estonia," *The Guardian*, 17 May 2007, available at http://www.guardian.co.uk/world/2007/may/17/topstories3.russia, accessed January 2009; and Pete Swabey, "US Department of Defense bans USB drives after worm attack," Information Age, 20 November 2008, available at http://www.information-age.com/home/information-age-today/814827/us-department-of-defense-bans-usb-drives-after-worm-attack.thtml, accessed January 2009.

15. See Brian P. Schmitt et al., "Recognizing and Responding to an Attack with a Biological Weapon," *Southern Medical Journal*, Vol. 94, Issue 11 (November 2001), 1048–1051, available at http://journals.lww.com/smajournalonline/Citation/2001/11000/Recognizing_and_Responding_To_An_Attack_With_A.2.aspx, accessed 27 September 2009.

16. This irreducible goal of crisis management is often overlooked. Much of the literature focuses on the mechanics of managing the consequences of crises, rather than the actual management of the event. Crisis management is more than just damage control. For this perspective on crisis management, see Eric Dezenhall and John Weber, *Damage Control: Why Everything You Know About Crisis Management Is Wrong* (New York: Portfolio, 2007).

17. Useful information on risk management in terror incidents can be found at the Rand Corporation's Center for Terrorism Risk Management Policy, available at http://www.rand.org/multi/ctrmp/, accessed January 2009.

18. For the official report on FEMA's response to this crisis, see US Department of Homeland Security, Office of Inspector General, *A Performance Review of FEMA's Disaster Management Activities in Response to Hurricane Katrina*, OIG 06-32 (March 2006), available at http://www.dhs.gov/xoig/assets/mgmtrpts/OIG_06-32_Mar06.pdf, accessed January 2009.

19. Richard Falkenrath, "Homeland Security and Consequence Management," in *The Challenge of Proliferation: A Report of the Aspen Strategy Group*, edited by Kurt M. Campbell (Washington, DC: The Aspen Institute, 2005), 131–138, available at http://www.aspeninstitute.org/sites/default/files/content/docs/aspen%20strategy%20group/ASGChallengeTextwCOVER.pdf, accessed 27 September 2009.

20. Criticism of crisis managers' actions in the aftermath of a crisis is ineluctable. Most recently, see the criticism of the actions of India's crisis managers with respect to the attacks in Mumbai. See, for example, Rama Lakshmi, "Cabinet Minister Resigns Amid Anger in India," *Washington Post*, 1 December 2008, available at http://www.washingtonpost.com/wp-dyn/content/story/2008/11/30/ST2008113001169.html, accessed January 2009.

21. See: FEMA at http://www.fema.gov/ and EMERCOM at http://www.mchs.gov.ru, accessed January 2009.

22. For an example of lead agency issues, see Kathleen Gereski, "The Department of Defense as Lead Federal Agency," *Homeland Security Affairs*, Vol. 2, No. 3 (October 2006), 1–21, available at http://www.hsaj.org/?article=2.3.8, accessed 27 September 2009.

23. In the United States, the Stafford Act and the Posse Comitatus Act both restrict how federal agencies may be employed in crises. See "Robert T. Stafford Disaster Relief and Emergency Assistance Act," Public Law 93-288, as of June 2007, available at http://www.fema.gov/about/stafact.shtm, accessed January 2009, and "The Posse Comitatus Act of 1878," 20 Stat. L, 145, 18 June 1978, available at http://www.dojgov.net/posse_comitatus_act.htm, accessed January 2009.

24. One of the great difficulties is knowing how much information should be given to the public regarding counterterrorist operations. The public requires reassurance and yet precise information regarding thwarted plots risks providing terrorists with valuable feedback regarding what the government may know about potential operations and modus operandi. An example of this was the announcement by the MI5 chief in London that the United Kingdom was tracking thirty terrorist plots. See "MI5 Tracking '30 UK Terror Plots'," BBC News, 10 November 2006, available at http://news.bbc.co.uk/2/hi/uk_news/6134516.stm, accessed January 2009.

25. This public desire is often referred to as the "CNN Effect," as it first surfaced in CNN reporting on the suffering in Somalia in the early 1990s, leading to a US response. For more information, see "'The CNN Effect': How 24-Hour News Coverage Affects Government Decisions and Public Opinion," a Brookings Institution–Harvard University Forum, 23 January 2002, available at http://www.brookings.edu/events/2002/0123media_journalism.aspx, accessed 27 September 2009.

26. For an excellent overview of decision making, see Paul C. Nutt, *Making Tough Decisions: Tactics for Improving Managerial Decision Making* (San Francisco: Jossey-Bass, 1989).

27. The charge of failure of imagination has been made in numerous sources, including the official government report of the 9/11 commission. See "Chapter 11: Foresight—And Hindsight," in National Commission on Terrorist Attacks Upon the United States, *The 9/11 Commission Report* (Washington, DC: US Government Printing Office, 2004), available at http://www.9-11commission.gov/report/911Report_Ch11.pdf, accessed January 2009.

28. The classic text regarding the use of images and cognitive obstacles to decision making remains Robert Jervis, *Perception and Misperception in International Politics* (Princeton, NJ: Princeton University Press, 1976).

29. Irving L. Janis's work on motivational factors in decision making continues to be of great value. See Janis, *Crucial Decisions: Leadership in Policymaking and Crisis Management* (New York: The Free Press, 1989).

30. For an analysis of the events leading up to the attack and the election, see "El 92% de los españos se opone la guerra contra Irak," Clarín.com, 29 March 2003, available (in Spanish) at http://www.clarin.com/diario/2003/03/29/um/m-537495.htm, accessed January 2009.

31. See, *inter alia*, Keith B. Richburg, "Spain Campaigned to Pin Blame on ETA," *Washington Post*, 17 March 2004, available at http://pqasb.pqarchiver.com/washingtonpost/access/580598271.html?FMT=ABS&FMTS=ABS:FT&date=Mar+17,+2004&author=Keith+B.+Richburg&pub=The+Washington+Post&edition=&startpage=A.01&desc=Spain+Campaigned+to+Pin+Blame+on+ETA;+Despite+Evidence+to+Contrary,+Basque+Group+Was+Focus+in+Blasts, accessed 27 September 2009. Another example might be the case made by the US and UK governments in the run up to the Iraq invasion of March 2003. Decision makers in many countries were persuaded that Saddam Hussein possessed WMD, even though the physical evidence was sparse. They were perhaps conditioned by their expectation and perhaps desire that he must have had them.

Unit 4

Case Studies

Ralf Roloff

The Limits and Opportunities of Effective Multilateralism:

Germany's Approach

Transnational terrorism has been a smoldering security threat in international politics. It represents one of the main challenges for the concept of comprehensive security or networked security, which has been promoted since the end of the Cold War. Combating terrorism has been a dramatic issue in Western Germany, especially during the 1970s—national and international terrorism at this time kept the country under serious pressure. The attack on the Munich Olympic Games in 1972 and the series of attacks and murders by the left-wing Red Army Faction (RAF)—culminating in 1977 in the so-called *DeutscherHerbst* (German Autumn) with the kidnapping and murder of Hanns Martin Schleyer, the hijacking of the Lufthansa airplane "Landshut," and the suicide of the imprisoned RAF leaders Andreas Baader, Gudrun Ensslin, and Jan-Carl Raspe—have been the peak points of this development.[1] The German security apparatus adapted during this period to the challenges of national and international terrorism, but given historical and constitutional restrictions, strong controversies always have appeared about the appropriate balance between civil liberties and security concerns.[2] The concept of *wehrhafte Demokratie* (defensible democracy or militant democracy) and Germany's political culture, with its strong emphasis on civil liberties and human rights, are deeply rooted in the society as lessons from the Nazi period (1933–1945). Thus, Benjamin Franklin's freedom-security dilemma[3] became a key feature in the development of Germany's counterterrorism approach.

The second key feature of Germany's approach to countering terrorism is the concept of networked security, with its emphasis on multidimensional, multilevel, and multilateral aspects of security.[4] Networked security has been promoted—especially after German reunification in 1990—as the appropriate approach for the country's security policy by almost all parties in the Bundestag. The basic idea of the concept is complex interdependence, multilateral cooperation, and integration of all relevant security institutions. Security thus became a cross-section area.[5] The interlocking of several institutions and policy fields creates a comprehensive understanding of security, which combines external and internal security matters. One of the most used terms in this context is the notion: "the borders between external and internal security are blurred" (Hanns W. Maull) and the second most used characterization is: "Germany's interests are interwoven interests" (Dieter Senghass).[6] A strong commitment to multilateralism, respect for international law, and European integration are therefore key to pursuing the strategy of networked security. In fact, this kind of engaging internationally has led to a multilevel system of governance that has created some concerns, dilemmas, or at least difficulties[7] with conflicting objectives in: domestic and foreign policies; multilevel governance in Justice and Home Affairs; fragmentation of the security apparatus; distinguishing security and defense policy; and conflicting interests among internal positions and interests and those of transatlantic and European partners.[8]

Countering transnational terrorism in Germany since 9/11 has shown these dilemmas and difficulties of networked security within a highly complex and interdependent political system. Accordingly, it may be asked, how effective is multilateralism, and how well does networked security policy operate to counter transnational terrorism? How does the freedom-security dilemma impact on the multilateral approach of countering transnational terrorism? These questions will be discussed in the following sections. I will start by analyzing the internal structures of Germany's combating terrorism apparatus. I will discuss the most critical points in terms of security versus civil liberties, which are related to the so-called counterterrorism packages, but also the multilevel governance in combating terrorism as well. The subsequent section will focus on Germany's multilateral engagement in countering transnational terrorism. The United Nations, the European Union, NATO, and the G-8 are the focal points here. What are the key issues in countering terrorism through these institutions? How effective are these multilateral instruments? What are the main contributions and the main concerns of Germany within these institutions? We will conclude by discussing the limits and opportunities of a multilateral approach towards countering international terrorism.

Germany's Internal Structure for CT: Vertical and Horizontal Differentiation

Germany's approach for countering terrorism before 9/11 was shaped by the threat posed by national and international terrorism. Countering terrorism was understood as a domestic affair. Legislation, law enforcement, and police measures were developed under this basic assumption: Terrorism is a domestic issue. This explains to a certain extent today's approach, which still treats countering terrorism more as a challenge for domestic security institutions than for external security institutions.[9] In the 1970s, several legislative antiterrorist acts were adopted. Between 1974 and 1978, three acts entered into force that criminalized the formation of terrorist organizations and the support and encouragement of serious violent crimes, strengthened the powers of prosecution, and limited the rights of the defense, especially restricting contacts between prisoners and lawyers. In 1977, the contact ban law was passed, barring contacts between detained and convicted terrorists with anyone else, including a block on written and oral contact with their defending lawyers.[10] The legal changes made during the 1970s opened a tremendous debate over the security-freedom dilemma and the question how far the *wehrhafte Demokratie* could and should go. The discussion considered the question whether the antiterrorist acts violated fundamental rights and freedoms or at least represented a severe challenge to the constitution.

These debates reached a first point of culmination after the contact ban law had been launched and affronted RAF prisoners and their liberal and left-wing supporters. Even after the Constitutional Court had decided in 1978 that the law was in line with the constitution, the debate about the security-freedom dilemma has been a key pattern in all political discussions on counterterrorism, up to and including today. Related to countering terrorism was the highly contested special regulation for principal witnesses (Kronzeugenregelung, 1989), which provided sentence reductions or amnesty in exchange for cooperation with the justice system and expired in 1999.[11] It came up in the discussion after 9/11 again; now the idea was to obtain information from Islamist extremists. Two additional measures on counterterrorism of that time need to be mentioned here as well because they were brought to the debate again after 9/11: trawl net search and grid search or scanning method. Trawl net search makes it possible to keep personal data or other information about people checked at borders and other control points, which may lead to the arrest of suspected terrorists. Grid search or scanning methods mean that databases were primarily used for identifying overlapping clusters of suspicious traits in parts of the population.[12] The computerization and modernization of police and intelligence were other consequences of the fight against terrorism of the RAF in the 1970s.

To understand the debates about the freedom-security dilemma, one needs to take into account that the structure of the German security apparatus has been differentiated and decentralized by purpose; it is both vertically and horizontally differentiated. This is a result of the historical experience of the Nazi period between 1933 and 1945, when a strong central security apparatus had been used to pursue inhumane and criminal activities. Ulrich Schneckener mentioned very correctly that "the word terror in German public discourse . . . refers often to the Nazi state and its inhumane and criminal activities."[13] The domestic security structure is organized to prevent a strong central security apparatus and it is based on three principles:

1. Police and other security organizations have to be organized according to the federal structure of Germany. That means each of the federal republic's sixteen Länder or districts has its own police, intelligence, and law enforcement institutions. The only federal institutions are federal police formerly known as the border guard and the federal criminal police office.

2. Between police and intelligence services there is a clear legal and political separation; this is imperative. This "separation clause" (*Trennungsgebot*) was imposed on Germany by the Western Allies after World War II.[14]

3. Between internal and external security matters there needs to be a strict distinction. This strict distinction can best be seen in the separation of police and military. Germany does not have any kind of *Gendarmerie*. Even more the military cannot be used for internal purposes. The *Bundeswehr* can only be used in a supportive role in cases of natural disasters, humanitarian purposes, technical assistance, and in a declared state of emergency (*innerer Notstand*). These principles had led to a very complex and fragmented institutional setting of approximately 39 different institutions and authorities plus a large number of ministries on the federal as well as on the Länder level.[15]

These federal institutions are politically supervised and controlled by different ministries: Interior, Justice, Defense, Finance, and the Federal Chancellery. This complexity and diversity of the security apparatus becomes even more complicated in everyday business because of the decentralization of the institutions. They are not all located in the capital, but spread around Germany.

German Internal Security Institutions

- **Federal Office for the Protection of the Constitution (*Bundesamt für Verfassungsschutz*),** plus sixteen Länder offices for the Protection of the Constitution, which operate independently from the Federal Office: Altogether they constitute the German domestic intelligence service. It is important to understand that the Federal Office has only a coordinating role. It cannot give orders or even supervise the Länder offices. The *Länder* offices are supervised by the ministries of the interior of each state.[16]
- **Federal Intelligence Service (*Bundesnachrichtendienst/BND*):** In charge of analyzing and gathering information abroad. The Federal Intelligence Service reports regularly to the federal government. The president of the Federal Intelligence Service is an ex officio member of the Federal Security Council/Cabinet, which is a committee of the security-related ministries.[17]
- **Military Counterintelligence Service (*Militärischer Abschirmdienst/ MAD*):** A part of the ministry of defense and of the armed forces. MAD is responsible for analyzing, gathering, and evaluating information on activities that threaten or undermine the constitutional order within the German Federal Defense Force and activities that are directed from outside against the German Federal Defense Force. Its emphasis is on espionage and extremist propaganda. On the federal level, the three intelligence services—Federal Office for the Protection of the Constitution, Federal Intelligence Service, and Military Counterintelligence Service—are coordinated by the Federal Coordinator for Intelligence, who works within the Federal Chancellery.
- **Federal Criminal Police Office (*Bundeskriminalamt/BKA*):** This is linked to the Federal Ministry of Interior and sixteen Länder criminal offices, and linked to the respective *Länder* Ministry of Interior. The BKA coordinates the work of the state Criminal Police Offices. It provides for information exchange and for central databases. The BKA has the right to conduct criminal investigations in cases of national and international interest. Since 1975, the BKA has a special antiterrorism unit. Its responsibility was extended during the 1980s to include dealing with international drug trafficking and transnational organized crime. It is also in charge of European and international cooperation in combating crime, especially coordination with Europol and Interpol. It has several liaison offices abroad.[18]
- **Federal Police, formally called Federal Border Guard (*Bundespolizei/ Bundesgrenzschutz*):** Since 2005, the former Federal Border Guard was renamed Federal Police. Key functions are border protection, railway-police duties, protection against attacks on the security of air traffic, police duties in the case of emergency or national defense, and the protection of German diplomats and missions abroad. The special antiterror squad GSG9, which was founded 1972 after the Munich Olympic Games terror attack, is also part of the Federal Police.[19]

- **Customs Criminal Office (*Zollkriminalamt/ZKA*):** This is the central office dealing with customs and intelligence. It coordinates, directs investigations in customs crimes, controls exports, and cooperates with police, fiscal, and trade authorities. The office is in charge of recording, evaluating, and coordinating information about the proliferation of weapons of mass destruction. It has the right to investigate drug trafficking, illegal transfer of technology, and money laundering.[20]
- **Office of the Prosecuting Attorney General:** The Office of the Prosecuting Attorney General is attached to Federal High Court of Justice. The Prosecuting Attorney General is responsible for investigations and prosecution in cases of severe criminal activities, which are directed against the internal and external security of Germany. This includes terrorism, espionage, and politically motivated crimes.

After 9/11, the federal government established a coordinator for counterterrorism who has to coordinate the activities among the different ministries and federal agencies. The coordinator is located within the Ministry of Foreign Affairs and has the rank of ambassador. He is not engaged in the everyday business but in coordinating the strategic lines of the counterterrorism efforts of the federal government.

After 9/11, the German government approved two so-called security packages, which aimed at five objectives: (1) destroy terrorist structures through comprehensive search and investigations; (2) repel terrorists before they can launch attacks in Germany; (3) enhance international cooperation in combating terrorism; (4) protect the German population and reduce the vulnerability of the country; (5) remove the causes for terrorism.[21]

The first security package focused on two issues: It led to the abolishment of the religious privilege (*Religionsprivileg*) in the act governing private association. As a result, the guaranteed special protection and rights of religious associations can be set aside if the purpose or activities of a religious association run counter to criminal law provisions, are directed against the constitutional order, or violate the idea of international understanding. This provision was in particular related to fundamentalist Islamic organizations. By this it was indeed possible to ban three fundamentalist Islamic organizations: Caliphate State (*Kalifatsstat*) (2001); Al-Aqsa International Foundation, a Hamas-related fundraising association (2002); and the network Hizb-ut-Tahrir (2003). The second issue in the first security package was a new paragraph in the penal code that criminalized the support and membership in a criminal or terrorist organization based in other countries.[22]

The second security package covered a broader range of issues. It was intended to strengthen the rights and capabilities of the security authorities, in particular by improving their information exchanges and the identification measures in visa applications, which would help to prevent terrorists from entering the country. It allowed for sky marshals from the Federal Police and the use of firearms by security officials on civilian airliners. It also attempted to improve border controls, as well as to detect extremists already in the country. The last point was the most controversial. Federal police institutions, intelligence services, and law enforcement agencies have the right to obtain information from various public and private services and to access telecommunication, mail, air traffic, bank accounts, money flows, and employment and university records of individuals and organizations that pose a threat to the "idea of international understanding" or the peaceful coexistence of the peoples. These provisions are subject to special permissions by the government and controlled by a parliamentary body.[23]

Additional amendments of the second security package are related to security checks and special identification measures in passports and other relevant documents. The immigration law has been changed to allow the authorities to deport people with a suspected terrorist background—as in the US and many countries. The aviation law has been changed in order to protect the airspace from terrorist attacks. A restructuring of the homeland protection took place as well. A program combating terrorist financing was issued by the Ministry of Finance. All these initiatives were accompanied by additional financial and human resources.

Nevertheless, the security packages and especially the extension of the rights of the security authorities in exchanging and gathering information have been dramatically reduced by several decisions and sentences of the Constitutional Court. The most prominent decision has been on the aviation security law, which has been declared as being "out of line" with the constitution because it violates the fundamental right of life.[24] In another preliminary decision, the Constitutional Court decided that gathering information via telecommunication and especially the recording and collecting of these data raises serious concerns, and therefore the court stopped essential parts of the execution of this law until its final decisions.[25] It seems that the Constitutional Court has a clear line of argument: *in dubio pro libertatis*. Laws need to address an appropriate balance between security interests and fundamental rights. So far, the Constitutional Court has drawn a clear line for the security apparatus—which forces the government to redefine some of the measures that have been taken immediately after 9/11.

The Constitutional Court's decisions have created a kind of straitjacket especially for the federal ministry of the interior and its efforts in optimizing intranational and international cooperation and coordination in countering terrorism. Thus, the Constitutional Court's decisions have reduced the room for maneuver not only of the federal Ministry of the Interior but for the federal government as a whole and its efforts at coordinating and cooperating. All of German government must account for the strong position of the Constitutional Court in favor of protecting fundamental rights. For the Federal Ministry of the Interior, the Constitutional Court's decisions have had an additional component: The Ministries of the Interior in Germany are in charge for the protection of the constitution. Public opinion now sees a kind of special division of labor between the federal Ministry of the Interior and the Constitutional Court: The Ministry of the Interior aims at optimizing security, and the Constitutional Court aims at optimizing fundamental rights and the provisions of the basic law. As in other political areas, the Constitutional Court's role as a political arbitrator has grown in the field of counterterrorism. These restrictions in balancing the security-freedom dilemma are getting even worse when it comes to international cooperation—the parameters for cooperation and negotiating are determined by the narrowly defined security-freedom linkage of the Constitutional Court.

Germany's International Engagement/Involvement

From the beginning, Germany has tried to embed its counterterrorism efforts into a network of multilateral institutions and fora. Multilateralism was and will be the key feature of German foreign and security policies. The multilateral component has been enshrined in German basic law as well. International and European law are constitutional parts of the federal law, and membership in international organizations and institutions—especially those pertaining to collective security—are mentioned in the basic law as well. In practice, Germany's multilateral imperative requires improving international law under the provisions of the United Nations, strong involvement in the European Union, a strong transatlantic relationship and commitment within NATO, engagement within OSCE, and finally a responsible role in the Group of Eight (G-8).

The German government has actively promoted an international approach in countering terrorism. The political mantra of the Red-Green Coalition under Chancellor Gerhard Schröder (1998–2005) as well as of the Grand Coalition under Chancellor Angela Merkel (since 2005) has been: The response to transnational terrorism must be an international network of countermeasures, and it must be a multidimensional approach engaging all relevant fields of policy. The networked security approach so far has resulted in a multilevel effort of countering terrorism with a mixed balance sheet. Multilateral approaches have been very successful in creating a common threat perception, but they have not been successful in creating a complementary approach in counterterrorism measures.[26] In addition, a kind of multilateral paradox has occurred. On one hand, the necessity of multilateral cooperation and exchange of information has been underlined. On the other hand, the more international organizations deal with the details in countering transnational terrorism, the more complicated international cooperation and finding international consensus become. States tend to restrict interference with national sovereignty, which undermines the efficiency of multilateral measures. In principle, the multilateral approach can be analyzed in terms of operational and structural measures. Operational measures are focused on countering existing terrorist structures, defending and protecting against terrorist attacks. These measures mainly engage police, counterintelligence, military, civil protection, border guards, custom services, and so forth. Structural measures are focused on the root causes of terrorism. They engage diplomatic, security, development, economic, financial, and cultural policies. Operational and structural measures create, to a certain extent, a tension of short- and long-term goals. Key to the success of multilateral approaches, therefore, is a balance between short- and long-term efforts. Another problem of multilateral approaches is the sheer number of different ways in which to approach multilateralism itself. Germany is following a clear approach of institutionalized multilateralism, which is known in the European Union as "effective multilateralism." The United States under the Bush administration, and even under the Obama administration, has been following the approach of selective or modular multilateralism. Formalized multilevel governance on one hand and "forum shopping" on the other hand make consensus on effective multilateral measures difficult. This leads to the general question as to whether multilateral structures are useful to deal with such a sensitive issue that reaches deep into the core of national sovereignty and national security. What are the implications of this multilateral paradox for Germany's multilateral networked approach? In the following sections, I will discuss limits and opportunities of the most relevant international organizations and international fora.

United Nations

The United Nations (UN) is important as the global institution for security and as one of the main sources for creating international law. Within the framework of the United Nations, international conventions have been developed and put into force. Germany has signed and ratified all UN conventions related to terrorism and is very active in codifying international law concerning terrorism. The main problem in creating international law within the UN is the lack of consensus on a common definition of terrorism.[27] This debate has two facets that have made consensus nearly impossible. The first facet is the old terrorist–freedom fighter argument that has driven the debate since decolonization in the 1960s. The second is the debate over to what extent measures undertaken by a state could also be understood as terrorist acts. UN documents often refer just to "terrorist acts," keeping the definition of terrorism open. This has especially been the case in UN Security Council resolutions, which have developed international law by treating terrorist acts principally as threats to international peace. In September 2006, the UN General Assembly devised a Global Counter-Terrorism Strategy and a Plan of Action based on five "Ds": dissuading, denying, deterring, developing state capacity, and defending human rights.[28] The action plan is not very consistent; in particular, it does not reflect how state actors can be deterred from supporting terrorist groups. Neutral and nonaligned countries especially resisted accepting any formulation that could bring states to the attention of the Security Council. The UN has treated counterterrorism as a broader issue, which has led to overlaps, bureaucratic dysfunctions, and the politicization of decisions. The burden of implementing operative measures mostly lies with the states. This shows a general problem in the UN efforts to counter terrorism: Decisions of the Security Council are often not supported by all member states, at least as long as reform of the council has not taken place. Thus, the limits of the UN approach are obvious in the fields of sensitive national security issues and of vital interests of the member states. For Germany's networked approach, the shortfalls of the UN system represent a serious limitation in implementing an effective multilateral approach. The competitive advantage of the UN in comparison to other international organizations is the norm setting capacity—despite the aforementioned political and institutional limitations.

European Union

The European Union (EU) represents the most important framework for Germany's multilateral approach of countering terrorism. The EU's main focus is "to face the networks of terrorism with networks countering terrorism."[29] Based on the European Security Strategy from December 2003, the Council adopted in December 2005 the European Union Counter-Terrorism Strategy, which covers four areas: prevention, protection, pursuit (prosecution), and response.[30] The EU's approach is therefore focused on operative rather than on structural measures.

One of the most important problems of implementing the EU counterterrorism strategy is the national caveat of many member states concerning their individual sovereignty. This reduces the efficiency of the EU policy. Countering terrorism within the framework of the EU covers a range of activities, and it covers all of the three pillars of the European Union. Furthermore, its activities reach out beyond the framework of the Union.[31] Since

2003, the largest five EU members (Germany, France, Great Britain, Italy, and Spain) created a network of closer cooperation among their intelligence services; in 2005, Poland also joined the group. This has started a Europe *à deux vitesses* in countering terrorism. Beyond the EU's framework, the so-called Bern Club, all EU member states plus Switzerland and Norway, are working closely together in intelligence cooperation. With Europol becoming a member of the Bern Club, the linkage between non-EU and EU members will be established.

At least three problems have occurred during the establishment of a European network: a lack of implementation of European law into national law; a lack of financing for EU counterterrorism activities; and a lack of coherence and interlocking of pillar three (cooperation of domestic and judicial policies) and pillar two (common foreign and security policy) of the EU structure.

From a German perspective, these problems occurred in the implementation of European Law when the German Constitutional Court decided that the European Arrest Warrant is not compatible with the German constitution because it violates the fundamental rights of its citizens. Problems also occur in the field of cooperation among intelligence and counterintelligence services; cultural as well as judicial differences make cooperation more difficult. The German separation clause comes more and more under pressure given the European provisions for information sharing and exchange. Finally, the debate on the use of armed forces for countering terrorism on the European level is not over, particularly as to internal uses of force. In particular, the internal use of forces is quite open. This became an issue when in 2004 the solidarity clause of the constitutional treaty was introduced on an intergovernmental agreement. The solidarity clause guarantees that all member states will support each other by all means (including military) in the case of a terrorist attack against any one member state.[32] Two important structural instruments need to be mentioned: (1) all development aid of the EU contains an antiterrorism clause, which has been introduced since the revision of the Cotounou agreement in June 2005; and (2) the individual action plans within the framework of the European Neighborhood Policy put a strong emphasis on countering terrorism. Creating European networks of countering terrorism has made progress. The usual problems of horizontal and vertical coherence and flexible integration occur in the field of countering terrorism as well and thus undermine the EU's effort of effective multilateralism.

North Atlantic Treaty Organization

"Broad in rhetoric but operationally thin"—that is the assessment of Markus Kaim on NATO's engagement in countering terrorism.[33] NATO's counterterrorism engagement has spanned four operations. Operation Eagle Assist in 2001 and 2002 helped to control the US airspace. Operation Active Endeavour has, since October 2001, patrolled civilian and military ships in the Mediterranean. The International Security Assistance Force (ISAF) in Afghanistan since summer 2003 is stabilizing Afghanistan and performing counterterrorist measures as well. Finally, NATO has performed smaller operations on the Balkans to fight against local terror groups that are connected to the al Qaeda network. NATO has also a strategic concept that was presented at the Prague Summit in 2002: The Military Concept for Defense Against Terrorism. Four main tasks are mentioned in this concept: defense against terrorism, consequence management, active counterterrorism, and military cooperation.[34] NATO also addresses counterterrorism through its partnership programs, including Partnership for Peace, Euro-Atlantic Partnership Council, NATO-Russia Council, Mediterranean Dialogue, and Istanbul Cooperation Initiative (with the countries of the Gulf Cooperation Council). The different action plans are nonbinding, and the declarations at the operational level are very vague. The implementation of the several action plans is subject to the individual states; controlling or even sanction mechanisms do not exist. Conferences on implementation and on developing the action plans have not taken place. Due to the differences in the approach of the Bush administration vis-à-vis most of the European partners of the Alliance—that is, selective multilateralism versus structural multilateralism—NATO's profile in countering terrorism remains low, except in the aforementioned operations.

Markus Kaim has identified three areas of conflict: the role of military violence as part of counterterrorism strategy, the role of multilateral organizations and international law, and short-term versus long-term strategies, specifically with regard to operational or structural strategies.[35] The differences among the members of the alliance concerning these three subjects lead to a more supportive role of NATO in the counterterrorism efforts of the United States, which puts more emphasis on the Group of Eight (G-8) and on UN efforts. From Germany's perspective, NATO efforts are complementary to those of the EU and UN. The Alliance is not the main institution for countering terrorism, but it can support the initiatives of the UN. The impact of NATO in countering terrorism for the German government will grow with NATO's changing role and engagement in Afghanistan.

The Group of Eight

The Group of Eight (G-8) has become a relevant actor in countering terrorism.[36] The group is relevant because of its potential to establish, improve, and link standards, guidelines, and best practices in the operational fields of counterterrorism. The G-8 has a long tradition in countering terrorism. In 1986, the Expert Group on Terrorism was founded. In 1989, the Financial Action Task Force on Money Laundering was established that consists of thirty-three members today. The Lyon Group on transnational organized crime was founded in 1995, and there is as well the new Counter-Terrorism Expert Group. A third group that is dealing with organized crime and terrorism—the so-called Rome/Lyon Group, plus a set of subgroups—started work in 2001. The Nuclear Safety and Security Group, the Experts on Transport Security, and the Global Health Security Action Group, which were founded in 2002, are focusing on important targets of transnational terrorism. In 2003 the Counter-Terrorism Action Group (CTAG) was founded and has eleven members: the G-8 plus Spain, Australia, and Switzerland.[37]

With its comprehensive approach on operative measures and its pragmatic and flexible approach concerning membership, the G-8 has become an agenda-setter in countering terrorism. The format of the group as the leading western industrialized countries allows the G-8 to act in a concerted manner based on a broad consensus. This concerted action and consensus-based cooperation is possible only because the G-8 consequently excludes matters of dissent. The Eight currently exclude questions of structural measures in countering terrorism; perhaps this is becoming inappropriate, given that at the Summit in Heiligendamm in 2007, the body initiated the so-called Heiligendamm Process, which initiated dialogue between G-8 member states and the five most important emerging economies—Brazil, China, India, Mexico, and South Africa. This Group of 13 is by far not as homogeneous as the core Group of Eight (except Russia). Germany is a strong supporter of the G-8 and the Heiligendamm Process. It is interested in extending the role of the G-8 and its global reach beyond the core group.

During the global finance and economic crisis the G-8's primacy as the leading international forum has been challenged by the so-called Group of 20 (G-20). How far this larger and newer group may replace the G-8 in managing international political economy (and in consequence in international politics) depends on the perception of legitimacy and efficiency of both groups. In terms of efficiency, the G-8 has proven itself, especially in the field of counterterrorism. The proof of legitimacy depends on the success of the extension of the G-8 in the context of the Heiligendamm Process. Germany has verbally supported the G-20, but it can articulate its positions and interests much better within the G-8 framework.

Conclusion: The Limits of Multilateralism

Multilateralism is a key factor for Germany's approach to counterterrorism. It has opened a lot of opportunities for international cooperation on the structural and operational levels. Nevertheless, the effectiveness of German counterterrorism efforts is therefore restricted by the limitations of the current shape of multilateral cooperation. First, multilateralism has not yet created a consistent system of coherent multilevel global governance. Different approaches of governance within the multilateral context have led to inconsistencies between the global, the regional, and the minilateral formats of cooperation. As long as these shortfalls among the different layers of the multilevel system exist, Germany's multilateral approach of countering terrorism will find itself in a multilateralism trap. How far this consistency can be realized in the future will determine the success of "effective multilateralism" and "networked security." The paradox of multilateralism thus is one of the main obstacles in a successful countering terrorism strategy for Germany. Multilateralism on the one hand and the freedom-security dilemma on the other are influencing and constraining each other. The great challenge for future German counterterrorism strategy, concept, and policy will be in finding ways to minimize the negative implications of the paradox of multilateralism. This is necessary or even more a condition *sine qua non* for finding a satisfying balance in the freedom-security dilemma. This seems to be the postmodern Gordian knot for Germany's security policy.

Ralf Roloff Dr. Roloff began teaching at the Marshall Center in 2003 and is now its senior German professor. Dr. Roloff's academic experience is in international relations, international security, and international political economy; European integration; and German foreign and security policy. He was acting professor of international and European politics, University of the German Armed Forces, Hamburg, from 2000 to 2003, and in the prior year taught international politics at Johannes Gutenberg University, Mainz. He was assistant professor and executive officer at the Research Institute for Political Science and European Affairs at the University of Cologne from 1994 to 1999 and lecturer and assistant to the Director of the department of political science, University of Trier, from 1991 to 1993. Ralf Roloff completed his Habilitation in 1999 in Cologne and his Dr. Phil. in political science at the University of Trier in 1994. He earned his Master of Arts degree in political science and German literature and linguistics from the University of Trier. He has also been a Robert-Schuman-Fellow in the European Parliament (1992) and a Fulbright Fellow at New York University (1995).

Recommended Readings

Der Spiegel news magazine.

Dobson, Christopher, and Ronald Payne. "Terror in Europe," part 3 of *The Never-Ending War: Terrorism in the 80s*, 115–196. New York: Facts on File, 1989.

Fernandez-Sanchez, Pablo Antonio. *International Legal Dimension of Terrorism*. Leiden: Martinus Nijhoff, 2009.

Hauser, Dorothea. *Baader und Herold: Beschreibung eines Kampfes*. Hamburg: Rowohlt Taschenbuch Verlag, 2007.

Klose, Gerhard J. "The Weight of History: Germany's Military and Domestic Security," Ch. 3 in *Armies in Homeland Security: American and European Perspectives*, edited by John L. Clarke. Washington, DC: National Defense University Press, 2006.

Merkl, Peter H. "West German Left-Wing Terrorism," Ch. 5 in *Terrorism in Context*, edited by Martha Crenshaw. University Park, PA: The Penn State University Press, 1995.

Schneckener, Ulrich. "Germany," Ch. 3 in *Counterterrorism Strategies: Successes and Failures of Six Nations*, edited by Yonah Alexander. Washington, DC: Potomac Books, 2006.

Wilkinson, Paul. *Terrorism versus Democracy: The Liberal State Response*, 2nd ed. London: Routledge, 2006.

Notes

1. Stefan Aust, *Der Baader-Meinhof–Komplex* (Hamburg: Hoffmann und Campe, 3rd ed., 2008); Tim Geiger, "The 'Landshut' in Mogadishu: The International Crisis Management of the German Federal Government Against the Terrorist Challenge in 1977," *Vierteljahreshefte für Zeitgeschichte*, Vol. 57, No. 3 (March 2009).
2. Johannes Hürter, "Counterterrorism Policy: A Comparison of Germany and Italy, 1969–1982," *Vierteljahreshefte für Zeitgeschichte*, Vol. 57, No. 3 (March 2009).
3. See Jeremy Waldron, "Security and Liberty: The Image of Balance," *The Journal of Political Philosophy*, Vol. 11, No. 2 (2003), 191–210.
4. Federal Ministry of Defense, German Whitepaper, Ch. 1.4. Networked Security Berlin 2006, pp. 29–30.
5. On the concept, see Barry Buzan, Ole Waever, and Jaap de Wilde, *Security: A New Framework for Analysis* (Boulder, CO: Lynne Rienner Publishers, 1998).
6. Hanns W. Maull, "Zivilmacht Bundesrepublik? Vierzehn Thesen für eine neue deutsche Außenpolitik," in *Europaarchiv* 10/1992, pp. 269–278; Dieter Senghass, "Verflechtung und Integration," in Karl Kaiser and Hanns W. Maull, eds., *Die Zukunft der deutschen Außenpolitik* (Bonn, Oldenbourg, 1993), 35–52. On the development of Germany's Foreign Policy since unification, see: Siegmar Schmidt, Gunther Hellmann, and Reinhard Wolf, eds., *Handbuch zur deutschen Außenpolitik* (Wiesbaden: Verlag für Sozialwissenschaften, 2007).
7. See Ulrich Schneckener, "Germany," in Yonah Alexander, ed., *Counterterrorism Strategies: Successes and Failures of Six Nations* (Dulles, VA: Potomac Books, 2006), 72–98.
8. The most evident case is the Iraq crisis of 2002–2003. The different positions within the alliance but as well within many countries led to a paralysis of European Foreign Policy and brought NATO very close to a "near death experience" (Nicolas Burns); see on this: Ralf Roloff, "Grundlagen und Grenzen der GASP: Der Fall Irak," in Peter-Christian Müller-Graff, ed., *Die Rolle der erweiterten Europäischen Union in der Welt, Schriftenreihe des Arbeitskreises Europäische Integration*, Vol. 57 (Baden-Baden: Nomos, 2006), 225–240.
9. Schneckener, "Germany," n. 7.

10. Schneckener, "Germany," n. 7, pp. 82–83.
11. "Van Essen: FDP warnt vor Einführung der alten Kronzeugenregelung," *Portal Liberal*, 26 October 2005, available at http://old.liberale.de//webcom/show_article.php/_c-567/_nr-239/i.html, accessed 29 September 2009.
12. One brief description of this is in Richard Clutterbuck, *Guerrillas and Terrorists*, of which the first edition was Ohio University Press, 1980.
13. Schneckener, "Germany," n. 7, p. 80.
14. Alexander Dorn, *Das Trennungsgebot in verfassungshistorischer Perspektive,* (Berlin: Duncker & Humblot, 2004).
15. Schneckener, "Germany," n.7, 80ff.
16. See *Bundesamt für Verfassungsschutz*, available at http://www.verfassungsschutz.de/, accessed 29 September 2009.
17. See *Bundesnachrichtendienst*, available at www.bundesnachrichtendienst.de, accessed 29 September 2009.
18. See *Bundeskriminalamt*, available at http://www.bka.de/, accessed 29 September 2009.
19. See *Bundespolizei*, available at http://www.bundespolizei.de, accessed 29 September 2009.
20. See *Zollkriminalamt*, available at http://www.zoll.de/d0_zoll_im_einsatz/h0_zollfahndung/a0_zka/index.html, accessed 29 September 2009.
21. Bundesministerium des Innern, "Nach dem 11. September 2001, Maßnahmen gegen den Terror," Berlin 2004.
22. Bundesministerium des Innern, "Nach dem 11. September 2001 Maßnahmen gegen den Terror," Berlin 2004.
23. Bundesministerium des Innern, "Nach dem 11. September 2001, Maßnahmen gegen den Terror," Berlin 2004.
24. See the decision of the Constitutional Court, available at http://www.bverfg.de/entscheidungen/rs20060215_1bvr035705.html, accessed 19 October 2009.
25. See the decision of the Constitutional Court, available at http://www.bverfg.de/entscheidungen/rs20080311_1bvr025608.html, accessed 19 October 2009.
26. Ulrich Schneckener, ed., *Chancen und Grenzen Multilateraler Terrorismusbekämpfung*, Stiftung Wissenschaft und Politik, Studie S14, Berlin, 2007.
27. Christian Schaller, "Völkerrechtliche Rahmenbedingungen und die Rolle der Vereinten Nationen bei der Terrorismusbekämpfung," in Schneckener, ed., *Chancen und Grenzen*, 13–30.
28. For the text of the UN Resolution and Plan of Action, see "United Nations General Assembly Adopts Global Counter-Terrorism Strategy," United Nations website, available at http://www.un.org/terrorism/strategy-counter-terrorism.shtml, accessed 30 September 2009. For analysis and description of the five "Ds," see Javier Ruperez, "The UN's fight against terrorism: Five years after 9/11," ARI 83/2006, Real Instituto Elcano (Spain), 6 September 2006, available at http://www.un.org/terrorism/ruperez-article.html, accessed 30 September 2009.
29. Quoted in: Annegret Bendiek, "Europäische Union: Netzwerke bilden, um Netzwerke zu bekämpfen," in Schneckener, ed., *Chancen und Grenzen*, 31.
30. Council of the European Union, "The European Union Counter-Terrorism Strategy," Brussels, 30 November 2005, available at http://register.consilium.europa.eu/pdf/en/05/st14/st14469-re04.en05.pdf, accessed 30 September 2009.
31. See on this: Bendiek, n. 14 and pp. 31–42.
32. The Solidarity Clause reads: "The European Council welcomes the political commitment of the Member States and of the acceding States, taken as of now, to act jointly against terrorist acts, in the spirit of the solidarity clause contained in Article 42 of the draft Constitution for Europe." See Bulletin EU 3-2004, "European Council Statement on Combating Terrorism," Bulletin of the European Union, available at http://europa.eu/bulletin/en/200403/i1029.htm, accessed 30 September 2009.
33. Markus Kaim, "NATO: Möglichkeiten und Grenzen militärischer Terrorismusbekämpfung," in Schneckener, ed., *Chancen und Grenzen*, 43–52.
34. See "NATO's Military Concept for Defence Against Terrorism," NATO website, October 2003, available at http://www.nato.int/ims/docu/terrorism.htm, accessed 30 September 2009.

35. Kaim, n. 16 and p. 47.
36. See Ulrich Schneckener, "G 8: Terrorismusbekämpfung in Form von 'Club Governance'," in Schneckener, ed., *Chancen und Grenzen*, 53–64; and John J. Kirton, "From Collective Security to Concert: The UN, G 8 and Global Security Governance," paper prepared for the conference on "Security Overspill: Between Economic Integration and Social Exclusion," Centre Etudes Internationales et Mondialisation, Universite de Quebec-Montreal, Montreal, 27–28 October 2005, available at http://hdl.handle.net/1807/4904, accessed 29 September 2009.
37. Ulrich Schneckener, "G-8: Terrorismusbekämpfung in Form von Club Governance," in Ulrich Schneckener, ed., Multilaterale Terrorismusbekämpfung (Berlin: Stiftung Wissenschadft un Politik, 2007), 55.

Peter Lauwe

The Protection of Critical Infrastructure Within Germany

Critical infrastructures can be seen as lifelines in our world. These lifelines enable the supply of our society with vitally important services and products and lay the foundation for economic prosperity. Thus, we all depend on the functional capabilities of critical infrastructures. However, in the recent past, terrorist or criminal attacks and natural catastrophes have inflicted casualties and caused unprecedented physical and economic damage. In particular, energy and transportation infrastructures were significantly affected by these events. Interdependencies can cause local breakdowns to cascade through different sectors and regions, sometimes having international implications. In November 2006, for instance, the shutdown of a single power supply line in the northwest of Germany led to a short-term power blackout in large parts of Europe.[1]

In the past, a sector-specific focus on critical infrastructure protection was common. This does not seem to be the right answer in a modern world. There is need for a strategic and methodical reorientation. Stakeholders from the various ministries, industry, and science must be brought together to concentrate their expertise and provide the best protection possible for critical infrastructures. Critical infrastructure protection can be seen as a mix of threat and hazard prevention activities, reduction of critical infrastructure vulnerabilities, preparation for crisis situations, and then actual reaction during crisis situations. This chapter outlines a national, cross-cutting approach to critical infrastructure protection and focuses on vulnerability reduction and, hence, the adaptation of critical infrastructure to a changing risk situation in the twenty-first century. For actual implementation of such an approach, this chapter takes examples from contemporary Germany.

Framework for Operating Critical Infrastructures

The framework for operating critical infrastructures has been changing dramatically. Security experts worldwide try to analyze and understand the changes to be able to use these results for adapting strategies and concepts. The following paragraphs summarize briefly the most important changes over the past years.[2]

Hazards and Threats in the Twenty-first Century

In recent history, natural hazards, health hazards, technical and human failure, and terrorist or criminal attacks caused significant damage to critical infrastructure. In 2007, a winter storm affected the electricity and transportation infrastructure all over Germany. It is assumed that with the climate changing the intensity and the frequency of severe weather hazards will increase. In some regions the impact on critical infrastructure will intensify.[3]

In 2009, the H1N1 influenza virus began transferring from human to human, causing thousands of infections and spreading worldwide. Next to affecting human beings directly, severe pandemics may have an indirect impact on our society by disabling critical infrastructures. Personnel will be unable to report to work either because they are infected themselves, they have to care for infected relatives, or they are frightened to leave the house. In the case of a severe pandemic, the absentee rate might rise to 50, 60, or 70 percent, potentially leading to a shutdown of critical functions within infrastructure systems.

A major challenge in the twenty-first century will be protecting critical infrastructure in the face of international terrorism and organized crime. The attacks on the subway in Tokyo in 1995, the regional trains in Madrid in 2004, and the subway in London in 2005 show the threat. In 2006, terrorists tried to explode suitcase bombs in two regional trains in Germany. In 2007, the so-called Sauerland-Gruppe (Sauerland Group) sought to attack several sites in Germany, including the international airport in Frankfurt, but were prevented.[4]

The Crisis and Risk Network (CRN) and the Center for Security Studies (CSS) at the Swiss Federal Institute of Technology in Zurich published their first *Focal Report on Critical Infrastructure Protection* in October 2008. They pointed to an increasing amount of terrorist attacks on energy infrastructure worldwide during the years 2000 to 2007.[5] One example of such an incident is the attack on the Abqaiq oil facility in Saudi Arabia in 2006. The oil facility is one of the largest processing plants worldwide. The attack was repelled by Saudi security forces, but the news caused oil prices to jump more than $2 a barrel.[6]

Economic Framework

The economic pressure on critical infrastructure operators increases through privatization and the liberalization of the markets. Investing in security measures becomes more difficult because a direct return on investment can often not be determined. Operators focus on the regulation requirements. Although regulators include security in their policies, the focus is consumer price. Incentives to build reserve capacity do not exist in a sufficient amount.[7] There are operators that decide against additional security measures like building redundant facilities. Some operators even dismantle existing redundant facilities.

Structural Framework

Today, infrastructure systems are larger, more interconnected, more interdependent, and more vulnerable than in the past. Most modern telephone systems, for example, depend on an external power supply and stop functioning shortly after a power blackout. Voice over Internet Protocol (VOIP) telephone systems depend additionally on the internet.

In case of disruption or destruction of infrastructure elements, interdependencies can cause cascading effects. That means local damage can lead to a loss of function in regions and sectors that have not been affected by the original impact of an attack or a natural catastrophe. It is impossible to identify all interdependent functions within critical infrastructures. It is also impossible to accurately quantify interdependencies and the potential damage of an extreme impact through an *ex-ante* analysis. This knowledge gap makes the identification of critical and vulnerable elements within critical infrastructures more difficult. However, identifying these elements is an important step in developing effective and efficient security measures.

International Aspects

In a globalized world, various critical infrastructures operate internationally. The operations are enabled by technical and logical networks like power supply lines, ship routes, or the internet. These networks span large parts of the world and are interconnected to a certain extent. Disabling elements of networks like these would almost certainly affect several countries.

International trading partners as well as transnational organizations like the European Union (EU), North Atlantic Treaty Organization (NATO), or Group of Eight (G-8) have realized the importance of international critical infrastructures and reacted by launching programs to protect them.

In the framework of the European Program for Critical Infrastructure Protection, the EU decreed, in December of 2008, Council Directive 2008/114/EC "on the identification and designation of European critical infrastructures and the assessment of the need to improve their protection."[8] According to the directive, EU member states will identify elements within their energy and transport infrastructures that are critical to at least one other EU member state and the disruption of which would cause damage that exceeds certain thresholds. The thresholds have been agreed upon via a discussion process in the past years. The operators of European critical infrastructure elements will carry out risk analyses for these elements and designate a Security Liaison Officer who functions as a point of contact to the relevant member state authority. The objective of the directive is to implement a high security level for cross-border infrastructures in Europe and reduce cross-border effects resulting from interdependencies between interconnected infrastructures.

Lord Jopling, rapporteur to the NATO Parliamentary Assembly, describes NATO's involvement in critical infrastructure protection in 2007:

> Studies and activities from NATO on critical infrastructure protection were initiated by the specialized planning boards and committees working under the Senior Civil Emergency Planning Committee (SCEPC). In 2003 SCEPC adopted a Concept Paper on critical infrastructure protection as well as a road map for the following areas of work: promoting information sharing among states; assisting in the development of training and education programs; contributing to the identification of critical infrastructure; identifying research and development projects to support critical infrastructure protection; and streamlining critical infrastructure protection in field exercises.[9]

G-8 working groups have addressed energy infrastructure and chemical plants by putting together best practice examples for their protection.

Guidelines

Modern societies depend more and more on critical infrastructures, sometimes without realizing the actual degree of dependency. The threats and hazards that can disrupt critical infrastructures have changed in the last decades. Some sources point out that specific sectors—for instance, the energy sector—are targeted more frequently by international terrorists in the past few years. This trend might continue in the future. At the same time, climate change will produce weather extremes that will have a more disruptive impact on critical infrastructures in the future.

Incentives to install redundant facilities are either nonexistent or insufficient. In some cases, redundant facilities are being dismantled. Infrastructure systems are becoming increasingly complex, with infrastructure networks and cross-sector interdependencies rapidly growing. In case of local or regional disruption, interdependencies can trigger large-scale cascading effects, thus causing widespread damage.

The international dimension of critical infrastructure protection is steadily getting more important. Energy, information, communication, and transport infrastructures provide transnational functions. In Europe today, power supply relies on a transnational power grid. Therefore, the disruption or destruction of elements within this power grid may cause blackouts in all parts of Europe.

The general framework for operating critical infrastructures in the twenty-first century asks for adaptation and additional protection measures. Evolving risks need to be identified at an early stage and minimized. Critical infrastructure operators need to be able to react flexibly during crises. Additional protection measures have to bring an added value to the infrastructures. The responsibility to adequately protect critical infrastructures rests with the operators. However, the approach to protecting critical infrastructure needs to be broad, cross-sectoral, and interdisciplinary, and should have a transnational dimension.

Strategic and Methodical Foundation

In the past, critical infrastructure protection was very much limited to the individual sectors. Even today, different sectoral regulations and protection measures often coexist without referring to each other. The need to bring the different sectoral approaches together, to create a strategic frame for critical infrastructure protection and to coordinate all stakeholders of the different sectors, was not met for a long time. Laurent F. Carrel writes in his book *Leadership in Krisen (Leadership in Crisis Situations)*: "Sector-specific thinking and communication problems between the different stakeholders are gaining ground. No one knows about the big picture, however from a sector point of view everyone is doing the right thing."[10] A national strategy that addresses a framework for operating critical infrastructures in the twenty-first century can provide the foundation for a holistic, cross-sectoral, and modern approach to protecting critical infrastructures. The following paragraphs outline some of the key elements that build up such a strategy.

Strategic Principles

A strategy to protect critical infrastructure is based on three principles that aim at bringing together all different stakeholders and canalizing their different interests. Protecting critical infrastructure includes stakeholders from the government, industry, and science. In some countries, the majority of critical infrastructures are operated by private industry. The industry operators know their systems best and can bring a substantial amount of expertise into discussions about how to protect the infrastructures. Scientific institutes can support cooperation by providing in-depth analysis of complex matters such as interdependencies, thereby enhancing the understanding of the infrastructure. Such a cooperation can be institutionalized by implementing discussion groups on different levels (local, regional, national), by implementing working groups, or by starting joint projects. The cooperation also needs a coordinator who can bring together the various existing initiatives and regulations to protect critical infrastructures and place them under the roof of a comprehensive strategy to protect a country.

In times of limited financial and human resources, protection measures should focus on highly critical elements that face high risks, particularly single points of failure—the disruption of which could lead to broad loss of service, and the protection of which can raise security levels significantly.

Methodical Foundation

Protecting critical infrastructure seems to be best incorporated into a risk management process. A variety of publications provides methodical principles on risk management in general and risk identification in particular. All of these publications define risk as a function of the probability of a specific event and the potential consequences of this event. In 2007, a working group in Germany, including representatives from various companies and public offices, compiled a risk management process for critical infrastructure operators based on the analysis of several national and international publications on risk management, some of which are listed in the reference list at the end of this chapter. In terms of consequences, a key element of the German risk management approach is a focus on the vulnerability of critical infrastructure elements. Assessing and evaluating the vulnerability of critical infrastructure elements automatically leads to potential security gaps and, hence, to potential options for protecting critical infrastructure elements. This notion of the German approach is based on the idea of reducing the amount and consequences of loss of critical services.

The results of this analysis were published by the Federal Ministry of the Interior in 2008 as guidelines on risk and crisis management for critical infrastructure operators.[11] The risk management process outlined in the guideline starts with formulating protection goals that describe a level of security that needs to be achieved. The next step addresses the identification of critical elements within the various infrastructure systems and the risk assessment for these elements. Based on the risk assessment, additional security measures are being formulated and implemented. The aim of security measures is preventing threats and hazards, mitigating vulnerability, and improving crisis management until the initially formulated protection goals are achieved. An extensive documentation of the risk management process is essential and a starting point for evaluating the process on a regular basis.

Infrastructure elements at risk can be personnel, facilities, apparatus, data, documents, and materials. The actual risk for the infrastructure is determined by the criticality of the elements at risk, the intensity of the threats and hazards that have the potential to disrupt or destroy infrastructure elements, and the vulnerability of the elements at risk. These three risk factors are being determined by *ex-ante* analysis, thus prior to potential attacks or natural catastrophes. Infrastructure operators carry out the risk management process on a local level. The government can support this process by providing information on hazards and threats. Additionally, the government leads the activities to assess the risks to infrastructure systems due to interdependencies between the different sectors and different countries.

Risk Factor 1—Criticality

Criticality of infrastructure elements can be understood as the element's relevance in respect to the consequences the disruption or destruction would have for the overall service an infrastructure provides.[12] Infrastructure customers or employees are critical at all times. Next to human criticality, there is the notion of functionality of services. The disruption or destruction of critical elements might lead to loss of essential services like energy and water supply or health care services and thus can cause further casualties and damage. The more critical an element, the higher is the risk for the infrastructure.

Risk Factor 2—Threats and Hazards

Threats and hazards create a more or less intensive impact on infrastructure elements with the potential to disrupt or destroy them. The more sophisticated a terrorist group or the more severe a storm, the higher the risk for potential targets. In 2007, terrorists known as the Sauerland Group in Germany were able to obtain large amounts of basic material to produce explosives. If not stopped, the effects of the planned attacks may have been more severe than the ones in London and in Madrid.[13]

In addition to threat and hazard prevention, the challenge of *ex-ante* analyses of threats and hazards in the context of risk mitigation and crisis preparation is formulating reasonable scenarios. The following questions need to be answered: What is a reasonable impact on a site? What is the probability for this event to happen? Police and intelligence actors can help answer these questions with respect to terrorist attacks. Weather services, scientific institutes, and environmental agencies can help formulate natural hazard scenarios.

Risk Factor 3—Vulnerability

Vulnerability can be defined as susceptibility of infrastructure elements to threats and hazards.[14] Infrastructure sites with reduced exposure to the public and with robust or redundant facilities are less vulnerable than others. At first glance, this proposition seems to be trivial. However, comprehensive vulnerability assessments for infrastructure sites are complex and expensive. Therefore, many existing weak spots are not identified in the course of *ex-ante* vulnerability assessments. Often weak spots are detected only when the damage is done. Key elements of a vulnerability assessment are analyzing interdependencies, identifying single points of failure, and estimating the robustness of facilities and equipment. In addition, there is the need for assessing the degree of redundancy and the capacity of backup systems like emergency power supply or mobile water treatment equipment.

Examples of National Strategies and Plans

In 2006, the United States of America bundled different strategies for protecting critical infrastructure by publishing the National Infrastructure Protection Plan. This outlines objectives, responsibilities, methodical fundamentals, and the resources for protecting critical infrastructure.[15] The plan is supplemented by sector plans that add sector-specific aspects to the overall program.[16] On 17 June 2009, the German Cabinet approved the National Strategy for Critical Infrastructure Protection.[17] Further examples for critical infrastructure protection strategies or plans can be found in several countries, including the United Kingdom, the Netherlands, France, Canada, and Switzerland.

Guidelines

A modern strategy for protecting critical infrastructure provides a policy for a public-private cooperation, including stakeholders from the government, the industry, and science. Within the strategy, a moderating and coordinating point of contact is required. The point of contact helps to place different sectoral initiatives in a common framework, assess gaps, and identify the need for action.

A strategy outlines key terms and definitions to provide common ground for all stakeholders. Protection measures deliver the best leverage when implemented with the most critical infrastructure elements undergoing the highest risks. Therefore, a strategy provides methodical fundamentals and details on implementing a comprehensive risk and crisis management for critical infrastructure.

Strategy Implementation Aspects in Germany

As a result of changing risks for operating critical infrastructure, different stakeholders from the German government and industry joined ranks to face new challenges in protecting critical infrastructure. This section shows some examples of the implementation of key strategic aspects in four fields of action: threat and hazard prevention, vulnerability mitigation, crisis preparation, and reaction. Again, the focus of this chapter is vulnerability mitigation and crisis planning through adaptation of infrastructure systems and their management. Therefore, most examples will concentrate on these two topics. The topics of threat and hazard prevention and reacting during crises will be outlined briefly.

Threat and Hazard Prevention

Threat and hazard prevention reduces the potential for critical infrastructure disruption or destruction at the earliest stage possible. It is certainly one of the most important responsibilities a government takes for its citizens. Threat and hazard prevention is based, for instance, on foreign policy, defense mechanisms, internal security, environmental protection, and health care. Aspects like diplomacy, military intervention, and internal security measures can reduce threats originating from terrorism. Environmental protection can cut down on severe weather hazards. Health monitoring and protection standards like those we see being implemented with influenza pandemics can curtail health hazards. As for terrorism prevention, Federal Criminal Police in Germany have been given additional authority by the implementation of new legislation. There are now additional instruments at hand for federal police to fight terrorism.[18]

Vulnerability Mitigation

Despite all best efforts, threat and hazard prevention cannot be expected to be 100 percent successful. Therefore, in addition to threat and hazard prevention, there is the need for adapting critical infrastructure to withstand potential impact. The aim is to reduce the effect of threats and hazards. This means primarily making critical infrastructure elements more robust and more tolerant to disruption. Effective control of access to facilities, enclosure of sensitive spots, and installing redundancy and backup capacity can reduce vulnerability. German critical infrastructure operators are responsible for implementing security measures of this kind supported by the Federal Ministry of the Interior.

In 2005, several companies and public offices participated within the framework of a public-private cooperation to draw up a baseline protection concept. Based on several checklists, the concept formulates a baseline protection standard that can be used by critical infrastructure operators of all sectors to compare against the security measures within their facilities. The baseline protection concept can be obtained free of charge in German, English, Russian, and French.[19]

In 2008, the German government published a risk and crisis management guide.[20] This was developed with the support of several companies, public offices, and a science institute. It outlines a structured approach to implementing or extending risk and crisis management procedures within a company or a public office. This guide illuminates the complete process chain, starting with implementing a risk and crisis management working group, identifying and evaluating risks, and deciding on effective and efficient security measures. It can be obtained free of charge in German, English, and French.

Both publications are meant to be used in all critical infrastructure sectors. The aim is to establish a nationwide minimal standard for the protection of critical infrastructures, thus creating a solid and broad effect in raising security.

In 2005, the *National Plan for Information Infrastructure Protection* was published as a strategy for protecting information infrastructure.[21] Since 2007, the implementation of the plan is carried out by four public-private working groups (WGs) coordinated by the Federal Office for Information Security: WG 1 Emergency and crisis exercises, WG 2 Crisis response and management, WG 3 Maintaining critical infrastructure services, and WG 4 National and international cooperation.[22,23,24] WG 3 puts an emphasis on vulnerability reduction by protecting critical information technology processes within critical infrastructures. Further sector-specific working groups have already been implemented—for instance, in the power supply sector—and others are planned for coming years.

Crisis Planning

Despite threat and hazard prevention and the implementation of vulnerability mitigating measures, crisis situations can arise. Public and private stakeholders should prepare for managing crises by informing about their activities, implementing joint crisis management instruments, and training together.

The German Federal Office of Civil Protection and Disaster Assistance has developed a web-based information management system called deNIS II plus. Stakeholders from the federal and state (Länder) level as well as critical infrastructure operators can be connected to it with the right to read from the system and insert local information. A joint federal-state situation center also feeds the system with regional and national information. The system provides a joint operational picture in crisis situation including the information on resources. Logging in is password-controlled.

In the framework of the 2005 information infrastructure plan, so-called single points of contact (SPOCs) on government and operator sites have been installed, which allow for immediate information exchange between government representatives and critical infrastructure operators in the case of cyber attacks.

Since 2004, government representatives on all levels (federal, state, and local) as well as critical infrastructure operators practice crisis management and collaboration every two years in a national tabletop exercise called LÜKEX. Each exercise is based on a different scenario to address different aspects within the crisis management. So far, scenarios have ranged from a severe winter storm, to multiple terrorist attacks, to an influenza pandemic. The next exercise, including several hundred participants, will take place in 2010. The exercise is planned, organized, and controlled by the Federal Office for Civil Protection and Disaster Assistance.

Reaction

Reacting in an effective way during a crisis situation depends primarily on the quality of the crisis planning, the resources at hand, and the leadership expertise of decision makers. Selected preparation aspects have been outlined in the previous paragraphs. Requirements to the actual operation in a crisis and the necessary capabilities of decision makers are outlined in detail in Carrel's publication *Leadership in Krisen*.[25]

An example of the need for substantial resources can be drawn from an event in Germany in 2005. An ice storm in the northwest of the country led to the collapse of several poles carrying power lines. The destruction of parts of the grid infrastructure caused a regional power blackout that lasted up to seven days in some areas. To implement a temporary emergency power supply for the region, several hundred emergency backup generators were needed. The situation was handled by deploying equipment from the regional power utility, various fire departments, as well as federal capacity from the federal technical relief agency (*Technisches Hilfswerk*) and the armed forces (*Bundeswehr*).

Limitations to a Public-Private Cooperation

There are certainly limits to a public-private cooperation, and open questions remain. A substantial amount of information that is exchanged in cooperation is supposed to be classified and protected. There is a need for an effective information transfer procedure. Despite arrangements for exchanging and handling classified information, critical infrastructure operators are reluctant to exchange certain critical information. Therefore, in terms of information there will be blank spots on both the government and industry sides.

Measures to mitigate vulnerability can only be effectively implemented by critical infrastructure operators themselves. Only operators have the sufficient expertise and know-how about their systems available to implement security measures effectively. For this reason, government representatives depend on the willingness of the industry to cooperate. It can be expected that some operators will not cooperate sufficiently. However, enforcing cooperation with a legal framework can solve the potential problem of unwillingness only to some extent.

Some questions that come up in public-private cooperation need special attention. What is the level of security government and industry stakeholders can agree upon? Immediately connected to the aspect of security level is the challenge of finding a way of how to pass on costs of security measures. Who is responsible for the financial investments and to what extent? Answering this question is for most critical infrastructure operators a prerequisite for serious cooperation. This applies particularly to critical infrastructure operators from the industry. At the end of the day, the general public has to cover additional security measures either by paying higher fees for critical infrastructure services or by paying higher taxes. Also, citizens have to cope with any residual risk that is not being addressed by either the government or the critical infrastructure operators. Therefore, including the public in the discussion on security levels seems imperative.

Conclusion

Critical infrastructure protection in the face of terrorism and natural or health hazards can be seen as a joint task of public and private stakeholders working in threat and hazard prevention, vulnerability mitigation, crisis planning, and handling crisis situations. In terms of such threats and hazards, the German focus in the past has been on threat and hazard prevention and the actual handling of crisis situations by state representatives. Vulnerability mitigation and preparing critical infrastructure management for dealing with the impact of extreme threats and hazards have been neglected more or less until the late nineties of the twentieth century. Since 2009, a new strategy on critical infrastructure protection in Germany helps bring together various public and private stakeholders in order to implement new protection measures and, hence, make critical infrastructures more robust and more flexible than in the past.

The framework for operating critical infrastructures has changed drastically in the last decades. This applies specifically to a changing threat and hazard situation, the increase in complexity of critical infrastructure systems, and the changes in the economic framework. Macroeconomic changes that have been introduced by globalization and liberalization of the markets force companies to further reduce costs. Talking to representatives of companies shows that investing in security measures seems more difficult. These changes need to be realized, analyzed, and taken into account when developing an approach to protecting critical infrastructures.

A strategy provides the core principles for protecting critical infrastructures. Three core principles seem to be absolutely essential. First, for protecting critical infrastructures, we must include all relevant stakeholders from government, industry, and science. Second, it is important to identify a coordinator on the national level who can bring together all initiatives and place them into a common framework. Third, the resources to protect critical infrastructures are limited in general. Therefore, additional security measures should be placed where most effective. This means concentrating on critical elements facing high risks for disruption or destruction.

The basic idea of identifying and mitigating risks for critical infrastructure elements is to simulate what might happen in the future and to implement protective measures long before the actual impact of real threats and hazards. Therefore, critical infrastructure elements need to be identified, threat and hazard impact scenarios developed, and weaknesses (vulnerability) assessed. There are several instruments available that help implement a risk management process for critical infrastructure protection. One such instrument, addressing critical infrastructure operators, is a risk and crisis management guideline published by the German Federal Ministry of the Interior.[26] However, it is important that science continue to improve these instruments and to make them more feasible.

Implementing strategic and methodological principles by public and private stakeholders will result in exchanging critical information, developing protection concepts and guidelines together, or participating in joint tabletop exercises. Although it is essential to include all relevant public and private stakeholders in such activities, cooperation on critical infrastructure protection including various stakeholders will have to face diverging interests and, hence, limitations. Some limitations might only be lifted over the long run, or not at all. Therefore, it is important for all stakeholders to accept a certain degree of uncertainty.

Peter Lauwe Mr. Lauwe is a graduate from Darmstadt Technical University in Germany. After graduation, he worked as a civil engineer in Germany. From 2004 until 2007, he served as desk officer at the Federal Office of Civil Protection and Disaster Assistance (BBK) in Germany, concentrating on critical infrastructure protection. Since February 2008, he has headed the BKK's section that manages the "National Hazard Register: Critical Infrastructure Protection Concepts." Key elements of the section's tasks are scenario development, vulnerability analyses, and protection concept development in cooperation with critical infrastructure operators and associations. Peter Lauwe represents his federal office on national committees, as well as at NATO and the EU.

Recommended Readings

Bouchon, Sara. *The Vulnerability of Interdependent Critical Infrastructure Systems: Epistemological and Conceptual State-of-the-Art*. EUR 22205 EN Office for Official Publications of the European Communities, 2006.

Federal Office for Information Security, Federal Republic of Germany. *Analysis of Critical Infrastructures: The ACIS Methodology*. April 2008. Available at https://www.bsi.bund.de/cae/servlet/contentblob/476040/publicationFile/28242/acis_paper_en_pdf.pdf, accessed 18 July 2009.

Howard, Russell D, James J. F. Forest, and Joanne C. Moore. *Homeland Security and Terrorism: Readings and Interpretations*. New York: McGraw-Hill, 2006.

Klose, Gerhard J. "The Weight of History: Germany's Military and Domestic Security," Ch. 3 in *Armies in Homeland Security: American and European Perspectives*, edited by John L. Clarke, Washington, DC: National Defense University Press, 2006, 37–62.

Rinaldi Steven M., et al. "Identifying, Understanding, and Analyzing Critical Infrastructure Interdependencies," *IEEE Control Systems Magazine*, December 2001, 11–25.

Robert, Benoît. "A Method for the Study of Cascading Effects within Lifeline Networks." *International Journal of Critical Infrastructures*, Vol. 1, No. 1 (2004), 86–99.

Notes

1. Maria Sheahan and Francois de Beaupuy, "Power Failure in Germany Triggers Blackouts in Europe (Update 1)," Bloomberg.com, 5 November 2006, available at http://www.bloomberg.com/apps/news?pid=20601085&sid=a4J9_1zeDuEo&refer=europe, accessed 1 October 2009.

2. Peter Lauwe and Christoph Riegel, "Schutz Kritischer Infrastrukturen—Konzepte zur Versorgungssicherheit," Informationen zur Raumentwicklung, *Infrastruktur und Daseinsvorsorge in der Fläche* Issue 1 (February 2008): 113–125.

3. Intergovernmental Panel on Climate Change, Climate Change 2007: Synthesis Report, IPCC Plenary XXVII, 2007, available at http://www.ipcc.ch/pdf/assessment-report/ar4/syr/ar4_syr.pdf, accessed 18 July 2009.

4. Uta Rasche, "Anklage gegen 'Sauerland-Gruppe' erhoben," FAZ.NET, 2 September 2008, available at http://www.faz.net/s/RubF359F74E867B46C1A180E8E1E1197DEE/Doc~E51 1A4C749F34406FA368113692AB478E~ATpl~Ecommon~Scontent.html, accessed 18 July 2009.

5. Crisis and Risk Network, Focal Report 1: Critical Infrastructure Protection, Center for Security Studies, ETH Zurich, 21 October 2008, available at http://www.crn.ethz.ch/publications/crn_team/detail.cfm?id=94902, accessed 18 July 2009.

6. Khalid R. Al-Rodhan, The Impact of the Abqaiq Attack on Saudi Energy Security, Center for Strategic and International Studies, 2006, available at http://csis.org/files/media/csis/pubs/060227_abqaiqattack.pdf, accessed 18 July 2009.

7. The State of the Nation: Defending Critical Infrastructure Institution of Civil Engineers, 2009, 11, available at http://www.ice.org.uk/downloads//ICE%20State%20of%20the%20Nation%20-%20Defending%20Critical%20Infrastructure.pdf, accessed 18 July 2009.

8. European Union, "Council Directive 2008/114/EC of 8 December 2008 on the Identification and Designation of European Critical Infrastructures and the Assessment of the Need to Improve Their Protection," 2008, available at http://eur-lex.europa.eu/LexUriServ/LexUriServ.do?uri=OJ:L:2008:345:0075:0082:EN:PDF, accessed 18 July 2009.

9. NATO Parliamentary Assembly, "162 CDS 07 E rev 1—The Protection of Critical Infrastructures," 2007, available at http://www.nato-pa.int/Default.asp?CAT2=1159&CAT1=16&CAT0=2&COM=1165&MOD=0&SMD=0&SSMD=0&STA=0&ID=0&PAR=0&LNG=0, accessed 18 July 2009.

10. Laurent F. Carrel, *Leadership in Krisen* (Zurich: Buchverlag Neue Zürcher Zeitung, 2004), 118.

11. *Protecting Critical Infrastructures—Risk and Crisis Management: A Guide for Companies and Government Authorities* (Federal Ministry of the Interior, Republic of Germany, 2008), available at http://www.bbk.bund.de/cln_027/nn_398734/SharedDocs/Publikationen/Publikationen_20Kritis/Protecting-Critical-Infrastructures,templateId=raw,property=publicationFile.pdf/Protecting-Critical-Infrastructures.pdf, accessed 18 July 2009.

12. Wolfram Geier, "Verstehen wir uns richtig?—Definierte Begriffe für eine klare Kommunikation." *Notfallvorsorge* Vol. 3 (2006): 32.

13. Rasche, op. cit.

14. Protecting Critical Infrastructures—Risk and Crisis Management, A Guide for Companies and Government Authorities, 41.

15. National Infrastructure Protection Plan: Partnering to Enhance Protection and Resiliency, United States Department of Homeland Security, 2009, available at http://www.dhs.gov/xlibrary/assets/NIPP_Plan.pdf, accessed 18 July 2009.

16. "Sector-Specific Plans," United States Department of Homeland Security website, 2008, available at http://www.dhs.gov/xprevprot/programs/gc_1179866197607.shtm, accessed 18 July 2009.

17. "National Strategy for Critical Infrastructure Protection," Federal Ministry of the Interior, Republic of Germany, 17 June 2009, available at http://www.bevoelkerungsschutz-portal.de/cae/servlet/contentblob/598738/publicationFile/34423/kritis_englisch.pdf, accessed 18 July 2009.

18. "Gesetz zur Abwehr von Gefahren des internationalen Terrorismus durch das Bundeskriminalamt," Bundesgesetzblatt Vol. a, No. 66 (December 2008), available at http://www.bgblportal.de/BGBL/bgbl1f/bgbl108s3083.pdf, accessed 18 July 2009.

19. "Protection of Critical Infrastructures—Baseline Protection Concept: Recommendation for Companies," Federal Ministry of the Interior, Republic of Germany, 2005, available at http://www.bbk.bund.de/cln_007/nn_398882/SharedDocs/Publikationen/Publikationen_20Kritis/Basisschutzkonzept__engl,templateId=raw,property=publicationFile.pdf/Basisschutzkonzept_engl, accessed 18 July 2009.

20. *Protecting Critical Infrastructures—Risk and Crisis Management: A Guide for Companies and Government Authorities.*

21. "Nationaler Plan zum Schutz Kritischer Informationsinfrastrukturen (NPSI)," Federal Ministry of the Interior, Republic of Germany, 2005, available at http://www.bmi.bund.de/cae/servlet/contentblob/121734/publicationFile/13577/Nationaler_Plan_Schutz_Informationsinfrastrukturen.pdf, accessed 18 July 2009.

22. "Appendices to the Concept of IT Emergency and Crisis Exercise in Critical Infrastructure," Federal Ministry of the Interior, Republic of Germany, 2009, available at http://www.bmi.bund.de/cae/servlet/contentblob/560090/publicationFile/27810/kritis_1_eng.pdf, accessed 24 July 2009.

23. "Early Detection and Mitigation of IT Crises," Federal Ministry of the Interior, Republic of Germany, 2009, available at http://www.bmi.bund.de/cae/servlet/contentblob/560094/publicationFile/27813/kritis_2_eng.pdf, accessed 24 July 2009.

24. "Federal Ministry of the Interior of the Federal Republic of Germany, IT Emergency and Crisis Exercises in Critical Infrastructures," Federal Ministry of the Interior, Republic of Germany, 2009, available at http://www.bmi.bund.de/cae/servlet/contentblob/560098/publicationFile/27811/kritis_3_eng.pdf, accessed 24 July 2009.

25. Carrel, *Leadership in Krisen.*

26. *Protecting Critical Infrastructures—Risk and Crisis Management: A Guide for Companies and Government Authorities.*

Jean-Paul Raffenne and Jean-Francois Clair

The French Counterterrorism System

France unfortunately has broad experience in dealing with terrorism, having been exposed to it for many years. Without going so far back as the anarchist movements of the late nineteenth century, it would be safe to say that during the terrible war in Algeria from 1954 to 1962 the country learned the meaning of mass terrorism aimed at urban civilian populations and designed to instill emotional and severe psychological shock.

Since then, it has known other dramas and other victims of terrorism. This is due to its geographical proximity to the Arab Muslim world, its political engagements—most notably in various conflicts in the Middle East—its historical links with certain countries, and its readiness to play a role on the international scene. It is also appropriate to note how some extremist groups that use or have used terrorism to support their political demands have affected the domestic scene.

Nonetheless, it bears mentioning that every time France has been dealt a severe blow, it has sought to learn lessons from these actions in order to better protect itself. This is why France has gradually built a very efficient police and judicial structure specialized in fighting terrorism and founded on an original body of law specific to this fight, with reliable support by its armed forces. In spite of the ever-present terrorist threat, France prides itself on this growing success, even if those successes may be considered silent victories. This does not obviate the urgent need to continue reinforcing the antiterrorism arsenal in order to prevent new attacks on French soil or within the territory of its neighbors, friends, and allies, at least to the extent it is possible to do so in this sphere.

The objective of this work is to amplify the French experience in antiterrorism. It consists of four parts:

1. The emergence of urban terrorism: aims, operational techniques, and lessons learned
2. Various kinds of terrorism to which France has been exposed from the early 1970s to the present
3. The country's response to the evolution of the terrorist threat
4. The need to enhance present-day tools and advance current projects

A brief conclusion will touch upon the originality and specificity of the French system.

The Emergence of Large-Scale Urban Terrorism

We begin with events that have left a strong imprint on the French psyche and have had terrible consequences for the country: the war in Algeria (1954–1962) and its cruelest and most tragic episode from the standpoint of urban terrorism—the Battle of Algiers in 1957.

In August 1956, the National Liberation Front (FLN) decided to take armed rebellion to the heart of the Algerian capital by systematically resorting to urban terrorism with indiscriminate brutality.[1] The objectives were clear: create an irreparable divide between the Muslim and European communities; engage young urban Muslims, particularly the commercial bourgeoisie and intellectuals, in a revolution that had thus far seemed too exclusively peasant-based; exploit the formidable reverberations generated by large-scale organized urban terrorism; and use international opinion to increase the audience for the rebellion. These goals would be rapidly achieved, forcing the French authorities to take extraordinary retaliatory measures in order to counter a totally new phenomenon that proved terribly destructive both psychologically and politically.

A Serious Dilemma for French Authorities

It is difficult if not impossible for a democratic country lacking specific (and extraordinary) laws to effectively counter indiscriminate terrorism. With the monthly number of terrorist attacks in Algiers reaching the astronomical number of 116 for January 1957 alone, the government called upon the military to restore order and civil peace and to eradicate terrorism "as quickly as possible and by any means." As of 7 January 1957, General Massu, commander of the 10th Airborne Division, was granted all civil and military powers in the Algerian capital. Within a few months, Massu's paratroopers had totally destroyed the clandestine organization that had been indiscriminately hitting the civilian populace in high-traffic areas of the capital. The horror of these blind attacks, their frequency, the targets (young people, women, and children), and the resulting psychological impact seemed to justify use of morally reprehensible measures without real judicial controls. The "enhanced interrogations," the brutality of the paratroopers' actions, the disappearances, and the arrests made it possible to achieve rapid tactical success. After a few months, terrorism in Algiers disappeared entirely until the end of the conflict. But at what price and with what consequences?

Serious Consequences

The "Battle of Algiers," as it has been called, is not comparable with the battles of Verdun or Stalingrad. But the army's victory resulted in serious consequences for the moral reputation of the army itself and for the country. They can be summarized under four aspects.

The attention of the country and of opinion makers in Paris was drawn to what was happening in Algiers. The reality of the conflict was exposed; this contributed to the war in Algeria being opposed by an ever greater majority of French citizens. On the international stage, as observers witnessed what was unfolding in Algiers, the attitude of many countries—"nonaligned" nations as well as our allies—turned against the French policy, sometimes profoundly. The army became deeply divided and politicized. The divide grew between those who favored brutal measures, arguing for their effectiveness, and those who supported the idea that terrorism cannot and should not be fought and eradicated using solely military means. This remains a sensitive subject in officers' canteens even to this day, a half-century after the battle of Algiers. Finally, the moral reputation of the country was seriously damaged. A mere twelve years after the end of the Second World War and its horrors, France was employing the same methods from which the country itself had suffered so greatly.

Could One Have Acted Otherwise? Can One Act Otherwise?

There is no question that the novelty and extent of the large-scale urban terrorist threat came as a surprise to the authorities of the time. Terrorism also hit the homeland ("metropolitan France") hard during the war in Algeria. From January 1956 to November 1962 nearly 13,000 terrorist attacks resulting in 4,176 deaths and 8,813 injuries were recorded in France proper. It bears mentioning that mostly Muslims were affected[2] by these attacks (3,957 dead and 7,745 wounded). These were the results of aggravated rivalries among three major groups struggling to gain supremacy in the insurrection. Moreover, the general context of the Algerian conflict was creating a specific framework (Cold War; communist threat; the dream of French Algeria). But it should be recognized that the political authorities took no specific measures of a legal or administrative nature at the time, outside of making the military authorities responsible for civilian affairs, which led to the politicization of the army.

The lessons learned, still of value today, can be summed up as follows: French authorities as well as French public opinion discovered that the armed forces are not the main and most efficient tool in the fight against terrorism. But considering the power and resources at their disposal, they can be of considerable help in the fight. Conversely, a specialized police force, trained for that purpose and having an appropriate legal framework at its disposal, is indispensable. Moreover, the availability of specialized judges, with national jurisdiction and working in close cooperation with the specialized police forces, is an absolute necessity. Of course, close and well-organized coordination of the three aforementioned elements is critical. And finally, France discovered that the use of illegal or immoral techniques and methods inevitably draws universal condemnation of the country that uses them. Unfortunately it would take France coming under numerous additional attacks for it to establish the system it now possesses to protect itself from the scourge of terrorism.

The Terrorist Threat and France: An Ongoing Phenomenon from 1970 to the Present

After the exceptional events of the war in Algeria, France has been faced with terrorism from the early 1970s to the present day. This terrorism is of very diverse characters, as one may observe in other countries as well. Two major patterns emerge:

Internal (or "domestic") terrorism, which may be separatist or of other political sorts in character, is generally less lethal in France than in Great Britain (Provisional Irish Republican Army, or PIRA) or in Spain (Basque Fatherland and Freedom, or ETA). Nonetheless it remains a persistent threat.

The second major pattern is from international terrorism, which affects not only French territory but also French citizens or French interests abroad. For the last twenty years this type of terrorism has been tied nearly exclusively to the problems of the Middle East and has involved organizations that are often well structured and supported by countries that, while they themselves do not practice state terrorism, have no qualms about utilizing such organizations. This terrorism then changed its character in the early 1990s, globalizing and using radical Islamism for its call to arms. Until the attacks in Madrid (2004) and London (2005), this type of terrorism would prove more deadly for France than for its neighbors. We now consider these two major patterns.

Domestic Terrorism

In the past, separatist terrorism in France was associated with the Bretagne region, and certain overseas territories and provinces, but has remained marginal. Corsican terrorism remains the primary problem: Thousands of attacks have been perpetrated since the early 1960s. They have rarely been lethal. The assassination of the prefect of Corsica in 1998 left its mark on everyone. This terrorism is aimed mostly at the property of non-Corsicans or at government and public buildings (i.e., banks). It is fair to say that it has seriously hampered the island's economic development.

France's own Basque terrorism has had very limited, although sometimes fatal reach. The Basque area of France, where there is some solidarity with the separatist cause in Spain, has served as a rear base for the ETA, which in addition is presently using—in total secrecy—other regions of France to hide its activists and materiel and to attempt to procure explosives. The Provisional Irish Republic Army has also used French territory on numerous occasions to hide materiel destined primarily for use in actions against British military interests in Germany. Thus, even "domestic" separatist terrorism has international dimensions at times.

This is true for other reasons, such as France's geographical proximity to the Arab Muslim world, and its political engagements in various conflicts in the Middle East—its historical links with certain countries, and its readiness to play a role on the international scene. It is also appropriate to note how some extremist groups that use or have used terrorism to support their political demands have affected the domestic scene.

Every time France has been dealt a severe blow, it has sought to learn lessons from these actions in order to better protect itself. This is why France has gradually built a very efficient police and judicial structure specialized in fighting terrorism and founded on an original body of law specific to this fight, with reliable support by its armed forces. This is the reason that in spite of the ever-present terrorist threat France prides itself on its growing success, even if those successes may be considered silent victories. This does not obviate the urgent need to continue reinforcing the antiterrorism arsenal in order to prevent new attacks on French soil or within the territory of its neighbors, friends, and allies, at least to the extent it is possible to do so in this sphere.

There are, of course, many types of political terrorism. France has not been exposed in recent decades to extreme right-wing terrorism. But after the events of May 1968 (student riots against the backdrop of a general strike), like many of its neighbors, it felt the effects of extreme leftist terrorism, which raged for years, and lasted as long as 1986, when the last clandestine cell was arrested. This was the final year of operations by a most active group, Action Directe, which assassinated many individuals. This tactic was less widespread than in Italy. Still, the security service must remain vigilant, as there still are protest groups with "free agents" willing to commit acts of sabotage (such as the group detained in

---

Case Study: Emergence of a New "Anarcho-Autonome" Threat?

Four cases of sabotage of the high-speed TGV rail line occurred on the night of 7–8 November 2008. In each case, the saboteurs placed a concrete hook on the electric supply cable (*catenary*), causing the cable to become dislodged when the first TGV train passed.[3] This paralyzed the line in question and halted traffic for many hours. Several months prior to this, the police had noticed the reemergence of an *anarcho-autonome* movement. Fires at the offices of the National Employment Agency; fires at the Union for a Popular Movement offices (Nicolas Sarkozy's party) during the 2007 presidential campaign; excesses during some public demonstrations, and so on. In this context, attention focused on, among others, Julien Coupat, a known "autonome" militant who since 2005 had been living with friends on a farm in Correze (a very rural French department). He was put under surveillance, but it was difficult to track him as the group, and he, in particular, took great precautions. On the evening of 7 November, Coupat and his girlfriend were being tracked when they "led" the police deep into the countryside. Due to deep mistrust of those involved, the police had to "widen the net" and were unable to determine what the couple did thereafter. It was only the next day that it became clear that Coupat had been lost near the railway bridge on the Paris-Strasbourg line where one of the hooks had been placed. The Coupat group (ten persons) was arrested a few days later under a counterterrorism procedure in which a confidential source had stated that even more serious acts were anticipated. By the end of the temporary holding term, the police search had revealed no incriminating elements (only the TGV schedules and some other clues were discovered) and Coupat refused to explain himself, acknowledging only that he had been in the area and that when he detected the police tail, he had deliberately led them into back roads in order to lose them. Coupat is still in custody, and the others were released, but remain under surveillance. The inquiry is being conducted in cooperation with foreign police agencies, most notably German and American (Coupat had attracted attention during a visit to the United States with his girlfriend in January 2008). French authorities fear a slide toward "autonome" terrorism such as occurred during the 1970s with the creation of Action Directe, dismantled in 1986.

---

mid-November 2008 and accused of attacks on trains) that for the time being are directed solely against infrastructure. These groups could one day move toward doing violence on a larger scale.

International Terrorism

France is definitely among those countries most concerned about terrorism, and the threat from abroad has long been and remains high. Many foreigners' attacks have been committed within France; fortunately, many have been thwarted or only involved damage to property.[4] Many attacks have been prevented, especially after passage of a "Special

Law"(*Legislation Specifique*) in September 1986. None of great consequence has been committed since a December 1996 attack in the Paris subway.[5] Nonetheless, many attacks have been perpetrated abroad, where French nationals and French interests are struck under general principle of being from the West.

Distinct periods can be identified; we begin with terrorism linked to problems in the Middle East (late 1960s to early 1990s) and occurring on French territory. The earliest cases were discovered in France as early as 1971 with the arrest of a small group of pro-Palestinian Europeans who were bringing explosives of Middle East origin into France. This case was dubbed the "Easter Commando" as it was uncovered at that time of year. But it was the Black September Palestinians' bloody taking of hostages at the Munich Olympics in 1972 that would be the point of departure for international terrorist activities in France—with a bomb attack committed months later by the Israeli services in Paris against the Palestine Liberation Organization (PLO) representative. A device was planted in his telephone and then triggered remotely by a call from one of the authors of the plot. This was followed by numerous other actions. Some were settling of scores between states and organizations in the Near and Middle East, often with collateral victims; others specifically targeted the public.

There has also commonly been settling of scores between foreign parties. This sometimes involves operations conducted by states against dissidents or against the interests of a rival state or against militant members of organizations, sometimes these are attacks by organizations against state interests or against members of rival groups. Among the many actions committed, some merit special mention due to their significance to various fields.

A very significant case was that of a small family-based Lebanese group, the Lebanese Armed Revolutionary Faction (FARL), an offshoot of the Popular Front for the Liberation of Palestine (PFLP). From 1981 until its leader was captured in 1984, it killed one Israeli diplomat and one American attaché, missed two other American diplomats, and put a bomb on a US embassy car in Paris, causing the deaths of two police bomb squad technicians who were attempting to disarm the device. When the group was dismantled, it had begun to settle in Italy and was looking for a "base" in Spain. The chief of FARL, George Ibrahim Abdallah, still detained, admitted that the purpose of his group was to attack people from Israel and the United States.

For their part, Turkish interests were some of the main targets for terrorists of the time. Armenian organizations have been used in France much more than others for the purpose of attacking Turkish interests and representatives in the late 1970s and early 1980s. The Armenian Secret Army for the Liberation of Armenia (ASALA), based mainly in Lebanon with facilities in Greece and Iran and supported by Syria, was a main actor, producing a large number of collateral casualties. Already in 1973, a Turkish extreme leftist group that had established a base in the Parisian suburbs and had just received arms and explosives from Georges Habash's PFLP was identified and dismantled. This group's purpose was to commit attacks on Turkish interests in France. Syrian interests were also targeted, although less frequently. For example, the Syrian Muslim Brotherhood had put together a cache of arms and explosives in the Paris area to be used against the interests of their country within France. It was uncovered in 1986 before taking any action. During this period, Damascus and the Muslim Brotherhood, who were often notably supported by Iraq, continued their confrontations with one another.

Likewise, certain states in the Near and Middle East have directly or indirectly assassinated opponents in France, or attempted to do so. This mostly involved Iran, which "successfully" targeted five different individuals, was probably behind the murder of two others, and prepared several additional actions, which were thwarted. The most spectacular action was the assassination, after an initial unsuccessful attempt, of a former prime minister of the last Shah, Chapour Bakhtiar. For its part, Libya in the early 1980s attempted to assassinate the principal leader of the armed opposition as he was passing through France. Syria has also been involved. Damascus supported and used the organization of Carlos the Jackal, for example. In one case, when an attempt to use two of his terrorists failed, due to arrests for their suspicious behavior, Syria turned to its own services. In 1982, Syrian terror thus bombed the Paris office of a pro-Iraq newspaper, killing one passer-by and wounding others. Other examples demonstrate Damascus's operational interest in certain opponents, often supported by their common enemy, Iraq. For its part, Israel killed five Palestinian or pro-Palestinian activists between 1972 and 1992. The Iranian, Iraqi, Syrian, and Libyan embassies each maintained a stockpile of arms, explosives, and grenades for their own use or to provide to organizations linked to them. Many specific examples have been demonstrated.

The Population as Target in "Blind Attacks"

Aside from the targets noted above, terrorism quickly began affecting the population in the form of blind attacks. This would reach its culmination in the 1980s. Carlos and his revolutionaries have been responsible for several terrorist actions of this type. The organization mounted a grenade attack at a public establishment in 1974, resulting in two dead and numerous people wounded. Later, in 1975, it fired a rocket at an airplane parked at Orly Airport; fortunately, there were no casualties. Those operations were planned from Hungary where the organization was mainly staying at this period. Supported and utilized by Syria, as well, this group placed bombs in two trains and a station in 1982 and 1983, resulting in deaths and injuries. The objective was to put pressure on French authorities to obtain the release of two of their accomplices arrested for bombing the newspaper office in the case cited here earlier. Thus, Ilich Ramirez Sanchez (a.k.a. Carlos) killed two French police officers in 1975.

For their part, Palestinian organizations were involved in several "blind attacks," starting with a bomb in front of Rue Copernic synagogue in 1980, a "false flag" operation blamed on the far right at the time. The Abu Nidal Organization (ANO) raked a Jewish restaurant with gunfire in 1982. Abu Ibrahim organization put a bomb at a store entrance in 1985, causing many deaths and numerous injuries. This does not include attacks that, by chance, had no victims. But these three operations caused many victims. But it was the Lebanese Hezbollah that committed fourteen bomb attacks on behalf of Iran against numerous public places—large stores, transport lines, commercial malls, public services among them—from late 1985 to September 1986, causing numerous casualties. Fortunately, half of these attempts failed. The apprehension of the perpetrators by the counterterrorism services in the beginning of 1987 prevented a second wave of attacks.

Abroad, during the same period, France has been hit mainly in Libya and Africa, but in other places as well. From 1983 to 1988 (the end of the war with Iraq), Hezbollah, on behalf of Iran, committed numerous attacks of different sorts against states accused of being too active in assisting Iraq. France was among those most affected. Most attacks took place in Lebanon. The bloodiest was a suicide bombing in a French military camp in Beirut in 1983 with 58 French soldiers killed (at the same time 241 US Marines were killed by another device). It was again Hezbollah that kidnapped eleven French nationals during the same period and assassinated eight others from 1986 to the beginning of 1988, again on behalf of Iran and for the same reasons as the attacks committed in France and mentioned earlier. Parallel to this, two Air France airplanes were hijacked in Europe and an Air Afrique one in Brazzaville. French interests in Africa were hit by Libya several times between 1984 and 1989. A bomb attack was made in 1988 through a Palestinian organization in Djibouti in a bar frequented by French soldiers. In 1984, there was an explosion on an airplane belonging to the French company UTA at the airport at Njamena, although no one was hurt. In September 1989, the in-flight explosion of another airliner belonging to the same company produced 170 victims, 54 of them French. All these attacks can be ascribed to Libya as either the initiator or the silent partner. Nor should one forget the 1976 hijacking of an Air France aircraft to Entebbe, Uganda—which action ended in an Israeli special forces raid.

Islamist Terrorism Since the Beginning of the 1990s

France was one of the first countries to suffer from Islamist[6] terrorism, first abroad and then within its own territory. This situation was mainly linked to the evolution of the security situation in Algeria after 1991. The last attack occurred at the end of 1996; since then, more than a dozen cells and individual "actors" have been neutralized judicially (see next page). In the same period, many dozens of young men were trained in Afghanistan and a few fought in Bosnia; a group of them involved in violent criminal activities after its return was neutralized when they were caught preparing a terrorist attack against a French police station). Some others went to Chechnya, or stayed many months at the border in Georgia where they were trained in terrorist activities. More recently, French actions have made it possible to prevent many dozens of individuals from coming to fight in Iraq after the US offensive in 2003, although a small number nonetheless succeeded in reaching that country. Most of them are dead or were taken prisoner in the war zone or in Syria.

But the main threat for France is still linked to Algeria, where the leader of al Qaeda in the Islamic Maghreb (AQIM) has recently announced that his organization will strike in France. At the same time France is still accused by al Qaeda and its emulators of taking the side of the enemies of Islam.

After the 1991 disruption of the electoral process in Algeria and the advent of particularly bloody and indiscriminate terrorism in the country, it became clear that the French were becoming the favorite targets of the Armed Islamic Group (GIA), the main organization declaring international *jihad* and led partly by former "Afghans." Forty-three French nationals were killed during the time this organization was active, from 1993 until the end of the 1990s. The group also hijacked an Air France airplane in December 1994—an episode that could have ended dramatically if the four terrorists, who had already killed three passengers, had not been neutralized by the National Gendarmerie Intervention Team (GIGN).

Attacks Abroad Against French Interests and Citizens

Since 1970

13 September 1974. Taking of hostages at the French embassy at The Hague. Japanese Red Army.

June/July 1976. Hijacking of Air France airliner, ending at Entebbe (Uganda) with an Israeli commando raid. FPLP/SC.

4 September 1981. Assassination of Louis Delamare, French ambassador to Lebanon.

January 1982. Bombing of the French Cultural Center of Tripoli in Lebanon. Carlos group.

15 April 1982. Assassination of a cipher clerk and his wife at the French embassy in Beirut.

18/19 April 1982. Bombings at the French embassy and the Air France agency in Vienna.

24 April 1982. Bomb at the offices of the French Press Agency in Beirut.

24 May 1982. Car bombing at the French embassy in Beirut. Nine dead, twenty-four wounded.

21 July to 7 September 1983. Nine attacks against French interests in Teheran (embassy, Air France, attempted kidnapping of diplomats, some non-French individuals wounded) in response to the late July dismantlement in France of a group that had committed a bloody attack on the Turkish Airlines desk at Orly Airport. ASALA.

25 August 1983. Bomb attack on the Maison de France in Berlin. One dead. Carlos group.

27 August 1983. Hijacking of Air France airliner (Vienna-Paris flight). No casualties. Ended in Teheran. Pro-Iranian group.

23 October 1983. Suicide attack via a truck parked across from a French military compound (Drakkar) in Beirut. Fifty-eight dead. The action was by Hezbollah, which committed a similar attack that day on a US military compound, causing 241 deaths. Note: Many soldiers, especially from among the "white helmets" (observers), were targeted and killed during this period of French military presence in Lebanon.

19 December 1983. Attack with an automobile parked across from the French embassy in Kuwait. This was one of six attacks, one of them on the US embassy. Total of five dead. No French casualties. Hezbollah.

10 March 1984. Explosion of a DC-8 owned by the French company UTA at the N'djamena airport. One dead and twenty-four wounded. Libya is accused of the attack.

31 July 1984. Air France plane (Frankfurt-Paris flight) hijacked. No casualties. Ended at Teheran. Pro-Iranian group.

1985 to 1987. Kidnapping of eleven French nationals by Hezbollah. The last ones were freed in the spring of 1988. One died in captivity.

18 September 1986. French military attaché (Colonel Christian Gouttiere) assassinated by Hezbollah in Lebanon.

18 March 1987. Attack on the *L'Historil* bar in Djibouti, frequented by the French military. Many dead, many wounded. Libyan involvement. The terrorist was arrested.

24 July 1987. Air Africa flight from Brazzaville to Paris hijacked. One French national killed. Ended at Geneva; terrorist was arrested. He stated that he was acting on behalf of Hezbollah.

8 November 1987. Ship *Le Sylco* captured off the coast of Libya. On board was a Franco-Belgian family en route to Egypt. The terrorist group Abu Nidal held them, and later freed them in two groups in Libya and Beirut.

Late 1987 and early 1988. Several French nationals assassinated (four police officers, one priest, one engineer, one embassy employee). Attributed to Hezbollah.

September 1989. In-flight explosion over the Niger River of a DC-10 belonging to French airline UTA, caused by a bomb in a suitcase. This resulted in 170 dead, among them 54 French citizens. Attributed to Libya. Case litigated.

Since 1990

27 September 1990. Attack on the *Café de Paris* bar in Djibouti, frequented by French military. One dead, seventeen wounded. Attributed to pro-Iraqi Djiboutians.

Between 1993 and 1996. Forty-three French citizens killed in Algeria by the GIA (Islamic Armed Group). Most notable case: in March 1996, seven monks were kidnapped and found several weeks later alongside a road with their throats cut. Another case: during an attack in 1992 against an embassy employees' housing facility at Ain Allah a commando, after killing the security guards (five dead), left behind a light truck loaded with explosives, fortunately disarmed in time.

December 1994. Air France plane hijacked in Algiers by four GIA terrorists, who were killed by the GIGN in Marseilles. Three innocents, one of them French, were murdered. The ultimate objective of the attack was never established: possibly it was to crash the plane into Paris or into the Eiffel Tower.

2 August 1997. Four aid workers from the organization *Equilibre* kidnapped in Dagestan. Freed on 17 November that year.

18 November 1997. Hostages, two of them French, seized in Tajikistan. One of the two, a woman, was killed during an assault by security forces.

29 January 1998. French citizen Vincent Cochetel, sent by the United Nations for humanitarian affairs kidnapped in Chechnya. Freed on December 12 of that year.

1 October 1999. French journalist Brice Fleutiaux kidnapped in Chechnya. Freed on 12 June 2000.

Since 2001

8 May 2002. Suicide bombing against French technicians in Karachi. Eleven French fatalities. Attributed to an Islamist movement close to al Qaeda.

6 October 2002. Suicide bombing attack in open water in Aden against the French oil tanker *le Limbourg* (a small vessel loaded with explosives rammed the vessel). One fatality (non-French). Responsibility claimed by the "Islamist Army of Aden-Abyan," aligned with al Qaeda.

19 August 2003. Attack on a UN building in Baghdad. One French citizen (Jean Selim Kanaan) among the twenty-two fatalities. Islamist terrorists.

16 November 2003. French humanitarian aid worker affiliated with the United Nations assassinated in Afghanistan. Taliban.

20 August 2004. Two French journalists, Christian Chesnot and Georges Malbrunot, kidnapped in Iraq. They were freed on 21 December 2004. Islamist terrorists.

26 September 2004. One French expatriate killed in Djedda (by firearm). Islamist extremists.

5 January 2005. French journalist Florence Aubenas kidnapped in Iraq. She was freed on 11 June 2005. Islamic terrorists.

5 December 2005. Humanitarian Bernard Planchon kidnapped in Iraq. He was ultimately freed on 7 January 2006. Islamic terrorists.

26 February 2007. Four French nationals shot to death at Medina (Saudi Arabia).

3 April 2007. Taliban kidnaps two French aid workers in Afghanistan. Freed.

24 December 2007. Four French travelers shot to death in Mauritania. AQIM.

8 June 2008. French expatriate killed in a suicide attack in Algeria. AQIM.

22 February 2009. A female French tourist is killed by a bomb detonated in a Cairo market.

The threat to France again became manifest with founding of the Salafist Group for Preaching and Combat (GSPC), an organization of GIA dissidents formed in the late 1990s that in its early stages limited its actions against the Algerian forces. The GSPC aligned itself with al Qaeda in 2007 and decided to attack foreigners, primarily the French. French citizens have joined the ranks of other western victims that since 11 September 2001 have been subjected to attacks in a few countries, the great majority of them Muslim countries (Saudi Arabia, Morocco, Tunisia, Indonesia, and Egypt, where the more recent victim was a French woman in February 2009). And France was especially targeted in Karachi in 2002 (twelve French nationals were among the team of engineers and technicians working at a local naval facility).

In France

The counterterrorism services have been fearful of repercussions in France since the very beginning of terrorist actions in Algeria. Judicial action and intelligence information as well as targeted administrative measures (refusal of visas, expulsions) have made it possible to limit the threat and avert some acts.

Groups of male youths of Maghreb origin have nonetheless formed at the present time in France, and some have engaged in violence. Young men of Moroccan origin living in the Paris suburbs who had not been detected were recruited by two activists of a former small organization neutralized some years before. They were discovered when some of them killed two Spanish tourists in Marrakech in 1994 and were arrested. Accomplices were apprehended in France. Investigations showed that the majority of these people were trained in Afghanistan. Others were neutralized before being able to go into action, such as one, the Tunisian Islamic Front (FIT), in 1994 and 1995. Still, many dozens of young Algerians or people of Algerian descent who were implicated in 1994 and 1995 in acquiring materiel and providing it to the terrorist underground were arrested.

In the same period, several young Islamists of Tunisian origin, accusing the leaders of the organization El Nahda, which follows the Muslim Brotherhood line, of being too moderate, and in imitation of "their Algerian comrades," created a new organization, the FIR (Islamist Front of Tunisia). They were collecting weapons when detected by the French Services and arrested, 1994–1995. The Algerian Islamic Salvation Front (FIS) tried as early as 1992 to spread to France, but French authorities stopped it and prevented many known Islamists from settling in the country. In the meantime, the Algerian GIA, after several futile attempts in early 1995, succeeded some months later in sending two operatives to France. Using some young men who had not yet specifically attracted our attention, they committed a number of bombing attacks in public places during the summer and fall. They were arrested in November as they were preparing new attacks. Concerning the young people of Algerian origin, none of them went to join the guerrillas, but several dozen implicated in 1994 and 1995 were arrested. The French Services believe that the Algerian terrorist threat is more pressing than ever after recent statements of the AQIM leader threatening to bring terrorism to France. Systematic work on analysis and information (studying the risk environment, systematic identification and surveillance of "dedicated" internet sites, international cooperation) is thus more important than ever in order to find dangerous individuals and bring them to justice.

The Response: The French Antiterrorism System

During the war in Algeria, due to the extreme frequency of terrorism, particularly within Algeria but also in the homeland (13,000 victims), the authorities implemented certain measures provided for by the constitution and created a special judicial venue called the Court of National Security.[7] This jurisdictional structure, which significantly enhanced police powers in such matters (particularly holding in police custody for ten days) was maintained until 1981, although with certain limitations (in particular, custody was limited to six, then four days). It was used with satisfactory results for fighting terrorism during the 1970s, but was not true antiterrorism legislation adapted to international threats. Other than this, no specifically adapted legislation existed after 1981, while this type of terrorism was growing in effect, with the number of indiscriminate attacks and organizations implicated in acts of violence multiplying on our soil. In particular, it was impossible to neutralize individuals the counterterrorism services were convinced would sooner or later carry out violent acts. Indeed, it was necessary to be able to establish "commencement of execution."

A specific case serves to illustrate this problem: a bloody bombing attack (eight dead, dozens wounded) carried out in July 1983 by the Armenian ASALA against the Turkish Airlines counter at Orly Airport. At the very beginning of 1983, thanks to intelligence work, we learned of the arrival in France from the Middle East of a team of men who had come to replace an Armenian activist who had blown himself up while preparing a bomb. This person had previously carried out many attacks. The DST succeeded in identifying and locating them. The police were dealing with professionals: They had taken serious security measures, lived among the diaspora, and relocated frequently. As time passed, we gradually became convinced that they would strike sooner or later. The police ascertained that constant and effective surveillance was not possible. The judicial authorities, after consultation with the police, stated that it would be impossible to detain them until they had initiated actual execution (not just preparation). The Ministry of the Interior responded to the police inquiry as to whether we could deport them by stating that at this stage there were no grounds to believe that they constituted a threat to public order. They ultimately did take action before we were able to prevent them from doing so. Moreover, starting the next day we had to give the Criminal Investigation Department all the materials in our possession that would have allowed us to arrest the perpetrators and finally dismantle the group.

This unfortunate experience did not serve as an immediate lesson, as it took indiscriminate Hezbollah attacks in public places in France in 1985 and 1986 before real and efficient antiterrorism laws were drafted and passed in September 1986. By that time, the counterterrorism services no longer had any avenues of serious investigation, as the authors of the attacks and their accomplices had planned their affairs well by creating a number of smokescreens and decoys.

That 1986 law would be revised again and again, most recently in January 2006, when provisions were adopted to cover the most diverse areas (investigator access to a number of databases, requirement for internet operators to maintain data, video surveillance, protection of investigators' identities, measures against the financing of terrorism, etc.), but especially the toughening of certain judicial measures.

The Cornerstone of the Fight: The Law of September 1986

The September 1986 legislation has four major provisions. One, there must be a specific infraction: "offenders' association with a terrorist enterprise." Individuals with varying degrees of involvement in a process culminating in terrorism may be accordingly detained and prosecuted. There is no need to wait until the execution of an act has begun. Specific penalties have been provided that increased for some cases in January 2006. Two, special judges are to be used, at both the public prosecutor level (a dedicated section), as well as during judicial inquiry (the number of judges has now been increased to seven) and trial phases. These magistrates are centralized in Paris at the Tribunal de Grande Instance. Three, there is an ability to hold suspects for 96 hours; this was raised to 144 hours by the 2006 law. Lengthening this period enables certain crucial verifications to optimize hearings (use of telephones, internet, seized documents, etc.). And four, jurisdiction for French judicial authorities with respect to terrorist acts committed abroad when the victims are French nationals. This gap in the law was indeed very regrettable, as demonstrated by the attack on our soldiers in Beirut in 1983 where, as opposed to the equally affected Americans, we were unable to so much as collect evidence at the crime scene.

Whereas investigations following the commission of attacks are carried out by the Criminal Investigation Department as before, inquiries designated as "derived from intelligence"—that is, conducted following the services' detection of suspects—are generally assigned by the specialized court system to the Directorate of Territorial Surveillance (DST; since July 2008, the DST is housed within the new Central Directorate for Domestic Intelligence, or DCRI), which like the FBI in the United States has dual jurisdiction. This is valuable for fighting international terrorism, the most complex form. (As for domestic terrorism, criminal investigations for the time being always fall to the Criminal Investigation Department.)

This approach, based on long-standing and trusting relationships between the police and the "specialized" legal system, makes possible well-adapted and rigorous procedures that ensure reliable protection of information. This is of fundamental importance for an intelligence service and for its credibility, especially among its foreign counterparts. This arrangement has enabled us to effectively confront domestic and international terrorism.

For one who is second in command and manages to attract our special attention here, it is thanks to him that it was possible to solve attacks ordered up by superiors that struck public places in 1985 and 1986 and to prevent a new wave of violence in 1987. Continuity between intelligence and the judiciary worked perfectly, for it was intelligence that provided us with a good trail.

In the same way, many large caches of arms and explosives were discovered from 1986 onward due to this "arsenal" of means. These discoveries have prevented attacks from being carried out. This legislation has also enabled us to better conduct the investigations in France and in the countries concerned (especially in Africa and even in Libya) that followed the explosion of the UTA airliner in September 1989 and to solve the case.

But it was especially the emergence and the development of Islamist terrorism of the early 1990s against which the French legislation has been shown to be particularly well adapted and effective. The importance of unstable geographical areas having served as combat training locations for young Muslim men from everywhere and particularly from France (Bosnia until 1995, Afghanistan until 2001, Chechnya from 1999 until shortly after

2000, and more recently Iraq, beginning in 2003) has become abundantly clear. Some of them became involved in terrorist activities upon their return, as noted earlier.

The justice system has systematically opened investigations into each of these channels, making it possible to identify and detain the individuals involved, and more importantly, prevent attacks. In the case of Iraq, we have been able to prevent the departure of many dozens of individuals who would have been used as suicide bombers, like many who did manage to return to their homelands.

This legislation and the practices it engendered made it possible to identify the organizers of bloody indiscriminate attacks by the Algerian GIA against public places in France in 1995. These attacks showed for the first time in France that, at the operational level, terrorists had the technical capability to fabricate bombs entirely on their own, using commercially available products and techniques learned in Afghanistan. They have also involved young men from the suburbs, some of whom were former offenders used by the organization who could have then acted on their own initiative. This is precisely the kind of threat we are facing today—small independent groups of individuals, often referred to these days as "homegrown terrorists." It is the job of intelligence to find them among the population and then detain them as soon as possible to avoid incurring any risk. In this respect, combining the DST and General Intelligence in one organization, the DCRI, is an excellent move in terms of coherence and efficiency.

Thanks to the French system, since the year 2000 the DST has been able to neutralize more than a dozen organizations that were preparing or planning attacks on French soil. More than 800 persons have been detained. Elsewhere, our arsenal of legal tools allows us to counter appeals for violence. A number of imams and other preachers have been successfully expelled during the past ten years. However, the threat remains viable today and reconnaissance is more necessary than ever.

Antiterrorist legislation in effect in France and the practices developed since its inception have shown that the laws must be applied with moderation. As practitioners, the Police Services consider terrorism to be a set of criminal activities and nothing more. This guarantees objectivity, and for the most part the Muslim community approves of this approach. Of course, terrorism is a diverse phenomenon that stems from numerous causes, which the authorities and the international community must examine. But this is another subject.

The Need to Enhance Existing Tools, and the Projects in Progress

Despite the undeniable successes achieved in recent years in the fight against terrorism, the threat has yet to be eliminated. France believes that it is necessary to continue building up the assets utilized in this fight. The status of projects that will be implemented for this purpose was described in a recent white paper published on 17 June 2008 after a year of study and reflection by a special commission convened for that purpose. These projects can be summarized as follows:

- Development of a new, expanded general defense concept that combines issues of defense and security, both internal and external, in a close and consistent manner. Therefore, the operational linkage between the Ministries of Defense, Interior,

Industry, and Foreign Affairs will be developed considerably through a continuum of action.

- Development and implementation of the concept of "resilience" (an enhanced capacity to absorb blows), at both the national and the European level. Specifically, this means common planning, common exercises, and centralized actions between the different state actors and private companies that are critical for the protection of the population.

- Due consideration of the country's new vulnerabilities (possibility of dirty bomb attacks, ballistic or cruise missile strikes, attacks on our information system by non-state actors aimed at paralyzing the country, drug trafficking, and commerce in counterfeit goods used to finance terrorism).

- Creation of a permanent joint crisis management center from among the ministries of defense, interior, and foreign affairs.

- Enhancing the country's resistance to large-scale terrorist attacks by developing the necessary plans and exercises among the country's major economic actors at the state level and at the regional level.

- Creation of a national agency to protect information systems, as well as an advanced missile detection system.

- Creation of a supplementary strategic mission named ANTICIPATION. This mission seeks to base security on the identification, and therefore the advance detection of threats. It is dependent on intelligence. Intelligence capabilities will thus be significantly strengthened in the following manner:

  - Improved coordination between the various civilian and military intelligence services will be ensured by creating the post of national intelligence coordinator, placed near the president of the Republic (this authority has been selected and set up since September 2008).

  - A significant increase in human and technical resources allocated to the various intelligence services, both domestic and foreign, is in progress. In addition, a deep reorganization of those services is currently underway.

  - The budget for space and electronic detection means will be doubled.

  - The establishment of information exchanges with our allies will be substantially increased, as well as the technical cooperation in this field.

Thus, France, cognizant of the risks that the terrorist threat poses for our societies and our way of life, has resolved to reinforce, reorganize, and substantially reorient its defense and security arrangements.

Conclusion

France, due to its long and sometimes tumultuous history, has suffered from terrorism for a long time. From this painful experience, France has been able to draw some essential lessons from which the following points emerge: No country, no matter how powerful, can protect itself from the terrorist threat alone. Trusting and focused cooperation based on equality must be established among those of us who strive to preserve our freedom, way of life, and values. The fight against terrorism requires patient, prolonged, and persistent effort. It cannot be efficiently prosecuted solely through the use of military force, which is not the most effective means of detecting and eliminating the terrorist threat. Indeed, through its very power, military force has created unavoidable collateral damage that aggravates the civilian population and actually generates more terrorists. Action by western countries, the defenders of values we share, must be consistent with a code of law recognized by all. In particular, the use of torture for combating terrorism must be firmly and clearly rejected. Any deviation from this will tarnish our soul, our image, and our reputation for many years to come.

The conditions that allow a country to effectively carry on the fight against terrorism can, according to the authors of this chapter, be summarized as follows:

- Possess police and intelligence agencies that talk to one another and exchange information in an atmosphere of complete trust.

- Have permanent and centralized antiterrorism judges with national authority who specialize in matters related to terrorism and have good connections to police agencies.

- Maintain robust specialized units—police, gendarmerie, and military—specially equipped and trained to penetrate, apprehend, neutralize, and/or destroy terrorist networks both within and outside of national territory.

- Adopt specific legislation that is sufficiently powerful and flexible to provide judges and police with the authority necessary to prevent terrorist attacks before they can be carried out.

International Terrorism in France: Selected Plots, Thwarted Efforts, and Cells Preemptively Disbanded

The 1970s and 1980s

1971. Neutralization of a cell made up primarily of Europeans who were bringing explosives in from the Middle East and working for the Palestinians.

January 1973. Discovery and neutralization of a major Turkish extremist group that had established a base in the Paris suburbs and was about to receive a consignment of arms and explosives from the PFLP.

July 1974. Discovery and neutralization of a group in the course of infiltrating a small organization called the Japanese Red Army, with ties to the PFLP. The Japanese Red Army would later be responsible for various bloody attacks in many parts of the world.

January 1975. An individual fired a rocket from an embankment at Orly Airport and then fled. He was aiming at an El Al plane, but instead hit an aircraft belonging to a Yugoslavian airline. The rocket did not explode. It was later established that the person was a member of the Carlos group.

May 1978. Attempted taking of hostages, again at Orly Airport, by three Palestinians, who were killed in the attempt. One police officer was also killed.

21 August 1982. Unexploded bomb in an American diplomatic vehicle parked in Paris. Two police technicians attempting to defuse the device were killed by the Lebanese Armed Revolutionary Faction, seeking release of its prisoners in French jails.

23 February 1985. Bomb placed at the entrance to the Marks and Spencer store in Paris (store was closed). One dead. (Not claimed by, but attributable to an PFLP splinter organization). The perpetrator was later arrested and explosives ready for use were found at his residence.

3 February 1986. Bomb on level three of the Eiffel Tower. Did not explode. Part of a bloody bombing campaign in Paris conducted by the Hezbollah front "Committee of Solidarity with Arab and Middle East Political Prisoners" or CSPPA.

20 March 1986. Bomb at the RER Chatelet station. Did not explode. CSPPA.

4 September 1986. Bomb at the RER Gare de Lyon. Did not explode. CSPPA.

Since 1990

26 August 1995. Bomb on the tracks of the Paris-Lyon TGV. Did not explode. GIA. There have been previous and subsequent successful attacks on French rails by other terrorists.

4 September 1995. Bomb in a public toilet in Paris. Defused before exploding. GIA.

7 September 1995. Car bomb in front of an Israeli school at Villeurbanne near Paris. Thirty wounded. The terrorists were mistaken about the time, and the device exploded before the pupils were let out of school.

From January to March 1996, a group of young Muslims and converts to Islam who were known in a mosque in Roubaix (northern France) and had returned from Bosnia where they had fought in an Arab battalion, committed eight attacks on stores, and so on, using imported rocket launchers. They were noticed by the police as they were about to park a car in front of the police commissioner's office in Lille. The car had been rigged with explosives. The bomb was defused. The terrorists took refuge in a house, where they engaged in a battle of gunfire with a "RAID" team (National Police special commandos), leaving four of the suspects dead.

Since 2000/2001

No attacks have occurred this century in France, but a number of actions were prevented by making arrests. They were attributable to the Islamic terrorist movement, which declared allegiance to al Qaeda and *jihad*. The principals in these actions were the following:

2000. Mass-casualty attack plotted against the Christmas market beside Strasbourg Cathedral. The guilty parties were arrested in Germany and France; their chief was in London.

2001. Attack on American interests in France, targeted according to opportunities to gain access. The leader of the group was arrested as he was returning from Afghanistan with instructions.

December 2002. Arrest in a Paris suburb of a group trained in the Pankisi Gorge in Georgia on the Chechen frontier. They were preparing to place bombs against Russian interests in France, the Eiffel Tower, police stations, and the Jewish community. They had toxic substances in their possession.

2003. Arrest of an Islamist who was preparing to board a plane to Reunion Island, where under the guise of doing Islamic studies he was going to "case" tourist sites as possible future targets for attacks.

2005. Arrest of a cell formed in the prison where they were serving a sentence for their (secondary) role in GIA attacks in 1995. The group was formed by an Islamist who began planning attacks upon his release from custody. The planned targets were Orly Airport, the metro, and even the DST headquarters.

2005. Dismantlement of a group made up of criminals specializing in attacks on banks and "hardened" targets. They were planning attacks in France and Italy. A significant amount of arms and explosive, mainly originating in the Balkans, were found.

2005. A young man who had returned from Iraq after refusing to die as a martyr planned attacks with his accomplices. This network was supplying detonator systems to the Algerian GSPC (renamed AQMI in 2007).

2007. Arrest of a young and notorious Islamist who was acting alone. He had acquired over the internet a technical ability to fabricate bombs and was preparing devices to strike public facilities. He was seeking to make contact with AQMI, which because of the specific threat to France posed by its leader had attracted authorities' attention and response.

May 2008. Dismantling of a small group of logistical support for Islamic Movement for Uzbekistan (IMU). Similar arrests were made in Germany and the Netherlands.

2008. Arrest of a group planning attacks against various targets, including the headquarters of the newly operational Central Directorate of Interior Intelligence (DCRI).

Jean-Paul Raffenne Lieutenant General Raffenne (retired), coauthor of our study of French counterterrorism, served at the Marshall Center between 2005 and 2009 as Republic of France Chair and as Director of the Senior Executive Seminar program. A graduate of the Military Academy of Saint-Cyr, class of 1965, and the national war college of France, he has also taught at the Joint Staff College, the Joint Defense College, and the US Army's staff college at Fort Leavenworth, Kansas. He is a Marine, an infantryman, paratrooper, and parachute instructor, with some fourteen hundred jumps. He has served overseas, particularly in Chad, Djibouti, Lebanon, and the Indian Ocean islands of Comoros and Reunion. He commanded the Second Marine Infantry Parachute Regiment in Reunion from 1988 to 1990. The general has been the military attaché to the French embassy in Washington; plans and policy officer for the staff of the Stabilization force in Bosnia-Herzegovina; director of international affairs for the French Armed Forces Staff; military representative to the European Union's Military Committee; and head of the NATO Defense College in Rome. Lt. Gen. Raffenne holds such military decorations as the Legion of Honor, Commander of the National Order of Merit, and the Cross of Valor with four citations.

Jean-François Clair Jean-François Clair was an inspector general of police and spent a thirty-five year career in the French security service DST, or Directorate of Territorial Surveillance. He headed their antiterrorist branch for fifteen years (1983 to 1997) and was then appointed as Deputy Director of the service, a position that he kept from 1998 to 2007, at which time he retired. Mr. Clair is a graduate of the French High Defence College (IHEDN-session 1992/1993). He is now an independent consultant, and teaches at Sciences-Po-in Paris on international threat matters, and in another institute (IRIS) on security and intelligence. He lectures and participates in conferences widely in France and abroad, to include those focused on terrorism and security. Much engaged in research on the French administration, he writes articles for various publications such as the *Defense Review* of IHEDN.

Recommended Readings

Aussaresses, Paul. *Services Speciaux: Algerie 1955–1957*. Paris: Perrin, 2001.

Crenshaw, Martha. "The Effectiveness of Terrorism in the Algerian War," Ch. 11 in *Terrorism in Context*, edited by Martha Crenshaw, 473–513. University Park, PA: Pennsylvania State University Press, 1995.

Horne, Alistair. *A Savage War of Peace: Algeria 1954–1962*. New York: Viking, 1978.

Ministry of Defense, Republic of France. *Defense et Security National: Le Livre Blanc*. Paris: Odile Jacob, 2008.

Parmentier, Guilliaume. "France," Ch. 2 in *Counterterrorism Strategies: Successes and Failures of Six Nations*, edited by Yonah Alexander, 44–71. Dulles, VA: Potomac Books, 2006.

Shapiro, Jeremy. "France and the GIA," Ch. 5 in *Democracy and Counterterrorism: Lessons from the Past*, edited by Robert J. Art and Louise Richardson, 133–166. Washington, DC: US Institute of Peace, 2007.

Sifaoui, Mohamed. *Mes "Freres" Assassins*. Paris: Le Cherche Midi, 2003.

Notes

1. The FLN made its strategic decision to enhance violence at the Soummam conference in the mountains of Algeria in August 1956. On aspects of the Algerian war, a valuable source is Bernard Droz and Evelyne Lever, *Histoire de la Guerre d'Algerie, 1954–1962*, 2nd ed. Paris: Edition de Seuil [1982], 1991.
2. The Muslim victims of these half-century-old FLN bombings, both in Algeria and France, anticipate our own day in which far more Muslims than others are murdered by avowedly Muslim terrorists. Western public diplomacy usually failed to make an argument of this evident pattern in the first years after 9/11. See "Arguments Washington Has Neglected," in Christopher C. Harmon, *Terrorism Today*, 2nd ed. (London and New York: Routledge, 2007), 149; see especially "Deadly Vanguards: A Study of al Qaeda's Violence Against Muslims," Dr. Scott Helfstein et al., Occasional Paper Series (West Point, NY: Combating Terrorism Center, December 2009), 55 pp.
3. "Rail Chaos in France after Sabotage on Lines," Reuters, 8 November 2008, available at http://uk.reuters.com/article/idUKTRE4A71A020081108, accessed 4 October 2009.
4. A remarkable preemption came in December 1994 when an Algerian GIA hijacking was foiled on the ground at a Marseilles airport. The French news outlet *24Hueres* (on 16 October 2009) referred to authorities stopping five attacks in the last three years, including one against a former Moroccan minister, and another targeting the headquarters of French counterespionage.
5. "Significant Terrorist Incidents, 1961–2003: A Brief Chronology," U.S. Department of State, Bureau of Public Affairs, Office of the Historian, March 2004, available at http://www.state.gov/r/pa/ho/pubs/fs/5902.htm, accessed 4 October 2009.
6. Here, as elsewhere in this volume, the authors' term "Islamist" must not be confounded with "Muslim." On the contrary, "Islamist" refers to a peculiar blend of violence and religious ideology, often more akin to Leninist vanguardism than any normal and peaceable religion.
7. La Cour de Surete de l'Etat, later disbanded by President Mitterand.

4.4

Michael R. Fenzel

Defeating Taliban in Afghanistan:

A Nuanced Approach to Waging a Counterinsurgency

Every country that has invaded Afghanistan in the last twenty-three hundred years with the intention of bringing its own brand of order has met with various and tragic ends. International leaders are all too familiar with the anthropology of conflict in Afghanistan. Now the United States' efforts to increase the coalition commitment of forces to the counterinsurgency campaign in Afghanistan are colored by weary visions of Alexander the Great's epic difficulties, Great Britain's three separate failures, and the Soviet Union's quagmire in that same country. I will argue that the current counterinsurgency is dramatically different than these past imbroglios and that the prospects for a military defeat of the Taliban, the adversary of the moment, are very good if we strictly follow six principles and apply two microstrategies in our approach to maneuver and engagement.

The Taliban is an insurgent organization making systematic and calculated use of terrorism as well as guerrilla war, political activism, and diplomacy with established states. While fighting the Taliban is a business that extends to Afghanistan's borders, with six different countries and the coalition effort involving contributions of forty-two nations in vastly different capacities, the principal focus of this chapter is on the efforts of US and Afghan forces in eastern Afghanistan, along the frontier border with Pakistan.[1] Although there are many governance and development questions that must be answered at the national level, I contend that the first step in bringing about a stable country with a legitimate and widely supported government begins with the military defeat of insurgent forces. Unless and until security is achieved, there can be no truly effective governance and no large-scale transformative development effort. One of the tactical realities of counterinsurgency operations in Afghanistan is that in order to establish effective security in a given village, coalition forces must address the needs of the people simultaneously. Eight years into this fight, our soldiers are getting very good at addressing this need. The most strategically decisive contribution to success in Afghanistan over the immediate term is what occurs on the ground with coalition and Afghan troops. More specifically, the manner in which both these parties carry out operations and conduct themselves in the process will define the outcome of this conflict.

This chapter suggests that defeating the Taliban is achievable if six tactical imperatives are employed and administered effectively on the ground and two microstrategies are implemented with a firm commitment. First, prevent collateral damage to avoid swelling the insurgent ranks; second, focus the expenditure of development funds to heighten the impact of each dollar; third, ensure there is a persistent presence in the remote rural areas to deny insurgents safe haven inside Afghan borders; fourth, commit to the longer term effort of developing a literate and broadly educated population; fifth, demonstrate respect for Islam in an active and concerted way; and sixth, stop corruption at the lower levels with a zero-tolerance approach. These measures must be complemented with the implementation of microstrategies to expand the incidence of cross-border *shuras* (meetings with tribal elders and villagers) among tribal groups along the border and the careful positioning and construction of combat outposts along dominant terrain just inside Afghanistan.

The Threat Environment in Afghanistan

Any consideration of waging a military campaign must begin with a review of the threat. The nature of the insurgency in Afghanistan can be summed up this way: The insurgents in Afghanistan (whether Taliban or foreign fighters) are like rats, and coalition forces are like water. Wherever coalition troops go in significant numbers, the insurgents scurry away and then operate either where coalition forces are not present or where they simply do not go. This is an effective technique for the Taliban because there are just not enough troops on the ground currently to consolidate gains as they are being made around the country. And the Taliban is not simply targeting civilians who work with the coalition, they are intent on preventing any sort of international investment. As Tom Johnson and Chris Mason have described,

> The Taliban today is conducting a brilliant defensive insurgency. They have deployed enough low-level fighters to intimidate the NGOs and international organizations into the rural areas, speaking to village elders. They are fond of saying, "The Americans have the wristwatches, but we have the time." The simple message they deliver in person or by "night letter" is one of intimidation: "The Americans will leave, and when they do, we will come back to this village and kill every family that has collaborated with the Americans or the Karzai government."[2]

In 2007 alone, United Nations Children's Fund (UNICEF) reported over 228 attacks on schools around the country, which resulted in seventy-five deaths and 111 wounded, and the incidence of these terrorist attacks rose in 2008.[3] This approach to inciting terror and fear among the population is illustrative of a more insidious objective. Afghan International Human Rights Watch spokesman Nader Naderly expressed this objective succinctly: "The Taliban and Al-Qaeda forces follow the policy of burning schools as a long-term strategy to preserve Afghanistan as an [undeveloped] country."[4] The enemy in this case does not feel compelled to strike only military forces, but in addition counts intimidation of civilians and terrorist acts as key tenets of their broader strategy.

Despite the recent commitment of an additional 21,000 troops to the campaign and recent addition of a third brigade on the ground in eastern Afghanistan, until the bulk of these new forces are on the ground and established, the challenge associated with not having enough forces in enough places to counter the Taliban's campaign of intimidation will persist. Coalition maneuvers from 2005 through 2008 resembled the old cartoon reel where one drawer is pushed in and another one opens in response. This is what has to change with the introduction of additional forces and the redistribution of Afghan forces. The insurgents in Afghanistan will retain the operational advantage until there is a more favorable ratio of counterinsurgent forces to civilians, particularly in the rural areas where the Taliban are known to enjoy safe haven.[5]

There is no scientific answer or calculation to applying existing forces that can be made by national security analysts with favorable results. Countering the Afghan insurgency means having enough troops to accomplish the tasks that commanders on the ground know must be done. It means frequently spending extended periods of time with the villagers and leaders in the district(s) they patrol. It demands reacting quickly to problems in these established sectors as they arise. Formulas and assessments are acceptable guides to understand the breadth of the challenge, but each province and district in Afghanistan will demand slightly different troop-to-civilian ratios based upon a variety of factors like population density and type of terrain. As a guide, and using counterinsurgency doctrine to determine the appropriate ratio, one counterinsurgent for every fifty civilians in the rural areas would be appropriate. Napolean Valeriano and Charles Bohannan make the alternative argument in their seminal work *Counter-Guerrilla Operations: The Philippine Experience*[6]—that there should be up to two hundred counterinsurgents for every one insurgent in a nonpermissive environment. The essential point is that these Afghan security and coalition forces are working closely together to protect the population. In larger and more dangerous districts, this means a larger combined force to address the additional size and higher threat.[7]

There is a US component and an Afghan component to making the changes that are essential to preventing a continued "see-saw" struggle with the Taliban. The US component means more troops are required (more than the current commitment if they are to properly address a land mass 50 percent larger than Iraq and terrain that is vastly more difficult to negotiate). The Afghan component would require that Afghan infantry battalions (or KANDAKs, as they are called) move off the large forward operating bases and move into the district centers around the country and among the people. These general imperatives will provide the foundation and opportunity to defeat the Taliban.

The Taliban are making mistakes as an insurgent force that the coalition and their Afghan hosts must exploit. Johnson and Mason have made clear how the intolerant form of Islam is not compelling to the average Afghan, but that pressure on villagers is often too great to resist:

> The rural Pashtu south has its own systems of tribal governance and law, and its people don't want Western styles of either. But nor are they predisposed to support the Taliban, which espouses an alien and intolerant form of Islam, and goes against the grain of traditional respect for elders and decision by consensus.[8]

There has been a significant shift over the last two years in the way the Taliban behave as an insurgent force. The good news from a counterinsurgent perspective is that the Taliban are no longer concerned with how the people of Afghanistan view them, especially at the local level. The Taliban routinely punish villagers for working with coalition forces and bully or murder village elders who make commitments to the government of Afghanistan. As a result, there is a definite hesitation to work with coalition forces because Afghans rightfully fear that US and Afghan forces cannot protect them.

This does not sound like good news, but a review of recent history in the region puts it in perspective. In 2005, there seemed to be a more silent battle raging for the soul of Afghanistan. There were competing visions of democracy versus theocracy that were equally compelling to the people in rural Afghanistan. The Taliban has since abandoned this ideological tug-of-war and appears to have decided that the only way to regain power is to work closely with al Qaeda and anyone else willing to assist them in order to wage a full-scale offensive. It appears the Taliban has made a conscious decision to stop concerning itself with collateral damage or taking the time to explain why Taliban rule is preferable to democracy. The Taliban have undertaken a strategy of intimidation that now includes integrating specific acts of terrorism against villagers, which seems designed to demonstrate that the US coalition cannot protect the Afghan people. This is the essential point. Counterinsurgency history reveals why this is significant and an ineffective long-term strategy. David Galula wrote in his 1964 classic, *Counterinsurgency Warfare*,

> If the insurgent manages to dissociate the population from the counterinsurgent, to control it physically, to get its active support, he will win the war because, in the final analysis, the exercise of political power depends on the tacit or explicit agreement of the population or, at worst, on its submissiveness. Thus the battle for the population is a major characteristic of the revolutionary war.[9]

This fact alone would indicate to counterinsurgency experts that the Taliban insurgency will fail, but the question, of course, is how long it will take to defeat them. It is the clear preference of the average Afghan to live peacefully and without the theocratic oppression of the Taliban. The immediate challenge, then, is clear but no less daunting: figuring out how to defeat insurgent forces.

Any argument for how to best achieve a lasting military defeat of insurgents in Afghanistan, or elsewhere, will always identify the people as the decisive additive. Johnson and Mason have indicated the same is true in Afghanistan, stating "The Taliban are well aware that the center of gravity in Afghanistan is the rural Pashtun district and village, and that Afghan army and coalition forces are seldom seen there."[10] The military challenge on the ground is indeed not nearly as much about killing insurgents as it is rendering them and their losing ideology as unacceptable to the people. David Kilcullen's "28 Articles" lay out this counterinsurgency imperative:[11]

> Whatever else you do, keep the initiative. In counterinsurgency, the initiative is everything. If the enemy is reacting to you, you control the environment. Provided you mobilize the population, you will win. If you are reacting to the enemy, even if you are killing or capturing him in large numbers, then he is controlling the environment and you will eventually lose. . . . Focus on the population, further your game plan, and fight the enemy only when he gets in the way. This gains and keeps the initiative.[12]

Mobilizing the Afghan people has to mean more than gaining their acceptance and move beyond seeking a passive support role for them. Afghans must do their part in bringing about tactical advantage in their respective districts. When counterinsurgent forces finally bring villagers and their leaders into a tightly knit web of information and intelligence collection, then it will become extraordinarily difficult for insurgents to continue to function. This is to say nothing of the solidarity that will inevitably develop in parallel with such a commitment. Insurgents will then be forced to move to provinces, districts, and villages where there is either indifference to them or overt support for their cause. The key is to first deny a village, then a district, and follow up with the alignment of a host of districts against the Taliban to deny an entire province. However, this requires consolidating these minor gains before they are lost to an insurgent force that "scurries" to counter those gains. But getting to that point requires a systematic approach where the principles one follows as a counterinsurgent force are strictly applied. I suggest that there are six tactical imperatives and two microstrategies that have the potential to lead to Taliban defeat.

Six Tactical Imperatives That Lead to Strategic Effects

The first and most critical tactical imperative is preventing collateral damage. The US Army and Marine Corps' new counterinsurgency guide (*Field Manual 3-24*) identifies the far-reaching impacts of collateral damage, which go well beyond damage to property and civilian casualties. An errant bomb drop and mortar round that misses its mark creates the potential to face another ten insurgents in the future. There are definitive methods to prevent or, at the very least, limit the incidence of collateral damage that any military unit causes, but it must become every commander's priority to employ those methods and work intensely to prevent collateral damage. The manual makes this clear:

> Exercise exceptional care when using airpower in the strike role. Bombing, even with the most precise weapons, can cause unintended civilian casualties. Effective leaders weigh the benefits of every air strike against its risks. An air strike can cause collateral damage that turns people against the host-nation government and provides insurgents with a major propaganda victory. Even when justified under the law of war, bombings that result in civilian casualties can bring media coverage that works to the insurgents' benefit.[13]

One battalion from the US Army's 173d Airborne Brigade returned from a deployment to Afghanistan in 2007–2008 after firing 24,600 rounds of artillery and mortars and dropping 469 bombs in fifteen months of fighting and did not kill one innocent civilian.[14] This sort of track record must transition from being the exception to becoming the rule. Preventing collateral damage must become the highest maneuver priority in Afghanistan since it is inevitably a war for the support of the Afghan people. Civilian casualties will always be a liability in the critical battle for "hearts and minds" and contravene the principles of counterinsurgency, which align with one of the paradoxes of such wars: the more force used, the less effective it is.[15] Inevitably, too much force runs the risk of turning neutrals into enemies and replenishing the ranks of the insurgency.[16] In fighting an insurgency, the highest concern must be to protect the people and by extension separate them from the insurgents. This is not possible if innocent Afghan civilians are killed on even an infrequent basis. It is not just the tragic and emotional nature of these events that is at issue, but the far-reaching role that tribal dynamics play in the response to incidents of collateral damage.

The Pashtun tribal code of *Pashtunwali* makes clear that avenging the death of a loved one is directly tied to the honor of a Pashtun man. This is not the type of situation where apologies or a $2,500 *solatia* payment will always resolve the problem.[17] After collateral damage is done in a given sector, then the number of insurgents will certainly increase; the only question is by how many. Pashtun anthropologist Bernt Glazer has carefully studied the concept of *Pashtunwali* and its applications in Afghan culture, and he explains that ethnic and tribal identity is connected with strong emotions and therefore easily leads to particular aggressiveness when conflicts arise.[18] An Afghan male who loses a relative as a result of military action carried out by coalition forces is honor-bound to avenge the death of that family member. It is not enough to understand the emotional trauma associated with killing civilians; it must be equally well understood in operational terms the dramatic blow to the local counterinsurgency effort. Otherwise, revenge will manifest itself through the swelling of insurgent ranks.

The second tactical imperative is to initially focus development funds in a few critical areas, at least until momentum is achieved and progress is apparent to the local people. Development funds have been effectively used since 2002 in Iraq and Afghanistan as a counterinsurgency tool at the tactical level. Since this date and despite numerous good news stories, the most common problem in investing these funds on a local basis is a lack of focus and clear strategic purpose. It is important to note that, in a conflict environment like Afghanistan, the category of development funds that has the most impact is normally a commander's discretionary development funds (Commander Emergency Response Program, or CERP) because they are most readily available and give the tactical commander an ability to have an immediate impact in the operational area. In counterinsurgency environments, these discretionary funds are more important than bullets in bringing stability to a given area because they engender goodwill and potentially a commitment to support the counterinsurgency effort. However, these funds must either be linked to operational objectives or applied toward a grander strategic purpose. As an example, in Paktika province through 2007–2008, the focus of development funding was on agriculture, irrigation, roads, and education. If a proposed development project fell outside one of those categories, the maneuver commander would simply not approve it; instead, it would either be shifted to a development-centric institution for consideration or cataloged until after security was well established in that sector. The larger point is that in waging a counterinsurgency war, it is not possible to function and carry out initiatives sequentially. The very essence of such operations is to simultaneously implement as many different initiatives as possible when those opportunities present themselves. Commanders must seize operational advantage as it arises, much as Kilcullen suggests. In a post-conflict environment, the urgent need for such discretionary funds will give way to development professionals and the more deliberate pursuit of larger projects under the control of USAID or international organizations like the World Bank. CERP funding gives a commander in a conflict environment the ability to make immediate progress or demonstrate a commitment to bigger development challenges. This will also provide a bridge to strategic and larger-scale development.

In a province like Paktika, where 98 percent of the population works as farmers, the development focus must be on improving the lot of the farmers. As an example, moving water to the fields of district centers and providing agricultural assistance that increases per capita income can lead to significant attitudinal shifts that facilitate the development of operational advantage. Similarly, since Paktika's literacy rate is a staggeringly low 2 percent, the propaganda of the Taliban is all the more powerful. As a result, pursuing broader educational initiatives has the potential to lead to longer-term strategic gains. Finally, in a province where there were no roads in 2004 and only unimproved trails to negotiate the open *dashtas* (plains) and craggy hills in between, focusing development funds on connecting the district centers and bazaars with improved gravel roads becomes an extraordinarily clear sign of progress to every villager. It is also a threatening signal to the Taliban, which cannot compete with this brand of progress.

These are only a few examples of how to focus development funds at the maneuver battalion level; the essential point is that all development funds, whether they are commander discretionary, USAID, or World Bank, must be tied to a larger strategy to combat the underlying causes of discontent. The causes are different from province to province in Afghanistan. The root causes of discontent and support for the insurgency vary just as widely. Therefore, the solutions to these problems must be varied, intensely creative, and carefully tailored to specific needs. Once development priorities are established in close conjunction with provincial governors, then maneuver task forces must stick to those priorities until real progress is realized. The obstacle to real progress will be rationalizing moves outside the established priorities and imperatives. There will be competing demands and "good ideas" that transition from one leader's tenure to another, but the continuity of effort and resolve is the most critical element in the development realm of a protracted counterinsurgency effort like Afghanistan.

The third imperative is ensuring persistent force presence in remote areas. This is the greatest threat to the insurgency and more powerful even than a successful development effort. What does not work in Afghanistan is driving back and forth from forward operating bases, conducting four-hour *shuras*, and then leaving. Military forces cannot "drive to work" each day in their sectors and expect to achieve meaningful progress. Relationships cannot be built in a few hours in Afghanistan. It is a culture where trust must be earned. Moving to the places military forces need to move in the war-torn land is often just plain hard, given the challenges of terrain and threat of Improvised Explosive Devices (IEDs) and ambushes along the way. What maneuver task forces must start consistently doing is going to remote villages for much longer periods of time (at least two weeks at a time, with coalition and Afghan soldiers, Afghan police, and district governor in the lead). When this is done, the impact will often be immediate and significant.

Troops that do not follow this persistent presence approach may be extended "guest" status as a demonstration of hospitality consistent with the Pashtunwali tribal code, but that is not enough. On longer duration missions, soldiers should seek *gawandai* or "neighbor" status, which is every tribal elder's right to extend. This effectively makes the maneuver force part of their community. It is not just a cultural boon but also important to the future of the local counterinsurgency mission. The early warning network for military forces (coalition and Afghan) with *gawandai* status will grow faster than it would otherwise, and the faith of people in these remote areas in a democratic Afghanistan system will grow in concert.

The fourth imperative is committing now to the long-term development of a literate and broadly educated population. Long-term and enduring mission success in Afghanistan depends most heavily on this point. There is a myth and commonly held international misconception (developed since 2002) that the literacy rate in Afghanistan lies somewhere above 30 percent.[19] This myth has prevented a more energetic and committed international response to the educational needs of the country because the figure of 30 percent is somehow seen as a significant problem but perhaps not tragic. The reality is that in the major population centers such as Kabul, Jalalabad, Kandahar, Ghazni, and other university cities, the literacy rate is at 50 percent by most national estimates. However, in the rural areas survey data show that literacy is below 25 percent in all but ten provinces and closer to 5 percent in most remote locations.[20] The educational opportunities for children are usually limited to live-in madrassas in Pakistan or nothing, since the number of functioning schools in rural areas is roughly one for every three districts.[21] And for many children walking to school is not possible, since the nearest school may be over forty miles away.

Part of this problem is tribal, since education in the tenets of the *Pashtunwali* code is more closely related to social development and an apprenticeship of sorts, where children accompany their parents to tribal *shuras* and learn by watching their elders. Although in more densely populated areas like the nation's capital a liberal education may be a priority, in rural areas attending schools is important but not an urgent requirement. According to Bernt Glatzer, education is more about growing up as a person than it is about developing literacy or imparting knowledge beyond religious requirements:

> Education or Tura begins early, the education is non-authoritarian, and a father is considered to be an example, not a penal authority. Children are present everywhere, in guest houses, at tribal councils and wherever serious decisions are made. In this way they are introduced to Pashtunwali and to the traditional values and their practical applications.[22]

The result of this cultural education is a set of strong and ingrained values where honor, integrity, and courage are honed, but even rudimentary education is not included. This is why Taliban propaganda can become so compelling to the average Afghan—the largely illiterate population does not know what to believe.[23]

The rural populations in Afghanistan simply trying to lead their lives and avoid the cross-fire of violent conflict are vulnerable to myths and gossip about how the coalition is an occupier and persecutes those that practice Islam. In 2007, the University of Nebraska was contracted to assist a US Army maneuver task force to develop the Paktika province into a "Province of Education Excellence" for less than $300,000 over three years.[24] With the full support and encouragement of the provincial governor, the university set out to develop and carry out a teacher-mentor program with a goal of filling the province with qualified teachers in those three years. This is the same cost to pave three kilometers of road anywhere in Afghanistan. The point is that nothing will put an end to an insurgency with a losing ideology over the longer term like a broad education and a commitment to literacy that moves beyond tribal norms.

The fifth point is that any unit or agency that is functioning on the ground in Afghanistan must actively and in a concerted way demonstrate a respect for Islam.[25] The repercussions of disrespecting Islam are now widely understood by counterinsurgents; the Koran desecration in Guantanamo Bay and other examples of the ill-advised actions of a few inciting worldwide violence have made this clear. When a military force turns the tables and presses to demonstrate clearly how much they respect Islam, the effect is powerful. Microstrategies like targeting the support of communities and their mosques' "clergy" in a given district with things like mosque refurbishment kits and solar-powered speaker systems (for calls to prayer) create goodwill. This effect cannot be measured but is a powerful weapon in a counterinsurgency fight. These types of nuanced strategies take a powerful arrow from the quiver of the Taliban. There is compelling evidence from former low-level Taliban who have seen some of these strategies in action and then asked themselves why they were fighting since, in their words, there was no real enemy; the motivation of many such Taliban to carry out attacks on coalition forces comes from the mistaken belief that US soldiers do not respect the Islamic faith. This approach has been called "Operation Embrace Islam." In some corners of eastern Afghanistan, Operation Embrace Islam has become one of the primary ongoing operations. It is run by senior sergeants, which gives it credibility down to soldier level.

The final tactical imperative is to stop corruption at the district and provincial level. It is a commonly held view that some level of corruption must be accepted in a country such as Afghanistan. This is a dangerous belief that puts the entire counterinsurgency mission in a vulnerable position, since with corruption in Afghanistan there is so often a direct connection with aiding and abetting insurgent activity. If one agrees that corruption directly or indirectly aids an insurgency, then the facts on the ground in Afghanistan are alarming. In watchdog Transparency International's *2007 Corruption Perceptions Index*, Afghanistan ranked number 172 of 178 nations in the world.[26] This has not escaped the eyes of the country's leader, who sees the disastrous potential at both the local and national levels. President Karzai made pointed comments in this regard on 13 November 2007 in Kabul:

> All politicians in this system have acquired everything—money, lots of money. God knows, it is beyond the limit. The banks of the world are full of the money of our statesmen. The luxurious houses [built in Afghanistan in the past five years] belong to members of the government and parliament, not only in Kabul, but here and there. Every one of them has three or four houses in different countries. With the support of the world community—money, aircraft, and their soldiers—and with the full sympathy of the Afghan people, the Afghan politicians were able to return to their country. Unfortunately, I see now that they did not learn the lessons of the past. They should know that the Afghan people will rise against us [if corruption continues]. And this time, there will be no place [abroad] for us to flee.[27]

The slippery slope theory applies in this case and on a lethal scale at the local level. If one district police chief accepts a small bribe to allow a group of insurgents to transit a route in his jurisdiction this sets the conditions for future support. A zero tolerance policy for corruption is the only method that effectively prevents the insurgency from courting the *de facto* protection from Afghan officials. US maneuver forces are now assigned law enforcement professionals with the expertise to build case files against corrupt officials and develop indictments that follow the strictures of the Afghan penal code. When these cases are developed and presented to national leadership, it sends a powerful message to officials at all levels: "you will be held accountable." This effort cannot be carried out separate from a maneuver task force's other counterinsurgency priorities, it must be a primary tenet of any local counterinsurgency strategy.

Courting Operational Advantage Through Two Microstrategies

Two other stand-alone microstrategies have similarly powerful potential to more effectively address the historically tenuous situation along the eastern border with Pakistan. Systematic and dedicated efforts must be undertaken to: first, set the conditions for cross-border *shuras* among the tribes on both sides of the Durand line; and second, construct a network of combat outposts on the dominant terrain near the border in order to block infiltration of insurgents from Pakistan.

The first microstrategy is setting the conditions for tribes on both sides of the border to conduct regular cross-border *shuras* and facilitate security. Currently, the security of the Afghan-Pak border in eastern Afghanistan is left to soldiers of the three dedicated armies of Pakistan, Afghanistan, and the United States. When there are attacks in Afghanistan on US and Afghan forces, it is the Pakistan military that is scrutinized for not doing enough to prevent the movement of insurgents into Afghanistan. When US forces pursue fleeing insurgents into Pakistan with indirect fire, tensions between the US and Pakistan military usually, and understandably, increase. This is often followed by an emergency "border flag meeting" to defuse the situation.[28] The willingness to work hard to improve the tactical situation on the part of army representatives from all three countries is most always sincere, and the initiatives that are proposed and implemented are often innovative and effective. However, the militaries are not the most important players in bringing about a more secure border region and in denying safe haven to the Taliban and foreign fighters. Instead, it is the tribes that live on both sides of the border and who do not recognize the Durand Line as dividing their tribal homelands. In fact, it is not uncommon for Afghans living just inside the border to have their watches set on Pakistan time and Pakistanis living in the Federally Administered Tribal Area (FATA) to be on Afghan time. This is demonstrative of how cultural and familial ties define the structure of tribal life in this area. The primary authority in the eyes of people living on either side of the border is the tribal elders who still enforce *Pashtunwali* as the dominant and guiding influence in their lives.

A strategic effort of intensive engagement between the border tribes must be considered to deny the Taliban the border region. In order to effectively execute this strategy, the only role of the three armies would be to provide security to prevent the encroachment of Taliban before, during, and after the gatherings. It would be the tribal leaders on both sides who would determine how to bring about an enduring peace in these critical areas and identify what type of support is required to initiate the effort. In a land where tribal ties define the identity of populations, it is an inescapable truth that solutions to seemingly intractable problems must have a significant tribal component and, potentially, tribal lead through the process. This has not been embarked upon on a large scale, but where it has been attempted the results are heartening. The Khost province's southernmost district of Spera was one of the most significant insurgent infiltration lanes in eastern Afghanistan from 2001 to 2007. In 2008, tribal leaders took the lead in securing both sides of the border with US and Pakistan military "over watch." The economic impact of this "enforced peace" was overwhelming. In Afghan terms, the flow of traders and families back and forth from Pakistan increased from an average of ten groups a day to over two hundred. The remuneration for the traders and the goodwill developed among the tribal leaders were so great that these positive effects were the best defense against any potential for a renewed insurgent infiltration lane.[29]

The second microstrategy is establishing a network of well-fortified combat outposts in the dominant terrain just inside the Afghan border to block insurgent infiltration. Conventional wisdom associated with the war in Afghanistan suggests that the border of Afghanistan and Pakistan cannot be defended or effectively monitored. These are comments that are most commonly made by people who have not spent considerable time on the border they describe. It is absolutely correct that the terrain in a large percentage of the 2,250 kilometers that spans the Afghan-Pakistan border is mountainous and extremely difficult to traverse. Nonetheless, from a military perspective the challenge is not insurmountable. It is axiomatic within the infantry of any army that seizing the key and dominant terrain provides the force that occupies it with substantial tactical and, in the case of the border region, operational and strategic advantages. The US Army reconstructed combat outposts along the border that were poorly placed in low ground and repositioned them in dominant terrain that provided over-watch of all avenues of approach from Pakistan. These efforts required as little as one heavy engineer company building the outpost while a battalion of infantry carried out a simultaneous operation to provide the "space" to build without the distraction of sporadic insurgent attacks. The end result of careful planning and two weeks of coordinated engineer and infantry effort was an extremely defensible combat outpost on the dominant terrain. Each such outpost can effectively cover, through observation and interlocking fires, up to fifteen kilometers to its north and south. The focus of counterinsurgents can then transition to denying insurgents freedom of movement and access to supply lines, attack positions inside of Afghanistan, and the interior of the border provinces in Afghanistan. In pursuit of military objectives that have a direct connection to bringing about the defeat of the Taliban, "too hard" cannot be an acceptable assumption.[30]

Conclusions and Implications

In determining the way ahead in Afghanistan, security must be the priority before a substantial increase in the number of major development initiatives is seriously considered from nongovernmental organizations, international organizations, and donor nations. Until then the threat environment makes that scale of development impossible to safely manage. Establishing security is going to take considerable time and a significantly larger commitment of troops, treasure, and presence. Historically, it takes no less than ten years to defeat an active insurgency under the best of conditions. In Afghanistan, the United States is battling an insurgency in the most challenging terrain in the world and through a country with a foreboding history that overwhelmingly favors the insurgent. This Taliban-led insurgency is dramatically different than the insurgency in Iraq and the strategy undertaken with success in Iraq cannot be directly applied to Afghanistan. In an aphoristic sense, Kabul is not Baghdad and 'as goes' Kabul is not 'as goes' Afghanistan. It is quite the opposite. If districts in the Afghan countryside become stronger and district leadership becomes more trustworthy and dependable, only then will the faith of the people grow and their willingness to trust in their provincial and national leadership follow. The opposite trend has been developing from 2005 until now.

The young company commanders, platoon sergeants, and their Afghan counterparts must have the tools (development funds) and talent (Afghan talent) to set up the districts for longer term stability and success. Even the strongest company and battalion commanders cannot do much if they don't have strong Afghan leaders to work with closely. Two of the most significant problems in Afghanistan are the intellectual capital flight from the villages to the big cities and the dreadfully low literacy rate. Those are the things that are tamping true development and preventing real progress. Strong leadership at the local level is what will put the Afghanistan counterinsurgency mission back on the right path; so drawing the talent back from Kabul and abroad to the provinces and districts must shift from a tactical challenge to a strategic and political requirement. Nothing will change the course of the war more quickly than strong district governors, brave district police chiefs, and committed security forces living among the people, rather than in the relative comfort and security of forward operating bases. These shifts in momentum, coupled with a widespread integration of the six principles I have proposed and intensive application of the two microstrategies detailed here will set the conditions for success in this Afghan campaign. The alternative is to test the will of the American people and risk the success of the Afghan mission. The Taliban is depending on sustained casualties and continued fighting, coupled with the historical track record for conflict in Afghanistan, creating enough public pressure for the Obama administration to withdraw US forces. The operational objective of the Taliban is simply to continue their fight without interruption. Their strategic goal is to force US "wristwatches" to finally give way to insurgent patience and clear the way for a theocracy driven by *sharia* law and the Taliban's unique brand of cultural terrorism.

Michael R. Fenzel Mr. Fenzel is an active duty US Army Colonel, selected to lead a heavy brigade combat team of the US Army's 1st Armored Division. He served as an airborne battalion task force commander in Afghanistan (2007–2008) and as deputy brigade commander also in Afghanistan (2005–2006). For a year he was in Iraq as a battalion executive officer, after taking part in the initial parachute assault in 2003. Col. Fenzel served two years as Director for Transnational Threats on the National Security Council, overseeing coordination and implementation of US counterterrorism policy. He also served as a strategist for the Army Chief of Staff. Mr. Fenzel holds a BA in Economics from Johns Hopkins University and two master's degrees (focused on international security) from Harvard University and the US Naval War College. Mr. Fenzel was a Term Member with the Council on Foreign Relations, a former White House Fellow, and a founding member of the Council on Emerging National Security Affairs. Currently he is a PhD student at Naval Postgraduate School focused on national security studies.

Recommended Readings

Clayton, Anthony. *The Wars of French Decolonization: Modern Wars in Perspective*. London and New York: Longman, 1994.

Coll, Steve. *Ghost Wars: The Secret History of the CIA, Afghanistan, and Bin Laden, from the Soviet Invasion to September 10, 2001*. London: Penguin Books, 2004.

Galula, David. *Counterinsurgency Warfare: Theory and Practice*. New York: Praeger, 1964.

Haycock, Ronald, ed. *Regular Armies and Insurgency*. London: Croom Helm, 1979.

Keiser, R. Lincoln. "Friend by Day, Enemy by Night: Organized Vengeance in a Kohistani Community." *Case Studies in Cultural Anthropology*. Belmont, CA: Wadsworth/Thompson Learning, 2001.

Marston, Daniel, and Carter Malkasian. *Counterinsurgency in Modern Warfare*. Oxford: Osprey, 2008.

Phillips, Andrew. *War, Empire, and the Transformation of International Orders*. Cambridge: Cambridge University Press, forthcoming in 2010.

Rashid, Ahmed. *Taliban: Militant Islam, Oil and Fundamentalism in Central Asia*. New Haven, CT: Yale University Press, 2001.

Roy, Olivier. *Islam and Resistance in Afghanistan*. Cambridge: Cambridge University Press, 1990.

Synnott, Hilary. *Transforming Pakistan*. London: International Institute for Strategic Studies, 2009.

US Army, US Marine Corps. *FM 3-24, Counterinsurgency*. Washington, DC: Army Headquarters; Marine Corps Headquarters, December 2006. See especially Sarah Sewall's "Introduction" to the 2007 edition by University of Chicago Press.

Valeriano, Napoleon D., and Charles T. R. Bohannan. *Counter-Guerrilla Operations: The Philippines Experience*. New York: Praeger, 1966.

Notes

1. Jason H. Campbell and Jeremy Shapiro, *Afghanistan Index: Tracking Variables of Reconstruction & Security in Post-9/11 Afghanistan* (Washington, DC: Brookings Institution, 28 April 2009), page 11, available at http://www.brookings.edu/foreign-policy/~/media/Files/Programs/FP/afghanistan%20index/index20090428.pdf, accessed 25 May 2009. Contributing nations include: Albania, Australia, Austria, Azerbaijan, Belgium, Bosnia-Herzegovina, Bulgaria, Canada, Croatia, Czech Republic, Denmark, Estonia, Finland, France, Georgia, Germany, Greece, Hungary, Iceland, Ireland, Italy, Jordan, Latvia, Lithuania, Luxemburg, Netherlands, New Zealand, Norway, Poland, Portugal, Romania, Singapore, Slovakia, Slovenia, Spain, Sweden, the former Yugoslav Republic of Macedonia, Turkey, Ukraine, United Arab Emirates, United Kingdom, and the United States.

2. Thomas H. Johnson and M. Chris Mason, "Understanding the Taliban and Insurgency in Afghanistan," *Orbis*, Vol. 51, Issue 1 (Winter 2007): 87.

3. "Conflict threatens access to children by humanitarian organizations in Afghanistan," UNICEF Afghanistan website, 8 July 2008, available at http://www.unicef.org/infobycountry/afghanistan_44707.html, accessed 15 April 2009.

4. AIHRC spokesman Nader Nadery, as quoted in Golnaz Esfandiari, "Afghanistan: Militants Are Targeting Schools," Radio Free Europe/ Radio Liberty, 22 February 2006, available at http://www.rferl.org/content/article/1066060.html, accessed 14 May 2009.

5. "Twenty counterinsurgents per 1,000 residents is often considered the minimum troop density required for effective COIN operations; however as with any fixed ratio, such calculations remain very different dependent upon the situation." *The U.S. Army/Marine Corps Counterinsurgency Field Manual* (Chicago: University of Chicago Press, 2007), 23. The ratio of soldiers to civilians in Afghanistan in 2009 was one soldier for every 1,650 civilians, unacceptable by any measure.

6. Napolean Valeriano and Charles T. R. Bohannan, *Counter-Guerrilla Operations: The Philippine Experience* [1962], (Westport: Praeger Security International, 2006). Valeriano and Bohannan present the experiences and conclusions drawn from the experiences of both the insurgents and the counterinsurgents in the Philippines. Although they do not set out either to address the history of the insurgent fighting in the Philippines or to establish doctrine on how to fight guerrilla wars, they do well on both counts nonetheless. The book demonstrates a comprehensive treatment of guerrilla warfare as the authors provide some insight that has universal impact in describing the dynamics of guerrilla operations, the imperatives associated with understanding the capabilities of the force you pit against them (before initiating operations). They then provide a pithy review of the pillars of any counterinsurgency effort: a clearly understood mission, cultivating the support of the people, understanding the cultural underpinnings of the country, and seizing advantage as it presents itself.

7. The thrust of my argument is that since the population is central to the success of counterinsurgent forces in Afghanistan, it is the appropriate ratio of counterinsurgent forces to the population that is critical to correctly identify. My overarching point is that the population must be protected from insurgent forces, and this cannot be achieved without an appropriate number of counterinsurgent forces on the ground to address the dispersion of rural populations. This is a marked departure from traditional counterinsurgency theory, which has long been associated with a "ten-to-one" rule, suggesting government forces require that advantage over insurgents

in order to prevail. Noted counterinsurgent author and expert Sir Robert Thompson calls such a math formula "nonsense," instead suggesting that it is the appropriate application of the forces available that makes the difference rather than a universally applied ratio. Thompson writes in his book *Defeating Communist Insurgency: The Lessons of Malaya and Vietnam*, first published in 1966, "It is a persistently methodical approach and steady pressure which will gradually wear the insurgent down. The government must not allow itself to be diverted either by countermoves on the part of the insurgent or by the critics on its own side who will be seeking a simpler and quicker solution. There are no short-cuts and no gimmicks."

8. Thomas H. Johnson and M. Chris Mason, "All Counterinsurgency Is Local," *The Atlantic Monthly*, October 2008, 16–17, available at http://www.theatlantic.com/doc/200810/afghan, accessed 2 October 2009.

9. David Galula, *Counterinsurgency Warfare: Theory and Practice* (London: Praeger Security International, 1964), 7–8.

10. Johnson and Mason, "All Counterinsurgency Is Local," 17.

11. The historical antecedent to David Kilcullen's 28 Articles was the 1917 publication by T. E. Lawrence of his own 27 Articles defining his view on the cultural imperatives for advising Bedouin and Arab forces. The 27 Articles were published on 20 August 1917 in *The Arab Bulletin* and are available at http://www.d-n-i.net/fcs/lawrence_27_articles.htm, accessed 2 October 2009.

12. David Kilcullen, "28 Articles: Fundamentals of Company-Level Counterinsurgency," Edition 1, March 2006, page 11, available at http://turcopolier.typepad.com/sic_semper_tyrannis/files/twentyeight_articles_edition_1.pdf, accessed 18 April 2009.

13. *The U.S. Army/Marine Corps Counterinsurgency Field Manual*, supra, note 2, at Appendix E, paragraph E-5.

14. Task Force Eagle [1st Battalion (Airborne), 503d Infantry Regiment] served in Paktika Province from 9 May 2007 through 23 July 2008. The Task Force was commanded by the author.

15. Lara M. Dadkhah, "Close Air Support and Civilian Casualties in Afghanistan," *Small Wars Journal* (30 December 2008): 5, available at http://smallwarsjournal.com/mag/docs-temp/160-dadkhah.pdf, accessed 18 April, 2009.

16. David H. Petraeus, "Learning Counterinsurgency: Observations from Soldiering in Iraq," *Military Review*, January/February 2006, 5–6, available at http://www.army.mil/professionalwriting/volumes/volume4/april_2006/4_06_2.html, accessed 2 October 2009.

17. *Solatia* is money paid to an Afghan family as reparation for either damaged property, wounding of a family member, or accidental death of a relative as a result of coalition actions.

18. Bernt Glatzer, "The Pashtun Tribal System," Ch. 10 in Georg Pfeffer and Deepak Kumar Behera, eds., *Contemporary Society: Tribal Studies: Volume 5: The Concept of Tribal Society* (New Dehli: Concept Publishing Company, 2002), 265–282.

19. See, for example, "Afghanistan," *CIA World Factbook*, updated 24 September 2009, available at https://www.cia.gov/library/publications/the-world-factbook/geos/af.html#, accessed 3 October 2009. This source places the Afghan literacy rate at 28.1 percent.

20. Eight of thirty-four provinces in Afghanistan have an official rural literacy rate of below 5 percent, while twenty-four provinces maintain a rate at 25 percent or below. Available at http://www.mrrd.gov.af/AIRD/Literacy%20rate%20and%20primary%20education%20.pdf, accessed 15 October 2009.

21. In Afghanistan there are 396 official districts within the country's thirty-four provinces. Twenty-four of these provinces may be considered predominantly rural. For families living in these most remote areas, access to education is often not available at all. There are currently twelve thousand elementary, middle, and high schools in Afghanistan, and 50 percent have no permanent structure, with classes being held under tents or trees. In many of the country's smaller villages, access to a school, even a school with no permanent structure, is unavailable. McCanna, Shaun, "Afghanistan: Remote Communities Lack Schools," The Pulitzer Center on Crisis Reporting, 29 June, 2009, available at http://pulitzercenter.typepad.com/untold_stories/2009/06/afghanistan-remote-communities-lack-schools.html, accessed 15 October, 2009.

22. Bernt Glatzer, "Being Pashtun-Being Muslim: Concepts of Person and War in Afghanistan," in Glatzer, ed., *Essays on South Asian Society: Culture and Politics II* (Berlin, Das Arabische Buch, 1998), 7, available at http://www.khyber.org/publications/021-025/glatzer1998.pdf, accessed 2 October 2009.

23. Additional material on Pashtun tribal dynamics from Bernt Glatzer can be found in his 2001 work, "War and Boundaries in Afghanistan: Significance and Relativity of Local and Social Boundaries," *Weld des Islams*, Vol. 41, No. 3 (2001), 379–399, available at http://www.ag-afghanistan.de/files/war-a-bound.pdf, accessed 17 February 2009.

24. "Programs and Activities: Paktika Teacher Training and Leadership Program," University of Nebraska Center for Afghanistan Studies, available at http://world.unomaha.edu/cas/?menu=initiatives_=paktika, accessed 3 October 2009.

25. The definitive work on the role Islam plays in conflict and discontent in modern Afghanistan is by Olivier Roy, *Islam and Resistance in Afghanistan*, 2nd ed. (New York: Cambridge University Press, 1990).

26. Ron Synovitz, "Afghanistan: Karzai's Corruption Comments Could Lead to Cabinet Shakeup," Radio Free Europe/Radio Liberty, 16 November 2007, available at http://www.rferl.org/content/Article/1079143.html, accessed 2 October 2009. In this article, the author details that Afghanistan was designated a corruption index score of 1.8. The index scores range from 0 (highly corrupt) to 10 (highly clean).

27. Hamid Karzai, Conference on Rural Development, Kabul, Afghanistan, 13 November, 2007, details available at http://www.rawa.org/temp/runews/2007/11/15/karzai-criticizes-high-officials-deputies-for-corruption.html, accessed on 15 October, 2009.

28. "Border Flag Meetings" are the common military jargon for meetings of the Afghan, US, and Pakistan military to discuss border issues and initiatives. They occur alternatively in Pakistan and Afghanistan, and the purpose is to maintain a close relationship with one another in the midst of the ongoing war with the Taliban and other miscreants.

29. Author's personal experience in commanding Task Force Eagle (1-503d Airborne) in Eastern Paktika and the Southern Spera district of Khost province. A Company, 1-503d commanded by then US Army Captain Christopher Hammonds and subsequently by Captain Jason Wayne directed efforts locally from the Spera Combat Outpost within one kilometer of the Pakistan border. The author conducted three separate "border flag meetings" with Pakistan military officials to pave the way for freedom of movement and trade to continue.

30. Kent Harris, "Laying the Foundation," *Stars and Stripes*, 18 September 2008, available at http://www.stripes.com/article.asp?section=140&article=57614, accessed 23 March 2009.

Tom Wilhelm

Security Architecture:

A Case Study of Pakistan's Tribal Belt

In the Afghanistan and Pakistan theater, the part of that conflict associated with the cross-border militancy of Pashtun tribesmen underscores the complexity and criticality of understanding the local security conditions as they relate to operations for countering terrorism, insurgency, and other forms of armed conflict.[1] Operationally, there has been a lack of consistent, mutually acceptable, and synchronized military actions, and the conflict has intensified inside the Pushtun regions. Since 2001, most of the security focus has been on Paksitan's national government and the federal army with little attention paid to the indigenous nature of security in the tribal areas and those local Pakistani security entities that operate there. The result is that deployed soldiers, their leaders, policy-makers, and public back home are largely unaware of the broader array of actors and conditions related to counterinsurgency and counterterrorism.

Although enemy combatants in the Afghanistan and Pakistan theater do not emanate exclusively from Pakistan and the Pashtun tribes, this case study focuses on the identification of three critical factors in Pakistan's Pashtun tribal region. These factors are identification of: the broader range of potential counterinsurgents, the main cultural conditions and perspectives that apply to the local security environment, and the operational capabilities and limitations of the security actors. These factors as they apply to this particular region can be referred to as the security architecture.

In any place where non-indigenous, national, and other local armed forces operate in the same battle space, with indigenous forces, a comprehensive understanding of the security architecture is fundamental. Security architecture provides the schematic for enhancing counterterrorism and counterinsurgency cooperation as well as defining the obstacles and limitations to achieving military objectives. The process of identifying security architecture is an indispensible first step in developing and executing operations.

Security architecture is complex. There is not a ready-made handbook or checklist that adequately outlines the innumerable historical and cultural calculations that define a particular battle space and pertinent organizations, leaders, and conventions often do not exist or function as advertised. Identifying and working through the layers of security architecture makes rapid military decision making difficult. There is a tendency, therefore, to ignore security architecture or oversimplify its elements. Nevertheless, the local population is the center of gravity for counterterrorism and counterinsurgent efforts, and understanding partner structures and capacities in the local environment is a critical task. This chapter is not an operational analysis of conflict in the Afghanistan-Pakistan theater and it is not a policy recommendation paper. Instead, this is a study to demonstrate that, despite the complexities of the security architecture, a discernible and comprehensible structure can be sketched out. This understanding is a starting point for a more collaborative and coordinated approach to conflict in this area. It argues that such "architectural" work is a fundamental task in any combined counterinsurgency and counterterrorism planning.

Two Views

From the viewpoint of a western commander in Afghanistan, under a rocket attack or in an exchange of gunfire with an enemy from the borderland hills, and from the view of a broader worldwide audience, operations at the Afghanistan-Pakistan border are boiled down to a simple modality: Militants come across the border, attack, and slip back to sanctuary.[2] To the coalition commander on the Afghanistan side of the border, the force inside Pakistan should be an armed partner with common counterinsurgency missions, including pursuing terrorists and preventing other militant incursions at the border. For this commander, the enemy may come from differently motivated groups, but in the end it is simply any individual who acts out with violence against the commander's soldiers and his security objectives. From the perspective of military necessity, the coalition commander understands the security architecture at the border to be the Pakistani military anvil to the coalition hammer. Frustration occurs as both sides are reduced to inadequately coordinated counter-ambush operations. In order to broaden the scope of military options and enhance effectiveness in fighting, forces violate the border in "hot pursuit," either by actions on the ground or with air attacks by artillery and remotely operated weapons such as armed Predators. Success, then, is measured by numbers of terrorists, insurgents, militants, and their leadership killed.

From the perspective of the Pakistani commander in tribal regions of Pakistan, the local security architecture is nondoctrinal and more nuanced; this architecture is the dominant operational factor. To him, there are more indigenous layers of understanding and definitions of the threats and conflict modalities, and a greater scope of limitations when applying force in the Pakistani tribal belt. There are also a variety of forces arrayed on this important ground, and most do not have the capacity or structure that is expected by the coalition forces stationed often only a few kilometers away. Pakistan forces on this battlefield are not merely underequipped; they are not oriented on the same missions. Here, security is not expressed as much in the technical character of an alliance as it is in terms of a special, internal social system. The enemy identified by the coalition in Afghanistan is nonspecific—"Taliban," "terrorist," "insurgent," "anti-coalition militant," and even as the vague "enemies of peace and security"—while the Pakistanis view the militants as "foreign fighters, Afghan-based Taliban, and local criminals and miscreants."[3] While the results of Pakistani military calculations include winning and losing engagements, success is defined as influencing traditional tribal-based practices and loyalties. Whereas American forces seek to neutralize or eliminate a broadly conceived enemy, Pakistani forces see their actions as interceding with their own population, a population in which many of its members consider the Pakistani forces themselves to be foreign.[4] Only through examination of the local security architecture does an understanding of counterterrorism and counterinsurgency take shape in Pakistan's borderlands.

As a case model, the tribal belt associated with Pakistan's Federally Administered Tribal Areas (FATA) and Northwest Frontier Province (NWFP) presents the three main aspects of security architecture in a compelling manner. These key variables are the local geo-social conditions that form the security environment, unique historical legacies that characterize the applicability of security conventions and practices among the population, and the organizations and operational capacities of existing security forces.

A "Baffling" Battlefield

Pakistan consists of four provinces—Baluchistan, the NWFP, Punjab, and Sind—and other special regions or territories, including what are labeled in Pakistan's constitution as "tribal areas." The NWFP provisionally incorporates districts, subdistricts, and the Provisionally Administered Tribal Areas (PATA) in Amb, Buner, Chitral, Dir, Hala Dhaka, Shangla, Swat, Khoistan, Malakand, and the FATA. However, the FATA also retains a semiautonomous status in the country[5] with such features as tax exemption and separate representation in the national parliament. There is little federal presence in this region, which shares three hundred miles of border with Afghanistan.

The FATA is composed of seven titular agencies and six frontier regions (FR). FATA agencies include Bajaur Agency, Khyber Agency, Kurram Agency, Mohmand Agency, Orakzai Agency, South Waziristan Agency, and North Waziristan Agency: Its Frontier Regions include FR Peshawar, FR Kohat, FR Tank, FR Bannu, FR Lakki, and FR Dera Ismail Khan. The relationship between the FATA's agencies and frontier regions and the NWFP's districts and tribal areas is important. The administrative divisions may be viewed as transition zones between what is considered "tribal" and "settled" in Pakistan. Compared to the tribal-ruled agencies, for instance, the FRs and PATA have separate administration through the NWFP, which links them more closely with the federal government. These areas enjoy greater social and infrastructure benefits, such as roads, clinics, and schools. They have more normalized institutions for law and order associated with the fully settled districts of NWFP, and there is a greater expectation of federally provided security among the local inhabitants. The terrorist and insurgent attacks in the FRs, PATA, and subdistricts of NWFP signal something different than the militancy in the agencies as conflict in these areas directly challenges the writ of state. In these areas, the Pakistani military response is executed more urgently.

While the geographic and administrative descriptions of tribal areas account for some of its daunting reputation, it is the nature of the majority Pashtun tribes who live there that gives the security picture both its ferocity and complexity. For the Pashtuns, the consanguine relations with other tribesmen define their territory; the international border between Afghanistan and Pakistan does not. To them, all others but themselves are outsiders. Although there is much written about them and as a people they have been studied for centuries, exact demographic and other information sought by outsiders remains difficult to determine and is often conflicting. The indigenous tribesmen are the battlefield's most significant but enigmatic factor;[6] they function as a separate party to the conflict.

The last attempt at a census of the independent tribes and subclans of the FATA was conducted in 1998. However, figures for the population of the FATA are often distorted by the large numbers of refugee influxes from Afghanistan's decades of war and the intermarriages and births that followed. The estimates are given in a broad span from approximately 2.5 to 5 million, with the most standard figure of 3.2 million for the FATA.[7] The differential in calculating the flow of these people to Pakistan causes experts to conclude that the

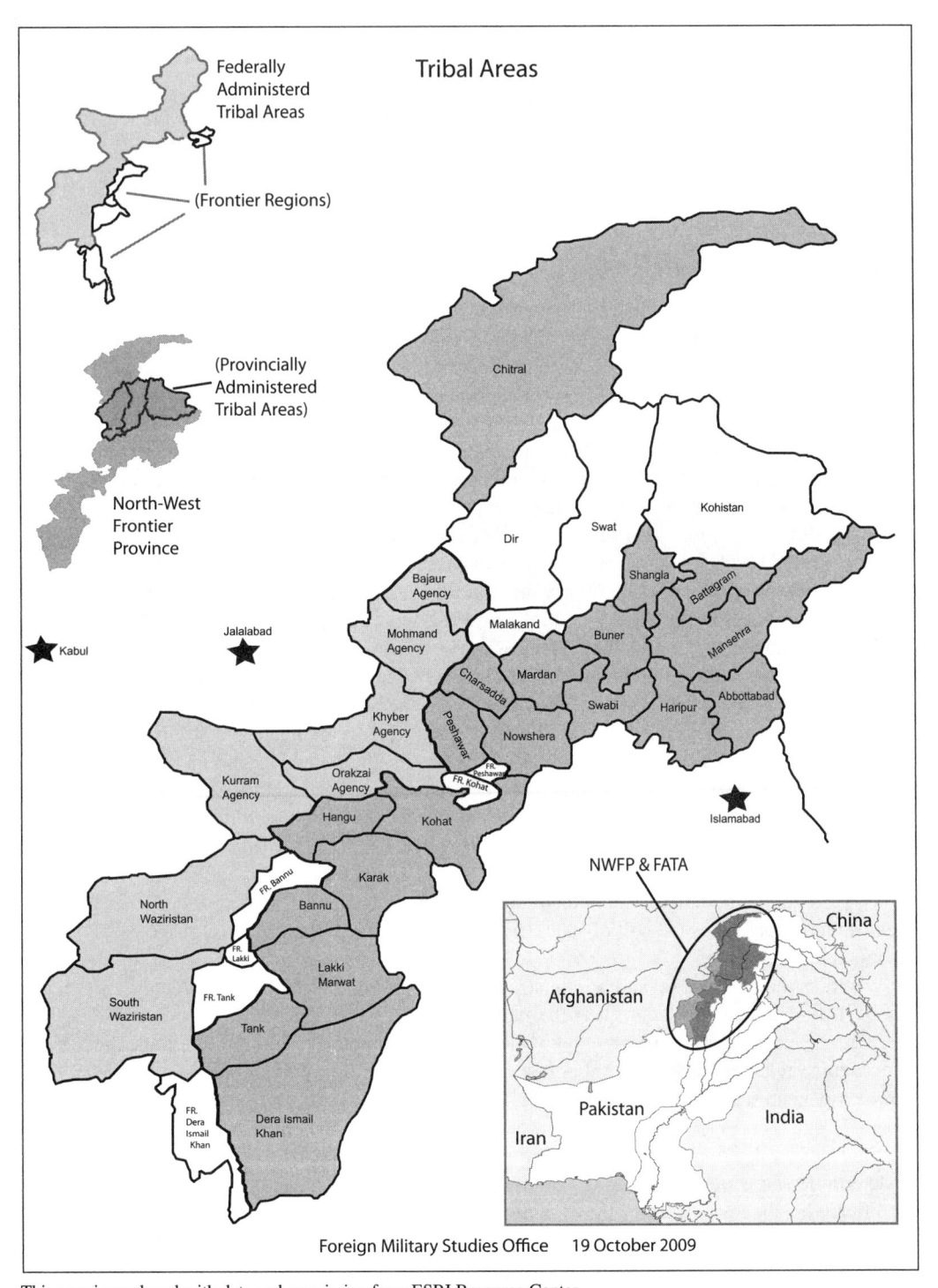

Tribal Areas

Federally Administerd Tribal Areas

(Frontier Regions)

(Provincially Administered Tribal Areas)

North-West Frontier Province

Chitral

Kohistan

Dir

Swat

Shangla

Battagram

Bajaur Agency

Buner

Mansehra

Malakand

Mohmand Agency

Mardan

Charsadda

Swabi

Haripur

Abbottabad

Khyber Agency

Peshawar

Nowshera

Kurram Agency

Orakzai Agency

FR. Peshawar

FR. Kohat

Hangu

Kohat

Islamabad

Karak

FR. Bannu

North Waziristan

Bannu

FR. Lakki

Lakki Marwat

FR. Tank

South Waziristan

Tank

FR. Dera Ismail Khan

Dera Ismail Khan

Kabul

Jalalabad

NWFP & FATA

Afghanistan

China

Pakistan

Iran

India

Foreign Military Studies Office   19 October 2009

This map is produced with data and permission from ESRI Resource Center.
ESRI, 06. 2008. Web. 19 October 2009 <http://resources.esri.com/arcgisonlineservices/> and Hijmans, Robert Free Spatial Data. DIVA-GIS, 02 04. 2009. Web. 19 October 2009 <http://www.diva-gis.org/>

Afghan refugees are not all refugees, not always in Pakistan, and not even necessarily Afghan.[8] In an area highly charged by armed conflict, the numbers and status of trans-frontier populations do matter. Language is another aspect that leads to difficulty in the identification of security actors and actions as well as general insularity of the inhabitants. In the tribal areas, there are dozens of dialects that are not mutually understood and issues of alternative self-identification among the Pashtuns themselves.[9] The role of security actors and the related lexicons varies across the region and invites arguments from observers and inhabitants alike, who often confuse and dismiss basic understandings. The term "Pashtun" itself has several other accepted variations or references—for example, Pakhtun, Pukhtun, Pathan, and, most confusingly, Afghan. Many of the Pashtuns of the FATA believe they have inhabited the region for thousands of years, but there is evidence that their habitation of the current homelands only dates back a thousand years, and the introduction of their language was only five hundred years ago.[10] This would account for the differentiation of historic narratives that bear on a variety of tribal security practices.[11] In security matters, for instance, a tribal militia infers different capacities when it is an *arbakai* in Afghanistan or a *lashkar* in Pakistan.[12] Communications about security issues and events, including among Pashtuns themselves, are subject to misunderstanding from the start.

With the exception of the Toori tribe in the Kurram Agency, the Pashtuns of Pakistan's tribal belt are overwhelmingly Sunni Muslims of the Hanafi school of Islamic jurisprudence, and they make up about 10 percent of the total estimated twenty-eight million Pashtuns in South Asia.[13] However, as an ethnic population spanning the national borders of Afghanistan and Pakistan, they represent more than 90 percent of the population of that particular area of conflict.[14] Equally important is the understanding that the Pashtuns count among the world's largest ethnic communities without an associated nation-state.[15] This sort of arithmetic might lead some to conclude that there is a "Pashtunistan" waiting to be brought into existence through insurgency. The militancy of the Pashtuns, however, is unlikely to be associated with the goal of secession and establishing a unified nation-state. If demographics help at all, it simply demonstrates that the Pashtuns of the FATA and NWFP dominate that area to a point of exclusivity, including from those groups that comprise ruling ethnicities in the national government and the army,[16] namely Punjabis and Muhajirs. This condition can account for local tribal perceptions of the national military force as a "foreign" or "occupation" force and why it is harder to apply national conformity and integration to military affairs, including counterinsurgency and counterterrorism policies and operations.[17]

Socialized in each tribal agency in the FATA are the twelve main tribal groups of approximately 350 clans, tribes, or *khels*.[18] A tiny 3 percent of the population is described as living in urban areas in the FATA, and there are relatively few kilometers of roads, paved or otherwise.[19] As a result, the homes and villages remain cut off in the mountainous areas, both from the settled areas and from themselves. The people of the FATA do not have the design or the social response of a modern, integrated society. Mass communications and social projects are difficult for both government and insurgent elements to implement. The many factions of the population also indicate natural fissures among the Pashtuns—indeed, in the historical context of conflict, the Pashtuns fight first and most often among themselves at the family and intertribal level.[20]

Overwhelmingly, the tribesmen of the FATA live in underdeveloped socioeconomic conditions. Only about 18 percent of the population is literate, and this includes

3 percent of all the FATA's females.[21] In the FATA, there is one doctor for approximately eight thousand people, and only 43 percent have access to clean water. Per capita public development expenditure—a measurement most certainly obfuscated by corruption—is at one-third of the national average.[22] The Pakistani government reports that 60 percent of the people in the FATA live below the poverty line[23] and further declares that there "are few livelihood opportunities. . . . Most households are engaged in primary-level activities such as subsistence agriculture and livestock rearing, or small-scale business conducted locally."[24] As for the character of the tribesmen in the security architecture, their general lack of education accounts in part for their religious conservatism[25] and, whereas their economic conditions have led some to describe a predisposition for "Talibanization,"[26] others point out that economic and religious-driven factors are much less connected.[27] Tribesmen are also a hardened human resource when it comes to security matters. They are accustomed to deprivation and the exceptional conditions of the area. Their ubiquitous weaponry is considered an indispensible status symbol, with more sophisticated arms endowing the owner with enhanced prestige.[28] They have been described as a "martial race" and a "powerful glue of tradition" that Pakistan attempts to capitalize for its military manpower.[29] All told, the physical remoteness, challenges of social conditions, and exclusionary geo-kinships in the region result in the Pashtuns considering their land to be *purdah*, or as a veiled woman, to be honored and defended with their lives.[30] This notion excludes the nuances of the internal administrative divisions or even the national boundaries. It signals an important motivation among an armed local population that is distinct and apart from a concept of national defense, and critical to affecting that human, counterinsurgent center of gravity.

Unique Security Legacies: Tribal Customs and Codes

In the FATA, there are no government police, courts, or taxation, and no weapon is illegal. Federal or provisional laws do not apply; the national manifest is exercised only by the Frontier Crimes Regulation (FCR) of 1901 and specific edict from the president and through the interaction of the state bureaucracy with tribal counterparts—essentially, by treaties with the tribes. For these reasons, the FATA has been described as indirectly ruled and "ungoverned" when considering access to arms, activity of organized armed groups, lack of border controls, and social and cultural resistance to change in these areas, including accepting the presence of other armed extremist groups and individuals.[31] Officially, the government of Pakistan recognizes this exceptional security environment when it delineates the areas in the region as either "protected areas" where the federal writ applies or "nonprotected areas" where rule through the tribes is the principal means of governance.[32] All of this, however, could lead to an inaccurate assessment that there is a security vacuum or no security architecture at all. Indeed, the opposite is true. Regarding governance in security affairs, there are two main features of the security architecture: tribal codes and customs and a draconian, colonial period system of law and order that is still in effect. The first feature is the customary practices related to the preeminent role of personal honor and conduct in society and the venues for arbitration and collective decision making in security affairs. These tribal practices are inherent in everything from settling local civil complaints to mobilizing militias and launching attacks.

Among the tribal customs, or *rewaj*, of the Pashtuns in Pakistan's tribal region and across the border in Afghanistan is a diversely practiced honor code called *pashtunwali*. Inherent in this practice are the most fundamental and indomitable aspects of the security architecture. Numerous historians, cultural anthropologists, and writers of all genres have provided explanations that describe this system of values. However, because this "un-codified set of rules" varies among the tribes and regions[33] and even among the individuals in the tribes and regions,[34] it is difficult to comprehend its relation to the security architecture and understand it in terms of broader military affairs. Nevertheless, "the Pathan is above all an individualist, despite the rigid behavior standards prescribed by clan membership,"[35] and the central feature of this honor system is the individual's personal honor, called *nang* or *izzat*.[36] Importantly, *pashtunwali* literally means "to do Pashtu" and is not considered passive in the way that those who live in civil societies with developed institutions of law and law enforcement might comprehend. The three required actions of *pashtunwali* that are most often described are *nawawati* (an obligation to provide sanctuary, the establishment of supplication, and the opportunity for forgiveness), *milmastya* (general hospitality and hospitality to the point of providing protection to any and all that are considered guests), and *badal* (obligatory vengeance).[37] This sort of active code of behavior accounts for many violent acts and militancy that take place in the frontier region and across the border, and includes events that occur internal to established paramilitary forces in the region. Pakistan security forces and other counterinsurgent actors must constantly gauge the undertow of *pashtunwali* within their ranks and make plans based on this. National counterinsurgency objectives must include a strategy for challenging or influencing the tribal code, but not ignoring it. In the FATA, there have been numerous incidents of both federal and militant religious competitions for enhanced position and dominance over this tribal code.[38] However, the people of the tribal belt remain disposed geo-spatially to be independent, self-reliant, and dominant.[39] This makes it difficult to instill conformity in standing up a force among the population and even the establishment of military leadership or hierarchical security decision making. Military actions must account for the individual Pashtun's need to satisfy his own requirements of honor. It provides an important fissure between the population and all others, including insurgents and counterinsurgents alike.

Because "*pashtunwali* is essentially self-enforcing,"[40] the foundation of the security architecture in the FATA is the processes whereby all adult males have an opportunity to deliberate and arbitrate their issues. There are numerous ways and corresponding interpretations of how such councils are conducted. The *hujra*, for instance, functions as a sort of central community forum for discussing local events, passing information, and resolving disputes. Food and tea are often served at *hujra* along with entertainment. It is as much a social gathering as a business venue. Also, the physical location can be used as a communal guesthouse. In the event that a decision cannot be resolved in the *hujra*, or for other reasons, a more specially focused *jirga* can be assembled. This counsel type functions simultaneously as the security advisory board, the leadership council, the judiciary, and the law enforcement institution. A *jirga* can be held at local, tribal, and federal engagement levels[41] and the process of discussion (in some lexicons called *salah-mashwarah*[42] or literally "advice giving and getting") varies among the *khels*. Given the preeminent status and active nature of the individual's participation in society, the fundamental source of conflict resolution and security application—from policing to war-fighting—comes from this local pageant of individual behavior in relation to the consensus of the group in these forums.

In the tribal lands, council resolution will often take the form of fines in livestock, property, or money, or even women. Response can also be the mobilizing and deployment of a local militia. The goal of the council resolution is not to emphasize individual punishment or an ultimate determination of guilt and innocence, rather collective justice to underscore the honor code and solidarity (elimination of discord) within the society. It is also an expression of independence from external authority and direction.[43] Gaining counterinsurgent support by reinforcing national identities is outside tribal conflict resolution. Decision making at this tribal level is not naturally aligned with expedient, linear, military-type decision processes. This does not mean that there is no efficiency to the process. Indeed, assembled *jirgas* of some tribes settle the vast majority of tribal issues,[44] and formidable tribal militias can be raised instantaneously to enforce these decisions.

Other key forms of councils in the tribal areas are the religious council, or *shura*, and the *sharia* court. Through these, the practitioners of Islamic law can also rule on and resolve disputes and impose penalties at the tribal level. Levying of fines is the most common method of resolution, even for major matters. *Jirga* and *hujra* decisions are sometimes expressly based on *sharia*.[45] *Sharia* courts can and do issue death sentences, whereas *jirgas* never do.[46] As with the formation of militias by assent of the tribal *jirga*, the *shura* process can declare *jihad* and raise forces, or *mujahedin*. It can also sanction the tribe's militia. While these tribal and religious systems can both support one another and be in competition with each other, there is no particular default that defines the dynamics of this relationship. Historically, when these systems are competitive, there may be strategic and even global security implications. Numerous political-religious uprisings, featuring tribesmen whom the British referred to as "Hindustani fanatics," started as early in 1858 in the areas where there are similar problems today. In 1897, a *jihad* in the Malakand region provoked pan-frontier conflict and a corresponding British strategic response. As World War I broke out, Islamic militant leadership in greater India conspired to get the Pashtun tribesmen to abandon their individualism for a pan-Islamic, second front against the British—a prequel to the 1980s US-Saudi-Pakistan manipulation of religious militancy on the Soviet-Afghan front. In 1936, Mirza Ali Khan, known as the Fakir of Ipi, instigated a war against the British that resonated until the establishment of Pakistan.[47]

By the end of 1979, General Zia ul-Haq promoted "the ascendancy of the Jihadi phenomenon,"[48] and the Hindustani fanatics of old became the *mujahedin* and Taliban of contemporary conflicts. These events, as occasionally as they may happen, describe a pattern of militant imposition of religious leadership and practice that co-opts local customs, followed by some level of confederacy or capitulation by the tribesmen, and then reactionary efforts to reinstitute customary practices.[49] British of the past described outside intervention in this pattern as the "primary role of keeping the peace, from a neutral stand-point, whenever inter-religious strife flared up."[50] Contemporary conflict in Pakistan's tribal areas is not a new phenomenon, and the security architecture shifts with the deleterious effects that it has demonstrated in the past. As evident from various proposals at different times to revise the FCR and to negotiate specific security accords in some instances, the Pakistan government recognizes that there is operational and strategic risk if it does not engage in tribal processes. In fact, military operations without discussion with tribal councils lead to charges of "undeclared war"[51] by the locals.

Unique Security Legacies: A Peculiar British Inheritance

Because "constitutionally, Islamabad has never maintained jurisdiction over more than 100 meters to the left and right of the few paved roads in the tribal areas,"[52] the most relevant security features of the FATA are inherited from the administrative system of the British Empire. These include the designated tribal elite, called a *malik*, and a plenipotentiary bureaucrat, called the Political Agent (and District Commissioner for Frontier Regions [FRs]), who has unique systems of empowerment available to him.

During the middle period of the British domination of the subcontinent (from about 1857),[53] the lands and tribes west of the Indus River represented a unique and heightened security challenge. British security policy responded to two key factors: the movement of Imperial Russia in the direction of British India, and a bloody mutiny of native forces inside British India itself. The intention of the British government was to develop the region of what is today's Pakistani tribal belt into a security zone with lines of communication between Afghanistan and the British Raj. This security approach was called the "Forward Policy" to distinguish it from the dissenting view not to overreach the Indus into the tribal belt with British troops and resources. The concept of considering the dangers of overreach into the volatile tribal belt was clear in 1887: "The opening of the country can only be affected in two ways, either by the use of military force or by endeavoring to draw the tribes into close and friendly relations with ourselves."[54] The policies and practices that extended from this realization are still the same nuts and bolts of the security structure today, and are the most under-considered aspect of counterterrorism and counterinsurgency coordination.

The British left tribal social institutions in place while creating enhanced conditions for security affairs that supported their interests. They approached the tribes through their existing systems of deliberation, particularly the *jirga*. To enhance their power and position in this venue, the British identified and paid individual, influential tribal members, the *maliks* (called by other titles in various tribes), to be interlocutors, counterparts, and local spokesmen. These individuals were provided resources and weapons.[55] This increased the local prestige of the *maliks* and enhanced their influence in the tribes,[56] helping shape support of British interests. The most significant departure from this came in the 1980s as the United States, Pakistan, and Saudi Arabia provided the Pashtun religious leaders with resources to recruit locals and fight against the Soviets in Afghanistan. This resulted in a shift from the *malik* to the *mullah* in terms of traditional tribal decision making and created the contemporary version of religious militancy, or "Talibanization," in the tribal areas. Exacerbating this evolving security disbalance are the large number of *maliks* who have been killed in recent times.[57] Nevertheless, *maliks* are still part of the security architecture but are not in positions of hierarchical leadership. Structurally, *maliks* do not have real decision-making powers in the tribe. Their power comes from the merit they are accorded from their fellow tribesmen.[58] This makes a difference when these individual leaders are engaged by insurgents and counterinsurgents alike. Their effectiveness when co-opted or their loss when removed is related mostly to the influence, resources, and benefits that the populace enjoyed. *Maliks* in the security architecture are not local decision makers or paramount leaders, but facilitators of access to those federal resources deemed useful by the tribes and as strategic symbols, the local face of cooperation with the federal government.

During the British India period, the chief administrator of the central government was the Political Agent (PA). The PAs established local networks of subordinate assistants, or *teshildars*, who came from among the tribesmen themselves, which enabled them to communicate, gather intelligence, and control benefits and programs. The PAs functioned through the *jirga* process to negotiate British interest and arbitrate disputes. Gradually, the PAs enhanced the British position in the security architecture. Because much of the British interest lay with maintenance of law and order in their own settled areas,[59] the PAs' principal power came from a special set of *jirga* rules: the Frontier Crimes Regulation (FCR). Compiled over decades from 1848 until 1901, the FCR contained draconian provisions. With this tool, the PA could levy community fines, create blockades, and seize and destroy community property for acts committed by individuals, pass sentences of whipping, detain relatives and associates of suspected individual perpetrators, and make arrests without warrant.[60] Although at different times in Pakistan history, proposals have been made to revise these regulations, the FCR remains essentially unchanged since 1901. What is not fully grasped by security planners today is that these rules still define the operational environment.[61]

Today, PAs are appointed by the NWFP governor and are often kinsmen of the tribes. The PAs, enabled with a corresponding system of assistants, are the direct representatives of the president of Pakistan, who, as of 1973, have discretionary powers to enact regulations in the FATA for "peace and good governance."[62] Whereas the laws that govern the NWFP and the rest of Pakistan are federal codes, such as the Pakistani penal code, criminal procedure code, civil procedure code, tax law, and so on, the process of governance in the FATA can best be described as treaty-making.[63] In practical terms, the PAs still hold the same enhanced executive, judicial, police, and revenue powers as during the colonial times. The relation of the state to the people of the FATA, when there is a working relationship at all, is the craft of the PAs in implementing and revoking official privilege and government programs with their clients, including *maliks* and clerics,[64] and wielding the FCR. This form of governance defines the relationship between the state and the tribal people in the FATA. The "indirectness" of this is a factor that cannot be dismissed or diminished in considering the centrality of the population in counterterrorism and counterinsurgency.

Kipling Would Recognize the Security Forces in the Tribal Areas

Paramilitary forces in the FATA and Pashtun lands have evolved against a backdrop of religious incitement, repelling outsiders, crime, personal or tribal grievance based violence and, even as noted in the 1901 FCR, the acts of "dangerous fanatics."[65]

The foundation of the security architecture in the FATA is the defense of honor and tribal custom. The *khel*, or local tribe, therefore, is the basic fighting system within a particular tribal boundary.[66] When formed as a militia, it is often called a *lashkar*. *Lashkars* may be small or in the thousands and tens of thousands. They can enforce small issues locally and they may deploy outside of their clan regions.[67] Another version of these tribal militias is as an *arbakai* (also called *salwishti*, or *shalgoon*). In this form, the tribesmen that compose the ranks perform duties that are more consistent with community policing and even peacekeeping missions.[68] Inherent in the tribal militia is a kind of "intelligence department," called *kishakee*, which detects threats and performs information collection.[69] Tribally formed forces are limited, however. They resist permanent leadership and structure because subordination in a military chain of command would be diminishment of the individual's status with regard to honor.[70] The *lashkar* and *arabkai* also do not conform to military doctrine other than through personal habits. They may be led by traditional leaders, and the other individuals may traditionally perform various military functions, but the principal design is to preserve social equality, the tribal code, and individuality. Tribal militias raised for religious or ideological purposes are sometimes referred to as *sipah* or *jaish*.[71] These militias theoretically are more enduring and have more hierarchical command structures.

Another feature of the security architecture in the FATA is the para-police: the *khassadars* and *levies*. The *khassadars* are tribal constables or watchmen. They were originally created by the British to ensure that Imperial representatives and forces would remain unmolested in the immediate areas along the lines of communication and in the frontier. In establishing these positions, the British related them directly to the tribal customs of providing protection for guests, with the individual or entire village performing this duty (called *naubati chaukidar* in some tribal vernaculars). Over time, the British codified this in the FCR, and thus grafted national requirements onto the tribal structure as obligations for providing "watch and ward."[72] Traditionally, *khassadars* protected roads and installations and provided armed escort. However, they also served in support of larger operations along with the central forces by performing limited military duties such as establishing checkpoints. The *khassadar's* area of operations is customarily limited by certain tribal boundaries where the *khassadar* can still be effective with his kinsmen.[73] *Levies* in the FATA function more as a police escort and local police for the PA and his *teshildars*. In the FATA, there are about six thousand *levies*, and they barrack in the PA's headquarters in each agency. Their range, however, is agency-wide.[74] Whereas the *khassadar* has largely become an inherited position, the *levy* remains a recruited billet. These local, counterinsurgent structures can serve as a keen source of local intelligence and are the visible, daily representation of security forces among the tribes. Both jobs are considered good employment by tribesmen, and when positions are available, they are eagerly filled. However, both are often un-uniformed, lightly armed, poorly trained, and unreliable.[75] While they are not a powerful force as an institution, as part of the security architecture, the *khassadars* are the first level of tribal-federal "village defense," and *levies* are initial tribal-federal defense of military "lines of communication."[76] Strategically, *khassadars* and *levies* are also important when determining the ratio of security forces to population.

Part of Pakistan's fifty-five-thousand-man national police force, the Police Service of Pakistan (PSP) serves in the NWFP. Another legacy of the British period, this force mans 217 stations in the NWFP, but does not operate normally in the FATA. The PSP unit leaders are Islamabad-appointed officers who are trained professionally at the national police academy. Junior officers come from provisional police services and are trained in separate local programs. While the national police represent the doctrinal force for counterinsurgency—bridging national security imperatives with indigenous security interaction with the population—they have not been effective in pursuing terrorist and militant organizations due to poor pay, lack of intelligence coordination with other agencies, lack of training, and lack of basic equipment. Hundreds of officers are killed every year in terrorist events.[77] Like the other tribal para-police forces, police training and operations are limited in terms of national capacity-building in counterterrorism and counterinsurgency.

Pakistan's Frontier Corps (FC) is the next feature of security architecture in the FATA. The FC is not a unit of the Pakistani Army, or even under the General Staff or Ministry of

Defense. Despite the FC's position in the border region and long military history of campaigns, its role is limited and determined by a peculiar legacy of development and relations with the federal authority and tribes.

The Frontier Corps evolved from tribal militias and scout units that were raised, paid, and led by the British government beginning in 1878. Originally, they were from the Afridi tribes near the Khyber Pass. They protected the critical line of communication between British Imperial India and Afghanistan against an encroaching Russian Empire and the local tribesmen. In addition to keeping the military road through the tribal belt safe, the FC conducted military operations in response to raids on the frontier settlements of the Raj.[78] Between 1800 and 1900, the British conducted over thirty major punitive expeditions in the tribal areas.[79] There were fifty-eight military campaigns between 1849 and 1939.[80] The formal paramilitary structure of the FC was constituted in 1907 by the Viceroy of British India and expanded by the government of Pakistan in 1947. The FC describes its establishment in the following way: "The main idea was to buy the loyalty of the tribesman and use their weapons against disloyal tribes."[81] Although there has been some shift in assigning more Pashtun officers to the FC, the vast majority of its leadership comes from the non-Pashto-speaking, non-tribal Punjabi military officers who are seconded from the regular army. The FC conducts limited types of missions and has fewer capabilities than the regular army, restricting features that are as much part of the legacy as they are contemporary characteristics.[82]

Today, there are actually two Frontier Corps—one for the NWFP and one for Baluchistan, both under the Ministry of Interior.[83] For FC-Northwest Frontier Province, there are between fifty-five and sixty-five thousand soldiers, affectionately called *jawans* or *sepoys*. At the end of 2006, there were twelve units in forty-six wings, with approximately eight to nine hundred men per wing.[84] In 2009, three more units were created in response to increased militancy and terrorism in the FATA and NWFP.[85] The FC has separate artillery batteries, an armored car squad, and companies of Special Forces.[86] The actual scope of the FC-NWFP is supposed to extend twelve hundred kilometers from the Broghil Pass outside the FATA and in Chitral to the Gomal Pass in the south. Clearly, it is a force not designed for rapid or sustained deployment throughout the FATA.

For most tribesmen, their military training and service is the only significant exposure that they have with other Pashtun and non-Pashtun tribesmen.[87] A force similar to the FC but much smaller in scope is the Frontier Constabulary (FCON). The FCON shares many of the same features of the FC, but its activities are mostly limited to the settled districts. The FCON does not have a writ in the agencies. Officers of the national police serve as FCON officers, which more closely relates them operationally to the PSP.[88]

Recruitment and service of the tribesmen in the FC and FCON are subject to collective representation. Recruitment is based on clan and village quotas and other demographics. Recruitment and service also include vetting at the village level to screen for past and potential violent actions of kinsmen related to the practice of *badal*.[89] FC squads and platoons are constituted with members of a single clan or village. Collective responsibility is also part of the custom, as all FC and FCON troopers form a particular group. They are all subject to dismissal or other punishment for the infractions of any one member.[90] Even when there is no military discipline issue, the tribesmen may collectively balk at operations that they perceive to be against their tribes.[91] For this reason, senior FC leadership notes that "trust" more than traditional military training is the most salient feature of performance of the FC troopers.[92]

FC troopers are organized around limited light infantry duties. The missions for the FC have not changed much over time. Peacetime missions include: maintaining vigilance along the Pakistan-Afghanistan border; conducting *gashts*, or patrols as show of force and combat patrols; conducting *baramptas*, or patrols specifically to seize or recover property or confine individuals; conducting anti-smuggling operations; and performing general law-and-order missions. In wartime, these missions are enhanced to include intelligence collection, sustained deployment in the border regions, protecting lines of communication, and defense of threatened areas. In a process called "regularization," the FC will conduct limited offensive operations in conjunction with the regular army, and assist the regular army in converting *lashkars* into tribal auxiliaries that can perform second-line duties.[93] Except for the very few new units that perform more sophisticated tactics specific to counterterrorism, the FC does not train or conduct joint operations that are part of modern warfare. Their tactics, techniques, and procedures are combinations of the basic mission sets of "post, picket, and patrol."[94] And while the history of the FC (and FCON) is the stuff of Kipling poems, another serious feature of the FC's organizational legacy is that "frontier campaigns must end in withdrawal."[95] In addition to the lack of inherent sustainment resources, this also underscores the preservation of autonomy that the tribes expect and applies today where these forces are placed in a counterinsurgent role.

While this chapter is not an examination of the Pakistan Army, units of the federal army are stationed and operate in the NWFP and FATA. Stationed in Peshawar, the capital of the NWFP and an FR itself, the Pakistan Army's 11th Corps serves as a strategic depth force for a broader regional conflict. Even so, until 2002, the federal army had never deployed to the FATA, resulting in a very significant "lack of formal state penetration,"[96] and, therefore, there was little federal integration into the security architecture, which includes the FC. During conflict, the army has control for tactical integration of FC elements. However, these missions are not closely integrated combined arms actions; instead, they are ancillary applications of FC's standard missions. In some of the operations against militants in Buner and Swat in 2009, the Pakistani Army forces provided the heavy punch with artillery, tanks, and air strikes, while FC units were used for the house-to-house and street fighting.[97] The advantage of this approach was keeping part of the lethal federal force at a distance from the locals. The critique was that it bypassed the local population and civil administration, isolating the local tribal leadership and causing collateral damage.[98] The local population may act in such a way that supports the army, the FC, or both (such as raising a *lashkar*), but they do not ultimately rally to the national cause.[99]

Compared to the national force, the FC is poorly equipped. FC tribal soldiers have a variety of old automatic rifles and antiquated crew-served machine guns, obsolete communications equipment, and ancient artillery pieces. The FC does not have body armor, modern helmets, night-vision devices, or advanced technology-enabled systems such as global positioning or communication devices.[100] Their uniforms—the prideful, cotton *shalwar-kamez*—are not as durable and utilitarian as modern combat uniforms. Much of the FC wears sandals instead of boots even during operations. In the winter, they only don a sweater over their garb.[101] The lack of medical evacuation capability impacts operational considerations to a degree often under-considered by a modern force. The FC has no night-fighting capability, limited mobility, no rapid deployment capacity, and limited firepower. For the FC, the missions at their border forts and elsewhere do not include counterterrorism tactics. The FC's tribesmen are "fiery and weapons-savvy"[102] and even a "martial race,"[103] but this disparity in equipment and training is a significant deterrent of effective independent operations and an impediment to closer integration in operations with the regular army and other potential counterinsurgent/counterterrorist partners.

Conclusion

The security architecture in any location is complex, with innumerable nuances of tribal practice and legacies. However, in Pakistan's Pashtun tribal belt, counterterrorism and counterinsurgency operations based on oversimplification of the natures of militancy and local security culture have not proven effective. Regarding this region, military planners must become more aware of the specific demographic and cultural conditions that shape the local population's resistance and acceptance of nontribal affairs. They must develop a starting point for understanding tribal security structures and customs aimed at illuminating both local security response and the opportunity for outside leverage. There must be an accounting of legacy security force structures and relationships in order to develop realistic operational expectations and schemes of enhancement. In Pakistan's tribal belt, a first draft of security architecture could look like this:

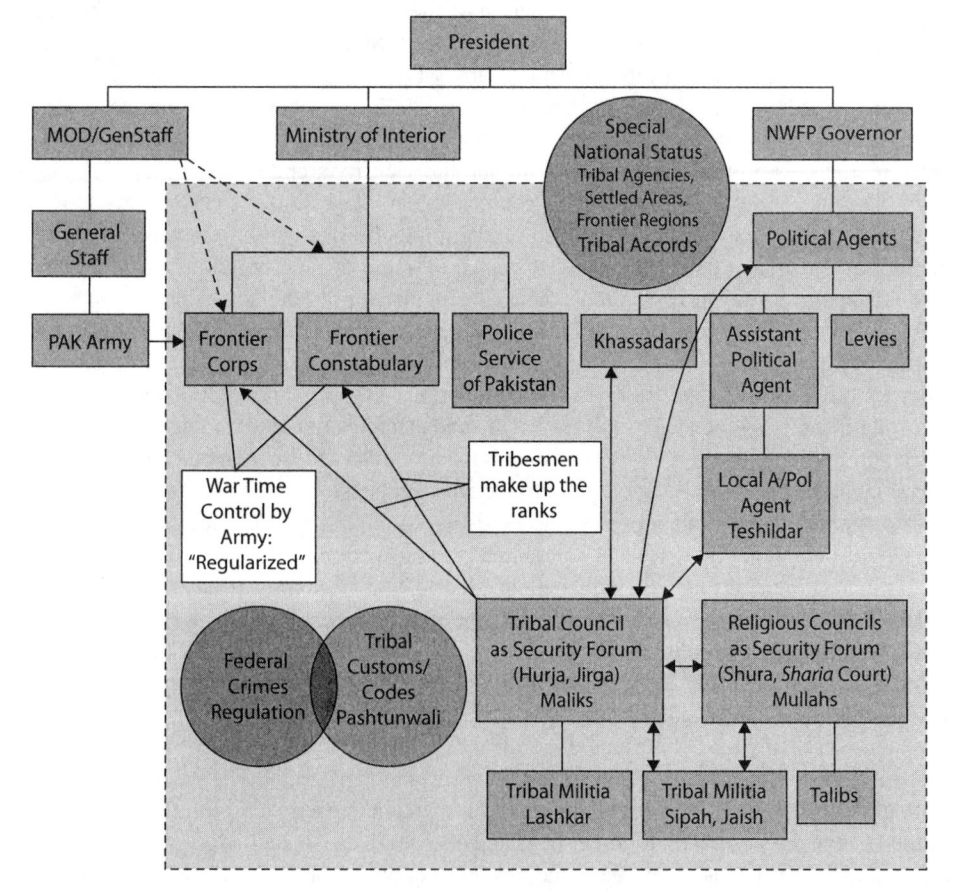

Tribal Areas: Security Architecture

These certainly are not all the details that define Pakistan's tribal belt, and these architectural components could be further developed. However, the practice of identification of these details is an important task in counterterrorism and counterinsurgency planning. The blueprint features of security architecture can also be extended to improve the planning and execution of social and economic development, institution and governance transformations, and other issues that shape the local population—the center of gravity in counterterrorism and counterinsurgency.

Tom Wilhelm Colonel (ret) Tom Wilhelm is the Director of the US Army's Foreign Military Studies Office an open-source research organization that focuses on foreign perspectives of defense and security issues. Tom Wilhelm was a past Associate Dean for Eurasian Studies and Military Professor for the Program on Terrorism and Security Studies at the George C. Marshall European Center for Security Studies. While on active duty, Tom Wilhelm served as the Director of Defense Resources for the Office of Military Cooperation-Afghanistan and Chief of Ground Forces Liaison with Office of the Defense Representative-Pakistan. He has participated as a guest of the Frontier Corps to study security forces in Pakistan's Federally Administered Tribal Areas and Northwest Frontier Province. Since that time, he has continued to examine this subject and lectures on it in a range of forums from deploying units to international academic venues.

Recommended Readings

Chalk, Peter. "Case Study: The Pakistani-Afghan Border Region" in Angel Rabasa, et al., *Ungoverned Territories: Understanding and Reducing Terrorism Risks*. Santa Monica, CA: RAND Corporation, 2007.

International Crisis Group. "Pakistan's Tribal Areas: Appeasing the Militants," *Asia Report*, No. 125. Brussels: International Crisis Group, 11 December 2006.

Johnson, Thomas H., and M. Chris Mason. "No Sign Until the Burst of Fire: Understanding the Pakistan-Afghanistan Frontier," *International Security*, Vol. 32, No. 4 (Spring 2008), 41–77.

Nawaz, Shuja. *Crossed Swords: Pakistan, Its Army, and the Wars Within*. Oxford: Oxford University Press, 2008.

"Pushtunwali-The Pushtuns' Tribal Code," *The Economist*, 19 December 2006. Available at http://www.economist.com/world/displaystory.cfm?story_id=E1_RPQVVPT

Shinwari, Naveed Ahmed. *Understanding FATA: Attitudes Towards Governance, Religion and Society in Pakistan's Federally Administered Tribal Areas*. Peshawar, Pakistan: Community Appraisal and Motivation Programme, 2008. Available at www.understandingfata.org

Trench, Charles Chenevix. *The Frontier Scouts*. London: Jonathan Cape, 1986.

White, Joshua T. *Pakistan's Islamist Frontier: Islamic Politics and U.S. Policy in Pakistan's North-West Frontier*. Religion and Security Monograph Series, No. 1. Arlington, VA: Center on Faith and International Affairs, 2008.

Notes

1. The term "insurgency" is meant to include all forms of militancy in Pakistan's tribal areas that impact national stability objectives of Pakistan.
2. See, for example, Phillip Smucker, McClatchy Newspapers, "U.S. Forces Face Afghan Dilemma," *Kansas City Star*, 24 May 2009, A1.

3. Rahim Faiez, Associated Press, "Fighting in Afghanistan Kills 39," *Kansas City Star*, 31 May 2009, and also direct comments to author from Pakistani and coalition senior and junior officers in Afghanistan and Pakistan, May–November 2004 and October–November 2006.

4. Comments to author by a Tochi Scouts post commander in North Waziristan, 10 November 2006.

5. Naveed Ahmed Shinwari, *Understanding FATA: Attitudes Towards Governance, Religion and Society in Pakistan's Federally Administered Tribal Areas* (Peshawar, Pakistan: Community Appraisal and Motivation Programme, 2008), 3, available at www.understandingfata.org, accessed 3 October 2009.

6. See, for example, Takht Bhai, "Fleeing the Battlefield," *The Economist*, 14 May 2009, available at http://www.economist.com/world/asia/displaystory.cfm?story_id=13649359, accessed 3 October 2009 and Smucker, A1.

7. For various figures, see Laila Bohkari, "Waziristan-Impact on the Taliban Insurgency," available at http://www.natiion.com.pk/pakistan-news-newspaper-daily-english-online/Politics/16-Jul-2008/Movement-routine-matter-ISPR, accessed 20 May 2009. (5.7 million); Thomas H. Johnson and M. Chris Mason, "No Sign until the Burst of Fire: Understanding the Pakistan-Afghanistan Frontier," *International Security*, Vol. 32, No. 4 (Spring 2008), 45. (3.2–4.0 million), and Imtiaz Ali, "Foreign Policy Challenges for the New President—Part I," *YaleGlobal*, 31 October 2008, available at http://yaleglobal.yale.edu/en/node/5011, accessed 3 October 2009.

8. Daniel A. Kronenfeld, "Afghan Refugees in Pakistan: Not All Refugees, Not Always in Pakistan, Not Necessarily Afghan," *Journal of Refugee Studies*, Vol. 21, No. 1 (March 2008), 43–63, abstract available at http://jrs.oxfordjournals.org/cgi/content/abstract/fem048v1?ck=nck, accessed 10 June 2009.

9. Johnson and Mason, 50–51.

10. "Pushtunwali—The Pushtuns' Tribal Code," *The Economist*, 19 December 2006, available at http://www.economist.com/world/displaystory.cfm?story_id=E1_RPQVVPT, accessed 30 May 2009; Jose Oberson, *Khans and Warlords: Political Alignment, Leadership, and the State in Pashtun Society: Anthropological Aspects and the Warlordism Debate*, master's thesis (Bern: University of Bern Institute for Ethnology, 2002), 13, and Shinwari, 12.

11. Johnson and Mason, 50 and Louis Dupree, *Afghanistan*, (Princeton: Princeton University Press, 1973), 343. Also this supports the notion that the Pashtuns are not an ethnic group at all, but only have some of the components that define ethnicity, as noted in "Pushtunwali—The Pushtuns' Tribal Code."

12. See, for example, Mohammed Osman Tariq, *Tribal Security System (Arbakai) in Southeast Afghanistan*, Crisis States Research Centre (London) Occasional Paper, No. 7 (December 2008), 3. Tariq argues that *arbakai* are not tribal militias. He defines *arbakai* as a "community policing system" and, therefore, different than a *lashkars*, which he says have varying definitions.

13. Ibid., and comments to author from US Army Colonel David Brigham, Peshawar, Pakistan, 11 August 2009.

14. Basic geo-social facts presented here are correlated from several sources, including International Crisis Group, "Pakistan's Tribal Areas: Appeasing the Militants," *Asia Report* No. 125 (Brussels: International Crisis Group, 11 December 2006), 3–4; "Pakistan," *CIA World Factbook*, updated 24 September 2009, available at https://www.cia.gov/library/publications/the-world-factbook/geos/pk.html, accessed 3 October 2009; and Johnson and Mason, 45, 47, 50, and 51. Note that the last census of the population of the FATA was taken in 1998, and its figures put the aggregate population estimate closer to 3.4 million, while there is some notation in the International Crisis Group report that indicates a spread from 3.3 to 7 million. Johnson and Mason put the number of clans at 350; other sources indicate 400 and 600.

15. Johnson and Mason, 50.

16. Tariq Mahmud Ashraf, "The Pakistan Frontier Corps in the War on Terrorism—Part I," *Jamestown Foundation Terrorism Monitor*, Vol. 6, Issue 15 (25 July 2008), available at http://www.jamestown.org/programs/gta/single/?tx_ttnews[tt_news]=5053&tx_ttnews[backPid]=167&no_cache=1, accessed 3 October 2009.

17. Brigham and Tochi Scouts post commander.

18. Johnson and Mason, 51. The terms for kin groups—i.e., clans, tribes, and *khels*—are used interchangeably here, except where otherwise qualified.

19. Shinwari, 19. There are 4,427 kilometers of road, of which about 2,500 kilometers are paved.

20. Thomas Barfield, Neamat Nojumi, and J. Alexander Their, *The Clash of Two Goods: State and Non-State Dispute Resolution in Afghanistan* (Washington, DC: United States Institute of Peace, November 2006), 2–3, available at http://siteresources.worldbank.org/INTLAWJUSTINST/ Resources/clash_of_two_goods.pdf, accessed 3 October 2009.

21. Shinwari, 1.

22. Ibid.

23. International Crisis Group, "Pakistan's Tribal Areas: Appeasing the Militants," 9.

24. Shinwari, 38 and 44.

25. Ashraf.

26. Shinwari, xvii.

27. Johnson and Mason, 55.

28. Shinwari, 3.

29. Shuja Nawaz, *Crossed Swords: Pakistan, Its Army, and the Wars Within* (Oxford: Oxford University Press, 2008), 3.

30. Ibid., 50.

31. Peter Chalk, "Case Study: The Pakistani-Afghan Border Region," in Angel Rabasa, et al., *Ungoverned Territories: Understanding and Reducing Terrorism Risks* (Santa Monica, CA: RAND Corporation, 2007), 61; International Crisis Group, "Pakistan's Tribal Areas: Appeasing the Militants," 3; and Johnson and Mason, 54, as a counter argument.

32. "Welcome to FATA," Official website of the Federally Administered Tribal Area, Pakistan, updated 2009, available at http://www.fata.gov.pk/index.php?link=3, accessed 26 December 2007.

33. Shinwari, 20.

34. Hassan Abbas, "Transforming Pakistan's Frontier Corps," *Jamestown Foundation Terrorism Monitor*, Vol. 5, Issue 6 (30 March 2007), available at http://www.jamestown.org/ programs/gta/single/?tx_ttnews[tt_news]=1056&tx_ttnews[backPid]=182&no_cache=1, accessed 3 October 2009.

35. Shinwari, 63.

36. Compare Trench, 284, who lists *izzat* as "honor" in the glossary, with Johnson and Mason, 62, who identify "personal honor" as *nang*.

37. Shinwari, 20, and Johnson and Mason, 63.

38. Some examples are in Johnson and Mason, 53.

39. Ibid., 50.

40. Johnson and Mason, 60.

41. Shinwari, 4 and 21.

42. Johnson and Mason, 60.

43. Ibid., 60–62.

44. "Pushtunwali—The Pushtuns' Tribal Code."

45. Shinwari, 3

46. "Pushtunwali—The Pushtuns' Tribal Code."

47. White, 24–25.

48. M. Ehsan Ahrari, *Jihadi Groups, Nuclear Pakistan, and the New Great Game* (Carlisle, PA: Strategic Studies Institute, U.S. Army War College, August 2001), 3.

49. For an example of tribal reactionary response, see Sabrina Tavernise and Irfan Ashraf, "Attacked, Pakistani Villagers Take on Taliban," *New York Times*, 9 June 2009, available at http://www.nytimes.com/2009/06/10/world/asia/10pstan.html, accessed 3 October 2009.

50. Geoffrey Moore, *Just as Good as the Rest: A British Battalion in the Faqir of Ipi's War in India N.W.F. 1936–37* (published by author, undated), 8. This work is the author's first-hand account.

51. Bokhari, 13. Bohkari also references Zaffar Abbas, "Pakistan's Undeclared War," *BBC News*, 10 September 2004, available at http://news.bbc.co.uk/2/hi/south_asia/3645114.stm, accessed 3 October 2009.

52. Johnson and Mason, 53.
53. The official beginning of British Company Rule is noted as 1757. However, due to the combined events of the encroachment of imperial Russia and the Indian Munity, from 1857 onwards may be viewed as a distinct period (the "Raj") in terms of security development in the tribal areas.
54. Punjab Government, *Report on Waziristan and Its Tribes*, 2nd ed. (Lahore: Sang-e-Meel Publications, 2005), 3.
55. International Crisis Group, "Pakistan's Tribal Areas: Appeasing the Militants," 4.
56. Trench, 189 and Anderson, 169. Anderson describes Ghilzai clan *khans*, which are comparable to *maliks* of other clans.
57. Brigham's comments to author. Brigham also estimated that approximately six hundred *maliks* have been killed by militants since the beginning of the current conflict.
58. Anderson, 170.
59. Ibid., 28 and 29.
60. A copy of the FCR is available in Shinwari, 122–142.
61. At various times after the establishment of Pakistan, amendments to the FCR have been made regarding non-FATA tribal areas, effectively converting police practice in these areas to Pakistani criminal codes. Other initiatives to amend or abrogate the FCR in the FATA have not succeeded.
62. International Crisis Group, "Pakistan's Tribal Areas: Appeasing the Militants," 4. This report references Article 247 (5) of the constitution.
63. Johnson and Mason, 53.
64. Carin Zissis and Jayshree Bajoria, *Pakistan's Tribal Areas*, Council on Foreign Relations Backgrounder, updated 26 October 2007, available at http://www.cfr.org/publication/11973/pakistans_tribal_areas.html, accessed 11 May 2009; International Crisis Group, "Pakistan's Tribal Areas: Appeasing the Militants," 4; and Chalk, 50–51.
65. FCR in Shinwari, 135.
66. Johnson and Mason, 63.
67. Trench, 28. Trench mentions 10,000 in a *lashkar* attacking Miranshah; Mukhtar A. Khan, "The Role of Tribal Lashkars in Winning Pakistan's War on Terror," *Jamestown Foundation Terrorism Focus*, Vol. 5, Issue 40 (26 November 2008) notes *lashkars* of four thousand raised by Bajaur tribes against militants there.
68. Tariq, 3. Tariq argues that *arbakai* are not tribal militias. He defines *arbakai* as a "community policing system" and, therefore, different than a *lashkars*, which he says have varying definitions.
69. Tariq, 2.
70. Johnson and Mason, 63.
71. For example, see, "Sipah, Lashkar Would Not Be Tolerated," *Daily Economic Chronicle*, 17 September 2004, 1.
72. FCR in Shinwari, 134.
73. Trench, 71 and 127. Trench indicates that *levies* is the Baluch word for *khassadar*, 71, and International Crisis Group, "Pakistan's Tribal Areas: Appeasing the Militants," 4.
74. Johnson and Mason, 44, and comments to author from Dr. Robert Baer, Foreign Military Studies Office, Ft. Leavenworth, Kansas, 9 June 2009.
75. Johnson and Mason, 44.
76. Major General Tariq Khan, interview, the *Economist*, 23 July 2009, available at http://www.audiovideo.economist.com, accessed 5 August 2009.
77. Hassan Abbas, *Police and Law Enforcement Reform in Pakistan: Crucial for Counterinsurgency and Counterterrorism Success* (Clinton, MI: Report for Institute for Social Policy and Understanding, April 2009) 7, 12, 15–17. Available at http://www.ispu.org/files/PDFs/ISPU%20-%20Police%20Reforms%20in%20Pakistan%20Report.pdf, accessed 3 October 2009.
78. For example, see *Report on Waziristan and Its Tribes*, 43.
79. Trench, 2.
80. Shinwari, 17.
81. *Headquarters Frontier Corps NWFP: Guide for Officers* (Office of the Inspector General of the Frontier Corps: undated), received by author at Bala Hissar on 17 November 2006, 9.

82. Hassan Abbas, "Transforming Pakistan's Frontier Corps," and Ashraf, 2.
83. Ibid.
84. Information provided to author by Frontier Corps-NWFP at Bala Hissar, 4 November 2006.
85. Tariq Khan, *Economist* interview.
86. Ibid.
87. Information provided to author by Frontier Corps-NWFP at Bala Hissar, 4 November 2006 and Trench, 70.
88. Information provided to author by Frontier Constabulary at Michni Fort, 13 November 2006.
89. Information provided to author by Frontier Corps-NWFP at Bala Hissar, 4 November 2006.
90. Ibid., and see also Trench, 63.
91. Nawaz, xxxiii.
92. Tariq Khan, *Economist* interview.
93. *Headquarters Frontier Corps NWFP: Guide for Officers*, 10.
94. Information provided to author by Frontier Corps-NWFP at Bala Hissar, 4 November 2006.
95. Trench, 27.
96. Chalk, 52.
97. For the role of the FC, see Tariq Khan *Economist* interview.
98. Nawaz, xxxiii.
99. See, for example, contemporary news accounts in Tavernise and Ashraf, and Takht Bhai, "Fleeing the Battlefield."
100. For example, when the author visited the FC post museum at Miramshah on 9 November 2006, the absence of a heliograph was explained by need for it at another FC picket site.
101. Author's observations and conversations with officers and soldiers during tour of FC in Kurram and North Waziristan agencies in November 2006.
102. Ashraf, 11 May 2009.
103. Nawaz, 545.

Afterword

Boaz Ganor

International Cooperation and the Dynamic Terrorist Threat

The terrorist attacks of September 11 were widely considered a "wake-up call" for the Western world—an international event that alerted the public and decision makers to the urgency of the terrorist threat. However, despite the subsequent action taken to combat the terrorist threat post-9/11, the world has yet to fully awaken to the most fundamental necessity of effectively defeating terrorism—international cooperation. Remarkably, almost nine years later, it seems that international cooperation in the fight against terrorism is as equally defined by its consistent reliance on the "snooze" button as it is on its achievements. In fact, while decision makers are seemingly sleeping, terrorist operatives and recruits are wide awake and taking "international cooperation" to a whole new level—developing complex and dynamic networks that span across continents.

In one recent case, an Atlanta court convicted twenty-three-year-old Ehsanul Sadequee, the US-born son of Bangladeshi immigrants, of conspiracy to materially support terrorists. Like many American twenty-somethings, Sadequee was internet-savvy. As such, he did not need to be well traveled to develop extensive international connections; out of Georgia, Sadequee communicated with operatives and extremists in Toronto, Sarajevo, Copenhagen, London, and Ohio. Through Islamic chat rooms, Sadequee made contact with like-minded peers—a Bosnian in Sweden, a Moroccan in London, and a Pakistani-American student from Georgia Tech. If it was not so reprehensible, it would be remarkable; with the simple use of internet technology, Sadequee established a loose network of like-minded individuals set on plotting attacks, joining terrorist organizations, and furthering their extremist ideology. In connecting North America, Europe, and South Asia, Sadequee could easily be a poster child for "international cooperation."[1]

So if they can do it, why can't we?

Given the unprecedented scope and severity of the threat of international terrorism, cooperation among counterterrorism officials, intelligence agencies, and local enforcement mechanisms—on a local, national, and international level—is simply nonnegotiable. More than simply boosting our cooperative efforts, however, the international community must seek to establish new international bodies designed specifically to address the increasingly international, networked, dynamic nature of the threat.

Defining the Threat

The challenge of international radical Islamic terrorism does not lie with one individual (Osama bin Laden) or with one single organization (al Qaeda). Rather, it lies in the question of how to defeat a vast international terrorist network with global reach. This network consists of activists from diverse backgrounds, living and working in Arab and Muslim nations, as well as western states and the developing world. It accepts individuals of all ranks and statuses—educated and non-educated, poor and wealthy, experienced and novice, Muslims and converts. It is in being such an equal-opportunity and expansive system that this terrorist network poses such an unprecedented threat, embracing a dangerous combination of unique characteristics.

One such characteristic is the fundamentalist belief in the divine command, which calls on the network's members to disseminate their radical Islamic worldview across the globe, through the use of extreme violence and terrorism—and increasingly, through propaganda and internet technologies. The belief in *jihad* (holy war) makes these activists particularly dangerous; after all, when advancing the will of God, neither argument nor compromise is acceptable. All-out war is thus their only option.

The network's global reach is based on a combination of various Islamic fundamentalist terrorist organizations, dormant and newly emerging cells, and individual actors inspired by the call to *jihad*. While activists like twenty-three-year-old Ehsanul Sadequee may be considered novices, members of radical Islamic networks are most often seasoned warriors with combat experience from the Afghan campaign.

It is also the methods employed by these groups that make them so dangerous. Members of this network do not hesitate to use suicide terrorism. Within the framework of their extremist Islamic ideology, these attacks are not seen as committing suicide, which is forbidden by Islamic religious law, but rather as an act of sacrifice for the sake of martyrdom (*ishtishad*), guaranteeing them eternal life in Paradise.

In addition to their proven capability to launch deadly and devastating attacks using suicide bombings and conventional terrorism, leaders of the international radical Islamic terrorist network have made it clear that they have no hesitations about using nonconventional means as well—chemical, biological, or even nuclear weapons. Among many examples, in a 1998 interview bin Laden declared that acquiring chemical or nuclear weapons "for the defense of Muslims is a religious duty" and "If I have indeed acquired these weapons, then this is an obligation I carried out and I thank God for enabling us to do that. And if I seek to acquire these weapons, I am carrying out a duty. It would be a sin for Muslims not to try to possess the weapons that would prevent the infidels from inflicting harm on Muslims."[2] If their statements aren't enough, a number of foiled attack attempts lend further support to the potential for nonconventional terrorist attacks.

It is on the basis of these characteristics that the radical Islamic terrorist network poses such an unparalleled level of danger to the modern world. This threat is so great, that the international community must stop simply *managing* it, and start really *preventing* and *defeating* it—which requires agencies around the world, from diverse fields and disciplines, to unite their efforts, combine forces, and formulate a new strategy to combat terrorism.

Defeating the Threat

Any cohesive strategy to combat the unprecedented threat of international terrorism must combine both military and strategic approaches, simultaneously addressing threats on a local and international basis. Military and law enforcement solutions are needed to directly and immediately suppress emerging plots, while the international community must attempt to strategically nullify the appeal of the radical Islamic ideology behind terrorism on a long-term basis. Several states have had considerable success in launching offensive measures against terrorist infrastructure, designed to disrupt the operational capability of terrorist groups. However, in many ways, what officials don't always realize is that such measures sometimes simply "buy time." It is the underlying motivation behind these groups' activities that must be addressed in the long term in order to defeat international terrorism.

The masses that support these terrorists, their ideological infrastructure, and the radicalization processes that attract new recruits all play a vital role in sustaining and expanding their abilities to launch attacks. Offensive measures, while clearly essential, might also add fuel to the motivation behind the radical Islamic terrorist network. That is why offensive and strategic counter-radicalization measures must be implemented simultaneously, on an international basis, and with calculated foresight.

Taking these factors into consideration, four primary elements must be included in an international campaign to combat the radical Islamic breed of terrorism we face today. First of all, offensive measures against al Qaeda and global and local *jihadi* groups must continue to play a substantial role in any counterterrorism program. As was initiated and largely successful in the months immediately following 9/11 with the US-led campaign in Afghanistan, al Qaeda's infrastructure must be destroyed, its activists arrested or eliminated, and its support base eradicated. Despite the relative success of the military campaign in Afghanistan, the international struggle, even on this fundamental offensive level, is far from over. Al Qaeda has since shifted its operational base from Afghanistan to Pakistan's Federally Administered Tribal Areas (FATA), which has emerged as the new "premier hunting ground for the al Qaeda leadership." From this new base, the al Qaeda threat has arguably proliferated, embracing new local groups and the support of the Pakistani Taliban.[3]

The second level on which the international campaign must be waged involves taking action against other radical Islamic terrorist organizations active around the Muslim world. Countering these groups should not be the responsibility of the western world alone, but rather a task for Arab and Muslim moderates, who must stand at the forefront of the campaign against radical Islam—for the sake not of the West, but rather of themselves. Moderate Muslim nations must prevent these radical movements from attracting public support by providing a constant supply of basic social welfare services, including health and education. They must fight to outlaw and shut down community centers opened by radical Islamic groups, and replace them with centers run by the central government, which will provide needed services without militant indoctrination and fundamentalist propaganda.

The third necessary step is international action against state sponsors of terrorism, which entails two fundamental prerequisites. First is the establishment of an accepted and objective international definition of terrorism, which would allow the international community to establish a normative international system. Such a system is necessary to, among many purposes, provide a framework for introducing international charters that can define the range of allowable and obligatory state action in an international war against terrorism in general, and against state sponsors of terrorism in particular. Second, nations across the world must place the battle against radical Islamic terrorism much higher on their list of priorities. The exceptional level of threat posed today requires a change in the balance of interests of such nations, with the war against terrorism placed at the top of the agenda.

Finally, the fourth sphere of activity is the struggle against terrorist cells and activists, who have either settled or been granted citizenship in countries throughout the western and developing world. The responsibility of dismantling these cells lies with the country that serves as their haven. These countries must adjust their laws accordingly, granting security forces the necessary tools to cope with these dangerous agents. Security forces must follow the illegal activities of radical Islamic activists, as well as verbal incitement both in the local language and in Arabic. Arrests and deportations may be necessary in this process, in order to weaken the tight grip these radical Islamic organizations have established.

This four-pronged program cannot be simply implemented by a state government alone—it requires a high level of coordination among both the public and the private sector, among academia and law enforcement, and most of all—between nations. It must be carried out simultaneously on a global level against all those who belong to or support the radical Islamic terrorist network.

International Cooperation and the "Joint Counterterrorism Campaign"

In order to ensure the kind of international cooperation essential to combating and eventually dismantling the radical Islamic terrorist network, the international community must first expand upon existing and traditional bilateral and multilateral cooperative methods, such as intelligence gathering, as well as the sharing of technological developments and "lessons learned." However, efforts cannot be limited to simply expanding and improving—an international normative legal platform for terrorism must be established, which would eventually lay the groundwork for an entirely new framework in the form of a "joint counterterrorism campaign."

The International Legal Platform

As discussed, the creation of a normative legal platform is dependent upon establishing agreed-upon common denominators—namely, an accepted definition for the term "terrorism." Such a definition must be as narrow and limiting as possible, representing the broadest possible basis for shared agreement. It must also make a distinction between the goals of terrorists and their modes of operation. Such a definition will allow for the development of international charters aimed at combating terrorism, potentially including:

- Provisions that require nations to dismantle the infrastructure of foreign terrorist organizations operating on their territory
- Charters that obligate nations to fight terrorist financing
- Charters that compel banks to divulge information to security forces regarding terrorist organizations or those suspected of involvement in terrorist activity
- Treaties for extraditing terrorists and their associates
- Treaties that prohibit membership in terrorist organizations and perpetrating various types of terrorist acts—suicide bombings, extortion attacks, killing, and sabotage

Establishing Joint International Counterterrorism Frameworks

While enhanced cooperation, as just described, is absolutely necessary in combating the threat, we must not simply stop there—that would be the equivalent of pressing the "snooze" button. The transition from international cooperation to a joint counterterrorism campaign is not merely a semantic change, but rather, it entails a new understanding of the essence of the struggle and the means needed for coping on an international scale.

In seeking to implement this fundamental change, international bodies must be established to address all aspects of the terrorist threat. One such institution would be an intelligence body that could channel real-time warnings and filter intelligence data concerning the movements, intentions, capabilities, and characteristics of terrorist operations.

On the defensive front, a joint intervention unit should be established, which would be available to carry out antiterrorist operations, including capturing terrorists, rescuing hostages, conducting negotiations, etc. Such a unit would have to have members well acquainted with aspects of radical Islamic terrorism, including the culture, language, religion, decision-making processes, and intellectual characteristics of its adherents.

Another necessary international body is an international court for terrorist crimes, since the International Court of Justice in The Hague is authorized to try any person—leader and common citizen alike—but only for criminal acts or war crimes, without any mention of terrorist activity.

Given the interdisciplinary nature of terrorism, an international academic research network that includes the finest minds in academia must be established and provided opportunities, through grants and other financial resources, to explore questions that are particularly relevant for terrorism prevention agencies. Also related to education is the need to develop informational and educational activities in nations facing terrorism in order to strengthen public resilience. An international framework of experts should also formulate joint public counter-radicalism and educational policies, especially in Muslim countries.

Finally, to promote effective action against terrorist organizations and the states that support them, a permanent, international antiterrorism institution must have authority to identify nations and organizations involved in terrorism, and determine sanctions and actions to be taken against them. Such an institution would have to function on a clear and approved mandate and include experts from around the world. After publishing an annual list of nations supporting terrorism, international sanctions could then be adopted against countries included on that list, in accordance with the scope of their support.

Clearly, this is an incredibly difficult task requiring broad international consensus on the definition of terrorism and of the range and scope of the different levels of involvement. While such efforts may seem rather unrealistic, perhaps some of these goals can be accomplished through the establishment of a new international alliance in the framework of NATO, which would expand to include many more countries—western, third world, and Muslim countries. This new international alliance should be constructed as a complex network of states, agencies, organizations, and experts, since "it takes a network to beat a network."

Conclusion

It is commendable indeed that nations are enhancing their counterterrorism programs, and, in many countries, establishing new and innovative approaches to address the many aspects of the dynamic threat posed by radical Islamic terrorism. However, many of the efforts undertaken by counterterrorism agencies around the world seem to be simply "buying time"—they have heard the alarm ring, but they are either pressing the snooze button, or ignoring it all together. For many nations, for the risk of terrorism to be fully addressed, it needs to be more tangible—which only occurs when a series of devastating terrorist attacks plagues a nation that has otherwise ignored the severity of the problem.

It is a matter of priorities, and unfortunately, nations may be waiting until "things get worse" until they take the initiative. Perhaps only then can we expect the nations of the free world to unite together in a genuine and uncompromising struggle against international terrorism. In the mean time, as decision makers seem to sleep in complacency, activists like Ehsanul Sadequee will continue to develop their international connections. But unlike Sadequee, some might succeed in forwarding their activities undetected and perhaps succeed in executing the next unfortunate "wake-up call."

Boaz Ganor Dr. Ganor is the Associate Dean of the Lauder School of Government and the founder and Executive Director of the International Institute for Counter Terrorism, Herzliya, Israel. He is also the founder and Chairman of the International Academic Counter Terrorism Community. In 2008–2009, Dr. Ganor was a Koret Distinguished Visiting Fellow at the Hoover Institution at Stanford University. A Senior Fellow at The Memorial Institute for Prevention of Terrorism (US), his other affiliations include: the International Advisory Council of the International Centre for Political Violence and Terrorism Research at the Institute of Defense and Strategic Studies, Nanyang Technological University, Singapore; The International Centre for the Study of Radicalization and Political Violence (US and UK); and the Regional Center on Conflict Prevention, Amman, Jordan. Boaz Ganor has been an advisor on counterterrorism to the Israeli Ministry of Defense, the Israeli Counter-Terrorism Coordinator at the Prime Minister's Office, Israel's National Security Council, the Israeli Ministry of Transportation, and Prime Minister Benjamin Netanyahu when the latter wrote his book *Fighting Terrorism: How Democracies Can Defeat Domestic and International Terrorism*. His publications include *The Counter-Terrorism Puzzle: A Guide for Decision Makers* (Transaction Publishers, 2005), a text used by many universities.

Notes

1. Sebastian Rotella, "Georgia Man Convicted of Aiding Terrorism Groups," *Los Angeles Times*, 13 August 2009, available at http://www.latimes.com/news/nationworld/nation/la-na-terror-trial13-2009aug13,0,4647485.story, accessed 2 March 2010.
2. "World's Most Wanted Terrorist: An Interview with Osama Bin Laden," by Rahimullah Yusufzai for abcnews.com, 28 December 1998; quoted in Michael Scheuer, *Through Our Enemies' Eyes: Osama bin Laden, Radical Islam, and the Future of America*, rev. ed. (Washington, D.C.: Potomac Books, 2006), 72.
3. Rohan Gunaratna and Anders Nielsen, "Al Qaeda in the Tribal Areas of Pakistan and Beyond," *Studies in Conflict & Terrorism*, Vol. 31, Issue 9 (2008), 775–807.

Index